E. L. B. Curtis
October 6, 1930

BISMARCK

BISMARCK

MAKERS OF THE NINETEENTH CENTURY
Edited by Basil Williams

BISMARCK

BY

C. GRANT ROBERTSON, M.A., C.V.O.

FELLOW OF ALL SOULS COLLEGE, OXFORD

LONDON
CONSTABLE AND COMPANY LTD

First Published 1918
Reprinted 1919
Reprinted 1929

Printed in Great Britain by
Lowe & Brydone (Printers) Limited, Park Street, Camden Town, N.W.1

GENERAL EDITOR'S PREFACE

No task is harder for the historian of to-day than to write in a manner worthy of his great calling on any subject even remotely connected with the war. It is close to us at every moment of our lives, our interests are so bound up with it and our affections are so involved in it, that the temptation to interpret every recent event solely according to its supposed influence on the war becomes nearly irresistible. And real disservice may come to the cause which we have at heart from yielding to this temptation ; for it leads to the selection of facts to accord with a theory, as opposed to the true historical method of building up the theory on an accumulation of facts. The pamphlet or book with a polemical purpose which results from the former method, however truthful and just, is never wholly convincing except to the man who requires no persuasion, and at best succeeds only in heartening the converted ; whereas the true history gradually moulds the opinion of the world.

No subject would be found more adapted for an easy polemic at this time than a life of Bismarck. But this volume is not of that kind. Mr. Grant Robertson justly claims that it is not a mere product of the war, but that it is based on exhaustive study and ideas already formed in the period of calm before this storm burst upon the nations. Here is a book that calls up Bismarck as a living human being, extenuating, it is true, none of his grossness or his arrogance, but nevertheless deeply appreciative

B.   a 2 of all that was great in him, and all that was tender and sincere. Based on such a foundation of insight and sympathy, it can pronounce a judgment on the value of his life to Germany and the world, which can no more be ignored by a German than by an Englishman. Nay more, history written in this spirit and on such a subject is, in fact, most illuminating in our attempts to form a sound judgment on these critical times and the causes of this war. For the upheaval of the last three years cannot be traced back simply to the events of a few weeks in July and August 1914, but to influences extending back for decades. Of these influences, the most powerful both on German character and statecraft, and on the conception of German policy held in other countries, is without question that of Bismarck.

BASIL WILLIAMS.

LONDON,
February 1918.

AUTHOR'S PREFACE

THIS book does not profess to be a history of Germany from 1815 to 1890, nor is it specifically a biography. It is a study, approximately in biographical form, of Bismarck's statecraft and of Bismarck himself as one of the Makers of Modern Europe and of the German nation and Empire.

It is in no sense a product of the war. My study of, and interest in, Bismarck began many years before there was a thought of war, and the conclusions and judgments expressed in the following pages were formed before August 4, 1914. The war indeed has retarded the completion of my task by the imposition of much work in no way connected with the historical research and literary labour required for a prolonged examination of the available material.

The origin of the book goes back to the lectures of Albert Sorel and E. Lavisse that I attended, after I took my degree, in the École Libre des Sciences Politiques at Paris and to various courses in the University of Berlin. Since then, repeated visits to Germany enabled me to pursue my investigations, to discuss with many—soldiers and politicians—who knew Bismarck well, and to study at first hand, and not merely in Germany, the Bismarckian system.

For no political figure, ancient or modern, does there exist original material more embarrassingly rich than for Bismarck. While in no way wishing to underrate the help obtainable from the leading secondary authorities, I have endeavoured throughout to base my conclusions on an independent study at first hand of the original sources. As the scope of the Series in which this volume appears does not admit of elaborate references, I must refer the reader to the Bibliography in an appendix for information as to the character, value, and extent of those sources ; but that bibliography by no means exhausts the evidence it has been necessary to examine. I have been obliged also to exclude much matter and to be very sparing of the critical discussions on which many of my conclusions are based. Judgments which take a few lines to express have frequently involved many months of sifting and reflection. Nor can the problems with which Bismarck was concerned be fully grasped if attention is confined to State papers, letters, memoirs, and diplomatic documents.

I much regret that the second volume of Sir A. Ward's *History of Germany* did not appear until my MS. was in the printer's hands, and most of it already in type. I have therefore only been able to refer to it in the Bibliography. The Master of Peterhouse will permit me the pleasure of saying that no living British scholar has a wider or deeper knowledge of German history (and not merely in the nineteenth century), and of expressing the hope that before long his third volume, covering the last twenty years of Bismarck's Chancellorship, will shortly be published.

It only remains gratefully to acknowledge the help of two friends. To Captain Basil Williams, author of the standard *Life of William Pitt, Earl of Chatham,* and General Editor of the Series in which this book is included, I am indebted for valuable criticisms and suggestions. Mr.

J. A. R. Marriot, M.P., with whom I was privileged to collaborate in *The Evolution of Prussia*, has found time amidst exacting Parliamentary and national labours to read my proofs and give me the benefit of his political and historical knowledge. But while I have profited much from the help of both these experts, they are not responsible for the judgments or statements in the pages they have read. For the Index I am indebted to another friend and former pupil, Miss M'Call.

C. G. R.

ALL SOULS COLLEGE,
February 1918.

CONTENTS

BISMARCK

CHAPTER I

GERMANY AND THE GERMAN PROBLEM, 1815-1848

BISMARCK was born on April 1, 1815, and died on July 30, 1898. His life and political career, therefore, cover the nineteenth century proper, reckoned from the final act of the Revolutionary and Napoleonic drama, with its consummation in the Congress and Treaties of Vienna. Bismarck as a figure in history has a twofold significance : by the accomplishment of German unification and the foundation of a German Empire under Prussian hegemony he succeeded, where so many had failed, in solving the German problem of the nineteenth century ; he altered the fundamental framework of the State system, as well as the map, of Europe. In 1871 the political capital of Continental Europe, hitherto either Paris or Vienna, was established beyond dispute at Berlin, and the European State system was remodelled by the creation of a Central German Empire expressed in the supremacy of a militarist and industrialised Prussia over a Germany unified on a federal basis. Each of these two results was a revolution. In combination they made a new Europe and a new world of political relations, thought and action. Bismarck's life and statesmanship, therefore, provide a study of the origins, principles, methods and consequences of this double revolution.

The nature of the historical problem is the essence of the story. It is easy to see the solution stamped on Europe in 1871, and to draw out its manifold moral. It is no less easy, and probably more tempting, to emphasise the logical character of each stage in the evolution, and the inevitability of the final result. Our generation forgets that, until Sedan had been fought and won, until the dramatic scene in the Galérie des Glaces at Versailles on January 18, 1871, had been played out and the German Reichstag with a German Emperor and an Imperial Chancellor had met at Berlin, no one, even twenty years before 1871, foresaw or could have foreseen, no one predicted or could have predicted, the precise form of the final result. It is easy to ignore the plain truth that the Germany of 1815 or 1848 or 1861 might have been unified at a different time in a different way with different objects, and with very different results, both for Germany and for Europe. The Bismarckian solution was not a predetermined and inevitable event in world history. The earnest and high-minded Germans of so many conflicting schools of thought, who from 1815 onwards worked so hard and sacrificed so much to achieve a German unity in fundamental contradiction to that established in 1871, no less than Bismarck himself, were aware that it was not the inevitable, but rather the unexpected, which ultimately came to pass.

Bismarck's career, indeed, illustrates throughout the truth, not too familiar even to historical students, that the chief difficulty of a scientific interpretation of events does not lie in an analysis of the solution, but in a reconstruction of the successive phases of the problem. In Bismarck's statesmanship, the man and the problem, and their subtle and continuous reaction each on the other—these are the marrow of the matter. And by non-German students who have not inherited the categories of thought and feeling, the traditions and outlook on life intuitive in the German mind, or experienced the political conditions in which the German people from 1815 onwards lived and aspired, the German problem of the nineteenth century has to be laboriously reconstructed. The lamentable absence of knowledge of the real Germany and the obsession of preconceived ideas in the France of the Bourbon Restoration, of the Orleanist Monarchy and the Second Empire, brought disaster to France. The no less lamentable ignorance of English statesmen, of our press that made public opinion, and of the British nation that did not wish to be instructed, if the instruction required a painful readjustment of accepted beliefs, was responsible for repeated humiliations, the misuse or loss of unrivalled opportunities and ultimately for a situation fraught with peril.

The British people, indeed, blind to the unperceived foundation of the British Empire in the intellectual toil of its best minds, and to the continuous influence of ideas on its political evolution, is impatient of all invitations to correlate, even in outline, the salient features of German political and philosophical speculation to the political history of nineteenth-century Germany. Fichte and Hegel, Humboldt, Savigny and Clausewitz, Novalis, Schelling and Schopenhauer, Haller, Ranke and Stahl, the *Kreuzzeitung* and the men of 1848, Dahlmann, Gervinus, Gneist, Blüntschli, von der Goltz and the young Treitschke—that vast and repellent mass of ' dead ' metaphysics, law, ethics and political philosophy so copiously produced by German minds and explored with the patience and zeal of national science by German erudition, the British mind instinctively feels has little bearing on Bismarck, the man of action, the apostle of ' blood and iron,' who solved by the sword a problem that would have been simple but for the metaphysicians, the professors and the pamphleteers. Bismarck, we are continually reminded, shared with Napoleon a supreme contempt for 'idealogues,' who darkened counsel by their nebulous fantasies—children in politics, fitted for academic class-rooms and the editorial camera obscura, incapable of governing or making the policy of States. Yet no one knew better than Bismarck that the theories and ideals of the aristocracy of intellect, the political programme of the university chair and the cry of the class-room made the Germany and the Germans of his day. The transition from the junker of 1849 to the statesman of 1862 lay in his discovery that the new Germany was the Germany that counted, and the new Germany was the Germany somehow to be unified. The master of a *Realpolitik* reckoned amongst the realities —the true *ponderabilia* of each successive situation—the German mind, as political speculation had made it and as a statesman responding to the ideals could exploit it. His debt to the 'idealogues' was greater than he ever publicly admitted. Meinecke, for example, in his *Weltbürgertum und Nationalstaat*—an illuminating study of the evolution of German political thought from Fichte to the new era of William II.—has proved how much of the alleged originality of Bismarck's federal solution in 1866 and 1871 was an adaptation from principles suggested by the despised Liberal leaders of 1848, and how impossible the Bismarckian adaptation would have been but for this intellectual travail of the 'idealogues' between 1848 and 1871. Countless memoirs, hundreds of pages of reports, the serried phalanx of Bismarck's letters and speeches, furnish proofs. From the spring of his irresponsible Junkertum to the magisterial utterances in the autumn of his Chancellorship —in the Landtag at Berlin, the Diet at Frankfurt, the Memoranda from the Embassies at Paris and St. Petersburg, the Reichstag of the North German Confederation and the Empire—Bismarck fought, dagger out of sheath, a truceless battle of ideas and of political and constitutional principles. He fought impartially with the Jacobins of the German Revolution, with Liberals, Unitarians and Federalists, with the conservative cosmopolitanism of the Holy Alliance and with the Prussianism of his dearest friends, with Catholic ultramontanism, secular liberalism and social democracy, with the conception of political parochialism (*Kleinstaaterei*) and local dynasticism, with Pan - German nationalism, and anti - German cosmopolitanism. These titanic collisions of ideas with ideas, the contests of informed wills with informed wills, the fifty years' struggle for the soul and mind of the German people, cannot be dismissed as an irrelevant battle of bloodless shades for bloodless shadows, nor blown to an empty air by the trumpets of Rézonville. The German mind had to be made and remade in a prolonged intellectual travail and an unending political duel before the foundations of the solid house that Bismarck's Germany acknowledged he had built for the German nation could be well and surely laid. *Tantae molis erat,* indeed. The picture of Bismarck as simply the demonic man of action is false

and unjust—unjust because it dwarfs the man and elim-
inates much that is most significant in his conception of
life and in his work—false because it unduly simplifies the
magnitude and complexity of his task. It is no less false
and unjust to the ideals of the defeated and to the conquered causes which pleased neither Bismarck nor, in the
end, the high gods.

The German problem, in short, was as much constitutional as political—and in the constitutional labyrinth
lurked theories, ideals and formulæ more formidable and
intractable than the institution and machinery which
made the Germany of 1815.

In 1815 Germany was constituted as a loose confederation (a Staaten-Bund) of thirty-nine States of very different
sizes, strength and system of government. The Federal
Act which defined the constitution was the result of, and
imposed by, the European Congress of Vienna. The
Settlement was a defeat alike of the unitarian and federalist
schemes of the Nationalists, either Prussian or in close
sympathy with Prussia. Its object was to provide the
Germany of 1815 with an organisation which would combine the preservation of the individual sovereignty,
independence and inviolability of each of the participating States with a guarantee of external and internal
peace for the confederation as a whole. The framework
of the Settlement of 1815 proved that the authors were
more influenced by the desire to provide securities against
the dangers of the past than to anticipate the evolution of the future. The Revolutionary and Napoleonic
period had proved the complete failure of the defunct
Holy Roman Empire to maintain the security and integrity of that Empire against foreign aggression, to prevent
its members from making war on each other, or from
entering into alliances with foreign Powers, detrimental
to the interests of Germany as a whole. It had permitted leagues such as the Napoleonic Confederation of the
Rhine, by which two-thirds of Germany passed under the

organised control of a foreign sovereign and placed its
military and economic resources at the disposal of a foreign
dictator. Hence, in the new confederation the Member-
States were forbidden to make war on each other, to conclude separate alliances with foreign Powers, while their
membership was conditioned by mutual guarantees of the
several territorial possessions included in the Union.

The Federal Act and the Federal Constitution implied
the existence of a common German interest, and the duty
of Germany organised in the League of Thirty-Nine
States to promote and defend it. It was not only a
German but a European duty. The interest of Europe
required the organisation of the German States for
certain common purposes ; the settlement arrived at in
a European congress recognised the interest of Europe in
providing the organisation and maintaining it.

There has always been a German problem. There
always will be. In 1815 the heart of the matter is reached
by two questions : How far did the new confederation
meet the requirements of Germany and of Europe ?
What provision, if any, was made for adaptation to future
and unforeseen needs or demands, either specifically German
or more generally European ?

It is easy to pile up a formidable indictment against the
German work of the Congress of Vienna, particularly from
the relentless criticism of a later generation, which reckons
the Settlement of 1815 as one of the *injuriae temporum*
inflicted by heartless diplomatists and malevolent European
Powers on a hapless and helpless Germany—and to show
that it had every imaginable defect.

It is not difficult to prove that the Settlement was a
galling disappointment to ardent Nationalists so different
as Stein, Humboldt and Arndt, and a cause of rage to
fierce Prussian Particularists such as Blücher. All these
things and much else—are they not written in the
chronicles of great and small German historians ? It is more
relevant to the purpose in hand to analyse than to indict.

The Federal Diet, whether in the ordinary session of
seventeen delegates, or in the plenum of sixty-nine representatives in which every sovereign State was represented,

was the one effective federal institution. The Diet was not a parliament but a congress of diplomatic representatives whose votes as defined by the mandates of their governments alone could alter the fundamental laws. It was presided over by the Austrian representative, who had a casting vote. Austria, therefore, was recognised as the head of the confederation.

We must further note that : (1) There was no federal executive to execute the Diet's decrees, a duty which fell on each Member-State; (2) no federal military force existed except on paper, and all efforts, notably by Prussia after 1815, to make a federal army a reality, broke down, not only in detail but in principle : for the question of the supreme command raised the insoluble dualism of Austria and Prussia ; (3) no alteration in fundamental laws, organic institutions, individual rights or religious affairs, could be made except by a unanimous vote, *i.e.* a *liberum veto* to block change was vested in every State, however petty; (4) the governments of the States were alone represented, and the governments meant the ruling dynasties. The German people were not directly represented, nor, unless they could influence the several governments, had they any voice in federal decisions and policy. The complete failure of the Federal Diet to realise even the most modest aspirations of nascent German nationalism and a growing liberalism, was due as much to the policy of the German governments as to the inherent defects of the constitution. Had those governments been ready to utilise the powers provided in the Federal Act, the thirty years between 1815 and the Revolution of 1848 might have witnessed a progressive series of moderate reforms, which would probably have averted that revolution with all its disastrous consequences. In their anxiety to avert revolution, the governments of Germany after 1815 stored up the forces which made revolution inevitable. The Diet fell under the control of Austria, which meant under the control of Metternich. It came to be a machine for either doing nothing or dutifully registering the decree of a reactionary system, based on a particular interpretation of German, Austrian and European interests. The suspension or mutilation of liberal constitutions in the German States, the denial of a free press, the interference with individual liberty and with the freedom of thought and teaching in the universities, the hostility to all change as necessarily democratic and revolutionary, have damned the Diet with a double dose of the original sin of Metternich himself. But Metternich, who imposed this policy on a willing Emperor and a despotically governed Austria, could not have imposed it on the Federal Diet without the ready complicity of the German governments.

The Federal Constitution did not make those governments what they were; but it provided them with an effective machinery for carrying out a reactionary, centrifugal and particularist policy. Popular representation and control were on principle excluded. But had the Federal Act set up a truly Federal Parliament and a truly Federal Ministry, it is practically certain that the quarrels between 1815 and 1848 would have been continuous and irreconcilable. So deep was the antagonism between the principles of the dynasties and the popular conception of government, so profound the economic and constitutional differences between the several States, so keen the jealousies and fears of the dynasties—so disunited were the nationalist or popular parties in political principles and ends—that Germany would have been rent by secessions or plunged into a civil war from which France, Russia and Great Britain could not have held aloof.

Federalism, as a system of political organisation, it must be remembered, and as a political solution for the administrative difficulties of modern States, was in 1815 in its infancy; Europe in 1815 had neither thought out the theory and principles, nor acquired the political experience required for its successful establishment. The literature and experience of 1917 are relatively rich in both respects; but even in 1917 there are obvious gaps which the political life of the United States, of the modern German Empire, of the Dominions of Canada and Australia, and the Swiss Republic do not automatically fill. And the Germany of 1815 was not only and necessarily poor in the philosophy, literature and experience of federalism : it had but recently revived its education in political philosophy and speculation. The new Germany was henceforward asking with increasing earnestness and thoroughness fundamental questions : What under modern conditions is a State ? What is its basis ? What are its rights ? Whence does it derive its authority, and over whom, and to what extent ? What are the relations of a State with other States ? What are the laws or principles of the evolution of States ? What is nationality ? What are the respective values of States based on civilisation (*Kulturstaat*), States based on political or governmental unity (*Einheitsstaat*), States based on nationality (*Nationalstaat*) ? What is the ethical and political import of citizenship based on cosmopolitan ideals (*Weltbürgertum*) as opposed to citizenship conditioned and restricted by the claims of race, the territorial State and the individual as such ? Hard questions, indeed, the answering of which might well tax the best brains and the ripest political experience of Germany for two generations to come.

The worst defect of the Federal Constitution was not its failure to realise conceptions of German unity, immature and limited by the exceptional experience of the Napoleonic and Revolutionary era, nor its curtailment of freedom of thought and political liberty, but its complete failure to provide a sobering and stimulating political education for the educated middle class of a loosely united German nation. The Germany of 1815 had passed through an abnormal ordeal since 1789. But the men of 1848, intellectually able, of a high sincerity and purpose, fired by an inspiring idealism without which no nation has ever achieved what endures, were as fettered by political inexperience as were the men who made the French Revolution. They had not learned what government demands, because all means for learning the lesson had been denied them, both on principle and as a fact. The Germany which produced scholars such as Savigny, Boeckh, Lachmann, Bopp, the two Schlegels, the two Humboldts, the brothers Grimm, and Gesenius; in science,

Ritter, von Baer, Gauss, Oersted, Liebig, Virchow and
Helmholtz ; in history, Niebuhr, Ranke, Waitz, Pertz and
Böhmer ; in theology, Schleiermacher, Strauss, Baur and
Döllinger ; in art, Rauch, Cornelius and Kaulbach ; in
music, Schubert, Schumann, Spohr, Mendelssohn and
Meyerbeer ; and in philosophical thought, minds so
powerful and original as those of Hegel, Schelling,
Schopenhauer, Herbart, Clausewitz and List—the Germany that witnessed the zenith and sunset of Goethe's
genius and the career of Heine, was singularly deficient
in statesmen of the first order and in the literature, as
distinct from the philosophy, of politics. It was a marvellous spring in a nation's intellectual growth, with the
pageant of its intellectual summer to come after 1848—
but the sources and masters of its political wisdom were
English or French.

It is no less striking how German statesmen from
Metternich to Bismarck and von Bülow, while extolling
the supremacy of German intellect, have denied to the
mass of their countrymen political capacity—forgetting
that the development of political capacity in a nation is
as much a question of opportunity as of ability. The
science and art of government are more exacting even
than the science and arts of the intellectual and imaginative life. If ability is a necessary condition, a free field
for its exercise, the remorseless tests of criticism, failure and
responsibility are even more indispensable for citizenship
than for thinkers, scholars and artists. The worst of all
schools for a nation's political life are irresponsible politicians appealing to a disfranchised, uninstructed, irresponsible and alienated public opinion. Nations generally pay
a heavier price for their sins of omission than for their
sins of commission. For the Germany of 1815-48 the
exclusion of its educated middle-class from an active and
corporate share in political life is the gravest indictment
that Metternich and the system of Metternich incur.[1]

---

[1] Hohenlohe (*Mem.*, i. 109) wrote : ' In south-western Germany the idea
of unity is regarded as a matter of life and death, and is the unceasing object of
anxious thought to politicians and eager excitement to the masses . . . the
true cause lies in the fact—more or less consciously recognised—that the greater
portion of the German nation has no voice in determining its destinies.' (1847.)

The political problems and difficulties of the German Confederation after 1815 were further complicated by the peculiar character of its component members. Luxemburg united to the ruling house of the new Netherlands kingdom was a member of the confederation : the King of Denmark as Duke of Schleswig-Holstein was represented for Holstein but not for Schleswig : Hanover until 1837 was united to the British Crown, and after 1837, though the personal union of the Hanoverian and British Crowns was severed, the connection with the British royal house was of the closest : Oldenburg was dynastically connected with the reigning house of Russia : the house of Saxe-Coburg in 1830 provided the new kingdom of Belgium with its sovereign, and in 1840 the British Queen with a Prince-Consort, reinforcing the British interest in and influence on German affairs : the whole of the kingdom of Prussia was not included in the confederation : and the Empire of Austria was only represented for ' the German ' parts of the Empire.

The Federal Diet, in consequence, was composed of diplomatic representatives from States purely Germanic and from States only partially so, the interests of which were frequently determined by non-German, or anti-German, considerations. The Diet, therefore, directly or indirectly, was brought into close relation with the most delicate and difficult problems of European policy. Apart from the European origin of the Federal Constitution, Austria, Prussia, Russia, Great Britain, the Netherlands, and Denmark had the right and the interest to intervene effectively in the deliberations and actions of the Diet, and such intervention would not spring from purely Germanic considerations. The history of the problems of Poland, Schleswig-Holstein, Luxemburg, of Slavonic, or Magyar, or Italian Austria, are a continuous commentary on this anomalous situation. In short, it was impossible to solve these problems either by the Federal Diet alone or without its co-operation.

One great European State alone, France, was excluded from all share—and its exclusion pointed unmistakably to a fresh phase of the historic struggle for the control of the Rhine. The creation of the German Confederation registered 'a Germany unredeemed' and a France unsatisfied. The refusal of the Prussian demand in 1814 for 'the restoration' of Alsace and Lorraine had been balanced by the removal of France from the Rhenish Provinces occupied since 1795. But the French flag on Strasburg and Metz, the federal flag on the fortress of Mainz, and the Prussian flag at Coblenz, signalised baffled ambition and inextinguishable ideals for French and German patriots. Neither France nor Germany could regard the Treaties and Settlement of 1815 as the last word. Any remodelling, therefore, of the Federal Constitution of 1815, any alteration of the composition or powers of the German Confederation, touched every live wire in the European State system.

The Settlement of 1815 had made the German problem an international problem. The unification of Germany, even more than the unification of Italy, could not be effected without a revolution in the European State system defined by the Vienna treaties.

No less could it be accomplished without an internal revolution in Germany and the formation of a new German mind. The system of Metternich had the merit of clearly conceived principles adapted to secure precise ends. The maintenance, moreover, of a *status quo* has all the advantages of the defensive in war. On the side of the conservative forces were vested interests, historic traditions, established institutions, the dynasties, and a bitter experience of revolution. Everywhere in Europe from the Neva to the Seine, from the Tagus to Copenhagen, fire and sword had done their fell work. Since 1789, the horror of war was subtly interlaced with the horror of revolution. A Europe emaciated in spirit and resources by twenty-five years of unbroken struggle, felt that peace was worth having at any price, and that liberty could be purchased too dearly. And Europe (excluding the Ottoman Empire) had peace for nearly forty years.

The succeeding thirty years accomplished much in formulating demands, and clothing them with precision

and clear objectives, which it is easier to appreciate to-day
than in 1848. The horror of war and the fear of revolution had slowly evaporated. The young generation
was open to persuasion that there were far worse things
than war : that peace could be purchased by sacrifices
too costly for individual, State and nation, and that when
other means were unavailable or futile, revolution was
justifiable and necessary. The solid achievements of
German brains in every department of human activity
had implanted in the educated German mind certain
potent convictions : that what had already been accomplished by German brains in philosophy, classical scholarship, in philology, literature, history, the physical sciences
and the æsthetic arts, was as nothing to what could be
accomplished in all these departments if German brains
could have a freer field and a purer air to work in ; that
in political no less than in the intellectual life, German
brains would show their creative powers ; that the future
lay open to the highest ' kultur ' nation, true to its mission
and the obligation to realise its civilised self ; that the
primacy in science and civilisation, once Italian, French
or British, was unmistakably passing to the German
nation ; and fourthly, that there was a causal relation
between the efficacy of a nation's form of government and
its efficacy in national science (*Wissenschaft*) in its finest
and broadest sense. No less significant, the renaissance
of the German universities were both cause and effect
of the renaissance of the German people. Prussia, in its
hour of humiliation after Jena, founded the University
of Berlin. The firm belief of the Prussian reformers,
building greater than they knew, was that the moral regeneration of the kingdom demanded no less imperatively
an intellectual regeneration ; Breslau in Silesia was made
a university town in 1815, and the re-hoisting of the
Prussian flag in the enlarged Rhenish Provinces was
emphasised by the reconstitution of the University of
Bonn. The foundation of universities as a memorial of
victory in the field and as indispensable organs of national
strength and unification, remains a remarkable element in
Prussian statecraft.

Outside Prussia, Heidelberg, Göttingen, Jena, Leipzig, Munich, Tübingen, were especially distinguished. A full generation before the Zollverein accomplished in 1868 the economic unity of Germany, the universities had achieved a unity of culture impressive as much for the solidarity of its foundations as for the tenacity of its grip on the German mind.

The brotherhood of German learning brought about the brotherhood of German learners. The Bavarian who came to Berlin to attend the courses of a Ranke or a Savigny, the Prussian who had heard Dahlmann at Göttingen or Droysen at Kiel, the Saxon who went to Strauss or Baur at Tübingen or Döllinger at Munich had realised that Germany was not a geographical expression, and that there were spiritual and intellectual bonds uniting all Germans which kings, diplomatists and treaties could not mar or destroy. In any young generation a settled conviction that ideas are power, the most potent because the most pervasive of all realities, will always develop a high-explosive political force. Epigrams on professors are as easy as they are popular ; and the German professoriate is the unfailing butt of the Philistine of every nation ; but in an epoch when young Germany was dreaming dreams and seeing visions, it was an inestimable service to the German mind that in the class-rooms of the universities German youth was taught by men who had a right to be heard the value of knowledge for knowledge's sake, and learned the lesson that national supremacy in science, whether of language, literature, history, or the physical world, could only be acquired by the severest self-discipline and the most exacting thoroughness —by toil, silence and endurance. The German professor had a German audience, outside his class-room, fit and certainly not few. Savigny's and Ranke's pamphlets, *France and Germany, The Division and Unity of Germany, The Great Powers,* are examples of the fermenting influences that could distil from an academic pen. And they could be multiplied at will. Carlyle said that the skins of the French aristocracy bound the second edition of Rousseau's works : it was not only the skins of

French aristocrats which bound the later editions of many German works of learning.

Through historical research, above all, the German nation rediscovered its past and read in it a guarantee of the future. The German people learned from the path-making science of the Grimms, Bopp, Pertz, Waitz, Giesebrecht, von Maurer, Gervinus and Dahlmann, how deep were their roots in the past, and what great intellectual and political achievements the German race had wrought. From the dim centuries of warring tribalism emerged the illumination of the Teutonic genius of Charles the Great, who combined the Central Empire, which formed the legacy of Imperial Rome, with the gifts of the Teutonic mind. Germany was bidden to march through the cycle of the Middle Ages, illustrious with imperial rulers—Carolingian, Saxon, Franconian, Hohenstaufen, Luxemburg, Habsburg—and to note how a Holy Roman Empire of the German nation had preserved for civilisation the religious, moral, political and intellectual unity of Europe under the wings of the Teutonic Eagle ; to recall the winning for Christ and the German conception of civilisation from Lithuanian, Wend, Slav and Avar of the Baltic lands almost to the banks of the Neva ; to ponder on Vienna and the marches of the East—barriers against Magyar and Turk. It was re-taught the inexhaustible services of the German Reformation and German Protestantism to the free and critical spirit of man ; it was invited to contrast the two centuries of internecine strife and political degradation ushered in by the Thirty Years' War and the bondage of the German nation to foreign masters, until Lessing and Winckelmann in the sphere of mind, Frederick the Great in the sphere of facts, pointed the way to a promised land beyond the wilderness in which they had wandered. Poetry, philology, comparative mythology and folk-lore, the comparative study of institutions, palæography and the archives, the philosophy of law—history in its widest streams, explored and mapped by the severest science—were exhibited to enforce a single moral—the greatness of the German contribution to the civilisation of the past, a greatness in proportion to its fidelity to its racial and national character, and the certainty that a similar fidelity in the future would produce no less momentous results for Germany and humanity. Arndt could proclaim that the healing of the world would be found in the German spirit.

The grandeur and unity of the German race sank deep into the hearts of a disillusioned generation. The German mind, it concluded, had been at its best when Europe had been politically organised round a German Empire, with West and East duly subordinated to the central framework. The 'natural frontiers' claimed by France were a denial of geography, and an insolent outrage on the natural rights of the indivisible German nation. Did not the renaissance of the German spirit require the racial unity of the German people to be expressed once more in a national and central political organisation ? Slowly but surely the mind of the new Germany became imbued with the doctrine and ideas of nationalism, rooted in the reinforced concrete of racial origins and the laws of political evolution, imposing as a corollary the duty of freeing all Germans from the servitude of non-German political or intellectual domination. Wherever Germans of a common speech, race, and literature lived, whether in the artificial Confederation of 1815 or outside it, wherever such Germans were prevented from realising their national and racial self—that was unredeemed Germany. The ideal of a national State in a free nation was thus built up, line upon line, precept upon precept. The doctrine of political salvation by fidelity to racial unity—the creed of the Nationalists—had its complement in the doctrine of salvation through political rights and personal freedom—the creed of the Liberals.

In its origins, liberalism and the liberal movement were separate from, and anterior to, the intellectual renaissance. French and English formative influences were jointly mingled. The theory of natural rights, intrinsic and superior to any other rights, however acquired, democratic government, the basis of the State not in authority, custom or prescription, but in the indivisible and inalienable sovereignty of the nation, law as the expression of an infallible general will—these and kindred basic ideas were mainly derived from the French Revolution and the principles of 1789. The study of English history and the English Constitution—the development of a kindred Teutonic race—provided a practical programme :—Limited State authority, representative institutions, a popular and statutory suffrage, ministerial responsibility, financial control of the executive by the representative chamber, government in accordance with the will of a majority, free to choose, a system of local self-government linked with the central government, an unfettered press, an independent judiciary and statutory guarantees for the liberty of the individual citizen against executive abuse of power. The liberal movement exhibited many forms and combinations from the extreme radicalism of the theoretical Republicans to the moderate programme of a limited monarchy of the English type. The movement was strongest in the southern States, which had been most deeply saturated with French revolutionary thought, but it was remarkably active also in the Rhenish Provinces, in Hanover and Weimar, and even in West and East Prussia, while the universities generally were centres of a powerful doctrinaire constitutionalism. English political development since 1832 was influential in shaping the ideas of the schools of Bunsen, Stockmar, the elder von Maurer and Gneist, and subsequently of National Liberalism. Three characteristics in particular are worth noting : the demand for a larger measure of personal liberty, secured by law ; the importance attached to fundamental constitutional rights (*Grundrechte*), generalised as principles but defined in a written constitution which should settle the character of the State ; the ideals of unification through a common law, and common and uniform constitutional rights. The liberal movement, whatever its variety or its source, thus linked hands with the nationalist creed. Both were incomplete unless the unifying forces they both represented were united for common ends in a common organisation. Unity on a racial basis required unity in the organs and powers of the State to satisfy scientific theory and practical needs.

Combined they met the argument of the earlier thinkers, such as Humboldt, that the particularism of Germany was an essential condition of a manifold cultural development, free from the obstacles of a rigid uniformity. For in the national and free polity of the future Rhinelander, Hanoverian, Prussian, Saxon, Bavarian and Franconian would develop his particular culture far more advantageously than in the cramped limits and restricted air of any single German State, however strong and self-sufficing. The national and sovereign authority of the unified German State would be the Universal Ordinary, deliberately permitting local variety and territorial differences, not incompatible with obedience to the fundamental laws of the unified whole.

Another and more potent change had been wrought. The philosophy of thought and action was ceasing to be purely speculative and becoming more definitely political, concentrating on political ends and means, as intrinsically more important and practical. The earlier conception of the functions and mission of the German race simply to be a 'kultur-nation' and organise a 'Kultur-Staat' was steadily superseded by the conception of a mission to be a political Power vested with the function to organise a State-polity corresponding to that high purpose : or, more accurately perhaps, the new conception was superimposed on the old. The conception of the supreme necessity and worth of the 'kultur'-nation and State was retained, but relegated to a secondary place. Deeper analysis and wider experience did not deny the duty of the German people to realise this spiritual and intellectual purpose : they enforced the conclusion that in the world-movement political power and the State as the supreme expression of power, right, law and liberty had a higher ethical value, and must be first realised in order to provide the full means for the development of spiritual, intellectual and moral excellence. For Truth, the philosophers emphasised, is only fully grasped not independently of, but through, a progressive realisation. Nationalism and liberalism effected the transition from the old attitude to the new, and in a reconciling synthesis would bring the activities and aspirations of young Germany on to the plane of development reached by the great political Nation-States, France and England.

But in the workaday world there were cruel burrs and briars, and, as Rosalind said, these were in the heart. First and foremost were the Federal Constitution and the Federal Diet. When the young Prince Hohenlohe, a cultivated Roman Catholic Bavarian noble, in 1847 called the Diet the bed in which Germany had slumbered for thirty years, when he noted that travels in the East were a humiliation for a German, because French, English, Russians, Austrians, even Turks commanded respect as members of powerful States, while the German had no State and no power as such, when he saw the British and French and Russian flags at sea, national flags symbolising national power, when, as Treitschke said, the German sailed the sea like a pirate without a national flag, he only voiced the inarticulate cry of millions of Germans, conscious of what they were accomplishing, but damned to impotence by the inertia and meanness of thought which the Diet incarnated. A fierce sense of political degradation, all the fiercer because it was combined with this consciousness of power within, and of achievement, had gripped the new Germany. Great empires and little minds indeed go ill together. The littleness of the minds in the Federal Diet exasperated a Germany aware that the great minds were everywhere except in the councils of the nation. The astonishing spring and summer of 1848 are only explicable by a passionate conviction that, whatever took its place, the Federal Diet and all it stood for must go; and go for ever. Germans had the right of other free nations to a share in their own government, to make a Germany and place her as a State on an equality with other States : they had a future and a right to determine it.

Secondly, the national enemy was France. Nothing is more arresting, alike in the thirty years that followed 1815 and the twenty that followed 1848, than the continuous revelation of the hatred and fear of France, ceaselessly simmering below the surface to break out with boiling force on the slightest provocation. Hatred and fear combined, shared by all classes, and for reasons frequently contradictory—hatred of what France had done, fear of what she certainly would do again.

Stein in 1815 wrote of France as ' the hereditary foe, the eternal, tireless, destructive enemy,' a sentiment shared by Blücher, Gneisenau and the Prussians baffled by Europe in their demand for a humiliating revenge. But the passions of the War of Liberation, nowhere so strong as in Prussia, continued to echo in the poetry of Arndt, Uhland, Uckert, Geibel ; and the map which left Alsace French vibrated with a perpetual challenge. In the international crisis of 1840 Germany was on the verge of war : three songs, Becker's ' Sie sollen ihn nicht haben, den freien Deutschen Rhein,' Hoffmann von Fallersleben's even more famous ' Deutschland, Deutschland über Alles,' and Schneckenburger's ' Die Wacht am Rhein,' passed at once into the national literature of the barracks, the schoolroom and the hearth. In 1842 the commencement of the completion of Cologne Cathedral was made a great demonstration against France. Political thought was no less anti-French. Haller, whose *Restoration of Political Science* was for a generation the Bible of orthodox conservatism, and who restated much of the authoritarian argument of French ultramontanes, such as J. de Maistre and Bonald, traced to French Jacobinism and French scepticism most of the sins and all the ills from which Europe suffered : Stahl, the brilliant Jew, who continued Haller's work and whose writings provided a philosophical basis for the romantic and pietistic conservatism of the Gerlach Circle, the *Brandenburg Political Weekly*, and the Camarilla of Frederick William IV., was no less denunciatory of French principles. Indeed, to Conservatives of all schools France was the mother of every social and political heresy, the architect of soul-destroying revolution. Even in the south-west the Liberals and Radicals repudiated their debt to French thought ; and Heine, whose *Buch der Lieder* had set all Germany singing through its tears and had inspired the marrying of immortal verse to immortal music, was held to have succumbed to the witchery of the

Gallic spirit, and lost his influence when he deserted Hamburg for Paris.

Germany, brooding over its wrongs, political, civic and racial, found in the rising forces of nationalism, so subtly fostered by Teutonic erudition, a fresh justification for the anti-French sentiment inherited from 1815. The glorification of Teutonic achievement involved that belittling of all other achievements, which is an indictment framed in self-flattery. History, whether ancient, mediæval or modern, recorded for German readers an inexhaustible catalogue of the wrongs done to Germany by alien, jealous and, in reality, inferior races and States. France was the chief author and inspirer of these crimes against Teutonic nationalism, and so there grew up in the heart of the German people the conviction, panoplied in the armoury of science, that, from the Treaty of Verdun in 843, which shattered the Carolingian Empire, to the wars and treaties of Napoleon, France and the French race were responsible for German disintegration and impotence : that until the robberies had been won back and the crimes expiated, Germany could not live in peace or enjoy her legitimate and God-given development. Even the most gracious qualities of the French mind were made items in the accusation : her literature, her philosophy and her art savoured of the diabolical. Already, thirty years before Sedan, a France frivolous, sensual, immoral, vain, sciolist, bloodthirsty and insincere, was contrasted with a Germany sober, profound, industrious, scientific, pious and peaceful, the guardian of the morals of the family and the hearth. The ever-growing demand for the extirpation of the ' Wälsch ' element in German thought, literature, the sciences and arts, rested on an exposure of the Latin races, and above all of France. Let two examples suffice : Mommsen's *Roman History* with its passionate and ill-concealed sub-current of contempt for Latin weaknesses, and Sybel's *History of the French Revolution*, which put the French nation in the dock of the *Weltgericht*. Sybel was an ardent Liberal, and Mommsen was expelled in 1850 from his chair at Leipzig for his share in the Revolution of 1848. If such was the green tree of academic science, what did not issue from the dry wood of journalists, pamphleteers and beer-garden politicians ?

The general hatred and fear of France was a strong sentimental force indirectly making for German unity. As a practical element in the German problem it was weakened by one momentous consideration. Previously and subsequent to 1848—when the simultaneous revolution in Paris, Berlin and Vienna created a unique situation in which France and Austria were helpless, a situation which alone made the Parliament of Frankfurt possible—a drastic revision of the Federal Constitution involved a general reopening of the whole Settlement of 1815, which was as galling to French as to German nationalism.

In the chancelleries of Europe, and most strongly at Vienna, the mere prospect created consternation. The Belgian question in 1831 had been localised and settled with extreme difficulty by Palmerston's dexterity and finesse, but Europe had been in measurable distance of a tremendous war. The avowed object of a general revision of the Federal Act was to make Germany stronger and more united : to prepare for a final and complete unification. That this could be carried through without reopening the question of the Rhine, 'the natural frontiers' of France, and the irreconcilable aspirations of Germany, was impossible. Belgium in 1839 had been placed under international guarantees. French expansion, blocked to the north-east, could only find its outlet in (German) Luxemburg and the Rhenish Provinces on the west bank of ' the free German Rhine.' One conclusion was certain. If Germany were strengthened, France would demand ' compensation ' ; and a completion of German unity without compensation to France spelled the decisive defeat of French ambitions and the definite elevation of Germany to a superior position. That France would accept such a defeat without war was unthinkable.

German particularism was, however, the obstacle to unification which contemporary opinion both inside and outside Germany probably regarded as the most formidable and insoluble. That particularism was a singular blend of facts ideals and sentiments, which can be disentangled but make a combination elusive and exceedingly difficult to measure. Already there was a legendary view of its origin. The German mind had persuaded itself that the 'Zersplitterung Deutschland's' was a comparatively modern fact, and that the mediæval and Reformation epoch had known a united and imperial Germany. The conviction was an erroneous conclusion from misinterpreted historical premises. And the *injuriae temporum* of the seventeenth and eighteenth centuries were injuries largely inflicted on Germany by the Germans themselves, and due to the irreconcilable racial and religious and social divisions of the old Reich and the Germans who composed it.

Particularism, in short, was a historical product and had the deepest roots in the stubborn characteristics of the German mind, which were its cause and effect. The reduction of the 360 principalities which made the map of 1789 to the 39 of the Federal Constitution, had strengthened rather than weakened the provincial territorialism which nourished a provincial patriotism; for the absorption of the pettier, and the secularisation of the ecclesiastical, principalities by the larger had enormously stimulated the ambitions and jealousies of States such as Bavaria, Württemberg, the Hesses, Nassau and Hanover, while the partition of Saxony was a menace which made the survivors in 1815 cling with the tenacity born of fear to their sovereignty and independence. Particularism was not confined to the south. The passions or prejudices it represented were as strong at Herrenhausen, Cassel or Dresden as at Munich, Karlsruhe and Stuttgart. It centred in dynasticism and the princely houses.

Bismarck in a famous chapter of his *Reminiscences*—a chapter eulogised by distinguished German historians—emphasised the existence and claims of these separate dynastic lines, each with a long history and traditions behind it, as one of the most stubborn forces for statesmanship to reckon with, and his argument is endorsed by the whole of German history before and after 1815.

German dynasticism was solemnly re-baptized at the font of legitimism in 1815, with the result that outside

Germany (as well as within) the maintenance of monarchical or princely rule was bound up with the principles of legitimate authority and recognised as providing a common basis for political conservatism in all countries and a barrier against revolution. The maintenance of even a petty German sovereign in his 'rights' appealed alike to the autocrat of all the Russias, the Pontiff of the Vatican, a Bourbon at Naples, and the constitutional sovereign of Great Britain, whose consort came from Coburg. But this dynastic particularism was the outcome and expression of deep-laid racial, cultural and economic differences. Prussian, Hanoverian, Westphalian, Saxon, Rhinelander, Franconian, Suabian, represented German types, the differentiation of whose original features had been heightened and deepened by the physical configuration of the German lands they lived in, internecine struggles, prolonged political rivalry and opposed economic needs and claims. The conception of sovereignty ratified in 1815, absolutely fatal either to a unitary or a truly federal Germany, implied the divine right of a Saxon or a Bavarian government to misgovern as against the illegitimate claim to be governed well by a 'foreign' though a German authority, and this principle was endorsed by the misgoverned.

The greater development of liberalism in the south-west than in any other region sharpened the resentment and stiffened the determination of more conservative states and rulers to resist the moral penetration of their territory by ideas made in Württemberg or Baden.

In the south-west and centre the memories of the Napoleonic Confederation of the Rhine were stronger than of the War of Liberation : although ideas in origin French did not really imply any desire for the restoration of French political domination. Prince Hohenlohe maintained that the undefiled fount of Germanism and of the present German race lay in Suabia and Franconia ; he always asserted that ' the true home of the idea of unification ' was in the south-west ; and it was a common criticism in the south that the best brains of Prussia had been recruited from non-Prussian territories : Struve, a strong republican and earnest political thinker, prophesied in 1847 that Prussia would, and must, disappear when Germany awaked to a new life. Particularism had a strong anti-Prussian side. If at Berlin the southern States were despised as mechanistic creations of Napoleonic policy, Prussia so radically different in type, structure and character from every other German State was criticised as un-German, artificial—the absolutist, militarist and bureaucratic polity in its most unattractive and dangerous form. Prussian power was a formidable reality; her absorbing capacity and appetite so plainly demonstrable; and her rulers, her administrators and her people were so occupied with justifying and proclaiming their merits and services to Germany that they forgot modesty, tact and sympathy. To the inefficient efficiency always makes an uncomfortable partner, and Prussian efficiency was heavily framed with an assertive Prussian egoism. The evolutionary beatitude—Blessed are the strong for they shall prey upon the weak—was a perpetual reminder to Prussia's neighbours that unless Naboth had powerful and disinterested friends his fate would be the fate of Silesia in 1740, of the Rhinelands and Saxony in 1815. There was only one Ahab—but there were so many Naboths whose vineyards marched with the black and white posts of the Prussian frontier.

Within the charmed circle of the Bund such a friend was to be found at Vienna alone. Clear-sighted thinkers at Stuttgart, Munich, or Karlsruhe recognised that Austrian policy was probably no less selfish than that of other States, and that Austrian growth was one long and historic appropriation clause; but in the hands of Metternich the egoism, mendacity, intrigues and duplicity of Austrian diplomacy lost through a high-bred courtesy and tact half their grossness. The King of Saxony remembered that Metternich had resisted the absorption of his kingdom and saved one half of it for its lawful owner; Bavaria, Württemberg and Baden that their sovereignty and territorial integrity were dear to the Austrian heart. The Foreign Office in the Ball-Platz at Vienna was a cave of Adullam, the doors of which were

always open to all legitimate German princes in distress
from Jacobin professors, university students afflicted by
the modern disease of reading and thinking, journalists
demanding that the press should be free, and politicians
deranged enough to regard a vote as a passport to the
millennium—above all to German princes in distress from
Prussian designs.

For Austria itself—if we could forget Prussia—epitom-
ised most of the elements in the German problem. Only
half the Austrian Empire was included in the Bund, and
that not wholly a German half, for Bohemia, Carinthia and
Carniola were not pure German, while Hungary, Galicia,
Dalmatia and the Italian provinces were excluded. The
Federal Constitution was largely her creation ; its maintenance on rigidly conservative lines had been one of the
chief objects of Metternich's policy, and the collapse
of the Federal Diet followed automatically when Austria
herself collapsed in the spring of 1848. Metternich's
copious Memoirs have drawn for posterity a full-dress
portrait of a good man consistently struggling with ad-
versity—a record of repeated success due to the victory
of high political principles over the forces of evil—of
failure inexplicably caused by the charlatanry of quacks
(such as Canning) masquerading as statesmen. Austrian
policy in Germany was indeed a subtle mixture of dynastic
pride, historic traditions, international and European
ambitions, reactionary political principles and unquenchable Austrian appetites. The unique character of the
Austrian Empire, coupled with the inflexible refusal of the
Habsburg House either to be cajoled by success or driven
by defeat from its determination to make a State out of
a European dynasty, necessitated a unique policy. The
territorial composition of the Empire, the product of a
long evolution, and the medley of races united only by
allegiance to a common sovereign which made the Austria
of 1815, brought it into the closest contact with all the
Powers and all the intellectual and political forces of
Europe. German, Italian, Pole, Czech, Little Russian,
Magyar, Rouman, Croat and Serb were combined and had
always been combined—and there is a world of significance

in the ' always '—ever since there had been an ' Austria.'
Metternich shared none of the ' delusions ' of these races :
an Italian or a German who obeyed his Imperial Master
was a good Austrian : a bad Austrian was the Italian,
Slav or German who opposed the Imperial will. Obedience, not race, was the criterion of citizenship. All the
new ideas from 1789 onwards Metternich regarded as
dangerous nonsense and frauds on a gullible European
public. It was the duty of statesmanship to expose the
fraud and extirpate the poison. But in the psychology
of Metternich's statecraft it is difficult to decide whether
Jacobinism and liberalism were bad because they threatened to destroy the historic Austria, or were destructive
of Austrian interests because they were intrinsically immoral. A professed realist in politics with his eye on the
object—before *Realpolitik* was the fashionable gospel of
representative assemblies—Metternich founded his policy
on the most incontrovertible of all realities—reason of
State—the reason peculiar to the peculiar Austrian State.
The interests of Europe were assumed to be identical with
the interests of the historic Austria. Germany was like
Italy, a geographical expression, a political distribution
of States with conflicting interests, and an Austrian hegemony over which was the form of political rule most
convenient to Europe, if exercised in accordance with
sound principles of conservatism, legitimism, and the
balance of European power.

Accordingly the Federal Constitution and the Diet were
admirably devised to achieve all these ends. They recognised the House of Habsburg in Austria as the heir to the
defunct Holy Roman Empire ; they maintained under
European sanctions the separate sovereignty and territorial independence of the German States ; they provided
an effective barrier to the west against France and to the
east against Russia, but without injuring them as great
Powers in the State system of Europe ; and last and not
least, they assigned an adequate but secondary rôle to
Prussia which shelved her illegitimate claims to equal
place with Austria in the management of Germany.
But if Austria had the hegemony, she did not demand

the institutions automatically working to impose an Austrian will on Germany. Jealous for her own, she was no less jealous for the rights of others. In the Diet, Austria, by herself, was in a hopeless minority. She could only work through and by the other members of the confederation. True, she had a veto on changes in the fundamental laws, but so had the pettiest of the federated members. Metternich, in short, relied on diplomacy, unswerving in its aim and unfettered by any scruples as to methods. His triumph over the German governments was complete enough to satisfy his exorbitant vanity. Most of his predecessors at Vienna had been able to hypnotise the electors, grand-dukes, landgraves and margraves, even when they became kings; but Metternich achieved what no Austrian statesman, neither Kaunitz, nor Thugut, nor Cobenzl, nor Stadion had achieved—he hypnotised Prussia. That accomplished, the task of imposing an Austrian policy on Germany was easy, and Metternich wisely remained content with the fact. Prussia was soothingly held up as a model of statesmanlike fidelity to correct principles. The hypnotisation of the subjects of the hypnotised governments could safely be left to the police, the censors of the press, the controlled universities and the schools. The revolutionary storm swept Metternich away, but not the ambition he represented. Metternich's successors strove faithfully to repeat his magic incantation; they even threatened with the magician's rod; but the will in Prussia to be hypnotised had been exorcised. Metternichism collapsed at Königgrätz under the blows of a Prussia which had deserted ' correct principles ' and returned to the immoral (Prussian) reason of State taught by Frederick the Great. In the new situation created in 1867 the parts were reversed. Henceforward Prussia was the hypnotiser, Austria the hypnotised. How this happened makes the ἀριστεία of Bismarck.

It was certain that as long as Austria was the Austria of 1815 and a great Power in Europe, no change could take place in the Federal Constitution without her consent, and that she would not permit changes which either challenged her presidential supremacy in Germany, or substantially altered the balance of power within the Diet, or introduced principles of government into the Germany of the federation which would detrimentally affect the administration of Austrian territories not included within the jurisdiction of the Diet. In the delicately equipoised system of checks and counter-checks, cogged into the central dynastic wheel, by which German, Italian, Slav and Magyar lands were set off against each other, the introduction into her German territories of representative institutions or democratic autonomy would create a demand for similar concessions in Hungary, Galicia and Lombardy; the concession to Germany of rights derived from the sovereign principles of nationalism involved the admission that Habsburg rule in Italy or Galicia was a violation of autonomy based on nationalism. Tested by a racial nationalism the Habsburg was an alien in three-fourths of his Empire. His rule could only be nationalised by identifying the Crown with one race and by oppressing three-fourths of his subjects in the interests of a single group. Austrian opposition, therefore, to nationalism and all its consequences was irreconcilable; it justified itself by a flat denial of the premises and conclusions of the nationalist creed and was compelled, if challenged, to suppress nationalism by force within the Austrian dominions and to resist its further recognition in the State system of Europe. The peculiar constitution and position of Austria confronted German Nationalists with an insoluble dilemma: the formation of a nationalist State of Great Germany (*Gross-Deutschland*) which would bring the whole of the Austrian dominions into a reorganised Bund, on the creation of a unitary and small Germany (*Klein-Deutschland*) from which Austria was excluded. The former solution violated the logic and sentiment of nationalism by the introduction of large blocks of non-German races into a German State; the latter sacrificed the sacred rights of the Germans of Tyrol and Austria proper to non-German and anti-German forces. It was no dilemma to the Habsburgs, for they denied the legitimacy of the demand, no less than they resisted either of the solutions suggested. Austrian interest prohibited the inclusion of the whole of the Austrian Empire within the jurisdiction of the federation, and Austrian interest and Habsburg pride peremptorily forbade the exclusion of German Austria from a German federation, however organised; and the interests of Austria were held to be the interests of Europe. Austrian policy, therefore, was a defensive maintenance of the *status quo* in perpetuity. Against the champions of every creed which demanded a revision of the system of 1815, Austria stood forward as the *Geist des stets verneint*;[1] and she entrenched her immutable negation in an organisation of cosmopolitan conservatism with common principles of universal validity registered in the public law and treaties of Europe.

In politics, time is not, as in war, on the side of a well-organised defensive, and increasingly is against it when the defensive is badly organised. The cynical advice of Prince Eugène to Charles vi. that the best guarantee of the Pragmatic Sanction was not the public pledges of the European States, but a well-drilled army and a well-filled treasury might have been remembered with profit by Metternich. The claims of nationalism and liberalism, if pressed, could not be stemmed by Carlsbad decrees, by ubiquitous police and obscurantist censors. Metternich's ignorance and neglect of finance was equalled by his ignorance and neglect of military science and administration. His blindness to the significance of a Zollverein under Prussian presidency was significant. Metternich's ignorant vanity prevented him from seeing the increasing importance of economic development, that in a policy of interests the economic may be the decisive consideration, that Prussia had stolen many marches on Vienna, and that in the near future the Austrianised middle and petty States would be driven to side with a Prussia they disliked rather than with an Austria they liked; in a word, that the Zollverein had placed Prussia at the head of an

---

[1] Beust in his *Memoirs* tells us (i. 283): 'For years the German courts were trained by Vienna and Berlin in the fear of God and of the Czar Nicholas'; and again (i. 363): 'I well remember what in the early days of my diplomatic service was the bugbear of Metternich's policy. In conversation every one feared to express a liberal opinion, as it might be reported at Vienna and ruin the speaker's future career.'

organisation which set the dualism between Austria and Germany in sharp relief. Within ten years of his expulsion from power the Austrian treasury was bankrupt, a Russian army had been required to suppress revolution in Hungary, and the shadows of Magenta and Solferino were lengthening out to the crowning doom of Sadowa. The Metternich system pointed a plain moral : conservatism and legitimism were identical with inefficiency.

Austrian supremacy in Germany rested on an identity of interest with the princes and the power of their governments. Of the deeper forces, running each year with a swifter current beneath the tessellated bed of the Diet, Metternich knew little and cared less. Of political thinkers he had a poor opinion and a poorer knowledge. They might be useful as the drudges and typists of the high diplomacy, hereditary in a hereditary aristocracy. At best, Gentz and Haller were intellectual flies on the great wheels of statecraft. Metternich was as incapable of appreciating a Humboldt, a Hegel, a Ranke, a Giesebrecht, a Grimm or a Pertz as he was of appreciating Gioberti, Mazzini or Manzoni. Hence, he never saw the increasing peril that beset the Austrian defensive in the manifold intellectual renaissance of Germany outside Austria, nor the combination of moral fibre and racial passion which that prolonged intellectual preparation was stamping on the German nation. 'They tell me,' said Napoleon, ' we have no literature. I must speak to the Minister of the Interior about it.' Literature, other than the belles-lettres of high-bred salons, was for Metternich an affair of the Minister of Education, working with a copious *Index Expurgatorius*. Universities, professors, pamphleteers, a public which read and thought—ideas as the forces which can make and unmake States and policies —scientific knowledge (*Wissenschaft*) providing the criteria and ends of political activity—these made the malady of the time, a time singularly out of joint. That Austria had lost the intellectual and moral sympathy of the Germany which worked outside the palaces and the bureaux of the princelets, and that Austrian apathy was daily digging a chasm between the governments and their subjects, Metternich did not grasp until the roar of the Viennese crowd shook the windows of his palace and sent him panic-stricken into exile. The ideal of Germany as a ' kultur '-nation he interpreted as many who had read Madame de Staël's *De l'Allemagne* and nothing else persisted in interpreting it till 1914—a nation blameless, bourgeois, pedantic and unpolitical—mainly composed of spectacled professors, philosophers as nebulous as the smoke of their tobacco, long-haired musicians and university students singing the ' Wacht am Rhein ' because the Rhine wine and flaxen-haired Gretchens had got into their sentimental heads—that old Germany on which Heine could lay the whip-cord of his affection because he knew that it no longer, and probably never had, existed. But to the new Germany the conception of a unified Teutonic ' kultur '-nation meant remorseless struggles for a presidential place in the Areopagus of civilisation, and its realisation was the pre-condition of a unified *Machtstaat* and a unifying *Machtpolitik*—the State and the policy that were German power.

Young Germany by 1840 was asking, ' What has Austria done for *our* German civilisation ; and what is she doing now to-day ? What is Austria contributing to *our* German literature, *our* ideas, *our* knowledge, *our* political philosophy ? What is the share of the University of Vienna in the intellectual life of Germany, compared with that of Berlin, Bonn, Heidelberg, Göttingen, Munich and Tübingen ? ' Vienna, indeed, could point to the dramatists Grillparzer and Benedix, Weber and a home for Beethoven (who was not an Austrian), the waltzes of the elder Strauss and Güngl, and the waning reputation of the Medical School. There was a splendid renascence in Bohemia and Hungary, but it was national, anti-Austrian and anti-German. Austria, in the eyes of many in Germany, contributed nothing of real weight to the serious criticism of life, nothing that guided through the darkness to the splendour of the dawn, breaking red on the horizon. In the majestic march of the German mind to conquest, Austria lagged with the vivandières and the camp-sutlers. Her institutions were obsolete ; her policy and ideas threadbare and poverty-stricken. Rancid reaction and ultramontanism were a sinister background to the new life of high endeavour, and not to be exorcised by a perpetual invitation to dance through a summer of roses and wine.

The national and liberal movements craved a leader and leadership. But past history and present realities proclaimed that the leader was not to be found at Vienna and in the House of Habsburg. A liberal Austria was as unthinkable and as impossible as a liberal Pope. Goethe's notable description of his youth, which all Germany read in the autobiography, *Wahrheit und Dichtung*, that seemed to sum up the spiritual experience and antinomies of the German mind, ' Fritzisch nicht Preussisch gesinnt ' (' In sympathy with Frederick but not with Prussia '), turned many ardent hearts wistfully to the bleak north. Might it not be written in the scroll of German destiny that the mantle of the great Frederick would fall on another and a greater Hohenzollern ?

No German State in the confederation had, since 1789, suffered more varied vicissitudes, had sunk lower or recovered more rapidly than Prussia. The Settlement of 1815 restored the Prussian kingdom to the full measure of strength enjoyed in 1805, but with a significantly different geographical configuration. Prussia surrendered much of the Polish territory acquired in the Second and Third Partitions, and in compensation received a part of royal Saxony and rich provinces in the west, which made her the guardian of the Rhine from Düsseldorf to the suburbs of Jewish and free Frankfurt. Yet her territories were not compact, for between the new Rhenish Prussia and the original nucleus of the Brandenburg Electorate in the Elbe basin lay Hanover and the Westphalian States, while East and West Prussia with Silesia made two huge salients with Poland in the re-entrant of the one and royal Saxony and (Austrian) Bohemia in the re-entrant of the other. Prussian patriots regarded the Settlement as an insult. They had desired to eliminate the Polish and Catholic elements of the Province of Posen, to absorb the whole of Saxony, and (with customary Prussian ' modera-

B.

C

tion ') to reduce their ' compensation ' in the west in return
for a consolidation in the centre. Prussia was to be a pure
German State, predominantly Protestant, while the black
and white flag and the double eagle would fly on an unbroken Prussian kingdom from Coblenz to Königsberg,
enveloping the north and making Hanover an enclave in
Prussian soil. The ambition was frustrated, but it remained an inextinguishable ideal in baffled Prussian
hearts.

For all that, Prussia was unquestionably the strongest
German State in the federation. And the consequences
of the Settlement operated at once on Prussian policy.
Much of the new acquisitions had never been Prussian,
and their assimilation into the Hohenzollern system was
essential; no easy matter, for the Protestant Saxons
resented the enforced separation from their former State;
on the Rhine a Catholic population with long-established
memories of the sovereign ecclesiastical princes of Cologne,
Münster and Paderborn, and saturated by French
thought and administration since 1795, resisted the supremacy of a sovereign civil state and the categorical
imperatives of the Prussian bureaucracy; in Posen the
aspirations of Catholic and Slav Poles were wholly with
their brothers across the highly artificial frontier that
divided a dismembered Poland from Prussia. And in
Brandenburg and Prussian Pomerania Junkertum retained
its grip on the government.

The next twenty-five years were a bitter disappointment to the dreams of the men of 1813. The ideal of
Gneisenau and Boyen, bred in the school of Stein, that
Prussia would establish a pre-eminence in Germany on ' the
triple supremacy of her army, her science, and her constitution,' withered under the blight of a reactionary sovereign. The royal pledge to complete the reforms of Stein
and Scharnhorst by the grant of liberal self-government,
with its apex in a central representative parliament which
would unite the whole nation in co-operation with the
Crown, was deliberately broken. Prussia was remodelled into eight administrative provinces and governed
by the central and reorganised executive, a bureaucracy,

decentralised local estates, and provincial diets so re-organised as to make the land-owning aristocracy supreme. Law was a royal ordinance; local, much less national, control over taxation and expenditure did not exist; the ministers and civil service were responsible to none but their royal master; the patrimonial manorial jurisdiction and administration of Junkertum in Brandenburg, Pomerania, and East Prussia, were practically untouched. Prussian unity, in short, was refashioned after 1815 on the lines of the military and feudal tradition, pieced together from the days of the Great Elector to the fatal day of Jena. The monarchy re-established its authority on the *rocher de bronze*—the prerogative; the bureaucracy was its executive instrument; the army and the administration were staffed and controlled by the noble caste, and the memorable law of 1814 completing the reforms of Scharnhorst, which made service in the army compulsory for all Prussian males, stamped on civil allegiance the ineffaceable imprint of military obedience to the supreme War-Lord (*Kriegesherr*), Lord of the Land (*Landesherr*), and the Commander-in-Chief of the Prussian nation in arms.

The world outside promptly decided that the new Prussia was simply the old Frederician State writ large. Superficially, this was true. But the new Prussia contained elements unknown to the Prussia of the eighteenth century, and these were developed even under the reaction of Frederick William III. Education, primary, secondary, and of the university type, was strenuously reorganised, and primary education was made as compulsory as military service. The Prussian universities—Berlin, Königsberg, Breslau, Halle, Bonn—were in the forefront of the intellectual renaissance; and by 1848 a professorial chair at Berlin was the recognised blue-ribbon of the academic career. Seldom, indeed, has a university had so much eminence in its professorial staff in so many departments of knowledge as that in the Prussian capital. The civil administration, despised by many of the Junkers, became extraordinarily efficient, and like the army it was carefully graded: the men at the top had passed by a severe apprenticeship through each stage in the official hierarchy.

They were experts, trained in obedience, and habituated to find their initiative in the higher command. The economic life was taken in hand. The Zollverein or Customs Union begun in 1819, in order to solve the difficulties of trade peculiar to a State with foreign enclaves that broke the Prussian frontier at countless points, had under Maassen's masterly management included most of Germany, outside Austria, by direct absorption or by tariff treaties with similar economic unions. Maassen was a follower of Adam Smith, and the tariff was low and simple, avowedly anti-Protectionist and on Free Trade lines. The economic advance was remarkable, thanks to sound economic science, the stability of the government, and the efficiency of the administration. If the new Prussia was in type autocratic, militarist, and bureaucratic —a kingdom governed by its Crown and aristocratic caste—its intellectual and economic activities made its social structure and political outlook a wholly different state to the Prussia of Frederick the Great. Between the governing nobility and the agricultural and industrial proletariat had grown up a solid middle class, prosperous, highly educated, very capable, versed in history, steeped in political ideas, who knew that their brains were indispensable to their country's increasing strength and mounting ambitions, and who resented their exclusion from an active share, not in executive tasks, but in shaping the policy and destinies of Prussia. If they served in the army, worked in the universities and industries, and paid more than half the taxation, they had an indefeasible right to the highest and most responsible duties of citizenship —a share in the government.

Thirty years of German and European evolution had reopened not solved the Prussian problem created by her history and the Settlement of 1815 ; and the difficulties shelved then and since remained unanswered. When Frederick William iii. was succeeded in 1840 by Frederick William iv., men felt that the dead could bury their dead, but that a new and critical epoch for the living was at hand. Would Prussia now obtain a constitution that would satisfy the Liberal party in Prussia ? Would

Prussian 'foreign' policy satisfy Prussian and German nationalism ?

The cleavage in the various parties and schools of ideas —the reaction of the internal on the external problem— made a most complex situation. Tradition, social environment, class bias, and the infiltration of new categories of thought operated with varying strength on varying groups. Prussia since 1815 had been brought into direct touch with Germany at many new points, and the contact tore gaps in the old tradition. Her political frontiers vanished in the sphere of knowledge. Her universities were recruited from the south and centre of Germany ; her own students went to Göttingen, Heidelberg, Leipzig, Munich and Tübingen. Trade, commerce, and industry, with the aid of the Zollverein, had created economic bonds throughout the length and breadth of the Federation. Railways were to carry the revolution much further—and it was a railway loan that precipitated the constitutional crisis. Liberals, Radicals, and Nationalists were demanding in Prussia what Liberals, Radicals, and Nationalists were demanding in Bavaria and Baden, and for the same reasons. In the struggle which raged for ten years in Rhenish Prussia between Catholics claiming the freedom and independence of their Church from the bondage of a supreme secular or heretical state—a forerunner of the great *Kulturkampf* of Bismarck's chancellorship—Protestant Prussia had learned that ultramontanism was a grave element both in the Prussian and German problem. The German 'Watch on the Rhine' was vested in a Prussia planted by the will of Europe as a strong barrier against French ambition. Polish Posen and East Prussia were a perpetual reminder of the Russian danger and the unsolved Polish question. Along the western flank of Silesia stretched Austria. Neighbours, neighbours everywhere, and no real frontier except the army and the Landwehr, with its immortal, if legendary, memories of 1813. Expansion outwards, consolidation within, were essential. But in what directions ? Save for Dantzig and Königsberg and Stettin—windows into a Baltic closed by Denmark and Sweden—Prussia had no harbours, no fleet, no colonies. Kiel was Danish, Hamburg a free city, Bremen another free city, Emden belonged to Oldenburg ; due north Hanover blocked the way to the German Ocean, and the mouths of the Rhine were Dutch.

History and the facts of everyday life taught all Prussians the unity and sovereignty of the State ; yet how could Prussia expand in Germany when the Federal Constitution guaranteed the inviolability of every German state, and the Federal Diet was notoriously anti-Prussian ? Only by smashing the Federal Constitution to pieces in her own and Germany's interests. The service of the Crown, in the army, the civil service, or the educational organisation controlled by and modelled for the needs of the State, was the ordinary career of both the noble and the middle class. Hence, the political theory of Hegel and the Hegelian school, with its insistence on the State as Power, bit deep into the Prussian mind, Conservative and Liberal alike. It supplied the philosophical basis for, and justification of, familiar facts ; it provided the reconciliation between the claims of the individual and of the community, for each would attain their consummate realisation through the supremacy of the unifying and omnipotent State.

No less important was the teaching of Clausewitz—a formative influence as powerful as the law of Military Service, which Treitschke has emphasised. War, Mirabeau had said, was Prussia's national industry : that Prussia had grown by war was a commonplace to every Prussian schoolboy. Clausewitz's *Vom Kriege* (On War) was a severely scientific study of war as a subject of knowledge, and a manifestation of life through a nation's will —a treatise based on deep thought and a masterly comparative method. The substance of his teaching that war is simply a continuation of the policy of the State by methods appropriate to its nature and for the achievement of the ends of the State, unattainable by the nature of things in any other way, bit no less deep into the minds of the governing and middle class. The relations of war to civil policy, and to the form, functions, and end of the State ; the exploration of first principles in close connection with their application; the severity and lucidity of the argument and the intellectual power of the author, made *Vom Kriege* a classic which marked an epoch in the scientific study of the subject. If Clausewitz summed up Prussian thought from Frederick to Scharnhorst, his mental distinction and grip of method were peculiarly his own, and they rested on the same characteristic that marked *The Wealth of Nations*, the intimate connection between the truth of the principles and their application in tested facts. To Scharnhorst he owed the inspiration of that intrepid and inspiring spirit, and in Napoleon he found the most convincing proof of the doctrines he expounded; but Clausewitz remained a great Prussian, the founder of the great Prussian school continued by Moltke and von der Goltz. His writings were never popular, even in Prussia : few outside Germany before 1871 had read him. Like our own Bentham he owed his profound influence to his mastery of minds which themselves became masters of science or affairs—to the brain of the Prussian army organised in the great General Staff, and to the application of his conclusions by the professoriate in the universities. The debates in the Prussian Parliament from 1858 to 1866 reveal the saturation of both political parties by Clausewitzian principles in this broader sense. And the greatest of his disciples was not Moltke, who acknowledged the debt, but Bismarck, who did not.

Not less significant in another sphere of thought was the work of List, who committed suicide in 1846, and of Röscher, first at Göttingen, and then at Leipzig. List's *System of National Economy* was the foundation of modern Protectionism ; Röscher was the pioneer of the historical, as opposed to the classical deductive school in economics.

The sum of List's teaching that the economic life and policy of the community were subservient to, and must be shaped to express, the will of the national State as Power, harmonised with Röscher's conclusions, based on historical analysis, that economic principles and laws had only a relative, not an absolute, validity, and were dependent on, and the exemplification of, national types of economic structure. Hence the argument that Germany

to realise its nationalism must have a German national
economy, and to achieve political freedom must first
attain a national economic independence. List and
Röscher, therefore, and their disciples provided a powerful
antidote to the influence of British thought, so marked in
Prussian Liberalism. Their greatest conquest was not
achieved until a full generation later, when Bismarck
broke in 1879 with the economic creed of his youth and
middle age, and the converted Imperial Chancellor hoisted
his flag in the camp of Protection.

Particularism was nowhere stronger than in Prussia,
precisely because all the essential ingredients of particularism were so highly developed in the Prussian State—
a dynasty the history of which was the history of Prussia
—a definite type of civic character reflected in the form
and character of the institutions—a proud record of
achievement due to the unity of a unified and centralised State on a racial basis. In a word, Prussia had bought
her freedom in Germany and Europe by fidelity to her
Prussian self, and at a great price. This Prussian particularism provided an obvious policy and programme of
the future. Let Prussia continue a rigid loyalty to her
traditions. By the union of her monarchy, her army, and
her civil service, in unquestioning obedience to the
Crown, she could always maintain her pride of place and
make a greater Prussia. Her duty to Germany was best
fulfilled by fulfilling her duty to herself—that State
egoism which Bismarck was to preach so effectively. Any
alteration in her historic institutions or principles would
shatter the secret of her strength and success—her Prussianism. The real danger lay in the desire of jealous
friends and baffled foes to ' mediatise ' Prussia, melt her
down in a common German mould, and dissolve a good
Prussian into a flabby German, State. In opposition
to this, Prussian Liberals based their programme on the
reform period of Stein and Scharnhorst and the new
Prussia created in 1815. Their object was to complete
the edifice begun after the downfall of Jena—a disaster
in their eyes caused by the isolation of Prussia from Germany, both in politics, thought, and ideals—to modernise

the Prussian State, while retaining all that was best in the historic Prussia, and to build up a real self-governing Prussian nation and government, in which all classes could share. It was folly, they urged, to ignore the demands of classes excluded from power, the character of the new age, and the intellectual movements in Germany and Europe. Prussia could lead the German renaissance, but she must first give practical proof of her identity with its principles and its objects. If she cut herself off from the great currents in the life of the German people, she would cease to be German ; she would unite Germany against Prussia, and experience a second time the bitter fruits of isolation. No other State had so strong a claim to be the successful champion of a German national movement ; no other State stood to gain so much by accepting, or to lose so much by refusing, this duty.

A remarkable development of Prussian conservatism, rather than of Prussian particularism, found its leaders in the Brandenburg Circle, which took its political philosophy from Haller and Stahl, its religion from a revival of Evangelical Protestantism, and its sentiment from a horror and fear of ' the Revolution.' It constituted the nucleus from which the Camarilla of the Gerlachs was evolved ; and in touch with it were many of the men who made the circle of Frederick William IV. both as Crown Prince and King. It exercised for thirty years a profound influence on Prussian and German history ; in its ranks Bismarck served his apprenticeship, and his breach with its principles was the first great formative fact in his career. The essential points of this aristocratic and pietistic creed—an offshoot from the Holy Alliance, tinged in its dreams and its aversions by the Romantic movement— can be briefly summarised : the maxim of their party was J. de Maistre's sentence, ' Nous ne voulons pas la contre-révolution, mais le contraire de la révolution ' ! The historic danger to all states and society lay in ' the Revolution ' ; the struggle between the Revolution and conservatism began long before 1789, and was continually taking new forms ; France was the main source of revolutionary principles, which either placed sovereignty in the people, or divided it between a hybrid and fictitious popular will and an emasculated monarchy; the political revolution was united with the intellectual, which taught the freedom and sufficiency of the critical reason and subjected everything to rational tests. Modern Germany was deeply infected with both the political and intellectual revolution, which unchecked would destroy all authority in government and be subversive of society and religion; hence it was the duty of Prussia to unite with all governments, based on legitimate principles, in order to maintain those principles and to combat the Revolution. Conservatism was not local or national; it transcended the artificial barriers of political, racial, and geographical division; and in practice the allies of Prussia were Austria and Russia; England after 1815 had deserted the true faith; France after 1830 was only a crowned bourgeois republic. In fine, the closest political and moral understanding between Prussia and Austria was the pivot of a sound German and European system: united with Russia, Prussia and Austria could save Europe. Separated from them she was a conspirator in a moral cataclysm.

Such a creed and such a policy differed essentially from the ideas of Prussian Junkertum; the Prussian polity was not justified because it was Prussian, but because it conformed to the tests of a universalist system, and in any collision between Prussianism and this orthodox conservatism the former must be sacrificed; but the Gerlach school shared with the Junker governing class the antipathy to all liberal reform. For Prussia to tread the path of England or France would be treachery to the cause of right. Opposed as these several parties were, they had two points in common. They accepted as an axiom the claim of Prussia to be a *Grossmacht*. They were profoundly dissatisfied with Prussian inactivity from 1815 onwards, which was an abnegation of her strength and European position. Prussia was the one German state in which patriotism was more than a rhetorical figure, and membership in which was a cause of pride and a basis of duty and service. Liberals, Particularists, or Conservatives demanded that the Prussian king and the Prussian sword should play a more independent part in the political life of Europe. Even to the Gerlachs the Austrian alliance, the *sine quâ non* of Prussian policy, caused obstinate questionings when it involved a submissive subordination to the secular and selfish statecraft of Vienna. Liberals felt more strongly the ' shame ' of Prussian obedience to the Carlsbad decrees, the reactionary measures of 1832, and the Prussian share in the suppression of the Hanoverian constitution. The alliance with Austria was in their eyes a surrender to reaction ; the Bund and the Diet were a national disgrace, and Prussia which could give the tone and the Liberal Law to Germany had become the tool of selfish and reactionary Austrian interests.

Prussian thought of all schools was inevitably driven back on the deadlock in the Bund. If Prussia continued to act with the Diet she was an Austrian instrument ; but how could she act in defiance of it without forfeiting her German position, and destroying the whole movement towards a common and more effective German organisation ? Nor could Prussian foreign policy be based on internal German interests. The Prusso-Russian *entente* had its roots in the established traditions of policy, gratitude to Russia for services in the past, and a deepseated fear of Russian power. Since Frederick the Great had learned the meaning of Russian enmity in the Seven Years' War, friendship between Berlin and Petersburg was a postulate of Prussian safety. Poland and the Polish question drove the conclusion home. The French danger was no less impressive. In Prussia, the memories of Rosbach and of Jena, of Napoleonic humiliation and partition, and of the War of Liberation, were in the national blood as nowhere else in Germany. The portrait of Queen Louisa, the royal saint and martyr, hung in the manor-houses of Junkertum and the cottages of the peasantry ; her tomb by Rauch at Charlottenburg was a national vindication of her sufferings at French hands ; and there were thousands of Prussians on both sides of the barricades in 1848 who had marched into Paris in 1814 after having liberated their country from French domination. The new King Frederick William IV. (born in 1795),

and his brother, the Prince of Prussia (born 1797), were
boys when the French entered Berlin in 1806, and they
had both served in the Prussian army of 1813. If France
was the hereditary enemy of Germany, she was the hated
and hateful oppressor of Prussia. Prussian Conservatives
and Liberals had common ground in their repudiation of
a French hegemony in Europe. It was the duty of
Prussian intellect to assist the superiority of Prussian
science, as it was the task of Prussian arms to maintain
intact the German territory in the west assigned to their
custody. A black cloud and the warning drops falling
anywhere in Europe, and Prussia instinctively faced to the
Rhine. War with France—long before Bismarck sat in
the Wilhelmstrasse—would always have set Prussian
nationalism aflame ; for deep and inarticulate in the
heart of every Prussian lay the desire to undo the work of
Louis xiv., which Europe, callous to Prussian services and
sacrifices, had forbidden in 1815, when Prussia was
' robbed ' of the fruits of her victories.

Prussian Liberals recognised, but underrated, the
difficulties of liberal reform. Emphasis on the logical
and historical connection of the new liberal programme
with the reformers of the Stein-Scharnhorst period ignored
the cumulative force of facts. The inertia of the monarchy and the obstinacy of its ally, Junkertum, were the
real reasons for the failure to complete the reforms of 1808.
The conversion of Prussia into a constitutional state of
the French or Belgian type, with rights guaranteed in a
written constitution, was a reversal of two hundred years
of development in a precisely opposite direction. Yet
the mere demand for the conversion showed the strength
of the new elements in the Prussian State. But it was
clear that it could only be accomplished with the consent
of the monarchy, or by a military disaster, or by revolution.
In 1840 a revolution seemed as improbable as a second
Jena. Hence everything turned on the character of the
new sovereign, Frederick William iv.

Like his ancestor, Frederick i., Frederick William iv.
was ' a Hohenzollern with his back broken,' who bewildered his subjects and himself by the obstinacy and

contradiction of his convictions. His pride in the army, his belief in his unfettered prerogative and the divine right of his Crown, his conviction that the Prussian sovereign in the scheme of human and divine things was appointed to be the instrument of his people's good, and earning their love and admiration, linked him with the past. Nature had endowed him with an acquisitive, sympathetic, and versatile intelligence, and no small share of oratorical and artistic gifts. Essentially pious, he was deeply stirred by the new religious forces at work in Germany; a strong Protestant, he desired the union of the Protestant churches both in Prussia and outside, yet could sympathise with the Roman Catholic revival, for he regarded religious belief and emotion as the basis and sanction of political and social development. As Crown Prince he had gladly cultivated the leaders of politics, philosophy, literature and art. The friends of the Crown Prince and King numbered personalities so various and so different as the Gerlachs with the orthodox Conservatives of the Gerlach circle, Radowitz, Bunsen, Rauch, Cornelius, the Munich leader of the Romantic movement in art, Stockmar, Humboldt and Ranke.

The rebirth of a national Germany, equipped with organs rescued from the Middle Ages and reshaped to express modern ideals, the reunion of Emperor and Church in a revived Holy Roman Empire, the reconciliation of modern Liberalism with historic Conservatism in the spiritual, intellectual, and political life of the German people, inspired the vision which haunted and fired his imagination. Of this *Restauratio Imperii* combining the fundamental unity of German culture with the unity of German religion, Austria and Prussia were marked out by Providence to be the co-architects and co-guarantors. The German Imperial Crown must necessarily be recreated as the hereditary prerogative of the House of Habsburg, but beside the Imperial Throne would stand the Hohenzollern sovereign as Captain-General and Arch-Chamberlain of the restored Empire, and round these two would be grouped the princes, dynasties, governments and peoples of Germany in an ordered hierarchy.

Frederick William IV. saw political realities through a magic and distorting screen of sentiment. His aversions were as strong as his ideals. Liberal principles were tainted at their source by French Jacobinism, and everything French he abominated. Obstinate and impressionable, he was always under the spell of characters with clearer and narrower conceptions and stronger wills than his own. ' I am not a Frederick the Great,' he pathetically confessed ; and when revolution and then reaction rent the web of sentiment asunder, he was helpless—the sullen and disillusioned victim of fate, the reluctant agent of a policy which, if it defeated the revolution, no less shattered the dreams and ambitions of the German and Hohenzollern king.

The summons to Berlin in 1847 of a united Diet—the concentration in a single assembly of the unreformed local Estates—brought to a head the issues between the old Prussia and the new. To the liberal demands the King replied that the royal creation of the united Diet redeemed the pledge of his predecessor, and that the constitutional reforms were now complete ; he added that his Crown was his by the grace of God, and that no written sheet of paper (a constitution) should ever intervene between his people and himself.

No less significant was the demand at Heppenheim in October, 1847, for an elected national German Parliament, repeated in a motion by Bassermann in the Diet at Baden (February 12, 1848), in which the reform of the obsolete and obstructive Federal Constitution was to be accomplished by and according to the will of the German nation. In Prussia and in the south the two Germanies —the Germany of princes and governments, the Germany of their subjects over whom the liberal and nationalist creeds were daily gaining a clearer mastery—were set in array. The nationalist issue could not be burked. Poland and the Poles within and without the German Confederation were in effervescence. From Schleswig-Holstein came the imperious demand of ' unredeemed ' Germans to be freed from denationalisation by Danish ' tyranny ' ; and Holstein, as a member of the German

Confederation, was within the jurisdiction of a federal execution. At Paris and Prague and Buda-Pesth, in Switzerland and Italy, the storm-cone was being hoisted. How long could the German princes resist the pressure from within ? How long could a representative public opinion acquiesce in an unrepresentative Federal Diet ? In 1847 Germany rang with the confusion of opposed creeds and programmes ; distinguished spokesmen there were in plenty in every state, but as yet neither side had produced a leader or a programme commanding an un-divided allegiance. Well might Stockmar write : ' A new epoch is in fusion, the particular metal and stamp of which cannot be divined.'

It was into this Germany of 1815-47 that Bismarck was born, and in it he grew up. It was in this Germany and Prussia, on the eve of revolution, that, as a member of the United Diet, he stepped on to the political stage, and into the political history of his country.

CHAPTER II

THE JUNKER POLITICIAN

§ 1. *Education and Entry into Politics*

OTTO EDUARD LEOPOLD VON BISMARCK-SCHÖNHAUSEN, born on April 1, 1815, in the feverish month of renewed war that followed Napoleon's escape from Elba, was the third son of Ferdinand von Bismarck and Wilhelmina Mencken. Of his two elder brothers only one, Bernhard (born 1810) survived, and a third brother (born 1819) did not reach manhood. Of his sisters only one, Malwine (born 1827) reached womanhood. Schönhausen, the ancestral home of his forefathers, lies to the west of Berlin in the Old March (Alt Mark) of Brandenburg, which was the original nucleus of the Electorate and the very core of the future Prussian kingdom and the cradle of the Prussian monarchy.

'Who are these Hohenzollerns ? ' Bismarck once demanded. ' We were in the March long before they were.' The claim that the Bismarcks settled in the March in the reign of Charles the Great rests only on the pious authority of the genealogical table hanging in the hall of the manor-house at Schönhausen ; but two hundred years before the first Hohenzollern, invested with the Electorate by Imperial hands, set to work to tame the lawless independence of noble and Junker in the March, the petty village of Bismarck gave its name to a Brandenburg family ; and towards the end of the thirteenth century the Bismarcks were established in the guild and government of Stendal, a township hard by. In 1345, as holders of the fief of Burgstall, they were definitely registered in the nobility of the March, and though they never reached the status of the great aristocracy, they were henceforward

48

one of the many noble families who constituted the governing class. In 1562 they were reluctantly obliged to transfer Burgstall to the Hohenzollerns and to take in exchange Schönhausen. Uninterruptedly in Bismarck's possession from that date, it gave the family the name— Bismarck-Schönhausen—which distinguished them alike from other Bismarcks—noble, middle-class, or plebeian.

On his father's side Otto's family record was that of most Brandenburg squires—military service in the electoral and then the royal army of Brandenburg-Prussia. Allegiance and devotion to the ruler were the traditional duty of the manorial lords; and the ruler's prerogative was reflected in the territorial prerogative of the servants of the Crown, who administered the land, led their peasants in battle, fought an unending struggle with Nature and their own passions, a caste to whom the State meant their Hohenzollern master and their own divine right to govern under his guidance. Otto's father had served, as usual, in the army; had seen Schönhausen (built in 1700 to replace the original manor-house, destroyed in the Thirty Years' War) in French possession after Jena, and the sacred family tree pierced by French bayonets. Love for the French was not, therefore, a maxim taught to the young Otto. The Old March nourished bitter memories of the French invaders, and inspiriting records of the War of Liberation, and these the young Otto imbibed as soon as he was breeched.

The tradition of the Menckens was very different. They were not noble, but they could point in their lineage to three professors of some celebrity in their day. Wilhelmina Mencken's father served in the Civil Cabinet of Frederick the Great and of his successor; was accused of Jacobinism and displaced, to return under a more liberal dispensation as Cabinets-chef of Frederick William III. His daughter seems to have inherited the civil, literary, and intellectual aptitudes of her race; she combined them with an extravagant love of building, of Berlin, and of the dilettante society of salons and fashionable watering-places—all of them, save perhaps the building, tastes detested by her son Otto.

B.   D

But until 1815 neither Bismarcks nor Menckens had contributed to the dramatic annals of Hohenzollern Prussia a statesman, a soldier, or a writer of the first, or even the second, quality. Both families had a long and creditable, but essentially parochial, record, research into which could be safely left to the county antiquarian, had the boy born in 1815 not made his name illustrious and his ancestry an interesting study in the origins of genius. These Bismarcks—and in Mendelian phraseology they were the dominating strain—for four centuries simply did their duty as squires and earnest Protestants, and they planted, tilled, fought, drank, duelled, married, served as sheriffs (*Landrath*), begat sons and daughters, and slept their sleep beneath their blazoned arms, ' In Trinitate Robur,' satisfied with being Bismarcks and Brandenburger manorial lords. They ended, in the mystery of human things, by producing a member of their ancient house to whom they bequeathed in treble measure their own fierce appetites, loves, and hates, an iron physique, a brain, ambitions, and a force unique in the history of the March and of their race.

In 1816 Otto's parents moved to Kniephof, the chief of a group of family estates, inherited in that year, and at Kniephof in Prussian Pomerania the little Otto grew up. It was the Paradise of his boyhood, and there the hereditary Bismarck link with the soil was forged. Towns and the life of towns neither the lad, nor the ambassador, nor the Imperial Chancellor ever liked. Streets were a prison, townsfolk an unpleasant riddle. Whatever else changed in Otto von Bismarck, the passion for rural nature—the hunger for the land and the life of the land, forests, moor, the blue spaces of an open sky, the wind across the pastures, the hard-bitten men who lived, worked, and hunted on the land—never changed. Pictures and sculpture do not figure in his letters : he confessed when he was an old man that once, only once, he had entered the Berlin Museum ; of books there is singularly little ; there is much of good food and good wine ; but the earth and its unceasing pageantry of beauty are never forgotten. Dawn and sunset, the maturing sunshine of midday, snow under moonlight, mountains, crags, and wooded dales—these things he always saw because he felt their message, their contact with, or memory of, his own home. The grey-haired Chancellor, with his wolf-hounds at his heels, striding with the watchful eye of a master amongst the sunlit glades of his oaks and beeches at Varzin or Fried-richsruhe, was happier in his freedom from the fetters of the State than the boy on holiday who galloped his pony over the monotonous demesne of Kniephof, stalked snipe and wild duck, or hunted hares through deep snow.

Otto's education was of the conventional German humanistic and literary type. At seven years old he was sent to a preparatory school (Plamann's Institute), and at twelve passed on to a gymnasium. At sixteen, as became a young noble and Protestant, he was confirmed by Schleiermacher, at the height of his celebrity, whose brief injunction : ' Whatever you do, do it with all your heart and as from the Lord,' is said to have made a deep impression. In 1832 he entered the University of Göttingen, where he spent two years, followed by one at the University of Berlin. Instinct and tradition suggested the army as a profession, but his mother apparently desired a civil career for this passionate, self-willed and robust son ; whether because she feared the life of an officer, or divined the power in her beloved Otto, is un-certain ; but she had her way, and after passing the neces-sary examinations he entered the civil service on its judicial side, and was attached for duty at the fashionable Aix-la-Chapelle and at Berlin. One year had to be given to military service, and this he spent with the Rifles of the Guard (*Garde-Jäger*).

Until 1839, when he lost his mother, abruptly ter-minated his State employment and, owing to financial difficulties of his family, took over with his brother Bern-hard the management of the family properties, his life had shown little indication either of ambitions or excep-tional abilities. As a university student, though not as idle as legend subsequently pictured, he had failed to find in academic studies either intellectual inspiration or prac-tical utility. Heeren's lectures made some impression, but neither Dahlmann, the glory of Göttingen, nor Savigny at Berlin can be reckoned as formative influences in his education as they were in the training of his contemporaries Windthorst and Beust. The truth is that then, as throughout his career, Bismarck revolted against discipleship or subordination of any kind. Life was the only teacher from whom he was willing to learn, and the lessons of life he hammered out for himself, and he refused to take them ready-made. He joined a famous duelling corps, the Hanoverana. Duelling, beer-drinking, and the riotous escapades of undergraduate youth, provided an outlet for his exuberant physical powers. In the punishment book of the university his name figures more than once. Friends he made in plenty, three in particular—Moritz von Blanckenburg, Motley, the American historian, and Roon, twelve years his senior. Little did either guess what the latter friendship would signify for the history of Prussia. There is a story that in 1832 he made a bet with an American student that Germany would be unified in twenty years ; but if he made the bet, he lost it. Forty, not twenty, years hence he could have asked from the Wilhelmstrasse for repayment. He detested and neglected his duties as a civil servant. The career of ' the animal armed with a pen' behind closed windows and under the orders of domineering, exacting, or ill-bred superiors, stirred his Junker pride and independence to mutiny. At Aix-la-Chapelle, crowded with fashionable pleasure-seekers of all nations, he plunged into gambling, debt, and dissipation. For four months he broke away altogether, travelled to Wiesbaden and Switzerland, fell in love with a pretty English girl, but whether he broke with her or she with him is uncertain. The sap was running strongly upwards, and in the dawn of superb physical vigour Bismarck, like many, sought in physical satisfaction an anodyne for an incurable unrest. ' Yesterday,' he wrote to his wife in 1851, ' I was in Wiesbaden. May it please God to fill with His clear and strong wine this vessel in which then the champagne of youth uselessly foamed and left stale dregs.' Neither politics nor religion came to his aid. He had ceased to pray ; he was practically an agnostic with a vague Pantheism simmering in a brain that demanded positive reality. Republicanism as a political creed had appealed to him, but the democratic excesses at the Hambacher Fest (1832) disgusted him with radicalism and all its works. Prussia had no public life to offer him. Service in the bureaucracy of an autocratic crown and the army were the only two professions available, and he had rejected the one and was too old now for the other.

He fell back gladly on the career of a landed proprietor. At Kniephof he was his own master, and his father's death in 1845 made little difference to his position. He acquired Schönhausen and lived there ; but from 1839 onwards he devoted all his brains and energies to the family estates and restored their prosperity. He studied the science and practice of agriculture in all its forms, revelling in his independence on the land that he loved, bending men and Nature into obedience to his will. Not the least impressive of the many personal touches that vibrate in his later speeches, are those which reveal the lessons he had learned in the management of his estates. It is instructive to remember that at this time, south of the Alps, another young noble, Camillo di Cavour, no less dissatisfied than Otto von Bismarck, was patiently serving a self-imposed and invaluable apprenticeship in statecraft on the estates of his ancestry. The Bismarck of later days, too, would have understood why Walpole in the most exacting pressure of his premiership always opened first every morning the report from his game keeper and bailiff. The Prussia in which the master of Kniephof and Schönhausen toiled was not the modern and industrialised state, which in 1841 was just beginning to develop a new economic life, but a kingdom of agriculture, of landed proprietors, farmers and peasants, in which more than seventy per cent. of the population lived on, and wrested their food from, the land.

But the cravings and unrest of Cavour and Bismarck were not, and could not be, satisfied with the breeding of beasts and making two blades of grass grow where one had grown before. The countryside of Pomerania rang with the dare-devil exploits, the dangerous tests of skill, nerve, and strength of 'the mad' and 'wild Junker' of Kniephof, ready to swim, shoot, hunt, or ride anywhere and in any weather ; no less ready and able to drink half a dozen lieutenants from neighbouring garrisons under the table. The gossip which represented him as a Herculean Lothario of coarse amours and a fabulous appetite is certainly exaggerated. But a host who could wake the tardy guest by pistol-shots through the windows, and whose irreligious views were more disquieting than his morals, alarmed the mothers, if they excited the curiosity of the daughters, in the manor drawing-rooms. Gossip, however, did not know that the mad Junker was devouring books—history, philosophy, theology, geography, and poetry : Feuerbach, Bauer, and Strauss, Schopenhauer, Lessing, Schiller, Rückert, Lenau, Freiligrath, Uhland, and especially Goethe, Shakespeare, and Byron. The effortless felicity of allusion in his speeches to Goethe and Shakespeare proves the grip that the imaginative realism of these two master critics of life had on his spirit. Yet nothing as yet could fill ' the unfathomable weariness and emptiness ' of which a letter speaks ; and Bismarck, like Cavour, left his estates to travel, now to Paris, now to the northern sea-coasts, now to England, completing his competence in French and English, noting, as always, the scenery, and storing his impressions of institutions and society in a retentive memory. ' I feel,' he wrote in 1845, when his sister Malwine married, ' more than ever my loneliness in the world.'

The gnawing at his heart, the flux in his ideas, the need of a sure anchorage in spiritual and moral realities, grew with the inarticulate ambition for a career wider than the duties of a manorial lord could provide. The answer came from an unexpected quarter, and Bismarck owed it to a woman's ideals. Through the wife, Marie von Thadden, of his friend, Moritz von Blanckenburg, the master of Kniephof and Schönhausen was gradually absorbed into ' the Trieglaff circle '—a group that had Trieglaff, the Thaddens' estate, for its centre. The Trieglaff circle linked hands with a more political group at Berlin, the most important members of which were

the Gerlachs and Stahl, the writer on political philosophy,
and in this way he began the memorable political friendship with General Leopold and his brother Ludwig von
Gerlach.   The blend of evangelical piety, prayer meetings,,
conservative politics, and sentimental literary dilettantism,
of spiritual tea-parties and picnics, at first amused and
then interested Bismarck.   It was a new type of adventure,
and he was to discover how much a resolute and high-
minded woman can accomplish when she deliberately pits
her strength against the will of a resolute man.   Marie
von Blanckenburg had divined the power in this erring,
loyal, and forceful friend of her husband's.   She made it
her duty to ' convert ' him.   She succeeded, though she
did not live to know her success and its results.   Her
premature death deeply affected the young man and completed the conversion.   He resumed the habit of prayer
and the study of the Bible ; Bauer and Strauss went into
the wastepaper basket ; his cynical and agnostic Pantheism melted like snow in the midday sunshine of April.
He returned to the unquestioning Lutheran faith of his
ancestors.   His mind was made up, and henceforward
his was a conviction impregnable to all the doubts, fears,
or disillusionment provided by the life that began in 1847,
and ended in the homage of a united Germany in 1898.
' I cannot conceive,' he wrote to his wife, ' how a man
who reflects and yet knows nothing of God, and will know
nothing, can endure his life for contempt and boredom.
I do not know how I formerly endured.   If I lived now
as I did then, without God, without thee, without children, I cannot think why I should not put life aside like
a dirty shirt.'   In 1870 he said : ' I know not whence I
should derive my sense of duty, if not from God : orders
and titles have no charm for me ; I firmly believe in a life
after death, and that is why I am a Royalist : by nature
I am disposed to be a Republican. . . . Were I not a
staunch Christian, did I not stand upon the miraculous
basis of religion, you would never have possessed a Federal
Chancellor in my person.'

Love and marriage consummated Marie von Blanckenburg's work.   An attachment to Johanna von Puttkamer,

the daughter of neighbours at Reinfeld, steadily deepened into passion. The father who 'had heard much evil and little good' of the suitor for his daughter's hand, was reluctant to consent; but Bismarck was not one to be thwarted when he had set his heart on success, and he had Fräulein von Puttkamer on his side. 'All right' was the brief announcement in English to his sister of his betrothal (January 12, 1847). His marriage followed on July 25, and a happy marriage it certainly was. In his domestic life Bismarck is seen at his best. What his wife was to him and what he was to her can be read in a correspondence which is real literature, and a precious human and historical document. 'I cannot,' he wrote from Biarritz in 1851, 'enjoy seeing so much beauty away from you.' 'My wife,' he said, thirty years later, 'made me what I am.' That adequately sums up an intimacy into which we need not pry further. There was a great place in 1846 waiting for a woman to fill. Johanna von Puttkamer showed her quality simply by filling it.

Fate had already tapped at the door. Between Bismarck's betrothal and his marriage (April 3 to June 24) the united Diet had met in Berlin, quarrelled with the Crown, and been prorogued. Bismarck was one of its members, confronted in a public capacity for the first time with the Liberal and National forces, to which in numerous utterances he opposed a defiant and unbending Conservatism. He denied that the national rising of 1813 had any constitutional significance, and had any other object than the natural Prussian desire to hurl the foreign invader from the Fatherland. The remark provoked fierce dissent from the Liberal benches. Bismarck pulled a newspaper from his pocket and read it, standing, until the assembly was quiet. He asserted that the Crown of Prussia was worn by the grace of God, not by the grace of the nation; he denied the right of Jews to hold office in a Christian State, rejected as irrelevant all parallels between Prussia and foreign countries, and maintained that abandonment of the Christian basis of the State would reduce it to a fortuitous aggregate of philosophical rights.

The young man of thirty-two was in collision with ideas

and with men he disliked on political and social grounds, and he opposed to them the traditions of the governing class to which he belonged, and which these rebels would destroy in the Prussia that the nobles had made. He gave vigorous expression to the creed of Prussian particularism. Nationalism was the traditional patriotism of Prussians, obeying an unfettered Crown ruling as it pleased through a hereditary aristocracy. Liberalism would destroy the historic Prussia, which must remain the Prussia of Frederick the Great, whom Gerlach noted Bismarck had already adopted as his model. In all these utterances there is no recognition that the strength of Liberalism lay in its mandate to represent forces within and without Prussia that could not be refuted by the rubric and articles of the crude conservatism of a caste, there is no appreciation of the gravity and complexity of the German problem or of Prussia's duty to Germany. The two impressive characteristics in these speeches are the unmistakable sincerity of the speaker's convictions and the undefinable atmosphere of independence which can grow into leadership. Bismarck spoke for himself, but he more than voiced, and men felt it, his party. He was pointing the way, and not merely tramping in the footsteps of others. Well might the Liberals already call him the champion of the Ultras; well might Leopold von Gerlach rejoice that here was an ally and a disciple after his own heart. The young Junker had made his mark. At his marriage enthusiastic friends hailed him as a new Otto the Saxon, a coming Otto the Great.

Allies and disciples of the old dispensation were needed. At Venice Frederick William iv. received Bismarck travelling on his honeymoon. Sovereign and subject next met after the Barricades in Berlin. Before the united Diet could renew its rejected demands, the Revolution of 1848 had swept over Germany and Europe.

§ 2. *The Junker Politician,* 1848-1851

The astonishing period from the March days in Berlin and Vienna to the Convention of Olmütz and the restoration of the fallen Federal Constitution and Diet of 1815, provides a panorama overloaded with bewildering and complicated events. The revolutionary spirit engraved her record with steel on hearts insurgent and scorched with fire. In the evolution of Bismarck's personality and the principles of his statecraft ' 1848 ' closed one chapter and opened another.

The main framework and background can be briefly disentangled. The first phase lasted from March 10 to November 1, during which Austria was crippled by continual riots and placed practically out of action. This gave the simultaneous risings in Germany the upper hand, and enabled the leaders of the Revolution to concentrate their efforts on the National Parliament at Frankfurt, and to work through a national assembly in Berlin for drastic reforms in Prussia. The fate of the Revolution depended on the capacity of this movement to make good its work before the Austrian government could recover and challenge its supremacy. The National Assembly met at Frankfurt on May 13, the Prussian Constituent Assembly on May 22 ; but by the end of June the revolution in Prague had been mastered, and on November 1 Vienna was in the hands of Windischgrätz, and the Ministry of Schwarzenberg, a determined foe to the Revolution, was set up.

A second phase began with November 1, and lasted until April 28, 1849, in which Austria, aided by Prussia, practically killed the Frankfurt programme. Hungary, with the aid of Russia, was reduced ; the battle of Novara (March 23, 1849) virtually crushed the revolution against Austria in Northern Italy ; in Berlin the National Assembly, removed from the capital, was dissolved, and a written Prussian Constitution, drafted by the Crown, was proclaimed (December 5). This was a blow at the Frankfurt Constitution-makers, whose success depended on the acceptance by the German States of the national unification, nearing completion at Frankfurt. The imposition by the Emperor of a new constitution on Austria (March 4, 1849) drove the Prussian stroke home. In April Austria practically declared war on the Frankfurt party. The Liberals had one chance left—to secure Prussia and pit her in alliance with Liberal Germany against Austria. The hereditary Imperial Crown of a Germany unified on a Liberal basis, guaranteed by the written constitution drawn up at Frankfurt, was offered to Frederick William IV. The Prussian government rejected the Frankfurt Constitution, and the King definitely refused the Crown (April 25). The Liberal Revolution had failed.

In the third phase, which lasted until October 5, 1850, the interest concentrates on the attempt of Prussia to make her own solution, an effort mainly influenced by the policy of Radowitz. While Prussian troops were suppressing the remnant of Republican irreconcilables in Baden and the south, the Prussian government endeavoured to form a union of the four kingdoms of Hanover, Saxony, Württemberg, and Bavaria with the petty states under Prussian leadership. The Union was to have a joint Directory, a common Parliament, and a constitution, to consist only of voluntary members, and to establish a close understanding with Austria, excluded from the Germany thus unified. The surrender of Vilagos (August 12) and of Venice (August 22) left Austria now completely free to deal with the Germany that would exclude her from all share in the Prussian Union. The Frankfurt Liberals decided to support the Prussian scheme, but by October 5 the four kingdoms, influenced by Austria, had seceded from the League. Austria had killed the original scheme of the Union. Would and could Prussia, with the petty States, carry the truncated scheme against the four kingdoms and Austria, and establish a union of North Germany under her leadership?

The fourth phase was closed by the Convention or Punctation of Olmütz (November 29, 1850). A Parliament of the Union met at Erfurt, approved a draft Constitution, and adjourned (April 29, 1850). Austria replied by demanding the revival of the old Diet. The Elector of Hesse-Cassel was at a deadlock with his subjects; Hesse-Cassel professed to be a member of the

Union, but the Elector appealed to the old Diet, and his cause was supported by Austria, Bavaria and Württemberg. A Federal execution was ordered. Resistance by Prussia meant war with Austria and her allies in the Diet, on behalf of Liberalism in Hesse-Cassel and the Erfurt Union. Behind Austria stood the Tsar Nicholas i., the spirit incarnate of legitimism and the counter-revolution. The Prussian Court was divided. Many Prussian Conservatives, including Prince William, the heir to the throne, were for war. Much as they disliked Liberalism, their Prussian pride could not brook the humiliation of surrender to Austria. The Austrian party at the Berlin Court, however, only desired to destroy the Revolution and to work with the cause of legitimism at Vienna. War by Prussia in alliance with Liberalism meant civil war in Germany, which must end either in the victory of the Revolution or the destruction of Prussia. Radowitz's resignation on November 3 proclaimed Prussia's refusal to take up the challenge of Austria. The Convention of Olmütz registered the abandonment of the Union and the acceptance by Prussia of the Austrian ultimatum. The Austrian School at the Prussian Court had vanquished alike the conservative Prussian particularists and Liberalism within and without Prussia.

The final phase ended on May 16, 1851. Austrian proposals to modify the old Federal Constitution in her favour failed. To the exile Metternich's joy, the old Confederation was revived unaltered. The position had swung back to that in February 1848, with one important qualification. Prussia accepted a secret alliance with Austria, by which in return for the maintenance of her territorial integrity she guaranteed the whole, and not merely the German part, of the Austrian Empire. The triumph of Austrianism was complete. The attempt to unify Germany through revolution and on the principles of Liberalism had collapsed. Nationalism had collapsed also. When Frederick vii. in 1848 succeeded to the Danish throne, the Duchies of Schleswig and Holstein demanded joint admission to the Germanic Confederation. The Duke of Augustenburg, who claimed to be the heir to the Duchies, was supported by Prussia, whose troops overran Schleswig. It looked as if the Duchies were to be won for Germany ; but Prussia (August 26) made the truce of Malmö with Denmark. Next year, when the Revolution had failed, the Danes compelled Prussia, unsupported by the European Powers or by Austria, to withdraw her troops. The Treaty of London of 1852, drawn up by a European Conference, guaranteed the integrity of the Danish Kingdom, provided for the succession to the Danish Crown, and restored the *status quo* in the Duchies. The attempt, which had the enthusiastic support of the Revolution to liberate ' unredeemed ' Germany from Danish control, and establish a German democratic government in the Duchies, had ended in a complete failure, for which Prussia was largely responsible.

Throughout these three years Bismarck developed a fiery energy. Fear was not a word to be found in his dictionary ; his will could dispose of an iron physique in the prime of manhood. From the March days when he scribbled a note to the King, urging him to stand firm, he was always ready to organise resistance, or, if need be, to head a *coup d'État.* He expressed his views with the brusque and vivid frankness which shocked and puzzled the courts and diplomatists ' du vieux pantalon,' and was a blow in the face of the Liberal benches. He was present in the Marble Hall of the Palace at Potsdam on that grey March evening in 1848 when Frederick William iv., pale and exhausted in mind and body, announced to the assembled officers, waiting for the command of the War-Lord to clear the rebel *canaille* from the streets of the capital, the order for the withdrawal of the troops—a capitulation to the Revolution. An angry clatter of half-drawn swords thrust back into the scabbards, and a growl of indignant mutiny, swept over the hall, ' such as a King of Prussia in the midst of his officers had never heard before and, I hope, will never hear again.' Though he had no part in the memorable Parliament of all Germany in the Church of St. Paul at Frankfurt, Bismarck was a member of the Prussian United Diet, of the Constituent

Assembly, and the National Assembly at Berlin, and of the Union Parliament at Erfurt. He spoke often, and always in uncompromising resistance to the Liberal programme. He took part in the so-called 'Junker Parliament' of August 1848—a conference of the Conservative Ultras organised in a league for defence of king and country. He was one of the group which founded and wrote for the *Kreuzzeitung*, henceforward the leading organ of the Conservative Party; throughout he remained in the closest touch with the Gerlach Circle, the organisers of the famous Camarilla, the unofficial secret ministry which utilised the social position of its members and political intrigues to undermine every minister tainted with Liberalism, and to force the vacillating and impressionable Frederick William IV. into obedience to the counter-revolution. No member of the Conservative rank and file worked harder than Bismarck to defeat the Revolution of the Barricades, the Liberalism of Frankfurt, or the Union policy of Radowitz. But he remained in the rank and file. The efforts of the Camarilla to secure office for him failed. Frederick William recognised the unimpeachable loyalty of this Junker subject, but to have given office to this ' red reactionary, smacking of blood, only to be employed when the bayonet reigns without reservation,' would have involved a breach with the Moderates as well as with the Liberals. The King probably saw in Bismarck the representative of the men who waged a truceless war on every effort to link the destinies of Prussia with a Germany from which Austria was excluded. The influence of Radowitz was predominant until Austria made it clear that the King of Prussia must choose between war and surrender. It is not improbable that Frederick William justly feared the influence of Bismarck's resolute will on his own obstinate irresolution. Nursing to the end the dream of a monarchical Prussia which should gather in a free union under its eagle wings the German kings, grand dukes, and landgraves, and build a golden bridge to meet an imperial and purified Austria, Frederick William shrank from the pitiless freelance, master of the flouting phrase that stuck, who amidst courts and national assemblies superheated with sentiment sought for realities and realities alone.

'I was a terrible Junker in those days,' Bismarck remarked long after. 'I grant,' he said in 1847, 'that I am full of prejudices; I sucked them in with my mother's milk and I cannot argue them away.' It is a trifle, but a significant one, that in 1848 he deliberately inserted in his public and private letters the 'von' in front of the Bismarck in his signature, which hitherto he had not used. As Frederick William said at Cologne, 'There are kings still in Germany, and I am one of them,' so Bismarck conveyed that there were nobles still in Germany and he was one of them. 'A terrible Junker,' yes, but not an unattractive one, though he lacked the higher graciousness. His superb physical vigour, his courage, his love of meat and drink and tobacco, his power to drink and enjoy the cup of life to the dregs, a buoyant geniality, and an amazing frankness, extorted admiration even from his bitterest opponents. The trenchancy of his principles was matched by the unrestrained recklessness of his tongue. He revelled in his irresponsibility and the power to castigate everything and every one he disliked. 'A handsome, muscular, and truly noble figure,' is the description of an eye-witness, 'in which is revealed in every feature the chivalrous courage and also the refinement of the landed aristocracy'; 'un gaillard avec le diable au corps,' summed up another critic. He was, in fact, the Bismarck of Kniephof and the United Diet, battling now in a Berserker lust for the fray with Revolution and anti-Prussians. To be young was good, to be strong was better, to have your adversary in your power and crush him was best of all. 'Every courtesy,' he told the Liberal von Vincke at the buffet in the interval of a heated debate, 'every courtesy as far as the gallows,' and he meant it. The Minister-President of the 'sixties, who could not sleep because he was hating all night, could assuredly boil with passion and disdain at thirty-two. Yet Schönhausen and his wife and the children now being born to him, were always in his mind. He yearned for his manorial hearth, for the sonatas of Beethoven, when the day's work in the field or

forest was over, and he could smoke his long pipe in the
corner by the great stove. At Erfurt in the spring of 1851
he would leave the Parliament to despatch tender inquiries
about measles or headaches, to stroll for hours through the
pine woods in the sunshine, watching the birds, noting
the cattle in the field, and reckoning the value of the
timber, or lie smoking countless cigars staring up at the blue
sky and reflecting that a landowner's life was freer and far
more enjoyable than these accursed politics, made worse
by the nerveless ministers who ought to drink a bottle
of champagne at every meal to give them some courage
and grit.

His political creed was as lucid as the terms in which he
expressed it. It was idle, he said in April 1848, to regret
the March days. The monarchy had itself thrown the
earth on the coffin. He could have had some sympathy,
he remarked, with the Revolution if it had proposed to
plant the German flag on the cathedral of Strasburg ; it
only proposed to fasten on the healthy body of Prussia
the Nessus shirt of Gallican Jacobinism. Similarly, the
Prussian Constitution of December 5 (limited as it was)
went further than he wished, but it was a free gift from
the Crown, and it must be accepted and worked because it
came from the Crown and not from the gutter. All attempts to deduce from it principles contradictory to the unfettered prerogative of the sovereign were illegitimate, and
must be resisted. Two points he never tired of pressing :
first, the specific and unique character of the Prussian
State ; secondly, its incompatibility with the Liberalism
which would dissolve the historic independence of
Prussia in a mongrel German unity. ' What has held us
together,' he said on September 6, 1849, ' is exactly our
specific Prussianism. It was the residue of the decried
Prussianism which survived the Revolution—I mean the
Prussian army, our Prussian treasure, the fruit of long
years of intelligent administration and the living instrument that stands between the Prussian king and his
people. . . . That people from which this army is drawn,
and of which the army is the truest representative, has no
desire to see its Prussian monarchy drowned in the putrid

yeast of South German anarchy. . . . We all desire the Prussian eagle to spread its guardian and governing wings from the Memel to the Donnersberg, but free will we see him, not fettered by a new Parliament at Regensburg, not sheltering under the feathers of the levelling vulture from Frankfurt. . . . Prussians we are and Prussians we will remain. I know that I express in these words the creed of the majority of my countrymen, and I hope to God we shall remain Prussians long after this piece of paper has been forgotten like a withered autumn leaf.' A dozen similar passages to the same effect could be quoted. Bismarck rejoiced over the rejection of the Imperial Crown offered by the Frankfurt National Parliament.

' The phantoms,' he said, ' of the theorists at Frankfurt have cost us in six months more blood, money and tears than thirty-three years of despotism. . . . The Frankfurt Crown may be very brilliant, but the gold which gives reality to the brilliance must first be won by melting down the Prussian Crown, and I have no confidence that the recasting will fit the form of our Prussian Constitution. My Prussian patriotism and so-called antediluvian point of view are as precious to me as a refuge from the flood in Noah's ark.'

' I fear,' he exclaimed, ' the whimpering sentimentality of our century, which discovers a martyr in every fanatical rebel and in every discontented fighter at the barricades.' And he stated his own theory of political government when he said :—

' History provides us with the most brilliant and grand, though not the most beneficial, phenomenon in a special degree under the mark of absolutism, but we can find more numerous examples of lasting political prosperity and power in States subject to the influence of a hereditary aristocracy . . . the brilliant memories of the German Empire point to a powerful Imperial nobility. The mediæval prosperity of our cities began to wither at the time when the patrician families went down before the pressure of the Guilds . . . England trod a happier path ; she had no Richelieu who cut off the heads in which a hereditary wisdom resides to an exceptional degree. The character of the English Revolution is Freedom, of the French, Equality . . . French Equality is the will-of-the-wisp, daughter of Envy and Greed, pursued without success by that richly gifted nation for sixty years through blood and madness. Let us refuse to join in that pursuit on the false supposition that it is popular.'

Radowitz's resignation and the collapse of his policy filled Bismarck with such joy that he danced on his chair round his room three times. The humiliating convention of Olmütz occasioned the most weighty and remarkable speech he had yet made. Nothing was easier, he pointed out, than to make war ; but, with an indirect allusion to Frederick the Great :—

'The one sound basis of a great Power which differentiates it essentially from the petty State, is political egoism and not romanticism, and it is unworthy of a great State to fight for what is not connected with its interest. . . . Woe to the statesman who at this time has not sought a reason for going to war which after the war will no less stand the test.'

He rejected the idea that honour required Prussia ' to play the Don Quixote all over Germany on behalf of sickly demagogues, who imagined their local constitutions in danger.' And then he came to close grips with his real gravamen against the whole policy of the Erfurt Union.

The Union involved nothing less than the destruction of Prussia's independence, not by the princes, but by the parliaments of the petty States. A war by Prussia to maintain the Union could only recall to his mind the Englishman who overpowered the sentinel in order that he might vindicate the right of every free Briton to commit suicide in the sentry-box.

In this speech Bismarck, for all its lucid trenchancy of expression, was groping his way to settled principles of foreign policy. It was not the interest of Prussia to fight ' as the shameful ally of democracy ' against Austria : she could attain her objects by co-operation with, not by opposition to, Austria, and the identity of Prussian and Austrian interests made war unjustifiable in 1850. Bismarck was also answering in advance the critics who have

urged that twenty years later it was this same Bismarck
who practically carried out Radowitz's programme—the
unification of North Germany under Prussia's presidency
—and only carried it out at the price Radowitz was not
allowed to pay in 1850, war with Austria and her allies,
the German kingdoms. The criticism ignores the deep-
seated grounds of Bismarck's opposition to Radowitz's
policy. In 1850, Prussia's one possible ally was Liberalism
in Germany : a Prussian victory would be not a victory
for Prussia's independence and position as a great state,
but for Liberalism. The Liberals, not Prussia, would give
the law to Prussia and Germany. But war was only a
continuance of policy—a policy based on specific Prussian
interests—to enable Prussia to establish the relations on
which she wished to live in peace with her neighbours and
rivals. The last thing that the Bismarck of 1850 or of
1866 desired or regarded as a real Prussian interest, was
the triumph of Liberalism. Moreover, in 1850 Radowitz,
in Bismarck's judgment, miscalculated. Behind Austria
and her German allies stood the sinister strength of a
Russia which had struck down Hungary, and was about to
impose its will in Schleswig-Holstein. Across the Rhine
was a revolutionary France, ready to intervene. In 1866
France's neutrality had been secured, a crippled Russia
was benevolently neutral, Italy was Prussia's ally. A victorious Prussia would annex Schleswig-Holstein and more.
In brief, between the statecraft of Radowitz and that of
Bismarck there was no identity in temper, methods,
principles, or aims. The two men interpreted the interest
of Prussia and of Germany as differently as two opposed
minds could.

In 1850, his whole argument hinged on the contention
that the Union of Erfurt was a false step in the wrong
direction, and rested on the fundamental and explicit
assumption that the historic Prussia could secure ' her
interests and her honour ' by the loyal co-operation of
Austria and Prussia. The words were Bismarck's, but the
voice was the voice of the Gerlachs and the cosmopolitan
Conservatives who saw in a renewed Holy Alliance with
Austria the salvation of Prussia and the defeat of the

Revolution. In 1850 ' the terrible Junker ' had not penetrated to the heart either of Germany or of Austria, nor had
he defined for himself, except in a superficial and conventional way, ' the interest, the egoism ' which ought to be
the sole basis of Prussian policy. But, as yet, he was not
aware that his knowledge was very limited and his interpretation shallow and retarding.

Generally for Germany, the restoration of the old Diet
in 1851 registered two decisive defeats—the defeat of the
Revolution, and of Prussia. Liberalism in alliance with
Nationalism set out, through revolution, to achieve unification, and to create a truly federal organisation with
democratic and responsible parliamentary government,
under an imperial and limited monarchy, the whole defined and embodied in a written constitution. The
Liberal majority in the National Assembly at Frankfurt had
rejected the programme of Radical Republicanism. It had
also rejected the programme of the Great German Party
(*Gross-Deutschland*). The German provinces of Austria,
included in the old Bund, were excluded. The organisation of the excluded Austria was left to Austria, and the
political and fiscal relations between the new German
Empire (*Klein-Deutschland*) and the reconstituted Austrian
Empire were reserved for later diplomatic arrangements.
But the authors of the Constitution of 1848 contemplated
not merely a political alliance, but a spiritual and moral
union wider and deeper than the formal bargain of a
treaty—the creation of a central Germanic Europe, finding
its expression in the material framework of constitutional
and economic organisation, and guaranteed by a community of purpose in the intellectual and political life of
two self-governing and democratic empires.

This comprehensive scheme, the work of high-minded
and able men, was a noble and imaginative effort in constructive statesmanship, which bears the stamp of the
idealism and an inspiring belief in the capacities of a race
for achieving salvation when men build on the uplands,
and not the lowlands, of human endeavour. What constructive statesmanship, indeed, has ever achieved permanent results on the theory that the spiritual and in-

tellectual consciousness of nationhood can be satisfied or stifled by economic and material well-being alone ? Had the unification of 1848 been given a fair trial it would have moulded the German mind and directed German destinies and ambitions into paths of self-development of incalculable benefit to Germany and the world. Its failure was a tragedy for German and European civilisation.

That failure is commonly ascribed to the academic amateurism of its authors, who wasted their time in threshing out fundamental rights when apparently they should have been cutting off heads or shooting down opposition, or lynching the King of Prussia. Such criticism is really amateur, Philistine, and ignorant of what revolution by Liberal methods from an old to a new system implies. As if the task of devising a federal unification of the Germany of 1848 and of solving the German problem could have been accomplished by any brain or any action in a few weeks, least of all by force.

In 1866, Bismarck with the experience of 1848 and twenty years of earnest constructive thought by many brains at his disposal, with Austria and her German allies prostrate, with a Prussian monarch wholly on his side and a victorious Prussian army at his beck and call, took ten months to work out, impose and bring into operation a unification, not of all Germany, but of the north alone—and Bismarck had been preparing for the task for four unrelenting years.

The remarkable feature of 1848, in reality, was the rapidity with which in the smoke and dust of a bewildering revolution the liberal majority hammered out by argument and under the conditions of government by public meeting, a scheme of unification that probed deeper and was more complete than the constitution of 1867. The men who could accomplish that, in spite of their lack of training in public affairs, were not unfitted to be leaders and teachers in self-government, or to make the policy and control the destinies of a great nation.

What they did lack was an army and the executive organs of government, and before they could create them they were crushed not by Germany, nor the princes, but by Russia and Austria—the two foreign States to which Liberalism and Nationalism, as Germans understood them, were anathema. The hero of the reaction was Nicholas i., without whose aid Schwarzenberg and Windischgrätz could not have mastered Prague and Vienna, nor dictated the surrenders of Vilagos, Olmütz, and Novara. Liberalism went down. Radical Republicanism does not appear again as a force to be reckoned with, except perhaps in sporadic and convulsive efforts in Württemberg. But Liberalism was not killed, neither was its twin, Nationalism.

The defeat and failure of Prussia—also at the hands of Russia and Austria—was the second outstanding fact in 1851. Prussia, unlike the Liberals of Frankfurt, had both an army and executive organs of government. Unlike Austria and almost every other German State, she had not been mastered by the Revolution. The strength of the monarchy and the grip of the royal autocracy on the army and the governing class were as convincingly revealed, as after the disaster of Jena. But from the March Days until Olmütz Prussia was hopelessly divided. The Liberals under G. von Vincke, the Moderate Conservatives under Brandenburg, the Constitutionalists led by Radowitz, the Junker Camarilla, under the Gerlachs, the Militarists thirsting for a *coup d'Etat* in the manner of Schwarzenberg, Windischgrätz and Haynau, the pure Particularists exemplified in Prince William, ' the Cartridge Prince,' the heir to the throne, to whom first and foremost Prussia was a *Grossmacht*, which must fight for honour and independence, the Poles in Prussian Poland crying out for national independence, the clericals from the Rhenish districts to whom the secular omnipotence of the autocracy was as dangerous as the secular atheism of the Revolution, and the Communists of the *Vorwärts*, founded by Karl Marx from Prussian Trier and Engels from Prussian Barmen—the men who created both the socialism of Lassalle and Bebel —all these whirled in vortices of varying strength round the King, who could have led if he could have made up his mind, or could have been deprived of a mind to make up But Frederick William persistently refused either to frame a policy for himself or to carry through a policy ready-made by any one else. The result was that Prussia failed to satisfy any single party at home, or the German dynasties and Austria without. The monarchical state cut a sorry figure in the March Days, in the Schleswig-Holstein fiasco, in the imposition of a badly drafted, inconsistent, and mongrel constitution, in the refusal of the Imperial Crown, in the hasty and ill-prepared Union schemes, in the Hesse-Cassel business, in the desertion of Radowitz, in the defiance of, and undignified surrender to, Austria at Olmütz. Prussia, in short, failed everybody in turn, and all parties had to drink of the bitter cup that her monarch ceaselessly brewed. Her prestige both at home and abroad had sunk to a low level, and the fall was not arrested in 1851.

These three years had, moreover, laid bare three impressive facts : the categorical refusal of Austria to allow Prussia either to usurp the Austrian leadership or to exercise an independent initiative in a limited and defined German sphere, the jealousy and fear of Prussia felt by the middle States in particular, the appeal to Prussia, as the sole hope, by all to whom the old system was intolerable. All three were the expression of forces and ambitions, separate in their origin and ends from the struggle between Liberalism and Conservatism, or between the ideals of the national and the dynastic and territorial State. Hanover, Bavaria, Württemburg, and Saxony—the four kingdoms —did not take up and then desert the scheme of the Erfurt Union from fear of Liberalism or attachment to Conservatism. The denunciation of Prussia as aiming at a League of Secession (Sonderbund) was made, curiously enough, in the name of German unity—unity through the dynasties—but Austria and the middle States increasingly felt that the Union would only end as the Zollverein had done, in an organisation controlled by its most powerful member. While Bismarck saw in the scheme the stain of a sinister surrender to democracy, the Four Kingdoms saw in it the sinister supremacy of the militarist police State of Prussia—an instrument for mediatising the political independence of the sovereign princedoms ; and the truculent pride of Prussian Junkertum was more terrifying than the levelling doctrines of Prussian Liberals and South German Democrats.　It was not only on the Liberal benches of the Landtag that Bismarck's stark Prussianism was neither forgiven nor forgotten, and his defiant prediction that the day would come when Prussian Junkertum would justify its claims, was not a day desired at Dresden, Munich, Herrenhausen, and Stuttgart—least of all at Vienna.　The Liberals had turned a suppliant appeal for Prussia's strength.　To the profound relief of the middle States and of Austria, Prussia refused to fight either for herself or for anybody else.　She meekly agreed to re-enter the restored confederation, and to accept as a principle of conduct that co-operation with Austria, which since 1815 had been simply a euphemism for subordination and self-effacement.

The Austrians and the middle States miscalculated, because they ignored the Revolution and its results.　The Prussia that re-entered the dynastic family party, termed the Federal Diet at Frankfurt, was not the Prussia of 1847. Since 1851 Prussia had a written constitution, a Parliament of Two Houses, a franchise, if a restricted one, a budget which had to be voted by the Lower House, even if she had not been given a ministry responsible to the Landtag. In a word, she had the organs through which the constitutional party could organise, develop, and focus the shattered Liberalism of 1848 and link it up with the shattered Liberalism from the Memel to the Donnersberg.　And neither the Camarilla nor the Haynaus, neither the Stahls of the *Kreuzzeitung,* nor a Schwarzenberg, nor a Bach could prevent the Prussian intellectuals from thinking, or could muzzle the Lehrfreiheit and Lernfreiheit—the freedom to teach and to learn—of the universities, or prohibit men like Gneist, Sybel, Virchow, Vincke, Forckenbeck, Unruh, from working and corresponding with a Bennigsen, a Roggenbach, a von der Pfordten, a Bassermann, or a Stockmar in Hanover, Bavaria, Baden and Coburg.　More dangerous still, they could not keep even the Junkers from reading and thinking, and one Junker in particular, Otto von Bismarck-Schönhausen.

It was no less a miscalculation to infer that the European situation would retain the features of 1848-51—a happy and 'healthy' antipathy to revolution and a magic power to re-establish reaction, that Russian absolutism would invariably be proof against Austrian ingratitude and treachery, that Italy would fail to produce a statesman, and always end in a Novara, that the young and new Emperor of Austria, Francis Joseph, would exchange dynastic selfishness for wisdom, that Prussia would always be governed by a Frederick William iv. and a Manteuffel, and be hypnotised by a Camarilla, and that the Eastern Question and Schleswig-Holstein would not again trouble the Chancelleries. Liberalism and Nationalism were like the gout, always causing local pains, neglect or mistreatment of which would drive them into attacking the heart.

In May 1851, Germany could read that his Majesty the King of Prussia had been pleased to appoint Herr von Bismarck-Schönhausen to be Councillor of Legation, and on July 15 to be the Prussian federal representative and plenipotentiary, at the Frankfurt Diet. Germany knew little and cared less about the revived Diet. It was on the point of forgetting Bismarck. That an irreconcilable Junker should represent reactionary Prussia in the obsolete Federal Diet was in the nature of things. The making of a statesman who would solve the German problem was the last result Germany looked for from Junkertum, Prussia, and Frankfurt.

CHAPTER III

THE MAKING OF A STATESMAN, 1851–1862

§ 1. *Bismarck at Frankfurt,* 1851–1859

THE eleven years from May 1851, when Bismarck was sent to Frankfurt, to September 1862, when he became Minister-President of Prussia, are not great years in the history of Prussia, but they are great years in the history of Europe, in which the stage was prepared for the drama in which Bismarck made himself the leading figure. In the development of his personality, the crystallisation of the principles of his statecraft, they are the central, critical, and decisive period.

Emphasis of this conclusion does not imply that in 1862, when this second phase ended, Bismarck had already reached the mastery of technique and the maturity of experience and conviction which high and responsible office alone could consummate; nor that in 1862 his development was arrested and that he had nothing more to learn; still less that he came into power with a cut-and-dried programme, and merely required the opportunity and the political authority to carry it out. Such a conclusion would ignore the opportunism, which he rightly and proudly regarded as one of the most conspicuous features —one of the *idées maitresses* of his statecraft—and rob of all significance another and no less justifiable claim that he was a learner all his life.

The results of this decade must be sought in the subtle, gradual, but profound changes in Bismarck himself. They can only be measured by comparing the man who went to Frankfurt with the man who deliberately accepted the challenge that the Minister-Presidency thrust upon him in 1862. Frankfurt provided the

indispensable experience for interpreting the full significance of the German problem for Germany and Prussia.
The ministerial posts at Petersburg and Paris enabled him
to complete the experience by correlating it to the knowledge of the political conditions of the European situation.
This knowledge of the tides, rocks, shallows, and winds he
had hitherto conspicuously lacked. To-day we are able
to trace from original and unimpeachable sources the
process of its acquisition and the sediment of conviction
that it slowly deposited. By 1862 he had decided that
there was a German, and not merely a Prussian, problem
to be solved ; that the negative and defensive Junkertum
of 1848-51 would not do, and that Prussia must find a
Prussian solution that was also applicable to Germany.

A new diplomacy, new principles of action, a new attitude of mind, and a new interpretation of Prussia's interest
therefore, were imperatively required to rescue her from
the blunders of the past and the menace of the future—
surrender to Liberalism or surrender to Austria.

Last and not least, the man Bismarck became inspired
with the ambition to devise and execute the new policy.
The growth, scope, and quality of a man's ambition are
always as decisive as the increase of his knowledge and the
development of his intellectual powers. In 1862, Bismarck had attained the supreme conviction that he could
both save his beloved Prussia and solve the German problem, and that no one else could do both. Character and
creed harmonised in a final union.

The European framework throughout this critical phase
of development is important. In 1851, the *coup d'État* at
Paris and the proclamation of the Empire in the following
year made a violent rupture in the stratification of Europe.
Henceforward the seismographs of the Chancelleries were
nervously watched for the red record of further upheavals
that would test the stability of every State. The advent
of Cavour to office and the inauguration of the Risorgimento at Turin, were even more important than the downfall of the French Republic and the inauguration of the
neo-Cæsarism at Paris, but ' the man of December,' the
sphinx without a secret, held Europe spell-bound. The

greatness and significance of Cavour were ignored or underrated and misinterpreted until his death revealed what
Italy and Europe had lost. The watershed of the nineteenth century was, in fact, crossed in the Crimean War,
in which the sound British fear of Russian autocracy and
of the terrorism of Europe by Nicholas I. leaped into
flame. The struggle between a Liberal West and the
Russia of 1854, fought out in the Crimea, not merely involved Great Britain and Russia in bitter antagonism for
two generations, but thrust the Near Eastern Question
into a prominence that it never again lost ; it broke up
the *entente* between Austria and Russia ; it brought Great
Britain and Italy together, and, curiously enough, made
an Anglo-French *entente* very difficult to maintain. Most
important as an immediate result was the crippling of
Russia's strength and ability to buttress up the monarchies,
legitimism and autocracy of Central Europe ; the Crimean
War, the Treaty of Paris, the death of Nicholas I., and the
internal situation in Russia deprived Alexander II. of the
desire or the capacity to repeat the policy of his inflexible
predecessor.

At the Congress of Paris the diplomatic salute was taken
by Napoleon III., though Cavour compelled the nervous
diplomatists of 1856 to recognise that the Italian Question
was a malady, calling for surgery, and not for opiates and
soothing poultices. Every Foreign Office in Europe, including that of the Vatican, was now ruefully aware that
the Near Eastern Question brought the Habsburg dynasty,
ruling over its mosaic of denationalised and submerged
races, in whom the memories of 1848 continued sullenly
to glow, into irreconcilable collision with Russia. No
Foreign Office was more painfully aware than that of the
Vatican (except, perhaps, the series of distracted ministers
who came, tried and failed at the Ball-Platz in Vienna)
that the Italian Question opened up issues far wider and of
deeper import than maintenance of the Treaties of 1815,
the continuance of the Austrian flag on the citadel at
Milan and on the Piazza di San Marco at Venice, or the
barbarism of a Bomba at Naples. Ultramontanism was
the weapon of the Papacy, and was rightly so named, for

its strength lay beyond the Western Alps, where it had
planted itself in the Tuileries, and had its unofficial legate,
the Empress, at the table and couch of the Emperor ;
beyond the Northern Alps, its roots were deep in the
separatist and clerical Bavaria, in the mediæval ' Priests'
Alley ' of the Main, in Rhenish Prussia, and in Prussian
Poland, whose nobles rubbed shoulders with the Prussian
Junkers in the cabinet of the King, and whose ladies whis-
pered in the drawing-room of the Queen of Prussia.
Across the Eastern Alps, in the city of St. Stephen, what
more devoted son was there than the Habsburg who was
Apostolical King of Hungary ? In these years the offen-
sive strategy was being constructed that leads from the
Proclamation of the Immaculate Conception of the
Blessed Virgin in 1854 to the Syllabus of 1864 and the
Vatican Decrees of 1870.

Liberalism and Nationalism, in their slow, but steady
renaissance from the débâcle of 1848, had the constructive
and reconstructed reply of the counter-Reformation to
reckon with sooner or later. Prussia had already crossed
swords with the claims of the Roman Catholic Church as
a cosmopolitan organisation in her Rhenish Provinces in
the decade between 1830 and 1840, and had failed to
secure a decision in favour of the omnipotent and secular
State. The *Kulturkampf* of 1873 lay, not in the logic of
history so much as in the logic of the humanist mind, once
Austria and Austrianism had been overthrown and the
Tuileries were in flames, Napoleon an exile at Chislehurst
and the Bourbons nerveless *emigrés* at Frohsdorf. Liberalism, Nationalism, and Prussianism in combination made
the *Kulturkampf* a foregone conclusion. But it was
Cavour, the Risorgimento, and the Liberal unification of
Italy—with the Rome of the Papacy omitted, but dependent henceforward on the stability of the Second Empire
—that opened the battle by challenging the alleged right
of an ecclesiastical sovereign to bar the consummation of
Nationalism in a modern State.

The compact of Plombières led to the Annus Mirabilis
of 1859. Magenta and Solferino, despite Villa Franca,
followed by Garibaldi's expedition of The Thousand, and

the collapse of the dynasties in Italy, set every Liberal and Nationalist pulse beating feverishly throughout Europe. At Kiel and Rendsburg, in the Duchies of Schleswig-Holstein, at Posen, Warsaw, Cracow, and Lemberg in dismembered Poland, at Bucharest and Jassy in the Danubian principalities, at Buda-Pesth in Hungary, no less than in the universities and capital of a federated but disunited Germany, the vital spark of faith and hope burned in reply to the beacons lit in Turin, Florence, and Palermo. 'Italy's year' coincided with a change of sovereign at Berlin, when Prince William became regent for his brother (October 26, 1858), and with the advent of a Liberal Ministry in Great Britain, whose action quietly but decisively checkmated an Austrian counter-stroke against the unification of the Italian South with the North.

The intellectual movement was no less impressive. It was the period when the modern mind of the nineteenth century was being made. The year 1859 is memorable for Darwin's *Origin of Species*, but between the years 1854 and 1870 the annals of Europe are studded with famous names and remarkable achievements in every department of intellectual and imaginative effort—Tennyson, Browning, Swinburne, Stubbs, Herbert Spencer, Carlyle, Lister, Clerk-Maxwell and the Pre-Raphaelites in England, Pasteur, Victor Hugo, Taine, Flaubert, Sainte-Beuve and the Barbizon School in France; Virchow, Helmholtz, Mommsen, Sybel, Droysen, Wagner, Brahms and Karl Marx in Germany. And if the United States had done nothing but produce Abraham Lincoln, Grant and Lee, it had accomplished much. Had the United States not proclaimed in memory of 'its honoured dead . . . that we here highly resolve . . . that government of the people, by the people, for the people shall not perish from the earth'?

Europe since 1849 had been gripped in the years of Arctic reaction. Warm water was once more steadily flowing beneath the frozen surface, and great fissures were now cracking through; the floes, loosened and sapped from beneath were grinding, packing, breaking away, and toppling over. 'The God of battles,' Bismarck had predicted in 1849, 'would throw the iron dice that would decide.' The first casts of those iron dice had been thrown at Inkerman, the Malakoff Redoubt, and at Solferino.

Prussia since 1851 had endured a drab and fatigued re-action, administered by timid and second-rate ministers. The hand of the police and the Minister of the Interior was heavy on personal liberty, the freedom of the press, and everything and everybody suspected of Liberal views, which were identified with revolution. But, despite every discouragement, the constitutional Liberals retained their hold on the middle class, and in the Lower House of the Landtag they consolidated a critical and earnest oppo-sition, which in both sections of the party—the Moderates and the Radicals—was affiliated by a common programme with Liberalism in Hanover, the Saxon principalities, Baden, and the more democratic South. As in Italy under the Risorgimento official Liberalism, though without office quietly shed the idea of reform by revolution.

The dividing lines in the opposition to the dominant system were determined rather by the differences between a moderate Liberalism and a drastic Radicalism; the old revolutionary party was substituting economic Socialism for political Jacobinism, finding its inspiration not in the school of Mazzini, but in that of Marx, and transforming the struggle for political rights into the class war, the piti-less contest of an exploited industrial proletariat against the organisation of society under capitalist direction and for capitalist ends. Constitutional Liberalism tended more and more to be the creed of a middle class, the importance of which was enhanced by economic development; it steadily aimed not at overthrowing the dynasties but at converting them, at victory by persuasion and moral pene-tration, at unification by agreement expressed through all the organs of the national life, the universities, the parliaments, the press, the machinery of parties, and an irresistible public opinion, disciplined into the possession of a common will. It was this programme and method on which Bismarck poured contempt.

Frederick William iv., who had never owned a will, was now rapidly losing his mind. The Regency of 1858 under

Prince William, inaugurated the ' new era.' The repressive internal administration was relaxed : a ministry with strong Liberal leanings under Prince Anthony of Hohenzollern was formed ; and on August 14, 1859, the German National Union, founded by Bennigsen of Hanover, issued from Eisenach an authoritative programme for the united constitutional and democratic parties. It demanded a national and independent German foreign policy, a strong and constitutional central administration for the whole of Germany in the place of the Diet ; and, most significant of all, it insisted that this Central Power, vested with military and diplomatic control, must be in the hands of Prussia, and that the initiative to establish it must come from Prussia. All Liberals and Democrats were urged henceforward to work for the establishment of German unity on a constitutional basis under Prussian direction and control—a Prussia to be Liberalised by its assumption of the directorship.

The Nationalist passion, vibrating in this remarkable document, is no less noticeable than its stress on constitutional rights. In 1859, Liberalism and Nationalism looked with eager hope to the Prussia of the ' new era.' Two appointments, however, might have given pause to all who dreamed of the Prussian army as an instrument for the Eisenach programme. In 1858, Colonel von Moltke had been appointed Chief of the General Staff—though not yet the important office it subsequently became—and Albrecht von Roon, the intimate friend of Bismarck, and an unflinching Conservative, replaced the Liberal General Bonin as Minister of War. Moltke, though the public did not know it yet, was the ablest of the Clausewitz School. Roon as a minister regarded himself as the Greek horse introduced by Providence into the Liberal Troy. And he was determined, like our George II., to keep the army free from the interference of the scoundrels in the House of Commons.

The National Union concentrated public attention on the urgency of national unification, the abolition of the Federal Diet, and a national and united foreign policy in view of the danger from France and the attitude of Austria.

The cry from Schleswig-Holstein was becoming louder every year. What the Danubian principalities were to the Eastern Question, the Duchies were to the German problem. They concentrated the local malady in a European framework, and no single European Power could move without tripping over treaties and conventions, and without stirring the jealousy and fear of every other Power. The Danish Radicals at Copenhagen were bent, like the Sublime Porte, on playing off the Powers against each other, and by the equilibrium of a skilfully poised selfishness achieving their own ends. Bennigsen, Duncker, Brockhaus, and the other distinguished signatories of the Eisenach Programme agreed with the diplomatist who said that the reform of the Diet was like cutting off the hump on a hunchback—fatal to the hunchback and useless to the surgeon. By ending and not mending could Germany alone obtain a truly national and vigorously executed foreign policy on behalf of German interests. When the National Union traced the root of all difficulties to Vienna they went to the heart of the matter.

Amongst the bad sleepers of Europe none slept so badly as Francis Joseph, and on his dynastic bed the Habsburg ruler threshed restlessly from left to right and from right to left, and could find no repose. Within his dominions it was indeed constitutions, counter-constitutions, reconstitutions, order, counter-order, disorder. The Crimean War placed Austria at the parting of the ways; the compact of Plombières and the war of 1859 aggravated the dilemma. The retention of her supremacy in Italy conflicted with the retention of her presidency in Germany; jealousy of Prussia demanded an understanding with France; Milan and Venetia involved her in war with Turin and Napoleon; she broke with Russia in order to keep in close touch with the Western Powers and prevent a Russian protectorate of the Danubian principalities and the Balkans; but German Nationalism demanded opposition to France: the middle German States expected Austria to save them from a Prussian hegemony; German Liberalism called for the abolition of the Bund and the Diet, and would only support Austria if she made concessions

fatal to her control in Germany and suicidal in Italy and
Hungary. 'There is only one statesman in Europe,'
Metternich had said in 1856, ' M. de Cavour, and he is
against us.' Cavour was the most brilliant and effective
Liberal statesman in Europe since Canning : his death in
1861 was a tragic blow to the whole cause of Liberalism
on the Continent; and it came at the unhappy moment
when Liberalism in Germany needed genius outside
Germany as an ally. Russell and Palmerston were not a
compensation for Cavour. Nor did Cavour's death bring
relief to Austria. Had Metternich lived to 1861 he might
have repeated his judgment : ' There is only one statesman in Europe, Herr von Bismarck, and he is against us.'

Bismarck asserted more than once that when he went to
Frankfurt in May 1851, he was ' an Austrian with the
political views that I brought, so to speak from my home,
sharpened by the struggle with the attacks of the Revolution of 1848 against principles that I valued '; and he
maintained that his personal political convictions coincided with his official instructions in the determination
to carry out the policy outlined in his Olmütz speech.
Prussia was to accept the presidential authority of Austria,
and to co-operate loyally on terms of equality with Austria
in all German affairs, on the basis of common Conservative
principles with common Conservative ends. The character of this union and the calculable results of its efficacy
reconciled him to the ' surrender ' involved in the Convention of Olmütz. But Bismarck in 1851 was not an
' Austrian ' in the sense that he was prepared to sacrifice
the interest of Prussia to Austrian supremacy. His
Prussian Junkertum and the unlimited independence of his
own personality would have forbidden the surrender, even
if he had not clearly indicated that the egoism and interest
of Prussia must be the sole basis of her policy. Equality
with Austria within the Diet was an essential for Prussia ;
she was not a Hanover, a Saxony, or a Bavaria, still less a
Baden or a Hesse-Cassel.

The eight years at Frankfurt were for Bismarck a period
of continuous disillusion and enlightenment—disillusion
as to the interpretation that Austria placed on the co-

operation of Prussia, enlightenment as to the principles which Austrian policy implied. The successors of Schwarzenberg at Vienna, not unnaturally, calculated on the humiliated Prussia of 1851. Austria lived in the past because it was impossible to live for a new future without jettisoning the only principles that kept the Empire of Francis Joseph together. But the Ball-Platz did not reckon on Bismarck. As early as 1851 a dispatch to Berlin struck a note of warning. Bismarck was at the outset inferior to the Austrian representatives in knowledge of the ground and in technique ; he had not at his disposal the public or personal prestige, the machinery and the countless levers—ultramontane, dynastic, Conservative, and social—by which Austria, entrenched in an historic ascendancy, worked the middle and petty States to her will.

The two famous incidents of the cigar and the shirt-sleeves delighted all the gossip-mongers of the higher diplomacy. Hitherto, no one but ' Austria ' dared smoke at the meetings ; but Bismarck lit his cigar at once, and before long even the petty States followed his example. Received by Count von Thurn in his shirt-sleeves, Bismarck pulled off his coat. ' I agree,' he said, ' it is a hot day.' These were trifles, but precious trifles. What was more important was the thoroughness with which he mastered his new profession. As with agriculture so with diplomacy, he was determined to penetrate to the heart of the business. ' No human being,' he wrote to his wife, ' not even the most malicious sceptic of a democrat, would believe the charlatanry and imposture hidden in this Diplomacy.' His power of work was inexhaustible ; his physique responded to any strain he chose to put on it, and his brains were far superior to those of his rivals. It is clear from his official reports, written with a verve, vividness, and command of the subject-matter that have made them classical documents in German history, and from his private correspondence, that he was reading, studying and reflecting on much outside his official duties.

Frankfurt was not an education in itself ; most of Bismarck's contemporaries there learned little that they did not know already, and most of which was useless, or forgot what they had already learned ; but Bismarck by self-imposed toil turned the sand of routine into the gold of political experience. He studied everything—men, women, machinery. His dispatches are filled with vivid vignettes—penetrating miniature and character sketches of the diplomatists who made the Frankfurt world—descriptions of a ball or a reception, in which he will note how the celebrated actress, Henrietta Sontag, now the Countess Rossi, has improved her face-powder since he saw her in Berlin ; or, with brief scorn, point out that the morals of this or that figure in their society offends his German standards. Bismarck knew that whatever the malicious gossip of idle and irresponsible tongues might say of himself or his political methods his private life and personal probity were invulnerable. His zeal and industry set him tracking down Austrian intrigues in hidden bypaths and the green-rooms of the political stage. It was at Frankfurt that he learned to look for the ubiquitous and secret hand of clerical and ultramontane wire-pullers, and to understand how public opinion could be manipulated through newspapers, if skilfully worked. This side of his activities laid bare many sordid secrets, and the acquisition and the experience weakened his belief—never very strong—in human nature. The marked contempt of later years for the sincerity of public opinion, for newspapers, for journalists, who could always be bought, for all the dark magic of an official press bureau, for diplomatic *reconnaissances* by the circulation of lies, for lashing up public sentiment by dictated paragraphs inserted in avowedly independent journals—the whole sinister and dirty stock-in-trade that exploited the servility and cunning of a Busch or subsidised with appropriated funds a Counter-Reptile-Press—all this can be traced to his Frankfurt period. The vengeance that a policy of reality —*Realpolitik*—exacts from its disciples is the necessity of using an unclean world as it would use you, and of assuming that the psychology of a nation is that of Tammany Hall. Yet unquestionably as Bismarck was tainted and degraded by the development of the coarser and more brutal fibres in his autocratic personality, he never him-

self mistook intrigue for diplomacy, nor made the coining
of phrases a substitute for a policy.   He evinced at Frankfurt one of the most striking and permanent of his characteristics.   Passionate by nature, with a nervous system
that strung itself beyond the pitch of every affair or crisis,
he always remained uncannily cool in thought.   His brain
worked as if packed in ice, when feeling within was red-hot,
and the words were ready to flow like lava.

He enjoyed his life, and he enjoyed his work, which
sharpened and heightened his physical appetites.   Motley,
his Göttingen friend, has described the large and generous
geniality of the Bismarcks' house in Frankfurt—the un-
assuming but lavish hospitality, the freedom of the house
where the guest became a member of the family, incited to
call for meat and drink in any quantities at any hour, the
children running in and out or sprawling on the floor,
books, papers, music, flowers, scattered about, the hostess
smiling and self-possessed, and her lord striding in and
out, sitting up half the night at his desk, yet as alert and
buoyant as if he had slept the clock round, always ready
to eat, drink, smoke, discuss politics or the merits of North
or South German cattle, dream through a Beethoven
sonata, or swim in the summer moonlight in the Main.
In a word, the German domesticities set in the atmosphere
of the grand manner.   Bismarck did not have to pose in
order to be the aristocrat who belonged to a class born and
bred to command.

His travels were partly official, but largely voluntary.
In three years he saw most parts of non-Prussian Germany.
We find him at Darmstadt, Cassel, Hanover, Dresden and
Munich ; he was twice in Vienna, stayed in Ostend, bathed
on the North German coasts, toured in Northern Italy,
and paid two visits (in 1855 and in 1857) to Paris.   He
invariably met the men who had made, or were about
to make, the Europe of his day, and formed his judgment
on their ability and nerve.   Gortschakov, Beust, Bach,
Schmerling, Rechberg, the Duke of Augustenburg, Prince
William at Coblenz, Persigny, Napoleon III., and many
others came into the record.   He presented himself to
the ex-chancellor, Metternich, at Johannisberg, and the

Princess notes both her own and her husband's pleasure at the wit and sound Conservative principles of the tall and soldierly Prussian noble. It was fitting that the veteran Austrian who had known all the great men of a wonderful past should place the wasted hand of the old diplomacy in the relentless grasp of the new. In that polished drawing-room, haunted by the ghosts of vanished empires and the fair women whom its owner had loved and lost, the Imperial Chancellor to come paid his homage to the Imperial Chancellor fallen and an exile, and listened with cynical deference to the political wisdom of ' a garrulous old gentleman.' Cavour was the one European statesman of the first rank whom Bismarck never met. An Imaginary Dialogue between the Minister-President of Sardinia and the Prussian Plenipotentiary at Frankfurt, with Austria and Liberalism as its theme, would be a fitting tribute to Landor. But Napoleon III. he had already come to know at the Tuileries. They were to meet often, these two, between 1855 and 1870, and for the last time at the weaver's cottage on the Donchéry road on the grey morrow after Sedan.

Bismarck's interest in the home politics of Prussia steadily evaporated. He fought a duel with G. von Vincke, and presently declined re-election for the Lower House; and though in 1854 he was created by the King a member of the Upper House (Herrenhaus), he did not often attend its debates. The growing alienation from the creed and methods of *Kreuzzeitung* and Gerlach Conservatism completed his reluctance to waste his nights on countless cigars in stuffy trains to and from Berlin. Not in Prussia under Manteuffel were the lessons and the realities of life to be found. One official task after another was laid upon his shoulders. He endeavoured, but without success, to persuade the Diet to accept and guarantee the Protocol of 1852, which settled for ten years the fate of Schleswig-Holstein, and which Bismarck himself was later to fling into the waste-paper basket; he strove to interest the Diet in the creation of a German Navy, and the effort ended in the sale by auction of the ships in existence; he wrestled with the question of a Federal Army

and was defeated by the fear of Prussia and the jealousy
of Austria and her allies. The renewal of the Zollverein brought him into the centre of the German
problem.

Austria, under the able guidance of Brück, aimed at
either securing her admittance into the Customs Union,
which Prussia had formed, or at persuading the Southern
Union to break away and unite with the Austrian Empire.
It was the ever-recurring riddle in an economic form of
German organisation. Austria in the economic, no less
than in the political, sphere demanded that the whole of
the Habsburg dominions must be included or she would
break up the inner unity achieved or demanded by
Prussia. The economic creed of the protectionist Austrian
Empire conflicted both with the free-trade policy of the
Zollverein and the tightening bonds between the Southern
and Northern Unions. Bismarck had the unravelling of
the tangle, and at Vienna he met the Austrian ministers
in their lair. It was his first struggle in big affairs, and he
won his first victory. The Austrians intended to isolate
and then coerce Prussia, by seducing the South from its
economic union with the North. Bismarck met the
Austrian menace with a courteous, but firm defiance.
Prussia would maintain the Zollverein at all costs. The
Southern Union was thereby left to choose between the
Northern Customs Union and Austria. Bismarck correctly reckoned that economic self-interest and not sentiment would decide the issue. Prussia had more to offer
to South Germany than Austria ; she was strong enough
to stand on her own feet. Headquarters at Berlin were
timid, nervous, and irresolute. Bismarck brushed the
charge of disloyalty and anti-German separatism aside ;
even if the charge were true, which it was not, the interest
of Prussia was the decisive criterion. This plain attempt
to sacrifice Prussia to Austrian manufacturers and agricul-
turists, and to rob her of the political influence behind the
Zollverein, must be defeated. And it was. Prussia made
one concession. Twelve years hence the arrangements
were to be reconsidered. In 1863, Bismarck was Minister-
President, and the power to determine Prussian policy was

in the hands, not of a Manteuffel, but of Austria's most relentless foe.

The whole affair set Bismarck thinking with renewed energy on cardinal problems—the principles of Prussian foreign policy, the meaning and consequences of Austrian ambitions, the relations of Prussia with the middle and petty States, the defects of the Federal Diet as an organisation for Germany. Under the stimulus of events he was exploring and appreciating the European framework, the new groupings of the Powers, the new forces manifestly at work. Facts, and reflections always drove him back on one supreme question : Was it possible for Prussia to co-operate loyally with Austria ? And if it were not, what must be the consequences of a rupture for both States ?

There is no need to question the sincerity of Bismarck's desire in 1851 to maintain an alliance between Austria and Prussia for common ends. The policy and the principles of the alliance satisfied his political creed and outlook ; antagonism to, and a breach with, Austria involved the abandonment of a traditional creed and instincts, estrangement from the friendships and ideals of his manhood, a drastic and dislocating rearrangement of his political faith, and the patient, painful, and perilous groping after a new policy in an unmapped and shifting future. We can catch in the more personal documents many glimpses of doubt and genuine regret. It would be so easy to renounce intellectual independence, remain an obedient and unquestioning servant of the monarchy, take the appropriate reward for obedience in ribbons and stars, or retire to Schönhausen, and under the blue sky of summer or the wintry sleets cast off this festering world of politicians and intrigues and live and die a Bismarck as his ancestors had done. Opportunity, said Disraeli, is more powerful even than conquerors or prophets. A demonic time-spirit moulded Bismarck's environment and his character. ' I am not a man,' pronounced Napoleon, ' I am a force.' Bismarck hacked out his daily way, because he was a fierce and proud Prussian, and because he was also becoming a great German. In the air all round him the German atmosphere vibrated with indefinable national aspirations, and his spirit responded unconsciously to the spiritual inspiration that fired his heart and steeled his brain. And it was the decree of Providence. He believed in a God Whose will ordered the world and chose the human instruments of His purpose.

The Crimean War was a disconcerting searchlight in an obscure night. The German intellectuals, no less than the German courts, were bewildered : for in every party sentiment was in antagonism to principles. The Conservatives were torn between their hatred of the crowned Jacobin at Paris, their distrust of Great Britain, which had yielded to democratic reform, their horror of a rupture with Conservative and Legitimist Russia, and their anxiety to be the ally in shining armour of Austria, the other great pillar in the Holy Alliance of the Three Monarchies. War on the side of Austria meant war with Russia and a hateful alliance with the Liberal West. Nationalism clamoured for settling with France and active support to Austria, the champion of Germanism (*Deutschtum*), but the opponent of nationalist rights and ideals. The Liberals, as passionately anti-French as Conservatives or Nationalists, could not forget Frankfurt, Vilagos, and Olmütz ; Russia was reaction and autocracy combined ; yet Austria placed a permanent veto on unification and constitutional government. The Prussian Court and government were in the sorest straits. Hohenzollern and Romanov were linked by the closest dynastic ties : a breach with Russia imperilled the eastern frontier, a breach with Austria imperilled the southern frontier ; it involved ' a family civil war ' (*Brüderkreig*) in Germany ; yet refusal to join France and Great Britain would be followed by a blockade of the North German coast by the British fleet on its way to the Baltic. The ' Watch on the Rhine ' was met by the demand for a Watch on the Danube and Vistula.

In this chaos of conflicting opinions, beneath which surged the demand of a Germany, conscious of its impotence to make its dynasties obey a national will which had no organs of expression, and thirsting to be a power in the world like other nations, Bismarck grew cooler as German sentiment developed a heated fretfulness. His diagnosis cut right across all the parties and creeds. There was only one question : What was Prussia's interest, analysed without reference to any obligations of traditional honour, dynastic family feeling, or sentimental likes or dislikes of this nation or that ? Prussia had no interest in the Danubian principalities or the Balkans. Austria had, but that was Austria's affair ; and Austria was working to involve Prussia in an Austrian quarrel, success in which would bring all the credit and the profits to Austria and nothing to Prussia but Austrian gratitude, a more insidious danger than her open enmity. Prussia was really asked to strengthen Austria's power and weaken her own in the Diet. Why should Prussia break with Russia at Austria's bidding ? The English blockade was moonshine. England was not so foolish as to drive Prussia into an offensive alliance with Russia, which would compel the British ally, France, to divert reinforcements for the Crimea to the Rhine. 'But France meant to attack Germany.' If Napoleon attacked Prussia, the Prussian army would see to that, and France would not attack Germany. Why not bring ' the man of sin ' to terms ? The relations of States were determined by interests and not by misinterpreted and irrelevant ethical considerations. Utilise the embarrassments of your friends above all to secure solid advantage for yourself : do not let those embarrassments be a bad reason for sharing in them and adding to your own. In a word, let Prussia remain rigidly neutral : hold fast to a real friend, Russia, and by skilful diplomacy improve her relations with France and let Austria go— not to the Devil, but to Frankfurt. The indispensability of Prussia was precisely the opportunity for making Austria pay Prussia's price.

Bismarck could only argue and advise ; he could not secure the adoption of his advice. His fear that his government would be coerced into war on behalf of Austria against Russia, and thereby mortgage its future and freedom of action beyond all chance of liquidation, caused him many sleepless nights. ' The smart and seaworthy Prussian frigate,' as he expressed it, ' was to tow in perpetuity the water-logged and dry-rotted Austrian battleship.'

While Bismarck argued, Prussia vacillated irresolute, yet fiery, with the sword half drawn, threatening every State and giving ground to every minister who threatened her. She was saved for the time from her tardy and reluctant adhesion to the Austrian cause by the course of events, and not by the amateurish inaction and fear of the Prussian ministers. She earned neither the gratitude of friends nor the respect of her foes ; and when all was over Russia and Austria informed her with contemptuous politeness, that they would use their respective good offices to secure her an invitation to the Congress which would settle the affairs of Europe at Paris in 1856. Manteuffel, who represented Prussia at the Congress, amused the diplomatists by his air of the poor relation included at the last moment, because there was a vacant chair, and it might as well be filled by Prussia as by any other State. The next great Congress after 1856 which settled the Near East was at Berlin in 1878, presided over by Bismarck as Chancellor of a German Empire.

Bismarck's sketch of a policy and explanation of the principles underlying it pained and angered his friends. He threshed it out at length with Prince William at Coblenz—in three years to become the King of Prussia—and not only failed to convince him, but filled him with suspicion of the adviser's sanity and loyalty. The Prince, as in 1851, was ready to fight because the honour of Prussia was involved : to leave Austria in the lurch was desertion ; France was an irreconcilable national enemy ; Napoleon was a Jacobin disguised as a sham Cæsar. Bismarck's advice, he pronounced, was not that of a statesman but of an ignorant schoolboy.

That ignorant schoolboy was destined to have many arguments with the simple soldier before he succeeded in winning the surrender of the royal conscience ; and the respect which with Bismarck deepened in thirty years into a sincere homage, began at Coblenz with this sharp antagonism. William of Hohenzollern was not a great intellect, but he was a man, and he had the strength that character and simplicity of aim alone can give. In Bismarck's eyes that quality atoned for many defects. Independence he could both hate and love, but it always earned his respect.

Bismarck's ideas were slowly consolidating into a coherent system. The issues raised by the Austrian war were disentangling in his thought three cardinal and governing considerations—the indispensability of an *entente* with Russia, the necessity of coming to an understanding with France, and the impossibility of co-operation with Austria. To adopt Napoleonic language, in the strategy of her diplomacy Prussia was to manœuvre from a fixed point, and that fixed point was Russia. Prussia could safely pivot on that. Central Europe was her theatre of operations, and movements outside that decisive theatre were eccentric or quixotic. An understanding with France would first secure the benevolent neutrality of the most important Continental Power, secondly, prevent a coalition between France and Russia, and thirdly, leave Prussia with undiminished resources to settle her relations with Austria. Bismarck did not as yet contemplate an open rupture, still less war with Austria. He was perfectly ready to support Austria, provided that she would give guarantees, and treat Prussia as an equal and not as a rather larger Bavaria. He was no less clear that the traditional system continued by Manteuffel involved a humiliating and crippling subordination of Prussia to Austria's needs and supremacy.

These ideas of policy necessitated a revision of principles of political action, very clearly revealed in his remarkable correspondence with Gerlach. The trite image of the hen in consternation at the chicken fledged beneath her protecting wings now taking to the water because it was a duckling, is a faint picture of the pain and indignation with which Gerlach discovered the apostasy of his disciple. It was easy for Gerlach to concur in the necessity of an *entente* with Russia; but when it was plain that the result of the alliance was to be an *entente* with France and antagonism to Austria, he recoiled with horror. ' Cynical ' and ' unprincipled ' were colourless adjectives for such a policy. The stability of European society, and of Prussia in particular, depended, in Gerlach's view, on legitimate monarchical rule, and on the maintenance throughout Europe of Conservative principles which were of universal validity ; the moral duty of combating ' the Revolution ' was a necessity of existence, no less than an obedience to divine law and authority. Austria represented every sound principle as clearly as Russia : France was the negation of everything sacred and solid—she was ' the Revolution,' with Napoleon crowned on a throne picked from the Jacobin gutters and placed on his head by perjury and bloodshed. How could it be statesmanship and right—for a Prussian above all, loyal to his sovereign by the grace of God and freed from the superstitions of Liberalism—to desert and impugn Austria and to seek for an unholy partnership at Paris ?

Bismarck took up the challenge. In the tactics of statesmanship, interests, he maintained, were more important than principles : policy demanded flexibility and not rigidity of principles. Understandings were simply temporary bargains. Napoleon was not so bad as he was painted. Austria was a great deal worse than she professed to be. A bargain with Napoleon was not a surrender to the Revolution, but an exploitation of it for Prussia's interest. And, to secure Prussia's interest, if an alliance with the Devil were desirable, it should be made with a light conscience. All this high-faluting talk about Conservative principles of universal validity was irrelevant and unreal. There were no such principles, Conservative, Liberal or Revolutionary. Reason of state—for Bismarck the reason of the Prussian State—was the one abiding reality in a world of uncontrollable facts and fluctuating situations. The true statesman must be prepared to be Conservative at home and Liberal abroad, or vice versâ ; to be a Jacobin in Paris and an Absolutist at Petersburg, if necessary, and must seek to wring out of every opportunity the maximum of advantage for his country, otherwise he was a doctrinaire or a bungler, a professor or a bureaucratic automaton.

He invited Gerlach to study history impartially. The

Conservative interpretation of the origin and evolution
of legitimism and revolution would not stand the test of
facts.   All thrones and forms of government were in origin
revolutionary or founded on usurpation.   Even the Prussian monarchy had usurped the rights of those it had
dispossessed.   Legitimism was a new-fangled doctrine,
created as a result of the Revolution of 1789, to meet the
conditions of a once existent but now vanished situation.
It was this obstinate obsession of unverifiable assumptions
and this irrational refusal to recognise realities which had
ruined Conservatism in the past, and would ruin it in the
future.   It was time for Prussia to free herself from the
fetters of a system which clogged her independence and
to return to the sounder system of Frederick who had made
himself and his State great.   If it was right for Frederick
to ally with France and withstand Austria in season and
out of season, because Prussia's interest required it, the
same reason of State and imperishable interest no less
required it to-day.

The correspondence, in short, widened, while it demon-
strated, the gulf between the old Conservatism and the
new.   Bismarck had indeed travelled far from the standpoint of his youth : Gerlach had remained unchanged.
And Gerlach was correct in his assertion, that master and
disciple no longer spoke the same language.   Bismarck
was content to leave it at that.

The German problem slowly intertwined itself into the
problem of Prussia's true foreign policy.   Bismarck's
maturing thought, continually reinforced by freshets of
experience, groped its way through the thickets of youthful
prejudice.   The process can be traced in the State papers
(confirmed by his letters) which pressed upon his government Bismarck's weighed and tested conclusions.

In 1851 he wrote : ' I do not believe that the Federal
Diet in its present form can be the last word in our politics ;
rather I see in it only a shell within which can develop all
the sound and practical elements of the union (Erfurt)
policy, a shell that will drop off when the kernel is ripe.'
In 1853, he pointed out that ' unless Austria renounced
the policy of Schwarzenberg . . . sooner or later the

federal wagon, pulled by the Prussian horse forwards and
by the Austrian horse backwards, would go to pieces.'
From 1853 onwards dispatch after dispatch emphasised
' the restless effort of Austria to compel Prussia by the
organisation of a majority of votes in the Diet ' to accept
the will of Vienna.   Prussia was driven to a defensive
attitude. In the notable 'splendid report,' ' *Prachtbericht*,'
of 1856 he wrote : ' The Emperor Francis Joseph is not
master of his lands and subjects in the same measure as our
all gracious Lord. . . . Austria on the defensive I consider
weak, and at the first successful stroke of a rival the whole
of the internal artificial fabric of the centralised scribbling
bureaucracy of Bach and Buol would tumble in like a pack
of cards . . . the traditional policy of Austria and its
jealousy of us cannot be removed, and I would trust the
old fox in his new coat as little as in his summer bristles.
. . . I will express my conviction that in no long time we
shall have to fight for our existence against Austria, and
that it is not in our power to avoid the fight, because the
course of events in Germany admits of no other development.'

' Austria,' he wrote in 1857, ' does not wish us to increase our importance in Germany, and England cannot
favour our development either on the sea or in trade.   In
politics no one acts unselfishly, unless it is his interest to
do so.'   ' Your Excellency is aware,' he wrote in 1858,
' that the Federal Diet and our disadvantageous position
in it is Austria's best weapon . . . the whole of my seven
years' service at Frankfurt has been an unbroken struggle
with efforts of every kind and the relentless attempts to
exploit the Federal Diet as an instrument to aggrandise
Austria and humiliate Prussia.'   ' We must,' he urged,
' establish a Customs Parliament . . . our Parliament and
press must discuss tariff policy without reserve from the
Prussian point of view ; it will thus divert the exhausted
attention of Germany to itself, and our Prussian Parliament
will become a power in Germany.'   From Petersburg in
1859 he wrote to Schleinitz : ' The federal machinery in
normal times is an oppressive, in crises a dangerous, hand-
cuff for Prussia. . . . I believe we should take up the chal-

lenge and consider it no misfortune if we found in a resolution of the majority at Frankfurt . . . a breach of the Federal treaties.' This is precisely what Bismarck did in 1866. ' The word " German " for " Prussian " I would gladly see inscribed on our banners, if we had first a closer and practical unity with our other fellow-Germans than hitherto ; it loses all its charm if it is employed as now to support the Federal bond. . . . I see in our Federal relations a Prussian malady which sooner or later will have to be healed by iron and fire, if we do not in good time find another cure for it.'

In 1861 he wrote : ' The system of the solidarity of the Conservative interests of all countries is a dangerous fiction, so long as there is not the most complete and honourable reciprocity. Pursued by Prussia alone, it is pure Don Quixotism which weakens our King and his government in the execution of its proper duty. It brings us to the absolutely unhistorical, godless and lawless swindle of sovereignty in the German princes, which employs the Federal system as its pedestal, and with which the European Powers play to make it the darling of the Prussian Conservative party . . . we protect foreign prerogatives with more obstinacy than our own, and get enthusiastic for the paltry sovereignties created by Napoleon and guaranteed by Metternich. . . . So long as the folly of the present Federal system lasts, which is simply a forcing-house of dangerous and republican party struggles . . . we need a stronger consolidation of German arms as much as our daily bread ; we need a new and plastic establishment in the sphere of tariff policy to protect our material interests against the disadvantages arising from the unnatural configuration of our German frontiers . . . Moreover I cannot see why we should so coyly shrink from the idea of popular representation alike in the Federal League, the Tariff, and the Union Parliament; an institution which has a legitimate validity in every German State, which we Conservatives in Prussia could not dispense with, cannot be resisted as revolutionary.' [1]

[1] The student who wishes to master Bismarck's views should study in *Preussen im Bundestag* the dispatches of the following dates :—November 19, 1851, April 23,

The substance of Bismarck's thought and principles at this stage can be summarised. Prussia must find her own solution of the German problem ; she must combine a satisfaction of the claims of Germany with the satisfaction of the claims of the historic and characteristic Prussian State. A radical reform of the Diet brought about by Prussian initiative must be such as to guarantee beyond dispute the supremacy of Prussia in Germany and her position as a great Power. There must be an end to the system by which Austria could manipulate the middle and petty States into a permanent and hostile majority in the Federal Diet, and by which kingdoms or landgraviates, of inferior extent, population, military and economic resources, voted down Prussia, and ' mediatised '[1] her. The root of the mischief lay in the pretensions of dynastic particularism to political equality with Prussia and Austria, based on a ' swindling ' and mushroom theory of legitimist sovereignty. Co-operation with Austria, as Austria interpreted it, was impossible. In the interest of Germany and of Prussia, Austria must be resisted. Prussian foreign policy and the German problem were inseparable elements

---

1852, June 18, 1852, January 13, 1853, August 9, 1853, November 14, 1853, February 15, 1854, February 11, 1855, April 26, 1856, May 12, 1857, June 7, 1857, March 14, 1858, April 10, 1858. They are all too long to be quoted *in extenso*, and they should be compared with the Baden Denkschrift, printed in *Bismarck Jahrbuch*, iii. 193.

[1] *' Mediatised.'*—This term so frequently occurs in Bismarck's writings and German historians that, as there is no single English equivalent, it is desirable to explain it for those not familiar with its technical and derivative meaning. Technically, ' to mediatise ' was a term derived from the old Holy Roman Empire of the German nation which came to an end in 1806. The sovereign princedoms of that Empire—whether ecclesiastical or secular—were held to be *immediate* vassals of the Emperor. To ' mediatise ' them meant, therefore, to deprive them of the status of being immediate vassals, and to reduce them to the position of being ' mediate,' or secondary vassals, *i.e.* with one or more authorities between them and the supreme fount of imperial power—a process equivalent to reduction from being a tenant-in-chief to subordinate tenancy. By degrees the term ' to mediatise ' or ' mediatisation ' derivatively came to imply an act or a result by which a sovereign prince or state retained a titular independence, but lost, or was deprived of, the rights and powers of sovereignty. Hence, in Bismarck's time, the term was commonly used of a result by which a state lost its true political independence and initiative and became dependent on some power or powers, sovereign in theory and in fact. ' Mediatisation,' therefore, broadly implied the retention of a titular sovereignty which conflicted with the practical political dependence of the ' sovereign ' on other sovereigns or states.

of a single and larger unity. The benevolent neutrality
of France must be secured ; with the friendship of Russia
and the goodwill of Napoleon, Prussia could throw her
individual strength into the decisive theatre—Germany
and Central Europe—concentrate, in short, on the over-
throwal of Austria in Germany.

These were conclusions calculated to dismay Conservatives and Liberals alike, for they challenged the dearest
traditions of both parties. Bismarck did not either then
or subsequently speak out the whole of his mind. He did
not wish to alarm friends or cause his opponents to blas-
pheme unnecessarily. Much was deliberately hidden in
his heart. But much also he could not have spoken out,
for he saw, and he recognised it, through a glass darkly.
' The longer I live,' he said later, ' the more incalculable
the future in politics proves to be.' There are no indications of how or when or by whom precisely this programme
could be realised. Not a word of war or annexations. It
is the quintessence of his statecraft that the opportunity
would create the means ; that in policy as in war a lucid
comprehension of ends was the one indispensable pre-
requisite, and that the major and minor tactics must be
settled by the situation of the moment and the character
and disposition of the enemy's forces. Success would come
to the side that made the fewest mistakes. Opportunity
was everything. The right stroke at the right moment
would give the decision. A lost opportunity was worse
than a defeat, for it implied a failure of judgment in the
commander. No tactical skill could compensate for inferior intelligence in the supreme direction, and the
persistent will to persevere once the policy had been
made.

Bismarck's letters and memoranda are like Beethoven's
notebooks. In both we can trace a mind at work, the
patient elaboration of an idea, the jotting down of flashes
of insight which in due time may be developed into a completed composition. Some, however, are never worked
out ; time and life failed, or the idea failed because the
mood that gave it birth never returned : others give us
the genesis of a perfected scheme : others merely indicate

a thought, a premonition of what will come but in another form. Genius is talking aloud to itself in the workshop of the human spirit, and it is the prerogative of genius to be fertile in contradictions and to nourish its strength on inconsistencies : and the winged word and glory of emotion may never soar beyond that free, inner mansion of personality, never carry its message beyond the chambers of feeling that divide, into the kingdom of action that unites, all thought.

Bismarck had divined the real weakness of Austria—the vulnerability of her European position, the competition in her councils between the concentrated egoism of the dynasty and the dissipated interests of the Empire, the administrative dry rot, the lack of vision and the absence of moral imagination in her ministers, and the insoluble antagonism between the ambition for supremacy in Germany and her historic claims in Italy and Hungary. No less had he divined the strength of Prussia, economic, political, and military. Prussia so far had been handicapped by slavish adherence to a false tradition, by a sick and irresolute sovereign, and by ministers whose wills and courage were as weak as their intellectual powers. She had neither developed her strength nor unified it under a driving control. There already floated in Bismarck's mind the conception of a reorganised Central Europe in which Prussia should have superseded Austria in Germany, and the Austrian Empire would reconsolidate itself as a Danubian State between the twin capitals of Vienna and Buda-Pesth. 'Un maître des indiscrétions savantes,' as M. de la Gorce felicitously terms him, Bismarck was continually expressing ideas which ministers and diplomatists regarded as a bad jest or the gaucherie of an incurable amateur, but which were really sincere and intended to probe a difficulty, or indicate an end. At Vienna he said outright in 1864 that Austria should transfer its centre of gravity to Buda-Pesth. 'At Berlin,' he told Rechberg, 'we Germans do not consider Vienna as a German city, and what happens at Vienna as related to Germany. Of course, I know that Vienna is a city on German soil, but it is the capital of a non-German Empire . . . it is obvious that the Austrian monarchy is scarcely German . . . it would do much better if it rested on its true strength, the aggregate of the numerous races which compose its Empire, rather than pursue the dream of a German supremacy which we dispute, and to which it has no title. What is German will revert to Germany sooner or later: it is inevitable. It is not more difficult to govern Vienna from Berlin than to govern Pesth from Vienna—indeed, it would be much easier.' And he seriously meant it. There was not room in Germany for Habsburg and Hohenzollern, and Bismarck had shed his Great Germany views of 1848-51. He was now definitely on the side of the Small Germany party, as the Frankfurt Liberal programme had defined it.

Prussia, in his eyes, needed diplomacy and an army— precisely what the Liberals of 1848 had needed and failed to secure. Questions of right (*Rechtfragen*) in the long run became questions of might (*Machtfragen*). But an army would be as useless without the right diplomacy as diplomacy without a strong army behind it. 'Diplomacy without arms,' pronounced Frederick the Great, 'is music without instruments,' and Bismarck concurred without reservation in the judgment. But neither in 1859 nor later did he assert or believe that force alone, or force aided by a skilful diplomacy, would suffice. The higher statecraft required a subtler sympathy with the motives and ideals of human beings, a tighter grip on realities, economic as well as spiritual. The future Prussia and the future Germany could not be brought into existence by force alone, nor could they live and develop on force alone. Intuitively and unconsciously, he was separating the Nationalism with which he sympathised from the Liberalism which he hated and feared.

The cry for strength—the will to power—based on the ineradicable racial instinct of a Germany that was daily bursting the bonds of the past and cleaving new paths into intellectual and economic spheres of illimitable scope, could and must be satisfied, and Bismarck was at one with Prussian, Saxon, Bavarian, or Franconian in the fierce thirst for power and domination. But the defeat of Liberalism was the price that Nationalism must pay for its satisfaction. Once the new Germany had come into existence, the German mind would adapt itself to new categories of thought, and Liberalism, mutilated at the root, would wither in the original stock, and the life and vigour of the races would find their self-realisation in the new National State and the new Nationalist ideals of German power. For power, not self-government, supremacy not parliamentary control, would satisfy a Nationalist and unified Germany. How this again would happen Bismarck neither knew nor attempted to reckon as yet. But the certainty that it could and must be done inspired him with fresh ambition and a perpetually renewed strength. When Gerlach and the *Kreuzzeitung* mourned the lost leader and the disciple's apostasy, they judged from the surface. Bismarck had not ceased to be a Conservative because he exposed the unsound foundations of their creed or challenged the erroneous conclusions drawn from vicious premises. Roon had a truer insight. Bismarck now and subsequently puzzled and pained that unrepentant Junker and unquenchably loyal friend. But Roon felt that Bismarck remained in fibre and temper true to the faith of Prussian Junkertum and his forefathers. The Liberals and Radicals were no less right when they distrusted Bismarck at every step and saw in him the implacable opponent of all they held dear. The Germany that Bismarck would make and the Germany they were working for were in fundamental antithesis. They had their origins in an antagonistic interpretation of life ; they were rooted in contradictory tables of value, standards of judgment, and criteria of conduct ; and they aimed at opposed ideals of Statehood, and the place in, and the relation of, the individual to the organisation of society.

Lastly, Bismarck's programme implied execution by a Bismarck, and there was only one. The French ambassador said to him once : ' Your policy and ideas will bring Prussia to another Jena.' Bismarck replied : ' Perhaps, but why not to Leipzig and Waterloo ? ' ' I will make my own music,' he had said in 1849, ' or I will make none at all.' But in 1859 it looked as if Fate was to deny him the opportunity or drive him back to Schönhausen.

§ 2. *Petersburg and Paris,* 1859-1862

On January 29, 1859, Bismarck was transferred from Frankfurt to the embassy at Petersburg. On March 6 he left Frankfurt, and on April 1, his forty-fourth birthday, he was received in audience by Alexander II. and presented his credentials. The new appointment had its personal and political significance. Prince William had become Regent on October 26, 1858. ' The new era ' began with his regency. The ministry of moderate Liberals, under Prince Anthony of Hohenzollern and their master the Regent, were well aware of Bismarck's views, and it was not unnatural that, having in contemplation a gradual change in a Liberal direction both in foreign and home policy, they should wish to be represented at Frankfurt by an agent more in sympathy with the new attitude. Bismarck's pro-Russian sympathies, evinced since 1854, would commend him to the Russian Court; his impenitent Conservatism was very unpopular with the Liberals ; and his advocacy of better relations with France was distasteful in the highest degree to the Prince Regent. At Petersburg, in short, he would be honourably out of the way. The appointment was a mark of disapproval veiled in the customary pretence of promotion. Bismarck had expected a change. He wrote to his sister (November 12, 1858) that he was ready ' to take refuge behind the guns of Schönhausen, and, as the government were now relying on the majority in the Left (Liberals), to consider how to do his duty in the Upper House. Change is the soul of life, and I hope I shall be ten years younger when I find myself again in the same position to fight as '48-49. . . . It is all the same to me whether I play the part of diplomatist or of a country gentleman (*Landjunker*), and so far the prospect of a merry and honourable fight without the clogs of office has as much charm as the prospect of a continuous régime of truffles, dispatches and Grand Crosses.' But for all these brave words Bismarck was chagrined. He was in the very prime of his powers ; he was ready for more responsible work than the duty of executing a policy made by others ; he resented the veiled censure conveyed in his transfer, and he suspected that—as happened—he was to be cut off from confidence at headquarters. The chagrin was deepened by the course of events.

The year 1859 was a depressing one for Bismarck. Since January an old injury to his leg, incurred in shooting, was aggravated by reckless exposure and a chill. His health gave way, and in June he was seriously ill. His case was mismanaged, and for some days he sat on Charon's pier, wondering whether he would be called on to cross to the other side. But his superb constitution came to his aid ; like the famous Duchess of Marlborough he refused ' either to be blistered or die ' ; he threw off both the treatment and the malady, and took instead to punch in (Bismarckianly) moderate quantities. Removed to Berlin he fell suddenly ill again, and August had to be spent in a wearisome convalescence at Wiesbaden and Nauheim. Like most men who have enjoyed unbroken good health, Bismarck was a bad patient ; he had taxed strength and nerves to their utmost, and he resented their refusal to stand unlimited drafts on their powers. The illness made a permanent mark in his life. The nervous breakdown, coupled with rheumatic fever and gastric disorders, seriously affected a highly strung system. After 1859 he was never the man he had been before. An increased irritability and excitability, a morose and violent temper, aggravated by sleeplessness, became increasingly apparent, and constant returns of pain emphasised the unlovely elements in his character. The old freshness and joy in life evaporated ; but he refused to alter his habits of life. Roon in the campaign of 1866 notes how ' Otto ' persisted in sitting up most of the night at his desk and lay in bed till midday. Henceforward, particularly after 1862, he was continually on the edge of a breakdown. With his habits in eating and drinking, it is a proof of his marvellous physical vitality that he did not collapse completely.

His recovery was not made easier by his political anxiety. His revived interest in the domestic politics of Prussia testifies to the fear that the renaissance of Liberalism, now in full swing, would wreck his programme. Even more disquieting was the outlook in foreign affairs. The

Italian war of 1859, with France openly in the field against
Austria, the French victories, the Austrian defeats, the
demand for a revision of the system of 1815, were blows at
the citadel of Conservatism; they stirred Nationalism
throughout Europe, and Cavour had pinned his flag to the
cause of constitutional and Liberal monarchism. Germany
was in an uproar. Conservatives, Nationalists, Liberals,
the dynasties from Berlin to Munich, felt that the national
enemy in the west was in arms, defeating a German State
in Austria, about to destroy legitimist and sovereign
princes in Italy, and to reopen the question of the Rhine.
' Austria in danger ' was a potent cry. Her sins were forgotten in the common peril to German supremacy and
legitimist monarchy in Central Europe. It was the crisis
of 1854 repeated in an acute form. For France—a Napoleonic France—was attacking Austria, and it would be
Prussia's turn next. And in 1859 it was not an affair of the
Danubian principalities, nor of Austrian neutrality. At
Berlin, as usual, government and nation faced at once
front to the Rhine. The Prince Regent mobilised four
corps; his strong sympathies as a ruler and as a German
with Austria, his desire to prove his German patriotism
and lead Germany in a national struggle, brought a great
European war into sight. Even so cold a head and so self-
controlled a Prussian patriot as Moltke decided on cool
reflection that the time had come for Prussia to intervene
and strike a blow for Austria and Germany.

Bismarck was literally in anguish, and he was helpless.
At Petersburg or Wiesbaden he was removed from the
direct contact with German affairs he had enjoyed at
Frankfurt; he was not consulted; and he had not the confidence either of the Prince Regent or the ministers. The
winds of Liberalism were sweeping from the lemon groves
of Sicily across the Lombardy plains to the sands and
heath of Pomerania, the March of Brandenburg and
East Prussia. War with France would blow his policy to
the limbo of shattered ideals. Prussia would enter it as
the ally of Austria, and with Prussia would march every
Nationalist and Liberal heart. The issue would, and must
be, the defeat of France. Austria would recover her grip

on Italy—for what could Piedmont do without the red
trousers ?—and either Austria would impose her will on
Germany, and re-rivet her supremacy, or under the stress
of the fray Prussia and Germany would be mastered by the
Liberals, in combination with the Nationalists, and unified
on the anvil of war by the master spirits of 1848. Which
would be worse—a Germany unified on a Liberal basis, or
an Austria triumphant on the Danube, the Po, and the
Rhine, reorganising the German Confederation beyond
Prussian control ? Germany in the grip either of the
anti-Prussian princelets grouped round Austria, or of
the National Union of the Liberals under Bennigsen,
Duncker, Gneist, and the Coburg pro-English group ?
Everywhere Bismarck saw all the machinery at work
that he had tracked out at Frankfurt—the Austrian hand
manipulating the middle States, coercing the petty ones ;
the illuminated princelets dabbling with Liberalism and
striving to combine Nationalism with Particularism ;
Habsburg egoism appealing to Hohenzollern pride and
generosity, but determined that Prussia's army should
extricate Austria from her dilemma, sacrifice Prussian blood
to save Lombardy, Venetia, and Hungary, and receive
the reward of disinterestedness by riveting the Austrian
yoke on the Confederation; and all this was to be done in
the name of Conservatism, and the European solidarity of
legitimism against Jacobinism, Cæsarism, and the Revolution. 'Our policy,' he wrote to his wife, 'daily glides
more and more in the wake of Austria ; a shot on the
Rhine, and it is all over with the Austro-Italian war, and
in its place will come a Franco-Prussian war, in which
Austria, when we have lifted the burden off her shoulders,
will support or fail us as her interest dictates. . . . As God
wills ! It is only a question of time ; nations and men,
folly and wisdom, war and peace, come and go like waves,
but the sea remains ; there is nothing in this world but
hypocrisy and the jugglers' tricks.'

It was idle to urge, as he did, that Napoleon could be
secured by tact, or, if need be, by paying blackmail ; that
Austria's necessities afforded an unrivalled opportunity
for re-settling her relations with Prussia to Prussia's advan-

tage, and that if Prussian aid were required Austria must pay in advance, and that a wedge could be driven in between the middle and petty States and their Habsburg ally ; that Prussia could indicate she and not Austria would reform the Confederation. Such advice only deepened the distrust at the Berlin Court, angered the Gerlach Conservatives, and stirred the scorn of the Liberals. It was midsummer Machiavellianism, destitute of all principle, and Liberals and Conservatives alike stood for principles and the solidarity of their cause with the cause outside Prussia or Germany.

Bismarck was bitterly attacked from both camps. He could tolerate Radical denunciations, but the reproaches of the *Kreuzzeitung* cut into the quick. 'Write me down a devil,' he wrote, 'but I am a Teutonic devil, not a Gallic one.' His idea of securing Napoleon never involved the surrender of essentials. He had taken Napoleon's measure already. 'The itch with Napoleon,' he pronounced in 1855, 'to achieve the unexpected amounts to a disease, and it is nourished by the Empress.' 'He is no general . . . he will only seek a war when internal necessities drive him to it,' he wrote in 1857. 'His heart is much stronger than his head,' he decided in 1861. He meant to flatter his vanity, encourage him to wander on the misty peaks of dreamland—*les idées Napoléoniennes*—commit nothing to paper ; words could always be disavowed and unverified verbal promises explained away. In Bismarck's statecraft, as his advice about Austria revealed, the extortion of services from an embarrassed friend only added contempt for the deluded to dislike. His theory of international relations left no place for gratitude or generosity. The successful deception of France would only increase Prussian resentment at obligations incurred to an enemy, stupid or weak enough to believe in gratitude. Statesmen lent or borrowed the capital and currency of the political life. The needy must pay, and the affluent had a right to exact a high rate of interest because the needy were so needy. In the remorseless world of inter-State competition business was business. Ethical considerations could not apply in the markets of diplomacy ; for their

application ignored the real motives of State conduct.
Bismarck wrote to Roon that Prussia was committing the
folly of being Liberal at home and Conservative abroad.
Such a policy sapped the confidence of the sound elements
in Prussia and flouted the real forces at work in Germany.
Roon agreed in this diagnosis and the mischief of the ' new
era.' But the recommendation of a Conservative policy
at home and a Liberal one abroad, left him wondering
whether illness had not shaken ' Otto's ' sanity.

Bismarck in the meanwhile could only growl and moan,
and do his best to strengthen the bonds between Prussia
and Russia. The gods decided for him. The crisis of
1859, like that of 1854, was tided over by the action of
France and Austria. Napoleon shrank from the consequences of his own intervention in Italy. Magenta and
Solferino had not been victories in the manner of his uncle ;
the idea of a war on the Rhine sent shivers through him ;
Italy was breaking away into unforeseen revolutions ; the
Ultramontanes were applying a pitiless pressure on the
Tuileries ; and France was not prepared for a colossal
struggle. Francis Joseph, with Hungary simmering into
rebellion, Russia deaf and cold, and Great Britain swinging
over to Italy's side, was prepared to sacrifice Lombardy
rather than imperil Austrian supremacy in Germany. The
armistice of Villa Franca, which shattered the hopes of
Cavour, brought immediate relief to the tension in Germany. The Prince Regent in Prussia could face the
German world. He had mobilised, he had not truckled
to France, he had satisfied German honour and his own
conscience.

The European crisis was over, and Prussia had made
neither mistakes nor concessions. William 1. had now to
face his Liberal subjects. The Liberals no longer hampered
by the cry of ' Austria in danger ' and the ' Watch on the
Rhine,' took up the programme of constitutional reform
with renewed energy, and the war crisis indirectly brought
the domestic issues to a head.

The Prince Regent was a competent soldier, thoroughly
sound in professional technique, and intimately acquainted
with the administration of the Prussian army. As heir

to the throne, and now as virtually king and commander-in-chief, he had studied military science, and he had at his elbow first-rate military advisers on all army questions. Prince William had the expert's knowledge and framed his own judgment. The supreme command was his prerogative, and he was not prepared to surrender the control it conferred to any one, least of all to politicians and civilians who had neither his knowledge nor his militarist principles. The rights of the Crown over the army inherited from his ancestors and expressly guaranteed in the Constitution of 1851, were the *rocher de bronze* on which the Prussian monarchy was impregnably based. The crises of 1854 and of 1859 had revealed defects in the great military machine, while the economic development of Prussia had outstripped the system embodied in the law of 1814.

Three points called for immediate attention. First and least important, the technical and material equipment required modernisation and extension. Secondly, the twenty thousand men who annually escaped military service, because the increase in the population furnished an annual contingent larger than that originally prescribed, must be brought into training; thirdly, the relations between the active army, the reserve, and the Landwehr —the constitutional militia—must be revised. The royal and ministerial programme, finally adopted after earnest consideration, aimed broadly at (1) increasing the numbers of the active army by the creation of new regiments; (2) remoulding the reserve and the Landwehr so as to give a larger first reserve for bringing the peace establishment up to war strength on mobilisation, and a second reserve better trained and more closely incorporated with the first line; (3) a supplemental annual charge in money of nine million thalers. This programme required the assent of the Landtag because the additional cost must be voted in the budget, and because the abolition of the old, and the reorganising of the new, Landwehr involved fundamental changes in the law of the land. In figures the situation came to this : the old system approximately gave Prussia a standing army of 150,000 with a war establish-

ment (without the Landwehr) of 230,000 men; and with
the old Landwehr, approximately, 480,000 men. The
new royal plan, with three years' service, would give a war
establishment of 450,000 men, and with the remodelled
Landwehr a total of 756,000. The plan of the opposition,
with two years' service, reduced the war establishment,
approximately, to 400,000, and the total, with the Landwehr, probably to some 600,000.

The Liberals, who were in a substantial majority in the
Lower House, had their chance. They recognised to the
full the desirability of increasing Prussia's military strength
—Prussia was to unify Germany—but they met the royal
programme by demanding (1) the reduction of compulsory
service from three years to two; (2) revision of the new
Landwehr scheme; (3) the annual voting of the Army
Budget. For our purpose here the details of a complicated
problem—military, financial, and constitutional—are not
of importance. But the principles in collision were vital,
and it must suffice briefly and clearly to disentangle them.

Prince William, as a professional soldier and as a ruler,
resented the criticism of a civilian opposition on the technical aspects of the scheme; his military advisers and he
himself were convinced that military efficiency could be
secured by the royal programme alone. But these technical questions were completely overshadowed by the
constitutional controversy. The opposition did not dispute the prerogative of the sovereign, as commander-in-
chief, or the duty of every Prussian male to be trained in
the army; but they put forward three claims. First,
that as the obligation of military service affected every
man in Prussia, the nation had the legal and moral right
through its representatives to decide on what conditions
that service should be performed, and if Parliament chose
to reduce the period with the Colours from three years to
two, it had the right to do so; secondly, Parliament had
the legal right to vote or to refuse the taxes required for
maintaining the army; thirdly, the army estimates were
part of the annual budget, and the representatives of the
nation had the right annually to review this budget, since
without parliamentary sanction no taxes were legal for the

army or any other institution of the State. In so far as the army was dependent on statute law and taxation for its existence, the concurrence of Parliament was essential.

The importance of these claims did not lie in their legal validity, which was undeniable, but in the principles and consequences they involved. The Prince Regent and Roon quite correctly grasped that the opposition was determined to assert, through the annual revision of the budget, the principle of ministerial responsibility to the Lower House ; and that through the power of the purse the establishment of ministerial responsibility would lead inevitably to a general and unlimited control of policy and executive ministerial action. Prussia would cease to be a State in which the King governed through the legislature ; it would become a State in which ministers, dependent on the legislature, governed through the King. The army would be turned into a creation of the Landtag, and the prerogative of the sovereign would be legislated out of existence. In a word, the old conception of the monarchy was in irreconcilable collision with the new conception of parliamentary Liberalism. For the Crown, the power and character of the monarchy were at stake ; for the Liberals, the power and character of Parliament as a national institution of government. An issue had been raised on which compromise was impossible. Was there, or was there not, to be parliamentary and constitutional government in Prussia ? It was recognised that the decision would affect not merely Prussia, but the whole of Germany.

At the outset the struggle was embittered by an act of bad faith. The opposition temporarily voted the additional money required on the understanding that the ministerial scheme should be withdrawn and the whole question of reorganisation reserved for future consideration. But the War Office promptly created the new regiments ; colours were solemnly given them by the Regent ; and the revised budget assumed that the scheme had been approved. William, who had become king in 1861, peremptorily refused to disavow the accomplished facts. His acts as War-Lord (*Kriegesherr*) were not subject to parliamentary revision ; the money had been voted, and it was

within his prerogative to apply it. Rejection of the
budget and a dissolution of Parliament followed, with the
result that the Conservative minority was smitten hip and
thigh. The Conservative party numbered a tiny handful
in the new Landtag. The Crown was apparently confronted with surrender to the opposition or resort to a
coup d'État.

Bismarck rejoiced in the quarrel. He had had nothing so
far to do either with framing the scheme or the crisis that
arose out of it. In his judgment nothing could be better
than to strengthen the army, and it was for the soldiers to
decide how most effectively to do this. But even better was
the collision between the Crown and the Liberals. The
control of the army by an irresponsible Crown and ministers
responsible to the Crown alone, lay in the essence of his
programme. The demands of the opposition implied
everything that he hated and feared—parliamentary
government, the Landtag as a government-making, policy-
making organ, and ministers under the thumb of a majority
composed of professors, lawyers, journalists, and middle-class
amateurs. Even if the scheme were wrong, the Crown
must be supported and the opposition smashed into heel.

The King was desperately unhappy. His Liberal ministers saw no solution but to yield. How could the
government continue without a budget ? The country
at the general election had pronounced. The Crown
Prince had the gravest misgivings about a policy which
threatened to destroy national confidence in the sovereign,
perhaps even shatter the throne. Prussia was at this
moment insisting that the incurable autocrat of Hesse-
Cassel must obey his constitution and his legislature, yet
at home was defying the plain rights of the Landtag to vote
taxes and determine their application laid down in the
Prussian law of the land. Roon and the soldiers daily
reminded his Majesty that the army as a monarchical
institution was at stake, and a Hohenzollern who betrayed
the army betrayed himself. Surrender ? Civil war ? A
coup d'État ? Abdication ? Which was King William to
choose ? Roon also suggested that if his Majesty's
ministers refused to do their plain duty and defy Parlia-

ment, there was at Petersburg an experienced diplomatist who could be trusted to do the King's business. But William shrank at the thought. Bismarck would be loyal, but he would insist on carrying out his foreign policy, an *entente* with France and opposition to Austria. His appointment was burning the bridges and blowing up the magazines. The opposition might still be brought to an honourable compromise, but not by Bismarck.

The ' Baden Memorial ' (*Denkschrift*), drawn up by Bismarck for King William in July 1861, repeated the familiar analysis of the reasons why the existing federal system was ruinous to Prussia—the continuous deadlock, Austrian jealousy, the subordination of Prussian initiative and independence to the votes of petty States, organised by a non-German Empire at Vienna. Bismarck urged the King to put Prussia at the head of the unitary movement and lay before the Federal Diet a proposal to create a national Parliament, chosen by direct suffrage from all Germany, which would give Prussia the political direction that it had already in the Tariff Union. Skilfully devised, such a Parliament would enlist for Prussia popular sympathy throughout Germany and largely heal the internal strife in Prussia itself. The ' Baden Memorial ' marks an important stage in the evolution of Bismarck's thought. It assumed the existence of a strong Prussian army, and the will to employ it at the right moment in imposing a Prussian solution on all recalcitrants. ' Make me,' he said, with reference to the Hesse-Cassel affair, ' an Under-Secretary of Foreign Affairs, and I will produce for you in three weeks a civil war of the first quality.'

Throughout 1861 and the spring of 1862 gossip in the capital was rife with reports that the ambassador at Petersburg was to be given ministerial office. Roon kept Bismarck closely informed of all that was passing. More than once he was brought ' on sick leave ' to Berlin, to be ready, but nothing came of it. The King was fascinated and repelled by the idea. Audiences between Bismarck and his sovereign improved their personal but not their political relations. William felt that in this strong, frank, masterful man's hands he would be dragged whither he knew not. ' He goes furthest who knows not whither he is going,' pronounced the practical mysticism of Cromwell. And in Bismarck's surveys of the future there was always a grand and indefinable atmosphere, a consciousness of the vastness of life, and the illimitable potencies of the future floating over the concrete directness of his grip on realities. He knew not whither he was going—he did not wish to know. Forces beyond human calculation were driving Prussia, and he must march with them. The Time-spirit would provide the golden opportunities and reveal how they could be used.

Bismarck concluded that his transference (May 29, 1862) to the embassy at Paris signified a definitive refusal of a ministerial portfolio at Berlin. He had learned much at Petersburg : sounded and charted the European situation ; established a personal friendship with the Tsar ; and by meekly sitting at the feet of the vain Gortschakov had created a credit on which in good time he intended to draw. ' The hatred of Austria here,' he wrote from Petersburg, ' exceeds everything I had believed possible.' Paris was the political centre of Europe, and a pleasanter place than Petersburg. The Court of the Second Empire was at the zenith of its social brilliance. The Empress Eugénie and her galaxy of frail butterflies—fêtes, balls, fashions, and opera—would be an agreeable background to the serious political work of exploiting Napoleon. On June 1 he was presenting his credentials to the Man of Sin at the Tuileries, and before long intimately discussing the higher statecraft with the Emperor and his ministers, and suggesting with a delicious audacity that a tyro in diplomacy would be grateful for all the instructions he could receive from the French experts—Bismarck instructed by a Persigny, a Drouyn de Lhuys, a Walewski, or a De Morny ! He was also scribbling notes to Roon on the iniquities of the Liberal majority in the Landtag, and letters to his wife and sister describing the Parisian fashions, with touches on the vanity of French ministers, and the beauty of the Champs Elysées in a Paris midsummer. He dashed off to London to see the great Exhibition and met Palmerston and Disraeli at the Russian Embassy. An amusing fellow this Prussian Ambassador, every one agreed. His verve and racy recklessness delighted the company, and his sketch of how in a few years he would settle Europe and Germany was more exhilarating than, and quite as evanescent as, champagne. Disraeli judged more correctly. 'Take care of that man; he means what he says,' was a verdict no less accurate and prophetic than Bismarck's scribbled comment to Roon. ' I am just back from London. People there are much better informed about China and Turkey than about Prussia. Loftus (the English Ambassador in Berlin) must write to his minister much more nonsense than I imagine.' It was tragically true. Neither at the Foreign Office, nor in Parliament, not even in the office of *The Times*, or in the exalted circles of the Court, did they know the truth about Prussia and Germany, and it is doubtful whether they wished to know.

From Paris Bismarck visited Trouville, and then, restless and dissatisfied, went on a tour to the south. Not even ' the Lafitte, Mouton Rothschild, Pichon, Laroze, Latour, Margaux, St. Julien, Beaune, Armillac, and other wines'—the ' other ' is a pretty touch—which he noted as having drunk at Bordeaux, nor the beauty of dawn on the seashore and of sunset in the Pyrenees, described in letters to his wife, could appease his feeling that Paris after all was exile; that the world of action lay in Berlin, and that he was shut out from it. Life was slipping away. Was he to be an ambassador all his days, and never have the great political levers in his hands ? Ministerial office was hateful, yet he could not be happy without it. ' My furniture,' he wrote on September 12, 1862, ' is still at Petersburg and will freeze there; my carriages are at Stettin, my horses at grass near Berlin, my family in Pomerania, and I am on the streets.'

Three days later came a telegram from Roon : ' Come. The pear is ripe. *Periculum in morâ.*' He plucked an olive branch as he hurried through Avignon on his way to Paris, and was in Berlin on the morning of September 20. In the forenoon of September 22 he had a memorable interview with the King at Schloss Babelsberg. He persuaded William I. to tear up the abdication he had drafted, put himself unreservedly at his sovereign's disposal, and declared his readiness to fight for the rights of the Crown and the royal scheme of reorganisation of the army to the last. There could be no surrender. This was a fight for honour and existence and must be fought to a finish.

Next day (September 23) the *Gazette* announced the appointment of Herr von Bismarck-Schönhausen to office as temporary Minister-President. On the same day the budget for 1862, providing for the army in accordance with the royal scheme of reorganisation, was decisively rejected in the Lower House of the Landtag by 273 to 68 votes. September 23, 1862, is a red-letter day in the Hohenzollern calendar; it opened a new chapter, or rather a new volume, in the history of Prussia and of Europe.

CHAPTER IV

THE MINISTER-PRESIDENT, 1862-1867

§ 1. *The Constitutional Conflict, the Polish Question, and the German Problem*

On October 8, 1862, Bismarck's provisional appointment as Minister-President was definitely ratified. He took up his residence in the Wilhelmstrasse, which was to be his official abode for twenty-eight years. The new minister was in his forty-eighth year, and he had passed, without any ministerial experience, direct from an embassy to the highest office in the State. Both in Prussia and outside it men naturally asked, What did it mean ? What would happen next ?

Apart from the constitutional controversy and the deadlock created by the overwhelming vote of September 23—a situation grave enough to demand the undivided energies of the government—a series of critical questions in foreign policy pressed for solution. Schleswig-Holstein, the situation in Hesse-Cassel, Poland, the renewal of the Zollverein, the proposed commercial treaty with France, the German problem—each and all of these in combination threatened to become acute. They involved the relations of Prussia as a German Power with the middle and petty States in Germany, and her relations as a European Power with Austria, France, Great Britain, Russia, and the new but incomplete kingdom of Italy. Public opinion in Germany recognised the gravity of the crisis, and was aware that a false step in foreign policy would create an international situation which would leave Prussia isolated and confronted with a hostile coalition that would reduce her to a humiliating impotence.

Bismarck's appointment was clearly a challenge. I

116

provoked in different quarters indignation, amazement, contempt, amusement. As we look back to-day and deliberately forget the knowledge of what happened between 1862 and 1871, it is instructive to read in contemporary literature—the newspapers, memoirs, letters, pamphlets, caricatures and dispatches—the judgments and interpretations expressed in these critical years of 1862-66. Rechberg at Vienna in 1862 described Bismarck to Gramont as 'incapable de sacrifier une idée preconçue, un préjugé, une idée de parti, à n'importe quelle raison d'un ordre supérieur; il n'a pas le sens pratique de la politique, c'est un homme de parti dans la force du mot,' adding truly enough, 'ce n'est pas un ami que nous aurons là.' The new appointment was so clearly either a jest *pour rire* to cover a deliberate ride for a fall, a surrender to the opposition, and perhaps the King's abdication, or it was the gambler's last throw, the discovery of a Prussian Polignac which proclaimed a coming *coup d'État*. Capitulation or revolution? What else could it mean, when the King selected this Junker diplomatist, known only too well for his violent, reckless, and impenitent championship of Prussian Conservatism in its most particularist form? The constitutional crisis and the international situation demanded a cool, conciliatory, and experienced statesman. The King replied by appointing a red reactionary. In the chancelleries of Europe the statesmen *du vieux pantalon* shrugged their shoulders and made bets whether Bismarck would last three weeks or three months. To the Liberals, above all, in Prussia the King's action was a stinging affront, and a summons either to make a revolution or to capitulate.

Such judgments—and they could be cited by the page —were natural under the circumstances, for neither the official world at London, Paris, Vienna, Dresden, and Munich, nor the superheated public in Berlin knew the real Bismarck. They simply saw in him the Junker of 1848-51. When he had practically disappeared at Frankfurt from the public gaze the little that had emerged since 1852 confirmed the assumption that he had not altered, indeed, that he was more than ever the sworn foe of the causes he had opposed with such fiery audacity. The profound change in his views and the breadth and variety of his experience were unknown to most, and were even misinterpreted by the few who had the material for framing a correct judgment. In September 1862 no one had divined the intellectual power, the cool and calculating brain, the intensity of conviction, the political nerve, and the extraordinary strength of character and will stored up and disciplined in that titanic frame. As with Moltke, so with Bismarck, the revelation of the next eight years was to astound and hypnotise Germany and Europe.

And if men did not know Bismarck they were no less ignorant in 1862 of Prussia and Prussianism. Since 1815 Prussia as a German state and as a European Power had done nothing to justify her claim to parity with the other great Powers. She had produced competent internal administrators, distinguished professors, and ardent but ineffective politicians. Her statesmen for fifty years were mediocrities; her policy continuously tarnished by prejudice, timidity, and irresolution—reaction ruined by spasmodic and insincere repentance. The material and economic strength of the country had been enormously increased since 1815; in her organised civil service and her army, no less than her system of education, Prussia was in 1862 far ahead of every other German state, and superior not merely to Austria and Russia but to France and Great Britain. The generation born in the Napoleonic epoch, under the shadows of Jena and the sunlight of the great age of reform —the age of Scharnhorst, Stein, and the War of Liberation —had been patiently moulded and tempered in the chill school of work and disappointment to a capacity for sustained sacrifice and effort which only required leadership —a man and a cause—to evoke a single-minded co-operation. Here lay the secret of the strength of the opposition in Parliament, for it represented a Prussia which had broken with the historic tradition because the organs of that tradition—monarchy, ministers, and the executive— seemed blind to the greatness of the German renaissance, and ignorant of the moral and intellectual forces that compelled the true German mind to be Liberal and Nationalist. Deaf to the call of the future, Prussia had frittered for forty years the vigour of the nation on a parochial prosperity or the ignoble scuffles of the dynasties in the Federal Diet.

Bismarck was a child of the age that had produced 1848 and the constitutional crisis of 1862—lived, learned, and inwardly digested. Like the Liberals whom he detested he had divined the strength of Prussia, but, unlike the Liberals, he diagnosed the cause of Prussia's failure in one vital and fatal omission. The Frederician tradition had been successfully followed in domestic administration, but had been neglected or betrayed in policy, above all, foreign policy. The time had come at last—and not too late— to prove what a strong Prussia could do, when her policy was shaped and directed by a minister to whom nothing was sacred or unclean, prepared like Frederick, the master, to devote soul, brain and body to the service of Prussia, and determined to concentrate unflinchingly the whole force of the State on one end and one end alone, the greatness of Prussia—a man to whom parties, causes, principles, conventions, were either means to that end or empty phrases. Prussia herself and Europe had forgotten the principles and methods of Frederick the Great. The schools of Metternich and Canning, of Palmerston, Guizot or Nicholas I.; lingered on in the shibboleths of the middle-aged, who advised their governments from office desks in the Foreign Offices; the school of Cavour had come and gone with 1861; in the west at Paris reigned the sham Napoleonism of the Second Empire; at London were the statesmen of both parties who persisted in interpreting the Continent, if they interpreted it at all, in the terms of an obsolete continental or a complacent insular tradition, no longer in touch with realities. By 1871 it began to dawn on Europe that in Bismarck had come to life a reincarnation of the Frederick who had shattered the Europe of Walpole, Maria Theresa, and Louis xv., a statesman controlling an organised Prussia, far stronger relatively than the Prussia of Frederick the Great—a statesmanship that was a re-created gospel in action. The State as Egoism and the State as Power, directed by the genius of the illuminated despot, had made a new Europe and a new Prussia between

1740 and 1786; directed by the illuminated genius of
Bismarck it was to make a new Prussia, a new Germany,
and a new Europe between 1862 and 1890.

It was not therefore either the unrepentant Berserker
of Junkertum or a mere diplomatist trained in the conventional *manège* of Frankfurt, Petersburg, and Paris, who
at Roon's bidding had promised his sovereign in the garden
of Schloss Babelberg to lead a forlorn hope. Bismarck had
studied the men both at Berlin and all over Europe with
whom he would have to deal; he was convinced that in
a test of resource, nerve, courage, and tenacity of will, or
in mastery of the realities in any situation, it would not be
he who would fail. This bitter quarrel was none of his
making, and his first step, when he met the triumphant
majority of the opposition in 'The House of Phrases,' as
he called the Landtag, was quietly to lay on the table the
olive branch that he had plucked at Avignon, with the
remark that it was a present to the progressive party, but
the time for it had apparently not yet come.

Bismarck's desire for an honourable compromise was probably sincere. He desired to be free from internal complications in order to deal with foreign policy. However, it
was a fixed principle of his system, enunciated now and fifty
times in the next twenty-five years, that government by
a monarchy through a representative assembly must rest
on compromises, and it was the function of statesmanship
to frame and work them. The external situation was
critical; foreign policy would demand for the next two
or three years sleepless vigilance, and the difficulties,
sufficiently great in themselves, would be aggravated by
an embittered controversy at home. He was new to
office; his position would be enormously strengthened
if he could inaugurate his minister-presidency by a reasonable settlement. Neither now, nor at any time, was it his
habit to close the doors or drive an adversary to open war
until he was convinced that negotiation could not secure
the essentials. But he made his terms perfectly clear.
Let the controversy over rights on both sides be dismissed
as misleading juristic jargon. But the Crown must have
the money for the reorganisation of the army, and the

control of that army and of policy must rest with the King. Co-operation with Parliament by all means, government by a parliamentary majority—never. If the opposition chose to make the issue not a question of right but of might, between government by the monarchy and government by the Lower House of the Landtag, against the will of the King and the Upper House, the struggle must be fought out, and there would only be one end to it—the defeat of the opposition which usurped the lawful authority of the State, inalienably inherent in the Crown.

Bismarck calmly explained his interpretation of the constitution, and to this he adhered through the period of conflict. He quietly ignored the overwhelming endorsement of the action taken in the previous Parliament by the general election. The Lower House had the right, he agreed, to vote taxes or reject the budget, but the veto of the Lower House was not conclusive, for the budget was expressed in a law, and laws required the assent of the Crown and the Upper, as well as of the Lower, House. If the consent of any one of these were withheld, a deadlock was created which could, under the constitution, only be removed by the voluntary act of the organ concerned and by no other means. Failing such, the constitution expressly reserved to the Crown the residual right of government. The Crown was therefore legally entitled to carry on the administration during the emergency created by the deadlock. Otherwise it failed in its duty to itself as the head of the State and to the whole kingdom. The Crown, therefore, simply was driven to avail itself of the special powers provided to meet a temporary and exceptional situation. The King might challenge the wisdom or patriotism of the action which had produced the deadlock, but in exercising his special powers he was not denying the legal rights of the Lower House, which was similarly bound not to deny the legal rights of the Crown. The action of the Lower House amounted to a claim to compel the Crown to surrender its prerogative at discretion, and to make the King's government dependent on the fiat of one chamber of the legislature, or, if the Crown refused to give way, to make all government impossible.

Bismarck made it no less clear that as a minister he was not appointed, nor could be dismissed, by Parliament. So long as he had the confidence of his sovereign he would remain in office, no matter what Parliament said or voted. The government of the Crown must and would be carried on, budget or no budget. The taxes would be levied under the law of 1861 (as indeed they were from 1861-66) ; the necessary legalisation of this emergency government by prerogative could and would be procured later (as it was in 1866), by a law of indemnity, or—as Bismarck thought possible in 1863—by an alteration of the constitution. On September 29 he gave expression in debate to the famous sentence : ' Germany has its eyes not on Prussia's Liberalism, but on its might. . . . Prussia must reserve its strength for the favourable moment, which has already more than once been missed. The great questions of the day will not be decided by speeches and resolutions of majorities—that was the blunder of 1848 and 1849— but by blood and iron.'

Spoken with calm conviction, the phrase burst like a shell in a powder magazine. It roused a hurricane of indignation through Germany. No such language had been heard from a Prussian minister since 1815, and if men needed convincing that the Landtag was confronted with the Junker of 1849, the proof was surely there from the Minister-President's own lips. Later, Bismarck repeatedly explained that all he meant was that the German problem could be solved only by action, and the effective use at the suitable moment of the Prussian army, and that Königgrätz, St. Privat, and Sedan proved he was right ; that without ' the blood and iron ' of military force neither Austria nor France could have been overthrown and German unity achieved. But the famous sentence in 1862 went much further, and was intended to go much further, than this. It was a warning to Germany as well as to the Prussian Landtag ; it was a concentrated condemnation of all, and not merely the Liberal, methods hitherto employed ; it poured contempt on reform by ' moral penetration ' and government by consent of the governed. It was the summary of the creed that the State stood for power, and that in political problems force, not right, was the sovereign remedy (*Macht geht vor Recht*).

It was inevitable that the opposition should reject the olive branch. Holding as they did that the general election had given them a plain mandate, that the government demanded more for the army than efficiency required, that the period of service could be safely reduced from three years to two, that the levying of taxes without the consent of the Lower House was a plain violation of the constitution, and that a compromise involved acquiescence in the illegal acts of the government, which would permanently destroy the power of the Lower House ever again to modify or refuse the financial demands of any ministry, —in a word, that the future of parliamentary and constitutional government was bound up with the successful assertion of their principles, the majority could only meet the challenge of the Minister-President by inflexible adherence to their decision. A surrender in the autumn of 1862 would have been a victory for reaction and a defeat for the principle of popular government through representative institutions throughout Germany. Accordingly, the Lower Chamber by 251 to 36 votes condemned the illegal expenditure incurred by the government, and demanded that the budget for 1863 should be submitted for approval. When (October 10) the Upper House accepted the condemned budget of 1862 by 114 to 44 votes, their action was condemned unanimously by the Lower House as ' contrary to the clear sense and text of the constitution.' Parliament was prorogued ; when it met in 1863 (January 27) an address to the Crown, accusing ministers of having violated the constitution, was passed after a passionate debate by 255 to 68 votes.

The breach was now complete. The Lower House was in plain conflict with the Crown, the Crown's ministers and the Upper House, and the struggle, in which feeling outside was as violent as within Parliament, soon spread to other issues than the reorganisation of the army and the budget.

The struggle was no mere juristic controversy over disputable and conflicting clauses in the written constitution

of 1851. It focussed in the clearest light the fundamental
and irreconcilable antagonism between the principles
and methods of policy, government, and the character of
the State represented by Bismarck and the opposition.
When Bismarck ignored the undeniable mandate of the
Prussian electorate to its representatives in Parliament,
and when he admitted that the levying of the rejected
taxes was an executive act which would require an
indemnity to bring it within the letter and spirit of the
constitution, he proclaimed that the struggle was not a
question of law, but of power. Was the Crown, as head
of the executive and of the army, to enforce its will on the
nation, and to retain a final and irresponsible judgment
in all questions of policy ?

'The Prussian Monarchy,' he asserted on January 27,
1863, 'has not yet completed its mission ; it is not yet
ready to become a purely ornamental decoration of your
constitutional Parliament House ; not yet ready to be
manipulated as a piece of lifeless machinery of parliamentary government.'

Bismarck was fighting with his back to the wall for an
issue more important in his eyes than the preservation of
the legal prerogatives of the Crown in Prussia. The personal monarchy, as an organ of government, was the indispensable condition of success in the task he had set himself.
A constitutional sovereign, in the British sense, not only involved ministers responsible to Parliament, but a legislature
the chief function of which would be to determine the
ends, the character, and the methods of policy. Hence
his unrelenting opposition now, and to the end of his life,
to government by and through representative institutions
was the subtle product of ingrained personal feeling and
a recognition of the fundamental antagonism between his
political convictions and the champions of parliamentary
government. He could be the loyal servant of a king
whose office incarnated the history and character of a
specific type of State, but to be the servant of a Parliament,
accountable to, and holding his place at the pleasure of,
a fortuitous majority of professors, lawyers, journalists,
tradesmen and tinkers, was intolerable to his aristocratic

pride and independence. He would take orders from no one save the King and God, and he served God as he served his royal master, on terms of devotion defined and interpreted by himself.

On political grounds he both feared and despised his opponents in Parliament. He told them roundly that they were ignorant, prejudiced, unpractical—dreamers without political sense—helpless children in affairs of State. Had he been perfectly honest he would have added that diplomacy, as he conceived it, could not be conducted with the blinds up, and that no representative body of responsible men of high character would sanction either his principles or his methods, and that for the realisation of his aims absolute control of all the resources of the State and an unfettered discretion were indispensable, and that it was easier to manipulate and hoodwink a king than a nation and a Parliament. The reorganisation of the army, the steady preparation for war by a militarised bureaucracy, the budget question, the Polish problem, the conquest of Schleswig-Holstein, the manipulation of the European situation, the understandings with Russia and Napoleon III., the Italian Treaty, the breach with Austria, the campaign and peace of 1866, and the formation of the North German Confederation—the Bismarckian solution of the great questions of the day—could never have been carried out, as Bismarck carried them out, by a minister under a system of constitutional monarchy and responsible parliamentary government. The conscience of Prussia and Germany in 1862 made, in Bismarck's eyes, for political cowardice. Nor were the Germans who created the National Union under Bennigsen as yet prepared to sacrifice everything to the State as Power, and to adopt as their sole criterion of policy the State-egoism of an unreformed and militarised Prussia.

In 1862 Germany was ripe for great changes. Under the pressure of the internal development, assisted by the course of events in Europe, most notably in Italy, the demand for the extension of political rights on Nationalist and Liberal lines could no longer be burked or denied. It was apparent in every quarter, and in every German State.

The dynasties and their ministers from Vienna to Liberal Coburg or reactionary Hesse-Cassel were responding, reluctantly or readily, to the movement which had Germany in its grip. The passionate manifestation of German public opinion in the Polish problem, and the Schleswig-Holstein question from 1863 to 1866, the execration which Bismarck aroused in non-Prussian Germany, have an historic and tragic significance. Bismarck had divined the force and direction of the currents now reaching their flood-tide, and he tacitly agreed with the leaders of the National Union that the key of the future lay in Prussia. The failure to secure Prussia in 1848 had destroyed the Liberal revolution. A second failure to capture Prussia in 1863 would have the same wrecking result. And as in 1848, so now, success or failure would determine not merely the fate of Germany and of Prussia, but the German mind and the future development of Continental Europe.

The strength of the Liberal opposition in the Prussian Parliament lay, first, in its devotion to constitutional law and right ; secondly, in a profound belief in the efficacy of orderly self-government through representative institutions ; thirdly, in the deep Prussian and German patriotism of the leaders and the rank and file ; fourthly, in their insistence on the complete identity of Prussian and German interests alike in home and foreign policy ; fifthly, in their recognition that the old order in Prussia and Germany had failed, and would continue to fail, to satisfy the deepest and most legitimate aspirations of the German people, and that a new departure on new principles was essential ; and lastly, in their sympathy, partly conscious, partly unconscious, with the great currents and forces moving elsewhere than in Germany—in the United States, in Great Britain, in Italy, in the Austrian Empire, in south-eastern Europe and the Balkans, in France, and even in Russia. It was a bitter duty for the leaders of the opposition openly to challenge the King, but they faced it because they had consciences and a deep love of Prussia. The ignorance in England of the true character of the German movement, the blindness of our statesmen, our press, and our public opinion to the significance for our nation and national destinies of the struggle fought out between September 1862 and July 1867, were more damning than the lamentable division in our councils and the fiasco of our statesmanship in Europe. In these years Great Britain was given a matchless opportunity to assert a moral and political ascendency, not based on power, but on the qualities and elements of national development of which the British State is the expression and the trustee, and she threw it away, as she very nearly in the same epoch threw away her birthright in the issues raised by the American Civil War.

But the Liberal opposition had two fatal defects, which Bismarck with a demonic intuition fully realised. The renunciation of reform by revolution, and of the right of resistance, and the adhesion to procedure by purely constitutional methods reduced his opponents to impotence. Constitutional weapons are helpless against force : argument is futile against an opponent who derides the impotence of speeches and pamphlets. Bismarck could not be driven from office by votes of the Lower House, but only by a revolution. He calculated that opposition would be confined to resolutions in the Lower House, public meetings and the press, and that he would not be driven to a *coup d'État* by refusal to pay illegal taxes or to serve in an illegal army. We may be quite sure that he would not have hesitated to employ shot and shell, but a civil war in Prussia which would have involved the whole of Germany and of Austria was the one thing that he knew he need not fear. With consummate irony he subsequently utilised the reverence for law and order that inspired the constitutional party as the clinching proof that German unity could not be achieved by any other methods than his own. Had the men who overthrew Charles I. and James II. limited themselves to passive protests, recorded in the *Journals* of the House of Commons, the house of Stuart would have been reigning to-day in Whitehall, and the palace of Westminster would have been replaced by a national memorial to Strafford and Father Petre. But Strafford had to work with a Charles I. Bismarck had King William and the Prussia made by the

Hohenzollern sovereigns. In the second place, the opposition were not dealing with a pure reactionary, determined to maintain, as Nicholas I. and Schwarzenberg had been determined in 1848 to maintain, the *status quo*, and to stamp out every obstacle to its maintenance. An infuriated public opinion saw in the Minister-President the arch-enemy of unification and the champion of Junker particularism. It was quite wrong. Bismarck was as profoundly convinced as every Liberal that the German problem must be solved and on Nationalist lines ; and his conviction was steeled by the knowledge that the future of Conservatism and Prussianism would be permanently assured by the capacity to achieve such a solution. He was as passionately in earnest as any Liberal in Germany, and he despised as strongly as any Liberal the rancid reaction of the Conservatives. In men, conscious of titanic powers, personal ambition is an immeasurable driving force, and everything he cared for, including his own career, was at stake in the contest to which Bismarck now deliberately committed himself. He meant to justify himself to the Prussia which he loved and the Germany which so heartily hated him. He would succeed because he must. The one thing that divided him from the Liberals was his interpretation of life, but that was vital and nothing could bridge or obliterate it. A Prussia and a Germany such as the Liberals desired to make, and would, unless they were decisively defeated, succeed in making, were to Bismarck the negation of everything that made life worth living.

At this stage in Bismarck's career two conclusions are fairly certain. He had no cut-and-dried programme when he came into office ; his difficulties were so formidable as to be almost insuperable. The marvellous march of events, in which each stage seems to slip into its pre-appointed place, stupefied not unnaturally contemporary opinion, and has perverted both the historical and moral judgment of German and non-German alike. The quality and characteristics of his genius are more, not less, impressive if we ignore the sequel, and endeavour patiently to reconstruct the situation from year to year, and realise the essential difference between an opportunism of ends and an opportunism of means. When he repeatedly called himself an opportunist in politics it was the latter, not the former, that Bismarck really meant.

No man had a clearer conception of the ends he had set himself to achieve; no man more deliberately on principle left the means to be determined by the conditions and possibilities, the realities and *ponderabilia*, of each situation as it arose. He was always playing for the next stroke; but it was the stroke of the moment that exacted the concentration of all his powers. His freedom from scruple was on the same titanic scale as the rest of his intellectual gifts. His conscience never caused him one of the many sleepless nights which the nervous torture of his brain so abundantly produced. The fear that he had miscalculated an opponent's strength or misinterpreted the resources at his disposal, that the King, the soldiers, or a subordinate would fail him, or that he himself had let a chance slip was with him night and day. To errors of judgment he pleaded guilty with an engaging and disarming frankness; to the commission of wrong, never; and for the simple reason that the ethical standards and criteria of private life were ruled out of politics by his creed and code of public conduct. In the sphere of statesmanship right and wrong were decided for Bismarck by the needs and interests of the State for whose destinies he was responsible, and by no other considerations, ethical or material. Hence he did not do what he plainly regarded as wrong in order that good might ensue; he did not salve a seared or rebellious conscience by the comforting illusion that ends justify means. The methods he employed were intrinsically justifiable or not at all, and the appropriate tests were drawn from the same sources as those properly applicable to the ends themselves. In a dozen crucial instances Bismarck was prouder of the methods than of the results of his diplomacy. He scornfully rejected the white sheet in which so many statesmen have appealed to the absolution of a posterity, grateful for their achievements, but as perturbed as the statesmen themselves by the immorality of their statecraft.

Between 1862 and 1866 the Minister-President was a

new man in office for the first time. As with Moltke, his collaborator of genius, the prestige and personal ascendancy which he enjoyed in increasing measure after 1867 had yet to be won. The constitutional conflict imposed a terrible responsibility. The opposition fought neither with small nor with great, save only with the minister who had intervened to arrest an otherwise certain triumph. Outside Prussia, the political relations of Berlin with the other German governments were poisoned by the fear that his antecedents and utterances aroused. At Paris and Petersburg he had created credits on which he intended to draw, but Napoleon and Gortschakov were chary of committing themselves to this audacious adventurer, whose fortunes were in so perilous a position. At Vienna, the Ball-Platz had good reason to know that the new Minister-President was no friend to Austria. To London Bismarck was an unknown quantity : in our Court, better informed, he stirred a deep-seated and justifiable aversion. At Berlin, the Conservatives, routed at the elections, welcomed the minister as an instrument to chastise democracy, but his principles, particularly in foreign policy, caused the gravest misgivings, and his haughty and brusque independence alienated and offended the phalanx of the *Kreuzzeitung*. The soldiers at headquarters soon discovered that to Bismarck the army was an organ of the State, not an end in itself ; soldiers, in his view, were bad masters but good servants ; he had no intention of becoming a political tool of the General Staff, and he brooked no interference with the higher political direction. The organisation of the army was the soldiers' business, policy was his. Indeed, in 1862, began the friction between the civil Minister-President and the army chiefs.

In a State, saturated with militarism, such as Prussia, in which an unbroken tradition had created an ethos that dominated the personal monarchy, a civil minister determined to control policy was bound to offend the military chiefs, habituated to regard the claims of the army as paramount. In Roon he had his one staunch friend. But Roon was a soldier first and last. He had brought Bismarck into power to prevent Prussia from being overwhelmed 'in the sea of mud called **parliamentary** government.' Otto's conduct of affairs sorely tried Roon's loyal affection and simple Conservative faith. For the scope and increasing growth of Bismarck's genius were beyond the limited political vision of Roon. Yet the friendship of these two, Prussian in every drop of their blood—that intimate 'du' in their letters—dating from the hot ambitions of youth, weathering and deepening through all the crises of the heroic age from 1848 onwards to the grey maturity that has achieved, warms and illumines the stark and gnarled loneliness of Bismarck's life. His wife, his sister, his children, Roon and the King—outside these lies a formal waste filled with countless figures, who belong to Bismarck, but Bismarck does not belong to them.

In 1862, everything turned on the King. The constitutional conflict had flooded the royal hearth and the steps to the throne. The Crown Prince and his circle, in close touch with the intellectuals of Liberalism, such as M. Duncker, Samwer, and Bernhardi, indicated unmistakably their disagreement with the minister's policy and methods, and their genuine fear that a reckless gambler was imperilling the future of the dynasty, pledging the monarchy to an irreconcilable breach with the nation, and destroying the moral primacy of Prussia in Germany.

King William was, indeed, desperately unhappy; the pressure of contradictory counsels was almost intolerable; adjured on one side to authorise negotiations with the Landtag over Bismarck's head, which would save his honour, and satisfy the opposition, on the other to stand firm and save the Crown and army from the men who insulted him by accusations of violating the constitution. Bismarck has vividly described the King's fear that he would end like our Charles i. on a scaffold, erected on the wreckage of the hereditary monarchy, and his appeal to the King that if it needs must be so, better to die at his post than surrender. He, at any rate, would not desert him, for he preferred the fate of Strafford to a craven submission. It is one of the many penalties of service under an autocracy that the security of tenure, assured by a representative legislature, is dependent on a single personality, and at the

and the distribution of ribbons and decorations to avowed
Absolutists could always raise the necessary steam in the
boilers of Liberalism. Foreign policy, finance, and military administration provided inexhaustible material for
baiting the opposition into violent rhetoric and resolutions
passed by overwhelming majorities. Roon's temper was
of a military shortness when he dealt, as Minister of War,
with civilian amateurs. Bismarck allowed him to provoke
quarrels in the Landtag, and then with magisterial im-
partiality, poured vitriol on the parliamentary critics.
The Minister-President proved that the Junker of 1848,
with his vivid utterance and racy brutality, was a master
of the studied insult, the barbed innuendo, the cynical
contempt, the phrase that cut down to the bone and
stuck. Indignation vexed him as a thing that is raw.
And he could lose his temper, too, when nerves and endurance cracked under the burden that he carried, virtually
alone. 'The House of Phrases' simply provided loqua-
cious passengers in a coach, the driving of which without
their ignorant interference imposed an almost impossible
task on the coachman. Bismarck was as little able as
Frederick the Great or Richelieu to share government
with a representative assembly. He did not understand,
or wish or try to understand, the secrets and mechanism
of a system repugnant to his feelings and a permanent
hindrance to the achievement of his ends. The time
spent in futile debates and logic-chopping controversies
was sheer waste. Every ounce of his strength, every hour
of his overworked day, were needed for the real partner in
government—the King—and the multifarious business of
the State. Not on the floor of the Landtag, but in a
correct judgment of political realities, lay the secret of
statecraft, and for the judgment of his opponents, Conservative or Radical, ignorant of the European theatre of
politics, and worshippers at the shrines of all the Idols of
the Tribe and of the Market-Place, he had a pitying contempt. Salvation would come from action—the patient
manœuvring for the strategic points, and then the decisive
stroke—the State as the incarnation of power and statecraft
as the expression of its disciplined force.

From the very outset he gave Germany a taste of the
' Bismarck touch.'   The constitutional and chronic im-
broglio at Hesse-Cassel was settled by a curt ultimatum.
The reactionary Elector recognised that the new minister
meant what was said and surrendered.   Public opinion
was bewildered at this example of Satan rebuking Sin.
For here was a ruler advised by his reactionary minister,
Hassenpflug, in conflict with a rebel legislature over his
prerogative, and compelled to admit the claims of the
rebels by a minister who was a Prussian super-Hassenpflug.
It forgot that Hesse-Cassel was not Prussia, that the struggle
was in Bismarck's eyes a nuisance, the continuance of which
strengthened the Progressives in Berlin, and that surrender
on a word from Berlin was a proof of Prussian strength.

That strength was more effectively exemplified in the
matter of the French Commercial Treaty and the renewal
of the Zollverein's Tariff Treaty with Austria.   The
French Treaty was an important step in promoting a
better understanding between Prussia and the Second
Empire.   Austria, as in 1851, desired either to break up
the Zollverein and thereby damage the political and
economic supremacy in non-Austrian Germany exercised
by Prussia, or to secure the inclusion of the Austrian
dominions in the Tariff Union on terms favourable to her
peculiar economic needs.   The French Commercial Treaty
had stirred serious opposition within the Tariff Union, and
at Vienna there was good hope of driving one or other,
perhaps both, of the wedges into the Prussian system.
The foundations of Bismarck's system were threatened.   In
Delbrück he had the coadjutor he needed, for Delbrück
had first-class ability and a complete mastery of the economic facts, and behind Delbrück stood Bismarck confident
in Prussia's strength.   The French Commercial Treaty
must go through.   Austria could renew with trifling
modifications the previous agreement.   But her inclusion
in the Customs Union was impossible.   And if the Zollverein refused the Prussian proposals, then it must break
up.   Prussia would go her own way and make her own
tariff arrangements, for she was strong enough to stand
by herself.   She peremptorily refused to sacrifice her

economic interests to South German particularism or
Austrian selfishness. Let the middle and petty States
choose between a Prussia which desired to be their friend
and ally and an Austria that aimed at exploiting them.

They chose. Austria secured neither the rejection of
the French Treaty, nor the dissolution of the Zollverein,
nor her inclusion within the Tariff Union. She had per-
force to accept simply a renewal of the fiscal treaty with
the Zollverein, that included the whole of non-Austrian
Germany and as a fiscal unit to stand outside the German
ring fence. There was more in this settlement than the
incompatibility of Austrian Protectionism with German
economic development, and a correct judgment that
material interests would defeat political sentiment in the
rivalry between Prussia and Austria for the economic
leadership of the middle and petty States. Bismarck had
struck for and obtained three results. First, the independence of Prussia; secondly, the right to settle with
France on his own terms; thirdly, clear proof that Austria
was not, properly speaking, a true German State. The
essential preliminary to a settlement of the political unification of Germany on the lines of the Small and not the
Great Germany conception was the establishment of an
economic unification which drew an unmistakable frontier
line between the Austrian Empire and the rest of the
Federal organisation. The Great Germany party, as
Bismarck fully realised, was by no means dead, either at
Berlin or outside it. The first step to the final defeat of
the Great Germans was taken with the successful conclusion of the complicated and highly technical negotiations in economics, and Bismarck took care to indicate
a helpful moral at Paris. Prussia had deliberately preferred an arrangement with France to an arrangement
with Austria. The identity of interest, he commented,
between France and Prussia was not necessarily confined
to tariff duties and the most-favoured nation clause.

At the snarling criticism on Prussia's anti-German and
unbrotherly Prussian selfishness towards Austria Bismarck
shrugged his shoulders. It was the privilege of the defeated to snarl. The spring of 1863 enabled the Foreign

Office in the Wilhelmstrasse to provide Germany and Europe with another example of Prussian independence and egoism that stirred a tempest of denunciation.

The Polish rebellion of January, 1863, precipitated a European crisis. The sympathy of Western and Central Europe, alike in the governments and their people, with the Polish effort to secure national unity and administrative autonomy—freedom as a race from Russian tyranny —is very remarkable and profoundly significant of the grip of Liberal and Nationalist ideals on the temper of the age. In London, Paris, Turin, and Vienna, the Polish cause was acclaimed with enthusiasm. The Poles were fighting for the inalienable right of a nation to work out its salvation and establish its civilisation as a self-governing unit in the fraternity of European National-States. The disintegrated Germany of the Federal Bund and denationalised Austria were no whit behind the new Italy, France, and Great Britain in their Polish sympathies. The contrast, indeed, is striking between the manifestation in 1863 of public opinion in Prussia and non-Prussian Germany, in support of the Poles, and in sincere reprobation of the terrible severity with which the defeated rising was crushed by the Russian autocracy, and the cold-blooded equanimity with which Germany and the Magyarised Dual Empire of 1876 and 1896 condoned, when they did not positively approve, the more terrible treatment of the Balkan Slavs and the Armenians by the Ottoman autocracy. Only by such a contrast can we realise the strength of the Liberal movement and of the moral forces behind it, with which Bismarck wrestled in 1863, and register in 1896 the atrophy of a nation's conscience and the withering of its ideals, when for two generations it has been drugged by the doctrine that the great questions of the day can be decided only by blood and iron.

Bismarck at once recognised the gravity of the Polish issue and the opportunity that the Polish question provided. His attitude to the problem of Poland, and Prussian Poland in particular, never altered since 1848, when he first denounced the danger of Polonism to the Prussian State, through the *Kulturkampf* to the anti-Polish legislation of his chancellorship that he left as a wasting mortgage to his successors. He told General Fleury in December, 1863, that the question was one of life and death to Prussia : ' I would rather die,' he said, ' than permit our position in Posen to be discussed at a European Congress : I would rather cede our Rhinelands.' He had no sympathy with the Nationalist principle, outside Prussia and Germany ; it was simply a force in a political situation, to be exploited as such ; and if a force that threatened Prussian hegemony one to be extirpated. The eighteenth-century partitions of Poland were the well-merited fate of a State too anarchic to resist the strength of its neighbours. The dream of a reconstructed Poland on Liberal lines in 1863 was simply a childish chimera. The independence of Russian Poland under the suzerainty of the Tsar would lead to a demand for the freedom of Prussian Poland, a result absolutely fatal to the Prussian position in the East and on the Baltic. The demand for autonomy and political liberties sprang from the same delusions about government that tainted the progressive and democratic parties in Germany. Concessions to Polish demands within Prussia were intrinsically inadmissible, and would embarrass the good friend, Russia. The Polish rebellion was a domestic affair of the Tsar's government, interference with which was an impertinence that the Tsar would justly resent.

Prussia's interest must be the sole criterion of Prussia's policy. A rebellion on her borders was a serious danger ; there were disquieting signs that the conflagration would spread. The sooner it was stamped out the better for every one concerned. Bismarck, in short, only cared to extract the maximum of political advantage from an affair which he examined with icy impartiality. The blood of Polish martyrs, for whose sufferings he did not care a groschen, might become the seed of Prussian domination in Central Europe. Through General von Alvensleben he promptly (March 8) concluded a convention with Russia, by which the two countries undertook to establish a military cordon on their respective frontiers in order to stop their respective Polish subjects from aiding the rebel lion, and to prevent the escape of rebels from lawful authority. The action of the parliamentary opposition in the Landtag only confirmed Bismarck's determination. Interpellations, denunciations of the convention, resolutions by sweeping majorities, he brushed aside as irrelevant attempts to interfere with the royal right to conclude treaties by prerogative, and to make the foreign policy of Prussia conform to the folly of ignorant idealists or crazy demagogues. He told the Lower House roundly that the making of war and treaties was the right of the Crown, and roused its fury by the emphatic assertion that he would make war or abstain from it without their approbation or consent, and that his duty to his sovereign and Prussia would never be influenced one hair's-breadth by their votes or their attacks.

When the governments of Great Britain, France, and Austria, under the pressure of public opinion agreed to present a joint note formulating six demands [1] to the Russian government, and invited the concurrence of Prussia in this diplomatic pressure, Bismarck firmly refused, and for four chief reasons. A close understanding with Russia was, and had long been, the *sine quâ non* of his system. Refusal to sign the note was the most practical proof he could give of friendship to Russia. The alienation of Russia, still suffering from the humiliation of 1856, and threatened with the boycott of Europe and the moral condemnation of the civilised conscience, was for Prussia in 1863 midsummer madness. Secondly, he disapproved of the six demands. If Russia conceded them, the National Union and the Radicals throughout Germany would utilise the concession to harass the government of Prussia already plagued with the charlatanry of Progress. Thirdly, rejection by the Russian government of the joint note must be followed either by more exacting pressure, and if necessary, war, or by a painful rebuff at Petersburg. Bismarck did not believe in a diplomacy that invited humiliation, and the idea of war on behalf of the Polish rebels

---

[1] The six points were briefly: (1) an amnesty; (2) a Polish parliament; (3) a Polish National Executive; (4) Polish language in official communications; (5) religious freedom; (6) legal recruiting.

was idiotic. Fourthly, he foresaw the failure of this singular union of Great Britain, France, and Austria, and he
desired it to fail. The ill-assorted partners would quarrel,
and from their quarrel Prussia would derive advantages
that could be left for future exploitation. The separation
of Austria and of France from Russia was worth all the
joint notes and all the Polish lives in the world. As early
as 1860 Bismarck had expressed the fear that France would
ally with Russia, isolate Prussia, or drive her into a hateful
dependence on Austria. He had laid it down that in a
Franco-Russian alliance Prussia must be the third member.
Great Britain could be soothed or neglected as circumstances indicated. The British army did not exist; and
the British fleet was useless in this business. Fortune had
now given Prussia an unexpected favour. France by her
stupid sentimentalism would alienate Russia. Prussia
could first secure Russian friendship, break up the Franco-
British *entente*, then work for a French benevolent neutrality, and Austria would be left to face an irreconcilable
Italy and an independent Prussia secure on both her
flanks. Here, indeed, was a game for the Titans.

Bismarck might well gaze into the baffling face of the
Time-spirit. The Schleswig-Holstein question was threat-
ening an ugly crisis. It is significant of the minister's
exploratory and prescient vigilance that while Nation-
alists and democrats were crying aloud for Germany and
Prussia to act, he gave no sign that he was earnestly
sounding all the depths and shallows in a rock-sown sea.
He contented himself with a pointed reminder to the
Danish government that Prussia was a signatory to the
Convention of London of 1852, and a sharp rap on the
heads of the 'noisy' journalists and politicians who desired
Prussia to go to war with all her neighbours because of
alleged grievances. *Toujours en vedette!* The motto of
Frederick, the Master, was more than ever the watchword.

Neither menaces nor caresses from London, Paris, and
Vienna induced Bismarck to modify his refusal to join
in the combined intervention at Petersburg and, as he
foresaw, the joint note was a complete failure. Assured
of Prussia's support, the Russian government in effect bade

the signatory Powers mind their own business, and proceeded to extinguish the rebellion in blood and flame. Napoleon was intensely chagrined at the result, the blame for which he threw chiefly on Great Britain. Our Foreign Office had used the strong language that should precede strong action, but it now covered its retreat to the wired trenches of a good conscience in the smoke-clouds of a parliamentary Blue-Book. At the Tuileries the need of a real diplomatic success somewhere was being seriously felt. Paris was seething with sentiment and ill-defined ambition. Napoleon's disillusioned eyes turned to Berlin. In the Wilhelmstrasse, not in the Ball-Platz, lay the keys that could unlock the doors to the Rhine ; and Napoleon knew that the hunger of France, gnawing at the vitals of the Second Empire, could be appeased, and only appeased, by the Rhenish provinces.

The true author of the Polish fiasco was Bismarck. Had he made Prussia a signatory to the Note of the Six Demands, the Russia of 1863, isolated and in grave difficulties, would have been obliged to yield to the Concert of Europe. Had Prussia been a country with responsible self-government Bismarck must either have met the overwhelming demand of the Landtag or been driven from office. With Prussian support it was well within the compass of practical diplomacy, without firing a shot, to have extorted a charter of liberties for Russian Poland and prevented the cruelties that added one more chapter to the blood-stained record. The moral and political effect of such concerted action would have been of incalculable advantage. But a Canning in London or a Cavour at Berlin were needed. Instead, there was Bismarck on the one side, and on the other Napoleon and the clever mediocrities of the Quai d'Orsay, the organised hypocrisy of Vienna and a Palmerston, no longer the man of 1839, and permanently suspect to a hostile court. Public opinion in Prussia and Germany was impotent against Bismarck. While it raged, he sided with Russia, thereby revealing to the Triple Entente that without war they were helpless, and that the strategic position of Prussia and the strength of the Prussian army made the suggestion of war without Prussia ridiculous and

impossible.   It was in Bismarck's power, and he knew it, to
meet the storm in the last resort by an appeal to Prussia
and Germany to forget the exaggerated woes of Poland
and concentrate on the Ahab of Europe—Napoleon.

Bismarck, it must be remembered, in these years was in
a dangerous temper : he was fighting for the life, honour,
and greatness of Prussia, as he interpreted them, and he
had thrown his all into the struggle.   Even more truly
than Cavour from 1852 onwards he was gambling for
tremendous stakes.   Not once but fifty times in the next
few year she indicated his determination, if the gods failed
him, to move Acheron.   What could not be done by the
Conservative forces, could be done by calling in the Revolution.   His heart within was white-hot with the same
emotion that mastered the German of his day, and no
man could let loose more skilfully the whirlwinds of
national passion, or rejoice more triumphantly in riding
the storm.

But in 1863, as always, he had himself in hand.   The
hour assuredly had not come : the situation must be developed much further and with a remorseless caution.
He could not afford to make a single mistake.   The Prussian army was not ready.   Like his diplomacy it needed
time.   And it was of the essence of his system, as of
Frederick the Great's, that so far as preparation and calculation could ensure it, victory must be a certainty.   The
Statecraft that is Force betrays the State that is Power if
it ignores or misunderstands the character and conditions
under which Force works in the world of human things.

Bismarck had secured the friendship of Russia.   His
confidence that Prussia could rely on her strength and independence had been justified.   The initiative in policy,
lost in the period from 1815 to 1862, was being quietly
recovered.   While the members of the temporary Triple
Entente were abusing Prussia, and still more heartily, each
other, Bismarck was drawing up an edifying balance-sheet.
He could remind his royal master of two sound lessons—
the indispensability of the Crown's unfettered control of
policy, the futility of ' moral penetration,' as a solution
of European problems.   The relevance of both to the

constitutional crisis was obvious, and the sequel was to
drive the argument home with cumulative power. King
William was, Bismarck discovered, eminently teachable ;
but he eminently required to be taught. Time was even
more necessary for the instruction of the Crown than for
the development of the European situation. An autocrat
who takes the bit in his teeth will dash the chariot of State
to pieces more quickly and disastrously than a nation that
loses its head. If William's conscience or prejudices
drove him to break loose, Bismarck would share the fate
of Metternich.

The quality of Bismarck's judgment was never better
illustrated than in his refusal of Gortschakov's suggestion
that the Russo-Prussian understanding should be converted
into a formal alliance. It was a tempting proposal ; and
we can well believe that he weighed it in every scale before
declining. Treaties, it is true, were not more sacred than
other, less formal, engagements. They were, in Bismarck's eyes, no more than the summary of a particular
situation, and their observance was always conditioned by
an implicit clause—*rebus sic stantibus*—things being as they
were. Nor was it the fear that a treaty would limit his
initiative or freedom of action. A virtual alliance with
Russia was the fixed point on which Prussian policy
was henceforward to pivot. The identity of interest—
dynastic, governmental, political—between the Russia of
the Tsar and the Prussia of William I., was practically
complete. Nor did Bismarck fear the accusation at home
or elsewhere that the Holy Alliance was being revived.
He had faced that when he made the Alvensleben Convention, and proved that he could ignore public opinion
in Prussia and the criticism of foreign governments. His
real reason for the refusal of Gortschakov's offer lays bare
an essential principle of his statecraft. To the Prussia of
1863, convalescent from a prolonged locomotor-ataxy, and
not yet cured, Russia was more indispensable to Prussia
than Prussia was to Russia. Bismarck's judgment of
Russia's strength was extraordinarily sane and impartial.
He shared with Gustavus Adolphus and Richelieu the
sense of limits, which is one of the finest and rarest, if not

the finest and rarest, gift of the highest statesmanship.
Russia, he pronounced with customary vividness, would in
such an alliance sit on the longer arm of the lever. All
that was needed in 1863 could be distilled gradually from
the informal but close understanding already established.
Every alliance, he remarked at another time, implies a
horse and a rider. The function of diplomacy is to secure
that you are the rider and your ally the horse. Because
he correctly judged that in 1863, Gortschakov would be
the rider and he, Bismarck, the horse, he put the offer
politely and with many assurances of affection, personal
and political, on one side.

While the Polish Rebellion was still running its appointed course, the German question also had developed
a crisis. The demand that something must be done, and
done now, to reshape the indefensible travesty of a political
mechanism, called the Bund—that precious monument
the restoration of which in its anachronistic nudity had
marked the grave both of 1848 and of Conservative constructive statesmanship. For ten years every German
mind had been labouring with the problem and putting on
record, to the embarrassment of that age and the despair
of the seeker after truth in the next two generations, its
perplexities, fears, hopes, dreams and solutions. State-
papers, diaries, letters, pamphlets, caricatures, memorials,
note-books, and minutes of clubs, unions, leagues—the
archives of the chancelleries, the waste-paper basket of the
patriot, and the scrap-heap of the lecture-room—which
German research has by no means exhausted, testify to the
deep-seated and universal discontent. Nationalists, Radicals, Clericals and Ultramontanes, Conservatives, bureaucrats and professors, hummed like bees in the swarming
season from the frontier of Schleswig to the forelands of
the Alps. The flower of the universities, professorial and
undergraduate, linked hands and pens with the politicians
—Bennigsen, Droysen, Samwer, M. Duncker, the Coburg
group, and the unitarian enthusiasm of the Grand-Duke
of Baden. Already the trumpet of the young Treitschke
was blowing its earliest clarion calls.

When the butchers meet in conclave because something

must be done for the sheep, we may be sure that it is not the sheep but the butchers who fear the future. In 1863, the Habsburg Emperor felt the cruel coercion of a Germany out of joint, and the unpleasant necessity of putting it right before worse befell. The dynasties from Dresden to Munich leaped to the suggestion from Vienna that disinterested patriotism could be concentrated in a Congress of Princes ready to confer benefits on their subjects. To the adroit Beust at Dresden, as fertile in diplomatic resource as in conversational epigram, the opportunity was exceptional. Beust, like every one else, had his scheme, or rather half a dozen schemes, in pigeon-holes, and another half dozen producible if required, like the magician's rabbits, for any audience, and from any diplomatic bag—and Beust was by far the cleverest of all the political conjurers in the middle States who desired a tripartite Germany—Austria, the middle States, and Prussia—regrouped in a new Federal structure. To Beust and to the Triad party, the supreme merit of this solution, the details of which were simply a drafting matter, lay in its recognition of the equality of non-Austrian and non-Prussian Germany as a collective unit with Austria and Prussia. Such equality would fairly meet the Prussian demand for parity with Austria and the Austrian reluctance to surrender her historic hegemony; it would no less fairly remove the fatal objection to all dualistic schemes which imposed on the middle and petty States an obligatory choice of being absorbed either in a Prussian or an Austrian system, an absorption damaging to the general interests of Germany, historically unjust, and repugnant to the legitimist sovereignty of the dynasties.

Concessions must, of course, be made to the people as well as to the States of Germany. Bismarck's failure was assumed to be a practical certainty : Prussia would then succumb to the liberal majority which would adopt the programme of the National Union and achieve a unitary and democratic solution under Prussian leadership. Once the citadel in Prussia had fallen to the parliamentary opposition, the rest of Germany would lynch its dynasties into acceptance of the unitary and liberal plan. And

Austria, racked on a series of Procrustean beds, called constitutions, with Italy on one side and Hungary on the other, and Russia sullenly hostile, could not expect to repeat in 1864 the miracle of 1849. Now, if ever, was the moment to drive an Austrian dynastic, anti-Prussian, and particularist programme through.

The problem was first to combine the minimum of real concession with the maximum of outward homage to democratic demands ; and secondly, to arrange the Federal machinery in such a way as to grant in theory the Prussian claim to parity with Austria, while refusing the substance —an easy matter, for equal voting powers between Austria and Prussia must always leave Prussia in a minority when non-Prussian Germany made equal either to Austria or Prussia voted (as it would) with Austria. The Austrian government accordingly produced its specious plan. A new Directorate of six States (Austria, Prussia, Bavaria, and three others chosen in rotation) under Austrian presidency was to be created, together with a Federal Council of 21 votes, a Federal Tribunal of Law, and a Federal Assembly of 302 Delegates elected, not by direct suffrage, but by the various parliaments of the Federated States.

Rebellious German democracy was, in short, to be remanacled in a new Federal cage, and Prussia was, through her King, to mediatise herself for the benefit of Germany on the altars of dynasticism. The Emperor Franci Joseph met King William at Gastein. The crises o German history always begin or end at a bathing resort The two sovereigns talked and agreed that the busines could be settled by a Congress of Princes at Frankfurt It was fitting that the rulers, by personal negotiations should settle the affairs of Germany in a royal and famil conference ; and their ministers were to be in close attend ance, but take no part in the august deliberations. Whil their princely masters worked, they could copy letters dine, dance, and arrange for the exchange of decoration On August 16 the Congress met ; only one importan sovereign (and his minister) was absent. The surprise an dismay were universal, for the absentee was the King c Prussia. They sent to fetch him. The King of Saxon was the courier chosen to remind King William that a Congress of Princes, headed by Cæsarean Majesty from Vienna, begged the honour of his company. Delay and much anxiety. Then the King of Saxony came back. The King of Prussia regretted his inability to accept the invitation. Indignation, expostulation, consternation, prevailed: then after a few days, the Congress ruefully broke up. All that it accomplished was to repeat the invitation (by letter this time) to Prussia and to 'leave open' the question of the Presidency 'for further discussion.' The proposal to proceed, without Prussia, was indeed suggested, but crumbled into pieces at once. 'We will have no confederation without Austria,' said the Bavarian minister, 'but likewise none without Prussia.' A reorganisation of Germany which omitted Prussia was ridiculous. The coercion of Prussia would, in the state of public opinion, probably end in the revolution with the Prussian army at its disposal. And when the Prussian government officially published its reasons for abstention—the patent inadequacy of the proposals of the Princes to meet the rights of Prussia and the needs of Germany was glaringly and painfully evident. 'A national Parliament,' said the Prussian memorandum of September 15, 'was an essential of any Federal reform. The interests and claims of the Prussian people are intrinsically and inseparably identical with those of the German people.' The argument was repeated in the Note of September 22, sent to all the members of the Congress of Princes. Prussia laid it down that: (1) She, as well as Austria, must have a right to veto a declaration of war by the Confederation; (2) her position in the Confederation must be equal to that of Austria; (3) she could not accept an enlargement of the functions of the Confederation limiting Prussian independence; (4) there must be a German Parliament, representative of the German nation, and elected directly by it.

At a word from Prussia the Austrian plan and all others of the same kind went, unhouseled, unanointed, and unannealed into the limbo reserved for the acrobatics of pseudo-statesmanship. The Congress of Princes summoned to consecrate the consummation of a new German

Confederation, was suddenly turned into the funeral of the Greater Germany party.

Henceforward, there were only three possible alternatives—a unification under Austria imposed on a defeated Prussia, a unification under Prussia imposed on a defeated Austria, or the unitary Empire of the National Union, in which Prussia was dissolved in a Germany, from which Austria was excluded, a unification to be imposed on Germany by the triumph of National Liberalism. In the autumn of 1863, though we to-day find it hard to believe it, and before the year 1864 had revolutionised the European situation and German public opinion, the last of the three alternatives seemed far the most probable. One conclusion, however, is certain. The author of the fiasco of the Congress of Princes, the man who administered the *coup de grâce* to the Greater Germany party, was Bismarck.

' Lord ! ' says Puck, ' what fools these mortals be.' The sacred simplicity of the diplomatic or royal ostrich provokes a deeper laughter of Jove than the perjuries of lovers. The supposition of Rechberg and Beust and all the sham and pigmy Machiavellians, princely or ministerial, that the Minister-President at Berlin, who had served seven gruelling years of apprenticeship at Frankfurt, would not see through the patent trap of the Austrian plan must have provoked the grimmest humour of Bismarck. The idea that the Prussian monarchy was meekly to strip to the skin in the imperial city of Frankfurt, and put on a Nessus shirt patched up by kings and grand-dukes in the workhouse at Vienna was too delicious even for the grand diplomacy. Did Rechberg, Beust, and their company seriously imagine that the Minister-President was risking all in the struggle with the Landtag to sacrifice the cause of Prussianism at the bidding of a mob of princes ? Their action proves that if they knew themselves and their tricks, at least they did not know the Minister-President at Berlin. ' Stripped of its coat,' Bismarck said, ' the Austrian poodle is distinctly meagre.'

Yet the reality of the German situation was profoundly disquieting to Bismarck. National Liberalism was, and remained, a tremendous and dangerous force. The time

had long passed when the German people could be fobbed
off with a hollow sham and be manipulated in blinkers into
a series of dynastic pens, renamed a Unified Germany.
The essence of the problem lay in the demand in all parts
of Germany for the nation to be included in the task of
government, so that legislation, taxation, policy would be
expressive of a nation's will, character and ideals—a Germany for the Germans by the Germans. Hence any
reconstruction to be practical politics, must be organic.
The Austrian and princely programme was the old Diet
and Federation, with a few new and useless wheels added,
some of the old grit and rust cleaned out, and the whole
recoloured with a thin coat of democratic paint, intended
to fade.

For Bismarck, the problem was not how to combine a
minimum of concession to democracy with a maximum of
princely and particularist independence and autocracy,
but how to combine a maximum of concession to the
demand for self-government with the unity of an efficient
and irresponsible executive. Bismarck had here penetrated to an abiding reality in the German heart. If the
Germans passionately desired a share in the government
of a unified Germany, they no less passionately desired
power. The National Union and National Liberalism were
the outcome of both desires. The old system satisfied
neither. Germany was impotent in the world. It was
simply shameful, every German felt, that a great country
could not, or would not, prevent a third-rate State like
Denmark from violating its obligations, defined in the
public law of Europe, and could not protect Germans in
Holstein from illegal oppression, and the reason was that
policy was determined by a group of conflicting dynasties,
and power was dissipated in an antiquated and contemptible
political mechanism. Ending, not mending, that system
would alone meet the demand for power—the power of the
National State—and provide the organs of power. The
foreign observer can indeed see in the evolution of National
Liberalism the Nationalism, fierce, deep, and continuous.
It is the Liberalism or the absence of it that puzzles him.
Bennigsen's speech in 1867 on the Luxemburg question,

applauded from one end of Germany to the other, is saturated with the doctrine of, and demand for, power, the German National State as the expression of German power. Yet in 1863 Bennigsen was Bismarck's most formidable opponent, because Bennigsen was a Liberal as well as a Nationalist.

The explanation is really simple. National Liberalism grew to its strength as a movement for self-government through representative institutions, and as a national protest against the inertia and apathy of the dynastic sovereignties that ruled Germany. Up till 1861 no German *government* had evinced any sincere desire to subordinate dynastic or particularist interests to the cause of Germany as a whole. The homage of the dynastic and diplomatic lip in all the Courts to the cause of Germany was copious ; but when it came to action, Austria, Prussia, Bavaria, placed Austrian, Prussian or Bavarian selfishness first, and Germany was forgotten. Hence the Liberals were convinced that, while self-government was intrinsically desirable, a unification of Germany on a democratic basis, that swept away the State sovereignties, alone would provide for the realisation of what the German people demanded—a single German State, playing its part as a European Power in the European system. Such a State would represent the totality of German brains, wills, ideals, and material resources ; and it would pursue a German policy made by the German people. Nothing but real representative institutions, with a Parliament that made policy because it was a government-making organ, would enable the Germans to be a single nation, with a national will working through organs automatically effective. Hence the stronger the Nationalist passion, the stronger with the Liberals was the insistence on the necessity of democratic self-government. Power through representative institutions was the complement to parliamentary self-government as the instrument of National power.

Bismarck might have said in 1863, ' Almost thou persuadest me to be a National Liberal.' He did not, however, believe, on principle, in the efficiency of constitutional monarchy and responsible parliamentary government. He was convinced that ' the English system ' was wholly inapplicable to the German character and the historical conditions in which it had been developed through many centuries. And the closer he studied Great Britain the more strongly he inferred that parliamentary government did not make for executive efficiency, continuity of policy and strong administration. The correctness of this judgment is not the question. That Bismarck thought so there can be no doubt. Unity achieved by moral penetration and persuasion he regarded as a pure delusion. Neither the dynasties nor the Liberals would give him the army that would smash Austria, nor the time, uninterrupted by party strife, to devise a foreign policy and prepare in secret for the day of decision. He did not doubt the German patriotism of the German people. He trusted it indeed far more than he did the dynasties, as his proposal for a National Parliament as an essential part of Federal reform proved ; but what he did doubt most gravely was the readiness of the Sybels, the Gneists, the Twestens, Virchows, Laskers, Dunckers, and Bennigsens to will the means no less than the ends of national unity. They aimed at power, but they shrank from force. They were, in his judgment, political cowards, and therefore in his view lacked the higher statesmanship.

The one system that would give him what he wanted existed already in Prussia. It was being tested now, and it was standing the test. Its retention, therefore, as the nucleus of the new Germany was indispensable. Just as in foreign policy Bismarck's system pivoted on an understanding with Russia, so in the German problem his solution pivoted on the Prussian monarchy, the irresponsible director of the Prussian nation in arms.

The National Liberals would mutilate or destroy the executive nucleus of a policy of power. But Bismarck was ready now to foreshadow the lines of his own programme. Once the Congress of Princes was killed, the publication of the official statement of Prussian policy, already cited, was a tactical move in the higher strategy ; for Bismarck often acted on Palmerston's dictum : ' I tell ambassadors the truth, because I know they won't believe it.' The Prussian

memoranda of September 15 and September 22, 1863, were
the last nail in the coffin of Austrian Greater Germanism.
They were also intended to be the first in the coffin of
the National Liberals.

Bismarck's victory over William 1. when he refused the
invitation to Frankfurt, was a signal personal triumph
greater even than the ratification in 1879 of the alliance
with Austria. Of the many struggles with his sovereign,
these two in 1863 and 1879 were the most critical and decisive, for in each case the central principle of his system
was in jeopardy ; and in 1863 Bismarck had yet to win,
not as in 1879 simply to retain, his ascendancy. William
wished to go to Frankfurt. Heart and brain, combined
in favour of accepting the invitation. All his relatives,
male and female, urged him strongly to accept. Indeed,
how could he as the King of Prussia refuse to meet his
brother sovereigns when refusal meant personal discourtesy,
and the rejection of the unique chance of demonstrating
to the German world the unity and patriotism of the
German dynasties, and their earnest desire to make a free
gift of Federal Reform from their united prerogative.

The dynasties as the initiators and executors of Reform !
' Thirty princes,' cried William, ' sending an invitation and
the courier a king ! How *can* one refuse ? ' Bismarck
guessed that William would be argued or trapped in
that tainted company into fatal concessions ; his royal
honour would be pledged. A counter demonstration of
the independence of Prussia and the power of the Minister-
President was imperatively required in the summer of 1863.
He appealed to William's pride. It was for Prussia to lead,
not to follow, to impose her own, not to accept the dangerous plans of others. The mediatisation of Prussia
would be the result of the Frankfort Congress, brought
about by Prussia's sovereign. But if the King went to
Frankfurt his Minister could not accept the responsibility and must retire to Schönhausen. The conflict of
wills, which lasted several days, exhausted ruler and minister.
Bismarck won. His secretary found him after the final
interview with the King, and after he had handed the
letter of refusal to the King of Saxony, alone in his room.

In reply to a question he hurled a plate and some glasses to pieces against the wall. ' I felt,' he said to the astonished subordinate, ' that I must smash something. Now I can breathe again.'

Germany busied itself in the autumn of 1863 with feverish activities and plans for unification. Negotiations arising out of the abortive Congress dragged on between Berlin, Vienna, and the German Courts. The *National Verein* and the *Reform Verein* discussed with unabated energy the scheme of the Congress of Princes and the Prussian memorandum of September 22 ; the honesty of the latter was contested by all reformers whether of the Great or the Small Germany camps. The Prussian Landtag was dissolved ; no budget had been voted, and the ' constitutional conflict ' was quite unsolved ; but despite the severity of the recent Press ordinance and the electoral efforts of the bureaucracy the Conservative party could only increase their numbers from eleven to thirty-eight. The new Landtag was as solidly hostile in foreign and home policy to the government as the old, that had rejected the Army Budget ; and the unpopularity of Bismarck was greater than ever. ' Men spat,' he said, ' on the place where I trod in the streets.'

A graver crisis than any Germany had faced since 1848 was at hand, the problem of Schleswig-Holstein entangled in all the barbed wire of a complicated international situation. On March 30, 1863, King Frederick VII. separated Holstein from Schleswig by granting it a separate legislature, budget and army. Schleswig was subsequently to be united by a common constitution with Denmark. This policy, the work of an overwhelming Radical majority at Copenhagen, angered the Duchies, which claimed to be autonomous and inseparable, and infuriated Germany, which saw in it the Danish determination to absorb Schleswig in the Danish kingdom. The Federal Diet, which was not a party to the London Convention of 1852, that regulated the succession to the Danish throne and the relations of the Duchies to the Danish Crown, passed a resolution (July 9) calling on King Frederick to rescind the ' March charter ' and restore the conditions defined in the Convention. The Danes ignored the resolution, and the Danish General Council passed the Joint-Constitution for Denmark and Schleswig on November 13, 1863. Frederick VII. declined to sign the Patent, bringing the constitution into operation, on the ground that he was a dying man and could not fairly prejudge the action or tie the hands of his successor in a matter of such gravity. On November 15 Frederick died. His heir, under the Protocol of 1852, was Christian IX. of Sonderburg-Glückstein, who now succeeded to the Danish Crown and to the dukedom of Schleswig and Holstein, integrally united to Denmark under the terms of the London Convention. Christian, threatened by the Danish ministry that refusal to sign the Patent would cause a Danish revolution and endanger his throne, signed the Patent (November 15). At once the Duchies and Germany were in an uproar. Frederick, Duke of Augustenburg, the son of the claimant of 1852 whose claims had been ruled out by the Convention, appeared in the Duchies and proclaimed himself at Kiel as the lawful duke. His claim was supported with enthusiasm by the Duchies and by all Germany. The *National Union*—the organisation of Liberalism—and the *Reform Union*—the organisation of the 'Great Germany' party—combined to promote the Augustenburg claims. The Federal Diet ordered a Federal execution, in the duke's support, and Hanover and Saxony were commissioned to carry it out.

All eyes were turned on Prussia. Germany would now see whether Prussian declarations of the identity of her interests with those of Germany were a reality or a sham ; whether the reactionary Bismarck, who had publicly laid it down that the German people had a right to be represented in German affairs, was a hypocrite or a German statesman. Action at once was required, and action would reveal this Bismarck in his true colours. Bismarck probably agreed. Action was required, and it would reveal himself and a good many others in their true colours. The sharper the challenge the more coolly and confidently he braced himself to pick up the gauntlet flung in his face by fate. He did not know what Prince Hohenlohe was writing in his diary at this time : ' Every one in Germany is conscious of the profound significance the Schleswig-Holstein question must have for our internal policy. Every one knows that with that question the German question, too, will be decided. . . . The Schleswig-Holstein question is therefore to the people a question of rights, a question of power to the governments, and a question of existence to the Confederation, that is the middle and petty States.' But he would have agreed, heart and soul, with the judgment. We may be sure also that another conclusion was recorded with Bismarckian satisfaction. Fortune had decided that Frederick VII. should die three months too late for Austria. Had the unhappy King of Denmark, who had escaped from the deluge which now threatened to submerge his no less unhappy successor, died in August 1863 when the Congress of Princes was in full conclave, Francis Joseph, the kings, and the princelets would have had such a chance as comes to a vaulting ambition but once. Not all the king's horses and all the king's men could have kept William I. from going to Frankfurt, and from concurring either in compulsion on Christian IX. to refuse his signature to the Patent or in the adoption by the Congress of the Duke of Augustenburg, William's relative, a Coburg Liberal of the circle of the Crown Prince of Prussia, as the lawful heir to the Duchies amid the tumultuous applause of dynastic, Conservative, Liberal, Particularist, and Ultramontane Germany, and the probable assent of Great Britain and France—perhaps Russia too. The Austrian programme of Federal Reform would have slipped into existence as a by-issue in the enthusiasm of that happy day. ' What an escape ! ' as Victor Emmanuel ejaculated, when the warning victories of Wörth and Spicheren cancelled the intention to throw in his lot with Napoleon III. in 1870. What an escape ! Bismarck's luck became proverbial. In 1863 the stars in their courses saw the Congress of Princes killed and buried before they released poor Frederick VII. at the right moment for Bismarck and the wrong one for Austria. Whom the gods love do not die young. They live to thank the loving gods for the gift of action in the summer

of their powers, and to meet in the golden autumn of
fame the inevitable summons with the serenity that
achievement alone can bestow.

§ 2. *Schleswig-Holstein, the Treaty of Vienna, and the Convention of Gastein, 1863-1865*

The labyrinth of the historical, legal, and ethical controversies buried in the slag-heaps of four centuries has
resulted in a formidable library on Schleswig-Holstein.
Palmerston said with more wit than accuracy that only
three persons in Europe were completely acquainted with
the truth, the Prince Consort who was dead, a German
professor who was in a lunatic asylum, and himself—and he
had forgotten it. Bismarck justly regarded his diplomacy
and achievement in ' the Schleswig-Holstein campaign '
as perhaps his most masterly performance. Genius, military, political, scientific, or imaginative, as the judge of
its own efforts is always instructive, though not infallible. But certainly no other episode in Bismarck's career
more convincingly summarises the pith and marrow of
Bismarckian principles and methods, the union of personal
character and intellectual gifts, the fixity of aim, and the
inexhaustible opportunism of means, ending in a dramatic
and unexpected triumph than his conduct of Prussian
policy from November 1863 to August 1865. Working on a
larger scale in a grander manner for greater ends, Bismarck
achieved elsewhere and later grander results. But as a
finished model of Bismarckian statecraft it was and remains
a masterpiece, and in the evolution of his career and the
perfecting of his technique the Schleswig-Holstein campaign was to Bismarck what the Polish campaigns were
to Gustavus Adolphus, the Silesian wars to Frederick
the Great, and the Egyptian campaign to Napoleon—the
apprenticeship of genius in the service of its profession.

Stripped of irrelevant detail, the problem of 1863 was
comparatively simple, but it raised issues of far-reaching
consequences and a baffling complexity. The Duchies of
Schleswig and Holstein had been united since 1460 by a
personal union through the Crown of Denmark with the

Danish kingdom. The King of Denmark was the king-duke who united in his person the hereditary right to the Danish Crown and the succession to the combined Duchies. Europe and Denmark had come to regard the Duchies in fact as an integral part of the Danish kingdom, while re-cognising, if it was reminded, that the two provinces had an autonomy and rights arising from an historic existence independent of Denmark. The dukedom was, in short, a separate principality contained and governed within a larger whole. But the prerogative of the king-duke was conditioned in these Duchies by his authority as duke, and the Duchies accepted his rule as their duke, not as King of Denmark. Hence the system of government for Den-mark was determined by the Crown in the Danish Riksdag, for the Duchies by the duke in the Estates of the Provinces. The law of Denmark would only be binding if accepted by the Provincial Estates.

The desirability of a complete incorporation—the abolition of the personal union and the fusion of the Duchies with Denmark under a single ruler and a single parliament—was obvious. But the Duchies clung to their historic autonomy with tenacity ; the law of succession to the Danish Crown was not the same as the law of succession to the dukedom. The underlying cause of this rooted objection to the extinction of their autonomy was racial. Holstein was predominantly German, Schleswig probably (here an insoluble controversy is opened up), though not so predominantly, Danish. To Holstein incorporation with Denmark meant de-Germanisation and Danisation, and, in addition, while the autonomy of Holstein was for four centuries connected with that of its partner Schleswig —the two together made the unity of the Duchy—Holstein had always been part of the Holy Roman Empire of the German nation, Schleswig had not. This historic anomaly was confirmed in 1815. The King of Denmark, as Duke of Schleswig-Holstein was a member of the German Con-federation for Holstein (but not for Schleswig) over which, therefore, the Federal Diet had a limited Federal juris-diction. So long as the dynastic problem was not reopened, and so long as the Nationalist principle was not inflaming sentiment, this anomalous tangle of cross purposes and contradictory allegiances would work, just because it was customary. Its maintenance turned on the equipoise of forces, balanced by the inconsistencies of tradition and habit.

Fate and the developments in Europe after 1815 destroyed the equipoise. Fate decided that the male succession in the direct line to the Crown of Denmark should fail; the growth of the principle of nationality steadily accentuated the ambition of the German and the Dane to secure the Duchies for the German or the Danish race. The incorporation of the Duchies, so long associated with Denmark, was opposed by the German ambition to sever them from Danish assimilation, and establish them as an autonomous German principality under a German duke, and weld them into the unified Germany of the future. But the 'unredeemed Germany' was also an 'unredeemed Denmark.' The dynastic problem was solved by the Protocol of 1852. The Duke of Augustenburg, regarded by Germany and the Provincial Estates as the heir *de jure* to the Duchies, was compelled with the other claimants to surrender his claims in favour of Christian, later the ixth, who was chosen by the Powers to maintain the integrity of the Danish kingdom and continue, as king-duke, the historic association of Schleswig and Holstein with the Danish Crown. Had the European Powers been wise, they would have repeated the lesson of Belgium in 1839: severed then and there German Holstein from Schleswig, and incorporated the former with Germany and the latter with Denmark. In all probability, when Christian succeeded in 1863 the fifteen years of separation would have habituated both Germany and Denmark to the situation, and there would have been no further trouble. But it was the age of Nicholas i., who regarded the Schleswig-Holsteiners as rebels; and the severance of Holstein from its legal duke (who was also the legal King of Denmark) would have required more unity and greater prevision in the Concert of Europe than the statesmen of 1852 were endowed with.

The maintenance of the historic integrity of the kingdom of Denmark was deemed of the greatest importance in the balance of European power, and the collapse of the Revolution of 1848, with the reaction that followed, seemed to the short-sighted diplomacy of Conservatism to destroy the forces that had made a crisis out of Schleswig-Holstein. The Convention of London, by placing the settlement under the collective guarantee of the European Powers, was held to provide an indisputable authority for its maintenance.

But that convention, like the Treaty of Paris of 1856, had the flaw fatal to all such solemn manifestations of the public law and will of the Powers. It assumed that the men and the States responsible for its maintenance would continue to be of the same disposition as those who originally made it—a large and historically unjustifiable assumption. It had also the defect that it was imposed on the Estates of Holstein and Schleswig, who were not parties to it; that the German Diet was not a party to it and retained its Federal rights in Holstein; that the son of the Duke of Augustenburg was not a party to his father's renunciation of his rights. It made no allowance for a more Nationalist and Radical Denmark or a more Nationalist and Liberal Germany coming into existence; it created no automatic and effective machinery to prevent provisions, so solemnly defined, from being broken before the vacancy to the Danish throne, filled by Christian's succession to Danish Crown and the Duchies, occurred. It left Denmark a sovereign State, yet with a mortgage on its sovereignty. It provided neither for the removal of a Nicholas I. nor the emergence of a Bismarck.

Two conclusions are fairly clear in 1863. The Convention of London required Denmark to observe the historic *status quo* in the Duchies. Dispassionate examination cannot avoid the verdict that the acts of the Danish government from 1852 to 1863 were a breach of the Convention—certainly of its spirit, and probably of its letter. They constituted a cumulative effort to separate the Duchies and incorporate one of them in the kingdom, and to present Europe with a *fait accompli* before the accession of Christian IX. This might have succeeded had

Frederick VII. lived six months longer. Frederick's death
before his signature as the sovereign who was incontestably
de jure king and also *de jure* duke could be obtained wrecked
the attempt.   Secondly, Christian IX., the new King, had
on the day of his succession to decide at a moment's notice
either to provoke a revolution at Copenhagen or a revolution at Kiel.   Had he been wiser, he would have referred
the issue to the concert of the Powers signatory to the
Convention of London, and invited their decision and
their support, if need be, to carry out that decision.   He
was their nominee ; they were bound either to tear up
their own convention or loyally to see he did not suffer for
being the instrument of their policy.   The coercion of
Copenhagen or of Kiel was the moral duty of the concert.
Christian, unhappily for himself and for Europe, did not at
once throw the responsibility on the Powers.   In his
excuse it must fairly be said that the rejection by Great
Britain of Napoleon's proposal for a Congress made it very
difficult for him to do so.

It is not possible here to write the history of Europe nor
to discuss the policy of all the European States in this complicated controversy.   We are concerned primarily with
Bismarck and his policy.   But it must not be forgotten
that the Danes and King Christian had a case, for which a
good deal can be urged.   In 1852 the Concert of Europe
had decided, on broad grounds, that the integrity of the
historic kingdom of Denmark was an essential element in
the Balance of Power.   The severance of the Duchies from
Denmark—apart from the juristic problem in the disputed
succession—was a grave violation of that Balance, for the
strategic position of the Duchies was of immense value.
Schleswig had a large Danish population, and there were
many Danes also in Holstein.   If there was a danger that
the Germans might be oppressed by the Danes, there was
no less a danger—which events fully bore out—that the
Danes would be oppressed by the Germans.   The forcible
Danisation of Holstein was less likely than the forcible
Germanisation of Schleswig.   Schleswig had never been
part of the Holy Roman Empire of the German nation, and
the attempt to annex it to the Germany of 1863—with

the avowed object of Germanising it—was neither historically defensible, nor racially just, nor politically justifiable. The claim of the Federal Diet that because it was not a party to the Convention of 1852 it need not therefore regard it as binding, was fairly met by the indisputable fact that the two greatest German States in the Diet—Austria and Prussia—were solemn parties to the Convention, and could not therefore support the Diet's repudiation without violating their signatures and pledges. The Germany therefore of the Federal Diet was a Germany minus Austria and Prussia : a Germany, in short, which claimed to have a more important voice in overriding the public law of Europe, to which the two most important German States had publicly agreed, than Europe and those two great German States. Moreover, the Federal Act of 1815, which defined the powers of the Diet, gave it no legal or political right to interfere in cases of a disputed succession, to decide questions of succession or enforce a decision, if it illegally attempted to make one. Yet in virtually supporting the Duke of Augustenburg the Diet was precisely doing this, and therefore acting *ultra vires*. Politically, the claim that one-third of Germany could override the rest of Germany and all Europe was absurd.

The succession question had been settled in 1852. In 1863 there was or could be only one lawful successor to the Danish Crown and the Duchies—Christian IX. Any denial of this indisputable fact was a declaration that the Convention was no longer binding without having obtained the prior consent of those who made it and were responsible for its maintenance. The Federal Diet was not a party to the Convention, precisely because the Federal Diet was not legally entitled to have a voice in deciding the succession in the Duchies, and still less in the kingdom of Denmark. The Duke of Augustenburg's claim in 1863 was a declaration that the Settlement of 1852, which ruled out his father and was accepted by him, was a wrong decision to which he had not been a party, and was therefore not binding on him. But if the sons of fathers against whom a decision has been given can always plead that the decision does not affect the son, no throne in Europe would be safe or secure. Bismarck recognised this from the first. And the subsequent decision of the Prussian Crown lawyers (p. 184) clearly laid it down that Christian IX. was the *de jure* successor both to the Duchies and the Danish Crown. The Prussian professors argued from the first that because the Duke of Augustenburg *ought* to have been made the heir in 1852, his son *was* the heir in 1863, all law and facts notwithstanding. And the argument, that because conceivably the Constitution of 1863 was *ultra vires* the whole Convention of 1852 became invalid, was as good as an argument that because the Federal Diet in 1863 acted *ultra vires* the whole Federal Act of 1815 ceased to be valid.

The Danes made serious mistakes from 1852-64. But the responsibility for those mistakes was largely that of the European Powers also. Long before the situation of 1863 arose it was the duty of the Powers in concert to tell Denmark that it was not strictly observing the Convention. That duty the Powers did not perform. Because they did not perform it, the Danes naturally inferred that the Powers would accept the Danish policy—a policy which had the support of probably a majority in Schleswig and a minority in Holstein. Condemnation of Danish ambition or Danish blunders may be necessary, but that does not involve approval of German policy and ambition—as indefensible as the extreme Danish claim. The sequel proved up to the hilt that the Powers allowed Prussia to commit a wanton aggression, to crush Denmark, to denationalise Schleswig, and to disregard even the scanty pledges of justice and fair treatment laid down in the Treaty of Prague. The Danish case against Prussia—as distinct from Germany—is so strong as to be practically irrefutable

The true gravity of the situation lay in the new forces at work. Public opinion in Germany repudiated the Convention of 1852. It was universally regarded as the act of a reactionary coalition to which not even the Federal Diet and still less Germany, was a party. The reversal of the decision of 1849, which had destroyed the unification of Germany and the demand for German self-government carried with it the reversal of the Convention. The

' liberation of the duchies ' was a very precise item in a
far-reaching programme of Germany for the Germans.
The claims, therefore, of the young Duke of Augustenburg combined with a dangerous felicity the demand for
the autonomy and inseparability of Schleswig and Holstein, the principle of hereditary legitimism, the rule of a
German prince, and the new Liberalism of the enlightened
dynasties; and his programme at Kiel in 1863 stood for everything that Germany now passionately demanded for itself.

All this was recognised in the chancelleries of Europe.
But the newest and gravest element in the situation—the
Prussia of 1863—was wholly unappreciated in the autumn
of 1863. The Prussia of 1848 had taken a brave line in
using her leadership of the German cause in the Duchies,
and had then at the first threat of European coercion
collapsed. Here, as in other matters, the impression persisted within and without Germany that Prussia was the
lath painted to look like iron. Bismarck shared the contempt and the indignation. He came into office to prove
what Prussian strength could do when efficiently directed
by a diplomacy that had shed the shibboleths which had
sapped the political and moral efficiency of the kingdom.
The geographical and strategic position of the Duchies
was for Prussia unique. In hostile hands they turned the
military frontiers to east and west; they opened a back
door by land to the capital at Berlin; and, more dangerous
still, they provided everything that sea power required for
the effective coercion of Prussia : as a bastion both on the
Baltic and the North Sea they were indispensable to Prussian power and expansion. The silent chief of the General
Staff, the ' library rat,' as men called him, gnawing his way
in prolonged toil to the heart of strategy, the strategy of
the State as Power, could furnish a memorandum convincing in its conciseness of the supreme strategic value of
Schleswig-Holstein to Prussia. Bismarck had studied as
hard as Moltke and with as fruitful results. Let the rat
continue to gnaw. When the time came to put in the
rat, the sharper its teeth the better. Instruction in the
truths of strategy and the inseparable union of strategy
and policy, was not needed in the Wilhelmstrasse. But it

was sorely needed in Downing Street and at the British Admiralty, at the Quai d'Orsay, in the Ball-Platz, and the fly-blown offices of the Federal Diet.

Moreover, Bismarck foresaw the character of the coming struggle—a real trial of strength between the diplomacy and methods of the statecraft of power against the old diplomacy of the State as the champion of right; between the old system of the Concert of Europe with its 'paradox' of the Balance of Power and the revival of Prussianism with its doctrine of force. The result must indicate conclusively the efficacy and superiority of the Bismarckian system; and Bismarck had this enormous advantage. He knew the methods of his opponents, but they did not know his. Obsessed by tradition and misled by ignorance of the real Germany and Prussia, they were in the position of generals fighting according to the red-tape of a conventional warfare against a foe who had superior science and used it to devise high explosives and asphyxiating gas. The true moral of the Schleswig-Holstein campaign, in which Europe was signally routed, is not that the statecraft of blood and iron must always win—men drew that false conclusion from imperfectly framed premises—but first, that the State which stands for right (*Der Staat als Recht*) in death-grips with the State which stands for power (*Der Staat als Macht*) must have better brains and a clearer mastery of realities; and secondly, it must not mix a sham copy of its rival's methods with its own, and then bay the moon because real force, applied by genius, beats sham force that lets 'I dare not wait upon I would.'

When Christian's action precipitated a crisis several solutions were possible. The Powers might at once insist on the withdrawal of the March Constitution as a condition of upholding the Convention; they might have decided that the whole situation was so completely altered as to require a new settlement, and have severed the Duchies from Denmark and recognised the claims of Augustenburg; or they might have severed Holstein from Schleswig; or they might have supported Christian and Denmark at all costs. All these and other courses were possible and arguable in November 1863. But they al implied that the Concert of Europe responsible for the Convention of London would act as a concert, and would act promptly; and that was precisely what Bismarck guessed they would not do, or intended to prevent. Bismarck started with Russia practically on his side—Russia that in 1852 was responsible for the coercion of Schleswig-Holstein and the integrity of the Danish monarchy. Four against one—Prussia against the other European Powers—in 1852 was a hopeless position; but two against three raised a practicable issue. When it had been converted into three against two the business would settle itself.

The two fatal blunders for the Powers to commit were, first: to allow an isolated and excited Denmark to be entangled in a war with one or more members of the Concert of Europe which were the guarantors of the integrity of the Danish kingdom; and, secondly, to delude Denmark into resistance by encouraging her belief that she would have allies in the last resort, when no ally was prepared to give more than the ' moral ' support of diplomacy. Such moral support is generally a euphemism for truly moral cowardice and selfishness, and always an insulting travesty of the real strength of the moral element in human affairs. Both these blunders were committed. And there was a third. In diplomacy, as in war, the statesman who trifles with time is a criminal; doubly so, if he is pitted against an adversary who puts time on his side. Throughout Bismarck reckoned that while Lord John Russell's pen would be blackening many sheets of paper, and Napoleon was flickering from one Napoleonic idea to another, the Prussian army could cover a good many miles into Holstein, and it would not meet the British fleet at Kiel. Both King William and Queen Victoria had consciences which made them obstinate, but it was easier to deceive King William than Queen Victoria, and to prove to the royal satisfaction of Prussia that black was white. The Queen of Great Britain had an alternative to the ministers in office, who were also not united. King William had no alternative to Bismarck (who had really no colleagues) but surrender to the opposition. So manifold in Bismarck's view were the advantages of being the Prussian minister of a Prussian king, who governed as well as reigned. The appeal of the Congress of London in May, 1864, to Prussian good feeling when the Prussian army had fleshed a victorious sword on the obstinate Danes was as helpful as an appeal to the good feelings of a terrier with a live rabbit in its mouth. The Congress simply enabled Great Britain and France to desert Denmark with all the phylacteries of diplomatic Pharisaism unsoiled : it justly incurred the impotent contempt of Denmark and the very potent contempt of Bismarck. Worst of all, it taught Europe that right only differed from might in the inefficiency of its State-egoism and selfishness. The nadir of British moral power in Europe was foreshadowed in the action of our Foreign Office ; the bankruptcy of the Second Empire was first proclaimed not at Queretaro nor by the guns of Königgrätz, but at London in 1864. For us British it is tragic that the Power which in 1860 by a single dispatch silenced Austria and enabled Cavour to complete the work of Garibaldi should have denounced, defied, and deserted in 1864. Bismarck and Gortschakov took the hint, and enforced the initial lesson in 1870. Dry powder and disbelief in God, said Europe, is a better creed than belief in God and no powder at all ; and Providence, said the cynics, thought with them. Were the cynics really so wrong ?

The one solution that no one in November 1863 contemplated was the annexation of the Duchies by Prussia for Prussia, apart from ' the folly ' of crediting her with the power to defy Europe, had no better title in law or history to the Duchies than the President of the United States or the Negus of Abyssinia. One title she could create, the title of Frederick the Great to Silesia or Polish Prussia—the title of the invincible sword, accepted by Europe because it disbelieved in its capacity to invalidate it. We know that Bismarck from the very first, perhaps before he took office in 1862, steadily kept annexation before his eyes as the most satisfactory solution. Indeed his diplomacy is inexplicable otherwise. But prudently recognising that the ideal is not always the attainable he was determined to prevent a settlement that would block the greater ends, to which the annexation was at best only a stepping-stone. The worst that could happen would be the severance of the Duchies from Denmark and their incorporation under their ' lawful ' duke, the Augustenburger, in the tessellated mosaic of Federal Germany. Another petty State under a Liberal prince, hand in glove with ' the Coburg gang,' voting in the Diet against Prussia, and working in Germany as a perpetual balsam of Liberalism and a mustard-plaster on the back of Prussia, was intolerable. The enthusiasm of Austria, the dynasties, and the National Liberals for the Augustenburger—the ominous conjunction of everything and everybody anti-Prussian—was quite sufficient to condemn that solution in Bismarck's eyes. Better the complete incorporation with Denmark than that.

Yet what easier and more tempting than to proclaim the leadership of Prussia in a great German affair, and employ the Prussian army to rip the Convention of London to tatters, in the sacred name of nationalism and Germany ? Why not liberate the Duchies from ' Danish degradation,' and end the constitutional conflict in Prussia with a demand that the Prussian Parliament should expunge its votes and expiate its rebellion by a doubled grant to a doubled army, henceforward wholly to be at the uncontrolled disposition of the Crown for Germany and Prussia's needs ? William 1. would have kissed his minister on both cheeks, the Crown Prince would have begged his pardon, the opposition would have voted sackcloth and ashes for themselves and a laurel wreath for the minister, and Germany, now burning Bismarck in effigy, would have kneeled at his feet, had he announced such a policy. Bismarck deliberately rejected the temptation, for it meant an alliance with National Liberalism in which he would be the horse and the popular forces the rider. Instead, he embarked on a course bristling with difficulties, and exposed to the gravest perils, which drew upon himself a concentration of hatred and indignation from Conservatives outside Prussia and Liberals within it. He defied a passionate public opinion and ran the serious risk of uniting Europe against Prussia. Every one in Germany was against him —the leaders of the Federal Diet, the Prussian Landtag, the Duke of Augustenburg, the Germans of the Duchies themselves, the Crown Prince and his circle, the princes of the middle and petty States. The Prussian Landtag refused the special grant demanded, whereupon Bismarck replied that he would take the money where he could find it. The Prussian Liberals had concentrated on three points—the desire to act legally and in support of Augustenburg's ' lawful ' claims, the absolute identity of Prussia's interest with that of all Germany, and the fear that Bismarck's opposition to German Liberalism and Nationalism would isolate Prussia and repeat the humiliation of 1849. His royal master, on whom everything turned, was an Augustenburger, gravely perturbed by his minister's tortuous, halting, and dubious proceedings, and by the arguments of Bismarck's critics to which he had no satisfying answer. Yet he could not dismiss Bismarck and face the cyclonic onset of the popular forces, concentrated in a Landtag that regarded the constitution as doubly violated by the treason to Germany and Prussia expressed in the minister's foreign policy. Bismarck did not dare to tell his royal master the truth. Until the inexorable drip of one accomplished fact after another wore away William's conscience it was better he should doubt his minister's sanity than be convinced of his iniquity.

Bismarck's extreme caution at every stage is remarkable. More than once he clearly was in grave perplexity as to the next move, and his own simile of the method of stalking woodcock in marshy ground is illuminating in its appositeness. Every step must be tested before the next is taken. If the ground gives, or a stone waggles, wait until a better foothold is found by patient exploration. Do not fire until you have both feet on firm ground ; otherwise you will miss your shot, scare the game, and be bogged into the bargain.

The successive moves of the next few months, viewed as a whole, present very clearly the general framework of Bismarck's strategy. The Danes must put themselves in the wrong, and be manœuvred into remaining in the wrong : driven to resist and then defeated. Once Prussian blood had been spilt, a claim for Prussian compensation could be set up. Germany as far as possible must be kept out of it. The Convention of London was an international document. It was easier to manipulate the European than the German situation, and to drive wedges between the Powers than to create discord in Germany. Hence the controversy must be pinned down to the Convention of London. Once that was torn up, the Powers resumed—delicious phrase—their individual liberty of action, and Bismarck guessed that none of the Powers was prepared to make a European war on behalf of Denmark. Why should they? They could not annex the Duchies. Prussia could. She had a definite and material gain for which to fight, in the last resort. Hence, combined action with Austria was essential. That broke the unity of the Concert, and the alliance of Vienna with the middle and petty States. It left the Federal Diet practically helpless. A skilful diplomacy working on the strained relations resulting from the Polish fiasco, could probably separate England and France. On a calculation of forces, England and Denmark were not strong enough to win. England would not risk it. The Duchies would be severed from Denmark. The final disposition of them opened up a much bigger problem—the settlement with Austria and the settlement of the German question.

Behind this diplomacy throughout stood silent and obedient—the Prussian army. The crude Junkertum of Roon, conscious of Prussian strength, grew very impatient with Bismarck's finesse and haggling with politicians armed only with a pen and phrases. ' The question of the Duchies,' he pronounced, ' is not one of right or law, but of force, and we have it.' Roon and all his school, who saw in history nothing but the blessing of Providence on the big battalions, failed to penetrate the secrets of the real statecraft of power, Bismarckian or otherwise. Moltke and Treitschke saw deeper. The big battalions must first range themselves on the side of Providence, before they can hope to extort the blessing. The maximum of effort can only be secured from the monarchical State as Force when sovereigns and subjects have a good conscience, convinced that their cause is lawful and right.

Bismarck undertook the apparently impossible task of convincing his sovereign and countrymen that in 1864, 1866, and in 1870 they were fighting, not an aggressive, but a defensive, war. Neither Moltke nor he himself believed that—quite the contrary. But it was essential that the King and Prussia—the professors, the lawyers, the bourgeois at his desk and the peasant in the fields—should believe it. And they did—in the end. The professors, who backed Augustenburg to a man, were the first and the most easily converted. For the disciplined and patriotic intellect must harmonise appetite with reason, and the carnal appetites of intellectuals are generally as irrational as their minds are rational. Bismarck relied on ranging the moral forces in Germany behind the strength of the Prussian army. But the moral forces must first be chained up in the Æolus cellar of the Foreign Office, and only let loose at the right moment. The key of the cellars and of the barracks must not be in the keeping of the Landtag, but in the pocket of the Prussian monarch, *i.e.* of his Minister-President.

How could this Bismarckian plan of campaign have been met? Only by first keeping Denmark in the right; secondly, by a complete understanding between France and Great Britain; thirdly, by making an Anglo-French *entente* the basis for a complete understanding with Germany other than Prussia. The isolation of Prussia was the true diplomatic objective, as clearly as for Bismarck was the isolation of Great Britain. It was essential to inform Denmark categorically and at once that she must withdraw from an untenable position, and place her cause unreservedly in the hands of her friends, or face Germany by herself. Nor was it enough to maintain the Convention of London and the *status quo*. The ambitions of the Danish Radicals were a grave danger for the future. The German demand had to be met frankly and with sympathy; for the German population in the Duchies had genuine grievances; and effective guarantees must be provided that the Schleswig-Holstein question did not continue to poison the situation in Europe. The distinction between Germany and Prussia (under the control of Bismarck) was real and deep. A true alliance with Germany other than Prussia, and with the powerful anti-Bismarckian forces in Prussia, was well within the scope of diplomacy, which could thus have divided Prussia and isolated her in Germany. But such a policy implied the sympathy and comprehension that only knowledge and mastery of the realities could give. The one thing needful was the one thing conspicuously wanting. English public opinion condemned Germany no less than Prussia, just because the Liberals in Germany were dead against the Convention of 1852. It broke the hearts of the few Englishmen and the many Germans who recognised the gravity of the issues at stake for England and for Germany to see the blindness, apathy, and ignorance on our side, and the squandering by our ministers of opportunity after opportunity. Great Britain deserted much more than Denmark. The alienation from Great Britain of Nationalist and Liberal Germany and Prussia—the commencement of the estrangement that was to deepen into opposition and solidify into an irreconcilable hostility—dates from 1864. Our policy, skilfully exploited by Bismarck, was the foundation of the conversion of Prussia and Germany to Bismarckianism. Yet if ever there was a British cause, the defeat of Bismarckian statecraft in 1864 was that cause.

British statesmanship had gravely handicapped itself. The rejection by the British government in November 1863 of Napoleon's proposal for a Congress was a criminal blunder which had greatly angered the Emperor. The rooted distrust of Napoleon III., and the exaggerated estimate of his ability and strength, which Bismarck had long ago abandoned, prevented a sincere Anglo-French union. Napoleon, as usual, wandered in the twilight of phrases which he mistook for principles. He was heavily committed in Mexico, he was not prepared for war, and he had had one damaging lesson from Poland in the blunder of empty threats. When Great Britain proposed in June 1864 that France should join with her in an agreed line of partition in Schleswig and make it an ultimatum, Drouyn de Lhuys replied that with Poland before their eyes such a step was, as Napoleon said, to invite another *gros soufflet*, and unless Great Britain were ready to go to the bitter end, *i.e.* make refusal to accept the ultimatum a *casus belli*, France would not join in the proposal. Great Britain was not ready for that, and the proposal came to nothing. The conception of Prussia as a representative of nationalism, strengthened in the north to make an equipoise to Austria in the south, fascinated Napoleon's ebbing imagination. He has received sympathy because Bismarck blackmailed him deliberately. But the truth is that Napoleon, like the gambler who fears the honest banker and borrows from an unscrupulous moneylender, hoped to get the money and evade the sixty per cent. He desired to win an imposing success without striking a blow or risking a French life. The Danes blew up their bridges and burnt their boats, and then expected Great Britain single-handed to intervene in their behalf.

The British Court, as has been revealed, had much sympathy with the Augustenburg claims; and the Queen was absolutely determined that her country should not be involved in war to save the Duchies for Denmark.[1] But the real cause of the mischief and the real responsibility for our failure lay with the nation and its leaders. The ignorance of ministers throughout the whole business was equalled by the ignorance of the organs of public opinion and of the nation they claimed to instruct. The newspapers— *The Times*, in particular—surpassed themselves in the winter of 1863-4 by the insufficiency of their knowledge and the self-sufficiency of the lectures they poured out on Germany and Prussia.[2] We were quite unprepared for war. The nation was not willing to go to war, for it

[1] Yet, curiously enough, in 1866 Queen Victoria desired 'to interfere by force against Prussian designs in the Duchies' (*Clarendon's Life*, ii. p. 311)— a pretty clear proof of sympathy with Austria and the Augustenburg claims. The ministers were wholly against the Queen.

[2] This is a deliberate judgment based on a careful study of the files of *The Times*, and other British newspapers for 1863 and 1864: the cumulative impression of such a study cannot be verified from a single reference. But I will cite three examples of knowledge, political judgment, and prescience as samples: 'The grievances of her (Denmark's) German subjects seem puerile or groundless' (*Times*, November 16, 1863): 'We have ourselves as a nation little interest in the question' (November 24, 1863): 'We believe that even now (February 6, 1864) Prussia is anxious to leave the Danish state untouched.' How Bismarck must have enjoyed reading that divination of

scarcely knew where Schleswig-Holstein could be found
on the map, but we were ready to threaten what we had
no intention of performing, and we hectored every one
with the complacent superiority that deserves the title of
insular. The gravity of the German and European situation was quite unappreciated, because there are none so
blind as those who do not wish to see. The language of
responsible public men, and not merely of Palmerston, of
politicians, and of 'Society,' naturally misled the Danes,
who made the pardonable mistake of supposing that
England meant what she said, and of interpreting ignorant
bluster as moral conviction. 'I wasted several years of
my life,' Bismarck remarked, 'by the supposition that
England was a great nation.' The price that we paid then
and subsequently was the price that we deserved to pay.
A nation with responsible parliamentary government is
not the victim but the author of its government's blunders;
and if it seeks to transfer the responsibility to politicians
and a party system, or some other scapegoat, it is guilty
of the lie in the soul.

Bismarck's first step was to secure Austria. It did not
escape his attention that Austria, compared with Prussia,
was in a very unfavourable position for effective military
and political action in the Duchies. Austria, humiliated
by the Polish fiasco and the failure of the Congress of
Princes, was only too ready to listen to the Prussian overtures. The rejection by the Federal Diet (January 14)
of the Prussian proposal, that Austria and Prussia, in virtue
of their international position, should occupy Schleswig
in order to secure the observance of the Convention, was
tantamount to a declaration that the Diet repudiated the

his policy and aims. The effect of these utterances on public opinion
at Copenhagen, throughout Germany, and at Berlin and Vienna, is not a
question of speculation. Morier and others saw with pain how our newspapers
encouraged the Danes, angered while patronising the German Liberals, inflamed
the tension, and were carefully studied by Bismarck, who was accurately informed of the ignorance and bluster in London. 'England,' said a Prussian
deputy, 'is always full of consideration for those who can defend themselves.'
And the England of 1863-64 also seems to have been convinced that (a) the
British fleet had only to appear and Prussia would retire in humble fear;
and (b) still more characteristic, that military states would conduct their
military operations as our Government and War Office had conducted the
Crimean War.

Convention; it compelled Austria to accept the Prussian alliance. 'We recognise,' said Bismarck, 'in King Christian the heir both of the rights and the wrongs of his predecessor; our fidelity to treaties must be open to no impeachment.' The Treaty of January 16, 1864, bound Austria and Prussia to determine the future of the Duchies by joint agreement and to decide the succession question only by common consent. It ruled out agreements with a third party, and it made the two States, as guarantors of the Convention and Protocol of 1852, a single State to all intents and purposes. Austria could henceforward only oppose Prussia or act with the Federal Diet, or another European Power, by tearing up the treaty, which proved, as Bismarck intended it to be, a millstone round Austria's neck. It was to be the connecting link between the German question and the question of the Duchies. Had the Danes now accepted the Austro-Prussian ultimatum of January 16, to withdraw the new constitution and place the situation in the hands of the Powers, there must have been at least delay, and time would have been brought on to the Danish side. The Danish government knew, as every one did, that Great Britain had previously rejected the reference to a Congress. The British government was of opinion that King Christian's claims to the Duchies could not be questioned. The ultimatum was accordingly rejected.

Bismarck afterwards smilingly admitted that a Danish acceptance would have been a serious upset to his plans; but he added, probably with truth, 'I had ascertained that the Danes would certainly refuse, otherwise I should not have taken the risk.' The Danes, moreover, were only given forty-eight hours to decide, and the Austro-Prussian army crossed the frontier at once. The Prussian note of January 31 virtually proclaimed that Danish resistance had torn the Convention of London to shreds and tatters. And Danish resistance was openly applauded in England —which expected to see 1849 repeated in 1864. So much did England know of Prussia and of Denmark.

The situation was certainly peculiar. Saxon and Hanoverian troops were acting for the Federal Diet, whose jurisdiction was limited to Holstein. The Austrian and Prussian troops, representing two signatories to the Convention of 1852, could coerce Denmark, for the Convention applied to the whole kingdom and not merely to the Duchies. France, Great Britain, and Russia had an equal right with Austria and Prussia to intervene; and Austria and Prussia by themselves could not draw up a new, or restore the old, Convention. A Congress was inevitable. The Prussian General Staff, on its mettle, recognised that the pace must be forced. The storm of the Düppel lines (April 18) drove the Danes to accept reference to a Congress at London, and the armistice of April 18 left Austria and Prussia in practical possession of the Duchies. Germany was jubilant: 1848 was avenged. It only remained now for Europe to sever the Duchies from Denmark, install the Duke of Augustenburg, and the business was over.

'The business,' Bismarck had decided, was only beginning. The Prussian Staff would not be whistled off its prey by journalists in Printing House Square or Fleet Street; the King, who flattered himself that he had faced a scaffold in Unter Den Linden for the army, felt it was good to be a Hohenzollern; and even the most rebellious Prussian Radical had pride in the soldiers of Prussia. 'It will not be amiss,' Bismarck concluded, 'if we enter the Congress in possession of the object in dispute.' But the floors of European Congresses are notoriously slippery. Bismarck, represented by Bernstorff in London, was determined to make the Congress end in a stalemate. He could always block what he did not want, and then propose what he felt sure would be rejected by others. The blood and iron of the Prussian sword could then bring the curtain down on the first act.

War was only a continuation of policy, a means to give you the terms on which you wish to live with your neighbours; and Bismarck had three fine cards to play. A settlement against the will of the Duchies was no settlement (that appealed to Napoleon with his itch for plebiscites); the restoration of the Duchies to Denmark would be violently opposed by Germany, and every Augustenburger in Europe (that was for the Queen of Great Britain, the widow of a Coburg prince) ; a partition could probably be wrecked on its details (that was for himself). Where in the Duchies did the Danish fringe end and the German begin ? Bismarck had a crushing answer to the proposals of his opponents in London. If he was thwarted he would resign, with the result that Prussia, in the hands of the overwhelming opposition in the Landtag, would join the Diet and the princes in supporting the Duke of Augustenburg, and Europe would be confronted with a united Germany, holding the Duchies in its possession and determined to fight for their retention. He kept his hand on German nationalism, and now opened the throttle to let the superheated steam out. From the Wilhelmstrasse he invited the journalists and the professors to lash public opinion into a frenzy. ' Let the whole pack go,' he commanded ; and ' the whole pack ' let themselves go with German thoroughness and rhetoric. As a corrective he encouraged Russia to revive the claims of the house of Oldenburg, passed over in 1852. Nor—he quietly insinuated—were the dynastic claims of a Prussian claimant to be wholly overlooked.

The interest of the Congress does not lie in its tedious details of proposals[1] rejected by one or other of the parties, but in the steady sapping and countermining by Prussia, so as to bring about a deadlock. Clarendon penetrated the blocking tactics. It was then too late. British public opinion, confronted with a disinterested war by Great Britain alone for two wretched Duchies on behalf of an unreasonable Denmark, which rejected every compromise, had not the vision or the knowledge to grasp the significance for Europe of Schleswig-Holstein, and the situation had been so bungled by the British government and so skilfully engineered by Bismarck that war on behalf of Denmark was war with Liberal Germany. Our Court was determined to

[1] The proposal to return to the position defined in the Convention of 1852 was rejected by Germany, Austria, and Prussia ; the proposal to install the Duke of Augustenburg in the Duchies, separated from Denmark, made by Austria and Prussia, was rejected by Denmark and Great Britain ; the British proposal to divide Schleswig at the line of the river Schlei was rejected by Germany ; the Danish proposal to make the river Eider the frontier was rejected by Prussia.

keep England out of war, and the ministers, divided amongst themselves, shrank from involving the Crown in a ministerial crisis, in which it was very uncertain that public opinion would support them. The government had not decided in advance whether it was a British interest to fight, and, if it was not, what line of action would spare Great Britain from a humiliating rebuff and treachery to friends it had deceived. Napoleon, ' the Man of Sin,' was playing with the idea (suggested by the Arch-Tempter) that the most reasonable solution was to recognise the Nationalist principle and assign the Duchies to Prussia as the representative of that principle—of course for a compensation to be defined later. The policy of disinterested idealism and the policy of *pourboires*—the policy of the benevolent heart and the policy of the calculating brain—are hard to harmonise at any time, but the harmony is impossible for a muddled head and a heart suffering from valvular disease.

While the Congress wrangled Bismarck was clearing a difficulty of his own out of the way. Through the Crown Prince and M. Duncker he gave the Duke of Augustenburg an interview at Berlin (June 1). The King and the Crown Prince were apparently confident that it would result in the adoption by Bismarck of Augustenburg as the candidate of Prussia. It is impossible to reconcile the narratives of that memorable scene, which come first hand from Bismarck and the duke. Recent German critical scholarship has held that the duke's story is the more trustworthy, which is quite probable, but the controversy, though a fascinating study in evidential sources, does not affect the result. When the two men parted at midnight of June 1 Bismarck had decided that he had finished with the duke, and the duke recognised that he would be installed in the Duchies only by Bismarck's expulsion from office. Bismarck expounded the difficulties, legal and political, of enforcing the duke's claims ; but if the duke were prepared to agree to certain conditions, which would place the Duchies in the military and administrative control of Prussia, he would work on his behalf. The conditions

B.   M

were such as to establish a virtual Prussian protectorate, under which the duke would be nominally sovereign, but in all essentials he would simply be the President (*Regierungs Oberpräsident*) of a Prussian province. The Duchies were, in short, to be the ducal scabbard of the Prussian sword. The duke rejected the conditions, as incompatible with his independence as a sovereign prince and his desire to be an autonomous and Liberal ruler. When he walked out into the summer night, he was walking out of history. Upstairs the Minister-President was shrugging his shoulders. Liberals never would see that half a loaf was better than no bread. It was now quite clear that annexation to Prussia was the only tolerable solution. Annexation? How? Would Austria consent to a Prussian annexation?

The Congress broke up on June 25 on the deadlock that Bismarck desired. Its debates registered three results : first, that the Convention of 1852 had gone into the wastepaper basket ; secondly, that no alternative settlement had been arrived at ; and thirdly,—the really momentous result—that Bismarck had smashed the Concert of Europe into fragments. Henceforward one of the main principles of his policy, not merely in the Schleswig-Holstein affair, was to prevent the fragments from re-uniting. German sentiment supported this policy. As long as the European Powers fell out, Prussia and Germany would come by their own. The next six years provided the proof. Beust—the representative of the Federal Diet at London—whom defeat always prompted to epigrams, said happily enough : ' The conference closed after some very animated debates, as a Black Forest clock sometimes stops after ticking more loudly than usual.' ' You came,' said Clarendon to Bernstorff, ' into the conference as masters of the situation, and as masters of the situation you now leave it. Have a care how long *that* will last.' Bismarck appreciated the compliment from an experienced statesman. As for the threat, he had the care to see that ' *that* ' lasted from 1864 to 1890. The disappointment at Windsor Castle was even more bitter than Clarendon's disgust. The failure of the Congress was a grievous blow to dynasti

Liberalism in Germany.[1] Our Court agreed with another
remark of Clarendon's : ' Je ne veux plus jamais rien avoir
à faire avec cet homme sans foi ni loi qui s'appelle M. de
Bismarck, ni celui qui est son nègre M. de Rechberg
(the Austrian Prime Minister).' Clarendon was to have
another bout later on with the man without faith or law,
and to fare no better.

Hostilities were resumed. The Danes saw the security
of their islands smashed in when Alsen was captured
(June 29) by the skill of the Prussian Chief of the Staff.
The miracle of British help, for which to the last they had
hoped against hope, was not vouchsafed. On August 1,
to avoid the fall of Copenhagen, preliminaries of peace
were signed. The Duchies were handed over in full sovereignty to Austria and Prussia conjointly, who in accordance with the treaty of January 16, would now conjointly
determine their ultimate fate. The major military operations were over ; but the major strategy of diplomacy had
simply closed the first phase of the campaign. ' We were
quite ready,' Bismarck remarked later, ' once we had
liberated Schleswig and Holstein to leave poor King
Christian in peace.' For Bismarck the annexation of the
conquered Duchies was only a part, and not the most important part, of the great problem—the solution of the
German question in accordance with Prussian principles
and interests. The enemy in that vast field was Prussia's
ally Austria. And until Austria was as decisively defeated
as Denmark Prussia could not impose her terms.

The Prussian army had had a dress rehearsal in the
Danish campaign. It had justified itself. Let the
soldiers now see to it that the experience was used to prepare the army for the much more serious trial that lay
ahead. ' The occasion for such a war,' Bismarck wrote in
December 1862, ' can be found at any moment, when our
position with regard to the great Powers is favourable for
carrying it on.' But the tremendous task imposed on the
director of Prussian policy was how to force a war upon

[1] 'The Queen cannot but think that this country . . . has no other course
t to withdraw, and to refuse to take any further part in this lamentable
ntest.' (Mem. to Lord Granville, June 27, 1864. *Life*, i. p. 475.)

Austria, and at the same time convince King William, Prussia, Germany if possible, and Europe, that it was Austria forcing the war on Prussia ; how also to link the interests of Germany with the essential interests of Prussia, and how to secure the European situation that would leave Prussia to fight in a closed ring fence with Austria, and garner undisturbed the fruits of victory. A Congress of Paris, London, or Vienna to rearrange the map of Europe and the organisation of Germany would be fatal to a Prussian settlement. Bismarck's diplomacy in the next eighteen months reveals his interpretation of the situation : first, the settlement of the Duchies must be kept open ; secondly, the key of the international situation lay at Paris ; thirdly, that so far from quarrelling with Austria in 1864 the benefits of the alliance were by no means exhausted and must be exploited a great deal further. ' So long,' he said, ' as we—Austria and Prussia —remain united no one of the great Powers will move a finger to disturb the *status quo*.' What Bismarck really intended was that they should not move a finger if Austria and Prussia fell out—as they were bound to do.

From September 1862 (and earlier) until September 1870 at least, a repetition by Francis Joseph of the Diplomatic Revolution of 1756 was perpetually in his thoughts. France and Austria had then laid aside their historic antagonism to unite against the troubler of the peace—Frederick the Great. Bismarck realised that in autocracies, such as Austria, Russia, or the Second Empire (as in the Europe of the *ancien régime*) policy could be shaped by the sovereign entirely against the popular wish or sentiment, and Bismarck's handling of Russia both before and after 1870 explicitly rested on his hold not on Russian sentiment—as he told the Reichstag in 1888—but on the Tsar. Great Britain was quite different ; for there you had to deal with a nation that could coerce, and could not be coerced by, its government. In diplomacy the power of the autocracies had great advantages, but also one great disadvantage. The autocratic State might be quickly switched off into a new orbit to suit the policy of its governor. The psychology of the

statecraft of power reveals one simple categorical imperative of state-reason : never let others do to you what you
would do to them, and it is one of the supreme penalties
of that statecraft, imposed on its disciples, invariably to
expect foul play as the riposte to foul play. Statesmen.
who spend half their lives preparing to force war on their
unprepared neighbours invariably spend the other half
in meeting the wars they are convinced their neighbours
intend to force upon them. The incapacity of a de-
bauchee autocrat is, therefore, a better security of the
peace of Europe than the ambitions of genius. The sovereign who covets his neighbour's wife is less harmful in
the long run than the Minister-President of an autocracy
who covets his neighbour's lands.

For Bismarck it was not necessary to secure France as
an accomplice—and he could not have secured *France*—
but it was essential to secure Napoleon. That the policy
of which Napoleon was to be the accomplice was wholly
opposed to the interests of France, indeed was to be the
basis of France's ultimate ruin, was obvious to Bismarck ;
and, in his mind, ought to have been obvious to Napoleon.
Yet, if the interest of Prussia could only be gained by the
ruin of France, it was the duty of a Prussian statesman to
ruin France. For Bismarck the ethics were irrelevant :
the real problem was of a wholly different kind—how to
secure the essential neutrality of Napoleon without paying
for it except in vague promises that could always be
repudiated, or in a good will which he did not feel. The
compact of Plombières could now or at any time be repeated by the compact of Biarritz. But pride and national
sentiment were far too strong for so simple a solution. He
was not Cavour, nor was Prussia the kingdom of Sardinia.
He said, truly enough, that in listening to Napoleon's overtures he felt like Joseph tempted by Potiphar's wife ; and
the cession of German territory, even if it did not belong
to Prussia, as the price of French support stirred genuine
and fierce resentment within him. For to Bismarck, as to
all the Germans of his day, France was the one irreconcilable foe with whom Prussia and Germany had a long account to settle. For Napoleon himself Bismarck seems

to have had a liking, dashed with pity and contempt. But Napoleon was France, and there was a quintessence of satisfaction now in the task of making France, whom he hated, the dupe of his diplomacy, and the engineer against her will of her own downfall.

While the legal points involved in the Duke of Augustenburg's claims were referred to the Prussian Crown lawyers (who might safely be trusted to examine them with Prussian impartiality) Roon was sent to France to attend the French manœuvres—a fairly clear hint to Austria that Prussia had friends elsewhere than at Vienna; and in October Bismarck's health required him to pay the second of three momentous visits to Bordeaux and Biarritz, where he met the Emperor, and on his way back discussed the situation and the future with the French ministers at Paris.

The principles of his policy were subsequently explained in an elaborate memorandum submitted to Napoleon (August 18, 1865) : ' Continental politics have for a long time been based on the close union of the three Eastern Powers, which, in the condition of things resulting from the Holy Alliance, took the form of a coalition against France . . . the policy of Prussia had for many years turned in this direction . . . and has forced her to follow Austria's South Germany and ' Entire Germany ' policies. . . . Opposed to this traditional view there is another doctrine which is founded upon Prussia's most vital needs. It is the doctrine of the free and independent development of Prussia and North German elements into an independent great power, which may feel itself secure. . . . Can the Emperor Napoleon consider it his duty to discourage Prussia . . . and force her back into the old defensive attitude of the Coalition. . . . This would be a certain proof that the traditional policy, pursued for fifty years, was correct, and that it must determine Prussia's conduct in the future.'

Bismarck was now carefully preparing the way for Napoleon's acquiescence in the annexation of the Duchies, the consolidation of Prussia in the north of Germany as an equipoise to Austria, and some unspecified compensation to France. But neither Napoleon nor his ministers had learned that Bismarck's unconventional frankness marked a diplomatic reconnaissance. The easiest way to evade committing yourself was, under the guise of friendship, to incite the other side to damaging revelations of greed or conquest. At present, until Austria had categorically refused a settlement satisfactory to Prussia, any definite engagement with France was dangerous. Neither the King nor German public opinion would in 1864 have tolerated a settlement of the Duchies by concert with France to the detriment of Austria.

The first step was to clear the Federal forces out of Schleswig and Holstein. The Saxon and Hanoverian troops were, therefore, peremptorily required to evacuate the Duchies, on the ground that they now legally belonged to Prussia and Austria. Moltke's correspondence proves that the Prussian Staff was ready to turn the Saxons and Hanoverians out by force, if needs be ; but it was not necessary. The Bund recognised its impotence, declared the Federal execution at an end, and the Federal troops were withdrawn (December 5). Two days later the triumphal return of the victorious army of Prussia was celebrated with much rejoicing in Berlin.

Public opinion both in the Duchies and without ceaselessly clamoured for the installation of the Duke of Augustenburg. At Vienna the blunder of concluding the alliance of January 16 was now fully recognised, and Rechberg's dismissal from office (October, 1864) proclaimed that the Ball-Platz was about to try a new line of policy. Bismarck was determined first to hold Austria tightly to the alliance, secondly, to make the administrative condominium of the Duchies quite unworkable. ' We stand,' he said, ' before the question of the Duchies like two guests before a delicious dish. One of them who has no appetite and will not eat rigorously forbids the other whom the delicacies tempt.'

The continuous drip of facts was eating away the hard rock in his sovereign's conscience and Prussian public opinion. William had begun to feel that Prussian honour was involved in a satisfactory settlement, and that ' coercion ' by Austria would land Prussia in a second Olmütz.

A very significant memorial, signed by Radicals so pronounced as Twesten, Jung, Mommsen, and others, emphasised the desirability of permanently securing the Duchies for Germany by incorporation on reasonable terms with Prussia. The report of the Prussian Crown lawyers proved first, that the Duke of Augustenburg had no legal claims ; secondly, that the title to the Duchies had been unquestionably vested in the King of Denmark ; and thirdly, that this title had been unquestionably transferred by the Treaty of Vienna to Prussia and Austria, who were now the *de jure* sovereigns of Schleswig and Holstein. If, therefore, Prussia consented to install the Duke of Augustenburg by agreement with Austria, the duke would be a delegate ruling on such conditions as the *de jure* co-sovereigns laid down. William's last scruples were thus removed. The settlement was not a question of the Augustenburger's ' rights ' but of policy, and the delegation of Prussia's rights affected the King's honour and trusteeship of Prussian interests. How could expert Prussian Crown lawyers possibly be wrong or biassed even if they flatly contradicted expert Prussian professors and historians ?

On February 22, 1865, Bismarck formally stated to Austria the conditions on which Prussia was prepared to join with Austria in establishing the Duke of Augustenburg in the Duchies. They were practically the conditions which the duke had rejected on June 1, 1864, and would have made the Duchies to all intents and purposes Prussian provinces, administered by the duke as a Prussian state official. The Schleswig-Holstein troops were, for example, to take the oath of allegiance to the King of Prussia : while Prussian control of the harbour of Kiel was guaranteed. The Austrian rejection of these terms was a foregone conclusion, and (March 27) the request of the Federal Diet, moved by Austria, for the unconditional installation of the duke was rejected by Prussia, as a matter beyond the competence of the Diet and also a breach of treaty by Austria. Bismarck was now able to convince his sovereign that it was not the Minister-President at Berlin who stood in the way of an honourable settlement. The suggestion of the pro-Austrians at Berlin that William should purchase Austrian acquiescence in a Prussian annexation by the cession of Silesia was deftly calculated to stir William's deepest resentment. The surrender of Prussian rights in the north, purchased by Prussian blood, was to be sealed by the surrender of Prussian rights in the south, purchased by the victories of Frederick the Great and the immortal heroes of the heroic epoch. William, in short, was finding, under guidance, his way to the conclusion that Austria—with whom he had passionately desired always to co-operate as a friend and ally—was utilising the situation to inflict a humiliation on him or drive him into a 'defensive' war.

The two secret Councils of State (March 9 and May 3), at which the Crown Prince and all the high military and civil authorities were present, revealed the gravity of the situation. Such secret councils in the history of Prussia are the invariable prelude to momentous decisions, and still more momentous action. The whole situation was surveyed, and the responsible opinion of the Prussian staff was earnestly canvassed. The Chief of the Staff spoke to men who knew what war, strategy and policy meant. The upshot was that the King, satisfied that the soldiers had correctly estimated the military position, decided that if Austria threatened war, Prussia would fight and Prussia would be right.

The tension in Prussia and Germany rapidly became acute. A civil war (a *Brüderkrieg*) was in sight, and all those influential sections of society to which war between Prussia and Austria was a disaster, subversion of the moral and political order, and the first step to 'the Revolution' were aghast at the cynical wickedness of the Minister-President, who betrayed the Conservative cause. L. von Gerlach wrote bitterly to the Minister-President at this cruel treachery to law and order. Bismarck's visit to France, the trafficking with Napoleon—the Napoleon of 1865 was generally held to be an arch-Machiavelli of Jacobin statecraft—the Augustenburg agitation, and the widening breach with Austria, inflamed and bewildered public opinion. The caricature literature of these tense years reveals the fears and execrations of Conservatives, Ultramontanes, Particularists of every shade, Nationalists, Liberals, and Radicals. Bismarck's policy had evoked the bitter denunciation of every party, and his unpopularity reached its height in the period from the spring of 1865 to the climax of the final rupture in July 1866.

But unpopularity did not trouble Bismarck. The crisis was of his own making. 'We have come,' he said to Austria, ' to where the road divides . . . our tickets take us upon diverging routes, nor can we in this trip enter the carriage that you share with others.' He anticipated correctly that, if he could achieve his purpose by the methods he judged suitable, reactionaries and progressives alike who now were ready to stone him as a traitor, would hail him as the saviour of Prussia and Germany, and his methods as the finest expression of efficient German state-craft. It is not surprising that his experience from 1849 to 1890 confirmed his contempt for public opinion, whether of the upper or the lower classes, and his belief that kings, princes, and nobles were even more ready than professors or tinkers to worship success. It is essentially characteristic of the man and his statesmanship that in the heated atmosphere of June 1865 he calmly weighed the forces in the situation, and decided to state, in the terms of an ultimatum drawn up at a cabinet council at Regensburg, the heads of a settlement. The Convention of Gastein (August 14, 1865) was the diplomatic expression of those terms. It was Austria, not Bismarck, who had given way.

The Convention provided for the transfer of the ad-ministration of Holstein to Austria, and of Schleswig to Prussia, with a joint share in the harbour of Kiel, the forti-fication of which was to be entrusted to Prussia. Prussia acquired Lauenburg by a money payment. The division of the condominium was remarkable. Holstein was now an Austrian enclave between Prussian Schleswig and the Prussian kingdom. The Austrian land route to Holstein was practically controlled by Prussia, and the Austrian fleet could only reach Kiel by a journey from Trieste to the North Sea, and before it ever got as far as Brest Bismarck intended it should be stopped or sunk—by an ally of

Prussia. The Duke of Augustenburg's claims went into the wastepaper basket, as also did the sacred and inviolable principle, which all German historians, Conservatives and Liberals, had regarded as a greater certainty than the law of gravitation, that the Duchies since 1460 were 'one and indivisible.'

The Convention was accepted by William 1. and the Conservatives with profound relief as 'a bloodless victory' —peace with honour. The shame of a war with Austria or of a second Olmütz had been triumphantly avoided. But in the Duchies, in the middle and petty States, and in the Nationalist, Liberal, and Ultramontane parties the agreement of the two great German Powers roused deep indignation. The cause of the duke, of Nationalism and Liberalism were surrendered in a common betrayal. Popular meetings at Frankfurt condemned the Convention as a violation of public law and right which could not be binding on the Duchies, whose autonomy was so cynically overridden—and by Austria, the avowed representative of moral order and legitimism.

Bismarck's view of the Convention is quite clear. The Napoleonic military maxim 'Engage everywhere and then see' summed up his action. Bismarck had engaged 'the enemy' along the whole line; the Convention enabled him now 'to see.' On July 13 he had written to M. von Blankenburg that 'war with Austria is only a question of time,' and after the Convention had been settled he remarked : 'I could never have believed that I would find an Austrian diplomatist who would have signed such a document.' He was quite willing to postpone the struggle to a more favourable occasion. Neither the Prussian nor the German nor the European situation was entirely moulded to his liking. On July 21 he had telegraphed both to Goltz at Paris to conclude a treaty of neutrality with France, if the Austrians rejected the ultimatum, and to Usedom at Florence to inquire officially what the attitude of Italy would be in the case of war. France and Italy—these were the two harassing uncertainties.

Nor was the German question, apart from the Duchies, adequately worked up. Bismarck had not yet been able to link up a precise Prussian programme of Federal reform with the issues raised in Schleswig-Holstein, and thereby proclaim that Prussia was fighting for greater ends than the mere acquisition of the Duchies wrested from Denmark. A letter to his wife briefly alludes to the cruel and increasing burden of work and responsibility that the preceding twelve months had thrust upon him. Daily dispatches from and to Rome, Florence, Vienna, Munich, Paris, the direction of foreign policy aggravated by the internal difficulties, the tangle in the Duchies, the military and financial problems and the necessity of controlling and directing his ministerial colleagues, and of keeping the King fully informed and true to the straight course—such were some of his chief cares, and the Minister-President found the task almost beyond even his powers, while behind the unending toil lay like lead the consciousness that a false step, an error of judgment, a miscalculation would wreck both Prussia and himself. His irritable and highly strung nerves conspired with the white-hot passion within to rob him of sleep, and to make him brusque, dictatorial, and harsh. Yet he could always find the necessary half-hour, when away from his home, to scribble a few lines to his wife, and in these letters his truest thoughts and many of his happiest descriptions and judgments are enshrined with a vivid and unforgettable brevity. Bismarck had a genuinely German contempt for women who meddled with politics, and for men who allowed themselves to be influenced in political affairs by women, whether wives or mistresses. But to Frau von Bismarck he wrote always as to one who had a right to know and on whose judgment and sympathy he could implicitly rely.

Austria was certainly not ready for war. The Habsburg primacy in Germany was at stake and could not be risked simply on the Schleswig-Holstein question. Bismarck, in the last resort, was determined to buy Napoleon or ally with 'the Revolution'—to fling, if needs be, the whole 'system of 1815'—treaties and principles, frontiers, and balance of power—into the conflagration, conscious that Prussia by her military strength and the exploitation of National Liberalism, would emerge master probably of

Germany, as defined in 1849. But Austria, with a hostile
Russia to the north and a mutinous Hungary in the east,
could not buy Napoleon. Still less could she face ' the
Revolution.' Austria's two deadliest foes, within and
without, were Nationalism and Liberalism, and the irony
of the situation in 1865 was summed up in the truth that
Austria's only genuine friend was Bismarck. Since 1849
Francis Joseph, a true Habsburg, blindly following the
star of the dynasty, and sacrificing all to the principle that
Austria was not a State but a family, had thrown away
opportunity after opportunity. As Richard III. was
haunted in the grey hours of the night before Bosworth
by the procession of the victims of his ambition, so now
Francis Joseph, on the eve of Königgrätz, could see the
procession of dismissed minister after minister sacrificed
to a dynastic obsession. The list was by no means complete in August 1865 ; the finest opportunities and the
most loyal servants were still to be thrown away. But
had Francis Joseph been gifted with a spark of the imagination without which all statecraft shrivels at the touch of
reality into the tricks of the diplomatic card-sharper, he
would now have purchased from Bismarck a Prussian
defensive and offensive alliance against all and sundry.
Except as pieces in the mighty game of Prussian ideals,
Bismarck did not care a groschen for Napoleon, Victor
Emmanuel, and Italian Nationalism or for Deák and Magyar
autonomy. The withdrawal of Austria from the Duchies,
acquiescence in a Prussian hegemony north of the Main,
together with a real parity in a reconstructed Federal organisation would have saved Venetia and much else besides for
the Habsburgs, and anticipated (under far more favourable
conditions for Austria) the system of 1879, perhaps even
have revived in a new form the Triple Alliance of 1819.
A big brain and a cool recognition of realities could have
made the Convention of Gastein a treaty that created a
system, not an armistice that simply called a halt, and
thus led up to the foundation of a Central Europe, more
justly poised between Berlin and Vienna than the system
of 1871. Whether such a treaty would have been better
for Europe as a whole it is idle to speculate. At least, it

would have spared the Continent the triumphant vindication of force as the sovereign remedy for 'the great
questions of the age' that the war of 1866 provided ; it
would have left Bismarck to face the difficulties of the
internal situation in Prussia without the conclusive argument that ended the constitutional struggle in Prussia,
and began the steady perversion of National Liberalism
from the gospel of Rights to the gospel of Power.

But Francis Joseph, in 1865, did not feel the need of
imagination. He only felt the need of time. Bismarck
needed time too, and he was confident he would make
a better use of the respite than the men who had tried
to bluff him and then shrank back at the counter-threat
of a Prussian mobilisation. Bismarck was neither the
Radowitz nor the Manteuffel of 1850, nor was William i.
a Frederick William iv. Austria was no longer represented by a Schwarzenberg. 'The Convention,' Bismarck
pronounced in a memorable phrase, 'simply papered over
the cracks.'

William was grateful for being spared war—as he
thought—by the achievement of a resounding diplomatic
stroke. On September 15 the Minister-President and
his descendants were promoted to the rank of Counts
(Graf). 'In the four years,' wrote the King, 'that have
passed since I called you to the head of my government,
Prussia has gained a position which is worthy of her
history and promises her further fortune and glory.'

§ 3. *The rupture with Austria—The Treaty of Prague,* 1865-1866

The ten months from the Convention of Gastein to
the final rupture on June 23, 1866, when the Prussian
troops entered Bohemia, make a very complicated chapter
in European history. Full justice to the diplomatic
moves and countermoves would require a large canvas
and elaborate detail. In France, Austria, Italy, and the
German States, the directors of policy continuously en-
visaged contradictory aims and alternative lines of action.
German public opinion was in greater bewilderment than

ever : fearing and detesting everything that Prussia did, yet mastered by an intuition that in Prussian strength and purposeful egoism alone lay all hopes of a permanent decision. Germany had indeed dragged its anchors, and was drifting into the storm.

The main lines of Bismarck's statecraft stand out in the sharpest relief against the blurred and shifting kaleidoscope. A letter from the devoted Roon, himself toiling at full concert pitch, to have the Prussian army ready, speaks of 'Otto's herculean industry day and night and his reckless demands on his physical strength. . . . He has now to reckon with the rebellion of his truest and most submissive subject, his stomach, and is so irritable and sensitive, particularly over petty matters, that I am full of anxiety, for I know what is at stake.' Roon adds truly, 'complete freedom of mind, a deranged digestion, and tortured nerves are hard to reconcile.' But for all his difficulties, political, mental, and physical, Bismarck exhibited the one clear and resolute will, the one clear and unshakable aim in the universal confusion. He was determined to settle the fate of Prussia and Germany by the appeal to the sword.

Roon, Moltke, and the Prussian Staff were of the same determination. Men then and since have convinced themselves that the war was inevitable, that it lay in the alleged logic both of history and the situation, and that after August 14, 1865, the two major States of Germany, Prussia and Austria, simply slid slowly down inclined planes to an unavoidable collision. A close study, however, of these ten months does not support the general conclusion that wars are unavoidable, and that this particular one exemplifies such a philosophy of history or statesmanship.

It would be a complete misreading of Bismarck's policy, principles, and methods to assert that either before or after the Convention of Gastein he so completely lost his grip on the Prussian rudder that he was forced into fighting. Bismarck may not have believed in 'preventive wars,' though the definition of a 'preventive war' would have to be very carefully drawn before either he or his disciples could accept so complete a repudiation; he certainly did not believe in wars merely for conquest or glory, and no statesman of the nineteenth century had a deeper sense of the responsibility that plunging a State into war imposes on those who direct policy. But in 1865 and in 1866, as in 1870, or in 1864, he willed the war and he deliberately worked for it.

The secrets of his statecraft will be completely missed if we do not recognise two elemental postulates—first, that in 1865 he rejected every opportunity by which war might be avoided; secondly, that he worked with steadfast patience to remove the obstacles to war, as the final conclusion of the matter. He could, for example, have taken up Napoleon's idea of a Congress, and with the help of Russia (and certainly of Great Britain) have opened all the festering abscesses in the operating theatre of the European Concert. Such a course would have been welcomed by the best minds in Germany and outside it. But a Congress would not have given him what he held with passionate conviction was alone worth winning.

War alone, he concluded, would do his business, and briefly for three reasons. Defeat, peremptory and conclusive, alone would drive Austria out of Germany and extort the recognition not of Prussia's parity with herself —the time for that had passed—but of Prussian supremacy; Prussian supremacy in Germany required territorial additions to the Prussian State (not merely Schleswig and Holstein), without which her mastery of the new German organisation would be incomplete, and such annexations could only be secured from the defeated and justified by victory in war : the constitutional conflict in Prussia and the terms of the new organisation could only be settled if the Prussian monarchy could dictate its will ; war alone, not diplomacy, would confer the dictatorship. It was not in 1865 any more than in 1864 or in 1870 the end—the unification of Germany on certain principles and for certain ends—justifying the means. To Bismarck the State, whose end is Power, does not justify the means, that are Force. More correctly, the means are simply the end in process of realisation. The stages through which the purposive life of an organised community passes, he would have argued, are not means to an end, they are the successive manifestations of the purpose. Each successive manifestation is linked with the preceding one, and the sum of the manifestations is not separable from the end, and does not require a justification different from that for the totality of the result. What justifies life as a whole justifies its successive manifestations or means of realising itself, and no other justification is admissible or necessary. Had Bismarck desired or conceived of a unified Germany consummating the National State which stands for Right, his methods would have been as different as the result would have differed from the Prussia and Germany he created. But then he would not have been the Bismarck of history, and his interpretation of life-values would have been the opposite of what it was. The impressive conclusions that his action has stamped *ferro et igni* on the Germany and Europe of his generation are two—first, that when a strong State is determined to find in war a solution of political difficulties and will accept no other solution, war will result, however unwilling other States may be to go to war; and secondly, that while the Germany of 1865 (and Bismarck knew it) did not want the Bismarckian solution, the Germany of 1890 had been convinced by Bismarck that no other solution in 1866 would have succeeded or satisfied what Germany had been taught to recognise as her real ambitions and needs. The one problem in statesmanship that Bismarck did not solve for his or any other generation before or since his time, and had no desire to solve, was how to defeat the statecraft (that is force) of the State (that stands for power) without recourse to force or without repudiating the principle that the State stands for Right not Might, or without accepting the poison distilled in the doctrine that ends justify means.

As previously, his first and permanent difficulty lay with his sovereign. William's education by his minister in the gospel of Bismarckianism had to begin over again after August 1865. Once his sovereign's ' conscience ' had been reilluminated, the King would readily misinterpret the appeal of military honour as the categorical imperative of royal and civic duty.

The Liberal opposition in the Prussian Landtag must, therefore, be provoked to continue its attacks on the Crown and its advisers. Surrender, therefore, would be surrender to ' rebels.' As on June 13 (before Gastein), so on February 3, 1866, when there were full-dress debates on the foreign policy of the government, Bismarck taunted the Progressive leaders with their political futility, ineptitude, and parliamentary insolence. Their criticisms on the conduct of affairs he dismissed as the interference of ignorant trespassers on the prerogatives of the Crown. This autocratic attitude in ' The House of Phrases ' was largely tactical. Not there, but in France and Italy, were the keys of the major political strategy.

Italy, in August 1865, had signified that it was impossible for her in a Prusso-Austrian war to remain an idle spectator. A Prussian alliance with Italy was dangerous ; committal to the Italian programme opened serious questionings ; behind Florence lay Rome and the Papal problem. The year 1864 had seen the issue of the famous Syllabus which seriously perturbed the intellectuals of German Liberalism and heated the Clericals in South Germany and in France. The parties in Germany were, in fact, marching to the *Kulturkampf.* Bismarck rightly feared that Napoleon might, in his resentment at a Prussian treaty with Italy behind his back, come to terms with Austria, secure Venetia for Italy, in return for compensation in Germany to Austria at Prussia's expense, and compensation to himself in the Rhenish provinces. The possibility of an anti-Prussian coalition was no idle chimera of an overstrained mind in the Wilhelmstrasse. Had there been a statesman of the first rank either at Paris, Florence, or Vienna, a very ugly turn indeed could have been given to the situation. As it was, Bismarck had to deal with Napoleon, Drouyn de Lhuys, La Marmora, and Mensdorff. The price that nations pay when their destinies are in the hands of the intellectually second-rate is set out with damning precision in the next four years.

Napoleon had to be brought to a definite understanding. On October 1 Bismarck was in Paris, and on October 3 at Biarritz—the third of three momentous visits. By November 7 he was back in Berlin. He had threshed out the difficulties both in the Villa Eugénie at Biarritz, and at St. Cloud with Napoleon and his ministers, and had virtually accomplished the difficult task of securing Napoleon's benevolent neutrality, without any awkward promissory notes, which could be presented for payment at sight at some future date. Prosper Mérimée has put on record his personal impression of the Minister-President—of his vigour and power and also of his irresistible charm (a quality we are apt to forget Bismarck possessed in a remarkable degree). But even in 1865 Mérimée did not take seriously the political ideas that Bismarck expressed with such disarming and genial exuberance. Like Napoleon, Mérimée thought the Minister-President was sometimes really not quite sane, a Prussian Gascon whose judgment was clouded by a misinterpretation of realities. These momentous conferences at the Villa Eugénie provide a dramatic contrast between the Prussian, in the zenith of his physical and intellectual powers, alert, adamantine, probing every weak point, and masking it all under an amazing frankness—and, on the other side, the Emperor, tired, puzzled, disillusioned, indecisive, yet clinging to his dreams which he mistook for profound insight into the Time-spirit. He was already suffering from the disease that killed him; already conscious that the noonday of the Empire had passed and that the shadows were falling, the shadows that came from the *coup d'État*.

Why Napoleon did not insist on a bargain in black and white, and on pinning Bismarck down to a definite compensation, is, indeed, a problem. Napoleon had a definite article to sell, French neutrality, which the purchaser, Bismarck, needed above all things. The experience of 1864 should have convinced the Emperor that he was dealing with a man whose verbal promises were worthless, and he should not have parted with French neutrality except for a bond in writing. Even if, as is probable, Bismarck had later repudiated the bond, Napoleon would have had it to convince France and Europe. Napoleon, it is true, was in a grave dilemma. He feared that Bismarck, foiled at Paris, might settle with Austria and re-establish the Triple Alliance of 1815 against France. The obvious reply to such a menace was a threat to unite with Austria and her South German Allies against Prussia. But the real crux for Napoleon lay, as always, in Italy. The Clericals would not let him evacuate Rome, and his own 'nationalism' drove him to desire to complete the work of 1859 by procuring Venetia for the kingdom of Italy. It was not so much that Napoleon did not know what compensation he really wanted as that he could not openly ask for it—the left bank of the Rhine or Belgium. The former brought him up against the dead wall of Prussia—the latter against the dead wall of Great Britain and the Treaty of 1839. Napoleon therefore postponed the decision. His 'compensation' was to be defined later. He trusted in his 'star' and on his calculation that a Prusso-Austrian War would be a bloody and indecisive struggle, in which France could intervene and dictate her compensation either on both combatants or on one by allying with the other. But the idea rested on two fatal errors of judgment, which Napoleon shared with most contemporary statesmen in Europe—an exaggerated estimate of Austrian strength and of the readiness of the French army—a complete ignorance of the Prussian army as remoulded by the Prussian General Staff. Bismarck and Moltke were in complete agreement that if Prussia could not make war she had better go out of business altogether.

Italy was now invited by Bismarck to conclude a commercial alliance with the Zollverein. Such an economic understanding, Bismarck told the Italian ambassador, would have a high political significance for the future. The negotiations were pressed, and by November 15 the treaty was ready for the respective ratifications (March 3, 1866).

The next step was to put the screw on Austria. Austria, of course, was 'behaving very badly' in Holstein —she was permitting the Augustenburg agitation to go on with Kiel as its headquarters. This was a plain violation of the Convention of Gastein, disturbing to Prussia in her occupation of Schleswig, and keeping open a sore that the Convention had healed. On January 26, 1866, Bismarck sent a rasping protest to Vienna. The Austrian administration of Holstein was intolerable ; the Augustenburg agitation must be promptly suppressed. Austria was making herself ' the champion of the Revolution.' The Austrian reply of February 9 informed the Prussian government that the alliance of 1864 was at an end. The position had reverted to the period before the Danish war, and Austrian relations with Prussia were neither better nor worse than with any other European Power. On February 28 a secret Council of State was held in Berlin at which the Crown Prince, the military chiefs, the Prussian ambassador at Paris, Goltz, specially summoned, and, of course, Bismarck and the King, were present. William decided that every diplomatic effort compatible with Prussian honour and safety must be made to maintain peace. ' After having prayed to God,' the King said, ' to lead him in the right path, he should consider the war, if it came, as a just one.'

On March 3 William wrote personally to Napoleon to propose a definite understanding ; next day the project of an offensive and defensive alliance with Italy was taken seriously in hand. At the Council of February 28, Moltke had expressed his considered judgment that with the neutrality of France, the military aid of Italy, and the consequent division of the Austrian army by war on two fronts, victory might be regarded as reasonably certain. With General Govone, sent from Florence, Bismarck now worked hard to conclude the Italian treaty. Not without great difficulty. Both sides thoroughly distrusted each other. The Italians, mindful of 1859, feared that Prussia would embroil them with Austria, and then either evade its share or settle the German quarrel at Italy's expense. Nor had they any confidence in Bismarck's honesty or honour. Bismarck, on his side, suspected that Italy intended to utilise Prussia simply to obtain Venetia, and was quite indifferent to the real issue—Prussian supremacy in Germany : he desired to tie Italy down to a specific engagement while leaving a free hand for himself. The project very nearly broke down on the crucial point, which of the partners was to pick the quarrel and open the fray. Each desired the other to make a war, in which its ally would then promptly join. But the difficulties were surmounted. Both Italy and Prussia needed each other too much to allow the negotiations to end in nothing. On April 8 the treaty was finished. It provided that, if a Prussian reform of the Germanic Confederation failed and Prussia was forced to take up arms, Italy was to declare war ; there was to be no peace or armistice without the consent of both States, but consent was not to be withheld if Venetia were ceded to Italy and an equivalent in Austrian territory to Prussia ; the Italian navy was to hinder the Austrian ships from reaching the Baltic ; and the treaty was to be valid only for three months unless Prussia declared war.

The treaty imposed on Italy obligations but no rights. It did not specifically provide for Prussian help if Austria declared war on Italy and kept the peace in Germany. But it secured three vital guarantees for Prussia. It made the *casus fœderis* dependent on the German question of Federal reform by Prussia (that was for William's conscience) ; it blocked Napoleon as protector of Italy from hostilities with Prussia (that was for the Tuileries) ; it reserved to Prussia the right to make war, when and if it chose (that was for Bismarck). Bismarck, in fact, was in a similar position to Cavour after the compact of Plombières. He had to provoke war within a definite period or lose the advantages of the treaty.

The international situation was thus cleared up, for Napoleon had replied to William's letter with an assurance of neutrality, the compensation for which was to be defined later—always later. Bismarck might well reflect on royal human nature, when he recalled that ten years earlier his master at Coblenz had repudiated, as a dishonourable temptation, the proposal that Prussia should come to terms with Napoleon, and had pronounced such an idea to be that of a schoolboy not a statesman

William's personal letter to the 'man of sin' recalls Maria Theresa's letter to the 'woman of sin,' the Pompadour, in each case to secure an alliance in order to annex. To what concessions will not 'conscience' compel honourable and royal men and women.

Austria had replied to the Council of February 28 at Berlin by a week of State Councils at Vienna (March 7-13), at which Benedek, who had prepared his army and campaigns in Venetia, was present. Poor, gallant Benedek, presently to be transferred from Venetia to Bohemia, in order that an archduke might win in Italy, while the general, assigned to command in a Bohemia that he did not know an ill-organised army that did not know him, was to be broken for his failure—the scapegoat's last services to the incompetence of a selfish dynasty. Such were the sacrifices that the Habsburgs expected and obtained from their best servants.

The Italian negotiations justifiably alarmed Austria : they caused consternation in the Conservative, fierce indignation in the Ultramontane, camp in Germany. Prussia had allied with 'the Revolution' at Florence, was playing fast and loose with 'the Revolution' at Paris, and was about to plunge Germany in civil war by a blow at Austria, the champion alike of Conservative and monarchical principles and of the Roman Catholic cause. The Italian treaty filled the cup of Bismarck's iniquities fuller than Germany suspected, for Bismarck had the audacity to assert on April 5 that it was far from the intention of the King to take active measures against Austria.[1] His next step, the Conservatives predicted, would be to proclaim 'the Revolution' in Germany.

[1] Still more remarkable is Gramont's telegram (June 11, 1866) to his government that the Queen of Prussia had written to the Emperor of Austria that the King of Prussia had given his word of honour that he had not concluded a treaty with Italy, and that the ministerial convention left him entire liberty to conclude a pacific settlement with Austria. Drouyn de Lhuys replied to Gramont that he knew the Prusso-Italian treaty bore the signature of King William. The accuracy of Gramont's telegram, denied by Sybel, is apparently accepted by the editors of Les Origines Diplomatiques de la Guerre de 1870, vol. x. p. 117. See their notes on the documents printed by them and also Ollivier's narrative in L'Empire Libéral, vol. viii. p. 169 et seq.

And it was. On April 9, the day after Italy had been secured, the Prussian representative brought forward in the Federal Diet an official resolution of the Prussian government for the reform of the Confederation. A national German Parliament elected by universal suffrage was to discuss with representatives of the States and dynasties the establishment of a new Constitution for Germany, from which it was implied Austria was to be excluded. The 'drop of democratic oil,' distilled not at Frankfurt but at Berlin, was to anoint a German Crown for the King of Prussia. It was the ideal of 1848 disinterred from the grave over which Bismarck in 1849 had read the burial service according to the use of Junkertum. The proposal was an ultimatum to Austria and the middle States. The issues of the Convention of Gastein had been transformed by a stroke of the reformer's pen into a battle for the future of Germany and the settlement of the German problem. Prussia challenged the Congress of Princes with an appeal, not to the middle-class Liberals of the National Verein, but to the democracy of Germany. She had Russia as her friend, Italy as an ally, France benevolently neutral—and the Prussian army. There was indeed a method in the madness of 'the madman of Biarritz.'

What friends or allies had Austria ? None of her own house, and in Germany only the dynasties and their disorganised armies. To Prince Hohenlohe's private comments in his Diary on the military chaos in the middle States the Prussian General Staff could have supplied precise footnotes.

It only remained to let loose 'the Revolution' in Europe. Napoleon's speech at Auxerre (May 8), in answer to a bitter attack of Thiers in the Corps Législatif on the foreign policy of the Empire, proclaimed his detestation of the treaties of 1815 and the impossibility of regarding them as a·permanent basis of the foreign relations of France and her position in Europe. An expectant France, a bewildered Germany—in hubbub over the Prussian proposals for Federal reform—and an alarmed Europe read the words as foreshadowing a French

onslaught to secure the left bank of the Rhine. But, unlike
Bismarck, Napoleon at cross-purposes with his ministers,
themselves divided in opinion, excited France and alarmed
Europe by proclaiming his ambitions from the mountain-
tops before he had considered whether he could or would
carry them into execution. And in Napoleon's mind at this
moment the lights and shadows were changing as rapidly
as the tints in a Highland sunset that precedes a
storm.

March, April, and May—the preludes to the great
war—were marked by snowstorms of diplomatic notes,
recriminations and counter-recriminations, mobilisations
and counter-mobilisations, and proposals and counter-
proposals for a settlement that would avert hostilities.
On April 21 Austria mobilised in the south against Italy.
The suggestion that Prussia should suspend her war preparations if Austria would do the like was met by Bismarck's
firm demand that the Austrian demobilisation must be
complete ; she must cease to threaten Italy as well as
Prussia. And the proposal broke down. Benevolent
intermediaries were prolific in schemes for a general exchange of territories. It was suggested that Austria should
cede Venetia to Italy and annex as compensation the
Danubian principalities, where a revolution had broken
out. But the acceptance against his father's wish of the
princedom by Prince Charles of Hohenzollern-Sigmaringen
(after an interview with Bismarck) and his rapid departure
for Bucharest checkmated the proposal, and placed, to the
disgust of France and of Austria, a Hohenzollern sentinel
beyond the Carpathians in charge of the destinies of a
Latin race.

Baron von Gablenz drew up an elaborate scheme for a
reconstruction of Germany under the divided leadership
of Prussia and Austria in a reformed Federal Constitution.
The Duchies of Schleswig and Holstein were to be placed
under a Prussian prince, while Prussia was to annex Kiel
and liberally indemnify Austria with a money payment.
But all such schemes, including variants on the idea of
ceding Silesia to Austria in return for the Duchies and the
cession of Venetia to Italy, have only a melancholy interest ;

they reveal an earnest desire for peace in many quarters, marred by a complete incapacity, as is usually the case, to realise the policy of Prussia and the will of her directors. Had Austria consented to withdraw from Holstein, and to give Prussia a free hand to reorganise a new Federal system, in which Austria renounced all membership, war might have been averted. But the opportunity for an imaginative statesmanship based on recognition of Prussia's primacy in North Germany, and on a wholly new conception of Austria's future and position in Central Europe, had passed with the Convention of Gastein. A great State such as Austria still was, with her historic traditions and imperial memories, could not abandon her allies in the German middle and petty States and renounce her past in the spring of 1866 at the threat of a Prussian mobilisation. The Federal Revolution engineered by Prussia was fatal to her German presidency. In April and May Bismarck's one fear was that war might be averted at the eleventh hour. Early in May Austria made a desperate effort to detach Italy by the offer of Venetia, through Napoleon, in return for Italian neutrality. Had the offer been made in January before the Italian treaty with Prussia had been concluded, it would have saved the situation. Sorely tempted, La Marmora refused. Italy was in honour bound to stand by her treaty. Well might Bismarck bid Govone good-bye with the words, ' To our meeting in Vienna ! '

Still more serious was Napoleon's next step. With Russian and British approval the Emperor formally proposed a Congress—magic word—to discuss in particular the three burning questions—Schleswig-Holstein, Venetia, and German Federal reform. Bismarck was in a grave dilemma for a Congress spelled the ruin of his policy. Nevertheless with a heavy heart he accepted, trusting to his goddess Fortune. And she did not desert him. Austria accepted also, but with the categorical reservation that the participating great Powers must renounce in advance all territorial aggrandisement. The reservation reduced the proposed Congress to impotence. The neutral Powers promptly withdrew their support. Benedetti was with

Bismarck when the telegram announcing the abandonment came in. The Minister-President sprang to his feet. ' It is war,' he cried : ' Long live the King ! '

His universal unpopularity had been checked by an attempt at assassination by Cohen-Blind in Unter den Linden on May 7. The prospect of war had stirred the military spirit in Prussia ; and next evening Bismarck received a great ovation from an excited crowd outside the Foreign Office. The tide of public opinion indeed was turning. It only needed some Prussian victories to set it swirling as fiercely in Bismarck's favour as it had hitherto run against him. Freed from the nightmare of a Congress, Bismarck now forced Austria to fight. He declared that Prussia, in consequence of the termination of the Convention of Gastein, had as much right to Holstein as to Schleswig. The Prussian troops were ordered to enter Holstein (June 6). The Austrians retired without resisting, as Bismarck had desired. A further provocation was therefore necessary. On June 10 Bismarck communicated to the Federal Diet a precise scheme of Federal reform explicitly excluding Austria and Luxemburg from all membership in the new organisation to be created. Next day the Austrian plenipotentiary pressed the Diet for a mobilisation of the Federal forces, with the exception of Prussia, on the ground that Prussia had violated the Treaty of Vienna and the Federal Constitution. In other words, Prussia was to be the subject of a Federal execution. The vote was taken on June 14, and the Austrian proposal accepted by nine votes to six. Baden abstained ; three *curiæ* only voted with Prussia—some of the petty States of the north and the cities of Hamburg, Lübeck, and Bremen : the rest voted with Austria. The Prussian representative at once declared that his government considered the Confederation at an end, and the sitting was raised.

On June 16, after a peremptory ultimatum, the Prussian troops entered Saxony, Hesse-Cassel, and Hanover ; on June 20 Italy declared war on Austria. Bismarck's fate and the future of Prussia were now in the hands of the military chiefs and the Prussian army. ' It is,' says Sybel, the one great and simple feature of the Prussian govern-

ment that at last it has always been the material and actual
considerations that have preponderated.' The King in his
Proclamation of June 18 asserted that ' as known to my
people and to God, Who sees the heart,' the war was a
defensive one, thrust upon him, in defence of Prussia's
honour, independence, and existence. But Moltke told
the simple truth (and gave the lie to his sovereign) when
in a few chiselled sentences he declared subsequently that
' The war of 1866 did not take place because the existence
of Prussia was threatened, or in obedience to public opinion
or to the will of the people. It was a war which was foreseen long before, which was prepared with deliberation
and recognised as necessary by the Cabinet, not in order to
obtain territorial aggrandisement, but in order to secure
the establishment of Prussian hegemony in Germany.'
Bismarck might be satisfied with his power to convert
He, too, now opened his Bible and read Psalm ix. 3-5
which greatly comforted him. Yet he also wrote with
perfect sincerity : ' We have good confidence, but we mus
not forget that Almighty God is very capricious (*seh*
launenhaft).' He recognised that he had thrown the iro
dice in a tremendous gamble, and that fate or fortun
might refuse the prize. At Königgrätz in those critica
hours when the Crown Prince and his army had not ye
appeared to turn the Austrian flank, it is related that Bis
marck reflected bitterly how for four years he had toile
to secure the international situation that victory required
and had succeeded beyond all expectation, and now thes
infernal generals were going to make a mess of it. He ha
decided that if victory fell to the Austrians he would di
in the last charge—a more probable resolve than the othe
he is credited with, that he would offer Napoleon the le
bank of the Rhine and call out the Revolution in German
He realised fully that to Germany he appeared a desperat
gambler. ' Had I failed,' he told the Reichstag later, ' th
old women would have swept me with a curse and the
besoms from the streets.'

The generals did not make a mess of it, nor did th
Prussian army fail them. The crowning mercy of Köni
grätz (July 3) was, as Roon said, the gift of the Prussia

soldier quite as much as of the Prussian higher command. Bismarck's inmost thought was revealed in his remark: ' The struggle is decided—the task is now to win back the old friendship with Austria.' A week later he wrote to his wife : ' Things go well ; if we do not exaggerate our demands, and do not believe that we have conquered the world, we shall get a peace worth the efforts we have made. But we are as easily intoxicated as we are depressed, and I have the thankless task of pouring water into the foaming wine, and bringing home the truth that we do not live alone in Europe, but with three neighbours.' The long strain, the concentrated excitement, the renewed pressure of multitudinous affairs, and the additional task of dealing with an elated King and triumphant generals, seriously affected his health. During the campaign Bismarck was really ill ; nothing but his superb constitution and his iron will kept him from a grave collapse. But intensely irritable and overwrought though he was, his judgment retained its mastery. ' The appreciation and import of military victory,' he said, with great truth, ' at the moment of its decision is one of the hardest tasks that statecraft imposes.'

The chief obstacles to the settlement that Bismarck desired were two : first, Napoleon ; secondly, his sovereign and the soldiers. Time is the one power with which statesmanship and strategy trifle at great peril. The longer the campaign lasted, the easier it would be for the European Powers to intervene with effect. The argument for a European Congress was indeed strong. The war had torn a great rent in the treaties and system of 1815. The signatory European Powers had as clear a right as, and an even clearer interest than, in 1856 or 1878 to insist on reviewing and completing the system to be substituted for the wrecked fabric. But Bismarck was absolutely determined to refuse either the arbitration of neutrals, or the revision of a Congress. Rather than submit to either, he was ready to provoke a general war. Fortunately for him Great Britain was in the throes of an internal struggle, far more interested in Franchise Bills than in the fate of Austria or Germany ; Poland and Schleswig-Holstein had been severe lessons in the futility of intervention, unless backed by ships, men, and guns. Russia under the mortgage created by Bismarck in 1863, was neither willing nor able to fight on Austria's behalf, was no less willing to let Napoleon have a severe snubbing, and was soon satisfied that Prussia did not intend to let loose democracy and Liberalism in Germany. Napoleon was the one grave difficulty, and Bismarck grasped at once that if he could satisfy or convert William I. to his idea of a settlement, he could deal with Napoleon.

The eleven days from July 11, when Benedetti suddenly appeared to Bismarck's intense anger at the headquarters at Zwittau, to July 22, when the armistices of Nikolsburg opened the discussion of preliminaries of peace, are packed with feverish telegrams, to and fro; but the principles of Bismarck's diplomacy stand out as clear and unwavering as in the months preceding the war.

'The world is collapsing,' said Cardinal Antonelli, watching the issues from an Ultramontane Vatican. 'It is France that is beaten at Sadowa,' pronounced Thiers with prophetic accuracy. Extraordinary as it now seems, Napoleon had concluded a secret treaty with Austria (June 12). Napoleon undertook to be neutral in the German war; Austria undertook for an equivalent in Germany to cede Venetia to Napoleon, and all changes in Italy or Germany, 'of a nature to disturb the European equilibrium,' were to be made by Austria and France in concert. Striking, indeed, that the curse of the later Bourbons, the secret diplomacy of Louis xv. against the declared policy, and behind the back, of the royal minister, should be repeated by the dynasty that claimed to represent the true France, that Bourbon dynasticism had ruined. The cunning of the Carbonaro was always unpicking by night the flimsy web of *les idées Napoléoniennes* woven in the day at the Tuileries. Napoleon, therefore, had faced the future with the assurance that he had bargained with both sides and was committed to neither. But the statesman who has failed to be ready for the collapse of his calculations commits against his country a graver crime than the general who plans an offensive for victory without providing the line of retreat in the case of failure.

On July 4 Napoleon suddenly found himself in a terrible position. France eagerly awaited the *coup de maître*, but the ulcer of Mexico had drained the military resources of the Empire ; the artillery lacked horses and armament, and the army was not ready ; the possible allies in Germany— the anti-Prussian States, Hanover, Saxony, Württemberg, Bavaria, Hesse—were in as poor a military way as France herself, and would be crushed before France could assist them ; national passion had flamed up, white-hot, in Prussia ; a neutral observer noted that in all classes there was one fierce conviction—' no French, no rotten peace.' Austria was on the verge of collapse, and Napoleon himself had no plan for immediate action. Worst of all, prostrating pain made him incapable of clear thought or prompt decision. The fate of France turned—that is the penalty of all autocracies, imperial or otherwise, at all crises—on the character and capacity of a single man ; and in those July days, that flooded the gardens of the Tuileries and the Champs Elysées, the orchards of Normandy, and the vineyards of the Garonne with their mocking sunshine, the decision had to come from a ruler tortured all his life by the disease of indecision, tortured now by physical agony. ' A grain of sand in a man's flesh and empires rise and fall.'

Napoleon at this point really did not know what he wanted ; he only knew that he did not want war and could not wage it. Bismarck knew precisely what he wanted ; he was ready to wage war, and knew how to do it. It difficult to judge what Napoleon should have done. Austria, Saxony, Hesse-Cassel were clamouring for the Emperor to intervene and save them. Thiers and every critic of the Empire were waiting to drive home the proof of their accusations ; Ultramontanes and Clericals, his only true if selfish supporters in France, were in consternation Austria's downfall. His ministers were as divided as their imperial master. The weak man who acts on the principle that ' something must be done ' is sure to do the wrong thing, and it is certain that Napoleon now did it.[1]

Bismarck was in a very ugly temper, with his back to the wall, fighting both with his sovereign and the military chiefs. 'Louis shall pay for it,' he exclaimed, when Napoleon's ambassador, Benedetti, unexpectedly appeared. For he neither forgave nor forgot those who acted on his own principle of applying the thumbscrews to an adversary in difficulties. Bismarck, indeed, at first, and not unnaturally, exaggerated both Napoleon's military readiness and his desire to press mediation at the point of the sword. The unfortunate Benedetti, however, was in no position to apply the thumbscrews. Bismarck made it quite plain that, first, he would not tolerate mediation in the sense of definition of the terms of peace by Napoleon; secondly, that no matter what the terms with Austria were, Napoleon could not have one inch of German territory as compensation; thirdly, that if Napoleon persisted in the idea of an armed mediation Prussia would take up the challenge. Moltke was ready with his plan of campaign. He would close the march on Vienna, assume the defensive in Bohemia, face front to the Rhine, and take the offensive on that line. The Chief of the Staff was confident that he could open the western offensive with a victorious Prussian army before Napoleon had mobilised and deployed the French army, and the Chief of the Staff did not promise what he could not perform. Incidentally the transference of the major forces of Prussia to the western theatre would crush the South German States into pulp. Bismarck went further. He warned Paris that he was

---

[1] On July 4 he telegraphed to King William announcing that Venetia had been placed in his hands by Austria, and demanding an armistice and negotiations, under his mediation, invited by Austria. On July 5 he rescinded his decision to summon the chambers and intervene as an armed mediator. On July 6 he formally requested Great Britain and Russia to support 'avec force' the proposed French mediation. On July 7 he ordered Benedetti to go to the Prussian headquarters and demand an answer to the telegram of July 4. From July 7 to July 14 Napoleon wavered between doing nothing, mobilising, negotiating between Austria and her German allies, despatching a French squadron to the North Sea, and harassing Victor Emmanuel with requests. On July 13 he received Goltz, and on the 14th accepted his terms. *C'est un cochon* said Victor Emmanuel when he received the telegram of July 4.

ready to call out revolution in Hungary,[1] even make peace on any terms with Austria, and then not crush the South German States, but demand their aid in a war of a united Germany against France—France that asked for the left bank of the Rhine alike from Bavaria and Prussia. This was not diplomatic rhodomontade, nor the exuberant defiance of Prussian Junkertum. Bismarck had not plunged Prussia into war merely to defeat Austria, but to lay the basis of a unified Germany under Prussian leadership. The scheme of June 10 presented to the dissolved Federal Diet and modelled on the revolutionary Liberalism of 1849 was not Prussian blackmail to a German democracy whom he intended to dupe. Through the smoke of Königgrätz the eyes of faith could see already the dim lines and shadowy shapes of a united Germany to come— with dreadful faces thronged and fiery arms.

Prussia, however, must not now embrace more of Germany than she could assimilate. The postponement of the ideal unity would assure to Germany within and without the driving power and the inspiration necessary to overcome the cold reaction that would certainly follow the war of 1866. Bismarck could probably have written out on June 1 his idea of a settlement—the exclusion of Austria from Germany, the annexation of Schleswig and Holstein, the formation of a Federal system under Prussia north of the Main, incorporating ' enemy territories ' (and the extinction of their dynasties) sufficient to secure an assured Prussian preponderance, the separation of the South German States, in an organisation of their own, but connected with the North by treaty arrangements, the ' gift ' of Venetia to Italy which would make Austria a purely Danubian State, and facilitate her dependence on the central German State. It was not by pure chance or for wholly military reasons that Hesse-Cassel, Saxony, and Hanover were selected for ultimatums on June 15. Their ' conquest ' was a political necessity to Prussia. Details

---

[1] On June 10 (before war was declared) he had seen at Berlin General Türr from Hungary and discussed the possibility of a Hungarian insurrection. They knew this at Paris, because Bismarck on June 11 suggested Türr should go to Paris and discuss the matter with the Emperor, through the mediation of Prince Napoleon.

could be left to the stage of negotiations, but the broad framework was in his mind before the war, and he adhered to it in all the complicated discussions of peace. King William at General Headquarters was in a fine moral and military indignation. The uric acid of Prussianism inherited by every Hohenzollern sovereign had attacked both his head and his heart. God was on his side ; and it was his duty to chastise Austria and the German princes for their presumption and wickedness in forcing war on peace-loving Prussia. The soldier chiefs—Moltke and Roon perhaps to a less extent—desired to make a clean business of the job and to keep Bismarck ' in his place.' But Bismarck would not be kept ' in his place.' He submitted a programme of peace—not a yard of Austrian territory, no annexations north of the Main, no depositions save in the territories necessary to secure a Prussian hegemony of the North. The proposal angered the King and the military chiefs. On July 7 the march on Vienna was resumed. Bismarck had threatened his sovereign with European complications to no purpose. He now opened a discussion with Austria ; but—a more decisive stroke—proceeded to threaten Napoleon with William I. Goltz conveyed to the Emperor the substance of Bismarck's scheme, with the veiled menace that mediation would be rejected unless the terms were accepted at once. Austria was to be expelled from Germany ; Prussia was to have a free hand in the North ; France would not be faced and hemmed in by a united German Empire, for the Southern States were to be excluded from the new confederation Prussia in the north would be balanced by an intact Austria (save for the cession of Venetia to Italy) and Southern Germany. The Prussian annexations were not specifically mentioned. Napoleon, to the indignation of his ministers accepted them later as ' mere matters of detail.' As a special concession to Napoleon, Saxony was not to be annexed, but to enter the new North German Confederation intact. Napoleon meekly accepted the proposal (July 14) and then transmitted them as his own to Austria and to Bismarck, who had inspired Goltz. M. Paul Matter's comment puts it concisely : ' Napoléon préten dant jouer le rôle de médiateur, il s'agissait de dresser un acte de médiation . . . Napoléon III., Empereur des Français, en laissa le soin à l'ambassadeur prussien. " C'est un fait rare dans les annales de la diplomatie " constate l'histoire officiel de l'Empire allemand : nul jugement ne peut être plus sévère que cette froide constatation.' Drouyn de Lhuys' comment was no less to the point. ' Maintenant il ne nous reste plus qu'à pleurer.'

Armed with this surrender of Napoleon, Bismarck was able to withdraw from Austria the more favourable terms he had previously (July 15) suggested. The Austrian acceptance had come just an hour too late. Better still, he now presented his royal master with an ultimatum. Acceptance of ' Napoleon's terms' would secure peace at once ; refusal meant the prolongation of the war, the possibility of French and neutral intervention and the hazarding of all gains of any kind. William consented,[1] after a prolonged struggle, in which Bismarck insisted on resigning, if his policy was rejected. Military head-quarters was on the King's side, but Bismarck found an unexpected ally in the Crown Prince. On July 22 an armistice was arranged ; on July 26 the preliminaries were signed, and ratified on the 28th.

It remained to settle with Napoleon. Hard pressed by Drouyn de Lhuys, the Emperor consented to renew the demand for compensation. The episode is instruc-tive, not so much in Napoleon's amazing weakness as in

---

[1] The dramatic narrative in Bismarck's Memoirs has been severely criticised by German and French scholars. Lenz, Marcks, Oncken, Philippson, Egel-haaf and Matter have pointed out the impossibility of reconciling the dates and assertions of Bismarck with the documentary and other evidence, and it is certain that Bismarck has both misdated and transposed in notable particulars the order of events. It is difficult to believe that he can have invented the famous scene in which the Crown Prince intervened. It is no less certain from the contemporary evidence of Bismarck's and Roon's correspondence, from the Memoirs of Stosch, Govone, Bernhardi, Abeken, Ernest of Coburg and other sources, that (a) Bismarck had prolonged difficulties lasting over a fortnight with the King and the military chiefs ; (b) that the King consented with great reluctance ; (c) the intervention of the Crown Prince on Bismarck's side was very influential. William and the soldiers desired in particular the capture of, or entry into, Vienna, and the annexation of all or most of royal Saxony (demanded and refused in 1814), together with Franconia, the cradle of the Hohenzollerns, to be ceded by Bavaria, and a heavier chastisement of Austria.

Bismarck's methods. Benedetti was foolish enough to write (August 5) to Bismarck, adding to his letter the *projet* of a secret convention. Bismarck then refused point blank (August 6) any concessions of German territory, and revealed the substance of the demand—the Rhenish provinces lost in 1815—and the explicit refusal to the French journal *Le Siècle*. Its publication proclaimed a fresh affront to the unhappy Emperor, prostrated at Vichy. Drouyn de Lhuys resigned ; the Southern States were furious, and Russia promptly abandoned the suggestion of a Congress. It would have been well had Napoleon remained content with the two severe rebuffs received since July 4. But encouraged by Goltz at Paris and other German agents of Bismarck's, the Emperor decided to demand Belgium—a demand Goltz asserted as ' legitimate in principle.' Once again the unfortunate Benedetti was instructed to submit in writing the project of a secret Convention (August 16) providing for the acquisition of Luxemburg and the armed aid of Prussia ' should the Emperor be required by circumstances to invade or conquer Belgium.' The document in Benedetti's handwriting was discussed in an interview with Bismarck, and amended (August 20). Nothing came of the demand except that Bismarck carefully retained Benedetti's original draft with the corrections inserted. The damning document now in his possession would be very useful some day when it was necessary to deprive France of the sympathie of Europe. And its subsequent reproduction in facsimile (July 25, 1870) in the official Gazette must have satisfied even Bismarck's implacable determination to punish those whom he had so completely duped. Napoleon in 186 could only fall back on a circular to France extolling her unity, moderation, and generosity in the crisis. 'C'est bon said a French agent, ' à calmer les estaminets de province

While the formal peace with Austria was being made Bismarck—a comparatively easy matter—was cleaning up the business by settling a series of peaces with the ' enemy ' German States. On August 2 hostilities were suspended in Germany and in Italy. Württemberg (August 13), Baden (August 17), Bavaria (August 22

Hesse-Darmstadt (September 3), obtained peace and the integrity of their territories on payment of an indemnity, except that the northern portion of Hesse was incorporated in the new Northern Confederation. Severally the Southern States agreed to renew the Tariff Union ; and to arrange in common with the north their railway system. Nothing seemed more generous or fair. But the generosity had been purchased by separate and secret treaties (*Schutz- und Trützbündnis*). These provided for mutual guarantees of territory, while in the event of war the troops of the contracting parties were to be united for common purposes, and placed under the command of the King of Prussia. In these negotiations Bismarck had confronted the Southern States with a confidential revelation, not minimised in the communication, of Napoleon's demands for compensation. He could satisfy Napoleon, if he chose, by acquiescing in the cession of Bavarian and Hessian territories to a France which the South had hoped to play off as a protector against Hohenzollern tyranny. The alternative was still more simple. Prussia in return for the signature of the secret military conventions would resist the cession of a single yard of German territory ; and if Napoleon, now or in the future, threatened Germany the Southern States would join with the Northern Confederation in a united resistance. The argument was irresistible. With the military conventions signed, sealed, and delivered, and Napoleon definitely disposed of, Bismarck could with an easy mind complete the formal treaty of peace that embodied the preliminaries of Nikolsburg.

The Treaty of Prague (August 23) opened a new chapter in the history of Prussia, of Austria, of Germany and of Europe. Austria agreed that the old Confederation should be dissolved and a new one, from which she was excluded, formed under Prussian leadership. The line of the river Main was fixed as the southern boundary of the new organisation. With the exception of Venetia, transferred, through Napoleon, to Italy, the integrity of the Austrian Empire was maintained. Schleswig-Holstein and Lauenburg were annexed by Prussia, while the Duke of Augustenburg subsequently abandoned his claims and

released his ' subjects ' from their allegiance. Napoleon
secured certain concessions. The kingdom of Saxony,
included in the Northern Confederation, retained its territorial integrity, and dynastic crown. The three Southern
States—Baden, Württemberg, Bavaria—and the southern
portion of Hesse-Darmstadt, were prohibited from entering the Northern Confederation, with which they could
make arrangements by treaty; retaining severally their
' international independence ' they were free to unite in
a separate confederation of their own. On the other
hand, Prussia was given a free hand in the North; and she
promptly prepared to annex Hanover, Nassau, Hesse-
Cassel, the northern portion of Hesse-Darmstadt, and the
former free city of Frankfurt, and to depose their several
ruling houses and governments. These annexations were
justified on the ground that the States in question had
made war as Prussia's enemies, and that ' by reason of their
geographical position they could embarrass Prussia beyond
the measure of their natural power.' In reality their
territories were required for military and strategic reasons,
and in order to secure for Prussia in the new Bund an overwhelming military, political, and economic predominance.
Bismarck desired also to teach a drastic lesson to dynastic
Particularism. Saxony had been spared to humour Napoleon, Austria and Russia, but the rulers of Hanover, Hesse,
and Nassau must be punished by extirpation. The new
League would contain no dynasty, other than the Saxon,
with either the tradition or the power of independence, and
Saxony after this object-lesson would give no trouble in the
future. In a word, Prussia emerged from the war enlarged
to the extent of some twenty-seven thousand square miles,
and four and a quarter million inhabitants. She had not
merely tightened her grip on the Rhine and consolidated
the connection between Berlin and her Rhenish acquisitions of 1815, but had secured an outlet to the North
Sea and the Baltic of supreme importance for the future.
The harbour of Kiel, in itself, was worth a king's ransom,
and the acquisition of Schleswig-Holstein with Lauenburg
would enable the canal from the Baltic to the North Sea—
so often planned in the middle of the century—to be

carried out as a Prussian enterprise. The sea-faring population of the Duchies would provide a splendid nucleus for the naval and mercantile marine that would complete Prussia's ambition to be a European Power on terms of equality with Great Britain and France.

The treaty was a signal triumph for Bismarck's statecraft of ' blood and iron.' Bismarck the man and Bismarck the statesman were now the foremost figures on the European stage, and behind Bismarck stood the new Prussia conscious of its strength. Prussia and the world were continuously reminded that fidelity to Prussian ideals was the secret of success. Prussia had saved herself by her efforts and Germany by her example. In 1867 Treitschke at Heidelberg as editor of the *Preussische Jahrbücher*, could begin to teach the lesson, driven home by his professoriate at Berlin (1874), that the Empire to come must be an extended Prussia. The clauses in the treaty which permitted the Southern States to form a separate union, and forbade the incorporation of that union or any member of it with the Northern Confederation were worthless. No treaty could destroy the intellectual, moral, and material bridges across the Main that a common German civilisation, embedded in a common speech, the intellectual fraternity of great German universities, and the economic bonds of an increasing trade aided by the tariff union, so richly provided, and the military bridges were already laid by the secret conventions. A German Empire was practically made by the Treaty of Prague. Its complete realisation in the future could only be prevented by destroying the framework which the Treaty of Prague had created. The first of these conditions was Prussia and Prussianism as Bismarck interpreted them.

But if the Treaty of Prague had gone a long way towards stamping on Germany a particular solution of the German problem—a solution which in 1862 had seemed so improbable as to be regarded as the fantasy of a political gambler—it had not solved the two formidable problems in foreign relations that the guaranteed form of German unification at once raised.

The new Germany, whether federal or unitary, whether

divided by an arbitrary line of demarcation, the river Main, or not, had to determine its attitude and policy towards a new Austria and an old France—an Austria, severed as the penalty of defeat from its historic membership in the German organisation, and with no historical or practical experience to inspire and direct either its policy, its status in the world of Europe, or its internal polity and framework—the old and undefeated France, whose flag flew at Metz and Strasburg, in whose heart the two most abiding and cherished convictions were the supremacy of France in Europe, and the peril embodied in a unified Germany. Thiers' indictment that Napoleon in 1866 had allowed the Empire of Charles v. to be revived was the phrase of a great phrase-maker, but it crystallised the fears of France in an epigram. For the Treaty of Prague, while most assuredly it did not threaten Europe with a revival of the Empire of Charles v., no less assuredly re-created for Germany and its neighbours the problem of Central Europe. On what principles, with what objects, and on what system of State life ought the territory between the Rhine and the Vistula, the Vosges and the Carpathians, to be politically organised ?

The Empire of Charles v. had attempted to solve that recurring riddle by the effort to re-adapt to the conditions of the Renaissance and the Age of Discovery the great mediæval conception of the unity of secular European Christendom under the continuance of the Holy Roman Empire of the German nation. The effort had collapsed with the rupture of the spiritual and moral unity of Europe, effected by the Reformation, and aggravated by the pressure of the territorial national State of which sixteenth-century France was the most potent expression on the Continent. Napoleon—the heir both of the Bourbons and the Revolution—had attempted to solve it by the practical abolition of Central Europe, the establishment of the Grand Empire Français of the West, resting on the alliance with the Eastern Empire of Russia and the allot-ment of the central area to a dismembered Prussia, an Austria expelled from Germany and cut off from the sea, and a League of the Rhine, militarily, economically, and politically dependent on the Empire of the West. Napoleon's structure was destroyed by Nationalism and sea-power in combination. The Congress of Vienna aimed at frustrating both Westernism and Centralism by a return to a modernised interpretation of the old theory of the Balance of Power. It remade a Germany that mirrored the European equilibrium ; it sustained the hegemony of a decentralised Austria, with a sub-centre of gravity at Berlin, as an effective counterpoise alike to Paris in the west and Petersburg in the east, and it revived the Concert of Europe. But the separation of Holland and Belgium, the unification of Italy, the renaissance of Prussia and the defeat of Austria had now wrecked the system of 1815. The problem re-emerged. What after Königgrätz was to be the new political framework of Central Europe ?

The Treaty of Prague did not register merely the substitution of Berlin for Vienna as the new nodal point of an old political system. That old system had explicitly rejected the unified national State as the framework of Central Europe. The unification of Italy was a victory for the national State ; and it was with the aid of the Italy made by Cavour and Napoleon, that Bismarck administered the *coup de grâce* to the wounded Austria of 1859. The removal of Austria left the central site clear for the erection of a national German State, the essence of which lay in the assumption that Central Europe belonged to the German race and must be so organised as to put the claim beyond question. The Italy of Cavour's policy combined Liberalism—government through representative institutions, ministerial responsibility, and a constitutional monarchy—with Nationalism—Nationalism as the foundation of the State that is Law and Right. But the Prussia that had annexed Schleswig-Holstein, absorbed Hanover, Nassau, and electoral Hesse, and defeated Austria was the State that is Power, whose organ is Force. And in the profound difference between these two expressions of Nationalism—the Italian and the Prussian—lay the deep significance of the emergence of the old problem of Central Europe. The doctrine of race in Germany had combined not with the gospel of Law but with the gospel of Power. The problem for Bismarck—the problem of Central Europe—was how to impose the new national German State, based on power, on the European system, and how to remodel that system to admit the new Germany. There now lay before him the task of internal reconstruction—the making of the new confederation— and the task of reconstructing Europe on the results of the victory of 1866.

The constitution of the new Germany must assist the solution of the problem imposed on foreign policy. The new Germany must be national in form and structure, but it could not be constitutional, parliamentary, or liberal, as England or Italy interpreted constitutional and liberal government. Nor could the new Germany realise its ambitions without a new orientation for Austria and a drastic alteration in the status and power of France. Not until Austria had transferred its centre of gravity (as he had predicted in 1864) to Buda-Pesth and accepted the rôle of a Danubian State, with a front facing to the south-east of Europe; not until France had been reduced to subordination in the west could the new Central Europe, with Berlin as its capital, be completed. Such a solution would be a fresh and decisive victory for the principles, enshrined in Prussian Nationalism, and the final defeat of the principles antagonistic to the State as Power.

If there was one certainty in 1866 it was that France would not allow without a struggle the North German Confederation to absorb the Southern States and ring France in with a German Empire stretching from the Memel and the Eider to the Alps. The claims of the old France could not be reconciled with the ambitions of the new Germany.

The interest therefore of the next three years in Bismarck's statesmanship lies in two directions : first, his determination to secure such a constitution for the North German Confederation as would practically ensure a State of the same character and under a similar irresponsible political control to those existent in Prussia ; secondly, an ultimate settlement with France that would establish the German Empire to come—a unified national State—as the dominating power in Central Europe. The connection between the character of the North German Confederation and the final victory of the Bismarckian solution of the German problem was vital. It provides an illuminating interpretation of the deeper issues and ideals of Bismarck's statecraft.

An ultimate reconciliation with Austria was clearly foreshadowed in 1866. But reconciliation with France was impossible in 1867, nor was it desired. Bismarck's policy required the defeat of France. The danger from France was not purely political or military—in the union of an undefeated France with a defeated Austria, a revival of the system of Kaunitz and the Bourbon monarchy of 1756. Rome and the papacy brought into the political conflict the battle of ideas. The syllabus of 1864 led logically to the Vatican Decrees of 1870. Papal infallibility was a victory of Ultramontanism. Against the sovereignty of the modern State, over all causes and persons, ecclesiastical as well as civil, throughout its dominions supreme, it arrayed the theory that in spheres of thought and action, defined not by the State but by the Church, the competence of civil authority ceased, and that the *jus dirigendi* and the *jus coercendi* passed to spiritual power, intrinsically and in the divine order of things, superior. France, Austria, and the patrimony of Peter, were the political strongholds of this creed and party. The defeat of Austria and France transferred the struggle to the floors of the Prussian Landtag and the imperial Reichstag. What would have been the issue of this tremendous struggle of principles, cutting down to the bone of civil life and the fundamentals of society, if France had won in 1870 ?

For the present Bismarck had to reckon with French and German national sentiment. On both sides of the frontier the high explosive of national passion was stored up in embarassing plenitude, and any political trifle might detonate the magazines. Napoleon's repeated and varying demands had proved not so much what the Emperor himself desired as what he knew France expected him to extort. The extreme irritability of French public opinion was caused by anger, humiliation, and fear, and the danger was all the greater because Napoleon's failure in Mexico and in Europe, in combination with the internal discontent, imperilled the dynasty and made it imperative for the Tuileries to re-gild its tarnished prestige with a striking success in foreign policy. France was corroded with the worst form of ignorance that can sap a nation's strength, the ignorance that is steeped in vanity. The boulevards of Paris and the *estaminets de province* did not know Prussia, and they refused to recognise the profound changes that had made the Germany of 1867 as different from the Germany of 1815 as that Germany was from the Germany of 1789. The France of 1867 was inspired with the axiomatic conviction that it was still the first country of Europe, the *foyer de civilisation*, first in science, letters, the arts and arms.

The irritability of German public opinion was due to pride and the consciousness of strength. Great things had been accomplished, but they were only the beginning. The supremacy in Europe was at last passing into German hands. The injuries of the past were not yet obliterated, and the one veto which German Nationalism was not prepared to tolerate was a French veto on the completion of German unity. After 1866 any French or German statesman could have made a war with ease in twenty-four hours. For things simply could not remain as they were in 1866. Neither Napoleon nor Bismarck could postpone indefinitely the collision without abandoning what neither could abandon. The maintenance of the French Empire and the imperial dynasty on the throne was Napoleon's, the completion of German unification was Bismarck's, task. For Napoleon the tragedy was summed up in the impossibility of refusing war if it was thrust upon him, since refusal meant another humiliation, and that spelled ruin. The Treaty of Prague placed the initiative in Bismarck's hands. Obedient to the opportunism on which his statecraft rested, he already willed the end in 1866; the means and the moment would be revealed by circumstances that could not be predicted in advance but might be made. It was Bismarck's deepest conviction that true opportunism consisted as much in creating opportunities as in seizing them when they occurred. But as in 1864 or in 1866 the war that lay ' in the logic of history '—a logic not made by chance or a blind caprice, but created by statecraft—must be strictly and essentially ' defensive.' War must secure, since policy could not, the conditions on which a German Central Europe could live for the future with its neighbours. The achievement of these conditions could on Bismarckian principles alone prove its justifiability and necessity.

CHAPTER V

THE CHANCELLOR OF THE NORTH GERMAN CONFEDERATION

The Making of the North German Confederation—The War
with France, 1866-1870—The Treaty of Frankfurt—The
Unification of Germany, 1870-1871.

THE conclusion of the treaties which established peace was
only part of the complicated and exhausting burden of
work that Bismarck had to shoulder. This enormous pressure of business could not be delegated, except in its details ; and even if delegation had been possible Bismarck
was not the man to permit, in so critical a situation, the
interference of colleagues, military or civil. The gigantic
labour fell on a man already worn out, living on shattered
nerves and an adamantine will. He had returned to
Berlin on August 4, and when on September 20 he took
part in the triumphal entry of the army, every one observed with concern the weary exhaustion in his face and
figure. He had in fact dragged himself from a sick bed
to ride with the generals, Moltke, Roon, Herwarth von
Bittenfeld, Steinmetz, and Vogel von Falkenstein, to receive the homage of a crowd, delirious with enthusiasm,
and the roses of the girls at the Brandenburg Gate. He
was, and he knew it, the arresting figure in the cavalcade ;
men and women along the route had their eyes on the
civilian in the cuirassier uniform, merely a titular general
of brigade, for he was the magician who had achieved the
miracle. To-day it was roses—roses, roses all the way
past the statue of his master, Frederick the Great—but
had the Crown Prince arrived too late at Königgrätz, it
would not have been even the besoms of the old women
or the stones of a duped democracy. He would have been
lying, face downwards, after the last charge.

The Landtag had been dissolved at the outbreak of war, and the elections of July 8 reflected the victories. One hundred and forty Conservatives had been returned, and had the dissolution been deferred till the end of July it is probable that the defeat of the opposition would have been decisive. Junkertum was jubilant. Now was the time to teach these pestilent Radicals a lesson. The King shared their views. But Bismarck thought otherwise. It was the hour for the olive branch that he had plucked at Avignon in September 1862. The opposition had had their lesson. National Liberalism—not Junkertum—was the true ally in the work of unification to come. Not even in his dealings with Austria and the defeated German South did Bismarck show himself more convincingly a masterly realist—the statesman who appreciates realities and bends them to his will—than in his treatment of the Landtag. ' I was in a position to carry out the boldest and most incisive policy of reaction,' he told the Reichstag in 1879, ' with the success and *éclat* which still attached to me from Königgrätz . . . if I had thought that absolutism in Prussia would have better promoted the work of German unity, I should most decidedly have counselled recourse to it.' For himself and for his policy the triumph would be all the more enduring if he could now hypnotise National Liberalism into servitude as a loyal agent of his will. The King, not unnaturally, resisted, supported by his military advisers, and Bismarck had a hard task, assisted by the Crown Prince, in persuading his sovereign to accept what he regarded as a personal humiliation and a public surrender. Bismarck wrote to his wife (August 3) :—

' Great controversy over the speech from the Throne . . these folk see nothing but their own nose and practice their swimming in the stormy flood of phrases. With our enemies we can settle up, but our Friends ! *They* all wear blinkers and see only a speck of the world.'

The Landtag opened on August 5, and the royal speech indicated that the government would throw a white sheet over the blue uniform with the red facings. The bill, introduced by Bismarck, provided an indemnification for the absence of a legal budget since 1862, and additional

credits for 1866. The Budget for 1867 would be submitted to the Lower House. It was a frank admission that
the government had acted illegally, but the Minister-
President invited the House to close the constitutional
controversy, and to recognise that if the government had
been ' technically' wrong it could not have acted otherwise under the circumstances, and that peace and pardon
were now necessary in order to proceed with the great
duties that awaited Prussia. Let bygones be bygones ;
neither Crown nor Landtag in the future would assail each
other's rights. The era of conflict was over—never to
return. ' The government,' he said, later, ' has gladly
grasped the opportunity to bring the conflict to an end,
in the conviction that it serves no purpose in constitutional
life to drive matters to extremities. Constitutional
government cannot be judged by mathematical, nor even
by juristic, rules. It is a continuous compromise . . .
the making of peace never satisfies every wish, never fulfils
every calculation.'

L. von Gerlach pronounced the bill a blow in the face of
Bismarck's best friends. The Conservatives received the
measure in morose silence, but it passed the Lower House
by 230 to 75 votes, and the Upper House without a
division. The irreconcilables of both camps refused the
olive branch, and from the Indemnity Bill dates a re-
grouping of Prussian and German parties which the organisation of the new Confederation definitely confirmed.
In September 1866 the Progressive party (*Fortschritts-
Partei*), which had been the core of the opposition, split up.
Fifteen of its important members, with eight from the
left centre, founded a new party, under Bennigsen's leadership, which on the dissolution of the Nationalverein
became the powerful National Liberal party. Its *raison
d'être* was to give the new government firm support in its
foreign policy, and to work for complete unity with freedom. ' Der deutsche Staat und die deutsche Freiheit
müssen gleichzeitig mit denselben Mitteln errungen
werden.' A similar split took place in the Conservative ranks. On October 27, 1867, the Free Conservative
party was founded on the principle that Prussia had

now entered 'the class of constitutional States.' 'The Time of Absolutism had passed.' The Free Conservatives pledged themselves to support and work for the 'Constitutional monarchy' defined in the Constitution of 1867. How active political thought and movement had become under the influence of the years 1866 and 1867 can be best judged by two other party manifestations : first, the notable Eisenach Programme which founded the Social Democrats in August 1869 ; secondly, the German Popular Party (*Deutsche Volkspartei*) of South Germany in September 1868, with its ideal of the complete democratic State and responsible parliamentary government. The Eisenach Programme, of which much was to be heard later, aimed amongst other ends at direct legislation by a popular legislature, substitution of a national militia for the standing army, separation of Church and State, abolition of ecclesiastical teaching in the elementary schools, complete independence of the judiciary, abolition of all press laws, legal recognition of trades unions, abolition of all indirect taxation, substitution of a single progressive income-tax, and regulation by law of the hours, remuneration, and conditions of labour.

During the short autumn session of 1866 Bismarck, exhausted as he was, astonished the Landtag by his persuasive geniality. The old rasping irritability and explosions of anger were reserved for the ministers of the South and for Benedetti ; it was all the more remarkable, as he was in daily pain and tortured by insomnia. But with Bismarck, as with the great Napoleon, anger, insolence, and menaces were storm-cones indicating that the situation was critical ; they were intended to drive an adversary into indiscretions. The surer that his grip on a situation became, the politer became Bismarck's manners.

The princes of the States north of the Main were summoned to Berlin to confer (August 4) ; they found a Prussian minister lavish in the amiability that is easy to the victorious master of many legions. It was a congress of roaches presided over by a benevolent pike. The basis of the new Confederation was laid (August 18) in fifteen treaties of alliance, in which the contracting parties

B.   P guaranteed the inviolability of their territories, and agreed to refer to a constituent Parliament, chosen as in 1849 by direct and universal manhood suffrage, the establishment of a Federal Constitution. One point alone was settled in advance. The troops of the allies were placed under the supreme command of the King of Prussia.

The Landtag ratified the annexations permitted by the Treaty of Prague. In the bill Hanover,[1] Nassau, Hesse-Cassel, Frankfurt, and Schleswig-Holstein were not ' annexed' but ' taken in possession' by the Crown. Bismarck however yielded with grace to the critics and agreed to annexation pure and simple. After voting a special military credit the Landtag was prorogued (September 27).[2]

Bismarck's endurance had given out. On September 26 he left for Pomerania, and for the next two months was seriously ill. His constitution and will were as usual better doctors than the physicians. Late in life he pronounced that a man should not die till he had smoked 100,000 cigars and drunk 5000 bottles of champagne. His wife hailed with joy the day, after many weary weeks of pain, sleeplessness, and black depression, when the Minister-President once more found joy in the Moselle and Hock specially selected by a princely host in the island of Rügen ; and with the appetite for wine and tobacco came back the lust for work and achievement. Devoted friends had been toiling in his absence on the new Constitution—Roon, Delbrück, Abeken—and Bismarck called in Hepke, Lothar Bucher, and Max Duncker. But their drafts failed to satisfy. In his solitude he, too, had been toiling to clarify his ideas, and on his return to Berlin, by a *tour de force* at a single sitting, he dictated to Bucher the scheme of a Constitution (December 13), copies of which were ready

[1] Hanover, like the other annexed principalities, became Prussian territory. It ceased to be an independent kingdom ; the dynasty was dethroned, and the reigning king became a 'legitimist' claimant to a throne he no longer possessed, who refused to recognise the validity of the treaty and the acts which destroyed his crown and turned the 'kingdom' into an administrative Prussian province.

[2] Saxe-Weimar, Oldenburg, Brunswick, Saxe-Altenburg, Saxe-Coburg-Gotha, Anhalt, the two Schwarzburgs, Waldeck, Reuss (younger branch), Schaumburg-Lippe and Lippe, Lubeck, Bremen and Hamburg. The two Mechlenburgs adhered on August 21, Saxe-Meiningen, Reuss (elder branch), and the kingdom of Saxony on October 21.

(December 15) for the Conference of Plenipotentiaries from the governments. The Conference lasted until February 7, 1867, when the amended draft was recommended by the governments for acceptance. The elections for the Constituent Reichstag were held on February 12, and on February 24 the Reichstag of the North German Confederation met to discuss the recommended draft. The Constitution was finally passed on April 17. The several governments accepted it, as amended by the Reichstag, and it was then submitted to the Parliaments of the several States. The Prussian Landtag agreed by June 1 ; the other States followed suit ; on July 1, 1867, the Constitution was duly promulgated.

The North German Confederation was now in existence ; one further act was necessary to complete the work. On July 14 Bismarck was appointed Federal Chancellor—combining the duties of the new office with the Minister-Presidency of Prussia. The task of making a Constitution and of unifying North Germany by a victorious Prussia, undisturbed either by enemies without or within, had occupied eleven months of continuous and hard work (August 4, 1866–July 1, 1867). The man of ' blood and iron ' had been as long over the task as the dilatory and un-practical professors, journalists, and idealists, who had toiled at a larger task in the Church of St. Paul at Frankfurt from May 13, 1848, to April 11, 1849. The critics, and they are not few, who assume that men of action can produce constitutions as easily as omelettes, and that the juristic, moral, political, and institutional problems that even partial unification of Germany provided could be solved by a triumphant sword in a few days, have failed to grasp the elements of history's lessons. One conclusion that is certain is, that without the noble and masterly work of the men of 1848, and the earnest co-operation of the finest minds and characters in Germany from 1849 to 1866, the establishment of the North German Confederation could not have been accomplished in double the time. ' There is spring in Germany to-day,' said a deputy ; but the intoxicating splendour of that spring had its dawn in the Liberalism of the Revolution.

The North German Confederation was not what National Liberalism desired, or for which it had worked so long and with such faith and loyalty. If Max Duncker might well remark, ' what a contrast between the seventy articles of the Constitutional text of 1867 and the twenty articles of the Federal act of 1815,' the comparison measures the profound change in the principles, temper, and ideals of the Germany made by Metternich and the Germany made by Bismarck. But what a contrast also between the Constitution of 1867 and that of 1849. The difference was due to Bismarck. The North German Confederation concentrates in lines precise and unmistakable the first of the two great chapters in the Bismarckian solution of the German problem. The text of the Constitution is stamped throughout with the imprint of his personality, genius, principles, and ideals.

The interest therefore of the eleven months' toil in constitution-making lies as much in what was rejected as in what was accepted, in the omissions no less than in the inclusions, in the extreme rigidity of some, and the extreme flexibility of other, parts of the framework. The three main organs were the Presidency (*Praesidium*), vested in the King of Prussia, the Federal Council (*Bundesrat*) and the Parliament (*Reichstag*). Legislation and taxation were shared between the Council and the Parliament, the concurrence of both organs being required for the validity of laws or taxes. The originality of the Confederation lay in the functions assigned to, and the relations established between, the Praesidium, the Council, and the representative Parliament. As President, the King of Prussia was not a sovereign in the ordinary sense. He was not a member of the Council, nor was his consent necessary to Federal legislation or taxation. He did not preside over the Council, the Chairman of which was the Federal Chancellor. But as President he summoned and dissolved the Reichstag, concluded treaties, declared peace and war, and represented the Bund in all external relations; he promulgated the laws, and in peace and in war was commander-in-chief of the combined Federal forces, to whom the oath of allegiance was taken. The Council was not an upper chamber of the legislature. It was a syndicate of governmental delegates, appointed in assigned numbers to the members of the Bund[1] who voted as units, representing the assigned vote, on the instruction of their respective governments. The Council was thus constituted not *over*, but *out of*, the States; its deliberations were secret; its decisions were taken on a majority of votes; it had the initiative in legislation, and it could reject bills passed by the Reichstag. Through its various committees, dealing with defined subjects, it acted as a semi-executive organ. The Parliament was an assembly of representatives sitting in a single chamber, and chosen by direct and universal manhood suffrage from equal electoral districts. It voted the Federal budget, and its consent was necessary to all legislation. The one Federal minister was the Chancellor, appointed by the Presidency, responsible to the Bund as a whole, and in his chancellery were concentrated the Federal executive and administration. The Chancellor was not responsible directly either to the Reichstag or the Bundesrat. He could not be dismissed as the result of a parliamentary vote, but he was intended to act as the spokesman of the Council in all matters of policy, administration, or legislation, and it was his duty to submit to the Presidency all matters in which the Praesidium was the executive organ, and to countersign all notifications in which the Presidency acted on behalf of the Bund.

This Constitution was, broadly, an adaptation of the old Federal organisation, fundamentally modified in four directions—the increased powers assigned to the Presidency, the creation of the Federal Chancellor, the inclusion of a popular and representative legislature, and the relations established between the Council and the Parliament. It was ingeniously organised to meet the two chief defects of the old system: the absence of real unity in consequence of the unimpaired sovereignty of the member-States, and the limited competence and lack of coercive power of the Federal organs. The new Federal system was a real unity; it could legislate for and impose its Federal will on the

---

[1] Seventeen votes were assigned to Prussia; twenty-six were assigned to the other twenty-one States which composed the Federation.

whole Bund in all matters defined in the Constitution as a Federal concern. It no less ingeniously combined the demand for popular representation and a share of all Germans in the government of the Confederation with the claim of Prussia to be the preponderant and directing power. It gratified the dynasties by the position assigned to the governments in the Council, which, although not a Congress of Princes, was a syndicate made from the princedoms ; it recognised local particularism by leaving the legislatures of the member-States intact in their diversity of franchise and institutions, and their powers only impaired by the transfer of defined Federal concerns to the dual central organ of Bundesrat and Reichstag. Lastly, and by no means least, it created a chancellorship with powers vague and ill-defined enough to satisfy the personality and ambition of a Bismarck. The position of Federal Chancellor was what Bismarck wished to enjoy. The office was the keystone of the Federal arch, and the whole structure was pieced together to maintain the keystone in its central position.

Bismarck's share, in speech, in writing, and in oral conferences in the prolonged discussions from December to June, would make more than a volume. He came to the creative task, not merely with the glamour of an acquired prestige, and the force of an overpowering personality, but with an experience unrivalled in Germany of diplomacy, administration, and knowledge of men and institutions. Bismarck was in the plenitude of his physical and mental powers in 1866-7—only a Titan could have carried the burden, and even he very nearly collapsed under it—and he revealed in the making of the Constitution the inflexible tenacity of aim and principle, the inexhaustible variety of resource, the complete absence of scruple, the combination of brutal strength, velvety suppleness, and Prussian mastery of detail that had marked his ministerial presidency. No man knew better that he was fighting now to impose the Bismarckian solution—to impose himself, his principles, ideals, and interpretations of life—on Germany It was the joy of achieving that supreme ambition, the consciousness of realising at last all that made life worth living, all the full-blooded sense of what it was to be a German and a Prussian, that inspired him to resist every party, principle, or proposal opposed to the German State he desired to establish.

Hence the procedure in the making of the Constitution. He first concluded alliances, as noted, with the States to be federated; then drew up the original draft, and on behalf of Prussia obtained the ratification of the text through plenipotentiaries by whom the governments were pledged. The constituent Reichstag was thus confronted with an agreed scheme, amendment of which in any fundamental sense was exceedingly difficult, for it must be made the occasion for re-reference to the governments behind the Reichstag. The Constitution passed by the Reichstag was finally submitted to all the legislatures, with the warning that emendation would involve a re-submission to every State and the Reichstag as a whole for its concurrence. Its final acceptance *en bloc* was thus secured. Apart from his personal authority in argument, Bismarck had two great weapons at his disposal. First, the power of Prussia. If Prussia would not agree, the proposal must come to naught; and Prussia was practically himself. The Lower and the Upper House of the Landtag would act as he advised. They were strong enough to veto where they could not create. Secondly, the critical external situation which made rapid decision urgent. Bismarck used this consideration both privately and in public with great skill. For while the Constitution was on the anvil the Luxemburg crisis and the danger of a war with France had to be faced and surmounted. The European situation had indeed the same driving influence that it had in 1689 on the English Revolution and the passing of the Declaration of Rights. 'Work quickly,' Bismarck said in a famous sentence. 'Put Germany in the saddle and she will soon ride.'

German pride, fed on its imperial history, lamented the absence of a Kaiser and a Reich, a sovereign and an empire. Prussian Junkertum deplored the emasculation of the Prussian monarchy, which it desired to see ruling North Germany as it ruled Prussia by direct authority and unquestioned prerogative. The tenderness to the petty States exasperated the fierce governing class, which would gladly have treated Prussia's allies with magisterial militarism. But above all, Liberals and Radicals strove to secure fundamental constitutional rights (*Grundrechte*), defined in the Constitution, a Federal ministry and an administration representative of, and responsible to, the Reichstag. The Bundesrat, dissevered from the Reichstag, ought in their view to be an Upper House the composition and action of which could be controlled, in case of conflict with the representative organ. But against everything savouring of parliamentary government and ministerial responsibility, in the British sense, against everything that would make the Reichstag a policy-making and government-making organ, Bismarck set his face like flint, and all such proposals were rejected.

There is not the slightest doubt that, had Bismarck so chosen, the Constitution could have conferred on the new Confederation responsible parliamentary government. The responsibility for the rejection, and the consequences in the history of Germany that followed from its rejection, rests with Bismarck ; and the reason for his refusal is plain. Parliamentary government in the Confederation would have involved a drastic re-writing of the Prussian Constitution, and a no less drastic reorganisation of the Prussian system. How could a responsible Federal Chancellor combine his office with the Minister-Presidency of Prussia, responsible only to the Prussian Crown ? Three things were essential in Bismarck's eyes. Policy and the responsibility for policy must be vested in organs outside parliamentary control ; the army must be withdrawn from parliamentary interference ; and behind the Federal Chancellor must stand a Prussia, the strength of which would be at the disposal of an unfettered Prussian Crown, supported by Prussian Junker tradition. He secured the first through the Bundesrat, the second through the alliances that preceded the making of the Confederation, and the clause in the Constitution that fixed for five years (*i.e.* until 1871) the composition and number of the Federal army, and placed it under the supreme command of the Praesidium ; the third by incorporating a Prussia unreformed, intact, and unrepentant in the Bund. Henceforward Moltke and the General Staff could work, unimpeded, on the army, and complete its preparation for its final task ; Bismarck could shape and direct policy, unhindered by Federal ministerial colleagues, and controlling a Bundesrat in which Prussia had seventeen votes out of forty-three, and the manipulation of which was withdrawn from public knowledge or parliamentary influence.

The democratic franchise occasioned deep misgivings in many quarters. It is very questionable whether Bismarck's later interpretation—that it was blackmail to democracy—really represents what he thought in 1866, or really felt until he retired. It seems more accurate to infer that he desired a representative assembly which would mirror as accurately as possible the German people, enable the government to gauge the currents in the nation as a whole, and provide an organ for the concentrated expression of national policy and for influencing public opinion. All these ends could be achieved with safety if the powers of the representative body, nominally large, were in reality checked and circumscribed, as they were in the Constitution at every point. Universal suffrage conferred a superb democratic glamour on a truly anti-democratic system. And Bismarck early in his career was convinced that the danger of Liberalism came not from the uninstructed masses but the educated and independent middle and professional classes. When he wrote his memoirs at the close of his life the industrial revolution had done its work and the democracy had largely been transformed into an urban industrial proletariat ; he wrote with twenty years' bitter experience of the weapon forged by Windthorst and the Clerical centre, by Bebel and the Socialist Democrats, from universal manhood suffrage. In 1867 Bismarck could understand and sympathise with the Socialism of Lassalle ; neither Prussia nor Germany were industrialised ; seventy per cent. of the population still lived in the country, and the framing and carrying of a restricted franchise for the Reichstag was, as he said, a matter so controversial and difficult as to prohibit its consideration. Universal suffrage was not ideal, but it was simple, popular,

and practical; its adoption in the Federal Constitution
would not involve the demand for its extension to Prussia
or other States, averse from it in principle. 'Direct
election and universal suffrage,' Bismarck pronounced, ' I
consider to be greater guarantees of Conservative action
than any artificial electoral law.'   Bismarck's conception
of a Parliament was that of our Tudors—a perpetual
royal commission to lay the wishes of the nation at the
feet of the throne ; a national organ with defined powers,
limited by the prerogatives of the Crown. The opinion
of Parliament could be ascertained and neglected, if
need be, but the Legislature could always be made a
grand ally for affixing the national seal on all enterprises,
where it was essential the Crown should appear both to
the nation itself, and to foreign states, as the representative
executor of a sovereign national will. Between policy
imposed on and endorsed by the nation, and policy
made by the nation, the difference was fundamental
and final.

July 1, 1867, when the Constitution was promulgated,
was the Königgrätz of Liberalism in Germany.   Foiled in
1848, thwarted in 1862, Liberalism and the Liberal programme had practically their last real chance in 1866-7.
The effort to renew the struggle in 1871 was the flash of
powder damped by disuse. The rejection in the Constitution of every vital element and principle of the Liberal
programme, coupled with the equally decisive failure to
modify the Prussian Constitution, provides a critical date
in the history of Germany and of Europe.   For ten years
Germany had been gathering itself at the cross-roads—
for four it had stood expectant, waiting for the decision
that would mark its route, and it now was set marching
towards unification indeed, power, opulence, discipline,
and the high places of the universe, but not towards the
ideals of character and law and self-government that were
the dream of the golden age of aspiration. National
Liberalism was enmeshed in the iron cage of the new
Federal Constitution ; it enjoyed a great political influence,
but neither political authority nor power, which were reserved to the Federal Council, and in that Council the

principles of the governing caste in Prussia achieved an invincible supremacy.

The real character of the victory won by Bismarck between 1866 and 1867 was concealed for ten years. And the reason lay in the dual programme of National Liberalism since 1848—unification and constitutional self-government through responsible parliamentary administration. The task of internal unification began with 1867 when the framework of the organisation had been completed, and to the achievement of this task the national Liberal leaders and their devoted followers contributed a driving power, ability, and work, that cannot be overestimated. Indeed, without the unselfish and patriotic labours of men such as Bennigsen, Lasker, Forckenbeck, Miquel, supporting the efforts of the ministerial chiefs of departments, Delbrück, Stephan, Falk, and Camphausen, Bismarck could never have achieved the remarkable results accomplished by 1880. Liberalism was endeavouring partly to find in legislation and executive action a compensation for the failure to obtain responsible parliamentary government; with the inevitable consequence that the bureaucracy, the guiding levers of which were controlled by the governing class, was enormously strengthened. Public opinion was steadily imbued with the conviction that liberty and law as character-building elements in national life, would be more rapidly and efficiently worked out through co-ordinated governmental action from above, than through the slow, disappointing, and patchworky progress of representative institutions and the friction of warring parties. The Reichstag, thus, was transformed into a legislative machine and a debating club, banked up against the dead wall of the Prussian Landtag in which the administration could always command, if its political authority was questioned, a solid Conservative majority. 'The Army' or 'the Crown' in danger played the part that 'the Church in danger' played in the evolution of constitutional government in England. For in each case first principles of the established State were the root of the controversy.

Hence with unification practically completed by 1879,

it was impossible for National Liberalism to resume in the industrialised and soaring Germany of 1879 the programme of self-government through representative institutions. It had itself assisted to build the breakwaters and the dams which barred the parliamentary waters from trickling into the reservoir of political power where policy was made. Its old ideals, mildewed by neglect, fell to the impotent Radicalism led by Richter, and the economic war of classes led by Bebel—both, and from one point of view, not unjustly termed 'enemies of the Empire' (*Reichsfeindlich*). For the aims of both could only be realised by taking down the whole imperial engine, riveted into the chassis of the Prussian State, and rebuilding it on a different pattern and for wholly different purposes. The specification of that imperial engine is written out in the text of the Constitution of the North German Confederation. The counter-specification had been elaborated in 1849.

One important consequence of the defeat of Liberalism cannot be omitted. The National Liberalism of 1850-66 had regarded England as its moral ally—the country which had inspired its programme and supplied the ideas, the precedents, and the example of constitutional self-government—and the Liberals, with no desire to make an English Germany, hoped that by realising the same ends in government and the same type of state as England, looked forward to a great political *entente* in which two great nations, working in their respective spheres and under a differentiated Nationalism, could achieve common ideals and purposes. The complete failure of Great Britain to understand the character of the struggle waged in Germany from 1850 onwards, and to grasp the meaning of 1867, the absence of sympathy, the obstacles placed by British policy in the way of German achievement, the hostile criticism, and, still worse, the patronising approval, killed the enthusiasm for England in the great Liberal camp. England, too, presently fell under the hypnotism of Bismarck in its attitude towards German affairs, in complete ignorance of what Bismarck and Bismarckianism really were, or what they meant for Great Britain and Europe. The old feeling and ideas continued to be con-

centrated in the court and circle of the Crown Prince and
Princess, but Germany steadily moved away from them.
The Franco-German war completed the disillusionment.
England had failed. Her principles and her ambitions were
as dangerous to the new Empire as the adoption of her
system of government would be disastrous. Industrialism
was superimposed on the political divorce: it made absolute
the decree *nisi* for the two countries. England and the
British Empire were regarded first as neutrals who had
betrayed, and then as rivals who would bar, the realisation
of the complete German programme. The extirpation of
'English' influence in every sphere—dynastic, political,
intellectual, and economic—grew to be the ideal of the
Nationalism that laboured for the Empire as the expression of Power—German Power.

The intellectuals and the universities slowly ranged
themselves on the anti-British side. The conversion of
a Treitschke, a Sybel, and a Mommsen to the new gospel
was far more significant than at first sight appears ; for in
the new Germany the universities were to be even more
potent in moulding the minds of the young generation
than in the epoch of the German renaissance. The influence of authority in the matters of spirit and intellect
more than kept pace with the increase of authority in
politics and administration. The organisation of intellect
came to be regarded as essential as the organisation of the
army, the civil administration, or the tariff union. To a
Realpolitik a *Realwissenschaft* is an indispensable element of
national power, since it controls the empire of man in the
universe of spirit, and provides the material weapons for
maintaining the control and extending its scope. When
Bismarck finally broke with the economic policy of Free
Trade in 1879, the last of the English chains which
'fettered' the evolution of a national Germany was
shivered. Cobdenism, Manchesterism, *Adam-Smithianis-
mus*, and the influence of the British school of individualism
were eliminated from State policy and economic action.
The emancipation of the German intellect was the corollary to the emancipation of the German nation from the
bondage of 'Wälsch' and foreigner. It gave a new

interpretation, and a new sphere, to the conception of a Teutonic Central Europe. Henceforward Great Britain —the incarnation of everything intellectual, political, and economic that was the antithesis of the German Empire— could by a subtle and inevitable transition in German thought be transformed from the rival into the enemy. Not until that enemy had suffered the fate of Austria and France would the German Empire be safe and the continent of Europe purged of political heresies.

Bismarck had not failed to grasp the position established in 1867. His virtual alliance with, and reliance on, the National Liberal party demanded great skill in political management lest Bennigsen and his colleagues should become the riders and he the horse. The Conservatives of the *Kreuzzeitung* were angered to bitterness with ' the lost leader,' and for the ten years after 1867 Bismarck was exposed to vehement attacks from the Right. The social and court influence of Conservatism was far greater than that of any other party, and the ramification and enlacement of its roots enmeshed every organ of authority—the Crown, the War Office, the General Staff, the Civil Service, and the local administration, above all, in the agricultural districts. For many years it was not possible to counterbalance the great industrials, because they were only in the making, as yet, against the powers vested in tradition, established institutions, and a social caste that provided the higher *personnel*. Bismarck could not shatter the sources of Junker authority without emasculating the Prussia by whose brute weight he controlled the Confederation, and, later, the Empire. His ally was the Crown, and his weapons were the doctrine of passive obedience as the life-blood of Conservatism and unwavering confidence in himself. He emphasised the principles of his youth. Conservatism, if it acted against the Crown and its government, was guilty of intolerable indiscipine, equivalent to mutiny and treachery. If it came to an open breach the Crown would act—and it did. In his private correspondence with Roon he could say what could not be said in public. Some characteristic and illuminating quotations will be relevant here : ' If the government has not at least one party in the country which does not support its principles and policy, then the constitutional system is impossible : the government will manœuvre and intrigue against the constitution ; it must either create an artificial or aim at a transitory majority. It succumbs then to the weakness of a coalition-ministry and its policy fluctuates, which is pernicious to the State, and especially so to the Conservative principle.' (February 6, 1868.) ' Every state which values its honour and independence must recognise that its peace and security rests on its own sword—I believe, gentlemen, we are all united on that point. . . . Just as a roof protects against the rain, a dam against inundation, so our army protects our productivity in its full measure.' (May 22, 1869.)

' The form in which our King exercises Imperial rights in Germany has never been of great importance in my eyes ; to secure the *fact* that he exercises them, I have trained all the strength God has given me. . . .' (To Roon, August 27, 1864.)

' I can emphatically maintain this : does not the Praesidium of the North German Confederation exercise in South Germany such an Imperial authority as has not been in a German Emperor's possession for five hundred years ? Where is the time since the first Hohenstaufen when there has been in Germany an unquestioned supreme command in war, an unquestioned certainty of having in war the same enemies and the same friends ? The name counts for something . . . the Head of the North German Confederation has in South Germany a position such as no Emperor since Barbarossa has had, and though Barbarossa's sword was victorious his power was not based on treaties and generally recognised.' (To Roon, February 24, 1870.)

' It is absolutely certain in my conviction that I have found the chief influence which I have been privileged to exercise, not in the Imperial, but in the Prussian Power. . . Cut away from me the Prussian root, convert me into a pure Imperial minister, I believe I should have as little influence as every one else.' (Reichstag, March 13, 77.)

One other remark reveals much. ' The stronger,' Bismarck said (March 28, 1867), ' the influence of Parliament on the State, the more necessary is it to maintain a stern discipline in the civil service.' He had learned in the constitutional conflict what an invaluable weapon the Prussian civil services could be in counteracting the Liberal opposition. The assimilation of the annexed provinces, the Prussianisation of the Confederation, was largely to be achieved through the organised *Beamtenstand*, disciplined and deployable under the Crown as efficiently as the army, and kept as free from parliamentary interference. The classical authority is the royal proclamation of January 4, 1882, which summarises the position as correctly in 1867 as in 1882 : ' Executive orders of the King require the countersignature of a minister . . . but it is incorrect and tends to obscure the constitutional rights of the Crown if their execution is represented as dependent on a responsible minister and not on the Crown . . . it is the duty of my ministers to protect my constitutional rights against doubt or misrepresentation. I expect the same duty from all officials . . . all officials who are entrusted with the execution of my governmental commands and are removable from their service under the law of discipline are required under the obligation of their oath of service to maintain the policy of my government even at elections.'

The future relations of the new Confederation with the South German States were a knotty problem. Bismarck's views are susceptible of very various interpretation. I is certain that he contemplated union between south and north, as the consummation of the work of 1867. I is no less certain that he recognised more deeply than many of his critics the external and internal difficultie in the realisation of such a union. It has been held by many then, and since, that the fluid and elastic element in the Constitution of 1867 was deliberately emphasised to permit a subsequent incorporation of Bavaria, Württemberg, Baden, and Hesse-Darmstadt without substantial modification of the main lines of the Federal structure It has, on the other hand, been argued that the Constitution of 1867 was deliberately provisional, and that Bismarck intended to recast the whole system on an imperial pattern. Bismarck can be quoted for and against both these interpretations. The truth would seem to be that he had not really decided, and could not really decide, when and how union with the south would be possible. The form would turn on the particular situation, European as well as German. 'It is impossible to see in advance with sufficient clearness the ways of Divine Providence.' (August 13, 1875.) When Miquel maintained that 'the line of the Main is no longer a line of separation, but simply a stopping station at which we draw breath, as an engine takes in coal and water, in order to proceed on our route,' Bismarck could reply that 'we all carry national union in our hearts; but for the calculating statesman the necessary comes first and then the ideally desirable . . . if Germany attains its goal in the nineteenth century, I should regard that as a great achievement; if it were reached in ten or five years it would be something quite extraordinary, an unexpected crowning gift from God. . . . I have always said to the National Liberals that I look on the matter with a hunter's eyes. If I lay a bait for game I do not shoot at the first doe, but wait until the whole herd is busy feeding.'

Apart from the obligations[1] implied rather than defined in the Treaty of Prague—which France regarded as a positive prohibition of complete union—and in the maintenance of which in all probability she would have the support of Austria, Bismarck recognised the grave internal objections and obstacles to union. Dynasticism, Particularism, Radicalism, and Clericalism were very strong in the south. The Wittelsbach monarchy in Bavaria had a historic tradition of independence that made its fusion in a truly Federal Constitution, and its subordination to a Hohenzollern presidency, virtually impossible in 1867; the Radicals were predominant in Württemberg and the Clericals very powerful in Bavaria. Representation of the south in the Reichstag of 1867 on the basis of universal

---

[1] Article 4 of the Treaty of Prague ran: 'H.M. the Emperor of Austria . . . also agrees that the German State to the south of this line shall form a union, the national connection of which with the Northern Confederacy is reserved for a more defined agreement between both parties, and *which is to maintain an international independent existence*.

suffrage would have made formidable additions to the National Liberals and Centre parties, and completely swamped the Conservatives. The Federal Council would have had an anti-Prussian majority ; and the parliamentary situation was sufficiently difficult already, without swelling the volume of discontent created by the dispossession of the dynasties in Hanover, Nassau, and Hesse-Cassel, and the overbearing efficiency with which the administrative incorporation of the annexed territories was being carried out by the Prussian bureaucracy.

French statesmen, it is true, were congratulating themselves and France that Germany was now definitely split into three clearly marked divisions—*les trois tronçons*, of which Rouher spoke—the North, the South, and Austria, and calculated that allies could be found south of the Main and on the Danube. This view of the south was a pure illusion, which sprang from an incurable persistence in interpreting German thought and feeling in 1867 by the light of a history that was as dead as Frederick Barbarossa or Louis xiv. The conditions that had made the policy of Richelieu and Mazarin, Louvois and 'the dance of the Louis d'ors,' even of Napoleon i. and the Confederation of the Rhine feasible, had vanished by 1848—never to return. It was the same fatal prepossession which had ruined Napoleon's Italian policy ; for it had led him to suppose that Italy in 1859 could be really carved out into a north, a centre, and a south, animated by a common sentiment of Italian Nationalism, but retaining the dynastic Particularism which could only exist on denationalisation propped up by foreign bayonets. At the Tuileries, in the Corps Législatif, on the boulevards, and in the 'estaminets de province,' Wittelsbach pride, the clerical press, and the Radical critics and caricatures of the south were regarded as proofs that the red trousers of the French army would receive a warmer welcome in Bavaria than the blue uniform with red facings from the north.

Bismarck entertained no such foolish illusions. The south he knew was as German as the north. But it was much more anti-Prussian. It had never come under the influence of Prussia to the extent that the non-Prussian

States north of the Main had; it had not assimilated the principles and postulates of the Prussian State, which were repugnant to all its traditions and outlook on life. But that repugnance did not involve any readiness to accept either French culture or political domination, still less the principles of the Second Empire. Quite the contrary. A Ludwig of Bavaria, a Prince Hohenlohe, a von der Pfordten, a Bray, a Döllinger, a Varnbüler, a Dalwigk, the representatives of the various warring parties —Unionists, Clericals, Radicals, Particularists, Democrats —that made the south such a tangle of conflicting aims and such a confusion of discordant voices, carried beneath their party robes as stout and patriotic German hearts as any that beat north of the Main. Because they were such good Germans they were so anti-Prussian, and had not yet learned to bow the knee in the house of Hohenzollern; they were not ready yet to accept incorporation on the terms of the North German Confederation, or to be de-Germanised in order to be baptized by platoons into Prussianism.

Bismarck on his side was decided in his refusal to sacrifice the assured Prussian hegemony in the north to South German dynasticism, Clericalism, and Radicalism. Had he been willing in 1866 to risk a war with France and Austria he would have overcome the external but not the internal obstacle to unification; had Germany been victorious in such a war, the unification that would have crowned the victory would have been very different to the loosely jointed settlement achieved in 1867. But Bismarck never took unnecessary risks, particularly to achieve ends not in themselves absolutely urgent. Everything therefore pointed to delay; but a halt implied that everything meanwhile must be done by practical administration and cautious diplomacy to improve the conditions that made for the ultimate acceptance of the Prussian solution by the south. The chart of the future was studded with rocks—many of them sunken, many just awash when the national tide was at its full—but Bismarck's navigation was in the next three years masterly. He had secured the substance in the offensive and defensive military conventions, in

themselves a shattering refutation of the dreams dreamed
at the Tuileries; the Unitarians must be sedulously
nursed and continuously denied; the economic bonds
must be tightened into a halter round the neck of the
south; France and Austria must be carefully cherished in
the conviction that union was neither desired nor possible.
The unitarian force of Nationalism could be trusted to
work of itself, all the stronger if it was drenched from
time to time with Prussian cold water. France, not
Prussia, must be represented as the obstacle to union;
France which coveted the Bavarian Palatinate, which
threatened Bavaria and Baden because it was the unlawful
occupant of German Alsace and Lorraine. 'You cannot,'
Bismarck said, 'ripen opinion in the south by holding a
lamp under it,' and when Baden, the most Unitarian of the
Southern States, and the friends of Baden in the Reichstag
repeatedly pleaded for its incorporation with the North
German Confederation, Bismarck put the demand on one
side with courteous firmness. The Treaty of Prague was
against it; it would be a breach of faith with Napoleon
whose heart was hard, and it would annoy Bavaria and
Württemberg, who ought not to be annoyed. 'Why,'
he asked, 'skim off the cream, and leave the rest of the
milk to go sour?'

But, above all, make Prussia strong. The new Prussia
was not ready. She had to be hammered together.
Time was required for the Prussian bureaucracy to Prus-
sianise the north, for the General Staff to impose Prussian
organisation on the Federal forces and screw them up to
the Prussian concert pitch, for Germany to accustom
itself to the Prussian praesidium of the Hohenzollern
monarchy, for himself as Federal Chancellor to acquire
the moral prestige over the north that had taken four
hard years from 1862 to 1866 to acquire in Prussia itself.
When the north was really unified—kneaded, moulded,
and hardened by the Prussian leaven—the anti-Prussian
south could be swallowed—perhaps. The damping down
of Junker Particularism, the quarrels with the *Kreuzzeitung* and the Conservatives, the *entente* with National
Liberalism that disquieted Roon and angered Prince

Frederick Charles and the fierce militarist Conservatives of the old guard, were not without their influence on the south. Bismarck, like other great Conservative leaders, whose political imagination is as strong as their fidelity to the essentials of the Conservative creed, had to educate a party that did not desire to be educated. He had not strained soul and body beyond endurance to win victories for Liberalism. He was leading a rebellious and incredulous Junkertum through the wilderness to the promised land of an assured supremacy. Their faith faltered ; why not be content with the flesh-pots of the old Prussianism ? The Junker camp swarmed with Korahs, Dathans and Abirams. Round the King the malcontents swarmed, and the King was at heart as Prussian as the most reactionary squire from the old March. He showed it by his resentment at Junker sedition. When Conservatives behaved as if they were middle-class parliamentary Liberals William turned his royal back on them at levées, or rated the rebels in the language of the Prussian War Book.

The strength of German Nationalist feeling was convincingly shown in the Luxemburg affair, that came to a head while the Constitution was still on the anvil. The establishment of the Confederation of the North had destroyed the legal and political status of the duchy in the dissolved Bund of 1815. Napoleon, obsessed with the policy of *pourboires*, grasped at the opportunity of acquiring Luxemburg, linked by a personal union with Holland through the house of Orange-Nassau. Bismarck maintained throughout that he would acquiesce in the annexation—it would please Napoleon and be no danger to Prussia—provided that France would settle rapidly with Holland and present him with a *fait accompli*. But he warned Napoleon that he could not, and would not, on behalf of the Confederation formally guarantee the transaction beforehand. In the spring of 1867, with the Constitution unsettled, he had no desire yet to quarrel with France, but he could not come to the Reichstag and confess that he had agreed to the cession of what Germany regarded as German territory. It is probable that this line of action was sincere, and that, in presence of a *fait accompli*, he could have persuaded the militant Nationalist Liberals that a war for Luxemburg was unjustifiable and not worth the cost. But Bismarck forgot that others had good reason to distrust his sincerity and his methods. The King of Holland, in fear of Prussian aggression on Limburg, was prepared to close with Napoleon, provided that the contract had been first approved of by Prussia. He not unnaturally was afraid of making a bargain that Bismarck could easily employ as an excuse for attacking Holland. And Napoleon, on the principle that the supper with the Devil must have a long spoon, feared a trap, unless Prussia formally consented prior, and not subsequently, to the agreement with France. The Quai d'Orsay had had bitter experience of Bismarck's verbal assurances. This time they would have a bond.

The negotiations were bruited abroad—perhaps deliberately by the Prussian Foreign Office—and at once the National Liberals were up in arms. They found solid support from Prince Frederick Charles and the Conservatives; Nationalist sentiment was no less stirred in France, and at the commencement of March Bismarck was faced with the alternative of yielding to French pressure or acting with the German Nationalists and defying France. He insisted that France and Holland had bungled the business and put him in a position where he had no choice but to resist. Be that as it may, he extricated himself with his usual mixture of menace and skill. On March 19 he published in the official *Gazette* the secret military conventions with the Southern States—a plain warning that France would meet a united Germany if it came to war over German soil; and it is practically certain that Bennigsen's interpellation of April 1 in the Reichstag was arranged by Bismarck with the full concurrence of the Conservative party. Bennigsen's fiery oration spoke out the thought of Germany, and is an instructive object lesson in the German Nationalism of the Liberals. Bismarck's reply was a disavowal of the idea that Prussia would consent to any infringement of German rights, coupled with the assurance that a pacific solution, honourable to all parties, could be found.

An International Congress at London devised the solution. Luxemburg had its fortifications razed ; the Prussian garrison which had occupied it as a Federal fortress was withdrawn ; and the duchy itself was neutralised under the guarantees of the great contracting Powers, signatory to the treaty. The whole affair was another rebuff to Napoleon—another feather in Bismarck's cap. Napoleon did not get his *pourboire* ; French national feeling was angered at a fresh humiliation, and the secret military conventions with the south ; German Nationalism was, if not triumphant, pacified by the influence it had exercised. It is not surprising that at the Quai d'Orsay Bismarck's conduct was interpreted in the most sinister light. He had lured France on in order to inflict a fresh rebuff. This man was neither to hold nor to bind—which was perfectly true. The Franco-Prussian negotiations, in fact, from July 5, 1866 to June 1867 explain, though they do not justify, the determination three years later to wring from the King of Prussia a categorical renunciation of the Hohenzollern candidature. Still more significant was the revelation of passionate feeling in France and Germany, which an incident far more trifling than Luxemburg could fire at any moment into an explosion. France felt she was being steadily ringed with a German girdle that only war could break ; Germany desired complete union, and was perpetually reminded that France vetoed it. In May 1867 a word from Napoleon or from Bismarck would have brought about war. But in May 1867 Prussia was not ready, and Napoleon was absorbed in the success of the universal exhibition, which made Paris the carnival of Europe.

Bismarck was in a genial temper. The Prussian Diet had assigned a large sum of money for rewarding the Prussian leaders in the victories of 1866, and the King, very properly, selected his Minister-President for distinction. He desired that the sum assigned (400,000 thalers) should be invested in an estate, perpetually associated ' with the fame of your name and your family.' Bismarck bought a property at Varzin, in the north of Pomerania, some five-and-twenty miles from the Baltic coast, and surrounded by the landed aristocracy which regarded itself as 'vassals of the Margrave of Brandenburg.' At Varzin he could live the life he loved, the life of great spaces, swept by the winds across the heather and through the woods, the life of the manorial lord, hunter, forester, agriculturist, the dispenser of a seigneurial hospitality in the old German manner, more interested, his wife pronounced, in turnips than politics. Around him, as at Schönhausen, were the estates of friends and kinsmen— the men who made the marrow and bone of Prussianism— and Bismarck flung himself into the task of ordering and developing his new property, planting trees, felling timber, fencing, draining, manuring, sowing, breeding cattle, creating outlets for his produce, buying in the cheapest, and selling in the dearest, market. The infernal toil of the Wilhelmstrasse, the perpetual audiences with the King, the daily flow and ebb of telegrams, deputies, ministers, ambassadors and the grinding pen-work intensified his passion for blue sky and the fragrance of the pine-woods with the salt of the Baltic in the north wind. Varzin was a better reward than the steady drizzle of crosses, stars, and orders, now descending on him from German kings or foreign potentates. But even at Varzin after a day on horseback, or in the marshes after snipe and woodcock, when the lights had been extinguished and the household slept, the lamp in Bismarck's study burned till dawn. The great Pomeranian boarhounds, asleep, but a symbol of Prussia *toujours en vedette*, knew that at his desk their master, freed from the day's routine, was hammering out, through cigar after cigar, the practical solution of the problems with which his brain never ceased to wrestle. It was in these lonely vigils that Schleswig-Holstein was annexed, Austria overthrown, Napoleon duped and chastised, the North German Confederation brazed together, the German Empire made—in the watches of the night that Bismarck would open his Bible and find the confirmation of his faith in a Divine Providence and a God Who ordered the world and chose the instruments of His inscrutable will.

All the world flocked to Paris. The reconciliation of France and Prussia was apparently sealed by the visit of

King William and the princes and elders of the Prussian congregation. The exhibition of 1867, like the exhibition in London of 1862 that preceded the American and Austrian wars, proclaimed to the Europe and the America that had witnessed Gettysburg and Königgrätz peace and goodwill, and an era of beneficent rivalry in the unrestrained quality of trade, commerce, and the arts. Paris has been, since the history of France began, a matchless creator of life's greater ironies. It surpassed itself in the summer of 1867, when Napoleon received his royal and imperial guests with balls, dinners, soirées, reviews, the enchantments of the exhibition, the galaxy of beauty at the Tuileries, fit to adorn the creative genius of Worth and the Rue de la Paix, and over all the carnal gaiety of *La Grande Duchesse de Gerolstein*, and the intoxicating romp of Offenbach's invitation to dance and dance again. ' Let us laugh, let us sing, and to-morrow we shall die.' What is life but an opera bouffe, the buzz of pleasure-loving insects in a brief circle of warm sunshine, the grey but rose-tipped dawn, the splendour of midday, and the annihilating darkness of night? What did it matter that Berejowski tried with his pistol to avenge the wrongs of Poland, that at Queretaro Maximilian had been shot, that Garibaldi had risen again and been wounded at Aspromonte, that the French chassepots had ' wrought marvels ' at the Mentana which denied Rome to Italy and reaffirmed the temporal power of the Papacy, that men and women were sweated and starved at Lyons, and that the ' red international ' was laying the basis of the commune in the hungry squalor of the faubourgs of St. Antoine and Belleville ?

With King William came Moltke and Bismarck, ready for a brief respite between the task of crushing Austria and crushing France. Moltke, more silent than ever, spied out the nakedness of the land, and in his morning walks studied the artillery positions from which this Paris, like the Florence of Charles VIII. only fit to be looked on in days of holiday, could be bombarded. It was Moltke's first visit, and he used it to make the next time a memorable one for himself and the world. Bismarck knew Paris well. He shrugged his broad shoulders at the hisses of the

patriots in the crowd. ' I am not surprised at my reception,' he remarked; ' we politicians cannot please everybody.' But for all that he conquered Paris by his gallant
readiness to drain to the dregs the cup that Circe daily
brewed for her guests. He walked and dined, drank and
supped, enjoyed the *féerie* at the Hotel de Ville, laughed
at the gala performances of *La Grande Duchesse,* with its
raillery of the morals, vanities, pettinesses, and pipe-clay
militarism of the small German courts. He danced.
Madame Carette records in her *Souvenirs Intimes* her waltz
with the Minister-President. ' Deign, madame,' he said,
offering her the rose from his buttonhole, ' to keep this as
a remembrance of the last waltz I shall dance in my life,
and which I shall not forget.' Nor did he omit to call at
the Quai d'Orsay, and with the barbed frankness of which
he was a master, half in jest, half in earnest, expose the
blunders that France had made in her diplomacy, and
suggest how the French Foreign Office could have put a
dozen nasty spokes in the Prussian wheels. Marshal
Lebœuf, immortal for his guarantee in 1870 that France
was ready to the last gaiter-button, divined the Prussian
heart when he solemnly conducted Bismarck and Moltke
round Versailles. ' Sire,' he related to Napoleon, ' I have
had a terrible day with two men who hate us with a mortal
hatred.' It was so true. But to Paris Bismarck appeared,
as Marshal Vaillant told him, a very human and fascinating
giant. ' Vraiment, c'est un bon bougre. Un gaillard qui
n'a pas froid aux yeux.' He promised to return—and
soon. Bismarck's next visit to Paris !

A year of patient work followed his return, bringing the
new Federal machinery into operation, but principally
occupied with completing the economic union of Germany.
The military conventions when submitted for ratification
to the Parliaments at Munich and Stuttgart provoked
obstinate criticism and opposition. Bismarck promptly
replied with a stroke at a vital and exposed part of the
Southern States. The renewal of the tariff union between
south and north was declared to be dependent on the
acceptance of the conventions. Threatened with economic ruin the Parliaments sulkily ratified the defensive

and offensive military agreements.   Bismarck now carried
the Zollverein far beyond the form and scope of the previous organisation.   A Tariff Parliament of deputies, chosen
by direct universal suffrage, and a Tariff Federal Council
(*Zoll Bundesrat*) on the model of the Federal Council of
the north, were created to authorise the economic legislation of the future.   The first session was held at Berlin
on April 27, 1868, and Germany, including Luxemburg,
had now a representative organisation at work, in which
south and north met in common conference for common
German purposes.   The economic, like the military union,
preceded the political by three years.

That first session of the Tariff Parliament was a notable
illustration of the forces at work for and against the maintenance of the divided Germany of 1867.   Ardent unionists north and south of the Main hoped to dovetail into the
Tariff Parliament powers to discuss political business
common to both Germanies.   But the proposal to extend
the economic authority of the new organ was defeated by
a narrow majority.   The prickly particularism of the delegates from the south took its revenge for the coercion
over the military conventions.   Bismarck wisely kept
aloof from the debates.   But in private he accomplished
much by frank intercourse with friends and critics.   The
economic machinery would have its effect in time.   The
inevitable union could be floated meanwhile in a flood of
good German Munich beer and Prussian hock, or en-
visaged with the eye of faith through the blue clouds of
after-dinner cigars.   A fine chance was given him, and he
grasped it at once.   Probst, a deputy from Stuttgart,
warned the Parliament against the union of north and
south, since it would involve a war to the knife with
France.   Bismarck replied that he could understand and
sympathise with the argument that the south must not be
coerced by the north—when union came, it must be the
free act of both Germanies—but the argument of fear—
as to that, he concluded with vibrating passion and amid
hurricane of cheers, ' the appeal to fear will never find an
echo in German hearts.' ˉ It was the note of power struck
on the keyboard of Nationalism.   In Bismarck's political

armoury it derived its tremendous force from the personality and achievements of the speaker, one who neither
feared nor flattered flesh.

Since 1867 the barometer of Unionism had been steadily
falling. Reaction had inevitably set in, and shallow depression after shallow depression drenched the two
Germanies. The formation of the Southern States in a
separate union, with an independent international existence, had not been established, and there was no likelihood
of its being carried through. The south felt that such a
union would facilitate incorporation with the north on the
terms of the north; Bismarck suspected that it would fall
under Austrian control, while Austria feared that it would
be a fresh sphere of Prussian influence, and France that it
would be a fresh obstacle to French ambition. Hohenlohe
summed the matter up : ' The reason why such a federation has not been consummated has hitherto lain in the
purely negative attitude taken by the governments of
Württemberg, Baden, and Hesse, and in the lack of any
sympathy with this idea among the people . . . and if the
Southern Confederation meets with insuperable difficulties
in Württemberg, you will admit that in Baden impossibility stares it in the face ' (*Memoirs*, i. 226 and 395). The
Bavarian feeling was no less strong in its indifference and
in its attachment to Bavarian autonomy. The failure was
all in Bismarck's favour. The independence of the four
southern States enabled him later (see p. 283) to negotiate
separately with each state and utilise the separate bargains
to compel acceptance of his terms. Had there been a
southern union in 1870, acting as a single unit, it would
have demanded and obtained far more favourable terms
as the condition of entering the Empire.

The real achievement of Prussia after 1867—the patient
manipulation of the Bundesrat, the unifying legislation
begun in the Reichstag, the remorseless assimilation of the
annexed provinces by the Prussian civil service, the solid
concrete of science, research, and political thought laid by
the intellectuals of National Liberalism and the flower of
the professoriate—was largely concealed from the foreign
public opinion outside the Confederation, which expects

to discover the soul, thought, and work of a nation in the columns of the newspapers with which its women light their stoves and the men their cigars. The entrenched Philistia of Great Britain, regarding universities as places where youths learned either to become gentlemen or book-worms, and science as a harmless recreation for literary institutes or the finger-staining drudgery of the apothe-cary, persisted in regarding the German universities, where the renaissance of the German mind was being completed, as centres of dreamy idealism or the dreary laboratories of an unintelligible theology. The apostle of sweet-ness and light, Matthew Arnold, writing the classical reports in which he foretold the coming supremacy of Germany because, like the Italian renaissance, it strove to combine the humanities with science, with 1866 staring him in the face, believed that the French army in 1870 would smash the Prussian. So potent even on priestly rebels of the House of Levi are the Idols of the Market-Place and of the Tribe. Colonel Stoffel, a tragic Cas-sandra, if ever there was one, for three years warned his government at Paris of what Prussia was preparing ; but the men like Maréchal Niel, who had divined the truth, either perished under the surgeon's knife or were impotent. The Second Empire had justly forfeited the confidence of thinking and toiling France ; and the ears of the Tuileries and the Quai d'Orsay were stuffed with clerical wax.

But the lower the barometer fell, the harder, with Bismarck's knowledge, did the Great General Staff work. Thanks to the Federal Chancellor, it was free from the interference not merely of journalists or irresponsible politicians but of a Cabinet which had never studied war or regarded it as an unexpected disease, to be dealt with on its symptoms when there could be no doubt it had broken out. To Bismarck there were two certainties, and only two, in an inscrutable world—the Prussian Crown and the Prussian Army. The Prussian King was his affair, and on him, as on the *rocher de bronze*, the compass of policy could swing freely in the dirtiest weather. The time of blood and iron had not passed. It was truer than ever in his interpretation that the greatest question of the age, the settlement with France, would not be settled by resolutions in the Reichstag and the Zoll Parliament, the speeches of Thiers, or the manufactured plebiscites of the Minister of the Interior at Paris. The surgery of war was needed to let the bad blood out in Germany. When some thousands of Bavarians and Württembergers had fallen beside Prussian, Saxon, Hanoverian, and Nassauer, the Empire would be made. The iron crown of the Imperial Hohenstaufen would not be picked up in the gutters of Frankfurt or Berlin—that was the folly of 1848 and 1866—but on a victorious battlefield in France.

The idea of disarmament had been in the air since 1868, and Daru at Paris, Virchow and the Radicals at Berlin were playing with it. But Lord Newton in his *Life of Lord Lyons* has kindly lifted the blinds for us, and the instructive episode in which the British government, inspired from Paris, confidentially invited in the spring of 1870 Prussia to join in a European disarmament can now be studied in its entirety. Bismarck maintained a grave courtesy—he was never gravely courteous with the realities of statecraft or of life—but the admirable essays of Lord Clarendon must have stirred 'the irreverent merriment' that he allowed himself when English pacifism was proved by the sale of an ironclad to Prussia and the readiness to sell another. These excellent insulars simply did not live in the world of facts, and Bismarck put them aside with the soothing firmness that self-control owes to a well-meaning but hysterical woman.

Clarendon in 1864 had protested that he desired no further intercourse with *cet homme, sans foi et sans loi*; he now appealed to Count Bismarck—'I am sure that a statesman so liberal and far-sighted will admit without regret'—a sentence the choice of the epithets in which is delicious. Bismarck replied quietly, 'that he did not dare even to name the subject of the letter to the King. . . . Coming from England it would make the worst impression on him.' He added 'that any weakening of Prussia's power, any disturbance of the Balance of Power in Europe, can hardly be for the interest of England'—and emphasised the formidable dangers that Prussia had to face from

France, Austria, Russia, and—a pretty stroke—Denmark. ' I saw,' wrote our ambassador, ' it was useless to pursue the question further.' In reality it was useless to have raised it at all.

This is not a case of superior wisdom after the event. When our Foreign Office suggested that Prussia should disarm, it was asking Prussia to cease to be the Prussia of Frederick the Great and Bismarck ; it was further asking that Prussia and Germany should abandon the ideal of unification on Bismarckian lines. There was substantial truth in Bismarck's contention that France was irreconcilably hostile to German ambitions, and that this hostility made the armed strength of Prussia a first condition of security, and, though he did not say so, of attaining her end in defiance of that hostility. If Lord A. Loftus had not categorically informed our Foreign Office that north and south would seize the first opportunity of agreement between the two parties to unite, he was writing, as Bismarck said in 1862, ' more nonsense to London than I suspected.' There was as little chance of the government at Berlin abandoning this ideal of union, as there was of England renouncing the union with Scotland and Ireland on the suggestion of Berlin ' in the interest of European peace and the Balance of Power,' or of the United States abandoning American unity in 1861 or 1867, because it suited the aristocrats of Great Britain and Europe. The suggestion of renunciation was to the German mind an impertinence which proved English jealousy. Lord Lyons, Ollivier, Daru, Napoleon III., the Empress Eugénie, Thiers, the young Gambetta, who had leaped into fame over the *procès* Baudouin, could all have told Clarendon that neither the Second Empire nor France would permit the union of North and South Germany—the establishment on their frontier of a military empire, controlled by Bismarck. Had our Foreign Office informed the Quai d'Orsay that the condition of disarmament was the acceptance by France of a German Empire from the Alps to the Baltic, the reply would have been truly enough that it was a command to Napoleon to abdicate. We had no answer to Bismarck's interpolation that he could have settled with Napoleon by letting him have Belgium and Luxemburg—Belgium, Palmerston's creation of 1839. From 1867 to 1870 our Foreign Office, like every other Foreign Office, was kept in a perpetual fret and fever by Napoleon's direct and indirect efforts to pave the way for annexing Belgium, and Belgium did not settle the problem of the Rhine. Alsace and Lorraine were to all Germans ' unredeemed Germany '; they were to German Nationalism what Rome was to Italian Nationalism. Nothing but French bayonets and the chassepots of Mentana kept Italy out of Rome. Nothing but the chassepots kept the French flag flying at Strasburg and Metz; nothing but German bayonets would get the Germans across the upper Rhine. If Lord Clarendon did not recognise these plain realities he and his colleagues at Downing Street were simply deceiving themselves. It was easy for a British minister and British public opinion—the combined expression of a triumphant Nationalism—to dismiss these distressing realities as the symptoms of the diseased mind. The poultice of disarmament did not and could not pluck from German and French memory a rooted sorrow, and the idea that it could was neither statesmanship nor even common sense.

The error went far deeper and much further back into the history of the European State system. Bismarck could smother the proposal in a tangle of detail : but the principle of disarmament cut down to the bone and marrow of the Prussian State. A progressive disarmament levied on the European States like a progressive income-tax, with a super-tax for all exceeding some fixed limit, ignored the fundamentals of the situation. Was Prussia expected to give up, or was she not, the law of 1814 and the reorganised military system of 1862-66 by which every Prussian male was required to receive military training ? How could Prussia ' disarm ' without abandoning this principle ? The Prussian army of 1867 was simply a scientific organisation to realise this fundamental of her civic polity, at a minimum of cost and friction to the civil population and the civil state. The Prussian State was the outcome of the principle—*Das Volk in Waffen*; the army was not as in Great

Britain a state mackintosh that could be thrown off in fine, and rediscovered from the national cupboard for use in dirty, weather. Yet Great Britain and Europe persisted in regarding the Prussian army—the Prussian nation in arms, achieving national aims by force controlled and directed by the Crown—as a luxury of the monarchy, and a dangerous but superfluous tool in the hands of unscrupulous ministers. The truest reply to the secret dispatch of Lord Clarendon would have been a volume of select extracts from the memoranda of Frederick William I., the writings of Frederick the Great, the documents of the Prussian reformers—vom Stein, Scharnhorst, the Humboldts—bound up with the salient passages from Clausewitz's *Vom Kriege*, and the correspondence of Moltke and Bismarck himself.

The evidence for the principles of Prussianism both in theory and fact had lain open for more than a generation to all who cared to study it. Carlyle's *Frederick*, which appeared between 1858 and 1865, was a noble and brilliant contribution to historical literature, but the connection between the Frederick portrayed by Carlyle and the Prussia of the age of Bismarck was not grasped by the generation that read Carlyle. The diplomatists of the Clarendon School, of Cobden and Bright, of Gladstone and Disraeli, continued to regard the Continent and the European State system with the eyes of tradition, insularism, or idealism. Yet Bismarck had been there since 1851. Since 1862 his speeches were reported and his acts were written out in language unmistakable. The North German Confederation was there in full daylight, and the Prussian General Staff and army had proved their principles and their power to carry them out. Morier in 1868 drew up for Lord Stanley a memorandum on the German situation, in which the truth is told with remarkable accuracy. A few sentences may be quoted here :—

' The motive power we seek resides, of course, in the Chancellor ; not however in the office, but in the individual Bismarck who at present fills the office. . . . The Federal Council, after the fashion of diplomatic congresses, works underground and away from the light of day . . . hence the work is *bona fide* got through at the

green table.   Under these circumstances, to those acquainted with
the personal prestige of Bismarck, his complete mastery of the
situation in the Federal Council is no matter of surprise. . . . He
is among his Federal compeers *facile princeps*, not merely in the
higher branches of statesmanship, but as a skilful workman in the
details of administration. . . . Certain it is that no law and no
measure comes out of the Federal Council in any other shape than
that the Federal Chancellor desires . . . The intrinsic vitality of
the national forces as compared with those opposed to them, the
recognition by Bismarck of this fact, and lastly, the accident of the
latter's Wolseyan lust for power ; for the more we penetrate into
the intricacies of the North German Constitution, the more we
become convinced that its whole framework is built up with reference to the exceptional and extraordinary position of the Chancellor . . . and to the concentration into his own hands of the vast
administrative power vested in the Federal Chancellor's department. . . . The government of North Germany is tending daily
to become as much a personal government as that of France. . . .
No man can be a *bona fide* leader of a great Liberal party without
faith in Liberal principles, and not one mustard seed of such faith
exists in Count Bismarck's nature.'—(*Life of Morier*, ii. pp. 103-23.)

Throughout Morier emphasised the secrets of Bismarck's
power—Prussia and Prussianism, and, secondly, National
Liberalism bent on unification.   Morier had been for
fifteen years a voice crying in the wilderness.   He was
hated and feared by Bismarck because he knew and told
the truth about Prussianism.   He was distrusted in
England at the Foreign Office because he told his chiefs
what they did not wish to hear, and had the embarrassing
gift of predicting failures and the reasons for them.

The real problem for the Europe of 1867-70 lay in the
undeniable antithesis between the State as Power, based
on the nation in arms, carrying out a policy in which might
made right, and the State as Right, striving to base international relations on law, morality, and the conscience of
self-governing democracies.   But the problem was neither
solved nor even simplified by a grotesque and unpardonable
ignorance of Germany's avowed ambitions and the sources
from which it drew its strength, or by the supposition that
Germany standing on the threshold of achievement would
listen for one moment to a suggestion of throwing down

the one weapon by which achievement could be made good.

Bismarck intended to unify Germany and alter not merely the Balance of Power but rearrange the Continent on a different system, the capital feature of which would be a German hegemony controlled by Prussia. In 1868, when Morier wrote, Moltke on foot had examined the Franco-German frontier from end to end. By 1870 the reorganisation of the Federal forces was practically complete; the strategic railways carried out; the military material collected, and mobilisation could be effected within three weeks or less. France swarmed with German spies. At Berlin every move in France was watched with the eyes of the hunter on his prey. The war with France was being as remorselessly prepared as the war of 1866 with Austria, and with all the benefit of the experience of 64 and '66. The Chief of the Staff knew that it would probably come on Prussia like a thief in the night. Character, personality, and power of work—these two men, Bismarck and Moltke, were the quintessence of Prussianism in the combination of these qualities. And they had at their disposal a nation brimming with capacity, fired with the faith that can move mountains, and ready to work itself to the bone in disciplined toil.

Two other quotations are relevant to the general situation. Lord Lyons wrote to Lord Clarendon on January 10, 1870 :—

' M. Ollivier was particularly alive to the importance of not exposing France to the appearance of being slighted ; in fact, he would not conceal from me that under present circumstances a public rebuff from Prussia would be fatal. Un échec," he said, " c'est la guerre ! " ' ' I could see,' wrote Lord A. Loftus on March 12, 1870, ' that Count Bismarck has no fear of the Russian policy towards Prussia, so long as the Emperor lives and Prince Gortchakov remains minister.'

After 1867 the external and internal situation was disquieting and depressing. In Bavaria Prince Hohenlohe, manfully striving against the Ultramontanes and the Particularists to find a form of union which would preserve the autonomy of Bavaria, was obliged to resign (March 7, 1870), and a clerical administration under Bray took his place. In Württemberg, a stronghold of Radicalism and the Deutsche Volkspartei, the anti-union opposition was so democratic that the Tsar Alexander ii. was seriously concerned for the throne of his kinsmen at Stuttgart. In the Reichstag there was much bitter criticism. Bismarck was so exasperated that he had recourse to his familiar device of tendering his resignation on the ground that one man could not reconcile the King, eight ministers, and three Parliaments. But his chief difficulties were not with the Reichstag but with the irreconcilable dynasticism of the deposed rulers—the Hanoverian in particular. The famous 'Reptile Fund' derived its name from the sequestration of a part of the royal property of Hanover to a fund for counteracting Hanoverianism. 'The reptiles must be pursued into their lairs.' Junkertum was a continuous stumbling-block. Edwin von Manteuffel, the chief of the military cabinet, was supported by a powerful party as likely to be a much better Chancellor. The Memoirs of Stosch and Bernhardi reveal the under-currents swirling round the monarchy. Bismarck retorted by attacks on feminine and English influence. The jackals round the lion yapped, with the lion's encouragement, in the press controlled by the Press Bureau and the Reptile Fund.

Foreign policy and the international situation kept Bismarck very anxious. The irrepressible Beust had transferred his services from Dresden to Vienna. Beust meant more mischief than Austria was capable of carrying out. German historians have sedulously built up the theory that between 1868 and 1870 Prussia was being steadily encircled by three hostile states. Hence the comfortable conclusion that the war with France was a defensive effort against an offensive assault, anticipated by Prussia and thrust upon her against her will.

In support of this view there are certain undeniable facts. In the autumn of 1867 Napoleon met the King of Württemberg at Ulm, the King of Bavaria at Augsburg, and the Emperor of Austria at Salzburg. Francis Joseph returned the visit at Paris. The *entente* between Austria and France was, however, confined to after-dinner toasts. Menabrea in Italy drew up the project of a triple alliance, and in 1868 and 1869 there was much discussion between Vienna, Florence, and Paris. The general belief at Berlin that an alliance between France and Italy had been concluded was erroneous. All that Napoleon had on paper was (September 1869) a letter from Victor Emmanuel and another from Francis Joseph approving of the idea of common action at some future date. He showed these letters in July 1870 to the Council at Paris that had war and peace in its hands, and they profoundly influenced the decision. The Council afterwards accepted Napoleon's interpretation —wholly unjustified, as the events proved—that they were equivalent to a solemn pledge. The visit of General Le Flô to Petersburg in 1869 caused much perturbation, but Le Flô discovered that Russia was only interested in the question of 'revising' the clauses in the Treaty of 1856 which closed the Black Sea to Russia. Bismarck truly told Lord A. Loftus that 'he attributed no importance to the reports of a Franco-Russian *entente*.' The permanent difficulty was Rome. Napoleon declined to give the one guarantee that would secure Italy's enthusiastic aid—the withdrawal of the French troops from Rome. The Archduke Albert, the victor of Custozza, visited Paris in the spring of 1870, and General Lebrun was sent to Vienna. Schemes of military co-operation were discussed, but when (June 15) Lebrun left Vienna no formal alliance had been drawn up, nor was there a military convention in existence pledging either France or Austria to combined action. No military convention with Italy was in existence nor had a formal political alliance been made. The danger of the situation lay in the critical position of the Napoleonic Empire, summed up in Lord Lyons' letter of May 6, 1870 :—

'It would be quite a mistake to suppose that this is a moment at which it would be safe to defy France. On the contrary, a war unmistakably provoked by Prussia would be hailed by many as a welcome diversion from internal difficulties. So far as I can judge, *Ollivier is not the man to shrink from one.*' (The italics are Lord Lyons'.)

So far, no evidence has been forthcoming to prove that Italy, Austria, and France had agreed to unite in an attack on Prussia or the North German Confederation. The 'conspiracy' to force an offensive war on an unwilling Germany had in fact not been made. The justification of Bismarck's action, wherever it may be placed, cannot rest on the defined menace of a Triple Alliance, ready to strike at an agreed hour for agreed objects by agreed and concerted action.

Bismarck was perfectly well informed of these facts. The intelligence departments of the Foreign Office and the General Staff did not accept the gossip of diplomatists and journalists as the basis of their policy and strategy, though they utilised it, with much embroidery, in the newspapers controlled from the Chancery to organise German public opinion. On the other hand, the evidence that Bismarck after 1866 regarded a war with France as inevitable and desirable is overwhelming, and he has completed it in his own Memoirs. After 1866 the political task was to isolate France, for the General Staff demanded the isolation of the foe as the condition of a crushing military decision. Bismarck started by giving Moltke the necessary time. For three years he sedulously damped down the Chauvinists in the Reichstag. For three years the Chancellor breathed peace and goodwill. The argument for unification through war was clinched by the course of events in Germany since 1866. Without war unification was either impossible or only attainable by pulling the North German Confederation to pieces and reconstructing it to suit the anti-Prussian feeling of the south. In the Reichstag the National Liberals, toiling at unifying legislation, had not abandoned the principle of achieving ministerial responsibility and responsible parliamentary government in a Federal and united Germany. In March 1869 Twesten and the Radical Left demanded the establishment of four responsible Federal ministers—finance, war, the navy, and commerce—to sit beside the Federal Chancellor as colleagues, not as the subordinate executive heads of Chancery departments. The proposal, which meant a re-writing of the Federal Constitution, was only defeated with the help of the Conservatives by seventeen votes. For three years Bismarck at Berlin and in the solitude of Varzin studied Germany and the problem. War alone would smash down, he concluded and rightly, the obstinate obstacles to the Prussian solution. So long as France was there, the south would be reinforced in its stubborn reluctance to enter the Confederation except on its own terms. War was necessary also as much to complete the defeat of Liberalism as to defeat France. In May 1870 Bismarck spoke in the Reichstag of the embogging of the work of unification in the sand of Particularism, of the States, and of parties, and of the German right to crush under a foot of iron every obstacle to the establishment of the German nation in all its splendour and power. The war of 1870 foretold the nadir of Liberalism in Europe.

Russia was in Bismarck's pocket. After 1867 Bismarck's system of foreign policy pivoted more surely than before on a close understanding with Petersburg. It is probable that in 1866 Russia's acquiescence in the Treaty of Prague had been secured by an undertaking to permit the revision of the Treaty of 1856 at a favourable opportunity. It is certain that Bismarck secured Russia's benevolent neutrality in 1870 by inviting Russia to denounce the prohibitive clauses : and the undertaking had probably been given in the spring of 1870, if not earlier. Such a denunciation would at once put Great Britain out of action ; it meant that Austria, a signatory to the Treaty of 1856, and bound by a secret alliance with England and France, dating from 1856, to resist the revision of the Black Sea articles by force, would have Russia on her back if she took action either against Russia or Prussia. Bismarck's refusal to intervene in the Italian problem was not due to indifference but to calculation. So long as France kept her troops in Rome a Franco-Italian alliance was out of the question. If circumstances required, Prussia could, as in 1866, buy Italy for a price ; on the other hand, the increasing volume of opposition to the Vatican Council in Germany offered the opportunity to gratify German

Protestants and Catholics by breaking with the Papacy. Bismarck therefore held his hand.

The neutrality of Belgium created a powerful lever on Great Britain. The General Staff at Berlin preferred for military reasons that Belgium should remain neutral. When Bismarck published in *The Times* on July 25, 1870, Benedetti's damning letter with its crude revelation of Napoleon's ambitions and proposals, and followed it up by a Prussian guarantee of Belgium's security, he practically obtained British neutrality. ' Louis ' was certainly going to pay dearly for his intervention in 1866.

So far then from Prussia by the spring of 1870 being hemmed in and isolated, it was France that was hemmed in. The only alliances Bismarck required were the military conventions with the south, and these had been secured in 1866. Moltke assured him that, humanly speaking, if a united Germany fought France in a ring fence victory was certain. The ring fence was practically complete.

It was not enough, however, to hem France in. She must be either coerced or lured into declaring war. The war could then be proclaimed a defensive one, on behalf of German honour, security, and independence. France the aggressor, pacific Prussia the victim of her vanity and ambition.

This attitude was essential. King William still had a conscience, even if, as Bismarck said in 1869, ' our master to-day has changed his tune from that in 1862 ; he has drunk from the chalice of popularity and refuses to break it.' But the south must be brought in, fired with the enthusiasm for ' Germany in danger.' Neutral public opinion must be influenced from the start to tolerate, perhaps demand, the chastisement of France. Bismarck understood as well as Lord Lyons that the Napoleonic Empire could not stand another rebuff. He knew the men with whom he had to deal : Napoleon, ill, vacillating, swayed by every group in turn ; Ollivier, high-minded, weak, and not master of his cabinet ; the reckless Duc de Gramont, ultramontane to his finger-tips, who replaced the cool-headed Daru in May ; behind them the Empress and the clerical camarilla, and in Paris the boulevard patriotism de café-concert, vain, ignorant, the dupe of its government and itself.

Spain could complete the isolation of France. Certainly Bismarck's luck was extraordinary, for just when Prussia needed a revolution the Spaniards obligingly provided one. In 1868 Queen Isabella abdicated. The Spanish throne was vacant. Who was to fill it ?

The complete story of the Hohenzollern candidature has never been told. It probably never will, for the secret may be concealed in the archives of Friedrichsruhe, but more probably was buried with Bismarck. But the main points are clear, and they conclusively contradict the Prussian version accepted for a decade because the refutation was not available. Whether Prim and Salazar started the idea of placing Leopold or Frederick of Hohenzollern-Sigmaringen, the elder or the third son of Anthony of Hohenzollern, and the brothers of Charles, ruler in Roumania, or whether the idea was inspired by Bismarck, is of historical interest but not of political importance. We know now that in February 1869 Villanueva came from Spain to Berlin and had a long interview with the Chancellor ; in March Th. von Bernhardi left for a special mission to Spain ; in September 1869 Salazar was introduced by Werthern, the Prussian minister at Munich, to Prince Anthony, and suggested the throne for Prince Leopold ; in February 1870 Salazar returned and pressed the candidature on King William and Prince Anthony, who were not favourable to the idea ; Bismarck on February 27 drew up a confidential report in which he strongly supported the proposal ; on March 15 a Council was held at which Moltke, Roon, Schleinitz, Thile, Delbrück, Bismarck, the King, and Prince Anthony and Leopold were present ; at this Council Delbrück asked Moltke ' Are we ready if Napoleon takes it ill ? ' and Moltke simply nodded ; the Hohenzollerns hesitated, attracted by the prospects, repelled by the dangers of so ambitious a stroke ; Bismarck sent Lothar Bucher and Major Versen on a secret mission to Spain in April; to Prince Anthony's deep regret, neither of his available sons would accept; the affair which seemed to be closed was renewed in May as the result of Bucher and Versen's mission, and thanks to a second mission of Bucher's, and Salazar's importunity, supported by Bismarck's persistent pressure, Prince Leopold finally consented probably by the end of May, definitely on June 19; and, lastly, on June 21, 'after a hard struggle,' King William also consented. So far the matter had been kept a profound secret. Olozaga, the Spanish minister at Paris, was quite in the dark; Prim, however, instead of carrying the business through and presenting Europe with a *fait accompli*, as Bismarck probably intended and Salazar expected, prorogued the Cortes till October 31. He seems to have lost his nerve at this point, and to have hoped to talk Napoleon over during the summer at Vichy. But the secret was either betrayed or deliberately let out, and on July 3 was definitively known at Paris. ·

Bismarck was perfectly well aware that France would not accept the Hohenzollern candidature. The King of Roumania duly noted in his diary the certainty of French opposition, as far back as December 9, 1868, and on the mere rumour of such a candidature in 1869 Napoleon (May 11) had sent Benedetti to Bismarck to indicate the attitude of the French government. It is certain that Bismarck intended to fling down a challenge to France, and that in procuring the acceptance of the candidature by his sovereign he was deliberately provoking a European war. The argument that a Hohenzollern prince at Madrid would drop his Germanism and become a Spaniard when he crossed the Pyrenees is worthless, and recent events in the Near East confirm its worthlessness. Bismarck himself can be put in the witness-box. In his report of February 2, he argued that among many advantages that acceptance of the Spanish throne would bring—the prestige of the Hohenzollerns elevated like the Habsburgs to a European position, the strengthening of the monarchical principle, the commercial concessions for German trade (as in Roumania)—the military aspect was of great importance :—

'If Germany and France were at war,' he wrote, ' and the position was that under Isabella, and if on the other hand a government in sympathy with Germany existed, the difference for us between these two situations may b calculated at one to two army corps. In the former, French troops would be released by Spain and be available against Germany; in the latter, France would have to detach an army corps to the (Spanish) frontier.'

In a word, Spain would complete the isolation of France and open the Mediterranean to Germany. It was a case of double or quits. If France acquiesced, Spain became a Hohenzollern satrapy, possibly an ally in a future war; if she refused, she must make the candidature a *casus belli*, and force war on Prussia.

Bismarck's contention that the whole matter was a pure family and dynastic matter is belied by his conduct and arguments. If so, why all the secrecy? Why was it necessary to discuss a pure family affair of a cadet branch of the Hohenzollerns at a Prussian Council, at which it was requisite to include the Federal Chancellor, the Chief of the General Staff, the Minister of War, the Director of the Federal Chancery, and the Under-Secretary of the Foreign Department? In Bismarck's confidential report the candidature was argued on grounds of high policy in which the interests of Germany and Prussia were deeply concerned, and refusal of the offer was represented to be politically detrimental to Germany. Bismarck repeatedly asserted that he had no *locus standi* officially to advise the King in a dynastic concern. Yet for twelve months he had used all his authority and power as Chancellor and Minister-President to press Prince Anthony and his sovereign to accept. Bismarck's denial of knowledge of the affair was a lie. In what capacity did he receive Villanueva, send Bernhardi, Bucher, and Versen to Spain, and correspond with the Crown Prince on the subject? The original introduction of Salazar to Prince Anthony was made by Werthern, certainly with Bismarck's consent and probably at his instigation. Men in the diplomatic service were broken by Bismarck for implicating the government, without the Chancellor's authority, in a policy that committed Prussia. Werthern would not have dared to do what he did, unless he desired to be treated as Arnim was later.

Bismarck's conduct throughout the affair was competent, dictatorial, and absolutely unscrupulous, and his behaviour was indicated in the letter, taken by Bucher to Spain on June 11, the authenticity of which can be accepted. He would maintain that officially he was not concerned. Why should the Spaniards not offer the crown to any one they pleased ? Accordingly, he retired to Varzin on April 14, and stayed there till May 21. Until June 8 he was in Berlin and then retired to Varzin to be out of the way, when ' the Spanish bomb ' burst, and stayed there till July 12. King William went for a cure to Ems, and the Hohenzollerns of Sigmaringen were at their country-house. Thile as under-secretary could therefore reply to French questions that ' the Prussian government was absolutely ignorant of this affair, which did not exist for it.' Thile who had been present at the Council of March 15 !

It is unnecessary to relate in detail the oft-told dramatic story of the French government's action when the news of the candidature became known. From July 3 onwards French public opinion was in a fever of excitement and indignation. The government recognised the challenge. By sending Benedetti direct to King William at Ems they succeeded in stripping the candidature of its family character. They deliberately fixed the responsibility on Prussia, and on July 12, when Prince Anthony renounced the candidature, with King William's acquiescence, France had won a striking diplomatic success. King William, indeed, confessed that the renunciation removed a load of stone from his heart. The French government feared, however, that Prince Leopold might imitate his brother Prince Charles in 1866 in the Roumanian affair, repudiate his father, and go to Spain. The Duc de Gramont and Ollivier knew the character of the Prussian government and of Bismarck, and were determined to stroke the t's and dot the i's of the renunciation ; they aimed at inflicting a personal as well as a political humiliation on the Hohenzollern sovereign and his minister. Like a weak man Gramont did not know where to stop. His insistence that King William must give a guarantee that the candidature would not be renewed, was made on his own responsibility without communication to the Prime Minister, or the Council of State, or, apparently, Napoleon himself. King William, who had behaved correctly so far, and was convinced that his acquiescence in the renunciation closed the whole episode, naturally resented the French demand as an insinuation against his royal good faith and as a deliberate attempt to pick a quarrel with Prussia. The message through an aide-de-camp that the incident was closed, and that he had nothing further to say, was somewhat curt but unobjectionable. It was not insulting nor intended to be an insult. Gramont had by his folly pledged France; much worse, he had given Bismarck his chance.

By July 12 Bismarck was very depressed. For the first time he had been worsted before Europe in a grave affair of diplomacy; and it is clear that he had not anticipated the French success in terrifying Prince Anthony into a renunciation. The game as he had intended to play it had broken down completely. He now had neither a defensive war nor the candidature. Public opinion both in Paris and Germany was very excited, but had the French government taken a strong and cool line on the 12th of July, informed France that as the result of French action the candidature was at an end, that the King of Prussia acquiesced in the renunciation, and that his royal words and pacific disposition could be trusted, it is difficult to see what Bismarck could have done. The Duc de Gramont's irresponsible and criminal levity ruined a great success. But it is impossible to acquit Ollivier, the Prime Minister, of culpable negligence, indecision, and weakness. A close examination of the evidence leaves an indelible impression that Ollivier wavered between several and contradictory lines of action, and did not supervise the action of the Foreign Office as he should have done. Gramont and Ollivier enabled Bismarck to represent France as insulted. The French government had now either to sit down under the insult or force a war in vindication of French honour. The famous 'dispatch from Ems'[1] which brought

[1] Late in life Bismarck remarked to Harden, the editor of *Die Zukunft*, who printed it in his paper: 'It is very easy, without falsification, but simply by

about the final rupture was neither a falsification nor a forgery. The King left to Bismarck's discretion the responsibility of publishing his intimation to Benedetti that he had nothing further to communicate. Bismarck saw Gortschakov on July 12 at Berlin, and probably then and there ratified Russia's benevolent neutrality in the case of war by agreeing to the denunciation of the prohibitive clauses in the Treaty of 1856 at a favourable opportunity; he was searching with ferocious earnestness for the opportunity to reopen the issues between France and Prussia and drive France into war. The edited version of the King's narrative which he authorised for publication was a brutalised and provocative message, true in the bare facts, but so worded as to convey a wholly different construction; it was deliberately intended to be ' a red flag for the Gallic Bull.' The Bismarckian version gladdened the gloomy hearts of Roon and Moltke at that memorable meal on the night of July 13. This meant the war for which they had prayed and worked. Roon said : ' Our God of old lives still and will not let us perish in disgrace.' Moltke smote his hand upon his breast and said : ' If I may not live to lead our armies in such a war, then the devil may come directly afterwards and fetch away the old carcase.' That night Bismarck said his prayers with unusual fervency. On July 14 Germany was singing ' Die Wacht am Rhein ! ' At Paris delirious crowds on the boulevards were crying ' À Berlin ! ' On July 15 King William issued the order for general mobilisation. On July 19 France declared war.[1]

Bismarck had won. The British offer of mediation (July 17) was politely but firmly rejected. France was isolated. Beust and Victor Emmanuel's efforts to settle

omissions and corrections, completely to alter the tone of a communication. I have myself once had experience of the task, as editor of the Ems dispatch . . . when by omissions and compressions I had edited it, Moltke exclaimed : " The original was an order to retreat (*chamade*), now it is a summons to charge (*fanfare*)."' The text of the King's message and the version, as edited by Bismarck and sent officially for publication and to all the Prussian diplomatic representatives, is printed in an Appendix (p. 496), where the exact character of the ' editing ' can be textually established by every reader for himself.

[1] The famous cartoon in *Punch* (July 30), one of Tenniel's best, in which the great Napoleon warned Napoleon III. to halt—' Beware ! '—published before the German victories bore the warning out, was a prophecy tragically true.

the Italian problem, with a view to armed mediation and subsequent active intervention on the side of France, broke down between July 19 and August 2. Even at the eleventh hour and in the extreme peril of the situation Napoleon could not, or more probably was not allowed to, bring himself to renounce Rome. He wavered, consented, and then withdrew his consent. By August 6 the German victories made the intervention of Austria and Italy or a Triple Alliance too dangerous to be seriously entertained further. Bismarck's political strategy, as in 1866, had given the German army its chance ; and the soldiers justified his confidence. Roon told King William on July 15 that mobilisation was easy, for everything was ready. Marshal Lebœuf had said the same at St. Cloud. Lebœuf's assertion was an ignorant boast, Roon's a summary of three years' relentless preparation. The German military machine worked with marvellous precision. After July 15 Moltke could find time to read French novels, until the troops had reached their appointed stations, when he left Berlin with his sovereign for Wörth, Spicheren, Mars-la-Tour, St. Privat, Sedan, and Paris.

Bismarck travelled with General Headquarters throughout the campaign ; his sons were serving in the army and took part in the desperate battles round Metz ; he himself was present at Sedan, and there at the weaver's cottage on the Donchéry road, on the morning of September 2, he met Napoleon. 'An emphatic contrast,' he wrote to his wife on September 3, ' with our last meeting in '67 at the Tuileries. Our conversation was difficult, although I did not wish to recall things which would painfully affect the man struck down by God's mighty hand . . . yesterday and the day before lost France 100,000 men and an emperor.' By October 5 Headquarters reached Versailles, and Bismarck resided in the Rue de Provence till March 6, 1871—Versailles he had last visited with General Lebœuf.

From the declaration of war to the ratification of the peace of Frankfurt, May 10, 1871, he was overwhelmed with work ; and, as in 1866, the strain imposed on his health and nerves by the continuous negotiations, the relations with the European neutrals, the necessity of keeping in close touch with developments and public opinion in Germany, and the perpetual crisis created by the war and the military operations, caused an excessive irritability, aggravated by frequent bursts of violent anger. 'The official files,' he wrote to his wife, 'make a pile higher than my head.' 'Dead tired as he is,' noted Abeken, 'he cannot sleep.' Every one from the King downwards had to endure his dictatorial temper, his explosions of wrath, and his rasping tongue, with its vivid, direct, unsparing, and bitter phrases. He was endured, because he was indispensable. His experience, prestige, inexhaustible resources, and amazing powers of work, the lucid grip on general principles and the mastery of detail, the personality and the temperament of genius, made him unique. There was only one Bismarck, and there were no three men at Headquarters or elsewhere in Germany who could combine his gifts and his qualities. 'The Bismarck touch' was revealed in the ten months that followed July 19, 1870, not once but fifty times. In truth, these Prussians, leaders and subordinates alike, were an iron race, tough of skin, lavish in all the relations of life of a stern brutality, and a full-blooded and unrestrained force, and meting out to each other no little of the militarist and graceless arrogance that defeated France had to endure. They were the victors, and they took care to let Europe as well as France feel it. Through all the events that make the history of these months so tragic for France, so intoxicating for Germany, so humiliating for Europe, there rings the gospel of the conqueror's sword. For pity, generosity, sympathy you will look in vain. The appeal is always to force. German power had brought the German armies to Paris —to Babylon—and Babylon was about to fall. Power was the one and only convincing argument, and Germany had it. No one else had.

From the commencement to the end of the war Bismarck's relations with the soldier-chiefs were more sharply strained than they had been in 1866. The soldiers—'the demi-gods,' as Bismarck called them—would gladly have left him behind at Berlin; his continuous presence at Headquarters, his 'interference' with the military direction and

decisions, his acrid criticisms, and his insistence on accurate
and complete information on all military matters, stirred
professional jealousy and the deepest personal resentments.
The war was a soldier's business ; and the generals wished
to make a military peace. 'It was a shame,' said E. von
Manteuffel, 'that a mere politician should have more
influence than a general.' And the soldiers did their best
to ignore the civilian, an attitude which simply infuriated
Bismarck. General Headquarters was a camp of continuous strife. Bismarck quarrelled with every one from
the Crown Prince downwards, and with Moltke at Versailles it came to an open breach, which the Crown Prince
failed to close. 'I am the military adviser of the King,'
Moltke said coldly, 'and I have no other duty to fulfil ;
I will not permit the decisions of Count Bismarck to lead
me into error.' Bismarck has laid down in his Memoirs his
general theory of the relations of policy and strategy—of
the civil and military powers in war—which is difficult to
refute :—

'The object of war is to conquer peace under conditions
which are conformable to the policy pursued by the State. To fix
and limit the objects to be attained by the war, and to advise the
monarch in respect of them, is and remains during the war, just
as before it, a political function, and the manner in which these
questions are solved cannot be without influence on the method
of conducting the war. . . . Still more difficult in the same line
is it to judge whether and with what motives the neutral Powers
might be inclined to assist the adversary, in the first instance
diplomatically, and eventually by armed force. . . . But, above
all, is the difficulty of deciding when the right moment has come
for introducing the transition from war to peace ; for this purpose are needed knowledge of the European conditions, which
is not apt to be familiar to the military element, and political
information which cannot be accessible to it. The negotiations
in 1866 show that the question of war or peace always belongs,
even in war, to the responsible political minister, and cannot be
decided by the technical military leaders.'—(*Reminiscences*, ii. 198.)

But in this argument, which practically identifies the
civil power with himself, Bismarck ignores two important
points. The decision, in a personal monarchy, lay with

the sovereign, who held the supreme command of the army. King William was the military and civil power in one, and as a soldier was likely to be profoundly influenced by purely military considerations. Secondly, the soldiers disputed the soundness of Bismarck's military judgments. Moltke was not prepared to admit that the Federal Chancellor's opinion should overrule the considered advice of the responsible Chief of the Staff. The admission would have reduced the Chief of the Staff to subordinate office in the Federal Chancery. He claimed, and not unjustly, that the successful conduct of the war frequently required policy to adapt itself to the military needs rather than strategy to adapt itself to policy ; the interpretation of the military situation he declined to surrender to any civilian, or indeed to any soldier other than himself. So long as the King kept him at his post, Moltke categorically refused to allow Bismarck to be both Federal Chancellor and Chief of the Staff. He gave Bismarck to understand that interference would be resisted and then ignored. Supported by all the generals, he met Bismarck's outbursts with an impenetrable silence. Moltke had a dignity and self-control extraordinarily disconcerting. He was the one man in Germany whom Bismarck could neither frighten, hustle, cajole, or ruin. Bismarck's wrath arose from recognition of this, and from the bitter knowledge that the King so often decided for Moltke and against the Chancellor.

In the conduct of war and the making of peace reconciliation of strategy with policy is the most difficult of al tasks for the civil power. The eight months from July 19 1870, to March 6, 1871, furnish the student of the Higher Command in the sphere of policy with ample material in the complexity and comprehensiveness of the problem As a training in the sifting and appreciation of evidence and in the synthetic construction of a fluctuating European situation, influenced by the military position, and reacting upon it ; in the function of history to provide a scientific criticism of life—its ends, its values, and the methods for realising the purposes of organised and self-conscious political communities—the Franco-German war is unsurpassable in the period from 1815 to 1878.

The intrinsic difficulties of war and peace were aggravated by two different sets of circumstances. Had it simply been a war and peace between Prussia and a stable Second Empire, the task would have been formidable enough. But the war and the peace were to make a unified Germany, and irrevocably to solve the German problem; they were to close one great chapter and settle the form and contents of another, in advance. Unification was to be the consummation of victory. No other result would justify the war in Bismarck's judgment. What kind of France, therefore, did German unification require? Everything turned on the answer to that question.

The collapse of the Second Empire, and the establishment on September 4, after Sedan, of a provisional government of National Defence, reduced the political and military situation to a bewildering flux. Where was France—at Paris, Metz, or Bordeaux? It was as difficult to find as 'the Europe' which Thiers sought. What was the government of National Defence? With whom was peace to be made? Where in France could be found the guarantees, who could give them, and what were they worth when given? The complications grew worse with every month, until they culminated in the struggle between the National government and the Commune. The tortuous dealings with Bazaine, the sinister episode of Régnier, the negotiations with Chislehurst, with Jules Favre at Ferrières, with Boyer, with the Comte de Chambord, with Thiers, the interposition of Gambetta, and the establishment of the National Assembly at Bordeaux, make a parallel column on the page, side by side with which the military events make another column, and the European situation a third. The three columns had to be daily written up, weighed and harmonised at General Headquarters—and all the time Germany, pressed by Bismarck, was writing a fourth column of greater importance than the other three in its decisive influence on the future. It is not surprising that in the Rue de Provence and in the Hôtel des Réservoirs at Versailles a tense irritability prevailed, and that these Prussians quarrelled with each other almost as fiercely as with the French. But Bismarck's luck was extraordinary. Had

Bazaine with 170,000 of France's finest troops at Metz fought like Colonel Denfort and the handful of heroes at Belfort to the last cartridge, man, and horse, France certainly would have obtained a reasonable peace. The Place Belfort at Paris with its unconquered Lion facing to the east and the simplicity of the inscription, ' A la défense nationale ! ' is illuminated to all time by the Duc d'Aumâle's cry at Bazaine's trial—' Mais il y avait la France ! ' Bazaine betrayed France. He deserved a monument in the Sieges Allee at Berlin.

Metz surrendered on October 27. The surrender settled the fate of the armies of the Loire and of Paris. On October 31 Gortschakov issued the note in which Russia formally declared that the neutrality of the Black Sea, defined in the Treaty of 1856, no longer existed. ' Idiots ! ' Bismarck exclaimed, ' they have begun four weeks too soon.' But Gortschakov was neither so foolish nor so vain as Bismarck would have us believe, either in that or any other transaction. He knew his Bismarck. He was not going to wait until the war was over, and his former pupil, with a treaty of peace in his pocket, could take an unembarrassed part in the Near Eastern question, and consider whether British and Austrian amity were not worth more than a pledge to Russia. We may be quite sure that Bismarck on July 12 had given no undertaking in writing. The understanding was purely verbal, and verbal pledges from Bismarck without corroboration were as difficult to prove as verbal offers of marriage without an engagement ring. The King of Prussia, the Reichstag, and German historians could always be trusted to accept, in a conflict of personal evidence, the word of a German Chancellor against all the words of all the statesmen in the world. When Bismarck lied, he lied as advised by one of the greatest of his countrymen—Luther. He lied *fortiter*, like a hero.

In reality Gortschakov's bomb burst at the happiest moment for Bismarck. Austria and Great Britain, considering with their hearts in their boots whether they could intervene in the west without being publicly insulted or of being drawn into a war, which they were determined

to avoid at all costs, were now flung into a whirlpool of
their own, from which it took them three months to extricate themselves with such bedraggled dignity as acceptance of the Russian ultimatum permitted. The Congress
of London accomplished the reconciliation of two contradictory propositions (March 13, 1871). It declared that
a solemn treaty, to which the European Powers were
signatories, could only be altered by and with the consent
of the signatories, and it registered in the Protocol the
successful violation of that principle by Russia. By the
time the Congress met (January 17) to insert the diplomatic and juristic patch in the document, torn up by
Russia, the German Empire was made and the preliminaries
of peace were practically settled. King William spoke the
truth in his letter to the Tsar, when he emphasised his
own and Germany's gratitude for Russia's invaluable services. Public opinion in England was hopelessly divided
between admiration for Germany, pity for France, contempt for the fallen Second Empire and determination to
remain neutral, *i.e.* the right to condemn both parties
without reserve, and the love of peace that is based on
military impotence. Carlyle's notable letter to *The Times*
did great service to the German cause. It is not surprising that Bismarck was not afraid of serious intervention from Great Britain and Austria. He could reply as
the friend of William the Silent replied, when he tested
his dagger on a protocol : ' I wish to see what steel can
do against parchment.'

To the making of peace Bismarck brought four fixed
principles : serious negotiations with any authority in
France that would grant his terms ; no submission of the
terms to a European Congress ; the impotence of France
for a generation to undo the settlement ; the foundation
of German unification on the impotence of France. A
France so bled and mutilated as to be an irreconcilable
enemy, and condemned to stare ' hypnotised at the gap in
the Vosges,' would be an incontrovertible argument for the
continuance of the Empire in arms. What Germany had
taken by force, she could only keep henceforth by force.
National sentiment and pride, and the perpetual danger

would prevent Prussia from 'falling asleep' as she did
after 1786 ' on the laurels ' of victory.

The evidence is sound that the first victories decided
Bismarck's intentions to annex Alsace and Lorraine, gilt-
edged by a swinging indemnity. Where exactly the
frontier line would be drawn would be determined by the
extent of the victories and the advice of the military
experts. Throughout the prolonged negotiations he
never wavered from these two conditions—the indemnity
and the annexations. After 1871 Bismarck ' confessed '
more than once that the soldiers were responsible for the
retention of Metz, and that he himself would have been
content with Alsace and a strip of ' German ' Lorraine.
The sincerity of such *obiter dicta* is more than questionable.
The contemporary evidence of 1870-1 points to a wholly
different conclusion. Bismarck was just as remorseless
as the most truculent militarist at Headquarters. His
insistence on the bombardment of Paris, his scorn at ' the
English catchwords of humanity and civilisation,' his
jeers at the sufferings of the civil population and the
children in Paris, the dinner-table ridicule of the appeals
and tears of Favre and Thiers—by these and fifty other
similar self-revealing acts recorded and gloated over by
Busch and the jackals of the back-stairs, he proved that he
neither wished nor intended to be generous. Generosity
would have been an unpardonable weakness. Behind the
impressive record of achievement lies an unforgettable
chronicle of envenomed pettiness and coarse brutality, and
the pitiable part of it is that Bismarck was unaware of the
depths to which he could sink ; and that the Germany of
Bismarck's Chancellorship could read and approve—even
praise—the qualities and traits revealed in these intimate
and degrading chronicles.

It is more probable that he agreed with the criticism
of the Junkers on his folly in not insisting on taking
Belfort as well as Metz and Strasburg. His remark that
had Thiers been the minister of an historic monarchy
France would have obtained easier terms, is illuminating,
but not convincing. In any case, he utilised to the full
the terrible dislocation which the demoralised and demo-

ralising Second Empire had inflicted on France. Every twist that the screw could drive home was utilised to the full. Napoleon, Bourbonism, Orleanism, republicanism, anarchy, the inexorability of Moltke and his sovereign, the national demand in Germany, the impotence of Great Britain and Austria, the connivance of Russia, were all in turn or together pressed on the unhappy French nego-tiators. Thiers and Favre had also frequently to suffer for the slights and jealousies of ' the demi-gods ' ; because Bismarck had lost his temper with the Crown Prince, or was exasperated at the obstinacy of Württemberg, or the insolence of Bavaria in the concurrent negotiations for the unification of Germany. In his hatred and contempt of France Bismarck was the incarnation of Prussia's stored-up passion. The preliminaries of Versailles and the Peace of Frankfurt—the annexation of Alsace and Lorraine, with Strasburg and Metz, worth in Moltke's judgment two army corps and an unrivalled *place d'armes* as a pivot for a future offensive, the indemnity of £200,000,000 and the occupation of French territory at French cost till the last franc had been paid, together with the guarantee that France would always accord to Germany ' the most favoured nation ' privilege in her tariffs—were the begin-ning of a new Europe.

It is idle to argue the thesis that Bismarck by another kind of peace could have reconciled France in a few years no less effectively than he reconciled Austria, and that such a reconciliation in the twenty years that followed 1871 would have enabled him to isolate Great Britain as completely as the most ardent champion of German Welt-macht could have desired. The ' might have beens ' of history are only valuable as a help to an interpretation of the actual. The thesis presupposes a wholly different Bismarck, and a wholly different evolution of Germany since 1815. Ranke's verdict that the war of 1870 was not a war with Napoleon III. but with Louis XIV. was the verdict of every German. There is every reason to conclude that if the National Liberals had established a constitutional monarchy and responsible parliamentary government in 1866 they would have exacted from France in 1871 terms as severe as those imposed by the preliminaries of Versailles. Bismarck correctly maintained that for the German armies or himself to return to an Imperial Reichstag without Alsace and Lorraine was impossible. The annexations were the 'liberation' of German territories wrested from a divided Empire in the seventeenth and eighteenth centuries, and without them the new Empire could not be made. It was not the terms, but the use made of them, which differentiated Bismarck from the National Liberals. With the exception of the tiny handful of Socialist Democrats, represented by the two votes of Bebel and Liebknecht in the Reichstag, every German man and woman believed that Sedan was the judgment of God (*Gottesgericht*), and that but for God and the German armies Napoleon would have come to Berlin, annexed the left bank of the Rhine, broken up the North German Confederation, reversed the verdict of 1866, and thrown back German unification for a century, perhaps for ever. Moreover, every German man and woman was convinced in 1870 that to Teutonic civilisation, and not to the decadent Latin races, belonged the future and the trusteeship of the higher humanism. Rénan's *La Réforme intellectuelle et morale de la France* and the two letters to Strauss with their dignified exposition of the qualities of the French mind and their subtle indictment of the Teutonic Gospel of Nationalism were as unintelligible to the German mind, as was their style unapproachable by any German pen. 'Ce qui nous a manqué, ce n'est pas le cœur,' Rénan summed up, ' c'est la tête.' In the difference between Rénan's *Letters* and Treitschke's pamphlet *What we require from France* was concentrated the whole bitter controversy.

It was easier to make peace than to make the Empire. The Unitarians had to decide what was to be the form of the new imperial organisation ; how and by what procedure it was to be brought about, and by whom ? Was there to be an Emperor (*Kaiser*), and if so of what ? What was to be the Empire (*Reich*) ? Were the Southern States to be invited to enter the North German Confederation, and on what terms ? or was the Northern Confederation to wait for

the request from the south ?   From whom was the initial
request to come, and to whom ?   How could Bavarian and
Württemberg ' independence ' be reconciled with the
Praesidium of Prussia and the unity of control in policy and
executive administration ?   Or was it desirable to scrap
the Constitution of 1867 and make a wholly new one,
federal or unitary ?   By whom was unification to be
made ?   By the King of Prussia direct on his own initiative,
or by the German princes in solemn congress, or by the
German peoples in a second constituent Parliament at
Frankfurt, Berlin, or even Versailles ?   Hard questions,
indeed.   So contradictory were the various views of warring parties in Germany, so sharp the clash of conflicting
ambitions at military headquarters, so inextricably intertwined were political principles with personal feeling and
petty intrigues, so entangled was the German problem
with the question of peace with France, that Roon in the
retirement where he mourned the death of his soldier
son felt that not even Bismarck would be able to thread
the labyrinth and reach daylight.

The south had swung into line on July 19 with impressive unanimity.   Bavarians, Württembergers, Hessians
and Badeners had fought as fiercely as Prussian, Saxon, or
Hanoverian.   Bismarck at Headquarters, watching with
anxiety the effect of the victories on the opinion of the
south, was rapidly convinced that the mould of unification
could be filled at once from the molten national passion
and the pride of victory.   Postponement until after the
war would bring the inevitable reaction, stiffen the stiff
neck of Particularism, give Liberalism time to organise its
forces, and confront the empire-builder with the justice
of satisfying the national demand for a real unity and
responsible parliamentary institutions.

Behind the military front and in Germany every one was
thinking and talking about unification.   The National
Liberals in the Reichstag discussed the idea of an address
requesting the King of Prussia to proclaim the Empire, in
the reconstitution of which a constituent Parliament
would subsequently play the decisive part.   Two conversations in September with the Crown Prince revealed

that the heir to the throne was working for the resur-
rection of the Imperial Crown and an Empire with an
Upper House of Princes, and a Lower representative
chamber with an imperial ministry and executive responsible to the Reichstag. The North German eonfederation
was strong enough, the Crown Prince held, to ' constrain '
the south, if it proved reluctant. The Crown Prince
voiced the ideals of moderate National Liberalism. On
the other hand, the King saw no need of any constitution-
making. The Prussian Crown was more glorious than
any imperial one. All that was necessary was to tighten
up the military alliances with the south, and secure beyond
all question the prerogative of the Prussian Crown in
policy and the army. An extension of parliamentarism,
or the interference of the German peoples in imperial
politics, was a return to the deplorable precedent of '48.
William had drunk of the chalice of victory as well as of the
chalice of popularity since 1862, and the military ' demi-
gods '. daily reminded him that but for the King's prescient
statesmanship in the constitutional conflict he and his
loyal Prussian army would not be at the gates of Paris.
The King, not Bismarck, the army, not the politicians,
were the authors of the unprecedented triumphs. If
there was to be a revision, it must be in favour of Prussia,
not in favour of parliamentary parties who would have
destroyed the Prussian army in 1862, and would destroy it
again, if given the power to do so. Bismarck rejected all
these ideas and methods. He was as firmly determined
not to have the Crown Prince's or the Liberals' solution,
as he was to take the settlement out of the hands of the
soldiers and to compel the King to accept the Empire and
the Imperial Crown. The national passion and demands
of Germany were a reality. They could be exploited to
drive through a Bismarckian solution. ' We must have a
contented Bavaria,' he asserted. But how to content
Bavaria, the king of which was more interested in Wagner
and the Decree of Papal Infallibility than in German unification, and who fled from politics to the enchantment of
his castles ?

But if the establishment of a unified and Imperial

Germany was not to be taken out of Bismarck's hands either by the military chiefs, the princes, or the popular forces in Germany, and a direction given which would permanently affect the final result, it was essential that Bismarck should get hold of the controlling levers at once. Bismarck, absent in France, desired first to master the facts and probe the situation, before committing himself. He promptly dispatched the ablest of his lieutenants, Delbrück, on a mission to the south. Delbrück justified the Chancellor's confidence in his diplomatic ability and firmness. In Berlin he first captured Bennigsen and the National Liberals for unity through the existing Confederation, and in the south he persuaded Bray, Varnbüler, and Dalwigk that modifications in that Confederation were the best way of combining unity with concessions to Munich and Stuttgart. Action on that line satisfied Bismarck. Concessions to Bavaria and Württemberg could be combined with the Praesidium of Prussia, the continuance of the Bundesrat, and an Empire controlled, as the North German Confederation had been, by an unreformed Prussia. By accepting the basis of the existing Confederation National Liberalism had in fact cut its throat. In its eagerness to promote unity, it was building a tomb for itself in the constitution of the new Empire.

The next step was to persuade the south to follow the Liberals and cut its throat also on the altar of patriotism. The idea of a Congress of Princes broke down on the impossibility of securing the attendance of the King of Bavaria. Instead of the princes, however, came their governments, and by October 26 Bismarck was negotiating with groups of ministers headed by Bray (Bavaria), Mittnacht and Suckow (Württemberg), Jolly (Baden), and Dalwigk (Hesse). Once the governments consented to negotiate at Versailles it was not difficult to deal with them separately, and play one off against the other. The strong unitarianism of Baden was a useful argument. True, the web of diplomacy was broken by the King of Württemberg's brusque reversal of a provisional agreement. Bismarck replied by concluding terms separately with Baden and Hesse (November 15) ; he isolated Württemberg by a special convention (November 23) with Bavaria embodying definite concessions to Bavarian particularism—' the free and independent administration ' of the kingdom, the retention of a separate postal service, the exclusion of the Bavarian army, in time of peace, from Federal control, and the presidency of a new Foreign Affairs Committee of the Bundesrat in which Prussia was not represented. Bavaria thus mollified with this tribute, illusory in fact, but impressive on paper, to its pride and importance, agreed to enter a Confederation, rebuilt on the Constitution of 1867. Bismarck was triumphant. ' Unity is made,' he exclaimed, ' and the Emperor also.' Württemberg could now only hasten to adhere (November 25), but without obtaining the special privileges of Bavaria. King Charles's vacillating obstinacy had simply prevented his ministers from exacting the price for agreement that could have been gained a month earlier.[1]

The several conventions were submitted to the respective legislatures for ratification. Both in the Reichstag of the north and the Parliaments at Stuttgart and Munich opposition to the terms was certain : in the Reichstag because they diminished the unity demanded by the National Liberals ; in the south because they conceded too much to Prussian supremacy. But Bismarck held the critics of both camps in an insoluble dilemma. Amendment or rejection would imperil the diplomatic contracts and postpone indefinitely a true unification. The conventions concluded at Versailles were not ideal, but they were the best obtainable. The Reichstag was accordingly menaced with larger concessions to southern particularism ; the south was warned that in a fresh negotiation the north would insist on far more stringent conditions. A delay of six months would imperil unification and perhaps ruin

---

[1] The evidence that Bismarck used the secret papers from Cerçay—captured by the Germans—to compel the Southern States to accept the Prussian terms, as alleged by Ruville and others, is not convincing. Such a method of political blackmail was quite in accordance with Bismarckian methods ; but we do not know the full contents of the papers, nor how far they were genuine. In the absence of more proof than has been so far vouchsafed, it is improbable that the Southern States had seriously negotiated with France in 1867-1870, or that the Cerçay papers contained matter which Bray and others were afraid to see published.

the treaty of peace with France. Delbrück's ability in securing from the National Liberals and the south the Constitution of 1867 as the basis of the new organisation had disarmed National Liberalism completely. It could now achieve its programme only by ruining an immediate unification. The National Liberal leaders consoled themselves with the argument that unification would prove its own reward. ' The lady,' Lasker said, ' is very ugly, but we shall marry her for all that.' The future was to show whether National Liberalism was justified in the Empire it had accepted but not made.

Bismarck had still two sovereigns to convince—the King of Bavaria and the King of Prussia. The latter he left to the last. William was to enjoy the fate of Ulysses in the cave of Polyphemus. But, acting on a happy suggestion, Bismarck persuaded the King of Bavaria to write to the King of Prussia, inviting him in the name of the German Princes to take the Imperial Crown and exercise as Emperor his Praesidial rights in the Confederation. On December 1, at Schloss Hohenschwangau, King Louis in bed and suffering from toothache, copied from Bismarck's draft the formal request ; and to prevent any slips the letter was dispatched hot-haste by special messenger to Versailles, and read to the King of Prussia on December 2. William proclaimed it to be ' as inopportune as possible,' and was very ' morose,' as was noted by the Crown Prince in his Diary : ' As we left the room Bismarck and I shook hands,' added the diarist ; ' with to-day Kaiser and Reich are irrevocably restored ; the interregnum of sixty-five years (i.e. since 1804), the Kaiserless, terrible time is past; this glorious title is a guarantee.' Bismarck could cordially shake hands. If the door had shut on a King of Prussia, indignant at being invited to convert himself into a German Emperor, it had shut even more decisively on the Liberal Empire of which the Crown Prince, the illuminated princelets of the Coburg group, and the intellectuals of Gotha had dreamed so ineffectually. William's fears were unfounded. Prussia was not about to be dissolved in Germany. Nor was the Prussian King to cease to be War-Lord of the German nation in arms. It was a Prussia, more Prussian than William himself, that was about to absorb Germany.

King Louis' letter drove home the argument for ratifying the conventions. The Reichstag accepted (December 9), and the other legislatures followed suit; Bavaria, true to its independence, deferring the decision beyond the day fixed in the Convention (January 1). The finishing touch was a visit to Versailles by a delegation from the Reichstag (December 16) to expound the popular demand for an Imperial Crown. Simson, the President, twenty-one years before, in 1849, had headed a similar deputation from the National Parliament at Frankfurt to Frederick William iv.; but, as M. Matter neatly puts it, ' Entre 1849 et 1870, Bismarck, Roon et Moltke avaient passé.' William boldly told the parliamentarians that the valid authority for conferring an Imperial Crown was not the Reichstag, ' but the German Princes and the Free Cities.' The implication that the Reichstag's function was simply to confirm decisions, made elsewhere, was true in fact. It was indeed the basis of the Empire which the Reichstag had agreed to accept. To the King, to the military chiefs, to ' the unemployed princes who made " the second step " at the Hôtel des Reservoirs,' and to Bismarck himself, the Thirty Delegates were either interlopers or superfluous. They could ratify, but they could not originate; they could praise famous men but they could not bestow Imperial Crowns. The dispensations of Providence stopped at the threshold of the Throne. They did not extend to the representatives of the nation. The deputies made known their wishes, and were treated very frigidly by the King, more warmly by the Crown Prince, and with cavalier militarism by the soldier-chiefs. Bismarck was as ' morose ' as his sovereign, and ' The Thirty ' returned to Germany effusive in their admiration for the King of Prussia !

For three weeks Bismarck wrestled with his obstinate sovereign. ' What have I to do with this honorary title ? (*Character-major!*),' William demanded sulkily. On January 17, when the final details of the coming ceremony were settled, he was so angry that he turned his back on those present and, like a spoiled child, stared out of the window until the business was settled. 'His reluctance,' Bismarck wrote later, ' was not unconnected with the desire to obtain an acknowledgment rather of the superior respectability of the hereditary Prussian Crown than of the Imperial Title.' William indeed was so ' morose ' that he wrote to the Queen, saying that ' he very nearly abdicated and handed over everything to Fritz ! ' An Empire and an Emperor required an Imperial Chancellor. Bismarck consented to accept the title and the office. 'They will put me in very bad company,' he said, ' for they will turn me into a Beust ! '

The final ceremony of January 18, 1871, in the Hall of Mirrors at Versailles—the anniversary of the assumption of the royal crown by the Electors of Brandenburg at Königsberg in 1701—proclaimed to the world the birth of a new State. The guns that salute the births of heirs to royal thrones added their welcome—they were the guns forcing capitulation on the beleaguered and starving Paris. The German Empire and German unity had their foundations laid in the defeat, dismemberment, and impotence of France.

It is commonly said that the Empire was not the creation of the German people, but of the German princes. Formally this is true : but the amended and expanded constitution of the North German Confederation was not the work of the princes. It was not the Empire desired, either by the King of Prussia, or the soldier-chiefs, or the dynasties. The compelling force to unity came from the heart and labours of the German people, and the princes who crowded the daïs on January 18 were the last to be converted—a Mahometan conversion in truth by the sword of the King of Prussia and his prophet, Bismarck. The structure, character, principles, and purpose of the new imperial polity and the new Federal Imperial State were the work of one man—Bismarck. Delbrück's services cannot be exaggerated, but he was a superb instrument, not a creator. The statesman who had defeated alike the dynasties and the Liberals, the Unitarians and the Particularists, the soldiers and the professors, was the new Imperial Chancellor. 'His Majesty,' Bismarck wrote in his Memoirs,

' was so offended at the course I had adopted that, on descending from the raised daïs of the princes, he ignored me as I stood alone upon the free space before it, and passed me by in order to shake hands with the generals standing behind me.' ' Standing alone '—Bismarck since 1852 had so often stood alone—in the presence of his sovereign and Germany, but he had always ended by bending men and affairs to his relentless will.   And never so completely as on January 18, 1871.

On March 21 the Emperor William expressed the verdict of Germany and Europe when he raised Count Bismarck to the title and status of a Prince in the Empire that he had made.

CHAPTER VI

THE IMPERIAL CHANCELLOR, 1871-1890

§ 1. *The Empire, the System, and the Chancellor*, 1871-1878

THE seven months from July 1870 to January 1871 registered five events of capital importance : the Declaration of Papal Infallibility (July 18), the virtual establishment of the Third Republic in France (September 4), the unification of Italy by the entry of the Italian troops into Rome (September 20), the fall of the Temporal Power of the Papacy, and the establishment of the unified German Empire (January 18, 1871). Of these five the two most momentous in their wide-world significance were the Declaration of Papal Infallibility and the abolition of the Temporal Power of the Papacy.

With January 18, 1871, secular Europe entered on the age of Bismarck. ' Germany in the Age of Bismarck ' was transformed into ' Europe in the Age of Bismarck,' the Imperial Chancellor of the new German Empire. From 1871 to 1890 Bismarck was the transcendent figure in Europ ean politics, with an influence akin to, but far surpassing, he ascendency of Metternich from 1815 to 1848. Metter-nich had equals and rivals who contested his supremacy nd defeated his policy—Castlereagh, Canning, Palmerston, Nicholas I. Bismarck did not meet a British Canning nor Russian Nicholas. Lord Odo Russell (Lord Ampthill), who weighed his words, wrote from Berlin in 1880 : ' At t. Petersburg Bismarck's word is gospel, as well as at Paris nd Rome, where his sayings inspire respect, and his silences pprehension.' And Lord Odo might have said the same ith equal truth of Vienna, Madrid, and Constantinople. n 1872 Lord Odo had informed our Foreign Office that ismarck's policy was ' the supremacy of Germany in

B.   T

Europe and of the German race in the world.' When
Bismarck fell in 1890 the author and upholder of a definite
political system ended his career. Every one asked the
question : Could the system continue without a Bismarck ?
Was a new system about to take its place, and, if so, what ?

Two broad conditions after 1871 materially assisted
Bismarck's policy and German supremacy—the weakness
and disorganisation of most of the European States, and
the character of the Germany of which he was the Chancellor. Although her recovery from the collapse of 1870
was astonishingly rapid, France had not securely found herself when Bismarck fell ; and her internal history during
his chancellorship is a chronicle of crises, from the struggle
with the Commune to the suicide of Boulanger on the
grave of his mistress at Brussels (1891). These were surmounted, it is true, but with great difficulty. The Dual
Empire of Austria-Hungary was a continuous prey to the
complications that had produced the Compromise of 1867,
and the consequences of that very provisional settlement.
Russia was swayed successively by the ideas underlying the
reform policy of Alexander II., a reversion to the absolutism
of Nicholas I., Pan-Slavism, the rise of Nihilism, and the
conflicting claims of the Near and the Far East. The
closer that Russian policy, within or without the Empire
in this epoch is studied, the stronger stands out the lack
of continuity and of insight, due to undeveloped resources
administrative disorganisation, internal and immature fer-
mentation, and contradictory conceptions and indecision in
the successive directors of the autocracy. Italy, ambitious
to be a Great Power at a stroke, but forgetting that though
salvation could not come without unification, it would not
come by unification alone, wrestled ceaselessly with
poverty, and the terrible consequences, moral, political
and intellectual, of three centuries of denationalisation and
misgovernment. And Italy suffered more than any other
European State from the inevitable opposition that the
Quirinal found in the Vatican.

Yet Italy, like France, was slowly finding herself, as she
groped her way through the valleys of disillusionment and
indecision. Spain was in no position to mark out a

independent orbit of policy, and the gravitation of Madrid to the German system, which would have been accelerated had Leopold of Hohenzollern crossed the Pyrenees in 1870, was steadily accentuated between 1870 and 1890. The Ottoman Empire and the Balkans were the Ottoman Empire and the Balkans, and they provided in the evolution of things many opportunities that Bismarck seized with a cautious but relentless grip.

The one exception to the continental States was Great Britain. Men of British speech analysing their politics with a microscope, and forgetting the telescope and perspective so essential to sane and long views, are prone to discover in these twenty years of British development from 1870 to 1890 either nothing but the repellent scuffle of parochial parties or an expansion of imperialism in which the insular record is an irritating blot. The critical function of history, however, like the critical function of literature, is not summed up in the scheduling and auditing of mistakes. Mistakes there were in plenty, but the connection between the external ' expansion of England ' and the internal development was intimate, vital, and decisive. The Empire that was being expanded and consolidated after 1870 rested securely, but not without many violent controversies, within and without the island, on responsible representative self-government for the heart of the system : and from that heart it could radiate in time slowly and surely to every part. It might well have been otherwise. There were not lacking influential voices within, responding to the powerful influences without, that demanded a different course leading to a very different result. Great Britain did not altogether escape the hypnotism of Bismarckian Europe. But the broad fact remains that she deliberately continued to toil up the steep and stony stairs of representative self-government. Though she did not recognise the full significance at the time, Great Britain preserved and strengthened a polity, an ideal, and an imperial State that were the antithesis in every respect of the German Empire. They were also the negation of the ultimate efficacy and value of German principles. Great Britain in the nineteenth, thus accomplished a work no less momentous than her achievement in the seventeenth, century. From 1603 to 1688 she cut herself adrift from the tremendous swing of tendencies on the Continent. From 1870 onwards she refused to surrender or betray the principles which had given her a unique position. The implicit antagonism of the British State to the monarchies of the Continent runs like a red thread through the diplomacy of Bismarck. Bismarck recognised the danger, but failed to exorcise or destroy it.

In comparison with Russia, France, Italy, Austria-Hungary, and Spain, and despite the severity of her internal struggles, Germany revealed a continuity of foreign policy clean-cut and self-conscious alike in principles and methods, together with an executive and an administrative stability, which contributed enormously to the riveting of a German supremacy on the Continent. The continuity and stability were not wholly due to Bismarck. The military, which preceded the political, ascendency of Prussia was laid on the granite, hewn and dressed by the German mind and German science. Bismarck had for his instrument in completing the political supremacy, which came last, a nation convinced that national like individual success must be won by sacrifice and self-discipline. We may both detest and admire the achievement of Germany, but it is only ignorance that fails to recognise the solidity of work on which German ascendency was based, and the futility of impeaching it except by a superiority in toil, concentrated purpose, and sacrifice.

In 1871 the grand lines of German unification and a new State-system, adjusted to the supremacy of a German Central Europe, were roughly made, but the mould required to be filled and adapted to use. Time and peace were the two essential requirements, which the Chancellor must provide. Foreign policy could provide peace—home policy must see that the time was fully employed. When Bismarck described himself as a *Friedensfanatiker*—a fanatic for peace—he was not so far wrong. But it was not peace in and for itself that Bismarck valued; it was peace imposed by the armed strength of the Empire, a peace by which Germany would develop every quality and char acteristic that established the State as Power, carrying out a policy the criterion of which was superiority in force. Between 1870 and 1890 Bismarck was not converted to the beauty and rationality of pacificism.   Quite the contrary. The last of his great speeches, February 6, 1888, was a passionate plea for an invincible German army as the arbiter in international disputes ; his theory of international relations assumed that fear, greed, and jealousy were the main motives of international life, and that a sharp sword was the true weapon of policy ; and the whole argument was a coda built up from the leading themes that his statecraft had continuously exemplified since 1862.

Bismarck returned to Berlin on March 9, and took part on June 16 in the triumphal entry of the victorious army. Between March 7 and May 10 the Chancellor's main task had been to translate the Preliminaries of Versailles into the definitive Treaty of Frankfurt.   On March 21 the Emperor had opened in state the first Reichstag of United Germany, to which the new Constitution was submitted. Bismarck might affect indifference whether the titles of Empire (*Reich*) or League (*Bund*) was to be assigned to the new polity, but at Versailles he had correctly maintained that the imperial title ' made for unity and centralisation,' and that ' in the term Praesidium lay an abstraction, in the word " Emperor " a powerful coercive force '—and the sequel proved that he was right.   Exception was taken in debate, more particularly to four points : the concessions to Bavaria emphasized by the militarists ; the virtual veto vested in Prussia (objected to by the Southern States), since rejection by fourteen votes of the Federal Council vetoed all changes in the Constitution, and Prussia had seventeen votes out of a total of fifty-eight ; the futility of the new Committee of the Bundesrat on Foreign Affairs (from which Prussia was excluded) ; and the requirement that for any but a ' defensive war ' the consent of the Federal Council must be added to the imperial declaration.   The reply to these criticisms was given in the Reichstag; the concessions to Bavaria rested on a treaty ratified by Bavaria, and it was too late at this stage to impugn its validity or its terms ; the military convention was more formal than real, since the Bavarian army would be organised in peace on the Prussian model and would pass under the imperial supreme command in war ; the Foreign Affairs Committee was a decorative luxury (as a matter of fact it has only met four times, in 1875, 1879, 1900, and 1910, and its influence on foreign policy has been absolutely *nil*) ; the negative veto of Prussia was an inevitable tribute to her complete predominance in Germany, based on her contribution to the Empire of from one-half to two-thirds of the total wealth, area, and population ; and finally, it was argued with delightful naïveté and prescience that Germany would never wage an ' offensive ' war, since the Foreign Office would always see to it that a war was, in name at least, ' defensive.'

The incorporation of Alsace and Lorraine provided an interesting problem. The anti-German feeling of the population foreshadowed years of hostility and alienation ; for, whatever ardent German historians and publicists wrote about the essentially German character of the annexed provinces, no one in Germany was ignorant that a plebiscite would have resulted in an overwhelming majority against the forcible dismemberment from France and annexation to Germany. ' French we are,' said the Alsatians and Lorrainers in the Assembly of Bordeaux, ' and French we will remain.' Treitschke spoke for German Nationalism when he asserted that ' we Germans know better what is good for Alsace than the unhappy people themselves . . . we will give them back their identity against their will . . . we invoke the men of the past against the present.' But how was incorporation to be carried out ? Annexation to Prussia would have stirred fierce jealousy, and would have planted Prussia on the flank of Bavaria, Württemberg, and Baden. Annexation to any others of the federated States was open to grave and obvious objections. The military chiefs and Bismarck were united in fearing the tenderer heart of the south in dealing with ' the unhappy people.' It was dangerous to split the annexed provinces and divide them amongst the frontier States which might subsequently compete in the severity of their coercion or the lenity of their humanity.

The method of 'giving the Alsatians back their lost identity' was therefore found in constituting the two provinces an Imperial Territory (*Reichsland*), placed, until January 1, 1874, under an administrative dictatorship, confided to the Emperor, whose legislative power was to be exercised with the assent of the Federal Council. At that date the Lorrainers and Alsatians were to receive such a degree of 'forced freedom' as they merited or circumstances justified.

This solution of the problem satisfied Bismarck, for it was practically his own. Alsace and Lorraine under Prussian administration were safe, and the treatment meted out would be more a matter of policy than of justice, or the 'English cant term' of 'humanity' and 'civilisation.' The Reichsland would be a convenient whipping-boy for the future delinquencies of France. The strategic value of the annexation justified a multitude of administrative sins to come. The Prussian staff accordingly set to work at once to construct strategic railways and fortifications based on Metz; it contemplated a future invasion, pivoting on the fortress won by Bazaine's military incompetence and political treachery; and Metz as the crow flies is only one hundred and sixty miles from Paris. The retention of an unwilling Alsace and Lorraine was an irrefragable argument for keeping the new Empire armed to the teeth. The use that Bismarck made of a French war of revenge after 1871 is one of the most instructive episodes in his policy; for when French feeling flagged, if German policy required it, he invariably lashed French patriotism into frontier incidents by a dose of severity to the Reichsland.

Most Germans in 1871 undoubtedly believed that a few years of German rule would make Alsace and Lorraine as contented as Bavaria. The widespread belief in the magic of their culture was so strong that, when the magic completely failed, they could only explain the failure by the assumption that the Latin, like the Polish race, was cursed with a treble dose of original sin. If it be true that anything can be done with bayonets except to sit on them, it is no less true that the forcible imposition of an alien civilisation,

even if it be superior, can never succeed when the subjects
of the imposition can immunise themselves by anti-toxins
from an antagonistic and living civilisation at their doors.
The extirpation of France might in time have enabled a
purely German Alsace and Lorraine to grow up, as the
extirpation of Russian and Austrian Poland might have
Germanised the province of Posen. The magic of German
culture in Alsace and Lorraine was defeated by the
counter-magic from across the frontiers of a France that
after 1871 renewed the genius of the French mind in a
marvellous renaissance. Germany was placed in a disagreeable dilemma. Justice to the annexed simply widened
the door by which French influence entered; injustice
strengthened the hold of the old allegiance.

Bismarck, probably, never entertained the illusions of
many of his nobler compatriots. He had not annexed
Alsace and Lorraine to convert good Frenchmen into bad
Germans. He accepted the historic argument of an
' unredeemed Germany' because it was a force in Germany that it was dangerous to ignore and useful to exploit.
Alsace and Lorraine were essential to complete the
unified Germany that was to make a Central Europe the
throne of German hegemony. Without Alsace and Lorraine the Rhine was not secure, nor was France reduced to
the subordination that German Centralism required. The
stubbornness of Alsace and Lorraine probably did not
surprise him; it certainly neither weakened nor strengthened his reasons for the policy he subsequently pursued.
Just as Prussian Poland was an absolute necessity to the
position of Germany in the east, so Alsace and Lorraine
were a consummation of Germany's position in the west.
And if the inhabitants of both territories were so stiff-
necked as to refuse to recognise that Germany's necessities
were Germany's law of existence and justification, so much
the worse for them. The State that was Power could not,
without denying the validity of its own title-deeds, admit
the validity of the title-deeds pleaded by Alsatian or Pole.
Might preceded right, and national safety outweighed all
sentiment. 'You are not a people,' Bismarck told the
Polish deputies to the Reichstag of 1871, 'you do not

represent a people; you have not got a people behind you; you have nothing behind you but your illusions and fictions.' The same reply was in substance given to the Danes in Schleswig as to the Alsatians and Lorrainers.[1] The force of nationality was in Bismarck's eyes ' an illusion and a fiction ' unless it was backed by a material power strong enough to enforce its claims. German Nationalism had produced 1848 and 1870. French Nationalism had failed to save Alsace, and would no less fail to recover it.

Another remark of Bismarck's (April 19) in the constitutional debates summed up a very significant view : ' I see,' he said, ' in the Federal Council (*Bundesrat*) a kind of palladium for our future, a grand guarantee for the future of Germany. Do not touch it.' The Reichstag was not allowed to ' touch it.' And the Imperial Constitution, ratified by the Reichstag, was simply a replica of the Constitution of the North German Confederation with such modifications as were required to admit the south, practically on the same terms that the Northern States had accepted in 1867. With that constitution before us, and Bismarck's continuous refusal to admit the slightest modification that would facilitate ministerial responsibility, it is astonishing to read, on Lord Odo Russell's authority, that ' on more than one occasion Prince Bismarck complained (to the British ambassador) of his imperial master for resisting the introduction of a system of administration under a responsible Premier, as in England, which he, Prince Bismarck, considered the best method of developing the education of the Germans, and teaching them the art of self-government.'—(*Life of Lord Granville*, ii. 113.) There is no reason to suppose that Lord Odo believed what Bismarck said, but the mendacity of the confession is very characteristic. When, in 1877, Bismarck had an opportunity of introducing ' a system of administration

---

[1] The clause in the Treaty of Prague (October 5, 1866) which provided that the populations of the districts of the north of Schleswig shall be reunited to Denmark, if they express the desire by a free vote,' was not carried out between 1867 and 1879, and in 1879 it was expunged, with the consent of Austria, from the Treaty. It had served its purpose in 1866—to deceive Napoleon and Europe. Prussia had never intended to put it into execution, and Denmark was not able to compel her. The rest of Europe, not being a party to the Treaty, could only note this violation of a solemn pledge.

under a responsible Premier, as in England,' he showed what he really thought of such a system. And the elaborate argument in the Memoirs is the best refutation by Bismarck himself of this amazing utterance to Lord Ampthill.

The results of the general election for the Reichstag conclusively revealed the distribution of political opinion with which Bismarck had to reckon in the next eight years. The National Liberals, numbering 114 out of 382 members, were the strongest party ; Conservatives of various shades made another hundred votes ; a new party—the Centre —formed from the Catholics and Clericals under the leadership of Windthorst, could reckon on sixty votes ; the remaining hundred members were divided between the old Progressive Radical Party (*Fortschritts-Partei*), the South German Popular Party (*Deutsche Volks-Partei*), under the leadership of Richter, and the handful of Guelphs, Poles, and Social Democrats (2). The inveterate tendency of German parties to split up and re-label their organisations makes the history of parties very confusing. This was partly due to the political impotence of the Reichstag as a government-making organ ; partly to the continuance of the deep-grained Particularism which gave to local claims a paramount importance ; partly to the inexperience of the German nation in political self-government which always fosters a group-system as distinct from a party-system ; and partly to the impact of new categories of thought in collision with the old traditions and names.

From 1871 to his fall Bismarck was confronted in the Reichstag with opposition and criticism, always strong and often bitter. A volume could be compiled from the passages in the Chancellor's speeches devoted to denunciations of the party spirit, the decay of patriotism, and the wrecking character of the parties represented in the Reichstag. The Chancellor was never weary of dilating on his own freedom from party partisanship, his single-minded fidelity to one principle—the welfare and interest of a unified Germany—and his unbroken record of party prejudice subordinated to the public good. Bismarck's tenacity of purpose is beyond challenge ; but, dispassionately considered, his claim amounts to nothing than a sincere conviction that the policy and measures he advocated were, and that the policy and measures of his opponents were not, identical with the best interests of Germany and Prussia as he conceived them. For much of the bitterness in debate Bismarck was himself responsible. He said of Windthorst that his oratory was not oil but vitriol on an open wound ; but as a debater his own vivid phrase could work like a fret-saw on raw flesh, and he was a master of the provocative lash and the studied insult. Above all, he lacked the sense of gratitude. ' You know,' he confessed to his wife, ' that my capacity for recognising services is not very large ' (November 17, 1870). It was painfully true. Colleagues, such as Delbrück, Bülow, Camphausen, Stephan, Falk, to whom he owed an unstinted devotion to duty ; opponents such as Bennigsen, Miquel, Lasker, Forckenbeck, Richter, Windthorst, and Bebel, to whose criticism many of the Chancellor's most celebrated legislative achievements owed a large portion of their success, were usually dismissed, not with faint praise, but an ugly reminder of their weakest points. Bismarck could be guilty of incredible pettiness and vindictiveness.[1] And outside the Reichstag the journalist hacks were in the pay of the Chancery Press Bureau to import, at command, into the discussion of home or foreign politics the temper, tone, and insinuations of the gutter and the blackmailer. It is impossible to acquit the Imperial Chancellor of frequently having poisoned the wells on the purity of which the dignity and decency of public life in Germany depended.

Bismarck's theory of government through, and not by, a Parliament was really very simple. It was based on the Prussian tradition in which he was born and bred. The initiative in legislation, as in policy and administration, was the prerogative of the Crown. The King in Prussia weighed the needs of his country and devised appropriate remedies, with the advice of ministers responsible solely to himself. In the Empire, the functions of the Prussian

---

[1] Witness, for example, the disgraceful refusal of the Chancellor in 1884 to communicate a message of condolence from Congress to the Reichstag on the death of Lasker at New York, on the ground that the dead Liberal leader had criticised Bismarck and the Bismarckian system in a hostile spirit.

Crown were allotted to the Federal Council, which was a syndicate of the federated governments. The Federal Chancellor, who was also Minister-President of Prussia, controlled the Prussian vote, and cast it in accordance with Prussia's interpretation of her interests. The decisions of the Council therefore represented the final harmony of the federated governments and the Prussian Crown ; in a word, the Federal Council was an imperial mechanism exercising an independent initiative corresponding to the authority of the Prussian King in Prussia. The Reichstag as a legislative organ could amend or reject the proposals emanating from this federalised prerogative ; but it could not compel the acceptance of an alternative proposal, nor could it in any way touch the independence of the governments composing the Council (which rested on the treaties antecedent to the Constitution) nor the position of the Federal Chancellor (appointed by the Emperor) ; still less could it impair the prerogative and power of the Emperor as King of Prussia. Prussia, very nearly two-thirds of Germany, was beyond the competence of the Reichstag altogether—except by imperial legislation, to which the Federal Council (controlled by Prussia) was a necessary party. A *resolution* of the Reichstag, even if unanimous, had as little influence on the royal prerogative and policy in Prussia as tickling the dome of St. Paul's would have on the Dean and Chapter.

In practice Bismarck argued that the government had a right to the support of the Reichstag. The Imperial Parliament was representative of all Germany, *i.e.* it mirrored the needs which it was the duty of the government to consider in deciding its measures. But it was for the Reichstag to follow the government, not for the government to follow the Reichstag. Criticism in the Reichstag should therefore be limited to criticism of detail, and amendment should be devoted to improving measures by practical suggestions, and not extended to disputing principles or opposing ends. Opposition to principles or ends Bismarck denounced as proof of a party spirit, hostile to the Empire. The monopoly of disinterested patriotism was vested in the government, *i.e.* himself. The charge of unpatriotic conduct can be dismissed as ungenerous and ridiculous. From Bennigsen to Bebel the party leaders were as stout Germans as Bismarck or Moltke. And they proved it by the ungrudging enthusiasm with which as representatives of the nation they shouldered the tremendous sacrifice that universal military service from 1871 imposed on every German. A close study of the programmes issued by the various German parties between 1871 and 1890—documentary evidence that fills several closely printed volumes—reveals a remarkable devotion in every class to the fundamental postulates of German unity and solidarity. The Federal Council and Bismarck himself could rely—as the general elections in 1878 and 1887 conclusively proved—on the patriotism of the whole population. But the fierce and prolonged controversies from 1871 onwards also showed conclusively that what Bismarck denounced as partisan parochialism or the relics of Particularism was in reality an opposed conception of the kind of Germany, the type of German citizenship, and the character of political rights and freedom held by German party leaders as earnest and sincere as himself. Bismarck desired to make a Germany closely resembling the Prussia that obeyed its sovereign ; his opponents desired to liberalise Prussia. And as soon as any party attempted to touch the structure of society in Prussia, or the independence of the Imperial Executive from parliamentary control, it found itself in danger of being crushed as ' hostile to the Empire ' (*Reichsfeindlich*).

Moreover, the Chancellor's increasing egoism and self-will more and more regarded criticism as a personal matter, which affected his honour. His position and character made this inevitable. Every one knew that, in fact, the government was Bismarck, and Bismarck was the government. But the sinister chapter of prosecutions for ' Bismarck-defamation ' (*Bismarckbeleidigung*) is more discreditable to the Chancellor than to the prosecuted. And down to 1880 far the bitterest attacks apart from the *Kulturkampf* (discussed in the next section), came from the extreme right, his old allies, the Junkers of the *Kreuzzeitung* and the Agrarian League.

In 1871 it was clear that an alliance with the National Liberals was essential, not merely because they were the strongest party, but because they were the one party ready to work with Bismarck in making the formal unity of the new Empire a working and living reality. The ability, knowledge, and enthusiasm of the serried ranks that followed Bennigsen made their co-operation indispensable. From 1871 to 1878 Bismarck therefore worked through the National Liberals, aided by one-half of the Conservatives —the Free Conservatives, who supported the government on principle—and the varying support of the Prussian and South German Radical parties. By this coalition the Chancellor had a good working majority with which the Centre, the Poles, the Guelphs, and other odds and ends could be decisively beaten. But the alliance was from the first a precarious *mariage de convenance*. Bismarck was not, and never desired to be, a National Liberal. But so long as the National Liberal crew were content to man the ship of State and to work at improving the engines, while the Chancellor stood on the bridge and directed the navigation, it was the most effective way for steering through the uncharted home waters.

The progress was rapid, allowing for the complexity of the difficulties. A common imperial currency was established (1871) ; an Imperial Bank was set up (1873), and the Banking Law revised and placed on a common statutory basis for the whole Empire ; the organisation of the Imperial Post Office was reformed and extended by Stephan with great success ; an Imperial Railway Office to co-ordinate the working of the railways (1873) was set up ; an elaborate code of Trade Law (*Gewerbeordnung*) was enacted in 1870, as was also a new code of civil and criminal procedure ; the criminal law was codified (1877), and a supreme Court of Appeal for the whole Empire established at Leipzig ; a civil code (*Bürgerliches Gesetzbuch*) was taken in hand, and when it finally came into force in 1900 was a monument of scientific jurisprudence of which its authors had every reason to be proud. In 1874 the system of military jurisprudence and of procedure in the military courts was also codified.

The driving force in these measures was National Liberalism, though their success was partly due to the zeal and efficiency of the civil service. The result was to give Germany, what she had never had even in the palmiest days of the mediæval Empire and the mighty Hohenstaufen, a uniform system of law, currency, communications, and military defence, crowned by a single imperial ruler, controlling a highly educated and organised civil service, and governing a nation represented by universal manhood suffrage in a unitary Reichstag. The cumulative effect of the devoted toil, mainly in the Committees of the Reichstag, on the conception and manifestation of the State as Power cannot be exaggerated, and can be traced in the debates, and in the speculative treatment of political philosophy by the universities and the professoriate. The theory of the State laid down in such works as Treitschke's *Politik* is simply an exposition in a philosophical form of the facts that Treitschke had lived through and saw developing fresh activities all round him—an exposition erected into a system of thought by deducing from the facts principles held to be inherent in the successive manifestations of spirit through the realities of Germany's political life. Treitschke and his school did not anticipate Bismarck and Bismarckianism. They harmonised the practical policy of the Chancellor with a philosophical explanation drawn from that policy and fitted together to justify and rationalise the experience of the ' average sensual German '—and from the acts of Bismarck and the Bismarckian State they built up a creed, treated as a series of principles of an universal validity.

The formative influence of this unifying organisation of a common purpose and a nation's power—intellectual, moral, economic—on Bismarck's conception of Central Europe and a system of international State relations for the Continent, can be traced in many directions in his foreign policy. The whole conception of centralism, based on Berlin, acquired a new content and outlook with the increasing organisation of German Power. If any man had reason to be grateful to the National Liberals that man was Bismarck, for the result of their efforts was to place in the Chancellor's hands a unity of authority and force, over which the Reichstag had little or no control. Without the National Liberals the Empire could neither have been made nor developed, nor could Prussian Particularism, the Centre, and Social Democracy have been kept in check.

In the alliance of the National Liberals with the government there were frequently difficulties and hitches. Bismarck's scheme for acquiring all the railways for the Imperial State was decisively defeated. The establishment of the Supreme Court at Leipzig, and not in the capital, was against his wishes, and was a deliberate step to remove the highest judicial authority from the pressure of the government. It is one of the few clear instances when the Federal Council defeated the Chancellor. The proposal in 1874 permanently to establish the strength of the army and to remove from supervision the annual financial votes was defeated in the Reichstag on the ground that it seriously diminished the right of the legislature annually to determine the Budget. The Emperor could not understand why the army should not be made as independent of the Parliament as the judiciary, but the Reichstag saw that if it surrendered its power to determine the number of men required and the cost of maintaining them, it might as well take a permanent holiday. It looked as if the constitutional conflict of 1862 was to be revived, and that in the middle of the *Kulturkampf*—for the General Staff with Moltke at their head were furious at the rebuff and very insistent. Bennigsen and the National Liberals saved the situation by a compromise, which granted the government's demands for seven years, when the system would come up for a fresh revision. Thus originated the 'Septennates.' As a matter of fact, the government won. The septennial revisions provided full-dress debates and much criticism from the Left. But to all intents the Reichstag might have agreed in 1874 to a permanent establishment. The relics of right reserved in the compromise adopted only revealed more tellingly the naked impotence of the Reichstag to bring either the strength, or the cost, or the character of the army under national control. Gneist, who had been one of the constitutional opposition in 1862, now calmly admitted that ' annual revision of the Army Budget was incompatible with the principles of conscription.' But had Bennigsen and his colleagues fought the issue to the bitter end Germany would have had a more violent constitutional controversy than Prussia had faced in 1862, one which might in 1874 have shattered the fabric of imperial unity. It was the votes of National Liberalism that defeated the Centre, the Progressives, and the Radicals. The party that in 1862 had fought the Crown and failed, now aided the Crown and disarmed itself.

The National Liberals were in more ways than one steadily building the tomb of their once powerful party. The strength they thrust into Bismarck's hands was before long to be used to destroy them. Bismarck chafed under the alliance ; but the Conservatives raged. The military chiefs who looked to E. von Manteuffel, the Court Liberals who clustered round the Crown Prince, and regarded General von Stosch as a substitute for Bismarck, derided the Chancellor's failures to coerce the Reichstag. The powerful agrarians from the centre and east of Prussia, to whom the Empire was only useful if it meant a Prussianised Empire with themselves in command, regarded Bismarck as a rene-gade who betrayed the interest of the governing class by truckling to middle-class Liberals. Roon had a hard time between his devotion to the old friend, his own dislike of his ' truckling to ' parliamentarism, and the anger of the Conservative party with which he sympathised. When the Prussian government so far forgot itself as to introduce into the system of local government in Prussia the principles of representation, and to lay profane hands on the sacred right of Junkertum to govern the country districts, the Upper Chamber of the Landtag threw the measure out. The Crown accepted the challenge. Opposition from the Conservatives to the will of the sovereign was an intoler-able defiance, and the creation of peers to ensure the passing of the measure brought the ' rebels ' to heel. The Em-peror was very angry and spoke plainly. But the ' rebels,' unable to touch the sovereign, and smarting under the

prerogative that they professed to regard as the one sound
institution of the State, turned on the Chancellor. The
Kulturkampf gave them their chance, and a solemn pro-
nunciamento—the *Declaranten* as they called themselves—
signed by names such as Gerlach, Senfft-Pilsach, Kleist-
Retzow and Blanckenburg, the men and the friends with
whom Bismarck had grown up at Schönhausen, Kniephof,
and Varzin, declared their public reprobation of the Chancellor's policy, and publicly withdrew their support from the
government of which he was the chief. The quarrel was
embittered by Lasker's exposure of corruption in railway
concessions in which blue-blooded Junkers were involved,
and which led to the resignation of Graf Itzenplitz, the
Minister of Commerce. The 'Arnim process' was also
provoking a violent controversy in the press. The Conservative party split up, and the press of the *Reichsglocke* and
the *Kreuzzeitung* rang with the recriminations of the old
Conservatives, the 'monarchical-national' party, 'the
Free' Conservatives, and 'the German' Conservatives.
Bismarck himself hit out freely in debate, and his henchmen
replied with scurrility to scurrility under his inspiration.

The unsavoury episode, however, only emphasised the
Chancellor's unique position. The Emperor had further
signalised his appreciation of unique services by the gift in
1871 to the new Prince of a princely estate—Friedrichsruhe
—in the duchy of Lauenburg, near Hamburg ; and the
development of this noble demesne, together with the
management of Varzin, was a fresh interest to the Chancellor worn out by the labours of the nine preceding years.
The only peace that he loved, the peace of a vast countryside, studded with oak and beech, and fretted with clear
streams, by whose pastures the cattle browsed, and where
the smoke, din, and pettiness of the crowded dirty town,
the hollow shams and splendour of courts and princes, and
the prison-house of parliament and politicians, could be
forgotten—that peace he found at Varzin and at Friedrichsruhe. 'When my political acts have long been forgotten,'
he said, pointing to an avenue he had planted, ' these trees
will be here to tell the world that I once existed.'

Nature was not cursed with ingratitude or jealousy : she

was lavish of her bounty to all who would toil with her—and she was free. No devilish diplomatists could wash the blue from the sky, falsify the inspiration of the dawn, or rob the night of its stars. Bismarck went back and slept in the room at Schönhausen where he had slept as a boy and dreamed of his life to come. Schönhausen—Kniephof —Varzin—Friedrichsruhe, to what an avenue of acts planted by himself and now attaining their maturity and splendour in the passage of the relentless years, did not these homes of Bismarck bear witness. Varzin, in particular, was associated with his wife; they had made it together in the period that preceded and followed the triumphs of the Franco-German War. It says much to those who would penetrate the depths and weaknesses in that passionately human but lonely heart, that dearly as he loved Varzin, the Iron Chancellor could not face its memories and its desolate hearth after the Princess's death in 1894. It was at Varzin that his wife was buried—until she was brought to share his grave at Friedrichsruhe.

Rest was essential. In 1871 and 1872 the Chancellor was repeatedly absent from Berlin; in 1873 he resigned the Minister-Presidency of Prussia to Roon and retired to Varzin for ten months. But the experiment was not a success. Roon, in his fierce old age, could not convert himself into a supple parliamentary hand, and Bismarck discovered the truth of his own prediction that separation of the Chancellorship and the Minister-Presidency in Prussia sterilised his power. At the end of 1873 Roon resigned the Ministry of War and abandoned political life. Bismarck sorely missed the loyal friend with whom ' he had fought shoulder to shoulder from 1862 ' against all the beasts of Ephesus. The vacant chair in the Council Chamber where Roon had sat reminded him ' that I once had a comrade.' He resumed his dual office, but in 1876—embittered by the Conservative split—he sent in his resignation, to which the Emperor replied on the margin with a single word, ' Never ! ' In the autumn of 1876 Bismarck took long ' leave,' and retired to Varzin for more than a year.

Men said that he was failing—the Clericals that Lucifer had fallen, never to rise again. He had broken Count

Arnim for insubordination at Paris ; [1] there had been a
serious quarrel with General von Stosch, the head of the
German Admiralty, in which the Emperor had refused to let
Stosch resign. In Bismarck's eyes the Court was a centre
of 'petticoat plots,' and he continually denounced the
interference of the Empress Augusta, the Crown Princess,
and the Liberal circle gathered round the Crown Prince—
'the royal women' who intrigued, the Chancellor alleged,
for Germany's enemies against Germany's interests. In
reality, Bismarck at Varzin was reflecting profoundly on the
whole internal political situation. The Chancery Office
had hitherto been largely organised under Delbrück, but
in 1876 Delbrück, the ablest of Bismarck's coadjutors, his
'Gneisenau,' as he called him, resigned for 'reasons of
health.' His resignation was an indication that a change of
policy was at hand in which he could not concur, and he

---

[1] Count Harry Arnim had been sent as German Ambassador to Paris in
1871. His political activities there greatly displeased Bismarck, who charged
him repeatedly with disobeying his instructions and with embarking on lines of
policy opposed to those of the Chancellor. Arnim appealed to the Emperor.
In March 1874 he was transferred from Paris to Constantinople. Statements in the Viennese paper *Die Presse*, based on confidential diplomatic
documents, were traced to Arnim's inspiration, and before he went to Constantinople he was placed on the retired list. He was then charged with retaining important documents belonging to the archives of the Paris Embassy, found
guilty, and sentenced to three months' imprisonment. The trial caused great
excitement in Germany owing to the high position of the accused, the nature
of the revelations, and the plain proof of a bitter quarrel between Arnim and
Bismarck. Arnim appealed to the Court of Appeal (1875), which increased
the sentence from three to nine months. A further inquiry in 1876 by the
Imperial Disciplinary Chamber resulted in his dismissal from State service.
Arnim published an anonymous pamphlet *Pro Nihilo*, for the publication of
which he was again (April 1876) accused and sentenced, as he failed to appear,
to five years' penal servitude *in contumaciam*, on the ground that he had revealed
State secrets detrimental to the Empire. He subsequently published two other
pamphlets, *Der Nuntius Kommt* and *Quid Faciamus Nos*, and died in exile at Nice
April 19, 1881. The 'Arnim process' formed part of the bitter controversies
that rent Germany during the *Kulturkampf* and the Chancellor's struggle with
the Junker Conservatives. Arnim's friends maintained that Bismarck hunted
him down because he was regarded as a strong competitor for the Chancellorship. Bismarck asserted at the time, and repeated it in the Memoirs, that had
Arnim been content with being placed on the retired list the matter would have
gone no further ; but that his pamphlets, in which he made use of confidential
State documents, were subversive of all discipline and a grave violation of all
the laws binding public officers of the State. It is certain that Arnim was
guilty of very serious indiscretions. How far Bismarck was responsible for the
prolonged judicial examinations, and was actuated by personal vindictiveness, is
a difficult question, the answer to which will vary with the view taken of
Bismarck's character.

was too loyal at once to join an opposition. Bismarck was not failing. On the contrary, he was about to give remarkable proof of an astonishing versatility and vitality. The year of retirement had renewed the lust of battle within him. His return to Berlin in the spring of 1878 was not caused wholly by the failure of the policy of the *Kulturkampf*, nor by the crisis that had developed in the Eastern Question. He returned to close the first phase of his Imperial Chancellorship and to open the second and last.

§ 2. *The Kulturkampf*, 1871-1878

From 1871 onwards Germany, and above all Prussia, was involved in the *Kulturkampf*, a name given by the ardent Radical and eminent pathologist, Virchow, to the struggle between the Papacy and the Civil State in Germany. It conveniently summed up the deeper issues involved between two antagonistic conceptions of culture or civilisation, and between two theories of the basis and competence of authority in a politically organised community and society. The abolition of the Temporal Power and the Declaration of the Infallibility of the Papacy were the climax to a great and well-marked chapter in the history of the Roman Pontificate. When the powerful movement of Conciliar Reform failed, in the first half of the fifteenth century, to heal the Great Schism and cure the evils of the Church of the Latin West, the modern Papacy began. Under Nicholas v. commenced a development which in the Council of Trent and the Tridentine Decrees not merely formulated the reply of the Counter-Reformation to the Reformation, but gave to the Pontificate a position, an organisation, and a title that distinguish the Papacy of the Renaissance and the sixteenth century from the mediæval Popes of the undivided Latin Church. The entry of the Italian troops into Rome on September 20, 1870, ended the political system on which the Papacy of the Renaissance and the Counter-Reformation rested. The nineteenth-century Papacy and the Roman Church throughout the world had now to readjust their title, organisation, and future—their claim to spiritual supremacy and to unlimited jurisdiction, and unquestioning obedience within the Roman Communion—not merely to a new Italy, but to a new Europe and a new world of international relations and intellectual and moral ideas. It was not accidental, but an essential feature of the processes that had made that new world, that the Vatican Council coincided with the world events of 1870. The first and most reverberating assertion that the new age had arrived was the Vatican Decrees. They were a challenge, a programme, and a publication of title-deeds in one.

The immediate origins of the embittered conflict that broke out in Germany, the first and severest phase of which broadly ended in 1878, had, as has been previously indicated, its roots in the evolution of thought and political action two generations prior to the establishment of the Empire. For obvious reasons the struggle centred in Germany, but the issues were raised in all the European States. Prussia had had a foretaste of the struggle in the newly acquired Rhenish provinces after 1815, which had ended in a compromise that did not settle any of the cardinal points at issue. Since 1848 the controversy had been concentrated in Bavaria; but it had also broken out sharply in Baden, where the control of the schools and of the training of the clergy raised the central principles in dispute.

The ' war '—for it was nothing less—was transferred from Bavaria and Baden to Prussia and the Empire in 1871. The concurrent promulgation of the Vatican Decrees and the establishment of the German Empire fused the political, ecclesiastical, and intellectual elements in the controversy into a single but complex whole.

The Declaration of Papal Infallibility of July 18, 1870, brought the matter to a head within the Roman Church, and the refusal of the Roman Catholic Professor Döllinger, ' as a Christian, as a theologian, as a historian, as a citizen,' to accept the Decrees at once raised the question : Would the State accept the determination of the Papacy to impose obedience on members of its own communion, priests, and laymen, or would it support those who refused in their right to exercise spiritual functions and jurisdiction, under State protection ? When the Archbishop of Munich published the Vatican Decrees without first obtaining the *Regium Placitum* required by Bavarian law, and when the Bavarian government turned to the Imperial government for assistance in the conflict, the answer was given by an addition to the Penal Code—the famous Pulpit Paragraph —forbidding priests in their official capacity to deal with political matters.

The Imperial government was thereby committed to a struggle with Ultramontanism. The claim of the Infallible Papacy challenged the nature, competence, and limits of the sovereignty claimed by the secular State over all persons and over all causes, ecclesiastical as well as civil, throughout its dominions supreme.

Döllinger stated the theoretical issue very clearly :—

' The ultramontane view can be summarised in a single, concise, and luminous proposition, but out of this proposition are evolved a doctrine and a view that embrace not merely religion and the Church, but science, the State, politics, morals, and the social order—in a word, the whole intellectual and moral life of men and nations. The proposition runs : The Pope is the supreme, the infallible, and consequently the sole authority in all that concerns religion, the Church, and morality ; and each of his utterances on these topics demands unconditional submission, internal no less than external.'

The Decrees involved the concentration of all ecclesiastical powers in the person of the Pope, whose utterances *ex cathedra* were declared by the Vatican Council to be infallible, and repudiation of which involved excommunication. They also enforced the claim that on the secular State was laid the duty of carrying out the decisions of the infallible spiritual authority, and that the definition and decision of what constituted a question of religion or morals lay in the ultimate resort with the Church, speaking through the person and office of the supreme and infallible Pontiff, by reason of the intrinsic, inalienable, and inherent superiority of spiritual to secular authority.

Bismarck and Germany had now to decide whether the

Empire would accept the doctrine and consequences involved in the Vatican Decrees. One example will suffice to illustrate the problem. When the Archbishop of Cologne excommunicated four 'old Catholic' professors of the State University of Bonn for refusal to subscribe to the Vatican Decrees, was the Prussian State to acquiesce in this jurisdiction over officers of the university who held their chairs under the authority of the State? The Prussian Constitution (Art. 12) guaranteed 'the enjoyment of civil and political rights independently of religious belief'; it stated (Art. 20) that 'science and its doctrines are free'; it laid down (Art. 22) that 'proofs of moral, scientific and technical capacity . . . to give public instruction' concerned 'the State authorities,' and that (Art. 23) 'public teachers had the rights and duties of State servants.' The action of the Archbishop implied that the Prussian State was to suspend or deprive its public servants of a right conferred on them under legal guarantees at the bidding of an authority, in itself only exercising jurisdiction defined by, and drawing emoluments under the protection of, the State. It followed that the Roman Pontiffs would, if the State assented unconditionally, determine what kind of teaching and by whom would be given in every university and school throughout Germany, and under what conditions teachers in State universities and schools, paid for and controlled by the State, would hold office or be liable to suspension, dismissal, or deprivation of their rights.

To Bismarck the problem at the outset was primarily political. The Second Empire and Napoleon III. had been the main supporters of the temporal power of the Papacy. Bismarck had refused to intervene prior to or during the Vatican Council. There is considerable evidence that the dominant party at the Vatican had contemplated completing the Decrees of Infallibility by a declaration that the retention of the temporal power by the Papacy should be regarded as a revealed article of faith, not a revealed dogma, but a truth guaranteed by the doctrinal body of the Holy Church. But if so, the course of political events quashed the intention. The immediate problem in the autumn of 1870 was whether Bismarck would take steps to restore the temporal power. True to his methods, the Chancellor first negotiated with Arch-bishops Ledochowski and Bonnechose. The support of the French Church, aided by the Papacy, in securing the peace with France that he desired might be worth buying. But Bismarck convinced himself in the negotiation that the Papacy lacked either the power or the goodwill or both to carry out a suitable bargain, and the general de-velopment of the international situation very soon proved that the restoration of the temporal power by Prussian diplomacy or arms would imperil the peace with France, the new Empire, and the completion of unification. All the Nationalist and Liberal forces in Germany would have allied themselves with public opinion in Great Britain and the Nationalist forces in Italy to repudiate and oppose such a policy.

There remained, therefore, the issues raised by the Vatican Decrees, separable from the question of the Temporal Power. The establishment of the Empire made a struggle inevitable. It could only have been avoided had Bismarck accepted the Decrees as binding on the Roman Catholic subjects of the Empire, and ac-quiesced in their enforcement by the active co-operation of the civil powers in the Empire and in Prussia. If that was impossible, as it clearly was, what was the Civil State to do to protect its authority, and how was it to treat ecclesiastical and spiritual persons who repudiated that authority or resisted the execution of its will ? Diplomacy between Berlin and the Curia could not effect a compro-mise in 1871. Those who controlled the policy of the Vatican were confronted by serious opposition within their own communion to the Decrees ; if they failed to enforce obedience, the Ultramontane interpretation of Papal power and ecclesiastical unity would be shattered. The Vatican Council of 1870 was a deliberate step in the policy of Ultramontanism : once the Roman Curia had pinned its flag to the Decrees the enforcement of obedience within its own communion and spiritual jurisdiction was a question of life and death. It was no less impossible for the Prussian Civil Power to place its secular authority unreservedly at the disposal of the Vatican and to acquiesce in the claim of the Roman Church to determine how far it would obey, and how far it would set aside as invalid, the law of the land defined by the Civil Power. The position in 1871 for Papacy and Empire was not that in 1878 or 1888 ; the validity of the Decrees was impugned by Catholics of the eminence of Döllinger, Rheinkens, and others, and in 1871 it was an open question whether the Vatican would succeed in enforcing its authority within the Roman communion.

Political and intellectual Liberalism prior to 1871, and notably since the promulgation of the Syllabus of 1864, combined in proclaiming the full sovereignty of the civil power ; it could reckon on the strength of the Protestant forces in a struggle with the Roman See. The opposition of the Clerical party to German unification, and its denial of the unlimited sovereignty of the Crown in Parliament, strengthened the determination of the Protestant parties in the broadest sense to impose the acceptance of that sovereignty. To the Liberal leaders, ' the intellectuals,' —such as Virchow and Bluntschli—the Vatican Decrees were illuminated by the Syllabus of 1864, which not only condemned without qualification the intellectual basis of modern society, but imperilled the free, critical, and scientific pursuit of truth ; and in the case of the German universities, which had made so notable a contribution to German civilisation, the policy of Pio Nono and Antonelli was, they held, a demand for the endowment and protection of obscurantism by the Prussian State. Because Döllinger refused to accept the Decrees he was to be hounded from the university chair that he adorned to die excommunicate, like a tainted wether of the flock. The *Freilehrheit* and *Freilehrnheit* of the German universities were challenged by such action.

The Liberal theory of State sovereignty was reinforced by the party which regarded the State as Power. If Prussia and the Empire could not be master in their own house, what was the meaning and value of Prussian power ? In Bismarck the Papal claims stirred the same feeling as in our Henry VIII. : ' Use not such language to me, I like it less than any man.' And Andrassy in 1873 has related how when Bismarck spoke to him of the *Kulturkampf*, ' his eyes flashed, his words poured out, he spoke of the Pope as a public danger, a revolutionary, an anarchist.' Bismarck deliberately told the Reichstag in 1874 that the war of 1870 ' was declared in agreement with Rome which securely reckoned on the victory of the French, and that the decision of Napoleon for peace was shaken and undone by the influence of none but the Jesuits.' After 1871 Bismarck rightly or wrongly feared an Ultramontane coalition against the Empire.

On the other hand, the Roman Catholics numbered a third of the German population, and the formation under Windthorst of the Centre party, of sixty votes, a party founded on a confessional basis, was a formidable reality, ' the most monstrous phenomenon in politics,' Bismarck said. The Centre denied the validity of the treaties on which the Empire was based, and demanded along with a more truly federal State and greater liberty for the federated States, the complete freedom and independence of the Roman Church within the Empire.

After an address to the Emperor, requesting the restoration of the temporal power, they opposed a resolute resistance to the unifying legislation and administrative action of the imperial sovereignty. Bismarck decided, with the enthusiastic support of the National Liberals, the Progressives and Radicals, to crush the Clerical opposition. Herr von Falk became Minister of Education in 1872, and between that date and 1876 a series of measures generally known as ' The May Laws ' (from the date of the first important batch of May 15, 1873) was passed in the Prussian Landtag. The Jesuits were expelled ; civil marriage was made compulsory ; the Catholic Bureau in the Ministry of Education was suppressed ; the inspection of schools was withdrawn from the Roman priesthood and placed under the control of State inspectors ; priests were forbidden to abuse ecclesiastical punishments, *e.g.* excommunication : all ecclesiastical seminaries were placed under State control ; every priest before being permitted to exercise office in the church was required to be educated in a German university and to pass an examination in German history, philosophy, literature, and classics ; all exercise of spiritual office by unauthorised persons was punishable by loss of civic rights, and the State was empowered to withhold from recalcitrant bishops the payment of the State endowment.

These legislative powers were enforced by drastic executive action. Cardinal Ledochowski, Archbishop of Posen, was fined, imprisoned, and then dismissed from his bishopric. The Archbishop of Cologne and the Bishops of Trier and Paderborn were imprisoned, and by 1876 more than one thousand three hundred parishes had no recognised and 'loyal' Roman Catholic priest. Thousands of Roman Catholics had been fined or imprisoned, while the Roman Catholics throughout the Empire refused to recognise the validity of the penal legislation, and were in open revolt. Germany, in fact, was rent into two bitterly opposed camps. The ferocity of the contending parties can only be appreciated by a prolonged study of the contemporary literature, the pamphlets, and the caricatures that flooded Germany from the Baltic to the Alps. ' Do not fear,' Bismarck had exclaimed (May 14, 1872), ' we will not go to Canossa either in body or in spirit.' The declaration, with its reference to the Investiture Contest with Gregory VII., rang through Germany. And in thousands of German homes, even to-day, portraits of the Chancellor, with these words as their motto, can be seen in a place of honour. ' I am,' Bismarck proudly claimed, ' from the Garonne to the Vistula, from the Baltic to the Tiber, the best-hated man in all Europe.' At Kissingen in 1874 Küllmann, a half-witted journeyman, who belonged to the Catholic society of Salzwedel, attempted to assassinate the Chancellor on the ground that he had insulted his party, the Centre. ' You may push away the man from you as you like,' Bismarck said to the Centre in the Reichstag, ' but he himself clings tightly to your coat-tails ' ; and the uproar that followed the taunt was a miniature of the internal situation in Germany.

Bismarck's decision to crush the Clerical Centre was

momentous.[1] After 1878 he argued that he was not responsible for the policy of the *Kulturkampf*, nor for the May Laws and their execution. The argument will not stand the test of facts nor of probability. In 1872, 1873, and 1875 he spoke repeatedly both in the Reichstag and the Prussian Landtag in defence of the coercive legislation and of the general policy of Prussia and the Empire in the controversy. He complained bitterly in private letters to Roon of the desertion of the Conservative party in the 'Catholic controversy'; he was responsible for the appointment of Falk, and supported him until 1878 against the attacks in Court circles. It is, in the absence of all corroborative evidence to the contrary, impossible to believe that Bismarck as Chancellor and Minister-President would have allowed a subordinate colleague to embark Prussia and the Empire by legislation and administrative action in a life-and-death struggle, which involved the most delicate and fundamental issues of high policy at home and abroad, without his complete concurrence. It is demonstrable that the correspondence between the Emperor and the Pope, which stated very tersely the Prussian attitude, was on the Emperor's side drafted by Bismarck ; the withdrawal of the German mission from the Curia—the rupture, in fact, of diplomatic relations—was Bismarck's act, and in the negotiations after 1878 Bismarck assumed that the May Laws would not be withdrawn unless the Vatican made substantial concessions. The later assertion (in 1878 and repeated in his Memoirs) that he regarded the struggle as mainly a recrudescence of the chronic problem of Poland was an afterthought, and the blame subsequently laid on Falk, as the author of the mischief and the failure, was a characteristic trait of ingratitude. A scapegoat had to be found, and Falk, the hero of the National Liberals and Radicals, served the convenient purpose of exculpating the Chancellor and affronting the parties with which Bismarck broke between 1878 and 1879.

In 1874 Bismarck told the Reichstag that since 1862 his

[1] Under-Secretary von Thile told Lord Odo Russell in 1872 'that Bismarck's determination to raise the storm and fight the Church was so sudden that he and Bismarck's private secretaries could mark the day and hour of the change that came over him like an inspiration.'

previsions and forecasts in all the great issues had been wonderfully accurate. The remark had a side reference to the *Kulturkampf*. But in 1871 Bismarck plainly mis-calculated. The diplomacy with which he had hitherto crossed swords successfully had not had the traditions, skill, fertility in resource, and pertinacity of the Vatican. The Roman Curia could and did pull many wires through-out Europe, and it could afford to wait. It had no capital that could be stormed, leaving the defence impotent. Its capital was everywhere, planted in the consciences of millions of its communion. Heads can be cut off, but the obedience of heart and will cannot be enforced by prison or the guillotine. Bullets or wristcuffs cannot kill ideas. The extermination of the faithful is not the same thing as the extirpation of a faith. Indeed, the seven years from 1871 to 1878 were an instructive object-lesson in the limits of power even when exercised by a State with the executive strength of Prussia. In the constitutional conflict in 1862 Bismarck had rightly assumed that the Liberals would not raise barricades, defy the laws, or refuse to pay taxes, and that, if they did, the whiff of grapeshot would settle the first outbreak. In 1872 he apparently calculated that the Catholics would either not resist, or, if they did, would soon surrender to a rigorous coercion. He was completely mistaken. When Cardinal Archbishops, with the applause of their congregations, defied the law and went to prison, the State as Power could only, as Windthorst remarked, bring in the guillotine—if it dared. For when a State by its own action converts law-breakers into martyrs for con-science it loses the sympathy of the law-abiding. The average German began to think as Pepys did when he saw oppressed Dissenters going to prison under the Clarendon code : ' I would to God they would conform or not be so well catch'd.' Universal suffrage proved a terrible weapon in the hands of the Centre party. At the general election of 1874 the National Liberals increased their numbers to over one hundred and fifty, but the Clericals polled a million and a half votes and returned not sixty but ninety-one members. Bismarck therefore had to face a National Liberal party stronger than ever and more

indispensable to the government, and a Centre opposition enormously encouraged by its success.

It was in the nature of things that on both sides the
struggle should extend far beyond the limits foreseen in
1871 : and the simple original issue, whether the Vatican
should or should not constrain opponents of the Decrees
to obedience, was by 1876 converted into an illimitable
controversy on the functions, basis, character, and ends of
civil government and its relation to ecclesiastical authority ;
it threatened to divide Germany into two great confessional camps, Protestant and Catholic, and to throw
back the newly born Empire of 1871 into the maelstrom
of Charles v. and the epoch of the Reformation, with the
passions of mediæval Guelph and Ghibelline, and of Empire
and Papacy superimposed. In the welter of conflict the
secession and formation of the 'Old Catholics,' a tiny handful of the combatants, became a neglected by-issue. The
fiery support of religious and political Protestantism, and
of the powerful secularist intellectuals who desired to see a
complete separation of Church and State in every German
State, and the extirpation of denominational endowment
and teaching, was fatal to Liberal Catholicism. The issues
raised by Vaticanism became an assault in many quarters
on the Roman Catholic Church : and the cry of ' Los von
Rom ' and the establishment of a German national Catholic
Church on Febronian lines, independent of the Papacy,
aided the Papal effort to represent ' the May Laws ' as a
Diocletian persecution, led by Bismarck into whom Satan
had entered.

To the Papacy, indeed, the *Kulturkampf* proved to
be an unqualified blessing. In 1871 and 1872 the anti-
infallibility movement within the Roman Communion was
a grave danger. But with an unerring eye the directors of
Vatican policy seized the weapon of their adversaries and
turned it against them. They closed the Roman Catholic
ranks as far as possible, and shifted the issue from the
narrower field of ' the May Laws ' to a trial of strength
between the Roman Church as a whole and its opponents
spiritual or secular. The more eagerly did those opponents mass for attacks on a broad front, the broader the

front on which the Vatican deployed its counter-attacks. Windthorst proved himself a consummate tactician and a polished debater. He placed large issues in sonorous phrases before the electorate in the programmes of the Clerical Centre—freedom of conscience, the independence of religion, the liberty of the individual German to worship as reason led him, an Empire based on justice (*justitia fundamentum regnorum*), taken from the mediæval law books—and by provocative taunts he understood how to seduce Conservatives, Liberals, Radicals, and Progressives into violent indiscretions. It required courage to stand up to Bismarck, but Windthorst smilingly removed the gloves and took and gave telling punishment with a finished equanimity.

The results by 1878 were disquieting. Lord Odo Russell's dispatches from 1873-77 indicate Bismarck's depression, irritation, and anxiety. The Clericals had built up a powerful and extraordinarily well-organised party; they had ample funds, an influential press, and a network of local machinery. It was the *Kulturkampf* which enabled the Centre to become in Bismarck's lifetime the best drilled, most obedient, and strongest single party in Germany. They drew their strength from every class— from cardinals and Polish magnates to the industrial democracy in the old ecclesiastical principalities. The stronger the executive action against them, the stronger they reacted against it. The disciplining of Germany for two generations told immensely in their favour. The Clericals, and later the Social Democrats, had in the German voter a man who had been drilled in a great military machine, to whom obedience to command was life. Given an organiser, a party with a real cause had organisable material ready to hand in the German electorate. The Roman Church was an organisation already made. Windthorst enjoyed its matchless and unlimited support. The decadence of National Liberalism after 1878 is largely accounted for by the absence of an intelligible cause, the halting and contradictory language of its spokesmen, and its dependence on a reservoir in a single social stratum, the middle class. The Clerical party had none of these patent defects.

The ministerial conduct of the fight was vitiated also by serious blunders. The punitive measures against the inferior clergy—the hard-working priest of the village and small town—threw hundreds of parishes, ignorant of the deeper issues of Vaticanism, into opposition. The government made no effort to enlist the sympathy of educated Catholicism with the cause of freedom of opinion. Instead of concentrating on the narrower issue of Vaticanism and assisting the German hierarchy, placed in a grave perplexity between two allegiances and influenced by a genuine antipathy to the more profound consequences in the Decrees and by a patriotic reluctance to defy the law binding on German citizens; instead of trying to find a compromise for the bishops coerced by Rome and menaced by the State; instead of rallying the Catholic laity to the support of its episcopate in the struggle with the Curia, the government struck right and left at high and low with the indiscrimination of brute strength. Falk fought with the ability of a trained lawyer who assumes that a juristic answer, expressed in well-drafted legislation, and backed by executive action, can settle every problem of life and conduct. Bismarck left the law to Falk, the administration to the Home Office, and thought of the higher politics alone. The limitations in his statecraft were at once exposed. This was not a case where ' one hand could wash the other.' The subtle yet deep intellectual and moral implications in the controversy did not interest him, nor had he the time, the inclination, or the accumulated knowledge to master them. And, as with Napoleon 1. in his struggle with the Papacy, the ingrained contempt for ideas as ideas, for 'ideologues,' and for men to whom ideas have a more inspiring import than material force warped his judgment and blinded his intuition. To Bismarck, as to Napoleon, the Church was a necessity of an ordered life, but its action and position must be strictly correlated to the ends prescribed by reasons of State. In the *Kulturkampf* Bismarck found himself in deeper water than his strength and skill could manage. He was to repeat the experience in the struggle with Social Democracy.

The shrewd Thiers predicted in 1873 that ' the iron

B.   X

Chancellor' would find himself in the position described in a story of Napoleon I. ' Sire,' said a wag, ' the enemy has lost thousands of men.' ' Yes,' replied Napoleon, ' but I have lost the battle.' At Varzin in 1877 Bismarck was ruefully reflecting that hundreds of priests had been driven from their altars, but that he was on the point of losing the battle.

For twelve months in the solitude of his estate the Chancellor calculated and probed. The Emperor was very unhappy, for he was at war with a third of his Empire. ' We have made enough concessions to Liberalism,' he kept on fretfully repeating. The Empress, the powerful Radziwills who represented at Court the Polish cause, the Crown Prince's circle, and the Conservatives who after 1876 had closed their split, were in different ways and for different reasons pressing for a cessation of the struggle. Strong Protestants argued that the State as Power might apply to the Lutheran Church the Erastian control applied to the Roman Catholics. The Conservatives hated the alliance with National Liberalism. The Centre might be intolerant and superstitious, but it stood for authority and social order, for religion and the Christian State, and not for secularism and a godless education. Bismarck's support of the law imposing civil marriage in the Empire—a recantation of the principles he had laid down from 1847-51—was denounced as a lamentable apostasy, forced on him by Liberalism. The governing class pressed for a return to a Conservative policy. In a word, the pressure in all the quarters most influential with the Crown was exerted against the Bismarckian régime from 1871 to 1877.

Bismarck felt the pressure, and lashed out perpetually at the insolence of the critics. But he recognised that the whole internal and parliamentary situation was crumbling into chaos. The financial position was critical. The unified Empire was proving to be very costly. The system of ' matricular contributions ' to the Imperial revenue from the federated States was a burden that aggravated Particularism. The failure to nationalise the railways cut off a valuable Imperial revenue. New taxation was imperatively needed. The government required a large expanding income, removed as far as possible from the control of the Reichstag. There was only one method available—indirect taxation by a tariff. Failure to provide the necessary Imperial revenue, except by trenching on the funds of the federated States, would inevitably cause a demand for a reduction of military expenditure. Yet, a comprehensive tariff meant a complete departure from the Free-Trade system. Would the Liberals—would Germany—agree to that ?

Since 1873 a series of commercial crises, aided by a wave of speculation and ' bubble companies ' and the artificial inflation caused by the milliards of the French indemnity swept over Germany. Bankruptcies became as familiar as funerals. German industry was hard pressed by international, and especially British, competition. The manufacturing interests cried out for protection, and the formation in 1876 of a ' central union of German Industrials ' (*Central Verband deutscher Industrieller*) on a Protectionist basis was a significant symptom. The industrial revolution, that had been coming for a generation, developed after 1871 with impressive rapidity. It was to convert Germany in thirty years into a second workshop of the world, in which the need of raw material and of expanding export markets, the rise of an industrial ' proletariat,' increasing with every decade at a remarkable rate, and the establishment of ' the grand industry,' were to be the decisive characteristics. The middle class was throwing up an industrial aristocracy drawn from the captains of industry—the financier, the manufacturer, the director of interlocking syndicates, cartels and companies—whose interests were those of a capitalistic society, freed from the interference of Parliament. Could not this new *Schlotjunkertum*—'the Junkers of the chimneys' that turned the romantic banks of the fabled Rhine into the Lancashire and Midlands of Germany— be allied with the old agrarian Junkertum in the struggle with individualist Liberalism inspired by Cobden, Mill, and the British ? With 1877 agricultural depression set in all over Europe, caused by the raising of the European margin of cultivation in consequence of competition in agricultural produce from the

two Americas and the cheapness and facilities of oceanic
transit. Rents fell as prices fell. Agrarian Junkertum
was being hard hit; no less serious was the future of
German agriculture, on which the structure of Prussian
society was based and the supply of the best recruits for
the army depended. Had Bismarck read Adam Smith he
would have agreed that for Germany defence was more
important than opulence, and defence meant the whole
system of government and the governing class.

The *Kulturkampf* had thrown much more than Vaticanism into the crucible. Socialist Democracy, fed by the
industrial revolution, and watered by the political confusion, was reproducing itself in the tissues, fibres, and
blood stream of the social and political organism with the
rapidity of the anthrax bacillus in an appropriate culture.
The Gotha programme of Social Democracy in 1875 re-
wrote the Eisenach programme of 1869 in italics : the
realisation of its aims was as deadly to the agrarian Junkers
as to the capitalist class ; its secularism menaced Catholic
Clericals, Lutherans, and Calvinists with complete impartiality. In 1874 the two Socialist members of the Reichstag
of 1871 had become 9, in 1877 12, representing half a million
votes, a third of the Centre vote. If it were not crushed,
what would Socialist Democracy be in 1887 ? Bismarck's
survey in short—the survey of a statesman who based his
policy on ' ponderable ' realities—suggested a complete
change of system ; and already in 1876 Roon, so often the
conservative periscope, hinted from his retirement that conservatives could begin to fatten the calf for the prodigal son
of Junkertum, emaciated by the husks of Liberalism.

It was not only in foreign policy that Bismarck's prolonged silences caused apprehension. From the woods
and glades of Varzin came rumours that rippled from the
lobbies of the Reichstag to the portico of the Vatican. Two
obstacles—the *Kulturkampf* and the National Liberals—
barred a bold bid for the governing classes of a future,
rather than the present, Germany, by a new, comprehensive and constructive policy—a policy of *pourboires* and
power. To Bismarck more than any man the road to
Canossa, the white shirt and shivering in the snow of

Henry IV., were hateful. But if the Papacy would share the shirt, forgo the snow and trudge half-way to meet him, a joint Canossa might be found at Kissingen or some other resort where foreign diplomatists cured their souls while they washed their bodies. If the Centre could be secured it would vote solidly and manœuvre at command like a regiment. As for ' the May Laws ' and Falk, ' we can always,' as Bismarck said to Augustenburg in 1864, ' wring the necks of the chickens we have ourselves hatched.'

The National Liberals were tremendously powerful— one hundred and fifty votes in the Reichstag—and they could rely in Liberal issues on the Progressives and Radicals. The Liberal *bloc* was at present the master of the situation, and intended to remain so. They held the road to Canossa or Protection in force. A hint came from Varzin. Bennigsen went to the lion's den and returned. When Bismarck came back to Berlin in the spring of 1878 it was clear what had happened. He had offered office to the Nationalist Liberal leader, but on condition of support in a new policy, vaguely outlined. ' I desired,' wrote Bismarck, in his *Memoirs* (ii. 198), ' sincerely to persuade him, as I expressed it, to jump into my boat and help me steer ; I was drawn up by the landing-stage and waiting for him to embark.' Bennigsen indicated that, if places were also found for two or three other prominent National Liberals, the proposal might be seriously considered. Bismarck refused. There was room for Bennigsen in the King's Council, but not for Forckenbeck, or Stauffenberg or any one else. Bennigsen then refused for himself and the others. When the Emperor, inspired by the Conservatives and soldiers, angrily remonstrated against this trafficking with Liberalism behind his Imperial and Prussian back, Bismarck was able to assure him, with perfect truth, that the last thing he desired was to ask his Majesty to confer office on National Liberals. Bismarck had hoped to split the Liberals by detaching Bennigsen and the right of the party. Bennigsen desired to introduce Parliamentary government—' a ministry *à la Gladstone*,' which as in Great Britain would be representative of the strongest party in the Legislature and make the policy of the future. The negotiation, however, was a complete failure. But while Bennigsen did not get office, Bismarck gave the *coup de grâce* to the last effort to introduce the system of responsible party government into the government of the Empire. It only remained now to crush the National Liberals.

It is commonly said that the Bismarckian policy in the *Kulturkampf* ended in a complete defeat—proved by the recantation of the next ten years. Three comments, however, are essential in this connection. First, the Liberal parties which passed and upheld ' the May Laws ' and the principles underlying them never recanted nor repented. On the contrary, they opposed and lamented, with good reason, the Chancellor's surrender. Secondly, the Vatican in 1878 was as tired of the struggle as Bismarck. It had not been defeated, but it had failed so far to secure amendment, much less the repeal, of ' the May Laws.' By 1878 the danger of serious schism within the Roman Communion had vanished. Ninety-nine Catholics out of a hundred accepted the Vatican Decrees, but the Roman Church in Germany was crippled by the Falk code. Had the National Liberals come into office, determined to fight to a finish, the Vatican would not have had an alliance to sell which gave it so commanding a position in the negotiations that followed the death of Pio Nono and the accession of Leo XIII. There is every reason to suppose that a strong National Liberal ministry could have continued the struggle and imposed a very different compromise to that dictated from Rome and accepted by Bismarck. Thirdly, Bismarck deliberately sacrificed victory in the *Kulturkampf* to victory in other issues, more important in his judgment. What those issues were the next twelve years revealed (see p. 451). The turning-point in the making of Imperial Germany was reached in 1878. The Germany of 1890 was essentially the product of Bismarck's policy in these twelve years imposed on the results previously achieved. But Bismarck was able to evade the Liberal ultimatum and accomplish the vital transition to the new era, only because the Reichstag was not a government-making, policy-making organ. The adroitness and intuition with which he created opportunities and utilised those provided by fate or fortune are very remarkable. The years 1878 and 1879 are essentially years, within Germany and without it, of ' the Bismarck touch.'

When the Chancellor returned to the Wilhelmstrasse in the spring of 1878 his first business was to deal with the Eastern Question and to preside at the Congress of Berlin.

§ 3. *Foreign Policy*, 1871-1879

The student of Bismarck's foreign policy after 1870 is perpetually confronted with the difficulty of ascertaining the truth. Sybel down to 1868 was permitted to use freely the Prussian archives, and his classical history, *The Foundation of the German Empire*, is written from original official sources and enriched by precious quotations, not available in other authorities. But for the period after 1868 Sybel found the archives closed. He was not sufficiently impressed with the duty of writing the history of Germany as a chronicle of Hohenzollern omniscience. Bismarck was lavish of explanations in the Reichstag, and in documents intended for publication, but the gaps are more conspicuous than the inclusions, nor do the explanations offered always tally in substance and fact. It is true that from British, French, Russian, and Austrian sources much new light has been shed on dark places, but the conclusion remains that the interpretation of many critical episodes rests on inferences from acts and events, with such other help as can be pieced together from stray sources. It is significant that Stosch's *Memoirs* stop at 1872, and that, critically tested, Hohenlohe's *Memoirs* obviously contain many excisions. The furious controversy over the Crown Prince's *Diary*, published by Geffcken, is illuminated by Bismarck's *Immediate Report*, the object of which was to deny its accuracy, combined with a virtual admission of its authenticity and a denunciation of the crime of publishing truth so damaging to the official version of the origin of the Empire. Bismarck's revelation in 1896 of the Re-insurance Treaty and its non-renewal terrified the Foreign Office. There were, obviously, a great many more skeletons in the cupboard, the key of which was kept by the relentless old man ; or, as Bismarck expressed it to Treitschke, ' you will not find our linen as clean as could be wished.' The official version of foreign policy for the public, and above all the German public, was framed in the interest of the dynasty and the government—as was its military history with all its parade of information by the General Staff. Such a publication as the French *Origines de la guerre de* 1870, dating back to 1863 with its complete set of documents, critically edited and annotated, has never been, and probably never will be, attempted by the Prussian authorities. Indeed, the closer one works on German foreign policy after 1871 the more certain is the conclusion that German official statements cannot be accepted as substantially true without independent corroborative evidence. And this is particularly the case with Bismarck himself.

Bismarck's conception of diplomacy was singularly like that of Metternich. Foreign policy should be handled as a confidential and personal transaction of State affairs by plenipotentiaries, able to bind their governments. Oral discussions permitted great freedom of intercourse, and a no less unfettered freedom of repudiation. The negotiations with Napoleon III. between 1860 and 1866 were models of Bismarckian methods. Similarly, after 1870 his dealings with Russia rested largely on personal engagements to, or from, Alexander II. and Alexander III. Hence his preference for autocracies ; business could be done with the autocrat, or, as in his own case, with the minister who had the autocrat well in hand. The continuity of the individual was more important than the continuity of the policy. Hence, also, his dislike of France after 1871. French statesmen came and went like partners at a ball, and the promise of the first might be good reason for infidelity in the next. Hence still more his dislike of Great Britain and the British system of publicity and ministerial responsibility : the more so because, unlike France, German threats could not cause the fall of a Gladstone or

a Beaconsfield, a Granville or a Salisbury.[1]   Above all, he
detested with a fierce detestation the British Blue-Book [2]
which brought government into the arena of public debate
and enlightened the public not with acts, which was all
that the public was entitled to know, but with methods,
which it was certain to misunderstand.   Bismarck's
hatred of the British Blue-Book was a blend of the
patrician superstition that foreign policy was a mystery
only to be mastered by the privileged class with a hereditary aptitude for its ritual—a superstition that still obsesses
the well-bred Levites of the cosmopolitan priesthood of
diplomacy—resentment at any government daring to do
anything without his permission, and the fear that if the
blinds of the temple were perpetually drawn up the plain
man would condemn the result because the methods were
so peculiar.   Bismarck knew well that the diplomacy which
annexed Schleswig-Holstein, which prepared the war of
1866, which laid the long mine of the Hohenzollern candidature and the 'defensive' war of 1870, and the revision
of the Treaty of 1856 did not cease with the Treaty of
Frankfurt.   Peace and those who ensue it have their
victories of lies, stratagems, plots, and counter-plots no
less than have war and the soldiers.

Peace after 1871 was the supreme need for the Empire.
Germany was now a 'satiated' country.   The 'injuries
of time' had been obliterated at last, and Germany, having
obtained by war the conditions on which she desired to
live with her neighbours, now wished for no more than the
maintenance of those conditions, and their development
into a permanent system.   It was inevitable that mutilated
and humiliated France should dream of the day when the
Treaty of Frankfurt would be revised—by a successful war

---

[1] Not that Bismarck did not attempt in Great Britain this particularly
German method of controlling policy.   There is clear evidence that Bismarck
between 1880 and 1885 tried to get both Lord Derby and Lord Granville dismissed, and their places taken by ministers more amenable to German
dictation.   The dismissal of Delcassé in 1905 was the Bismarckian stroke by
Bismarck's disciples.

[2] 'It is astonishing,' wrote Odo Russell to Granville, 'how cordially Bismarck
hates our Blue Books. . . . If he once takes offence at anything we publish, he
will take his revenge by making himself as disagreeable as possible for the rest
of his days.'—(Life of Granville, ii. p. 367.)

of revenge—but the France of 1871 single-handed could never accomplish that. A France without allies was a France condemned to accept 1871 as the last word in the great struggle for the Rhine. The task therefore was to keep France isolated. The surest way of accomplishing this was the organisation of Central Europe with the rest of the States in subordination to the new German Empire. The isolation of France and the German hegemony of the Continent were complementary aspects of the same problem and were complementary results of a single aim.

Bismarck set to work after 1871 to convince the leading continental States that it was their *interest* to accept the facts of 1871 and keep France isolated. The revival of the Triple Alliance of the three monarchies of Russia, Austria, and Imperial Prussia was the first step. 'There is always a chancellor in Europe,' says M. de Mazade in his illuminating study of Metternich. The difference between the system of Metternich and that of Bismarck lay in the transfer of the centre of gravity from Vienna to Berlin. But that was vital.

The material interests of the Empire, deduced from a system of political ideas maintained by Germany, with the nation in arms, as the guardian of both—such was the core of the Chancellor's system. Prestige in diplomacy also was a weapon of incalculable strength in Bismarck's hands. Prussian prestige after 1871 rested on two clearly defined and intelligible elements—a man and a nation's power. In 1862 the European chancelleries had felt like the Prussian officers before Jena. 'Your majesty,' they assured Frederick William III., 'has several generals superior to M. de Bonaparte.' In 1871 they felt what Goethe said of Napoleon I. 'You cannot beat him, the man is too strong for you.' Personal intercourse with the man heightened the hypnotism that Bismarck exercised. His personal diplomacy was a marvellous mixture of brutality, arrogance, and geniality, of patrician grandeur aided by the tricks of the card-sharper. A stab in the back came as easily from his vindictive rancour, as the great stroke that achieved a long-matured ideal. He might pretend to forget, but he could not forgive, and never pretended that he did.

The invincibility of Prussia, scientifically organised, so that her strength could be concentrated on a policy directed by an unflinching fidelity to a single purpose— on that assumption he had taken office in 1862, and that assumption after 1871 he taught Europe to regard as the first and last axiom of the State system of the Continent. The power of Germany, a Germany perpetually mobilised and ready to spring at a word from the Wilhelmstrasse, was burnt into the mind of Europe, and the German Foreign Office acted on the assumption in every transaction, great or small. ' Germany,' said Moltke in the Reichstag in 1875, ' must remain armed to the teeth for fifty years, in order to keep what took her six months to win.' The world studied and copied the Prussian army. Even at our Horse Guards the British military ' demi-gods ' began dimly to realise that the conduct of war required educated brains, and could not be acquired on the parade ground in the morning and the hunting or cricket-field in the afternoon. Moltke, however, was determined that for all the slavish copying of Prussian technique by Prussia's rivals, the real secret, ' the secret of the higher command ' should remain an inviolable Prussian monopoly. Other nations would produce soldiers, but Germany alone would continue to educate generals. And Bismarck in the Reichskanzlerpalais had the same determination. The secret of the higher command in policy, won by the blood and sweat of a lifetime, must be kept by the same blood and sweat. If Germany once allowed the quality of that right judgment in all things on which her prestige in diplomacy was built to deteriorate, disaster would follow. No material strength could compensate for an inferiority in the higher direction.

The confidence of Germany in the Chancellor as the director of foreign policy and the guardian of Germany's place in Europe was implicit. The bitter criticism poured on the successive phases of his home policy scarcely trickled into the sphere of foreign affairs. Gone were the days of 1862 and 1863, when professors and pathologists, publicists and pamphleteers, arraigned before an audience half-convinced in advance, the foreign policy of the Minister-President. The Reichstag listened and obeyed, at the feet of the Master. Bismarck studied and gave great weight to the volume of public opinion, as his handling of the colonial question subsequently showed. His speeches on the delicate problems of international relations were invariably stamped with the magisterial note, the recognition of the nation's demand for power, and the subtle personal appeal for confidence. ' Bismarck has,' said Lord Odo Russell, ' a prophetic *coup d'œil.*' He wove into his analysis autobiographic reminiscences and tantalising glimpses of the forces moving behind the scene ; and the vanity and egoism with which they were flavoured reflected the vanity and egoism of the audience. The German Reichstag was on these occasions, and it knew it, the Olympus from which Jove spoke to Europe. He made Germany feel its unity and grandeur. Such speeches, with their exposition of the realities, were a tonic and an inspiration. No German but drew deeper lungs after hearing these utterances of pontifical infallibility from the tribune of the Reichstag ; the speaker himself—that gigantic figure of the Chancellor, the civil Prime Minister of the Empire, in a military uniform with his sword at his side, the lionlike head, the flashing eyes, the gesture of command, even the hoarse, rasping, and hesitating voice that made the barbed phrase or the felicitous apophthegm more telling—the speaker himself was an arresting incarnation of Imperial power and of Prussian militarism.

In reviving the triple *entente* of the Central and Eastern monarchies Bismarck securely reckoned on the ill-will of Russia to Great Britain, so patent in the Washington negotiations and the Genevan arbitration, and the genuine fear of Liberal and Radical tendencies in France and Great Britain. ' The downward course ' of England alarmed Alexander II., who forgot that England had been going to perdition since 1815, and that some countries can even wax strong and prosperous on such perdition, and can be a far safer home for monarchs than the hearth of order at Petersburg. ' The sacred cause of Royalty ' was

declared to be imperilled ; 'Germany, Austria, and Russia
should hold together to resist those dangerous and evil influences of England, if order was to be maintained in Europe.'
Dynasticism and order were to be pitted against republicanism and the revolution.   The solidarity of European Conservatism—the familiar catchword took Bismarck back
to the age of Metternich in which he had grown up, and
the school of Gerlach that now proclaimed him a rene-
gade.   *Toujours ça change, toujours c'est la même chose.*
Bismarck now exploited the shibboleths of the dynasties to
rivet the Bismarckian conception of Central Europe on
Vienna and Petersburg, as he had exploited the shibboleths
of Gerlach to rivet Prussian supremacy on Germany.   The
sovereigns met in 1871 at Gastein and Salzburg—which
was ' the coffin ' of Beust, about to be dismissed and replaced by Andrassy—and in 1872 at Berlin, exchanged
kisses on both cheeks and showered decorations.   Bismarck
entertained the royalties and their staffs with diplomatic
reminiscences ; he was particularly pleased to dilate on the
tortures suffered by the French negotiators (1870-1), and
explained with genial humour how he had baited the hooks
to play with the fish before landing it.   The Emperor
William returned the visits at Petersburg and Vienna.
Königgrätz was forgotten ; the reconciliation prepared
by the peace of 1866 proceeded rapidly. 'No formal
treaty was concluded,' the Crown Prince wrote to his
cousin the ruler of Roumania, but the understanding was
intimate and complete.   In 1873 Victor Emmanuel also
came to Berlin. His readiness to join Napoleon in 1870
was forgiven and forgotten by his accession to the monarchical *entente*. Bismarck had secured the vulnerable flank
of Germany in the east ; he had withdrawn the constitutional kingdom of Italy from gravitating towards the
sister Latin race ; France was without an ally.   The Kings
of Holland and Sweden made a pilgrimage to the new
Mecca of royalism and order at Berlin, and Belgium was
compelled to alter her penal code, because Germany did
not think it adequate to deal with Ultramontanes or
Radical journalists. Beyond the Carpathians and in the
valley of the lower Danube stood the Hohenzollern

sentinel on guard. The intimate relations between Bucharest and Berlin, between the Hohenzollern cadet and the great Hohenzollern Emperor, are written in every line of the diary of Charles of Roumania.[1] The pacific penetration of Europe by a Germany, matchless in arms and science, had begun.

All went as happily as marriage bells, all except the course of events in the accursed France. Until 1873 France patiently explored the causes of her collapse, and heroically wrestled with the German indemnity and the re-making of her army. Thiers, by the Treaty of March 15, which ended the German occupation, earned the proud title of ' Liberator of the soil of the patrie,' and the Monarchical Right promptly rewarded him by hurling him from power (May 24). Bismarck viewed with profound resentment the recovery of ' the hereditary foe.' The military and financial convalescence was being speeded up beyond all anticipation. The restoration of a Catholic Bourbon royalty, whose legitimacy and lineage dated to an age when the mushroom monarchism of the Hohenzollerns had not yet sprouted in the sandy wastes of Brandenburg, might bring France back into the sacred circle of dynasticism, even become the centre of a Catholic coalition against Prussia. The *Kulturkampf* raged in Germany. What if ' Henry v.,' the *émigré* of Frohsdorf, proved to be the ' stone ' that Pio Nono proclaimed in his visions would ' issue from heaven and break the Colossus ' ? *Mit der Dummheit kämpfen Götter selbst vergebens*—one of Bismarck's favourite quotations—'Against stupidity even the gods fight in vain.' ' Henry v.,' like our ' James iii. and viii.' was not of the stuff to recover crowns lost by the folly of his ancestors. Bismarck's luck did not desert him. ' Henry v.' refused to make the great renunciation : an assegai in the South African bush killed the Prince Imperial (1879) ; Gambetta died from a poisoned hand in his forty-fourth year (1882) ; Skobeleff, who never could

---

[1] 'I am here alone,' wrote Prince Charles of Roumania in 1871 to King William, ' a solitary outpost, the sentinel of the frontier against the East . . but I am neither so distant nor so wearied but that I can heartily join in the acclamations for the German Emperor.'

decide which he desired the more passionately—to lead the Cossacks into Delhi or into Berlin—died in 1882 ; and Harry Arnim, who foretold the *Kulturkampf* from Rome in 1869—brilliant, unstable, and cursed with an ambition and the absence of all the qualities required to achieve it—was broken and hunted into exile. His place at the German Embassy in Paris was taken by Prince Hohenlohe, whose Memoirs reveal how odious to a refined gentleman was the task of hectoring and bullying France, laid upon him from the Wilhelmstrasse.

'A republic,' Bismarck decided, 'would find it more difficult to obtain allies than a monarchy.' German diplomacy therefore supported the republicans, while also aiding every party that would embarrass the republic. In the republican solution Bismarck saw a Nessus shirt for France : French Jacobinism clinched the argument pressed by the royal physicians of Law and Order for keeping the moral leper in a sanitary isolation.

The war scares of 1874 and 1875 are still an obscure episode. The argument of German historians and Bismarck hagiographers that Bismarck did not believe in 'preventive' wars, because he said so in two or three obscure and probably insincere sentences, is as childish as Bismarck's own explanation that it was a Stock Exchange manœuvre, inflated by the Chauvinism of the General Staff, the chief of which, Moltke, was a 'street Arab *gamin*) in politics,' and utilised by the vanity of Gortchakov to score an empty diplomatic triumph. Moltke was not a *gamin* in politics, and Gortschakovs do not win triumphs over a Bismarck if they have only vanity at their command. Considering what France had suffered she was perfectly entitled to make her army as strong as she could, and in doing so, she only acted on Bismarckian principles. The Foreign and War Offices in Berlin knew that a France with a strong army would be an ally worth having—at Petersburg, for example. The one black fear that haunted Bismarck—it dated back to 1854—was an alliance between France and Russia, in which Germany could not be a third and wrecking partner. Such an alliance meant the restoration of the Continental Balance of Power which it had been the work of 1866 and 1871 to destroy. It could be frustrated at the outset by threatening France with war—compelling her to suspend her re-organisation and driving her back on the impotence of a second-rate State. In the winter of 1874-5, Bismarck tried to pick a quarrel with France because the French bishops had endorsed the papal encyclical condemning the arrest of Cardinal Ledochowski, and provoked it by a violent and inspired press campaign on the menace involved in French armaments. German armaments, of course, were a proof of Germany's pacific intentions. Moltke—a real god from a real machine—was brought from his silence in the War Office to explain to the Reichstag the serious danger in which Germany stood. And Moltke explained with an emphatic brevity that sent a shiver down the patriotic spine of every German.

It is fairly certain that the famous article in the *Post*— ' Is War in sight ? '—was inspired by Bismarck, and that the Emperor had not realised the elaborate manœuvre going on behind his back. It is quite certain that the facts communicated to *The Times* by De Blowitz, primed by the Duc Decazes (May 4, 1875), the information sent from Berlin by Lord Odo Russell, by Lord Lyons from Paris, and by three German Embassies in three capitals, together with the information on which Alexander II. and Gortschakov acted, and on which Queen Victoria wrote her famous letter to the Emperor William, were substantially correct. But Alexander came to Berlin, and by May 10 Gortschakov was able to send his telegram ' *Now* peace is assured,' and the British government to say publicly that it had ' supported, as much as seemed necessary, the exhortations which the Emperor of Russia appeared inclined to make during his visit.'

Bismarck was very angry. The Prussian General Staff was quite ready to make a dozen preventive wars, but it is difficult to believe that the Chancellor meant more than to drive the Duc Decazes from office, and thus compel France to reduce her armaments, or possibly to coerce her into indiscretions in which the chassepots would go off of themselves. The cause of his anger lay much deeper than

resentment at a personal and public rebuff at the hands
of Gortschakov. He had been completely outplayed in
the diplomatic game. The Emperor told Prince Hohenlohe ' I do not wish war with France . . . but I fear that
Bismarck may drag me into it little by little.' The warnings to the Kaiser from the sovereigns of Great Britain
and Russia turned Bismarck's flank. He was confronted
with a European coalition, and Decazes, thoroughly terrified
as he was, as indeed were all the statesmen in France,
managed the episode very neatly. He remembered July
1870 and behaved with studied discretion. ' Decazes,'
Bismarck is reported to have said, ' is like a ball—if pricked,
he rolls away ; nothing goes in.' Bismarck knew, for he
had been pricking the ball assiduously in the hope that
it would not roll, but burst. An appeal from the French
government to Russia and Great Britain elicited a very
clear pronouncement that a war thrust on France would ' be
an iniquity' which Europe would not tolerate. Bismarck
realised that he was not dealing with the Duc de Gramont
or the European situation of July 1870. The leading strings
woven for the Triple Alliance of the monarchs did not
prevent independent Russian or British action. In a
word, the Europe that Thiers had ' failed to find ' in 1870
Bismarck ' found ' by colliding violently with it. Europe
earnestly desired peace, but not a peace based on the permanent obliteration of France. The whole episode was
a culmination of the perpetual bullying of France by
Bismarck, based on the assumption that the French
government must arrange its internal policy to German
dictation. Arnim, for example, on one occasion said to
the French Foreign Minister, ' Remember, I forbid you to
take Tunis—yes, I forbid you.' ' Bismarck,' wrote Lord
Odo to Lord Derby, ' is at his old tricks again . . . his
sensational policy is very wearisome.' Europe had not yet
grasped that a hectoring foreign policy was continuously
employed by the Chancellor to lash up German public
opinion and influence the Reichstag. In 1874-5 the
Kulturkampf was in a critical stage. But, with all allow-
ances, the weight of the evidence confidentially laid before
the Russian and British governments convinced them that

Germany would pick a quarrel, if it could, with the French Republic.

The eternal Eastern Question placed a far heavier strain on Bismarck's system, for at once Great Britain, reluctant in 1875 openly to take the side of France, stepped into the centre of the European stage. It proved indeed as critical as the Greek insurrection had been to Metternich's Holy Alliance from 1822-30. The revolts of Montenegro, Bosnia, Serbia, and Bulgaria, and the intervention of Russia, followed by the Russo-Turkish War and the Treaty of San Stefano, brought Europe within measurable distance of a European conflagration. Bismarck had endeavoured to meet the danger by the Berlin memorandum (May 11, 1876), which broke down because Great Britain, rightly or wrongly, refused to be a party to it. National passion was rising fast. It was Nationalism that had brought the Russian armies to the gates of Constantinople. Neither Great Britain nor Austria had forgotten Russian action in 1870, and the British fleet also was at the gates of Constantinople. Austria could not keep out of a war between Russia and Great Britain—her interest in the Balkans was too deep. What was Germany to do in that case : side with Austria or with Russia, or cut the sorry figure she had cut in 1854 ? If she sided openly with Austria or Russia it was certain that France would find an ally at once in Germany's enemy. In the winter of 1877-8 Bismarck saw the foundation of his system crumbling away. National ambitions were riving asunder the identity of dynastic interest expressed in the Entente of the Three Monarchies. At all costs, therefore, the war in the Near East must be localised and ended, and the European problem settled not by arms but by diplomacy.

Bismarck returned from Varzin on February 14. The preliminaries of peace between Turkey and Russia had been signed on January 31 ; on February 7 part of the British fleet had entered the Sea of Marmora and was within sight of the Russian lines. On January 14 the British government, supported by Andrassy, demanded the revision of the Russo-Turkish treaty by the Concert of Europe. On February 19 Bismarck reviewed the situation for the Reichstag—a masterly performance on a very slack rope. He emphasised the supreme need of peace, the justifiability of a European revision, and the disinterestedness of Germany. He quietly disclaimed all idea of dictating to any of the great Powers ; Germany, however, could perform one humble and efficient task—' that of the honest broker '—facilitating business between clients at cross-purposes, all of whom were the broker's friends. Beneath the speaker's cool analysis surged the deep bass of German power. It was because she was so strong that Germany could be so calm. But if she chose to throw her incomparable army into the scales, it would be decisive. Russia had no option but to submit. Her ministers, however, felt that here indeed was Bismarck's gratitude for aiding the refusal to submit the Treaty of Frankfurt to a Congress.

The Congress of Berlin under Bismarck's presidency testified to the primacy of the German Empire in Europe. In 1856 Prussia had been kindly allowed the vacant chair in the Congress of Paris. It was now shared between France and Turkey. The diplomatic salute that in 1856 had been taken by Napoleon III. was in 1878 taken by Bismarck. ' The honest broker ' did not merely act as a clearing-house and take a small commission. For two of the clients at least—Austria and Russia—if not for all, he wrote out the contract notes and settled the article to be transferred as well as the price. In 1878 the principle was quietly laid down that the business of Continental Europe must henceforward go through the Berlin Exchange in the Wilhelmstrasse, and transactions concluded without the Berlin official stamp would always be at the buyer's or seller's peril.

The details of the Congress belong to general European history and the particular States immediately concerned. But apart from the registration of Germany's hegemony, the Congress raises a pertinent and difficult question. At what precise point did Germany's and Bismarck's direct interest in the Near East commence ? If we were to believe the Chancellor's public utterances, that direct interest did not begin until at least a decade later, if then.

In 1876 (December 7, 1876) he pronounced, in a pictur-
esque phrase, that to Germany the Near East was not
worth the bones of a Pomeranian grenadier, and he continued to repeat the disclaimer with a monotony and an
emphasis that convey the quintessence of suspiciousness.
It is, however, not necessary to pick the locks of the
German and Turkish archives to prove that for some
years prior to 1878 German diplomacy had been working
with stealthy and steady persistence at displacing British,
Russian, and French influence with the Sublime Porte, and
quietly substituting a German replica of ' the great Eltchi,'
Stratford de Redclyffe, as the most important figure
at Constantinople. By 1878 Turkey had been already
taught to recognise that while Russia was an irreconcilable enemy, Austria at best a very interested friend, and
Great Britain a useless ally or an open foe, Germany would
be ready to preserve the integrity of the Ottoman Empire,
in return for political and commercial control. Such a
control was an essential corollary to a secure Central
Empire, and was perfectly compatible with an ultimate
Austrian advance to Salonica. The argument and the
opportunity were immensely heightened by the sequel
to the Berlin Congress—the blunders, in particular, of
Russian policy in the treatment of Roumania and Bulgaria.
But it is demonstrable that the subsequent and growing
resistance of the Ottoman Empire to the Concert of
Europe rested on German support which did not begin in
1879. The success of the European Concert at Berlin in
averting war, and its failure in assigning the Balkans to
the Balkan peoples, were largely due to Bismarck. A
truer perspective has taught us that not ' der alte Jude '
(Beaconsfield) but ' der alte Junker ' (Bismarck) was the
great figure at the Congress of Berlin.[1]

It is no less true that in 1878 Bismarck primarily en-

[1] To-day we can read many reminiscences by those who took part in the
Congress, and many and vivid are the stories related by eye-witnesses of Bismarck.
His temper throughout, we are assured, was ' vile.' We have the picture of his
fainting, with Gortschakov, who thought he was going to die, offering him a
glass of water, and the Chancellor's reply, ' Pas mort, mon cher, pas encore, mon
cher, pas encore !' or of his striding up and down at a private session and ex-
claiming—' Settle, gentlemen, settle, I insist—to-morrow I go to Varzin.'

visaged the problem from an Austrian angle. The assignment to Austria of Bosnia and Herzegovina with the Sandjak of Novi Bazar, which opened up the road to the valley of the Vardar, was certainly the result of a secret agreement between Austria and Russia, and was probably the result of a prior agreement between Vienna and Berlin. Tatischeff takes it as proved that as early as 1873 Austria was to secure such compensation in the Balkan peninsula, with Germany's approval, as would partially make good Austrian losses in Germany and Italy. Such a policy was the logical completion of Bismarck's Central Europe, based on Austria as a Danubian State, expansion of which would be south-eastwards. Agreements behind the back of an ally were part of Bismarck's methods, as the reinsurance of 1884 and 1887 proved. He was always ready to find compensation in territory that did not belong to Germany for a State that he had mutilated. The understanding of 1873 was a reinsurance against the *entente* with Russia of 1872. A Balkan sphere of control was a sop to the Magyar ascendency, and since Beust's dismissal in 1871 the reconciliation of Germany and Austria rested on an *entente* with Andrassy and the Magyars. Vienna and Buda-Pesth combined could be trusted to stem the tide of Panslavism in the Balkans and hold the passes until Germany had completed her diplomatic penetration and decided on her policy.

The international situation was very complicated. But from his central position at Berlin Bismarck by ceaseless effort and utilising every turn aimed first at maintaining the national antagonisms of Russia, Austria, and Great Britain, which enabled him always to have rival groups to bargain with; secondly, at continuing the isolation of France. The European Powers were to be grouped round Berlin, with Germany as the arbiter of their rivalries. A study of the evidence available suggests the suspicion [1]

[1] The student can study, for example, the evidence derived from the dispatches and memoranda in Crispi's *Memoirs*, vol. ii.; Lord Newton's *Life of Lord Lyons*, Lord Fitzmaurice's *Life of Lord Granville*, Wertheimer's *Life of Andrassy*, Busch's *Bismarck, some Secret Pages of his History*, Gontaut-Biron's *Mon Ambassade en Allemagne* and *Dernières Années de l'Ambassade*, the letters of General Le Flô published in the *Figaro* (1887), Prince Hohenlohe's *Memoirs*, and the unpublished documents cited by M. Hanotaux in his chapters on foreign policy in *La France contemporaine* (vols. i.-iv.).

that from 1872 onwards Bismarck continuously passed on the confidential information obtained from Vienna or Petersburg or London and used it to poison and inflame Great Britain against Russia, Austria against Russia, and all these against France. The Wilhelmstrasse became a laboratory of international quarrels, fomented by ' the honest broker.' ' They dislike me,' as Bismarck said of the petty Balkan States, ' but by a merciful dispensation of Providence they dislike each other much more.' It was the agreeable duty of the Chancellor to co-operate with Providence for Germany's untold advantage. The administrative occupation of Bosnia was the first instalment of a prior agreement, and a pledge of further favours to come—if Austria behaved properly.

After 1878 Russia, in Bismarck's view, got out of hand. The Nationalist party, led by Skobeleff and Katkoff, aided by a great wave of Panslavist feeling, proclaimed that Bismarck had instigated the Russian attack on Turkey (which is quite probable), in order to favour Austria and rob Russia of the fruits of victory. At Paris and Petersburg the desirability of a Franco-Russian alliance was openly canvassed. Schuvalov, the chief Russian plenipotentiary at the Congress, was compelled to resign, and the Tsar wrote a bitter letter to his relative, Emperor William. When Bismarck inspired Busch to open a counter-attack in the German press on Gortschakov and Russian Pan-slavism, the wire between Petersburg and Berlin was not broken but made red-hot with recriminations. ' Do not,' Bismarck said to Gortschakov in 1878, ' Do not compel me to choose between Austria and you.' In truth it was neither Gortschakov nor Austria, but France, that compelled Bismarck to choose. Russia by herself he did not fear, but France in conjunction with Russia—the war on the two fronts—weighed like lead on Bismarck and Moltke's minds.

While the Emperor William, much distressed by the Tsar's indictment of German ingratitude, met his angry relative at Alexandrovo, Bismarck met Andrassy at Gastein (August 27, 1879). From Gastein Bismarck went to Vienna, where the author of Austria's expulsion from

Germany received a triumphant ovation. Vienna, like Petersburg, recognised Germany's services to Austria in the Balkans. And without German support Francis Joseph could not face Russia. In a long confidential letter (September 10) to the King of Bavaria Bismarck explained the imperative reasons for an alliance with Austria. It was a dexterous move to invite in advance Bavarian support, which was given by King Louis without reserve, but Bismarck was really planting a powerful breaching battery on the flank of his own sovereign.

An alliance with Austria, avowedly against Russia, roused the anger and obstinacy of the Emperor William : for it was a violation of every precious tradition—the dynastic connection, the support of Russia in every Prussian crisis, and the solidarity of ' the system of order on a monarchical basis.' The Emperor roundly dubbed the proposed treaty a ' perfidy.' For six weeks the Chancellor wrestled with the conscience and limited political intelligence of his master. ' All my well-weighed arguments,' he writes in his Memoirs, ' were entirely without effect . . . I was compelled to bring the cabinet into play, a method of procedure extremely against my grain.' The Crown Prince once again supported the Chancellor. When the Emperor finally yielded on October 7, ' he was not convinced by the arguments of policy but . . . only because he was averse to ministerial changes.' In the autumn of 1879 Bismarck's place—for the Chancellor was determined to have the treaty—could only have been filled by Bennigsen. It was the last of Bismarck's historic struggles with his sovereign, which stand out with the arresting significance of obelisks on a straight road across an open plain, and each marked a momentous decision. In 1862 he had persuaded the King to fight out the struggle with the Liberal Landtag ; in 1863 he had prevented the King from going to the Congress of Princes at Frankfürt ; in 1866 he had induced the King to sign ' a shameful treaty ' with Austria ; in 1871 he compelled the King of Prussia to become German Emperor ; in 1879 he made the Dual Alliance. The last was probably the greatest victory of the five, and of a more pregnant import for the future of the two Empires and the European State system.

The treaty of October 7 was secret, and the text was not published until February 3, 1888, and then, naturally, without any of the secret clauses or conventions which unquestionably were attached to it. The nature and extent of these can only be estimated by careful inference from the course of German and Austrian policy after 1879. In the published text the alliance provided for three eventualities : first, if either party were attacked by Russia the other was to come to its assistance with its whole military force ; if either party were attacked by another Power than Russia (*i.e.* France), the other was to observe a benevolent neutrality, which, if Russia intervened, was to turn into an active support ; and if Russia increased her armaments so as to menace either of the contracting Powers, the Tsar was to be informed that an attack against either was an attack against both.

The treaty was in form ' defensive '—a distinction intended for the intelligent public that assumes that phrases are identical with the realities of international conflicts. But a war in which the formal declaration of hostilities comes from the side that has been diplomatically manœuvred into a position in which it must either declare war or accept a diplomatic defeat is technically for the other side a defensive war. Bismarck had never waged an ' offensive ' war, in the technical sense, and he never intended to bungle so badly as to be obliged to do so. The *casus fœderis* therefore of 1879 provided precisely what he required—an ally, should it be necessary to force Russia to declare war. On the other hand, he could always repudiate his Austrian ally on the ground that she was about to wage an offensive war, outside the scope and ambit of the contract. In other words, Bismarck retained the initiative and secured the control of Austrian *policy*, for it is policy that makes wars, not wars that make policy.

' I was not blind,' wrote Bismarck, ' to the perplexities which made the choice (of Austria) difficult.' All the evidence available fully bears out this measured judgment. The Chancellor weighed long and with a remorseless scrutiny the case for and against so momentous a decision. To-day, perhaps, when the Dual Alliance has lasted for thirty-six years and seems as familiar and inevitable a phenomenon in the firmament of continental policy as King Charles's Wain in the heaven of stars, we are disposed to ignore the problem that Bismarck strove to solve. The Treaty of 1879 closes a crisis in the evolution of Bismarck's statecraft. It marks a climax, but, like all climaxes, it turned a fresh page, the writing in which was determined by the character of the terminus.

What then were ' the perplexities ' ? It is clear on the evidence that Bismarck in 1879 could have turned to Russia and concluded a similar defensive treaty, with Austria as the foe to be neutralised. The cordial meeting of William and Alexander II. at Alexandrovo, which cleared up their personal relations, strengthened the German Emperor's desire to heal the political breach and renew the liaison established in 1872. William, indeed, failed to see that Austrian and Russian ambitions were in conflict after 1878, and that Germany could not support both, but must decide between them. Bismarck's deeper knowledge and ' prophetic *coup d'œil* ' had penetrated the logic of history, ' more remorseless than the logic of the Prussian audit office,' and for him the antagonism of Austria and Russia made the cruelty and inevitability of a choice. But why not select Russia—the champion of order and monarchical autocracy, the dynastic and political friend on whose support Prussian policy had pivoted since 1862 ? Why not by such a master-stroke close the Eastern frontier and permanently dissolve the nightmare of a Franco-Russian alliance ? Would not such an alliance have before long coerced Austria into renewing the Triple Entente of 1872 ? Powerful critics in 1879 and since have argued this thesis impressively, and concluded that Bismarck now made his first and biggest mistake. The road, it is said, to Petersburg via Vienna was impossible in reality ; but the making of a road to Vienna via Petersburg was not beyond Bismarck's great gifts. The alienation of Great Britain from Russia and the Anglo-Austrian *entente* in 1879 left, it is also argued, Russia isolated, faced by a hostile Germany,

Austria, and Great Britain, the Near East closed, and France alone as a possible friend. The Treaty of 1879, it is therefore concluded, made a Franco-Russian *entente*— the one result Bismarck feared—only a question of time. Yet, if Bismarck erred, he did so with his eyes open. He knew the arguments for a Russian alliance better than his critics, and he rejected them. Why?

Three central points take us to the heart of the system enshrined in the Austrian treaty. First, a sentence in the confidential letter to the King of Bavaria, unaccountably ignored by many students of Bismarck: '*The German Empire in alliance with Austria would not lack the support of England.*' Lord Salisbury, the British Foreign Secretary, confirmed this prediction by saying that the rumour of such an alliance was 'good tidings of great joy.' Would a British Foreign Secretary in 1879, 1889, or 1899 have said the same of a Russo-German alliance? Bismarck knew that an alliance with Russia must commit Germany to the Russian antagonism to Great Britain, as well as to the Russian antagonism to Austria. Neither in 1879 nor 1889 was he prepared to place such a wasting mortgage on German policy: for Bismarck had a sounder sense of British strength than many of his critics then or since. The alienation of Great Britain and of Austria in 1879 would almost certainly have involved a renewal of the Anglo-Austrian alliance of 1856, to which France in 1879, as in 1856, would have become a partner.[1]

Secondly, was Germany prepared to see Russia at Constantinople? Apart from any prior promises to Austria, not involving Constantinople but Salonica, that was a question of profound import for Bismarck in 1878-9. His answer as given in his acts is a decisive 'No'; not

[1] The Secret Treaty of April 15, 1856, which pledged Great Britain, France, and Austria to unite in resisting any attempt to tear up the Treaty of Paris of 1856.

[2] The extraordinary *obiter dictum* in the *Memoirs* (ii. 285) that Bismarck personally would have 'welcomed' the 'physical and diplomatic possession of Constantinople' by Russia cannot be taken seriously. It is contradicted by the argument in which it is embedded, and is belied by the action of Germany prior to, and after, 1879. Written late in life, it probably is a criticism on German policy in the Near East after the Chancellor's dismissal, and is one of the many similar 'confessions' suggesting that in matters of high military policy he was continuously overruled by the Emperor, or the soldiers, or by his colleagues, or by public opinion. *Credat Judæus Apella.*

because a Russian Constantinople rang out a sharp quietus
to Austrian ambitions, but because it ended all German
ambitions in the Balkans. Austria at Salonica was no bar
—rather a help—to German control of Constantinople and
the Ottoman Empire, the 'integrity' of which Beaconsfield
' consolidated' by annexing Cyprus, securing a tighter hold
on Egypt, and by handing over Bosnia to Austria, half
Bulgaria to a virtual Russian protectorate and the Armenian
frontier fortresses to Russia. But if a Russian alliance did
not mean Germany's acquiescence in the Russian advance
to Constantinople, it meant nothing. It meant, moreover, that either Germany must support Russia in her
Eastern quarrel with Great Britain or obliterate the
treaty; and if there was an excentric dissipation of German
strength it would be to sacrifice Pomeranian Grenadiers
in Europe that Russia might annex Turkestan or Afghanistan. Bismarck was confident that Austrian Chauvinism
could be controlled, but a complete German control of
Russian policy was not a practical proposition. Teuton
and Slav could not work together as Teuton and Magyar
could for a common interest.

Thirdly, a Russian alliance left the main gateway of
Central Europe—the Danube—in neutral, and probably
hostile, hands. The strategical and economic confor-
mation of Central Europe is moulded by three great river
basins—the Rhine, the Danube, and the Vistula. The
Rhine was now firmly in German hands : a Russian alliance
did not secure Germany the control of the Vistula, and it
left the Danube out of the central German control altogether. Without a control of the Danube basin as complete as the control of the Rhine, the political and economic,
no less than the military, conditions of centralism could not
be adequately realised. Moreover, Bismarck reckoned on
bringing Roumania with Austria's help into the system; and
thanks to Russian bungling, the Treaty of 1879 was promptly
followed by that close understanding between Bucharest
and Vienna which was certainly expressed in a precise contract, the text of which has never been published. The
Austrian alliance, therefore, closed the Danube from source
to mouth : it brought Serbia and Bulgaria on the southern

bank into the sphere of Austrian policy ; for it placed Roumania as a German outpost to the north, and an Ottoman Empire under German influence on their backs. Moreover, the Austrian bastion in Galicia, from Cracow to Czernowitz, left Russia controlling the Vistula only from Thorn to Ivangorod, with Prussia on one, and Austria on the other, flank, of the Russian Polish salient. In short, the framework of Central Europe was completed by the Austrian alliance. A Russian alliance, and Austria hostile, would have destroyed it. Bismarck's diplomacy from 1879 to 1890 aimed at filling the mould thus created with an organic and expanding system of political traditions, habits, and ideals—the full life of the allied States incorporate in the environment that gave them blood and air.

There were two other positive advantages of great weight—the maintenance of the Austrian monarchy, which coincided with the maintenance of the Prussian State régime, and the checking of Slav influence, working then and since so powerfully against Germanism. The German alliance gave to the Habsburg throne a support moral and political, difficult to exaggerate. How the Habsburgs would have fared without that support in the next thirty years can be as easily imagined as can the effect on the German Empire and the Hohenzollern throne if the Habsburg monarchy had been crippled as a monarchy. The alliance of 1879 was a compact with Buda-Pesth even more than with Vienna. It set the seal of German approval on, and assured the promise of German support to, the true construction of the Compromise (*Ausgleich*) of 1867—an alliance of German and Magyar to crush all non-German and non-Magyar elements (about one-half of Austria-Hungary) into subordination. Was Bismarck not right, from his point of view, in concluding that, so construed in action, the Compromise which he supported on principle in 1867 was worth an Emperor's ransom to an Imperial Germany determined to establish a German hegemony ? What would have been the result had he in 1879 rejected Andrassy's overtures, closed the door to Buda-Pesth, and opened the door that led to the Nevsky Prospect and Tsarskoe-Seloe ?

Two obvious disadvantages, however, perplexed Bismarck —the Polish question and the Austrian future in the Balkans. The denationalisation of the Poles and the continuity of the tripartite dismemberment of 1795, endorsed in 1815, was a question of existence for Prussia. Bismarck held, as had been already indicated, that the dissolution of the ancient kingdom of Poland by Frederick the Great and Catherine was the pre-condition of a safe and strong Prussia. The Polish problem was with him day and night, and it had flamed into a fresh crisis with the *Kulturkampf*. The relations and policy of the Dual Monarchy to the Austrian Poles provided a very thorny internal conundrum for the Ball-Platz, and Bismarck foresaw in 1879 that the interests of Vienna and Berlin in Polish policy were not identical, and might easily become antagonistic. The Vatican, with its trusteeship for Roman Catholic Poland, had an influence on Roman Catholic Vienna and Buda-Pesth that foreshadowed the gravest complications. Nor could the Dual Monarchy, in face of the Ruthenian population in Galicia, treat the Poles as Prussia treated the province of Posen. A liberal policy at Vienna towards the Austrian Poles went ill with the drastic oppression of Polish Prussia by Berlin. If Austria 'got out of hand' in this sphere of action the basis of the Treaty of 1879 might crumble away entirely.

There was a similar danger in the Balkans. If we knew the whole truth of what lay behind the innocent clauses of the Treaty of 1879, itself a further instalment of the system begun in 1872, it is quite certain that it would confirm one broad conclusion. Germany endorsed cautiously but deliberately the Austrian bill of exchange in the Balkans. The nature and extent of the commitment can only be roughly inferred from the tangled diplomacy that preceded 1879 and fills the next thirty years. But in 1879 Bismarck took a great risk—all his public utterances confirm the guarded language of the Memoirs—and he took it deliberately. The 'occupation' of Bosnia and Herzegovina was nominally a transitory arrangement : its conversion into an 'annexation' was a permanent bait to Austria, but Germany secured a powerful control, for she could always refuse to support the conversion. He placed an ally in shining armour behind Francis Joseph and the Magyar oligarchy : and the ally stood there, not in the interest of Austria but of a Prussianised Germany. The contention that the Treaty of 1879 made a Franco-Russian alliance inevitable rests on arguing back from 1896 to 1879. It is certain that no alliance between France and Russia took place before 1890. Diplomatic coquetry and flirtations are even less convincing evidence of alliances than glasses of wine and the toasts of monarchs (drafted by their ministers) at ceremonial banquets. The whole point of Bismarck's criticism of the policy of his successors after 1890 is concentrated in the indictment, that while he prevented such an alliance (which was true), his successors not merely permitted it, but by their diplomatic bungling actually brought it about. It is therefore neither fair nor historical to argue that the Dual Alliance of 1879 made a Russo-French alliance inevitable. Bismarck could and did argue that, so far from that result being inevitable, the Dual Alliance, properly handled, made an *entente* between Paris and Petersburg impossible.

Bismarck was a continentalist, and remained a continentalist to the end of his days ; that is, he held as an axiom that German supremacy must rest on mastery of the strategical and political situation in Europe. Efforts outside the central European theatre were an excentric and unjustifiable dissipation of German strength, the concentration of which was required on the major objective. Secure that, and the rest followed ; lose it, and no gains elsewhere would compensate the loss. Austria-Hungary and the Balkans—the two could not be separated, for the problem of south-eastern Europe was the problem of the Dual Empire—were essential to German hegemony and the sole avenue of continental expansion. The crisis of 1875 reinforced the lesson that Europe would not tolerate a further expansion westwards at the expense of France and Belgium. But an expansion to the south-east could secure British neutrality, if not active support, for it would be at the expense of Russia. To-day we are apt to forget that in 1879 Great Britain viewed Russia not with the eyes of 1908 or 1914, but of 1856 and 1870. How—Bismarck might well ask—was German trade to expand after 1879 if Great Britain, *the* sea-power *par excellence*, were driven by German action into the camp of Germany's foes ?

Nevertheless the gravity of the risk taken in 1879 is proved by the insurance against its exploding into an unlimited liability. Until 1890 Austria was never allowed to get out of hand. How precisely this was done we cannot say with certainty. But it was done. The control of the Wilhelmstrasse over the Ball-Platz was effective, for Bismarck had his personal prestige, unrivalled knowledge, and experience to help in the difficult task. These are qualities not acquired by intuition, still less by birth or hereditary succession, but by brains and the travail of a lifetime. Control of Austria was also assisted by positive counterchecks—the alliance with Italy and the continuous ring at the Russian front door. It is safe to conclude that Bismarck prepared for the inclusion of Italy in 1879, and that without the Dual Alliance Italy could not have been secured. We have Bismarck's word for it, and his judgment outweighs a dozen criticisms. For he had the whole of the facts before him, whereas his critics argue from edited documents written on one side only.

A further consideration is very relevant. Down to 1879 the isolation of France had been the prime object of German policy. The policy was breaking down. France, excluded from the Congress of London in 1870, took part in the Congress of Berlin in 1878. After 1879 the diversion of France became more important than her isolation : and with it went the diversion of Russia and the diversion of Great Britain—in each case the diversion being intended ultimately to increase the antagonism. But these developments open up a fresh section of Bismarckian policy, with an intrinsic character of its own. They lead to the Triple Alliance and the consequences of that consummation of the Chancellor's diplomacy.

Gastein in 1865 saw the making of a new Austria; Gastein in 1879 provided the new Austria with an alluring future and the means of realising it. Vienna was right in welcom-

ing Bismarck with a gratitude which deeply touched that
seared, proud, and sensitive heart. The Treaty of 1879
was a masterpiece.[1] It was signed by Bismarck and
Andrassy on October 7. On October 8 Francis Joseph
was graciously pleased to accept Andrassy's resignation—
for reasons of health. The treaty was cordially approved.
But the statesman who made it for Austria received the
reward of Beust, Benedek, Rechberg, Schmerling, Buol,
and Bach.

§ 4. The New Era—Home Policy, 1878-1888

The years 1878-80 witnessed a gradual but complete
change in the home policy of the Chancellor, culminating
in the establishment of the system which Bismarck maintained until his fall. In foreign policy, as has been
already indicated, the development of events prevented
the continuance of the alliance of the Three Monarchies
on the lines originally planned, and imposed on Bismarck
the necessity of a choice. In home affairs the necessity of
a choice was even more urgent. Bismarck practically
said to Bennigsen, ' Do not compel me to choose between
you and Windthorst.' And Bennigsen's reply was virtually to the effect that the choice must be made.

The several elements in the problems by the spring of
1878 were clear, but together they made a very complicated
situation. First of all, there was the Chancellor himself.
His health and strength were no longer capable of bearing
the continuous strain of mastering and directing the foreign
and home policy of a great and expanding Empire, in
which Prussia was the predominant partner. An imperial
ministry did not exist. The imperial executive was
organised as a branch of the Imperial Chancery, the secretaries of the various departments being simply depart-

---

[1] Prince von Bülow writes in his *Imperial Germany* (edition of 1916):—
'Prince Bismarck, a second Hercules, accomplished many great labours. . .
If I were asked which of these is the more admirable from the point of view of
foreign policy I should say without hesitation—the Austrian alliance.' The
whole chapter (v.), as indeed the whole book, bears out Mr. Headlam's considered judgment on its importance as an authoritative exposition of German
principles and a German interpretation of the meaning of Bismarckianism—
a meaning falsified by his successors, of whom Prince von Bülow is the ablest.

mental and executive officers, appointed by the Chancellor, and responsible as managers of sub-departments to him alone. Bismarck had stoutly resisted every effort to convert these departments into independent ministerial offices, with ministerial chiefs, colleagues in an imperial cabinet, and representing their several departments in the Reichstag; and his reason was not pure autocracy and personal jealousy—the determination to keep everything in his own hands—though they accentuated his refusal. The reasons went far deeper; an imperial cabinet, such as the Progressives and the Left Wing of the National Liberals had advocated since 1867 as an irrevocable advance to parliamentary government and were urging with persistence in 1877, cut at the root of the position of the Federal Council, and the interlocking machinery by which Prussia maintained her control of policy as a whole. For the Federal Council, like the Tudor Privy Council in England, was the real governing organ in the Empire, and combined legislative with executive duties (through its committees), and was essentially the organ which made policy. Although we are without exact information as to how Prussia, behind the closed doors of the Bundesrat, maintained her control, it is clear that it was exercised and maintained by the chairmanship of the Imperial Chancellor, who as Minister-President of Prussia cast the Prussian vote; and in the secret deliberations of the Federal Council, just as in the Tudor Privy Council or the modern Cabinet in England, there could be perfect freedom of discussion, and a complete representation of different points of view, while the decision arrived at was the decision of the organ as a whole, and the voting was unknown except to the initiated. A real Imperial Minister of Finance, for example, responsible to the Reichstag, would obviously supersede to a large extent the power and functions of the Federal Council and transfer them partly to himself and (no less important) partly to the Reichstag. The creation of such imperial ministers simply meant that in a few years the Federal Council would either shrivel into the position that the British Privy Council has shrivelled into, relatively to the Cabinet and the House of Commons; or, it would be transformed into a real Upper Chamber of the Imperial Reichstag, as had been in 1870 the ideal of the unitarians led by the Crown Prince and the intellectuals of the ' Coburg and Gotha ' school. But such a transformation destroyed the essence of the institution which was constituted *out* of, not *over*, the Federated *governments*.

No less serious (and to all Prussians of the Bismarckian and conservative type, far more serious) would be the effect on Prussia. The British student is apt to forget that beside the Federal Council (*Bundesrat*) and the Imperial Reichstag existed the Prussian Ministry, presided over by the Prussian Minister-President, and the Prussian Parliament (*Landtag*), and that Imperial Reichstag and Prussian Parliament were frequently sitting at one and the same time in Berlin. Indeed, a large number of Reichstag members (who were Prussians) spent their time between the two bodies, voting on and fighting the same issues in two separate legislatures. The *Kulturkampf* was essentially a Prussian affair, and the greater part of the ' May Laws ' was a Prussian, not an imperial, concern : just as the administrative execution of those laws was mainly the duty of the Prussian Minister of the Interior.

Prussia had, like the other federated States, her separate (and very narrow) franchise, ministry, and bureaucracy the only difference being that Prussia was very nearly two thirds of the Empire, and that behind ministry and bureaucracy stood a solid concrete wall of tradition and conventions, the parapet of which was the royal autocracy. There was a Prussian Minister, but no Imperial Minister of War ; a Prussian Minister of Finance, Education, and so forth, and the Prussian Foreign Minister was the Minister President who was also Imperial Chancellor : an Imperial Minister of Finance or War, not directly under the Chancellor's control, involved the dual system in a terrible dilemma. Either it meant the government of that imperial department by Prussia, or the government of the Prussian department by the Empire. The former would have led to a revolt of every non-Prussian State from the imperial system, the latter to the dissolution of Prussia in the Empire. Bismarck plainly told the Reichstag more than once that an independent Imperial Minister of Finance would have for his greatest antagonist the Prussian Minister of Finance. He might have added with even greater truth that an Imperial Minister of War would either have to swallow the Prussian War Office or spend all his time in fighting the Prussian Minister of War. Was the Imperial Minister to exercise the prerogative of the Prussian Crown, or only the much more restricted power of the Imperial Praesidium ?

The duty of correlating this dualism and ensuring its harmonious working was Bismarck's main task, and he did it by combining the office of Chancellor and Minister-President, by controlling the Federal Council, and by the domination of the conservative majority in the Prussian Landtag. As Minister-President he took care that the decisions of the Prussian Ministry broadly coincided with the policy of the Federal Council ; as Imperial Chancellor he took care that the Federal Council's decisions coincided with the broad requirements of Prussian policy. Furthermore, his control of the Prussian Ministry was ensured by the Cabinet order of 1852 by which the Prussian Ministry in its relations to the Prussian Crown acted through the Minister-President alone ; the Minister-President was in the same constitutional relation to the sovereign that custom has assigned to the Prime Minister in the British Cabinet. The Minister-President was the sole channel of communication with the Crown ; and Bismarck's immense prestige, personal gifts, inexhaustible powers of work, political tact, and commanding influence with the sovereign enabled him to accomplish a perpetual miracle.

From 1871 to 1888 it must also be remembered that Bismarck was the servant of a sovereign rapidly ageing. William I. was seventy-four in 1871, and he was content to leave Bismarck a very free hand. The King was not capable of doing the amount of work that autocracy and an intimate personal control implied. The autocracy was in fact shared by the King-Emperor with Bismarck. William's governing interest, the army, fell outside the shared power. Bismarck provided the legal basis and the money, and left the army to the King and the General

Staff, for in his eyes the army was simply a superb executive instrument of policy. The General Staff provided him, through its chief, with the information necessary for a correct judgment of any political situation, but he would have resented the intervention of the ' demi-gods ' in the office of the Wilhelmstrasse even more fiercely than Moltke resented the effort of the Imperial Chancellor to overrule in problems of strategy the chief of the General Staff.

The system therefore rested on the individual character and gifts of King-Emperor and Chancellor more securely than on the legal and constitutional relations established by the Imperial and Prussian constitutions. But if we assume that in 1878 the Cabinet order of 1852 had been repealed, and that in the place of William I., aged eighty-one, was a sovereign young, active, capable, able to do the work required, and with his own views of home and foreign policy, not necessarily identical with those of his Chancellor and Minister-President, the system would have begun to show widening fissures that no papering over by photographs, decorations, and eulogistic letters would cover. What took place in 1890 might have taken place at any time between 1878 and 1890. ' The older one gets,' said Frederick the Great, ' the more convinced one becomes that His Majesty King Chance does three-quarters of the business of this miserable universe.' In 1878, when a crisis had been steadily developed and Germany and Bismarck had reached the cross-roads of a great decision, had the bullet of Nobiling ended the life of William I. and put the Crown on the head of the Crown Prince, it is as certain as anything can well be that the history of the next ten years in Germany would have been fundamentally different. The fate of Liberalism in Germany might have been decided with a moderate Liberal on the throne. ' King Chance ' provided that it should be decided with an aged and very conservative sovereign, the two attempts on whose life profoundly influenced a critical general election. Had the Conservatives and the Clericals hired the half-witted miscreant who fired at the old gentleman to whom age, character, and service to Germany should have given a perpetual immunity, they could not have done a better stroke for their parties.

In 1878 Bismarck recognised that personally he could not carry on as he had done. The law which authorised the creation of a Vice-Chancellor (*Stellvertreter*) to act for the Chancellor, if required, was intended to relieve the strain but retain the system. In 1873 Bismarck had met it by resigning the Minister-Presidency to Roon, but that solution had proved a failure. The *Stellvertreter* law of 1878 was a deliberate effort to avoid the other solution— the creation of imperial and responsible ministers, who could be real colleagues to the Chancellor, and relieve him of half his work (and more than half his power). The debates on the law revealed the issues, and the law passed because Bismarck, for the reasons previously explained, categorically refused any other alternative. The Reichstag had to choose between Bismarck and an approximation to parliamentary government. No one in 1878 could face the possibility of governing the Empire and Prussia with Bismarck out of office and in opposition ; no one had any confidence in a foreign policy directed by any one but Bismarck ; for the Congress of Berlin, the antagonism between Russia and Austria, the renaissance of France, the policy of Great Britain, and the menacing problems offered by Italy, the Mediterranean, Greece, and the Ottoman Empire—unsolved by the Congress—made no other decision possible. In 1878 the Reichstag voted first for the man, and with reluctance, for his system. The life of States, as of families, was once more proved to be dependent in the great crises on the individual.

Bismarck now had to keep the system that he had created efficient. If it failed in efficiency, his own personal position would crumble away. It was not enough to direct foreign policy, anticipate and neutralise hostile coalitions, and rivet in that German hegemony which, as he said himself, had to face four fronts at one and the same time. The German at home must be satisfied by material proofs that Bismarckian government was the best both in theory and practice. In 1878 the Germans had begun seriously to doubt the adequacy of the theory and the benefits of the practice. It was openly asserted by friends and foes alike that Bismarck had done his work. The Reichstag was the crux. The irresponsible autocracy of the Federal Council that made policy must either work with the majority in the Reichstag or make a majority for itself. The Bismarckian system which in theory made the government independent of party could only achieve its purpose through the manipulation of the party vote. The perpetual creation of King's Friends in sufficient numbers to ensure 'the right' decision in the Lobbies was essential. The general election of 1877 proved that under no conceivable circumstance could the united Conservative parties command the majority required, or indeed now hope to win more than one-fourth to one-third of the votes. The Conservatives must therefore be united with another strong party. There were only two from which to choose—the Liberals or the Clerical Centre. Union with the Centre gave a working, with the Liberals a handsome, majority. Which therefore was to be secured ?

The whole point lay in the 'securing.' In Great Britain under similar circumstances there would have been a Coalition *Ministry*, representative of the fused parties. But in Germany the problem for Bismarck was to get the votes without admitting the voters to the control of policy. Hitherto, the National Liberals had solidly supported the government. The negotiations with Bennigsen revealed two interesting results : National Liberal support would be continued if the previous policy were continued, but a change of policy meant probably a struggle with National Liberalism. To the Liberals above all the maintenance of Free Trade, the issues involved in the May Laws, and ultimately parliamentary government, were the three cardinal items.

Conservatism combined with the Centre involved marching down the road to Canossa, and it was uncertain that the Centre would vote for a new fiscal policy. While Bismarck faced this troubled political situation, accident helped him partially to solve it. The death of Pio Nono, and the elevation to the Pontificate of Leo XIII., created a new situation at the Vatican. The new Pontiff could, without damaging Papal prestige, inaugurate a more conciliatory attitude ; Bismarck without disinterring a penitential white sheet could enter on an ' exchange of views.' Both sides, thoroughly tired of the struggle, indicated through appropriate channels that conversations would at any rate do no harm; and in the autumn of 1878 Bismarck sought a cure at Kissingen, which was also recommended as the one health resort in Germany that would help Monsignor Masella, the Papal Nuncio to Bavaria. Nuncio and Chancellor met by an arranged accident and exchanged views. They were really determining what they could buy or sell, and in 1878 the wares on either side were simply brought out and handled in a friendly manner.

More decisive for the present was the attempt (May 11) by Hödel on the Emperor's life. The government at once brought in a very severe bill which practically put the Social Democrats at the mercy of the Ministry of the Interior. For years the growing organisation of Social Democracy had been alarming the Conservative classes. Argument having failed, force alone remained. But the bill was so comprehensive in its severity that it threatened all political organisations not approved of by the government. Despite a denunciation by Moltke of Social Democracy as the enemy of God and society, Bennigsen and Lasker from the Liberal benches tore the measures in pieces, and it was rejected by 251-57 votes, the Centre voting with the Liberals. A few days later (June 2) Nobiling, a doctor of philology, attempted to assassinate the Emperor, and succeeded in wounding him severely. Bismarck heard the news at Varzin. He struck his staff into the ground. ' Now,' he cried, ' we will dissolve the Reichstag.'

The dissolution was decreed promptly by the Bundesrat (June 11), and the elections were held in all the excitement of panic, aggravated by indignation. Liberalism was aghast at the Chancellor's stroke : and the result bore out their fears. They lost thirty-two seats at least, and the united Liberal and Radical forces numbered 106 as against 176 in the old Parliament. The Centre gained a couple of seats, but the seats lost by Liberalism went to the

Conservatives, who now disputed with the Clericals the claim to be the strongest single party in the legislature.

The anti-Socialist law was promptly reintroduced, and passed by 221 votes to 149. Bismarck was obliged to accept some amendments from the National Liberals, for without their help the measures could not become law, and the chief concessions were two : first, the operation of the law was limited to three years (March 31, 1881) ; secondly, electoral meetings were excluded from its provisions. But, as passed, the discretionary powers granted to the government were tremendous, for it enabled the central authorities in the States to prohibit public meetings, dissolve political associations, suppress newspapers and books, and decide who was or was not a Socialist, what was or was not Socialist doctrine or objects calculated to undermine the State. Socialists could be banished from their homes, and a whole district could in case of urgent danger, decided by the authorities, be placed under a state of minor siege.

The debates were remarkable for three utterances. Bebel, in his attack on the bill, revealed the qualities which in ten years were to make him the most remarkable political character in Germany, after Bismarck himself. Richter the Radical leader told the Reichstag that he feared Social Democracy more under this measure than without it. The Chancellor, after explaining that Socialism sought a heaven in momentary and material enjoyment alone, and confessing that if he lost his own faith in God and a future life, he could not live a day in any peace of mind, urged all parties to unite in making a bulwark against the common enemy to the Empire. He also foreshadowed the necessity of counteracting the insidious poison of these pestilential foes by measures of social and economic benefit to the industrial proletariat.

The Radicals and Progressives, with the left wing of the National Liberals, gallantly fought the fight for freedom of opinion and liberty of political utterance and association to a finish. But the National Liberals by their action threw the earth on their own coffin. The programme of Social Democracy has always terrified middle-class Liberalism more than any other party. Chastened by the election the Liberals were in a sad quandary. Fearing the further loss of public support if they resisted the anti-Socialist law, and surmising that Bismarck could throw them over and secure the Clerical Centre, they supported the measure, not from conviction but on calculation. Persecution of the Socialists was a lesser evil in their eyes than driving the Chancellor into the arms of Windthorst and the Vatican. They therefore clung to the broad principle of supporting the government as the sole means of retaining their political influence. But in doing so they sacrificed the essentials of their Liberalism, and they virtually buried their party as an instrument of progress and political freedom. Bismarck was quick to recognise the weakness. He had forced them against the wall and they had refused to fight. Another sledge-hammer blow and they would break up. In political arithmetic that meant that he would get half their votes without any further concessions, and the other half would melt into coalition with the Progressives and Radicals. When National Liberalism had ceased to exist as a solid phalanx the way would be open for a reactionary Conservatism. National Liberalism was to learn the wholesome lesson that when parties prefer tactics to principles and opportunism to convictions, the funeral service with their antagonist as the officiating minister is at hand.

The anti-Socialist law was put into operation with drastic severity. ' Now for the pig-sticking ' (*Jetzt geht die Sauhatz los !*) Bismarck is reported to have remarked, and the Prussian police got to work with energies whetted by their failure against the Catholics. Everything that a strong executive can do, when directed by men to whom Social Democracy was the creed of the *canaille*, was done. Berlin was placed under the minor state of siege, as were later Hamburg, Leipzig, Stettin, and other city fly-belts of the plague. Every club savouring of Socialism was broken up ; newspapers were prosecuted, pamphlets suppressed. The police even forbade subscriptions for the unfortunates selected for banishment from their homes. Indeed, everything was done to provoke the broken into violent outrage, to be used as a justification for further severity. What the Chancellor felt about freedom of speech was shown in his proposal, first, that two Socialist members of the Reichstag should be delivered over to the police because they had dared to attend the Parliament to which they had been elected; secondly, that the Reichstag should by law take power to limit the freedom of speech within the House itself. Both these proposals were rejected. Every one, except Bismarck and the Conservatives, knew that the ' Muzzling Bill ' (*Maulkorbgesetz*), as it was speedily nicknamed, would be employed by the governmental majority in crushing all serious criticism. Criticism that is successful is always ' offensive ' to autocrats and bureaucrats. It would be better to close the Reichstag at once. Well might the most distinguished of living German historians, Mommsen, publicly say in 1881 that ' the Prussia we had, the Germany we believed we had, are at an end . . . the freedom of Germany will be lost for many years to come.'

The anti-Socialist law was thrice renewed by a compliant legislature (1881, 1886, 1888), and the results were remarkable. The Social Democratic party, thanks to wonderful leadership and organisation, grew under persecution. In 1877 it had twelve members in the Reichstag and polled half a million votes; in 1893 it had forty-four members in the Reichstag and polled more than two million votes. Twenty years later it was to be the strongest single party (one hundred and thirteen members) in the Reichstag, polling four and a quarter million votes, a third of the total electorate voting, and owning no less than eighty-six newspapers. Richter's prediction in 1878 was more than verified in Bismarck's lifetime.

The transient victory of 1878 did not solve Bismarck's problem. He could not reckon on an unsuccessful attempt at assassination every year. The anti-Socialist law did not give him a working governmental majority, nor did it bring in money, and he needed the latter more than the former. The new economic policy that began in 1879 was due to the needs of the imperial revenue. The Imperial government was not paying its way, and it was confronted with a stagnant or declining revenue and ever-increasing expenditure.

With characteristic thoroughness Bismarck planned a complete reconstruction of the fiscal and financial principles and machinery on which the Federal Empire had hitherto been based, to be followed by a new departure in the objects to which the revenue was to be devoted. The Reform period lasted from 1879-88, and involved the abandonment of the Free Trade principle of taxation for revenue alone; a return to a Protective tariff, increasingly severe in its successive emendations; a halt in the system of direct taxation and a large substitution of indirect for direct taxes; an attempt to establish gigantic State monopolies in articles of such general consumption as tobacco, brandy, and sugar, and a comprehensive legislative code creating for the industrial workers compulsory insurance by the State against accidents and sickness, and establishing old-age pensions. The broad result of these nine years of feverish effort and strenuous controversy was completely to alter the economic and political structure of Germany.[1] The essential details and progress of this comprehensive programme are noticed below, but it is desirable to envisage at the outset the problem as Bismarck evidently saw it and the solution that he provided.

First and obviously, the provision of an automatically expanding revenue was his main concern. The existing system had four main defects. It kept the Imperial government in dependence on the Reichstag. The annual Budget was voted by the Reichstag, and the discussion enabled any strong party to hold up the imperial authorities either by refusing a particular item or by amending or refusing the specified appropriation. The greater the need of the government the greater the leverage of the opposition. Bismarck foresaw that through the Budget the Reichstag would in time secure by continuous flanking attacks that parliamentary control which

---

[1] On the whole question see the Report (*Parl. Papers*, CD. 4530, *August* 1885) drawn up by Mr. Strachey, discussing the fiscal, commercial, political and other points at great length and with elaborate wealth of detail and statistics. The evidence for the prosperity of Germany both under a Free Trade and a Protectionist system is impartially examined.

it had failed to secure by a frontal onslaught. Secondly, the requisition that deficits must be made good by matricular contribution from the federated States was very unpopular with the contributories, and the opposition made itself felt in the Federal Council, where the governments could outvote Prussia and resist measures of policy that involved further expenditure with a corresponding increase in the *pro rata* matricular contributions to imperial revenue from the States. Hence the control of policy was threatened. Thirdly, an increase in direct imperial taxation was not practical politics. The several budgets of the federated States were dependent on direct taxation, and it was impossible for the imperial revenue either to add an imperial to the State tax or to remove from the State governments their main source of income. Fourthly, without much larger sums of money, unification and centralisation through the imperial executive would come to a standstill. Even more pressing was the cost of defence. Foreign policy and the general principles of the State polity necessitated the arming of Germany to the teeth. An expanding population automatically provided the men, and the Empire had to pay for their equipment. The more scientifically that an army is organised, the larger the amount of science that it brought into armaments, the more costly will that army be. Efficiency can only be purchased by increasing expenditure. If the German army was no more efficient, better equipped, and in advance of all rivals in the quality and amount of its *matériel*, the basis of Bismarckian foreign policy was shattered. ' It must never be forgotten,' wrote Frederick the Great, ' that distrust is the mother of security.' Bismarck's system started from profound distrust and fear of foreign States, and the assumption that distrust and fear made the foreign policy of all other States. He studied the omens of the international situation with the superstitious creed of the augur, profoundly convinced that the gods were jealous, malevolent, and implacable, and the human beings they influenced a debased copy of the gods. If the Socialist Democrat, according to Bismarck, interpreted life in the terms of a carnal and fleeting hedonism (which he did not, for he lived and throve on ideas and ideals), Bismarck for all his belief in God, Heaven, and a Hereafter, seems to have been convinced that the sole justification of Heaven and an after life lay in importing as much of the Devil and of Hell into international relations as were necessary to provide a deterrent to coalitions against Germany. The prestige of Germany depended on the universal conviction that Bismarck relied on force, and that the German army could be at the gates of its foe within ten days of a rupture. The army therefore must be provided with strategic railways and vast stores; and on the horizon there already grew out of the sea the little cloud that foretold an imperial navy no less efficient and ready. The navy was an imperial affair. As yet it was in its cradle, but even cradles are expensive, and those who rock them must be paid. The most fatal disaster to be apprehended was a limitation of German armaments imposed by a Reichstag that refused to tax the Empire any further.

The advantages of a new, were as conspicuous as the defects of the old, system. Bismarck saw the German nation, in consequence of its unification, its long intellectual preparation, its intoxication from victory, and its belief in its own disciplined, intellectual, and moral strength, growing in wealth, numbers, and solidarity. A tariff and indirect taxation would tap the expanding national reservoir and disguise the withdrawal of the wealth. In his eyes the supreme advantage of indirect taxation lay in the concealment of the tax. It would fall on the ignorant consumer, not on the taxpayer directly mulcted by the action of a government. A tariff was an arrangement that could not be annually revised, for it would rest on an economic code enacted for a period of years, or be largely regulated by treaty beyond the revising power of the legislature. Hence the revenues derived from indirect taxation would fall into the same category as the military Septennates, and pass from parliamentary control into the hands of government. More than ever policy would remain the monopoly of the Federal Council and Prussia, and the Reichstag be reduced to a debating society, incapable of interfering at any point with the central springs of power.

Already in 1879 Bismarck foresaw one further marked advantage. The existing structure of society was the core of the Prussian system. The real danger of Social Democracy did not lie in its opinions, for the executive could always ignore or crush opinions and ideas, but in the reconstruction of society that the Socialist programme avowedly contemplated. The Bismarckian system and the State which stood for Power could not exist on a different stratification of society to that established in Prussia. Social Democracy aimed at a social revolution, the political effects of which would be simply consequential to the economic and social redistribution. Apart, however, from Social Democracy, the existing structure was in 1878 threatened more insidiously and continuously by the operation of social and economic changes, not confined to Germany, though accentuated by the rapid industrial revolution that set in after 1871. Agricultural depression, if unchecked, meant that Germany would shortly be dependent, like Great Britain, on imported food ; but far more serious politically was the pauperisation of agricultural Junkertum. The squirearchy would be transformed from an independent landowning and governing class into a class no longer able to staff the army and the civil service, but divorced from the land and driven like the bourgeois to earn a middle-class living. Industrialism, too, was throwing up a new aristocracy of brains and money whose power rested on their capacity, their wealth, and their potent material interests. Sooner or later they would usurp the position occupied by the old Junkertum, because they were quite as able, worked as hard, and commanded a far greater share of the elements of material power. It is as hard to argue with the masters of industrial, as with the master of military, legions.

Bismarck's economic and fiscal policy from 1879 to 1888 has absorbed the analytical attention of the economist and the political philosopher, but the major premises from which he argued and the conclusion to which he marched with relentless energy, derive their deepest significance from their relation to the principles of his statecraft. For by his policy at the critical moment of development he gradually attracted the allegiance of the new elements of power to the Prussianised Empire. By so doing he saved the Bismarckian State, and he prevented all those formidable elements from being thrown into revolt against the existing régime. He did not love industrialism or its works ; all his sympathies were with agriculture, the landowner and the farmer and the peasant ; he did not argue from economic science, or from any devotion to an economic theory of freedom or otherwise. From first to last his inspiration and his objective were purely political, and intensely conservative. Contemporary and later critics alike have questioned the sincerity and disputed the meaning of Bismarck's 'conversion' to Socialism. In reality there was no conversion at all. Socialism as a theory of society, or of the economic life and functions of an organised community, he never accepted nor professed to accept. His view of the true type and character of social and economic stratification remained constant, and it may be questioned whether in 1879 or 1890 he had altered one hair's-breadth of the opinions he professed in 1849. But he was a realist and an opportunist, and he recognised that change must continually be taking place. The function of conservative statesmanship, if sincere in its allegiance to a defined table of social values and a defined social order, must continuously incorporate the ' ponderable ' elements, created by change, and employ them in shoring up the social framework and preserving the type. The problem was essentially one of political judgment, knowledge, delicacy of method, and an elastic adaptability—a perpetual compromise which conceded details but never allowed fundamentals to be questioned or weakened. Hence his deep contempt for the Metternich school or for the unbending Conservatism of the *Kreuzzeitung* type, which would let a conservative social order go to ruin because some conscientious shibboleth was erected into an inflexible principle. A Conservatism that lacked the political instinct and the true political judgment was as useless and dangerous as the Socialism of Bebel and Liebknecht. Had Bismarck been a conservative leader in Great Britain between 1820 and 1850 he would have put Eldon, George

Bentinck, and Wellington in the same category as he put
Gerlach and the tribe of Senfft-Pilsachs and Blanckenburgs.
He would not have waited, like Peel, for the destruction
of the landed aristocracy and a potato famine to be converted into a great betrayal and the ruin of his party.
He would have united the millowners and manufacturers
who were the backbone of Cobden's League in an
alliance with the old aristocracy, and compelled the
Whigs and the middle-class Liberals to share the fate
that he meted out to Bennigsen, Lasker, Forckenbeck,
and Stauffenberg.

Failing a *coup d'État*, which Bismarck regarded as a confession of failure and stupidity, parties in the Reichstag
had to be manipulated. The autocracy was yoked to a
representative legislature and lived under a constitution.
The new policy, as Bismarck foresaw, offered unrivalled
opportunities, first, for splitting the existing party distribution, and, secondly, for bargaining. The substitution of
interests for principles as the basis of parties was not the
least important result that accompanied and flowed from
the new system.[1] Bargaining over principles is always a
failure. Hence coalitions in a country where party sys-
tems rest on principles are usually failures, and always
hated by the country as a whole. But bargaining over
interests is simply an affair of political and economic
arithmetic. Conducted by a strong government with a
resolute chief it resolves itself into a simple problem of the
quantity of the article required conditioned by the price.
Bismarck, though he probably had never read an economic
text-book and could not have explained the meaning of
'final utility' or 'marginal value,' applied the principle
in the world of parliamentary politics in the same effective
way as M. Jourdain spoke prose. The final political
utility of Clericals, National Liberals, or any other group
was, in his eyes, simply the last quantity of votes that the
buyer was prepared to secure, and the seller willing to

[1] Cf. Strachey's remark (Report already cited, p. 45) as an example in
1885: 'No reason can be given why spun silk should be excluded from the
blessings of protection, except the conclusive one, that they do not form a
powerful interest, and that in spun silk, as in other things, "to be weak is to be
miserable." '

part with, at a given price. And the famous cartel which secured him a working majority was a political coalition, arranged precisely on the principles on which a big manufacturer coalesces with a group of rival but smaller firms. Bismarck, moreover, started from two fixed points, as intelligible to every one as to himself—he could move the government levers, and once he had broken with Liberalism he could always rely on the Conservative vote. King and Junkers, the social structure round the throne, and the Federal Council and the governments would fall to heel. They barked and bit (sometimes) and growled perpetually, but they knew when their master meant business.

In a word, the new policy of 1879 was a fresh manifestation, moulded by circumstances, of the State as the incarnation of Power. The Alpha and Omega of Bismarck's ' Socialism ' were summed up in the determination to make the Empire self-sufficing, stronger than ever, and still more dependent on the government, still more impotent to place the control of policy under responsible parliamentary institutions. Such measures were not really Socialism, properly defined, at all—the Social Democrats saw that from the first—except in the sense that every act of a State is ' socialistic.' It was the renaissance of the mercantilism of the seventeenth century adapted to the benevolent and illuminated despotism of the eighteenth century and the conditions of a militarist State, remoulded by the phenomena of modern industrialism. Hence its ultimate and unequivocal challenge to the principle of Free Trade, and the modern State built up on the principles of which Free Trade was but one plinth in the whole structure. Its *raison d'être* and end were power, directed by a fusion of the landowning and capitalistic classes that dominated a social organisation of a definable type. The so-called Socialism of Bismarck was a denial of the postulates and economic analysis alike of Lassalle, Marx, or Bebel. The academic Socialists of the Chair— the *Katheder Socialisten*, led by Wagner, Schmoller, and their school—wrote elaborate volumes on Bismarckian Socialism, and read into it a mass of theory which Bismarck

would have failed to understand, or dismissed as irrelevant
verbiage : so far as it had an ascertainable paternity, the
genealogy of Bismarck's Socialism can be found, not in the
writings and teaching of Karl Marx, but in the doctrines
of F. List. But the new programme was a wonderful
illustration of Bismarck's intuitive sensitiveness to change
and ideas, that he exploited for his own political purposes.

So long as Germany was rent by the *Kulturkampf* this
comprehensive programme could not be fairly discussed
or embodied in law. The *Kulturkampf* was essentially a
controversy over principles, which brought the theory and
functions of the civil power into the arena of conflict. The
Clerical Centre, as developed by Windthorst with the aid
of the Roman Curia, was first and foremost a confessional
organisation which united in a single party every class from
the princes and hierarchs of the Church to the industrial
proletariat in the great Catholic centres of industry, and
which subordinated all the separable class interests of its
members to a broad aim, the practical independence of
the Roman Church. The new economic programme involved a complete breach with Liberalism and Radicalism.
It could not therefore have any chance of success unless
the Centre were rallied to the side of the government.
The *Kulturkampf* must therefore be ended, as a preliminary condition to the new era. Bismarck's conversations
with Masella at Kissingen cleared up the situation. The
Vatican required the repeal of the May Laws and a return
broadly to the position in 1871. Bismarck required the
Centre vote on all governmental proposals. Both sides
had a valuable article to sell ; both sides were weary of
the struggle, and neither side dared openly to don the
white sheet and publicly reverse their explicit statement
of principles. Each side thoroughly distrusted the other
and with good reason. Windthorst feared that once
Bismarck had utilised the Centre he would throw them
over and reunite with the Liberals. Bismarck, uncertain
of how far Germany would accept the new programme
and aware that the Liberal and Protestant forces would
resent an advance to Canossa, and that repeal of the May
Laws was a damaging blow to his prestige, dared not make

the Centre master of the situation. The exchange of a Clerical control for the National Liberals was no gain but loss. For he wanted to be independent alike of Clericals and Liberals, and of the two the Clericals were more difficult to satisfy. Foreign policy entered into his calculations. Ultramontanism in France and Austria was a continuous and disturbing element in the European situation. Bismarck had to reckon with a possible Ultramontane supremacy in France upsetting the results achieved by the Dual Alliance of 1879. And there was always Poland—the eternal Poland, Catholic and Slav in one.

It was essentially, therefore, a case for a slow and gradual reconciliation, every concession being decided by the situation of the moment and paid for in advance by positive results. Bismarck began by heartening the Conservatives. In 1878 Camphausen, the Liberal financial minister, was replaced by Maybach, a Conservative; Eulenberg, the new Minister of the Interior, was a strenuous Conservative; Stolberg, the new Vice-Chancellor under the *Kanzlervertreter* law was not a National Liberal, but an unbending Conservative. On July 14, 1879, Falk's resignation was accepted. He left office with all the indications of dismissal. His health had failed; and to assist him in his recovery he was given a riband, a eulogistic letter, portraits and photographs, while his place was taken by Puttkamer, a fierce Conservative. On May 3 the members of the Reichstag who attended the Chancellor's parliamentary soirées, where Bismarck, cigar in one hand and glass in the other, arranged his parliamentary plans of campaign, saw with astonishment 'the pearl of Meppen,' 'the little Chancellor,' Windthorst, making his bow with the air of a *habitué*, and witnessed the genial cordiality with which the 'big Chancellor' welcomed the apparition expected by himself and no one else. Delbrück, Camphausen, Falk had gone, and in their place was Windthorst, polished, smiling, and epigrammatic. 'Every courtesy as far as the gallows,' Bismarck had said thirty years before to G. von Vincke. 'Every courtesy as far as Canossa,' was now Windthorst's silent comment.

It cannot have been a happy evening for Bismarck, though he made his new guest taste from the huge cask of the finest Franciscan liqueur sent him by the reconciled monks.

The fruits of the negotiations behind the scenes were laid on the table of the Prussian Landtag in 1880 in a governmental bill. The measure was roughly handled and drastically amended, and in its final form only passed by four votes (206-202), a convincing proof of the strength of Liberal feeling and voting power. As amended, the bill did not repeal any of the fundamentals in the May Laws, but gave to the government a qualified discretion in the enforcement of the penal legislation. It had been preceded by a Papal announcement (February 24) authorising the Roman bishops in Prussia to notify ecclesiastical appointments in their diocese to the Prussian government for approval (*Anzeigepflicht*). The bill was the first step towards a complete peace. The remaining stages were covered in the next four years. In 1882 (May 31) Roman priests were largely dispensed from the necessity and conditions of the State examination, prescribed in the May Laws ; in 1883 (July 11) Roman bishops were released from the obligation to notify ecclesiastical appointments to the civil authority, which simply retained a power of veto ; in the same year the Crown Prince visited Rome and had an audience with the Pope ; in 1884 the Roman bishops were introduced into the Prussian Council of State ; in 1886 Leo XIII. was invited by Bismarck to arbitrate on the dispute between Germany and Spain over the Caroline Islands, and in the same year a new law empowered the government practically to dispense at its discretion with the penal code set up between 1873 and 1875. On May 23, 1887, Leo XIII. was able to assure the Consistory that the *Kulturkampf* was at an end, and that the Roman Church had secured the essentials for which it had fought. Bismarck received the Order of Christ, the first Protestant to be given this Papal decoration, a portrait of Leo XIII., and a copy of the Pope's Latin poems. He did not forward in return a bound volume of his speeches in which he had laid it down that he would not go to Canossa either in body or in spirit.

'That journey,' as a distinguished German historian
said, 'nevertheless took place.' The argument that
Bismarck was not beaten, and that he did not surrender,
cannot stand the test of indisputable fact. Still less
tenable is the view that Bismarck made the surrender
willingly. He was not the man, after all his stout words
and the violence of the conflict in which Protestant and
Liberal Germany had hailed him as a second Luther,
nailing 'the May Laws,' like the immortal ninety-five
theses at Wittenberg, to the Throne and Parliament of
Prussia. The attempt to enforce the omnipotence of the
Civil State had broken down; the attempt to assert civil
control over the faith, discipline, and education of the
Roman priesthood had collapsed. In 1873 Bismarck had
plainly miscalculated the resources of the foe he had challenged, and exaggerated the strength of the weapons at his
disposal. He had beaten a retreat because he could not
hold the position that he had occupied in the battle :
but he had not retreated without securing compensation
adequate to the humiliation. The Clerical vote enabled
him to carry out a policy more important in his eyes than
the principles enshrined in the May Laws, and in the critical controversy in 1887-8 over the Septennate the Centre
came to his aid and secured the victory (see p. 451).

The Chancellor's surrender was a bitter blow to
Liberalism and Radicalism. To both parties the Clerical
Centre was, in Gambetta's phrase, *the* enemy, for Ultramontanism challenged every principle of importance in
the Liberal and Radical creed, and to them the victory of
Windthorst and the Vatican was a victory of obscurantism,
not merely in the narrow plot of theology and dogma,
but in the unlimited fields of intellectual and social life.
The far-reaching influence of the 'progress to Canossa'
between 1879 and 1887 on the German mind cannot yet
be fairly estimated, nor do they fall within the scope of
our subject, but its direct and immediate results were
obvious. It opened up an epoch of growing reaction in
home politics and administration, and the barometer of
Liberalism steadily fell. The Centre remained at a fairly
constant figure of approximately one hundred votes in

the Reichstag, and Bismarck's action made it the arbiter of the parliamentary situation. The full effect of that predominance was felt outside the period of Bismarck's Chancellorship, and he left it as a dangerous inheritance to his successors. They had to liquidate the bill incurred between 1879 and 1887.

The smashing of Liberalism was the other conspicuous result. Here again Bismarck reaped the direct advantage for himself, and left the aftermath to his successors. But when Bismarck broke the National Liberal party he left the Empire with no buffer between the government and Social Democracy except an uneasy marriage of convenience between Conservatism, which completely failed to grow any stronger in voting power, and the Clerical Centre—a coalition of interests, not a fusion of principles. The inheritor of the broken Liberalism was the Socialist Democratic party, and the growth of that party was a fresh proof that Bismarck had miscalculated its strength, the sources from which it drew its recruits, and the methods by which it could be successfully combated.

The gradual degradation of the Reichstag, and with it the deterioration of political life in Germany, began in 1879 when Bismarck for purely tactical reasons bought the support of the Centre. That degradation was perhaps inevitable, because the Reichstag under the Imperial Constitution was simply a part, and not the most important part, of the legislative machine ; and no representative body can retain its vitality, its dignity, and its self-respect —the three qualities essential to a healthy and self-renewing political life—when it is deliberately made a House of Phrases and nothing else. But unquestionably the deterioration was materially hastened by Bismarck's policy. Power and responsibility are correlatives in the life of organised communities, and the Reichstag was steadily deprived of the shreds of both that it once possessed. When the generation that had produced Bennigsen, Lasker, Forckenbeck, Miquel, and Richter had passed away, as they practically did in Bismarck's lifetime, the ideals and the effort to realise them which had been the life-blood of the heroic Germany from 1848 to 1870 were no longer there to inspire the new generation. An acute observer remarked at the time when Prince Hohenlohe's *Memoirs* were published, the painful disillusionment in Germany at the revelation of the atmosphere of intrigue poisoning the political world in which Hohenlohe had played his part, with increasing aversion to the setting in which he found himself. The disillusionment of the politicians began long before 1902. The lifting of the curtain on parliamentary history after 1879 reveals the Reichstag not as the centre of national life where the principles of a nation's policy are fought out in argument and open daylight, but as the market-place where an irresponsible government secured a more or less transient majority by the sleepless manipulation of the leaders and the purchase of votes by concessions to the rank and file. The real bargaining took place in the Federal Council, and as to its nature and terms our information is either non-existent or so scanty as not even to justify the speculative hypotheses of a *Privatdozent*. The function of the government was reduced to securing a majority in the Reichstag in order to place the legal stamp on decisions arrived at elsewhere. And this function Bismarck performed with remarkable skill, because he had an unrivalled personal prestige, and to the end he exercised a personal hypnotism over the men with whom he negotiated and the Germany that they represented.

Here again the results affected his successors more disastrously than himself. Surrounded by a network and an atmosphere of intrigue he was strong enough to defeat it, simply because he was Bismarck. But Caprivi, Hohenlohe, and Bülow—to take the story no further—had to wrestle with the system that Bismarck had created, and they were the victims of that system. In home as in foreign politics Bismarck did not wish to look beyond the immediate needs of the hour. He saw the storms successively rolling up, and he added one temporary lightning conductor after another to divert the destructive force from the main building. He had definite ends in view, but for their realisation he implicitly relied on the tactical situation, and even more on his own unrivalled power of extricating himself from any and every difficulty by an unerring use of opportunities.

He illustrated these qualities triumphantly in the great struggle from 1879 to 1888, which was the climax to his political career. The first step was the abandonment of Free Trade and the return to Protection, embodied in the measures submitted in May 1879. The corn duties were voted in May, and the new general tariff passed on July 12 by a majority of one hundred, the Centre voting with the government. Bismarck's interest and share in the policy was shown by his continuous intervention in debate. He spoke no less than eight times, and his speeches were a personal confession and the exposition of a comprehensive programme. He desired to return to the ' time-honoured ways of 1823 ' (when Prussia began to abandon its Protectionist system with the organisation of the Zollverein), and he asked the Reichstag to believe that in 1862 he had, to his shame, no ' economic tendencies ' at all ; for fifteen years he had been so completely absorbed in foreign policy that he had had no leisure to form independent opinions or an exhaustive investigation, and he had relied on Delbrück and others, whose opinions he had accepted. Delbrück's retirement in 1876 had compelled him to take up the matter for himself, and he had discovered that Germany and himself had been ' the dupes of an honest conviction ' (Free Trade) 'worthy of the honourable capacity for dreaming in the German race.' In a characteristic passage he argued that surgery based on experience had made brilliant progress, whereas medical science, unable to examine the internal mechanism of the body, had practically stood still : so with economics, ' the abstract doctrines of science leave me perfectly cold, my only standard of judgment being experience,' and experience showed him that Protectionist countries prospered and Free Trade countries were stagnant or retrograde. The unanimity of the professors for, was in itself an argument against, Free Trade. He concluded with his customary peroration that party considerations never influenced his patriotic zeal, and that in advocating the change he had but one motive, the prosperity and well-being of the Empire.

As an account of Bismarck's conversion the speech was as remarkable for its omissions as for its assertions, ignoring as it did the powerful pressure exerted by the agricultural and manufacturing interests. The passage on science must have highly diverted Virchow, and had Pasteur read it, would have caused him to raise his eyebrows in amused contempt. Still more naïve was the assertion that Free Trade was a cause of decadence, when it was precisely a Free Trade Great Britain whose competition was so distressing to German manufacturers. Windthorst, too, must have enjoyed the passionate protest that party considerations never entered into the Chancellor's calculations, for the night before he had been haggling with Bismarck over the price for the Clerical vote. The Chancellor struck the note of irresistible appeal when he invited the Reichstag to save agriculture and preserve the German market for German industry at all costs, and by a large addition to the revenue release the Federated States from the burden of the increasing matricular constitutions. He bid for the material interests, and they responded manfully to the invitation.[1]

The division was a personal triumph, and the aged Field-Marshal Moltke could be seen stumbling over his sword, caught in the rails, as he mounted the steps to the Chancellor's seat to congratulate him. Yet the triumph was not unalloyed. Bismarck had been compelled to accept the Franckenstein amendment by which all revenue, above one hundred and thirty million marks, derived from the new tariff was to be appropriated to the relief of the Federated States. His desire to obtain the sole use of the new revenue for imperial purposes was thereby frustrated, and this damaging amendment was the beginning of a series of disappointments and rebuffs.

For eighteen months the economic battle between Free Trade and Protection had been squarely fought out in Germany in the press, on public platforms, and in academic controversy. The vote of July 1879 decided the issue,

[1] 'The political constitution of the Empire, the highest personal influences, the most powerful industrial and commercial forces, some of the principal press energies, all are on the side of the (Protectionist) system.'—Report already cited, p. 75.

and the Centre gave the victory to Bismarck. The National Liberals broke over the controversy ; sixteen voted with, but the majority against, the government. Free Trade and a Free Parliament in a united and centralised Empire had been their programme since their formation in 1867, and in the attack on Free Trade the majority recognised a general assault on the whole Liberal creed. The suspicion was confirmed by the revision of the May Laws next year, and the party broke up. The *Secession*, which included the ablest and most vigorous members—Lasker, Forckenbeck, Bamberger, and Bunsen —endeavoured to establish, like the Peelites in England, an independent existence between the Conservatives, with whom the right of the party now acted, and the Progressives under Richter. But the general election of 1881 was a further blow. True, it went badly for Bismarck and the government, for the Conservatives lost a great many seats, but it made clear that there was no room for a divided National Liberalism, and it gave the gains to the Centre, the Socialists, and the Radicals. Bennigsen, worn out and disillusioned, retired from public life in 1883, and the *Secession* was driven to unite with the Progressives, and found under Richter's leadership a new party, the *Deutsch Freisinnige*—the German Free Thinkers. The remnant of the old party continued to exist under the old name, and to support the government, because it was national rather than Liberal. But between 1881 and 1883 the old National Liberalism really ceased to exist. It became under a misleading label a party moderately Conservative at home, and fiercely Nationalist in foreign politics. The old National Liberalism had been the most powerful intellectual, educative, and political force in forming a united Germany ; but when in 1867 it subordinated free institutions to unity, when in 1870 it accepted without a struggle the system of 1867 as the basis of the Empire, when it persistently helped the government by the Septennates to ruin the Budget control of Parliament, and when in 1878 it consented to pass the law against the Social Democrats, it destroyed itself.

Bismarck treated the party as he treated Napoleon III. ;

and he used the support it gave him to be the engine of its downfall. The middle class from which it drew its strength turned either to Protection, from which it could gain wealth, or to the Progressives who fought a hopeless battle with the entrenched governing class. Richter's party had at least an intelligible creed and an avowed aim —that of destroying the Bismarckian system and of substituting for it responsible parliamentary government at home, an economic régime not founded on prosperity for the landowner and manufacturer and State doles to the proletariat, and a foreign policy that did not rest on a continuous expenditure on armaments and the Prussian sword as the *ultima ratio* in international relations. After 1878 National Liberalism, as such, had no constructive policy to offer Germany. It resisted the conversion of Bismarck, but it had no practical alternative to meet the needs of the Empire it had largely created. It criticised with acerbity, and voted with docility in the government lobby, and its dissolution was a confession of bankruptcy. Bismarck and the Radicals acted as joint-receivers, liquidated the account, and distributed the business of a once-flourishing and powerful House into various and hostile hands. It was, indeed, the end of an old song.

The year 1880 was mainly occupied in opening the road to Canossa, but from 1881 to 1889 Bismarck laid down the main framework of the economic legislation that earned him the title of the Great State Socialist of the nineteenth century—the measure which provided for Employers' Liability in accidents, for insurance against sickness, and for the provision of Old Age Pensions. The feverish energy—*alles ging in galopp,* as he said—with which these measures were pressed is very remarkable, and still more remarkable is the Chancellor's personal share in their construction and in the task of carrying them in the teeth of bitter opposition in the Reichstag. In the autumn of 1880 he took over the Ministry of Commerce, adding it to the duties of Minister-President and Chancellor; he was then in his sixty-fifth year, and during all this period he carried alone the burden of foreign policy, in itself a tremendous task, and was also engaged in the complicated negotiations with the Vatican and the Centre which ended the *Kultur-kampf*. The expression that Bismarck was the government and the government was Bismarck conveys a very faint conception of the responsibility and labours that he shouldered. The Prime Minister of a modern Parliamentary State, such as Great Britain, carries no doubt an onerous burden, but he shares his responsibility with colleagues, while the party system relieves him of the duty of creating a majority that will loyally vote as required; because if the country refuses him the majority the burden of office is transferred across the table to a rival party leader. But Bismarck had to steer through the rocks, shallows, and eddies of the parliamentary seas, finding 'allies where he could get them,' and uncertain whether in a critical turn if the ministerial ship ' hung in stays ' the crew might not take to the boats. He had, moreover, as Chairman of the Federal Council to keep that essential organ united and compliant, and the Federal Council was not a Cabinet cemented by the ethos of collective responsibility and composed of members in broad agreement on the current questions of public policy. Mr. Gladstone or Lord Salisbury would not have relished working the Parliamentary System through a Cabinet of fifty-six members, only seventeen of which could be implicitly trusted to vote straight. It is not surprising therefore that Bismarck's performance from 1879 to 1888, in the autumn of a life, which had never spared itself from youth to old age, made an indelible impression on Germany. Compared with the ' Iron Chancellor ' the other public figures seemed indeed bloodless and fleeting shades. Every quality in the Chancellor's person was titanic—the physical frame, the head carved and moulded by a Berserker's hammer and chisel, the will, the temper, the appetites, the ambitions. The Empire that was Power was incarnated in that hypnotic personality.

In 1881, 1884, and 1886, the Trade Law (*Gewerbe-ordnung*) was substantially amended and extended; the structure and scope of Trade Guilds were reorganised with a view to strengthening artisans against the capitalist and the factory (and incidentally to minimise the power of

Trade Unions), and ' in diametrical opposition to the principle of *laissez-faire*, the abandonment of the weak to their own resources and to private help.' The measure providing for compulsory insurance against sickness was destroyed by criticism in 1881, was reintroduced in 1882, and carried against the Radicals and Socialists in 1883 ; it was subsequently extended in 1885 and in 1886. A bill for insurance against accidents was introduced in 1882 and became law in 1884 (July 6) ; it, too, was amended and extended in 1885, 1886, and 1887. The system was completed by the Old Age Insurance Law of June 1889.

Concurrently with these measures of vast scope Bismarck was engaged in an effort to recast the whole system of taxation, and to create an imperial revenue that would provide the funds for ' the socialism of the State.' But he met in this sphere with more defeats than successes.

The Stamp Tax of 1881 imposed a duty on Stock Exchange transactions, and the Usury Law of 1880 introduced legal rates of interest. But the proposal to tax all exemptions from military service was rejected in 1881, Moltke ostentatiously leaving the Reichstag before the division. The attempt to establish in 1882 a tobacco monopoly which was to provide the funds for Old Age Pensions broke down completely; and though an income tax was introduced for Prussia, the idea of imposing a separate Imperial Income Tax was dropped. The suggested monopoly in brandy was introduced in 1886 and decisively defeated, and the failure destroyed the idea of establishing a monopoly in sugar. The principles and aims of this programme were fully set out in the Royal Speech of November 17, 1881 :—

' We express our conviction that the cure of social ills must be sought, not exclusively in the repression of Social-Democratic excesses, but simultaneously in the positive advancement of the welfare of the working classes. . . . The finding of the proper ways and means is a difficult task, yet it is one of the highest of every Commonwealth which is based on the ethical foundations of a Christian national life.'

Bismarck's own views can be summarised by a few quotations from his speeches :—

' In my opinion we are behind all great European States in regard to the development of our system of Taxation, especially with respect to its reaction upon our economic conditions, and we have much ground to recover in this domain ' (February 22, 1878).

' In regard to exemption from taxation, I hold in general the principle that the man who has nothing but his two hands, that is untrained hands that have learned no industry, should be quite exempted from both state taxes and imperial contributions, and that the taxation should begin when a further capital exists ' (February 4, 1881).

' You know that I am an opponent of direct and a friend of indirect taxes . . . my ideal is not an Empire which must collect its matricular contributions at the door of the individual states, but an Empire which, having in its hands the principal source of good finance—indirect taxes—would be in a position to pay contributions to all the individual states ' (February 26, 1878).

' I regard it as one of the greatest superiorities of our life in Germany that a large part of our well-to-do classes live all the year round in the country, carrying on agriculture themselves . . . if you succeeded in destroying this race you would see the result in the palsying of our entire economic and political life ' (February 14, 1885).

' Give the working man the right to work as long as he is healthy, assure him care when he is sick, assure him maintenance when he is old. If you do that and do not fear the sacrifice, or cry out at State Socialism—if the State will show a little more Christian solicitude for the working man, then I believe that the gentlemen of the Social-Democratic programme will sound their bird calls in vain . . . yes, I acknowledge unconditionally a right to work, and I will stand up for it as long as I am in this place ' (May 9, 1884).

' I should like to see the State which for the most part consists of Christians—although you reject the name Christian State—penetrated to some extent by the principles of the religion it professes . . . I, the Minister of the State, am a Christian, and as such I am determined to act as I believe I am justified before God ' (April 2, 1881 and January 9, 1882).

' It is a tradition for the dynasty which I serve that it takes the side of the weak in the economic struggle. Frederick the Great said *Je serai le roi des gueux*, and in his own way he carried out this precept with strict justice . . . my present master is animated by the lofty ambition to secure to the weakest class of our fellow-citizens . . . confidence with which they can contemplate the future of the State to which they belong' (January 9, 1882).

'If you believe that you can frighten any one or call up spectres with the word "Socialism," you take a standpoint which I abandoned long ago, and the abandonment of which is absolutely necessary for our Imperial legislation' (March 1882).

'The popularity of a thing makes me rather suspicious about it than otherwise, and I am induced to ask myself, if it is also sensible' (June 12, 1882).

All these measures were not carried without bitter controversy, and the most strenuous pressure from the government. They were attacked from three different standpoints—individualistic Liberalism which feared the extension of State functions, and on principle opposed Protection as an economic system and for its ulterior political results; the political school that feared, and rightly, the immense accession of power to the centralised imperial executive, vested in irresponsible hands, and the Socialists who called the whole code 'bastard Socialism.' The latter were savagely attacked because of their opposition. But their answer was effective. Every effort that they made was futile to amend the legislation so as to deprive it of its character of being a material sop to the industrial working classes, and an instrument for diminishing the political power of labour by making it dependent on a State over which they could exercise no control. To Bebel and his party Bismarck's 'socialistic' policy was the minimum of blackmail that the ruling classes would pay in order to strengthen their own political power. Again and again they pressed (with some help from the Clerical Centre) for essential and complementary reforms —the regulation of wages and of the hours and conditions of labour, the amelioration of the status of the children, the lads, the girls, and the women in the factories and workshops of the New Germany, and for an extension of the powers of Trades Unions which would enable the worker to confront capital on equal terms. Without legislative regulation of these matters the State Socialism of the Chancellor was, they contended, simply a tax on labour aggravated by the effect of the Protectionist tariff. But they pleaded in vain. The principles of the Christian State which Bismarck set in the forefront of his programme did not apparently require that women and children should not be sweated, or that wages should be raised above the barest minimum of subsistence,[1] or that employers and the State should see that their employees should live under conditions which would ensure decency, health, and morality ; it did not even require that there should be one day of rest for the workers toiling in the factory. The worker was assumed to be a Christian and to belong to a Christian State, but he was not to be assured of the leisure to worship. The factory was to be his Heaven and his Hell.

The most damning criticism of the blots and defects— the most effective exposition of the purely political character—of Bismarck's policy was set out in the resolutions of the International Labour Conference of 1890, the meeting of which Bismarck did his best to prevent.

The plain truth is that Bismarck's programme was inspired by the same fear and distrust that underlay his theory of international relations; and much of his legislation was (apart from its money-producing effectiveness) a reinsurance scheme against the results of the manhood suffrage which made the electoral law of the Empire. In 1867, when he said that democracy would be more monarchical than middle-class Liberalism, he did not foresee the industrial revolution. He had in his mind an agricultural Germany, and above all an agricultural Prussia, where the peasant had been trained in a position of dependence on the landowner, with whose interests as a tiller of the soil his own in many respects coincided. But he never understood the industrial proletariat, the numbers of which increased by leaps and bounds after 1871 ; he disliked towns and towndwellers ; to the end he regarded industrialism as a gigantic excrescence to be exploited and emasculated of its strength, rather than assimilated, and his economics at bottom were saturated with the postulates of the eighteenth-century physiocrats ; while he forgot that the new

[1] 'One of the principal secrets of the expansion of the German export trade is the prevalence of wages, which, in some branches, are hardly two-thirds or half the British rates.'—Report already cited, p. 75.

and toiling Germany had no traditions, and no social mould ready-made and tempered by generations of development, into which it would steadily flow and be reshaped. On the contrary, it had its traditions and outlook on life to make in all the roar, dust, and fog of a vast economic revolution. Taking experience and facts alone as his guide Bismarck probed his way as best he could in the teeth of opponents who, like himself, thought more of ends than of means. There was no conservative Shaftesbury to strop a dulled moral conscience ; the bureaucracy at his disposal smothered him with figures and facts compiled in their offices ; he was in the hands of the political majority on which he relied, which resented the demands of labour as subversive of their own power, and his own system cut him off from utilising the help he might have got from those who really knew. A close study of his speeches reveals from time to time the note of despair— the complexity and ramifications of the problem were so great and so baffling—and his contempt for economic science led him into avoidable blunders and many political rebuffs. The repercussion and incidence of taxation, for example—subjects engaging some of the best economic minds in Europe—he more than once angrily brushed aside as the pastime of professors. The realist had neither time nor patience for such abstractions. If a tax would bring in money here and now, it had fulfilled its purpose, and the consequences could be dealt with later.

Volumes—a whole library indeed—have grown up round the economic problems with which Bismarck wrestled, and it is not possible to discuss issues which require a separate monograph for adequate treatment. It must suffice briefly to observe three or four outstanding features.

In two of his main objects Bismarck unquestionably succeeded—the provision of money, and the preservation of his political system. Whether the great expansion of German industry was largely due to the adoption of Protection need not be argued here, for it opens issues too large and controversial to be summarily decided ;[1] but,

[1] See the report, already cited, where much material is statistically examined and summed up.

unquestionably, the remarkable industrial expansion provided in the Chancellor's political lifetime an expanding
revenue from indirect taxation, which met the exigent
needs of Bismarck's policy. Secondly, the ten years of
social legislation deeply impressed Europe, and in this, as
in other developments of German policy, the great experiment was studied, praised, and copied. Germany
flattered itself that it was the pioneer as well as the model
of constructive statecraft, and Bismarck's legislation profoundly stimulated economic thought and political
practice far outside the limits of the German Empire.
Bismarck, ' the social reformer,' acquired a prestige devoid
of the dubious elements that discounted the fame of his
other political achievements. A later generation either
in or outside Germany, more accurately acquainted with
the motives, aims, and effects of the ' new era,' has not
been able to accept without serious qualifications the
eulogies so noticeable in the early nineties.

But in two notable respects the failure even in Bismarck's
lifetime was as conspicuous as the success. The spectre of
Social Democracy was not laid. Bebel, who had a good
right to know, told the Reichstag and the Chancellor that
the effort to put Social Democracy into a siding would
fail, and that the social legislation would be one of the
main causes of the failure. ' The bird call' became more,
not less, potent in its appeal just because the Christian
State did so little, when it could do so much ; and
he warned the Chancellor that if you could not kill the
Socialist party by the law of 1878 you would not kill it
by compelling the artisan, with some help from the
State, to insure against accidents, sickness, and old age
A compulsory and dilatory distribution of doles could
not extirpate a movement which had its roots deep in a
determination to secure political and social ends—politica
and social power—through the economic status of the
worker : and the more the State compelled the worker
to organise, the more certainly they would use the organi
sation for their own purposes. Bismarck recognised the
failure. But, unlike the *Kulturkampf*, he could not brea
off the action when victory was no longer within his grasp

He had committed the Empire to a course from which it was impossible to recede.

Nor did his fiscal experiments succeed in solving the problem of imperial finance. Within ten years of 1890 the problem of the matricular contributions and the deficits in the Imperial Budget threatened to be no less serious than in 1878-9. Bismarck could fairly say that had the Empire become the monopolist that he desired it to be in tobacco, brandy, sugar, and other articles of general consumption; had it nationalised all the railways and absorbed all the profits, even the great increase in imperial expenditure might have been met. But he never explained how in that case the Federated States were to balance their several budgets, or how a large increase in direct taxation, which he regarded as politically inexpedient and economically indefensible, was to be avoided. Armaments and State Socialism were the main causes of the steady increase in expenditure. Bismarck's system placed armaments outside the arena of discussion. The policy and principles were imposed on the nation—whose duty it then was obediently to pay the bill—and if the nation resisted, a general election with the main issue of 'The Empire and Army in danger and War in sight' invariably proved decisive.

These ten years from 1879 to 1889 made a decade of embittered home politics. The reactionary character of the Chancellor's system was revealed in many ways. Bismarck seriously suggested, for example, that biennial budgets and biennial meetings of the Reichstag would be a desirable reform; the prosecutions for Bismarck *Beleidigung* steadily increased, and when men like Bunsen and Mommsen were prosecuted (and happily acquitted) for indicting the government measures as 'immoral,' every one who cared for freedom of opinion and freedom of criticism had just cause for deep misgiving. Bismarck increasingly regarded opposition as a personal affair; to complaints of bribery and intimidation by officials at elections he invariably retorted by emphasising the character of the Prussian monarchy and the disloyalty of the Progressives to the Throne. 'I do not believe,' he said,

' in electro-plated royalism.' In 1886 he concluded one
of his speeches with unmistakable threats : ' We must aim
at becoming stronger ; we must show that we stand not
on feet of clay, but of iron. We must find a means of
becoming independent of the obstruction of the majority
of the Reichstag. I do not advocate such a step, but if
the Fatherland should be endangered I should not hesitate
to propose to the Emperor the necessary measures. The
Minister who will not risk his head to save the Fatherland,
even against the will of the majority, is a coward. I will
not allow the achievements of our army to perish by
internal discord, which I will find the means of counteracting.' (January 28, 1886, in the Prussian Landtag.)

Prussian Poland and Alsace-Lorraine were essentially
problems of home policy which illustrate the close connection between the internal system and the principles of
Bismarck's foreign policy. The failure of Prussia to
Germanise her Polish provinces inspired the Prussian
government to drastic action. Puttkamer, the Minister
of the Interior, in 1885 pointed out that, whereas the
German element had increased from one to five per cent.,
the Polish element had increased from eight to eleven per
cent. An Edict of May 5, 1885, expelled all Poles not
Prussian subjects, and no less than thirty-four thousand
were so expelled, bag and baggage, on the ground of State
necessity. Next year Bismarck brought in an Expropriation Bill. He told the Landtag that the incorporation
of the Polish provinces in 1815 was a strategical necessity,
but that the pledges then given were a blunder, which it
was against Prussia's interest in 1886 to fulfil. The bill
authorised the government to spend five million pounds
in acquiring Polish estates to be leased to German farmers,
bound to marry German wives ; it also transferred the
supervision of all popular education in the district to the
central executive. The necessity for this colonisation
was due, in addition, to the gradual submerging of the
Germanic element in the Near East, in Bohemia, Hungary
and elsewhere, and also—a very remarkable statement—
to the ' extraordinary tendency of the Germans to sympathise with everything that was not German.' Bismarck'

speech, breathing fire and fury, and the rapid acceptance
of the bill, were the most conclusive refutation of this
alleged German sympathy. ' You,' he said to the Poles,
' will never realise your ambitions except as the result of
a war, disastrous to Germany, when Prussia has been
smashed to pieces.'

To Bismarck the international aspect of the Polish
question was as dangerous as the existence within the
Prussian kingdom of an ' alien ' element that, despite all
persecution, resolutely refused to abandon either its language, its religion, or its culture. With 1863 in his mind
he told the Reichstag that it could not interfere in a
matter, reserved solely for the prerogative of the Prussian
King ; and, followed by all the Prussian members of the
Bundesrat, he pointedly walked out of the House when
an attempt was made to interpellate him. The reference
to Prussian sovereignty was intended for Vienna and
Petersburg quite as much as for the South German Liberals
or the Catholic centre. Poland and the Poles were a conclusive reason, even if there had not been others equally
exigent, why Berlin should have a control of the vassal
State of Austria, and maintain a close understanding with
Russia. But Bismarck's policy of voluntary, and then of
forcible, expropriation was a failure. It rested on three
false assumptions : first, that racialism and nationalism
can be extinguished by administrative action, aided by a
culture the superiority of which is not evident except to
those who administer it ; secondly, that the Poles would
not combine to defeat the policy ; and thirdly, that the
government could control completely the economic
situation. Neither Bismarck nor any one else could
obliterate the previous history of Poland. The Germanisation of Prussian Poland pursued by the government
virtually required that all Poles should become Protestants and German-speaking or remain celibate, and that
those who refused the Germanisation or the celibacy must
be evicted. So long as Polish men and women produced
more children than the Germans and brought them up to
be Poles in religion, speech, and ideas, there was no practical alternative between extermination and conciliation.

The futility of the law of 1886 was proved in 1906 when the government confessed that, while ninety thousand German colonists had been brought into the Polish provinces, the Poles had increased by two hundred thousand, and that the increase of economic prosperity produced by the State grants had only strengthened the economic capacity of the Poles to buy out the German faster than the State planted him in. Coercion, also, had made the whole Polish population far more ' disaffected ' than in 1885.

Bismarck's nationalism simply came to this : if the German Empire required for political, strategic, or economic reasons that certain areas should belong to Germany, no claim based on previous history, tradition, race, or religion could countervail the right. Necessity of State prescribed the end, that power enabled the State to realise. Condemnation of the iniquity and futility of Prussian policy in West Prussia and the province of Posen ought not, however, to blind the student of statecraft to the problem with which Bismarck was confronted, and the serious menace that the Slav race imposed on the German nation. For there was a measurable risk that in a large area the German race and language would become the distinguishing attributes of a dwindling minority.[1] The problem of government by a dominant minority raises one of the most formidable difficulties that modern statesmanship is called on to solve. It is immensely intensified when the minority deals with a majority whose civilisation is not qualitatively but only quantitatively inferior in consequence of previous historic injustice, an undeveloped economic environment, and the complications arising from the competition of other and more congenial civilisations across the frontiers. The true indictment of Bismarck's attempted solution of the Prussian problem of Poland is concentrated in the assumption that German civilisation

---

[1] In October 1914 it was authoritatively asserted on behalf of Germany that but for German 'militarism' German culture would have perished in Europe. Whether this means that all national civilisations depend on force for their existence, or that German 'culture' can only compete with other 'cultures' when it is enforced by the sword, does not call for decision here. Nor is it necessary to decide the validity of either or both meanings.

was superior, while it practically admitted that, unless it were imposed and maintained by force of the most drastic character, it could not hold its own. Every decade after 1886 clinched the conclusion that the Pole was successfully competing with the Teuton in all the qualities that makes a civilisation worth preserving. So far then from solving the problem, Bismarck's policy made it more formidable; worse still, it carried within itself a Nemesis the beginning, but not the end, of which he witnessed. It made all Poles, not merely Prussian Poles, the enemies of the German Empire. In his determination to localise the purely Prussian problem Bismarck internationalised the whole Polish question, since the principles on which he worked were no less disastrous to other races in a similar position both within and without the Empire. It was not only the Poles in whom the conviction deepened that the destruction of the Bismarckian Empire and its reconstruction on different principles might be essential in the interests of a true nationalism, of the European system, and of the whole world : and that without such a reconstruction progress in civilisation and an international system were impossible. When Bismarck deliberately pinned the maintenance of Germanism to the brute capacity of a German State to enforce it, he imperilled as well as degraded the claims of that civilisation whose champion he was. Nor did he ever seriously attempt conciliation of the Polish subjects of Prussia, based on an equality of rights and opportunity. There was a golden chance for such a policy in 1871. The Poles had fought bravely for Germany in 1866 and in 1870. Their reward was the *Kulturkampf*, a coercive bureaucracy, and the law of 1886, leading inevitably to the doubled coercion of 1906, a fresh crop of legislation, the flogging of school-children, and similar proofs of the proud claim that German civilisation aimed at ' freedom for all in thought and activity.' A policy of conciliation could not have been more unsuccessful than the policy of coercion ; conciliation, indeed, might have led to detaching to Prussia, ' the Liberator,' the whole of Poland. The Russian danger, which was a perpetual nightmare to Bismarck, Moltke, the National

Liberals, and the Radicals, might then have been thrust back behind the Dwina and the Dnieper, instead of which it was thrust forward from the Vistula to the Warta and the Netze. Bismarck's system, which identified the interest of Germany with the interest of the Russian autocracy, made all conciliation impossible, and for this the intensity of his own Prussian Nationalism, with its traditions and interpretation of life, was more responsible than his conception of the State as Power.

The limitations and dangers of that Nationalism were no less patent in Alsace-Lorraine than in Prussian Poland. It is true that in 1874 the military government of the Reichsland was theoretically ended and Alsace and Lorraine were represented by fifteen members in the Reichstag. These fifteen were simply an addition to the opposition ; and they might have stayed at home for all the practical influence that they exerted, while their united hostility to the government, a continuous protest against the annexation and the policy of internal coercion, provided a fresh argument for drastic repression. Edwin von Manteuffel's appointment as Statthalter in 1879 was a concession to the demand for autonomy, but Bismarck's jealousy of Manteuffel marred the use that might have been made of the Statthalter's great personal gifts. Hohenlohe, who was transferred from Paris in 1884 to succeed Manteuffel, had a doubly difficult task ; as a civilian he incurred the enmity of the governing chiefs of the soldier-caste, as governor he was continuously overruled by Bismarck. His Diary, carefully edited as it clearly is, shows that the Chancellor accepted the militarist view that the object of the annexations was not to make a contented Alsace-Lorraine, but to hold the Reichsland as a strategic glacis of the Empire. There can be little question that Bismarck had hoped in ten years or so to extort from France a renunciation of the idea of recovering the provinces lost in 1871, and the temptation to make such a renunciation had its part in the bewildering history of French internal politics and foreign policy from the fall of Thiers to the presidency of Carnot ; but he failed to secure it, and Alsace-Lorraine more than ever was employed to coerce

Germany by a great fear and provoke France by a perpetual humiliation. The German effort to assimilate the Reichsland broke on two unsurmountable obstacles—the refusal of France permanently to accept the position defined in the Treaty of Frankfurt; the claim of German Nationalism to hold by force what it could not hold by any other means. By 1890 Bismarck's system was steadily making the problem of Alsace-Lorraine of international importance. The Europe that had debarred itself in 1871 from intervening in the terms of peace, had begun to realise that the principles involved cut down to the root of the whole European system and raised the most fundamental problems of international relations.

At home after 1884 there was one compensation—the parliamentary situation became much easier for the Chancellor. The general election of that year resulted in a severe defeat for the new and reunited Radicals (*Deutsche Freisinnige*), and for the first time Bismarck had at his disposal a governmental *bloc* composed of Conservatives, the Centre, and the Conservative rump of National Liberals, which gave him a comfortable majority over all the other groups combined. This was even more marked in the Prussian Landtag, where the narrow franchise, ' the worst in the world,' Bismarck once said, left Progressives, Radicals, Poles, or Guelphs in an impotent minority. There was indeed but one shadow. The union of Crown and Minister-President, of Emperor and Chancellor, was the corner-stone of the Bismarckian system. In 1884 the Emperor was eighty-seven years old. Would his successor, whose accession could not be long delayed, accept the position developed between 1862 and 1884 ? In 1884 Germany speculated on the consequences of a trial of strength between the Crown and the Man. The trial indeed came very shortly, but neither in the form, nor with the results, anticipated by Germany and Bismarck.

§ 5. *Foreign Policy—The Triple Alliance—The Colonial Problem—France and Russia,* 1879-1888.

' For thirty years,' writes Naumann in his *Central Europe,* ' politics for us meant Bismarck.' He could have said, with equal truth, that for twenty years at least politics for the whole continent meant Bismarck. After 1878 Bismarck's personal position was unique. The Chancellor achieved the aim of the French king who desired that not a cannon-shot should be fired in Europe without the consent and knowledge of France and himself. The German hege-mony of the European State system rested on the power and prestige of Prussia, but it was a power and prestige interpreted by, and reflected in, the personality of a single man ; and if the revolving years strengthened the political ascendency consummated by the Treaty of Frankfurt, the Congress of Berlin, and the Dual Alliance—the main terms of which were known before the ink was dry on the signa-tures—they also emphasised the egoism and vanity of the ministerial autocrat. Bismarck demanded homage, and he expected incense, from all the statesmen and all the courts. Ambassadors at Berlin informed their govern-ments that they would do well always to consult Bismarck on every step, for if they acted without asking his advice, even in matters in which Germany could not be regarded as directly interested, they would soon discover that the jealous, suspicious, and vain Chancellor intended to make them pay for the neglect and the implied personal insult.

' His excessive sensitiveness,' wrote Lord Ampthill, ' is incomprehensible in so great a statesman.' He pointed out what a mistake ' Goschen had made ' in daring to go on a mission to the Near East without travelling via Berlin and seeking wisdom at Friedrichsruhe. Goschen rectified the error by returning via Berlin. ' Prince Bismarck,' Lord Ampthill wrote in 1882, ' has never got over or for-given Goschen's departure from the advice he was asked to give in the Greek question.' Gambetta therefore, in 1879, was right when he contemplated a secret visit to ' the monster.' The meeting, despite M. Lair's beliefs, did not take place, but an hour between Gambetta and

Bismarck might have made a world of difference to the French statesman. The greatness of great men is indeed a mysterious paradox. Bismarck's vanity had its paternal weaknesses. If 'a pleasant truth, a well-deserved compliment, publicly uttered by an English statesman had a magic effect,' still more magic was the effect of flattery or kindness to a son. In Herbert Bismarck the Chancellor was training up his successor, and the generous hospitality offered to the son when he came on special missions to London deeply touched the father's heart. It probably smoothed away the friction far more effectively than a dozen dispatches. Personal kindness to the limited few for whom he cared—and guns—these were the two arguments that Bismarck understood. And those who had not got the guns, or were afraid to use them, were well advised to go confidentially to the Chancellor, place their case in his hands, and ask for his disinterested offices and advice.

An element of grandeur sublimated this vanity. More and more the Chancellor absented himself from Berlin and conducted the foreign affairs of Europe from Friedrichsruhe or Varzin, and the men who combined business and homage in a visit to Bismarck enjoyed a patrician hospitality from the hands of a great patrician, who tried to forget on his own hearth or in the glades of the avenues he had planted, the methods so congenial in the Wilhelmstrasse. If, in addition, the visitor could prove that in his arteries ran the red blood of a fierce virility—that rich meat and drink, physical exuberance, and joy in the carnal framework of life and the passions of nature, appealed as much as the conclusion of a hard bargain—Bismarck was ready to make concessions that were not for the anæmic and the bookworms of the Chancery. The statesmen, such as Favre and Pouyer-Quertier, who could drain not their glass but their flagon, earned a personal respect as strong as the contempt meted out to his jackals such as Busch, or the spectacled pedant whose amusements were centred in a Kaffee-Klatsch and the gossip of women. Statecraft was an excrescence on the natural life of the healthy man, but as it was inevitable, let men bring into it not the weaknesses of the physically unfit but the qualities that made man the lord of the universe and of his own hearth.

Bismarck was never on the side of the angels—for in a dirty and sordid world he held that the angels by Divine wisdom prudently kept clear of human affairs—but he was never on the side of the apes. He was always ' on the side of the white man,' not ' the blonde beast,' of which so much has been written with so much profound igno- rance, but the white man who represented ' his idol, Authority,' the man of the master races whose very vices and brutality were the necessary correlatives of his virtues, and were a proof of his strength of brain, physical vitality, and appetite for order and discipline.

But beneath the elements of grandeur in Bismarck lay an inferno of personal feeling as passionate and intense as the manhood that he admired. His memory was relent- less. Lord Derby in 1884 and 1885 was the Lord Stanley whose share in the Luxemburg affair of 1867 was remem- bered and requited by Bismarck's determination to chastise him for thwarting his will. As Beust said, even the Chancellor's boarhounds turned their backs on the former Saxon minister and Austrian Chancellor. And from all the agents of his instructions and his subordinates in the Foreign Office Bismarck extorted a submissive obedience, as Arnim and others discovered, the sanction of which was dismissal and disgrace. Woe to the ambassador or the under-secretary who betrayed any independence. What men such as Holstein, whom many regarded as the ' Éminence grise ' of the Wilhelmstrasse, even in Bismarck's day, thought the world did not learn until after 1890, when official Berlin slowly realised that the terrifying master would no longer emerge from Friedrichsruhe to castigate and crush those who had dared in his absence to take their own line.

One chapter of this personal autocracy has never been, and never will be, fully written for this generation. Bismarck's devotion to his sovereign was limited to the King-Emperor. The dignity, self-respect, and patriotism of those concerned prevented the public, as distinct from a narrow circle of the initiated, from knowing the full truth of the Chancellor's conduct and relations to the Empress, the Crown Prince and Princess, their relatives and friends. But if that chapter is ever written, it will assuredly not weaken the certainty that in the man were elements of jealousy, vulgarity, meanness, pettiness, insincerity and unscrupulousness, ineradicable and detestable. And it is desirable to remember that the material for that chapter was piled up by Bismarck himself, who knew that it could not, and would not, be given to the world, in its repellent entirety, during his lifetime—perhaps never.

The Dual Alliance of 1879 had been intended to solve the critical dilemma thrust upon him between 1876 and 1879, and to provide a firm foundation for his system. But Bismarck doubtless felt that his object was identical with that expressed in 1872 when he pronounced that he had ' thrown a bridge across to Vienna, without breaking down that older one to Petersburg.' In 1879 ' the older bridge ' was hardly safe for traffic ; but Bismarck was determined to reconstruct it.[1] The Dual Alliance steeled this determination, while it provided an immovable point from which to work. After 1879 a new method is distinctly discernible, caused by the unexpected introduction of wholly new elements. The position and problems of Russia, to begin with, were fundamentally altered after 1878. The effort to effect by diplomacy and intrigue what the Treaty of San Stefano would have established by war and a treaty—the Balkan States controlled by Petersburg, and a Constantinople living under the fiat of the Tsar—the policy of Kutchuk-Kainardji (1774) and of Unkiar Skelessi (1833) gave a wholly new turn to the Near Eastern question. Such a policy, with Pan-Slavism behind it, cut right across the Austrian line of development and was wholly opposed to the ambitions of

[1] 'I have thus succeeded in carrying out the first stage in my political policy —that of placing a barrier between Austria and the Western Powers. . . . I do not despair of realising the second, that of the reconstruction of the Drei Kaiser Bund . . . an idea that I have followed all my life . . . they will never devise a political system offering greater guarantees for safeguarding all the Conservative elements in the modern world.'—Prince Bismarck to Prince Sabouroff, quoted in the (unpublished) memoirs by Professor J. Y. Simpson, *Nineteenth Century*, December 1917.

Germany, masked behind the Dual Alliance. It involved Russia in desperate and tortuous courses in which the weakness of her statesmanship was continuously revealed, witness the folly and blindness of her treatment of Roumania and Bulgaria, but it made a new and torturing problem for Bismarck. The antagonism of Great Britain and Russia was superimposed on the antagonism of Austria and Russia ; it had been recreated by the events of 1876-8, and henceforward was a standing menace to both countries. Russian expansion eastwards into the heart of Asia inflamed the old quarrel of the Crimean War and of 1875-8, and for Russia the expansion eastwards into Central Asia was inevitable, apart from its merits as a riposte to Great Britain, though it imposed a fresh drain on her resources, while it restated the old problem : Was Russia to concentrate on her Eastern Empire, or on establishing her position in Europe ? Pan-Slavism, voiced by Skobeleff, Katkoff, Ignatieff, and Pobodonostzev, could not decide whether it was better to proclaim the Holy War against the Teuton, and reach Constantinople via Berlin and Vienna, or ignore Teutonic ingratitude and establish the Slav in the capital of the Moguls at Delhi, and thereby destroy the British Empire. Skobeleff at one moment proclaimed the Eastern ideal, at another denounced the Germans and deplored the Russians ' as dupes of German policy, victims to German intrigues, and slaves to German strength, only to be delivered by the sword from the baneful influence of Germany.'

After 1878 Nihilism honeycombed Russia, and the assassination of Alexander II. on the banks of the Catherine Canal in 1881 terrified his successor, credited, as heirs to the throne often are, with Liberal sympathies, into terrorism. The necessity of an international union of dynasties and governments against the menace of revolution, sharpened by dismay at the unending surrender of Great Britain to democracy, and detestation of republics and republicanism, obsessed Alexander III. Nihilism, more than any other force, held France and Russia apart, poisoned the relations of Great Britain and Russia, and, in Bismarck's skilful hands, laid the basis of the compacts of

1884 and 1887. Alexander, swayed by Nationalism, religion, and ambition, was continually breaking away from the principle of a modern Holy Alliance of the Three Monarchies, and continually being lured back by the fear of revolution into the charmed circle of the magician at Berlin. Well-informed statesmen were convinced that in 1880 Russia was on the point of returning to the *entente* of 1872, when the assassination of Alexander II. and the confusion caused by a change on the throne and the internal peril to the autocracy, snapped for the time the 'new wire' between Berlin and Petersburg. The opposing schools of policy strove round the person of Alexander III., but it was not until death removed Gortschakov, Skobeleff, and Katkoff, and the Nihilist danger had been comparatively mastered, that Russia and the Tsar had both ears for Bismarck's arguments. Through all the evidence available runs a persistent principle—the desirability of uniting the monarchies on a common basis of resistance to democracy and revolution—the old principles of the historic Holy Alliance in a modern form. Apart from the political considerations underlying a German hegemony of Central Europe, this dynastic unity was a bulwark of the existing social order, and no one felt more strongly than Bismarck that his system at bottom in Germany and without rested on the maintenance of a defined social structure correlated to, and a guarantee of, a distribution of political authority and defined political principles. He could and did cordially agree with Alexander III. that the political evolution of France and the ideas underlying the Republic, together with the continuous lapse of Great Britain from aristocratic grace to democracy, constituted a real peril and set up a perpetual antithesis between the Liberal west and the Conservative and Monarchical centre and east. The danger of infection from the west was serious. For all the facts went to prove that the west might inoculate and sap the centre and east, but there was small prospect of the centre and the east curing democratic Great Britain and France of their deplorable heresies. Dual or Triple Alliances were of no avail unless they aimed at ends deeper and more substantial than a nicely and perpetually readjusted political equilibrium. A coalition of ideas and principles could be more fatal to German supremacy than a coalition of fleets or armies. The return, therefore, to a reactionary Conservatism, discussed in the previous section, was partly the reflex, partly the inspiration, of Bismarck's foreign policy.

The disturbing elements in the situation were not confined to Russia. Europe in 1880 was on the threshold of an era with a very different outlook and ambition. Five other characteristics can be broadly disentangled—the Eastern Question, the problem of the Mediterranean, the renaissance of France, the revived activity and policy of Great Britain, and the colonial movement. Their combination provided the problem for Bismarck, and his exploitation of them makes the history of his foreign policy from 1879 to his fall.

After 1878 the Powers were much concerned with the execution of the terms of the Treaty of Berlin. But the military occupation of Bosnia and Herzegovina, the question of Dulcigno—'Dulcigno far niente,' as was wittily said—and similar items of the Berlin programme, very soon faded into much larger issues—the Roumanian, Serbian, Bulgarian, and Greek questions; Egypt, Tunis, Syria and Tripoli. Was the liquidation of the Ottoman Empire to continue? Who were the lawful creditors of the estate, if from any quarter a petition in bankruptcy was seriously pressed? What was to be the dividend, and to whom and in what shares was it to be assigned? The Congress of Berlin had proclaimed the integrity of a ' consolidated ' and reduced Ottoman Empire, which like the immortal ' Peau de Chagrin ' was always being pegged out, and was always shrinking in defiance of every effort to prevent it. Bismarck, therefore, had to decide what was the interest of Germany in the Near East, and he found the decision very difficult.

If we may judge from events, everything strengthened his conclusion in 1879 that safety lay in a firm control of Austria-Hungary.[1] He could pivot on the Dual Alliance

[1] 'Germany in view of her own security could not possibly allow Austria to have any other alliance than with herself.'—(From the Sabouroff Memoirs.)

more securely than on any other nodal, strategic, and diplomatic point. The remarkable analysis at the end of his Memoirs, with all its obvious omissions and veiled allusions, shows how continuously and with what microscopic diligence he watched and weighed every symptom in Austrian policy. Austria was essential to Germany, for if Austria collapsed the Near Eastern Question threatened a catastrophe. The heart of the problem lay therefore in this issue : if it was easier to control Austria than to control Russia—and to secure Russia if Austria had been first secured—to what extent could Germany ' back the Austrian bill ' ? That Berlin must back the bill drawn at Vienna broadly was clear. But the analysis in the Memoirs and the crisis of 1890 reveal that Bismarck fully recognised very precise limits to the German credit placed behind the Austrian draft, and showed that he was not prepared to support ' an unreasonable Austria ' at the price of a complete rupture with Russia. He decided, in effect, that Germany and Austria might at some future date have to part company, under the pressure of events : and the decision brought him into sharp antagonism with the new school of policy which made an Austro-German alliance, *coûte que coûte*, the basis of German policy in the Near East. (See Holstein's criticisms in Hohenlohe, ii. 451.)

The main argument of that school was profoundly influenced by the growing ambition to substitute, also *coûte que coûte*, a German ascendency at Constantinople (with all its illimitable possibilities) for a Russian, a British, or French ascendency ; or, in other words, the integrity and the revival of the shrinking Ottoman Empire could and ought to be made a primary German interest. The Mayor of the Sultan and the Sublime Porte was to be the German Emperor, in close alliance with Austria. Bismarck between 1879 and 1890 was not prepared to go that length. He recognised that it involved, for all its advantages, an irreconcilable breach with Russia, and a serious antagonism to Great Britain. To the end, while recognising a deepening German interest in Constantinople and Turkey in Europe, he had his eyes on the West and France. The ' Austrian school ' at Berlin was really interpreting Centralism in a way that, in Bismarck's view, might imperil not merely Germany's interest in the East but the fundamental basis of German supremacy in Europe. For Bismarck an alliance of Russia and France, and the closing of the breach between Great Britain and Russia, spelled the ruin of a true system of European policy. The younger generation, in short, was distinguishing between Bismarckian Centralism and a *Weltpolitik*. They aspired to make Germany a *Weltmacht*—a World-Empire—and not merely a Continental Power, and they saw the main road winding from Hamburg through Berlin across the Balkans, through a Constantinople controlled by Germany to Mesopotamia and the Persian Gulf, with an entry to the seas not so closely controlled as the routes down the Channel or north of the Shetlands; they also saw it reaching across the Atlantic to the Pacific, expressed in the formula ' ships, colonies, and commerce.' And for this young generation the heart of the position lay in the closest offensive alliance with Austria. It made Great Britain, not France or Russia, the great rival of Germany. Bismarck's virtual reply to such an argument was a paraphrase of Beaconsfield's judgment on Herat and Candahar. ' The Key of East and West, of Centralism and Empire, was not in Belgrade or Constantinople or Zanzibar—it was in Metz, Berlin, and Thorn.'

In a more concrete form, the Near Eastern Question from 1879 to 1890 was summed up in the antagonism of Austria and Russia in the Balkans, and in the rivalry between Great Britain and France in Egypt. These two problems brought the Mediterranean into the main diplomatic theatre, and kept it there.

By 1878 the isolation of France was proving exceedingly difficult. The crisis of 1875 had shown that the European Powers would not tolerate a further reduction of France or French power; the International Exhibition of 187? picturesquely mirrored the remarkable extent of France' recovery from the collapse in 1870. Paris, as in 1867 was still a great, if not the great, *foyer de civilisation* the attraction of which was inextinguishable. The new France, working so hard to make good the blunders of th

Second Empire, would soon be, if she was not already, an ally worth having. But the Germany that had failed to crush her or to isolate her completely, and that must fail to reconcile her because of Alsace and Lorraine, might divert her gathering strength into directions that would involve her in a collision with all the possible allies of the new France. There were three such possible allies— Great Britain, Russia, and Italy. The colonial movement combined with the situation in the Mediterranean to give Bismarck a fine chance of checkmating the *rapprochement* so necessary to France and his diplomacy was equal to it.

After 1879 Colonial questions moved sharply and suddenly into the forefront of European controversy and ambition. Africa and the Pacific kept the chancelleries busy. For Africa was the one great area, of vast extent, and unlimited possibilities, a continent not yet properly explored, and not yet finally allotted to, or occupied by, any great European Power. With 1880 ' the scramble for Africa ' seriously began, and it behove the Powers that had started late in the foundation of colonies to be quick, or the one fine field left in a limited world would be overrun and mastered by the Powers which had started early, and were already settled at various points on the rim of the Continent. Everything combined to make the ' African appeal ' urgent and critical—the romance of exploration, the prose of business and trade, missions and religion, coaling stations, hinterlands and doctrines of international law, struggling to establish principles which distinguished spheres of influence, protectorates, treaty rights, and the nature of actual or virtual possession ; and with these mingled the claims of humanity and the slave-trade, the rights of races and civilisation, ' the white man's burden,' and the territorial ambitions that underlay the conception of the State as the incarnation of Power, or the State as the incarnation of Right and Law. Darkest and unknown Africa indeed summed up everything for Europe, from the selfless heroism of a Livingstone, the stubborn pertinacity of a Stanley, and the philanthropy of a Lavigerie to the imperialism of a Rhodes or the syndicates of gold and diamond companies, the provision of raw materials for the workshops of Europe, or the cruder claim to sell bad guns and the poison of potato-spirit in return for rubber extracted by the lash. And in Africa, with its harbours and mighty rivers and its stepping-stones, east or west, might not prescient statecraft call a new world into existence that would not merely redress, but completely upset, the balance of the old ? Africa was the whole which developed the rivalries of other and more purely local areas—for the Mediterranean was a localised form both of the larger African and the Near Eastern problems.

The diversion, as distinct from the isolation, of France, began in 1878. Whether Bismarck first, in the green-rooms of the Berlin Congress, where so many tempting whispers were uttered, suggested the idea of France occupying Tunis, as a compensation for losses elsewhere, or whether the suggestion fell from Beaconsfield and Salisbury, may be a nice question in the origin of things, the evidence for which is still incomplete ; but it is tolerably certain that France understood after 1878 that, if she did go to Tunis, Germany and Great Britain would not combine to make the occupation a *casus belli*, or an occasion for a humiliating rebuff. In 1881 France accordingly went to Tunis—with the results that Bismarck at any rate had foreseen and intended. Great Britain was already hard pressed by difficulties in Egypt ; her relations with France were becoming strained, and the new Foreign Secretary at London regretted the virtual pledge of his predecessor.

That France should quarrel with Great Britain was just what Bismarck desired, and the causes of quarrel could be extended by judicious diplomacy inflaming further French colonial ambitions in Africa, in Siam, Cochin-China, and the Pacific. The more that France spent in men or money on colonial expansion, the less she would have for her eastern frontier in Europe ; the more she stared across the seas the less she would be ' hypnotised by the gap in the Vosges ' ; she would not find European allies by expeditions to the Nile, the Mekong, or the Niger, but European rivals, whose ambitions would be reflected and refracted at London, Paris, Rome, Petersburg, Brussels, and the Hague : colonial policy and colonial failures have, moreover, always been since 1660 a fine dissolvent of ministries in most European States. French and British ministries would come to grief at home because French or British expeditions met with reverses on the Nile or the Niger : France must therefore be encouraged to suffer a perpetual *angina pectoris*, in which colonialism would be an irritant, very shattering to the Republic.

No less beneficial to Berlin and Central Europe, Tunis and French Mediterranean ambitions brought France at once into sharp collision with the sister Latin race in Italy. The kingdom of Italy desired colonies and a sure grip on the Mediterranean. The French occupation of Tunis was a bitter blow. How was France to be prevented from adding Tripoli to Tunis ? And if she had a *condominium* in Egypt, what was there left in the Mediterranean for Italy ? An isolated Italy studied the map and the diplomatic constellations. Her position was becoming desperate. She could not stand alone. But with whom could she act ? A confidential explanation from Berlin of the terms and meaning of the Dual Alliance of 1879, made one certainty absolutely clear. 'Unredeemed Italy' (*Italia irredenta*)—Trieste and Istria, the Alpine frontier of the Napoleonic kingdom of Italy of 1810, the Balkan littoral of the Adriatic were now postponed to the German Kalends. If Italy could not get these from Austria single-handed, she assuredly could not get them by a war in which Germany stood behind Austria. The Dual Alliance sponged from the screen of the future the Italian dream of rounding off the unification of 1859 and 1866 by the incorporation of unredeemed Italy or securing the Dalmatian coast of the Adriatic. And the exposed shores of the peninsula were vulnerable to sea-power and to French sea-power, located at Toulon, Corsica, Tunis, Bizerta—perhaps Egypt. Given the conditions of 1882, the accession of Italy to the Dual Alliance was—if the invitation were held out from Berlin—a foregone conclusion.

On May 20, 1882, Italy's accession turned the Dual into the Triple Alliance. The text of the treaty has never been officially published ; but it is certain that in 1882 Italy joined for five years, and that the treaty was renewed in 1887 and at subsequent intervals, with which Bismarck was not concerned. It is practically certain that the three signatory Powers gave a reciprocal guarantee for the integrity of their respective territories, undertook to assist each other in the case of attack by any European Power (*i.e.* France), and (probably by secret conventions) agreed to allot with precision the nature and amount of their respective military contribution to a joint effort. It is practically certain that no guarantee was given to Italy either by Germany or Austria of support in a colonial policy in the Mediterranean or elsewhere, and that Italy was in no way bound to support Balkan or other adventures of Germany or Austria. The maintenance of the existing balance of power in the Mediterranean, or the nature of any future rearrangement of the Mediterranean situation, probably did not fall within the scope of the engagements undertaken in 1882.

The wisdom or the inexpediency of Italy's action in 1882 do not call for judgment here ; but two other considerations, besides those mentioned, unquestionably weighed with Depretis and his successors. Alliance with Berlin was a powerful support to the Quirinal against the Vatican, and in 1882 the relations of Quirinal and Vatican were severely strained : if the Dual Alliance made ' unredeemed Italy ' an affair beyond redemption, the Triple Alliance made the restoration of the temporal power of the Papacy and the removal of the House of Savoy from Rome practically impossible. The annoyance and anger of Ultramontanism in Italy, Austria and France, and also in Germany, are the best-proof of this consequence of the Triple Alliance. Secondly, it did not prevent Italy from improving an historic friendship with Great Britain, and obtaining, if circumstances required, the assistance or protection of the British fleet, with one of its bases at Malta. The more strained Anglo-French relations became, the greater became the likelihood of such assistance ; the better Anglo-German relations became, the better would become the relations of Great Britain and

Italy. Italy was, and was desired at Berlin to be, a middle term between Great Britain and the new Triple Alliance.

To Bismarck the conclusion of the Treaty of May 20, 1882, was the culmination of his system. Henceforward German hegemony in Central Europe moved securely on the pivotal point of the Triple Alliance, which gradually and naturally grew into the one grand combination in the European State system, with which all other possible combinations or *ententes* had to reckon. And for Bismarck the accession of Italy had every advantage and no disadvantages. Italy from 1878 to 1882 was in a restless and excited state.[1] She might indeed precipitate a crisis which would upset the carefully poised equilibrium of Europe. Crises that arise from the action of strong States are often not as dangerous as the crises provoked by the recklessness of weak States. Italian policy in 1882 came under the control of the Wilhelmstrasse, and control was stealthily and relentlessly followed by the moral and economic penetration of the German bankers, cartels, syndicates, and commercial travellers. After 1878 the Ottoman Empire was similarly ' penetrated.' How deeply the penetration had pierced in both cases—how enmeshed had become the finance and the springs of trade by German wheels and cogs and ' controls '—Italy and the world learned in 1914. ' Trade followed the alliances, and the alliances followed trade.'

In 1882 the *Kulturkampf* was by no means healed. The agreement of ' May 20, 1882 ' was a potent schedule to ' the May Laws ' of 1873 and 1875. Prussia now had a rod, steeped in Italian brine, which it could use, if required. Crispi, who figures so prominently in the later phases of the story, had known and fought under great and hypnotic men—Garibaldi and Cavour. At Friedrichsruhe he met another hypnotic personality and succumbed. Bismarck and Crispi, exchanging their memories over cigars and wine at Friedrichsruhe, the old revolutionary of the red-

[1] ' This whole attitude shows that Italy must not be numbered to-day among the peace-loving and conservative Powers, who must reckon with the fact. . . . Every encouragement to Italian policy to join the bellicose and predatory Powers in Europe is contrary to *German* interests.'—Bismarck to Prince Reuss at Vienna, Jan. 28, 1880.—Busch, *Bismarck*, iii. p. 221,

shirts and 'The Thousand' and the veteran Junker who had denounced the journey to Canossa, overthrown clerical France and Apostolic Austria, were not a pleasant thought, we may be sure, in the Apostolic chancery of the Vatican.

But Bismarck, in concluding the Triple Alliance, was not thinking so much of the Vatican or the British fleet, as of Central Europe and France. The Triple Alliance completed Central Europe ; it closed the Alpine passes ; it barred the great gate to Vienna through which Napoleon had marched in 1796 ; it opened the Mediterranean to Germany ; it rent away from France the ally of the sister Latin race and made it henceforward necessary for her to keep two of her best corps to guard against invasion through the Maritime Alps. Best of all, it shivered the serious menace of 1869 and 1871. France, Austria and Italy, bound in a common war of revenge, had been a real danger. Austria had been secured as an ally in 1879 ; Italy was secured in 1882. It would take genius on the one side or bungling on the other to undo the Triple Alliance. Where were now the possible allies of France ? Great Britain ? Russia ?

In 1882, with the bombardment of Alexandria, the rebellion of Arabi, the fall of Gambetta (January 26), and the Anglo-Egyptian Campaign, war was more likely than an alliance between France and Great Britain. The Triple Alliance, in fact, largely undid the benefits to France of the benevolent hint to take Tunis and to take it at once. In the future Italy's claims in the Mediterranean might be much more serious, if Berlin found it convenient to give them ' moral ' support. Bismarck's ' moral ' support was unlike that of most European Powers. It was only given because he had decided that, if need be, behind it lay ' the immoral ' support of German force.

And there was another supreme advantage in Bismarck's eyes. If Austria kept Italy in check, Italy could be used to keep Austria in vassalage. There was little fear that Italy, the weakest of the three allies, would break loose, take the bit in her teeth, and defy Berlin and Vienna, while France was hostile, and Great Britain vaguely friendly. But there was always a real danger that the men in the Ball-Platz might lose their heads. Megalomania and folly were hereditary diseases in the statesmanship of Imperial Vienna. Modern history was a dreary record of Austrian blunders—from Charles vi. to Francis Joseph ; we are almost tempted to add from Charles vi. to Aerenthal, Hötzendorf and Tisza. Italy provided the Wilhelmstrasse with a very useful curb for keeping the Ball-Platz 'in hand.' In that unwritten chapter of the relations of Berlin and Vienna after 1879 the historical student of Bismarck's statecraft, provoked by the tempting glimpses revealed here and there, sighs indeed for a few weeks uninterrupted work in the archives of Vienna and the Wilhelmstrasse with an unrestricted general warrant, entitling him to examine all confidential documents. Such a search would not merely satisfy a hungry curiosity ; it would be invaluable in the scientific appreciation of Bismarck's statecraft. The use of Italy's aspirations in pruning the rank growth of Austrian appetites is an obscure chapter in Bismarck's system—but would be an illuminating one. It might, indeed probably would, furnish an instructive contrast between Bismarck and the post-Bismarckians.

Italy in 1882 was like Italy in 1866. She had concluded a treaty which imposed obligations, but conferred practically no rights. Bismarck had, to a certainty, refused in any way to endorse in advance the 'Italian draft' on the future. How far he had cautiously endorsed a very limited Austrian 'draft' is, as has been pointed out, very uncertain ; but Italian claims and aspirations in Albania or elsewhere, that so obviously conflicted with an Austrian programme, could be, and were, used after 1882 to keep Austria 'in order.' How far Bismarck's successors departed from the Bismarckian system—how far they gradually interpreted the articles of association in the very limited liability company that constituted Bismarck's Triple Alliance, as constituting a company of unlimited liability, how far they gradually came to regard it as practically a Dual Alliance in which Italy made a negligible third, who would not dare to break away, and at the

worst would observe a sulking and peevish neutrality—
it is neither necessary, nor possible, to decide here. But
to Bismarck, the Continentalist in feeling, thought, and
fibre, the Triple Alliance was of supreme importance, for
it secured the Continental position that made the marrow
and bone of Bismarckian Central Europe ; and if it was
never easy from 1882 to 1890 to prevent his two allies
from snarling at, or quarrelling with each other, such
management called for all the arts and skill which Bismarck
rejoiced to prove that he had. The position of arbiter
was precisely what he desired, and in the exercise of the
office he was consummate. The Triple Alliance, in short,
was an open re-insurance against the liabilities, deliberately incurred in 1879. But if we may judge from the
copious criticisms poured out in the *Hamburger Nachrichten* after 1890, Bismarck was convinced that very
little of his mantle and no double portion of his spirit
had fallen on his successors. It is no less certain that
had Count Herbert Bismarck succeeded in due course, as
his father intended, to the vacant desk in the Wilhelmstrasse that Hohenlohe and Bülow could have said with
unanswerable truth that the mantle and the double
portion of the Chancellor's spirit had not fallen on the son.

The Triple Alliance was, like all Bismarck's strokes,
aimed at France. It was the policy of isolation and diversion in one. There is substantial reason for believing
that in 1882 a serious attempt was made to include Spain
in the network of alliances. But the attempt, if it was
made—which would have completed the isolation of
France—did not come to a treaty. Spain was left to
' moral penetration ' by Germany—and it was effective.
Be that as it may, German emphasis was now laid on the
diversion of France. After 1882 the Republic was quietly
or openly encouraged from Berlin to pursue colonial
aims. In 1881 Bismarck compared Gambetta to a
drummer in the sick-room of Europe. But Gambetta's
fall [1] and death, which soon followed, ended the Gambetta
policy of cultivating the good-will of Great Britain, uniting

---

[1] 'Gambetta,' says M. Hanotaux, 'had to learn that one cannot in France
defend French interest with impunity.'—*La France Contemporaine*, 4.629.

the Latin races, and making a democratic Republic a power for democracy in Europe, while keeping the lamp of revenge at home polished and burning with a subdued and steady light that at the right moment could flame into a great national beacon. ' Ne parlez jamais de la guerre,' Gambetta had said, ' mais pensez y toujours.' Gambetta's radical republicanism quenched the ardour of Russian autocracy for a Franco-Russian *entente*.

After 1882 Ferry's policy in Egypt and the Far East steadily estranged France from Great Britain. The Nile and Tonkin, Madagascar and Siam, caused the French to forget their hostility to Germany in their hostility to Great Britain. And Bismarck took care to hold open the fissure between Great Britain and France. Encouragement to England in Egypt was balanced by encouragement to France in the Far East and the Pacific. The Foreign Office in Berlin and the German Embassy in Paris were prolific in their hints of ' the great man's ' sincerity in wishing France well, while his magisterial experience was readily placed at French disposal. The French consulted the oracle freely. The Ferry Ministry in 1884 could say publicly that not for two decades had the relations of France and Germany been so friendly. Such friendship with good reasons disquieted the Cabinet at London.

Bismarck certainly hoped that a few years of this conciliation by diversion would wring from a French government a stammering renunciation of *revanche*. A great and magnanimous speech in the Reichstag from the Chancellor could then have proclaimed that a generous and brave nation had wisely closed the account and henceforward with Germany's unqualified goodwill and assistance would march in a common work of civilisation—in which Great Britain must be compelled to yield to the legitimate rights of the new *entente*. But, instead of the stammering renunciation came Ferry's fall (April 2, 1885) : a colonial failure sharply awakened France to the truth that colonies might be colonies, but Alsace and Lorraine remained the monument of German victory and French defeat. French ministries henceforward grew like grass in the green spring and fell like leaves in chill October; and in the place of the great and unspoken speech that Bismarck desired to make, we have the Bismarckian orations of 1887 and 1888, in which France was held up to Germany as the hereditary, irreconcilable, and malignant foe in whose vile heart justice and conciliation only whetted the impotent lust of revenge. Worse still, the colonial movement, Egypt and the diversion of Russia to the Middle East brought on a severe Anglo-Russian crisis and involved Germany in sharp and dangerous friction with Great Britain. The year 1884 was a momentous one in French history. It was a far more momentous one in the history of Great Britain, of Germany and of Bismarck.

The relations of Great Britain and Germany after 1871 and Bismarck's policy are susceptible of various and contradictory interpretations. Bismarck's dislike of Gladstone and Gladstonianism is beyond question, for Gladstone's principles of foreign policy and theory of international relations, no less than his system of home politics, represented everything that Bismarck regarded as dangerous, detestable or futile,[1] and Gladstone's noted radical distrust of Bismarckianism, which was very apparent from 1880 to 1885, and was largely, if not mainly, responsible for the refusal of Great Britain to enter the German net, was no less strong. Bismarck seems to have held the view, adopted by many continental statesmen, that Great Britain as essentially a naval, maritime, and colonial Power was not, and ought not to be, concerned with the Continent of Europe. If, therefore, Great Britain actively intervened in 'purely continental affairs,' she was taking upon herself matters not properly *sui juris*, as well as introducing an unwelcome and incalculable element into a situation, already sufficiently complicated. Her very disinterestedness could be disconcerting: because it made it difficult to conclude material bargains by material bribes. British Liberalism, in particular,

---

[1] 'It is very apparent in the Sabouroff memoirs,' writes Professor Simpson, who has seen these unpublished papers, 'how uneasy Bismarck was at the prospects of a Liberal England.'—*Nineteenth Century*, December 1917.

introduced also into international relations ' cant ' phrases and formulæ—humanity, the Concert of Europe, the unity of European moral interests, arbitration, moral responsibility, Blue Books, amenability to public opinion, and ' nations rightly struggling to be free '—and had always done so from Canning onwards. Great Britain's intervention in 1875 had been more than disconcerting— it had led to a serious rebuff : and even more serious had been the sharp action of the Beaconsfield ministry in the crisis of 1877-8. A war between Great Britain and Russia over Constantinople and the Balkans would create an in-soluble dilemma for Austria, and therefore for Germany. The steady insistence of Mr. Gladstone's ministry in 1880 on fulfilling the pledges and terms of the Treaty of Berlin was very annoying. A Concert of Europe, manipulated by the Wilhelmstrasse, was one thing—a Concert of Europe led by Great Britain was another, and did not make for German hegemony and for peace as Bismarck under-stood it.

But for all his gibes or snarling innuendoes Bismarck did not underrate British strength. The British fleet, unlike the British army, could not be dealt with by ' calling in the police.' And Great Britain in some mysterious way had an uncanny gift for provoking the jealousy yet attracting the support of European Powers. Bismarck, therefore, after 1871, aimed mainly at encouraging British goodwill to Austria and Italy, at keeping France and Great Britain apart and Russia and Great Britain in strained tension, in which German good offices could be effectively employed to maintain the tension, yet prevent a complete rupture. Down to 1884 Germany and Great Britain could maintain in theory and phrase the friendliest of relations, for no direct or serious cause of quarrel between the two Powers existed. The two Powers might indirectly have divergent interests in many European questions in which these European States were largely concerned, but a direct antagonism in which Great Britain and Germany were the chief actors had not so far arisen.

The Egyptian question, with all the embarrassments arising out of the tangle or created by ministerial policy in

Great Britain, was just what Bismarck could have wished. It made Great Britain more dependent on German good-will, and, properly handled with the requisite air of im-partiality, could separate France and Great Britain and prevent an Anglo-French alliance. The evidence that Bismarck would have welcomed a loose Anglo-German alliance or *entente* between 1880 and 1890 is suggestive, but neither precise nor conclusive. Such an ' alliance ' would have been a triumphant codicil to the Triple Alliance, would have been warmly welcomed in Italy, and need not have damaged a separate understanding between Germany and Russia. The interests of Great Britain and Russia in many respects were not more divergent than those of Austria and Italy ; and it would have been a powerful aid in emphasising German arguments at Petersburg. But if Bismarck went so far as to make direct or indirect overtures, they broke down on Mr. Gladstone's radical distrust, and no less on the direct conflict of interest in colonial policy that came to a head in 1884. In that year Germany was caught up in the colonial movement.

It was inevitable after 1871 that Germany should begin to take an interest in colonial expansion, if for no other reason than that the most powerful of the Continental States had no colonies, and that colonial possessions were a proof and a guarantee of strength. German Nationalism, after 1815, as has been emphasised earlier in these pages, had found its deepest conviction and most stimulating nourishment in the consciousness of German impotence relatively to other great national States. The feeling that a united Germany could and ought to stand in the world as a Power, able to stand and speak for Germans as a whole in the gate of its rivals, and on terms of equality face France, Austria, Russia, and Great Britain, was overwhelm-ing and reasonable. Germany had now accomplished her unification, and the power of the German Empire after 1871 was an indisputable fact which satisfied to the full the passionate craving of the once impotent Germany of the Federal Diet. After 1871 the German nation, like its Emperor had ' drunk of the chalice of victory and would not break it.' It now desired to be an Empire like other great Empires—and the Empires with a future had colonies because the future lay with colonies. Leroy Beaulieu's remark, that colonies may not be signs of strength to-day, but that they hold the strength of the future, sums up the inarticulate German ambition. Just as a man who has made himself a millionaire by his own efforts desires motor cars, a fine picture gallery, or historic castles in the country, not for their intrinsic value, but because they prove that he is as rich and as powerful as other millionaires, so the German nation also desired colonies as the appurtenances and apparatus of Empire—to give them the external position and framework in the world enjoyed by other imperial nations.

After 1871 a decade was spent in completing unification into which the best energies of the German nation were thrown with enthusiasm. By 1880 the increase in population, wealth, commerce, and maritime trade, no less than the stability and strength of the administrative and military fabric was remarkable. The industrialisation of Germany proceeded by leaps and bounds. A still greater future awaited a further expansion. It was inevitable that the German trader should seek outlets for capital and markets outside Europe. He found them and developed them with the same energy and thoroughness that marked the work done by Germans at home in science, the army, civil administration and trade. But there was one humiliating disadvantage. The German emigrant was lost to Germany because there was no Germany outside Europe. The German trader had to explore and develop his trade either under the protection of a foreign flag or at his own risk. In Europe he could say ' *civis Germanus sum* '—a claim that no European State was likely to underrate—but in the Pacific or on the coast of East or West Africa the claim lost its force. The German found the white ensign of Great Britain everywhere ; the tricolour of a France which he had defeated and despised was being planted steadily outside France ; but the German flag did not fly, even where trade was in German hands or the unknown spaces of the earth had been explored by German effort.

Germany had obliterated, since 1815, the 'injuries of two centuries' in Europe. Unless she now girt up her puissant loins the world would be closed and time would have inflicted fresh and irremovable injuries.

The conversion to Protection at home clinched conclusively the sentimental and the political argument. That conversion, as has been pointed out, was a renaissance of seventeenth-century mercantilism interpreted in the terms of the later nineteenth century. The Bismarckian doctrine of power, developed from the renaissance theory of Reason of State, joined hands with the mercantilist doctrine of power, founded on a specific economic analysis of national power, of which F. List in his masterpiece *The National System of Political Economy*, a generation earlier, had given a penetrating and reasoned exposition. Cobdenism and Manchesterism, the disciples of List in Germany argued, had failed. The belief of the Cobdenites and the builders of the Zollverein that the future of the great economic and industrial States lay with Free Trade had proved a delusion. The world had slowly turned not to Free Trade but to Protection, to tariffs and tariff treaties, and Germany had now turned with it. The economic future lay with a new and scientific Protection, which was the basis of economic and political Power. The essential and logical corollary to the reservation of the home-market, and the home industries to the natives of the State, was the opening of the maritime markets to the products of modern industry on the grand scale. Germany as a workshop of the world—protected by a scientific tariff—required expanding markets and the reservation of the requisite raw materials which could not be provided in Europe. Unless these were secured beyond dispute German trade would either be mutilated in its upward expansion or be left dependent on the precarious goodwill and the certain jealousy of her European rivals. Her most serious economic competitors were also her most formidable political rivals. Markets and raw materials could, in short, only be secured by colonies and a fleet. Without colonies, the expanding mercantile marine and the nerves and sinews of German industry were exposed to an increasing jeopardy. Colonies, therefore, on this argument, the cogency of which was strengthened by every increase in economic efficiency and prosperity, were not a luxury, but an absolute necessity of power. In the early eighties the argument was being driven home by professors, newspapers, the industrial magnates and the increasing scramble for colonies, so notable after 1871. In 1887 *Die Deutsche Colonial Gesellschaft*, the union of two separate colonial organisations, was a significant proof of the solidarity of the movement; and the formation of a 'Colonial group' in the Reichstag as early as 1883, to press the demand, was the political expression of the forces at work.

Bismarck was not convinced. Like most men who have grown up and achieved great things under the influence of one set of conditions—men whose characters, convictions, and principles of action are strong because they are so set in their fibres and their blood that they are the men themselves—Bismarck was never very sensitive to new ideas and new forces which were the result of wholly new conditions and a new age. He was hostile to ' colonialism,' also, because it was not his own idea, the product of his own original and creative gifts. Unlike many statesmen, and most of his own countrymen, Bismarck had, with all his devouring ambition and pride of, and trust in, power, a fine and moderating sense of limits. Between the ideal and the practicable he continually drew a distinction that is the marrow of his statecraft. He was like Gustavus Adolphus or Richelieu energy indeed, but energy under restraint. And he never forgot what he wrote to his wife after Königgrätz—' we must not think that we have conquered the world nor forget that we have to live with three neighbours.' He recognised that the success of the German Empire had stirred the deepest jealousies and resentment ; it might and could be overthrown by coalitions ; Germany was not able, for all her strength, to defy the world.

His intuitional dislike of colonialism went deeper than mere sentiment, temperamental indifference to principles not his own, or a practical calculation of the limits of German Power. He was and he remained to his death

essentially a continentalist ; that is, he held as the core of
a true system of German policy that the German Empire
must be based on the complete mastery of the continental
conditions of supremacy. Germany must control Central
Europe ; without that control the Empire would either
be dissolved or be reduced to the second rate position of
his youth and early manhood. And the control of Central
Europe imposed the absolute necessity of an invincible
army, superior to that of any likely coalition of forces—
an army in fact on a two-Power or three-Power standard—
together with a foreign policy carried out by a vigilant
and invincible Higher Direction, concentrating on the
keys of power in Europe. The German army involved
a severe tax in manhood and money. Any dissipation of
strength on objectives outside the main theatre would
mean a proportionate reduction in the army ; and, no less
pernicious, a dualism in the higher strategy of the Wilhelmstrasse. No one realised more completely than Bismarck
the task that the maintenance of German hegemony in
Europe after 1871 laid on the Chancellor. Only by
prestige and a sleepless diplomacy had the successive
phases of the European situation been successfully met,
manipulated, and worked into the broad plan. The task
of watching and controlling Austria, France, Russia, Italy,
Spain—of anticipating the complications in the Near East,
in Poland, and the Mediterranean—became harder, not
easier, as the European Powers grew, penetrated or copied
Bismarckian principles and methods. The invitation
therefore to break out on a new objective—a great colonial
campaign—must be resisted. It was excentric to the
central issues, which in the nature of things constituted
the essentials of a true German policy.

Moreover, Bismarck foresaw that a successful colonial
campaign inevitably involved rivalries outside Europe
that would react on the European position. There were
two chief Colonial States in Europe—France and Great
Britain. Was Germany to compete with France, stop the
policy of diversion which dissipated French strength and
drive her back on concentrating on Europe ? And Great
Britain ? Competition here would not drive Great Britain

back on Europe—it was competition with a Power essentially colonial and only secondarily continental. At sea
Great Britain was supreme. What if Great Britain replied
by building up a European coalition against Germany ? The
antagonism of Great Britain was not lightly to be provoked.
Bismarck predicted that a really serious German challenge
to Great Britain in the colonial and extra-European
sphere would end in a Franco-British alliance and a deep
penetration of Great Britain into the continental situation—precisely the one object that he desired to prevent.
Bismarck had studied history as a great statesman should
study it—to learn from it the secrets of statecraft. History
was for him a study in statesmanship: precisely as to all the
great commanders from Cæsar to Moltke the study of military
history—the great things in war done by the great soldiers
—is the indispensable apprenticeship in the principles of
their science. And he saw, as his speeches and *obiter dicta*
prove, in modern European history that Great Britain had
always, and only, been formidable, when, in the task of
building and consolidating the British Empire, and in the
pursuit of British ends, she had been driven by the facts
and forces of a given situation to be the backbone and
the reservoir of a European combination. William III.,
Marlborough, Chatham, Castlereagh—did not these prove
that no European coalition had ever succeeded of which
Great Britain was not the backbone and the reservoir?
Thus, indeed, had Louis xiv., Louis xv., Kaunitz, and
Napoleon been overthrown. The Great Britain of Lord
North and George III., or of the ministries of 1864, 1866,
and 1870, without European allies, and either refusing to
find them or wilfully rejecting them—sulking or ignorantly
rejoicing in a splendid isolation—had brought disaster or
impotence on itself. Put Great Britain, Bismarck virtually
argued, with her back to the wall, because her imperial
interests are threatened, and if she had a statesman to
direct her policy, she would make a European coalition
and keep it going until her British ends—outside Europe
—were achieved. A Concert of Europe directed by Great
Britain spelled the end of German supremacy in Central
Europe. Germany would be not the first amongst equals,

but an equal among equals. Could Germany ever hope
to have an army of a continental three-Power standard
and also a navy equal or superior to that of Great Britain ?
The first was the essential of Continentalism, the second
the essential of Colonialism. Which was Germany to
choose ?

'Colonies,' said Bismarck in 1873, 'would only be a
cause of weakness, because they could only be defended by
powerful fleets and Germany's geographical position did
not necessitate her development into a first-class maritime
Power. Many colonies have been offered me. I have
rejected them.' This repeated what he had said in 1871 :
'For us in Germany this colonial business would be just
like the silken sables in the noble families of Poland, who
have no shirts to their backs.' In 1884, in the Reichstag,
Bismarck openly said he was 'no colonial man' (*Kein
Kolonial-mensch*) and in 1885 (January 10) he pronounced :
'The last speaker has told us that we must either abandon
our colonial policy or increase our naval strength to such
an extent that we need not fear any naval Power, or, to
speak more clearly, that our navy should rival that of
England herself. However, even if we should succeed
in building up a navy as strong as that of England, we
should still have to fear an alliance of England and France.
These Powers are stronger than any single Power in
Europe is or ever can be . . . from my diplomatic experience, I cannot see any reasons which can make
hostilities possible between Germany and England, unless
a Cabinet of inconceivable character should be in power
in England, a Cabinet which neither exists nor which
is ever likely to exist, and which criminally attacks us.'
And again (January 26, 1889) : 'I absolutely refuse to act
towards the Sultan of Zanzibar in opposition to England
. . . . English colonial interests compete with ours in
numerous places . . . the preservation of Anglo-German
goodwill is, after all, the most important thing. I see in
England an old and traditional ally. No differences exist
between England and Germany. I am not using a
diplomatic term if I speak of England as our ally. We
have no alliance with England. However, I wish to remain

in close contact with England also in colonial questions . . . if I should discover that we might lose touch with England I should act cautiously and endeavour to avoid losing England's goodwill.' It is asserted on good authority that German diplomatic agents were in the Bismarckian epoch instructed to ' Do all in your power to keep up good relationship with the English. It is not necessary to cable in cipher. We have nothing to conceal from the English, for it would be the greatest possible folly to antagonise England.'

Such an antagonism Bismarck foresaw jeopardised the Triple Alliance—the basis of his Continental system and the German control of Central Europe. In 1890 (January 13) an article written under Bismarck's inspiration laid down the following : ' Italy must be able to rely on the assistance of the English fleet, for the Triple Alliance cannot protect the Italian coasts. Hence Italy has to think of England, and consideration of England may conceivably limit Italy's freedom of action. As long as Germany, Austria-Hungary and Italy are united in the Triple Alliance, and as long as these three States may reckon on the assistance of English sea-power, the peace of Europe will not be broken.'

So far general principles. Active German intervention in the acquisition of colonies in 1884 was due to the pressure of a combination of forces. German relations with France were good ; Great Britain was gravely embarrassed in Egypt ; British relations with France were strained : Ireland and the Franchise question were additional burdens on an administration, the credit of which was gravely undermined, and the internal unity of which was sapped by ministers themselves ; a quarrel with Russia in the Middle East was brewing. The British government was not in a position to resist dexterous pressure. Great Britain was not able in 1884 to quarrel with Germany, unless she were prepared to abandon important commitments in her policy elsewhere. Public opinion in Germany was vociferous. It represented powerful material interests. The government was not too strong in the Reichstag ; a general election was imminent and the internal measures

of State Socialism had stirred severe criticism in some,
and bitter opposition in other, quarters. The government had to convince Germany that its policy was based
on true German interests. The closer Bismarck's policy
is studied the more apparent is the vital connection
between a stroke in foreign policy and the home situation.
Bismarck might affect to despise or ignore public opinion
in Germany—he frequently did, when it was essential to
his aims to do so—but he watched its course and weighed
its volume with vigilant care, and he always found a safety
valve to let the steam out and ease the pressure on the
ministerial boilers. As with the *Kulturkampf* and the
Vatican Decrees, so now with the colonial movement, he
saw the opportunity and gripped it with characteristic
firmness and dexterity. In the spring of 1884 he had been
able, as is indicated below, to secure an important understanding with Russia, endorsed in the autumn of the same
year. The embarrassment of Great Britain was the
Chancellor's opportunity to satisfy public opinion at
home, achieve what was necessary to satisfy public opinion
without sacrificing the essentials of his system, and do it
before the fall of Ferry's administration and the renaissance
of the inveterate hostility between France and Germany
made the opportunity no longer available.

It is not necessary or possible here to trace in detail the
swiftly developed plans by which Germany between 1884
and 1890 acquired Togoland, the Cameroons, South-
West Africa (but without Walfish Bay), the framework of
German East Africa, a third of New Guinea, and a share
of the Samoa group. The Anglo-German agreement of
July 1, 1890 (which brought Heligoland to Germany, but
ceded German claims on Zanzibar and Witu to Great
Britain) falls outside Bismarck's period of office, and was
concluded by his successor, Caprivi. The initial and
most characteristic stages in German colonial policy and
the Anglo-German conflict are described at length, and
from authoritative sources, in Lord Fitzmaurice's *Life of
Lord Granville*. It must suffice here to note that after
1885 a Conservative, not a Liberal, ministry in Great
Britain was responsible for the ' concessions ' and conven-

tions; that the German colonial party was by no means satisfied with the achievements of their government; that in 1885 the attempt to secure the Caroline Islands was abandoned when Bismarck referred the dispute to the arbitration of Pope Leo XIII., in order to conclude the *Kulturkampf* and secure the Clerical Centre; and that Bismarck bitterly criticised the agreement of July 1, 1890, which may be partly due to his determination to condemn as a blunder everything done after he ceased to be Chancellor. But the broad fact remains that the foundations of Germany's Colonial Empire were laid by Bismarck, and that unless we are to regard all his public utterances on the subject as deliberate insincerity, he accomplished a limited programme under pressure, with considerable misgiving and much reluctance.[1] He was severely criticised in the Reichstag and in the press, inspired by the Colonial Society, for being so apathetic, hesitating, and absurdly considerate of Great Britain, no less than for sacrificing Germany's future across the water to an obsolescent Continentalism.

In 1883 and the spring of 1884 Lord Ampthill warned our government that the pressure of powerful parties in Germany was greatly influencing Bismarck ' whose interest (in colonial policy) was increased by the prospect of a general election this autumn' (March 15, 1884). The German government was also indicating with unmistakable emphasis that German goodwill in Britain's Egyptian policy was dependent on British goodwill in German colonial policy. This plain hint was continually repeated in the next two years. ' I am in perfect despair,' Ampthill wrote (August 2, 1884), ' at Prince Bismarck's present inclination to increase his popularity before the general election by taking up an anti-English attitude. Compelled by the colonial mania . . . he has discovered

---

[1] 'For the sake of two million marks I cannot throw myself against the great impulse of the nation, or offer opposition to the will of the whole country. To this day I am not "a colonies man," and I entertain the gravest apprehension on the subject ; but I was compelled to decide upon yielding to the general demand of the nation. . . . If the locomotive of Empire has struck out a track for itself, I shall not be the one to throw stones in its way.'—(Bismarck in the Reichstag, January 26, 1889.)

an unexplored mine of popularity in starting a colonial policy, which public opinion persuades itself to be anti-English : and the slumbering theoretical envy of the Germans at our wealth and our freedom has awakened and taken the form of abuse of everything English in the press.' The remark apart from its special reference is deeply significant, for it confirms the trend in the development of German public opinion, emphasised (p. 275) earlier in these pages. The alienation of Germany from England, which was in truth the gravest feature for the future of both countries, had proceeded with great rapidity since 1870, and though Bismarck regarded it with misgiving, as he well might, he would have abandoned all the principles and methods of his statecraft had he not utilised it to the full when his policy required it.

The colonial chapter in his Chancellorship is, therefore, of deep interest, for it reveals all the secrets of his statesmanship—his eye for realities, his extraordinary mastery of his own peculiar technique, his recognition that a genuine and deep-seated German public opinion must not be ignored, together with an inflexible determination to maintain his Continental system and not to push the antagonism with Great Britain to measurable distance of a rupture. Great Britain could be harried and badgered ; she must understand that international relations were the result of bargains ; she must make concessions that could be represented as diplomatic victories for Germany ; but she must not be driven into the enemy's camp. And as the situation developed from 1884 to 1890, Bismarck relaxed or increased the pressure on the successive Cabinets in London, not thinking so much of the Colonies themselves, as of the prestige of his government, German relations with France or Russia, and the Triple Alliance, in which Italy's continued inclusion was not too certain.

The more clearly that the Anglo-German negotiations are studied in detail, the more clearly stand out those methods which this biographical study has continuously emphasised as truly Bismarckian. The German demand for colonies and the German movement towards expansion outside Europe were not intrinsically indefensible and were the product of forces beyond the control even of an Iron Chancellor. The supposition which underlay much violent criticism both of Gladstone and Salisbury from 1884-90 that Great Britain could have peremptorily vetoed all German colonial acquisitions, and could have done so without sacrificing British interests in Egypt or in the Middle or Far East—in a word, that Great Britain was strong enough between 1884 and 1890 to defy France, Russia, and Germany, or should have embarked on a policy which might, and probably would, have ended in a Triple Coalition against the British Empire, is not one which can be sustained by a careful study of a very complicated and critical European situation, combined in those years with a very critical situation at home. Great Britain had to choose between France and Germany, and France was practically under German direction. In these pages we are not primarily concerned either with explaining the origins and development of British policy, or with drawing up a balance-sheet based on a critical survey of mistakes, alternations and successes ; for the complete British balance sheet cannot be adequately set out here, nor the verdict based on the necessary cross-examination of the very copious evidence.

One conclusion, however, seems fully justified. It would have been easy for Bismarck, had he chosen to do so, to have picked a very formidable quarrel with Great Britain. Such a choice could have been made really popular in Germany. Bismarck, indeed, in a month, could have lashed Germany into a frenzy over colonies, at any moment after 1884 to 1890. His prestige savoured of the miraculous : his knowledge of his countrymen's passions was unrivalled and Germany's military strength was beyond question. It would have been no less easy to have lashed Great Britain and colonial sentiment, particularly in Australia, into the temper that makes either a complete diplomatic victory or war the only alternatives. The Pendjeh incident in 1885 proved the readiness of the country to respond to a strong lead against Russia. ' The Colonies ' would have been a far more formidable appeal to national passion than an obscure place on the Afghanistan frontier. But neither Bismarck nor the successive British governments embarked on a course so fraught with peril. Bismarck deliberately refused indeed to push Great Britain against the wall and the inference from his refusal is irresistible. For reasons, that may be bad or good, but to which he attached the greatest weight, he was ready to badger, even to insult, while insisting on concessions, but not to 'antagonise' Great Britain. German critics then and since have questioned the accuracy of his judgment and the validity of his reasons. In this country we can appreciate the reason for, and ratify the wisdom of, his decision. For Bismarck was convinced his policy secured the best interests of Germany. He was not concerned with the question whether it also made for British interests. But it made for peace in Europe—and peace he held was a supreme German interest in those years. That it was also a British interest, not lightly to be sacrificed, is demonstrable.

But if Bismarck's ends were and remain defensible, his methods were and remain quite indefensible. British ministers must plead guilty to lack of vigilance and errors of judgment; the Colonial governments cannot escape severe criticism; but whatever their mistakes, our Foreign and Colonial Offices acted in a straightforward and honourable manner; and in the beginning they credited, quite wrongly, the German government with similar intentions and methods. It would be, on the facts before us, impossible to pronounce but one verdict on German diplomacy. From the negotiations about Angra Pequena to the annexation of part of New Guinea, Bismarck's methods were marked by duplicity and a demonstrable intention to deceive the British government as to the true aims of the German government, to present our government with *faits accomplis*, snatched in defiance of soothing assurances or virtual pledges, and thus to make the whole situation doubly difficult. The German White Books were an incomplete, misleading, and, in places, positively inaccurate version of the negotiations; our Blue Books, which threw a very different light on what had happened, roused Bismarck's deepest wrath, and we can understand the reasons for his anger. The Chancellor utilised his unique position in Germany to work up carefully prepared explosions in the Reichstag, even publicly to suggest that the British government was hostile to, and jealous of, any German colonial acquisitions—which he knew was not true —and to make charges against both Lord Granville and Lord Derby which he was quite unable to sustain.[1] The public statements of the Chancellor were intended for a credulous German public opinion and an invitation to draw its own (and quite false) conclusions ; the withdrawal of the charges was either privately made or slurred over, after the poison had been allowed to inflame German feeling. The missions of Count Herbert Bismarck, whose reception in England by ministers and society deeply gratified a sensitive father's heart, were intended to do more than effect an amicable settlement. ' Count Herbert Bismarck,' wrote Sir C. Dilke, ' came over again. If at his former visit he had only tried to get us to dismiss Lord Derby, on this occasion he wanted us to dismiss Lord Granville and Lord Derby.' He failed. So gross and unwarranted an interference in our home politics, thoroughly Bismarckian in character, was calculated to produce precisely the opposite effect to that which Bismarck desired. All through this trying period Lord Granville, who acted as an honourable gentleman towards a great statesman, who in his diplomacy was never a gentleman, suspected that the cession of Heligoland was at the bottom of Bismarck's tortuous and dishonest methods. The possibility of the concession had been confidentially mentioned more than once to Lord Granville, but no formal or open suggestion on the subject was made, though Lord Granville was

---

[1] *I.e.* the charge that Lord Granville had betrayed confidential communications of Bismarck's to the French government (Granville's *Life*, ii. p. 370), and that the British government had failed to reply to an important dispatch of May 5, 1884, when as a matter of fact the dispatch had, by Bismarck's instructions of which he was well aware, not been communicated to our Foreign Office. ' I had a talk with Münster,' Lord Granville wrote privately to Mr. Gladstone, ' he was frightened out of his wits. He found the famous dispatch, but a telegram not to act upon it. He begged me to keep this secret.' And this our government did, to their honour (*op. cit.*, ii. p. 428). Münster was grateful. But Bismarck never repudiated his statement, and to this day it is believed in Germany—along with many other innuendoes and allegations, derived from Bismarck's speeches which were untrue in fact.

aware ' it was the intention of Germany to open a canal into the Baltic . . . for the security of which it would be necessary to give a good and fortified harbour to Heligoland.' The concession was ultimately made by Lord Salisbury on July 1, 1890, as part of the general Anglo-German agreement of that date.

It is impossible to avoid the conclusion that Bismarck threw away a great opportunity between 1883 and 1885, and threw it away deliberately. Had he frankly and openly approached the British government in 1883 with an explanation of the difficult position the German government was in, placed all the cards loyally on the table, invited our goodwill while emphasising the necessity of concessions on grounds of policy, and his readiness in return for such concessions to support us against Ferry and the French government, whose policy was to embarrass Great Britain everywhere by subservience to Germany, all that Germany subsequently obtained might have been gained and more, without endangering the good relations of both countries. Bismarck pursued a very different course : partly because such methods were not his idea of diplomacy, partly because he could not resist this opportunity to utilise the difficulties of Great Britain, partly because he conceived it necessary to mislead Germany by representing Great Britain as hostile, while representing that her hostility was only broken down by the skill and force of an invincible German diplomacy. Tactically he succeeded. The incompleteness of the German success was concealed from the German public : the embittered controversy was left to rankle in the German mind. Strategically, the campaign failed. There can be little doubt that Bismarck desired to draw Great Britain into the German net and the German system—to establish a general *entente* which would have placed the Triple Alliance beyond question and left Germany completely master of the European situation and of British policy, and put the British fleet under German direction, objects all the more desirable when the fall of the Ferry Ministry (April 1885) freed our policy from the continuous onslaught of a French premier, 'determined to stir up trouble for Great Britain in every quarter of the globe.'[1] The whole colonial episode left a deep impression on the minds of Mr. Gladstone, Lord Granville, and Lord Derby, and deepened Mr. Gladstone's distrust of any general understanding with Germany while her policy was directed by Bismarck and pursued by such Bismarckian methods.

Lord Fitzmaurice, for whose judgment and knowledge all who have worked over the same material must have a profound respect, is of opinion that 'the Berlin Act,' of February 24, 1885, 'may some day be considered the most remarkable event in Lord Granville's long tenure of the Foreign Office.' That Act finally defined and established under international guarantees the Congo Free State; it also defined the relations between Germany and the new state and the claims of Portugal and France; it provided for the suppression of slavery and the slave-trade, and for religious liberty; and it was the first international document formally to recognise 'spheres of influence' as distinct from territorial acquisitions. In a word, it went a long way towards solving some of the acuter problems of the Partition of Africa—and to solve them by a European Concert.

The Anglo-German Agreement of July 1, 1890, completed the negotiations begun in 1883, and laid the foundation of German East Africa. It was concluded by Bismarck's successor Caprivi. Bismarck criticised the agreement of 1890 with characteristic bluntness: 'Zanzibar,' he told Busch, 'ought not to have been left to the English. It would have been better to maintain the old arrangement. *We could then have had it at some later time when England required our good offices against France or Russia.* In the meantime our merchants, who are clever, and, like the Jews, are satisfied with smaller profits, would have kept the upper hand in business. To regard Heligoland as an equivalent shows more imagination than

---

[1] 'Ferry,' wrote Lord Granville, 'is certainly no loss to us. He arrived at the Quai d'Orsay quite ignorant of foreign affairs; and the more he learnt of them, the more subservient he became to Bismarck, and the more tricky to us.' —*Life*, ii. p. 435; see also Lord Lyons's *Life*, passim.

sound calculation. In the event of war, it would be better for us that it should be in the hands of a neutral Power.'

The criticism contains in a nutshell Bismarck's ideas and methods. The embarrassments of Great Britain were to be utilised, as opportunities arose, to extract concessions which would strengthen the prestige of the government at home, consolidate Germany's position in Europe and satisfy powerful sections of public opinion. German trade would succeed in and for itself, under the benevolent and careless ægis of the British flag, without committing the German government to a systematic colonial policy. Without a fleet adequate to protect the German colonies, those colonies would simply be exposed to British attack : and it was a profound mistake to put Germany in a position in which she might require the good offices of Great Britain, instead of having her own good offices to bargain with in a British competition with France or Russia.

Hence, from the first, Bismarck declined to incur Imperial responsibility for the administration or development of the territories acquired. His principle was to adopt the time-honoured British method of development by chartered companies, with assistance, not readily granted, of a subsidy to a steamship line. The Imperial government did not incorporate the acquisitions, a step which would have raised very difficult constitutional and financial problems. Were the colonies, for example, to be Imperial Territories (*Reichsländer*) ? What were to be their administrative relations to the Imperial government and the Reichstag ? Who was to be responsible, and to whom for their government ? How were they to be financed during the long period when they could not be self-supporting or policed, and so forth ? Technically during the Bismarckian régime they were simply 'Protectorates' (*Schütz - Gebiete*), *i.e.* the Imperial government undertook to 'protect' them from foreign aggression—a definition of a 'Protectorate' much narrower than that commonly accepted. But even, in Bismarck's day, this guarded and limited liability broke down. The Arab Revolt in East Africa of 1888 proved that the German East African Company (*Die Deutsche Ost-Africa Gesellschaft*), mainly financed by the German traders interested in the vast district, was unable to 'protect' the 'Protectorate' from native attacks or rebellions. Direct Imperial assistance had to be given. But even without the coercion of internal danger the Bismarckian policy was bound to fail. Behind the colonial movement worked the forces of a public opinion that demanded the full status of German sovereignty for the German 'colonies,' and the creation of a Germany beyond the seas, to become as essentially and integrally a part of the German Empire as Alsace or Mecklenburg. But the later development of German colonial policy, which led in 1907 to the establishment of a Colonial Office in the central executive, and the gradual transference of all the colonies to direct imperial administration fall outside the Bismarckian period. How far the development since 1890 has borne out Bismarck's original reluctance to embark on a systematic colonial policy, and how far it inevitably led to the one result that Bismarck feared from the first—an irreconcilable antagonism between Great Britain and Germany, spreading from the Atlantic and the Pacific to the North Sea and the heart of Europe —and how far colonial policy has been the main cause of the creation of a German fleet, sufficiently powerful to rival that of Great Britain, are questions of the profoundest significance to all students of the European State system in the quarter of a century that followed Bismarck's fall from power. But they can neither be discussed with advantage, still less adequately answered, by the student of Bismarck's statecraft alone.

The colonial movement, as a phenomenon in the revolution of the German Empire, does indeed enforce, with the same clearness that the history of Social Democracy brings out, one great truth, salutary alike for the pure historical student and the political researcher into the springs and causes of national development. The industrialism of Germany, with its concurrent features of a rapid increase of wealth and a marvellous expansion of

population, was not Bismarck's work, nor did he deliberately at any time in his career make it his task to promote
it, in and for itself. He endeavoured in 1862, and still
more in 1879, to utilise the economic ambitions and expanding material resources of Germany in achieving his
main political object ; he checked from time to time its
energies or directed them into channels approved by
himself. His success was certainly very limited even in
this limited programme. The forces were too vast,
too ubiquitous, and too complex to be controlled
within the mould of a policy which had originated
and attained a successful issue in a very different field of
action. And by 1890, when Bismarck departed, the
economic and industrial elements that made the new
Germany were beyond the power of any statesman to say
—'thus far and no farther; this we will have, but not
that.' Had Bismarck held his place until 1898 this conclusion would be more apparent than it was in 1890.
The Chancellor was, in short, experiencing the lesson that
eighteenth-century British history drives home. Neither
a Chatham, nor a Clive, nor a Warren Hastings could
prevent the ' expansion of England ' from taking a form,
a volume, or a direction which their policy had not contemplated ; and when the industrial revolution was
superimposed on the originally narrower colonial and
imperial movement, the government at home was obliged
to follow where the nation, mastered by its own internal
vitality, unconsciously led. England, often reluctantly,
was driven by forces within and without, which were like
the propulsive forces of life within a healthy and growing
human individual. So thin and obscure is the partition
in the lives of individuals and nations between appetites
and ideals. British policy in Europe was gradually
coerced by the colonial expansion into a new orientation
and a re-definition of the ends and methods of British
action in Europe.

So with Bismarck. He had taught his nation the
Bismarckian gospel of power and proved its efficacy. The
industrial revolution in Germany, superimposed on
unification and victory, inspired new concepts and a new

and deeper meaning in the principles of power as the end
and justification of organised State action.   The colonial
movement in Germany was at once both the expression
of the new interpretation of power—of which the German
nation was becoming more and more conscious—and a
demand for the realisation of that new power by the old
methods by which Bismarck had taught Germany the
gospel of the State that stood for Power.   Bismarck
felt, indeed, intuitively, that the German demand could
not be ignored.   What he refused to admit was that
the satisfaction of the demand must in the end result in
a re-interpretation of German policy in Europe and result in a new attitude to the problems of international
relations.   And until he fell he was really wrestling
with an insoluble dilemma.   He insisted on maintaining
the Bismarckian conception of Central Europe, with its
strategic and political conceptions, its delicate equipoise
of European State relations, derived from the Europe of
1848 to 1870, and its theory of alliances and preventive
combinations, directed chiefly against France.   But, as the
next two decades conclusively indicated, the colonial and
industrial movement in the civilised States of Europe, the
' armed peace ' resting on ' nations in arms,' more or less
Prussianised in their military machinery, and the new ideas
of power in conflict with the new ideas of political liberty,
law and right, had produced a deadlock in Europe by
1890.   The struggle had been shifted from the chancelleries with their obsolescent political conceptions to the
Europe beyond the seas, reacting on the new industrial
basis at home, and in turn influenced by it.   Hence in
1890 Europe as the result of forces, at best only indirectly
created by Bismarckian principles, was on the eve of an
effort to readjust the whole European State system and
the international relations of the armed nations to the
new ideas of power, and of empires based on a modern
colonial mercantilism.   Colonialism and industrialism
were destined to produce a new Europe and a new world ;
and for Germany in particular they were shortly not to
supersede, but to re-write, the meaning and value of the
fundamental conceptions of German hegemony, and to

re-interpret Central Europe in terms that Bismarck regarded as a departure, and a blundering departure, from sound policy.

The Chancellor, however, to the end adhered with impressive tenacity to his fundamental conception, and the final decade of his career witnessed a resolute effort to fit Russia into the system embodied in the Triple Alliance.

The new Tsar, Alexander III., had not the same dynastic connection with the royal house of Prussia that had so materially influenced the relations of Alexander II. and the Emperor William. He was torn between the desire to represent a powerful Russia in Europe and his fear of Nihilism, which by the assassination of his father had brought him to the throne. Liberalism and all its works were in his eyes only the inclined plane to democracy and anarchy. Liberal Great Britain and the democratic French Republic changing its ministries every few months were a public danger. The solidarity of the Conservative interest and the monarchical principle demanded the formation of a 'monarchical international' to combat the Socialist international—so formidable in Germany. Bismarck could work on this line of thought. Lord Granville openly recognised from 1881 to 1885 that a Liberal ministry, because it was a Liberal ministry, would be harassed, and that Bismarck would enjoy harassing it, because the German system required that the destruction of Liberalism in Germany should be followed by the destruction of it elsewhere. The world could have peace, but only if it first made a Conservative solitude. Accordingly Bismarck 'got at' the Tsar in the autumn of 1881 in Denmark. The Emperor William, so sincere, straightforward, and so eminently admirable in his simplicity, could be persuaded to employ the hypodermic syringe for 'doping' the Tsar into sanity. That autumn there was much discussion in exalted circles about the desirability of saving a perishing world by an international anti-Nihilist and anti-Socialist league. Great Britain was the trouble, of course, as Great Britain had been the trouble under Castlereagh in the earlier form of the Holy Alliance. Even a Conservative Great Britain was never at any time ready, at the dictation of Berlin, Vienna, or Petersburg, to wreck the constitutional system and to abolish its freedom of the press or abandon the right of asylum to political refugees. Fortunately for Germany Great Britain was in cruel difficulties and Alexander III. was amenable to influence. When the Tsar replaced the anti-German Ignatieff by de Giers (June 12, 1882), and when Skobeleff died, Katkoff lost influence, and it was clear the German wind was once more blowing steadily along the repaired wires from the Wilhelmstrasse to Gatchina and Tsarkoë Seloe. The Austrians were restive, for they suspected treachery at Berlin. They had not learned, even in 1882, that Bismarck refused alliances or conventions in which he did not sit on the longer arm of the lever. In the spring of 1884 (March 24) Bismarck could rejoice, for he had made his first 'reinsurance' (*Rückversicherungs*) treaty. In the autumn of that year, at a meeting of the three Emperors at Skierniewice, a verbal endorsement was given to the written compact of March 24. But, unless the evidence available is absolutely untrustworthy, there was no written understanding at Skierniewice. The convention in writing had already been made in the spring, and there was no adequate reason either for writing it out again or altering its terms.

The compact apparently was to hold good for three years : and provided that if one of the three contracting parties made war on a fourth Power, the other two were to maintain a benevolent neutrality ; that in the problems of the Balkan peninsula the contracting parties would consult their own interests, but in cases of disagreement between two Powers there was to be a casting vote with the third ; Turkey was to come under a kind of joint Protectorate which would be responsible for the execution of the terms of the Treaty of Berlin; while the occupation of the Balkan principalities was forbidden to all the three signatories.[1]

For Bismarck the treaty was a triumph. It is very

[1] See Appendix B for a further discussion of the Treaty of 1884-87, and the questions arising out of them. The Treaty of 1884 had been preceded by a treaty (dealing with the Near East) in 1881.

difficult to see, if the terms given above broadly represent the contents of the convention, why Alexander III. should have consented to become a party to such an undertaking. He gained on the face of it nothing, while he lost everything, including his independence of action. It is true that in the struggle, now approaching a crisis, in the Middle East between Great Britain and Russia the Tsar was freed from the fear of German and Austrian attack, should it come to war with Great Britain, but cool reflection should have convinced the Tsar that it was inconceivable that Germany or Austria would ever attack Russia to enable Great Britain to win a victory that would consolidate British power in the Middle or Near East. Bismarck was not likely to sacrifice the bones of Pomeranian grenadiers in the interest of a Liberal Great Britain. And had he been so inconceivably foolish, he would at once have brought about an alliance between France and Great Britain, which he feared even more than an alliance between France and Russia. A Franco-British Alliance meant that Italy would at once desert the Triple Alliance. Russian diplomacy from 1862 to 1890 (to proceed no further) is indeed a mysterious and fearful thing—so bristling with patent miscalculations, glaring blunders, and the inconsistent idiosyncrasies of mediocre autocrats, that the student is driven to suspect some rational but hidden explanation, the nature of which has never been revealed, to account for the mistakes. The truth, probably, is that in Bismarck's hands Alexander III. was a hypnotised stripling. Lord Ampthill's last letter to Lord Granville (August 16, 1884), however, repeats a familiar theme : ' the progress of democracy in England,' he wrote, ' is the cause of very serious alarm to the sovereigns and governments ; and they purpose to meet it by consolidating the Monarchical League.' If the Tsar was so impressed with the danger to his person, throne, and principles from the progress of democracy, led by a pestilent Great Britain, as to sacrifice his political independence and initiative and tie himself up in the meshes of the Compact of 1884, no sovereign ever made a more unjustified and foolish sacrifice to Conservative principles.

The Tsar interpreted the compact as giving Russia a free hand in Central Asia ; and certainly as the result of it he was enabled to conduct, under continuous German inspiration, the negotiations over the Pendjeh affair in a way that he could not have done, had he not been assured of German neutrality. But in so doing he was playing Bismarck's game to perfection. The diversion of Russia to Central Asia, a continuous and rasping antagonism with Great Britain, the diversion of Great Britain in Egypt or the Middle East, the alienation of Russia from France, and of France from Great Britain, the with-drawal of Russia from Europe and the Balkans, and the elimination thereby of a conflict between Austria and Russia, together with the weakening of Russian and British influence and the increase of German power at Constantinople, were results that in the glades of Friedrichs-ruhe and by the cigars smoked in serene reflection by the Chancellor's hearth seemed to be the gifts of Providence to the wise. There is every reason to believe that Bismarck supported (for adequate considerations) Great Britain in Egypt against France, and urged Russia to increase her Asiatic Empire. It was Great Britain not Bismarck who suffered from 'Mervousness,' and it is practically certain that in 1885 Bismarck used all his unrivalled influence and skill to keep open the breach between Russia and Great Britain, while dexterously suggesting to both parties that Codlin was the friend, not Short. He did not want an Anglo-Russian war; but he wanted the highest tension possible short of war, and if both governments in consequence lost prestige, or felt they must secure German goodwill in a political world in which they had no friend but Germany, the Wilhelmstrasse more demonstrably than ever became the central exchange of European rivalries. The 'honest broker' meanwhile took his commission in West Africa or New Guinea, best of all in shutting the doors of the Quai D'Orsay to all but the German Ambassador. A Liberal Great Britain, as the disturber of the peace of the world and the jealous foe of every one's prosperity, was an effective theme alike at Paris and Petersburg, and most effective of all in the Reichstag.

' Bizzimarck here, Bizzimarck there, Bizzimarck, Bizzimarck everywhere,' said Punch in a famous cartoon—and it was so true. Moreover, what an appropriate moral for sovereigns shivering in panic at Socialism—' To what impotence and embarrassments will not Liberalism bring deluded nations and ministers ! ' Gambetta, Ferry, and Gladstone compared with de Giers, Taaffe, and Bismarck.

The *entente* of 1884 was, as usual, primarily directed against France. The compact provided for the neutrality of Russia if any of the three partners came to war with a fourth Power (France). But it did much more than dissolve the possibility of a Franco-Russian Alliance (with the war on two fronts for Germany) ; it constituted Bismarck the arbiter and mediator between Russia and Austria. A quarrel between Russia and Germany in the Balkans was very unlikely ; but a quarrel between Russia and Austria was always on the horizon. Bismarck, by the compact of 1884, could decide whether he would support Russia or Austria, and the choice of the alternative gave him just the leverage he required to keep both his ' friends ' in order. The absorption of Russia in Central Asia immensely facilitated the task. But what Bismarck desired above all was to secure the requisite degree of control over Austrian policy. If Austria was ' in hand ' the diversion of Russia or the coercion of Italy was easy, and it is a fair inference that the compact of 1884 tightened, and was intended to tighten, the control of the Wilhelmstrasse on the Ball-Platz.

The unscrupulous ingenuity and dexterity of Bismarck's diplomacy may easily conceal the real source of his success —German strength. Germany could secure allies, not because her minister was a master of the technique of the higher direction, but because she was a State of such organised power. The Prussian sword was a permanent weight in the scales of the international Balance of Power. Europe in these days was steadily going to school in Germany. In German universities the foreigner could learn what organised work really meant, and it was a revelation that inspired justly a profound admiration and a no less wholesome fear. From 1870 onwards the mighty preparation of, and sacrifice by, trained brains from 1815 to 1870 was bringing its harvest safely home; and surely it deserved to do so. German science in its broadest sense had its origin in the universities, but by 1880 it had gripped the whole nation. The German mind might be un-political—which is very doubtful—but in commerce as in the professions it understood, as no other national mind in Europe understood, the meaning of science and the vital difference between amateurism and expert know-ledge. The most demonstrable manifestation of that national science was the German nation in arms—the German army as a political organ of the State that repre-sented Power. That army was neither a luxury nor a profession for the well-to-do and the rank and file who could not be fitted by an individualistic rule of thumb into the civil life of trade or agriculture. The foreign soldier who studied at Berlin became acquainted with a great national machine, the education and training of which was based on the severest science co-ordinated to political ends. Foreign soldiers in Europe realised that the German army was not merely large in numbers or well-equipped with guns and ammunition, but was trained for war. From the Chief of the General Staff, now one of the grand old men of Germany and history, to the lads of the Cadet-tenhaus the German nation recognised, not that the army must be ready (which it took for granted), but that it would win not only by its numbers but by its superiority in science—and that the science of war demands, as does every science, not merely the devotion of a lifetime but first-rate brains in politics who have grasped what an army is and implies. The chiefs of the German army, whose education did not cease until they were on the retired list, assumed that the political direction was in the hands of one, to whom war was a familiar subject, and who regarded war as a necessary manifestation of national life and power and the indispensable instrument of a national policy. How Bismarck used the German army to assist his policy, and how he manipulated his policy to increase the effective use of the German army is written on the record. What

Europe had not yet grasped was that since 1862 the Prussian army—the nation in arms—was also organised and employed by Bismarck (in conjunction with the General Staff) to be a political instrument, not merely for maintaining the Hohenzollern dynasty in power but for maintaining a defined type of polity in Germany, and for educating the nation in the principles and ethics of that polity. It would be instructive if we could have transferred him to London and seen how he would have used the sea-power of Great Britain now as an instrument, and now an end in itself, of policy. British sea-power was unique in its capacity to satisfy the ends of an Imperial policy and to achieve the British right to live and achieve national purposes. Bismarck would have taught us how to adapt our policy to the instrument, and how policy could have secured at each stage further and effective opportunities for obtaining the command of the sea and placing it beyond dispute. The period from 1815 to 1890 is fertile in illustrations of the just criticism that British foreign policy repeatedly incurs in the eighteenth and nineteenth centuries—that the British Cabinets were generally ignorant of naval or any other strategy and the essentially national and imperial purpose for which the British fleet justifiably existed; while the British Admiralty, at last and reluctantly compelled to regard (1887) a starved Intelligence Department as a necessary equipment of the Brain of a navy, was no less ignorant of foreign policy and its vital connection with naval strategy. Had the Wilhelmstrasse been ignorant of the relations of strategy to policy, and also been kept in one watertight ' political ' compartment, and had the great General Staff been ignorant of policy and shut up in another watertight ' military ' compartment, Königgrätz, Gravelotte, and Sedan would not have been won, nor would there have been a German Central Europe controlling the Continental State system from the assured basis of the Triple Alliance.

There were, however, two forces that Bismarck could not control, the national consciousness of France and the expanding nationalism of the Balkan races. The fall of Ferry recalled Alsace-Lorraine to the French memory.

After the death of the Comte de Chambord (August 23, 1883) the speeches of Manteuffel, the persecution of Antoine in Alsace, and the insult at Paris by the boulevard mob to the King of Spain, after he had been made colonel of an Uhlan regiment, showed what slumbered in the French heart, even while Ferry cultivated the friendship of Germany. From 1885 onwards Franco-German relations passed from friction to tension and from tension to serious strain. The theatrical but brief episode of Boulanger (1886-89) coincided with events elsewhere to make the years 1887 and 1888 critical.[1] In 1887 Boulanger was Minister of War ; the famous black horse on which he rode in the Bois de Boulogne and captivated the café-concert patriotism of the Boulevards seemed as formidable a menace to the Republic as was his advocacy of *revanche* and of a Russian alliance, openly discussed at Petersburg, to the Foreign Office at Berlin. The 'Schnaebele incident,' when a French police commissioner was lured across the frontier in Alsace, arrested and thrown into prison, almost brought matters to an open rupture.

In the Balkans the union of the two Bulgarias, the furious anger of the Tsar, the demands of Turkey, the war between Serbia and Bulgaria, the defeat of Serbia and the intervention of Austria on Serbia's behalf, the collapse of the Russian party in Bulgaria, and the failure of the German consuls to save the Russophil officers at Rustchuk, together with the active part played by the British government, had produced a situation from which, quite apart from the Franco-German embittered relations, a European war could easily emerge.

For Bismarck the gravity of the situation lay in two formidable possibilities : the Triple Alliance might crumble away—the understanding of 1884 with Russia might dissolve and be replaced by a Franco-Russian alliance, linking the quarrel of France with Germany to the avowed objects of a Russia, humiliated and frustrated, in the south-east of Europe. Pressure from Paris and Petersburg was being put upon Italy to detach herself

[1] Dilke (*European Politics in 1887*, p. 16) asserts that in October 1886 France refused an alliance with Russia and Austria an alliance with Great Britain.

from Germany and obtain her 'national satisfaction' in
a new Triple Alliance against Germany. Three important
contracts ran out in 1887 : the Dual Alliance of 1879, the
Triple Alliance of 1882, the Compact of 1884 with Russia.
Their renewal was an essential condition of Bismarck's
system, and on their renewal, in Bismarck's view, clearly
depended the peace of Europe, more than ever a German
interest. The crisis in foreign policy coincided with an
embittered and strained situation in home politics.
Bismarck therefore had to satisfy Germany's allies,
Austria and Italy, to satisfy Russia and thereby renew the
isolation of France, satisfy German public opinion, beginning to be as excited as opinion in France, Russia, and the
Balkans,—and also to crush the organised parliamentary
opposition at home. Nor could he forget Great
Britain. The retention of Italy was largely dependent
on British goodwill. Clearly it was not a moment to
harass Great Britain either about Egypt or colonial
acquisitions.

The years 1887 and 1888 were therefore the severest
touchstones of a German statesman's statecraft. Bismarck's performance was, when we appreciate the complex
difficulties, a consummate one. The master proved his
mastery.

How seriously the German government viewed the
situation was shown by the introduction (November 25,
1886) of a new Army Bill, augmenting the peace strength
of the army by forty thousand men, the increase to take
effect as from April 1, 1887. The expiration of the
Septennate in April 1888 was thereby anticipated by
twelve months. Opposition came from the Centre and
the Liberals. The aged Chief of the Staff addressed the
Reichstag (January 11, 1887) with the deliberate assertion
that if the bill were rejected ' we shall most certainly have
war. All political and civil liberty,' Moltke added, ' all
the results of culture, the finances, the State, all stand or
fall with the army.' Bismarck's speeches in 1887 and 1888
were, as he fully realised, delivered quite as much to
Europe as to Germany. As expositions of the Chancellor's system and policy they are amongst the *loci classici*,

and they deserve to be studied *in extenso*. Only a few quotations can be given here :

'Our relations with Russia afford no motives for this bill . . . we shall have no conflict with Russia unless we go to Bulgaria for the express purpose of provoking a war. . . . What is Bulgaria to us ? It is nothing to us who rules in Bulgaria, or even what becomes of Bulgaria. . . . The difficulty of our position is not to keep peace with Austria and Russia, but between Russia and Austria. . . . With words I can do nothing. Words are not soldiers, nor are speeches battalions. When we have the enemy in the Fatherland, and read them speeches they will laugh at us. The possibility of a French attack, which to-day is not imminent, will recur as soon as France thinks she is stronger than we are, either by alliances or being better armed. . . . In case of an unsuccessful war, the peace of 1870 would be mere child's play as compared with the peace of 1890. We should have the same French against us whom we met from 1807 to 1813, and who would again suck our blood so that we should be paralysed for thirty years. . . . We have interests which do not affect Austria, and Austria has interests which are far removed from us, and each must go therefore its own way.'—(January 11, 1887.)

'We cannot trust the existence of the army to a vacillating majority. If the status of the army is to depend on Parliament and Budget grants, we shall be compelled to say : " *videat Imperator ne quid detrimenti capiat Respublica* " and " *salus Reipublica* will become *suprema lex* " (January 14, 1887). On January 14, an amendment limiting the proposed increase to three years was carried by 183 to 154 votes, the Centre voting with the Liberals in the majority. Bismarck quietly drew a paper from his portfolio and filled in the date. 'I have,' he said to the Reichstag, excited by the results of the division, 'an Imperial Message to communicate.' He read from the piece of paper a decree dissolving the Reichstag.

Six weeks later the elections justified the Chancellor's prediction ' that I shall carry the Army Bill, because the Progressists are against it.' The Liberal opposition was badly beaten. The Liberals lost thirty-three seats, the Socialists sixteen, the Clerical Centre only two—but the reconstituted National Liberals, now really a branch of moderate Conservatism, gained nearly fifty seats, and the Government Party of a hundred and fifty-four was increased to two hundred and twenty. The Army Bill was reintroduced on March 9 and passed, the Centre abstaining from voting, for reasons discussed below. On April 28 Schnaebele was released. There had been a regrettable misunderstanding. It is difficult to avoid the conclusion that the ' Schnaebele incident ' was deliberately planned, possibly to provoke the French into a serious indiscretion, certainly to assist the passage of the Army Bill by driving into the German elector's mind the peril from France. The British reader will recall how in 1901 during the Boer War certain naval incidents were employed to emphasise the tyranny of Great Britain, and the impotence of the German Navy, in order to promote the passage of the Naval Bill, then before the Reichstag.

In the spring, Bismarck had succeeded in renewing the Triple Alliance (March 1887). Crispi, who had succeeded as Premier on the death of Depretis (July) in the early autumn, ostentatiously paid a visit to Count Kalnoky at Vienna (September 14), and had then gone on to Friedrichsruhe (October 2). On the return journey, he informed a German journalist of the *Frankfurter Zeitung* that Italy wished well to Bulgaria, but ' there can be no doubt that Italy, like every other European State, has every reason to fear Russia's advances to Constantinople. We cannot allow the Mediterranean to become a Russian lake.' This carefully prepared ' aside ' drew its significance from the peril that the situation in Bulgaria still involved.

The relations of Austria and Russia and of Germany and Russia were the crucial questions for Bismarck. He had provoked a storm of criticism at Vienna by deliberately revealing in the semi-official *North German Gazette* the agreement of January 15, 1877, between Austria and Russia by which the Austrian occupation of Bosnia-Herzegovina had been provisionally arranged in advance. Europe was as much puzzled as Austrian public opinion at the revelation. Why should Bismarck select this moment to let out secrets which embarrassed the Austrian ministry, and embittered the relations of Germany and Austria, and of Austria and Russia, when his avowed policy was to keep the peace between them—Germany as the *tertius gaudens duobus litigantibus* ? Had Bismarck not got the renewal of the Triple Alliance safely in his pocket ? The explanation is probably to be found first in Bismarck's desire to remind Austria-Hungary that her Balkan policy must be dependent on German goodwill ; secondly, in the relations of Germany and Russia, and of Bismarck and the Tsar. Austria had continuously to be kept in control, Russia convinced that Germany might, under certain eventualities, prefer a Russian to an Austrian policy in the Balkans.

The Compact of 1884 had run out in the spring of 1887 and had not been renewed. Since 1884 the Pan-Slavist, anti-German party in Russia had slowly regained its ascendency, in spite of Katkoff's death in the August of 1887. Count Tolstoi, General Ignatieff, Pobodonostzev and General Bogdanovitch (author of the pamphlet which caused a great stir, *L'alliance Franco-Russe et la Coalition Européenne*), utilising the crisis in Bulgaria and the Tsar's envenomed hostility to Prince Alexander of Battenberg, and marked disapproval of the election of Prince Ferdinand of Coburg in Prince Alexander's place, combined to produce a serious anti-German movement in Russia. The military preparations and movements of Russian troops on the Austrian frontier, replied to by military preparations and movements of troops in Galicia and Hungary, seemed to foreshadow a war between Austria and Russia ; and when the Tsar, at Copenhagen in September, pointedly omitted to visit the German Emperor at Stettin the warfare in the press on all sides became fiercer. The Tsar, however, did come to Berlin (November 18), and Bismarck has related how he convinced Alexander III. that forged documents were responsible for the Russian misinterpretation of German policy in Bulgaria. It is probable, indeed almost certain, that the ' Re-insurance Treaty,' the existence and non-renewal of which were revealed by Bismarck in 1896, was concluded (November 18, 1887) at this time.[1] But the conclusion of this pecu-

[1] See Appendix B.

liarly Bismarckian convention, behind the backs of his allies, Austria and Italy, did not diminish the tension in the Near East. The year closed with little relief to the strained relations of Austria and Russia, while the hostile relations between Great Britain and Russia were such as completely to satisfy Bismarck.

The German government took (December 16, 1887) another characteristic step. Not content with the Army Law of March 1887, another military Reorganisation Bill was introduced, which by the recasting of the period of service in the Reserve and the two classes of the Landwehr and of the Landsturm was calculated to add 700,000 men to the army, when mobilised on a war footing. Warned by the chastisement of the General Election of 1887, the opposition was naturally shy of resisting these fresh demands, involving a loan for military purposes of £14,000,000 (280,000,000 marks). Bismarck made the debate on the second reading of the Bill (February 6, 1888) the occasion for one of the greatest of his speeches—an elaborate review of German foreign policy and the European situation—a demonstration of Germany's unique military strength and a consummate proof of his own personal ascendency. The second reading of the Bill was passed *en bloc* without a division on February 6— a superb testimony to the Chancellor's unchallenged supremacy—and the enthusiasm of a delirious crowd repeated the homage of the Reichstag by escorting him home and continuing the demonstration under the windows of the Chancellor's residence. The third reading was passed on February 8, 1888. It was the zenith of Bismarck's career. Two years later he was on the eve of a compulsory resignation, forced on him by a conflict with his sovereign on the principles of German policy both in home and foreign affaiis, laid down in 1888.

The Reichstag heard, and Europe read, the speech, ignorant that behind it lay ' the Re-insurance Treaty,' which guaranteed the reciprocal neutrality of Russia or Germany in case either should be attacked by a third Power. This placed Bismarck precisely in the position that he desired, that of arbiter between Russia and Austria;

for to Bismarck's diplomatic fertility of resource nothing was easier than to prevent or secure, as German policy required it, Austria or Russia being the aggressor in the Eastern issues that continued to cause military councils, movements of troops, and increased armaments on both sides of the Galician frontiers. The secret convention tightened the control over Vienna, without relaxing the frailer control on Russia. It also prevented a Franco-Russian alliance. The third Power contemplated in the secret convention of November 18, 1887, might not be Austria but France. The Tsar, in fact, by making the convention really renounced the possibility of making France an ally, should Bismarck force a war on the French Republic. Yet, in Bismarck's deliberate judgment, a demonstration of German strength in February 1888 was desirable, and his speech of February 6 was preceded (February 3) by the official publication simultaneously at Berlin and at Vienna of the text of the Austro-German alliance of 1879, as renewed in 1887. It is significant that the text of the treaties on which the Triple, as distinct from the Dual, Alliance, was based, was not published, and it is fair to infer that the publication in question was not so much a hint to Russia as a warning to France and a skilful counter-stroke intended to deceive Austria, perturbed at rumours about what had passed at Berlin between Bismarck and the Tsar. Had the Ball-Platz been cognisant of the secret convention of November 18, 1887, the publication in the *Vienna Gazette* of February 3, 1888, would have been ridiculous. For the Dual Alliance precisely provided against the contingency that made the Secret Convention an operative agreement.

The great speech of February 6, 1888, is remarkable, not merely for its magisterial breadth of view, range of survey, felicity of phrasing, and pontifical sureness of touch— the qualities evinced in all Bismarck's considered expositions of principles in foreign policy—but also for its clear indication of the speaker's mind and temper. German relations with Russia rested, he told the Reichstag, not on the press, nor on a gullible and ignorant public opinion, not even on peace-loving or war-desiring ministers

but on the Tsar. ' In opposition,' he said, ' to the views
expressed by the Russian press, I have the unqualified word
of the Tsar Alexander himself ' (and, he did not add, his
pledge in writing). France, he pointed out with unmistakable emphasis, was unreconciled and irreconcilable. She
was more peaceful in 1888 than in 1887, as was proved
by Carnot's election to the Presidency, but ' no wars are
waged from mere hatred,' for 'otherwise France would have
to be at war with Italy and England and the whole world,
for France hates all its neighbours '—deliberate words not
intended to pacify France, and a passionate appeal to the
worst passions in the German heart. As for Bulgaria,
Germany's policy was clear. ' If Russia attempts to make
good her rights (in Bulgaria) I should consider it the duty
of a loyal German policy to hold purely and simply to the
stipulations of the Berlin Treaty. . . . If Russia makes
official application to us to support steps for the re-establishment of the situation in Bulgaria, as it was created at
the Congress . . . I shall have no hesitation in advising
His Majesty the Emperor to comply with the request.
This is demanded of our treaty—loyalty to our neighbour,
with whom, whatever his prevailing mood, we must still
cherish neighbourly relations, and make common cause
against the foes of Social and Monarchical order in Europe,
a task of which the Sovereign of Russia has a full appreciation.' The significance of these passages is unmistakable. They announced publicly Bismarck's share
of the bargain in the Secret Convention—a general support
of Russian policy alike against Great Britain or an unreasonable Austria.

The peroration was a finely worded summary of
Bismarck's gospel of power, evincing his grip on the
secrets of German strength and the indissoluble unity of
strategy and policy which made its ringing appeal a text
for every German household :—

'The European pond is too full of pikes for Germany ever to
become a carp. . . . Behind our army stand our reserves. It
must not be said "others can do the same." That is just what
they cannot do. We have the material, not only for forming
an enormous army, but for furnishing it with officers. We have

a corps of officers such as no other Power has. When we undertake a war it must be a people's war which all approve, as in
1870. If we are attacked then the *furor teutonicus* will flame out,
and no one can make head against that. . . . We base our
alliance on the strength of our army. If we have no cause to
use it, all the better, but we must make our arrangements with
the idea that we do use it. . . . Every country in the long run is
responsible for the windows broken by its newspapers; the bill
will be presented one day in the ill-temper of a neighbour. We
can be easily influenced by love and sympathy—perhaps too
easily—but by threats, never! We Germans fear God and
nothing else in the world; and it is the fear of God that causes
us to love peace and ensue it. . . . He who attacks the German
nation will find it armed to a man, and every soldier with the
firm belief in his heart that " God is with us." '

The most scholarly and accomplished of the French
biographers of Bismarck, M. Matter,[1] has held that this
speech was, for all its resounding success, a proof of failing
powers in Bismarck, and ultimately responsible for the
breach between Russia and Germany, and for the Franco-
Russian Alliance. ' Il avait brisé net l'alliance russo-
allemande et préparé l'entente franco-russe.' It is difficult
to concur in this judgment. The failure to renew the
secret Reinsurance of 1887 in 1890 was due to the Emperor
and Chancellor Caprivi, not to Bismarck. As is indicated
further on, Bismarck's quarrel with the Emperor was
partly the result of a fundamental difference in foreign
policy. Neither in 1890 nor in 1887 was Bismarck ready
to support Austria at all costs against Russia, nor to throw
away the opportunity of a close (if secret) understanding
between Berlin and Petersburg by backing Austrian policy
in the Balkans without reserve. The more closely that
the speech of February 6 is studied, the more clearly do its
veiled inferences stand out. It was intended to be, and
remains, a classic and magisterial review by Bismarck at
the end of his life of the principles of his policy that he
had followed since 1871. The action of the German

---

[1] M. Matter (*Bismarck et Son Temps*, iii. p. 524 *et seq.*), usually singularly
accurate, gives the date (pp. 538 and 540) of the great speech as February 8.
Bismarck did not speak on February 8 (the third reading). The correct date is
February 6, as is clear from any of the collected editions of Bismarck's speeches
and the accounts in the daily newspapers of that date.

government in 1890 was the first of a series of departures from the Bismarckian system both at home and abroad. Those departures may have been justifiable or the reverse, but Bismarck cannot fairly be held responsible either for their consequences in the Franco-Russian Entente of 1891 or for making that alliance inevitable when it is demonstrable that he resisted to the last the policy that inaugurated them.

The years 1887 and 1888, so crowded with crises, had witnessed another great Bismarckian stroke, belonging both to home and to foreign policy, which measured by its results was more momentous than the brilliant strokes that impressed Europe. In 1887 Bismarck was winding up the *Kulturkampf.* Elaborate negotiations in 1886 had continued between Berlin and the Vatican. On January 14, 1887, the Centre under Windthorst agreed with the Liberals under Richter to vote not for the Septennate, but for a limitation of the government demands to three years, and, as has been stated, the Centre and Liberals threw out the government proposal. If the government were to carry their measure in the new Reichstag the vote of the Centre was essential, for without the hundred votes of the Centre, whatever might be the result of the General Election, the military policy of the government must be defeated. It is generally supposed that Bismarck ' went to Canossa ' for the last time, and bought the support of the Centre by the Law of 1887, which was a fresh set of concessions to the Vatican, and that the Vatican thereby won its final victory. The Papacy sold, it is commonly asserted, the Centre vote for the Septennate in return for the Law of 1887.

Bismarck, the Curia, and Windthorst could have told a quite different story. On this occasion Bismarck did not go to Canossa. Instead the Papacy went to Friedrichsruhe. The Triple Alliance in the early spring of 1887, and with it the inclusion of Italy, came up for renewal. It was notorious in 1886 that the relations between the Quirinal and the Vatican were severely strained, and that both the Italian Monarchy and the Papacy were working against each other, and both in need of allies. And this

continued all through 1887. Bismarck saw his opportunity. His objects were purely political—the maintenance of his system. He had negotiated with the Vatican
all through 1886, and the word went out from the Vatican
in a diplomatic note (January 3, 1887), from Cardinal
Jacobini, the Vatican Secretary of State, that the Catholic
Centre was to vote for the Septennate. Windthorst
defied the command on January 14, 1887, and the Septennate was defeated. This was rebellion in the eyes of
the Curia. A second warning note from Cardinal Jacobini
followed (January 21). The German Catholic bishops
were ordered to throw themselves into the fray on the
government side against Radicals and Socialists; and they
did so with exemplary obedience. They organised a great
pro-government campaign. In the new Reichstag the
Centre were again ordered to vote for the government's
Bill. Windthorst had both resisted and resented the
orders from Rome in a purely political matter and the
consequent split between the ecclesiastical and lay forces
of Catholicism within the Empire. But the alliance of
Bismarck and the Papacy was too strong for him. He
regarded the Bill as fatal to the principles of freedom that
he had represented since 1871, and he distrusted profoundly
the bargain that the Papacy had made, because he distrusted Bismarck. Vote for the Bill he would not, despite
the Papal command. Vote against it he dared not ; so
with eighty-three of his ninety supporters he walked out
and took no part in the division.

Only seven of the Centre voted with the government.
Bismarck had won—and won completely. Henceforward
through the Papacy he would command the Centre Party.
The Government Bill of 1887 to end the *Kulturkampf*
was, as Windthorst knew or guessed, not the complete
repeal that the Vatican desired,[1] and Bismarck's speech
of March 23, 1887, in the Herrenhaus of the Prussian

---

[1] The Bill:
  1. Empowered the opening of seminaries for priests;
  2. Abolished the civil veto on the appointment of parish priests ;
  3. Restored the episcopal powers of discipline ;
  4. Permitted the return of purely religious, charitable, or contemplative
     Orders. The Society of Jesus was not included.

Landtag, in which he reviewed the general situation, is pervaded with a subdued note of triumph. The concessions to the Papacy he argued were reasonable and did not conflict with the authority of the State. What was important was that the Papacy had crushed the alliance of the Centre with the Radicals and had thrown itself on the side of law and order. 'Pope and Emperor,' he asserted, 'have an identical interest and must make a common front against Anarchy and Revolution. . . . I consider the Pope more friendly to Germany than the Centre. . . . The Pope is not a Guelph, a Pole, or a new Liberal, nor has he anything to do with Social Democrats.' The Triple Alliance was renewed. When Bismarck spoke on March 23 the order of the Black Eagle had been conferred on Count di Robilant for his share in the renewed inclusion of Italy. If the Papacy had hoped by going to Friedrichsruhe to obtain the complete repeal of the laws against the Roman Church, the unqualified readmission of the ecclesiastical orders, and the support of Germany against the Quirinal in Italy it was bitterly mistaken. The bargain had been dictated and interpreted by Bismarck, not the Vatican. No less significant was the undoubted fact that Great Britain had given specific pledges of protection to the Italian Kingdom—the preservation of the *status quo* in the Mediterranean and the defence of Italy from invasion by sea. 'Our position,' Depretis said in February 1887, 'is now secure both by land and sea.' 'Our friendly relations with England,' said the Italian Foreign Minister, as late as 1896, 'are in our view the natural complement of the Triple Alliance.'

Bismarck in 1887 might well feel triumphant. He had secured Italy on such terms that he virtually secured Great Britain also.[1] At Rome in the allied Italian Monarchy he had a powerful check on the Vatican; he had compelled

---

[1] See Chiala, 'La Duplice e la Triplice Allianza,' *Hansard* (1888), vol. 322. 1172, *et seq.*, and *The Times* for November 5, 1887. It was generally understood that the renewal provided, 1. If France 'attacked' Germany or Italy both were to join in defence; 2. If Russia 'attacked' Germany or Austria both were to unite in defence; 3. If France and Russia attacked any one of the three allies, all three were to unite in defence. The re-organisation of the Italian army in 1887 and 1888 (particularly after the visit of the Emperor William II. to Rome in 1888) was one of the consequences of the renewal of the Triple Alliance.

the Papacy to win a victory for the German government in Germany, which enormously increased the power of the civil and militarist government, and through the Papacy and the German Catholic bishops he had destroyed the independent and powerful political opposition of Windthorst and the Clerical Centre in the Reichstag. The Chancellor's political cartel was complete; it consisted of the Conservatives, the old National Liberals, and the Centre; and the union gave him a decisive and obedient majority.[1]

The year 1887, therefore, registered the final defeat of Liberalism, and not merely political but also intellectual Liberalism. Militarism and reaction won all along the line and the commander-in-chief of Militarism and reaction was Bismarck. The German Clerical Centre, like the old National Liberals, shed its last rags of independence, and became henceforward a party that stood for authority, despotism, and Pan-Germanism, corrupted by the favour of the government, demoralised by its dependence on the Vatican, and allied with the Pan-German party in Austria. The Papacy and its parties became the allies and agents of Prussianism, as Bismarck understood the term. 'The Anti-Christ,' denounced by Pio Nono and Antonelli had become the champion for whom Popes and Nuncios would work—and not only in Germany. The ring of interests that buttressed up the Bismarckian system was now completed by the alliance between the Conservative Lutherans of Junkertum and the Conservative Clericals of the Centre. Success, like misfortune, makes strange political bedfellows. The 'white international of the dynasties,' true to the solidarity of legitimate autocracy, was seconded by 'the yellow international of High Finance,' the *Kaiserjuden* and the Industrials (*Schlot-Junkertum*), and the 'black international of the Clericals.' After 1887 the penetration and capture of the Curia by the diplomacy of Bavaria, Prussia, and Austria, was only a question of time—proved up to the hilt when it became necessary to elect a successor to Leo XIII. Germany, says

[1] 'Peace with the Catholic Church,' Bismarck said, ' will strengthen our relations with foreign countries, especially Austria.'

Naumann, became 'a prosperous Spain.' A passage in Bismarck's speech of March 23 is very significant : 'The sharpest and bitterest opponents of the government,' he asserted, 'have been pupils of the German Universities, not of the Seminaries. . . . A seminary under a peace-loving, well-disposed bishop, with a good German mind, is far preferable to a course of study at a German University, where no one is responsible for the education with all its influences which uncontrolled mould the student.' In other words, minds made to order and on a pattern prescribed by the government for its own political ends are preferable to minds formed by free and critical inquiry. It is the prescription and the ideal of reaction and authority and always will be. But it was a sorry and sinister ending to the struggle for intellectual and political freedom with Vaticanism—an unexpected close to the conflict that Bismarck had commenced in 1873—and it opened a chapter in the intellectual history of the German universities and of the German mind, dreaded alike by Mommsen and Virchow—the two greatest figures in the German world of intellect. That chapter was not closed when Bismarck died in 1898. It is not closed yet. It was therefore wholly consonant to Bismarck's policy that in the spring of 1888 a new anti-Socialist Bill prolonged the exceptional powers conferred on the Central Executive until September 30, 1893. The power to deprive of civic rights all Socialists convicted under the law was enlarged, and the Minister of the Interior, Herr von Puttkamer, announced openly that the German Secret Police extended their efforts to Switzerland, and acted as voluntary agents in the struggle of Russian absolutism with Nihilists and refugees. The bill passed on February 17.

On March 9 the change long foreseen took place. The death of the Emperor William on that day opened the last phase for Bismarck.

§ 6. The Last Phase—Bismarck's Resignation, March 1888–March 1890

The death of the Emperor William I. removed the sovereign whom Bismarck had served for twenty-five years with a personal devotion, as sincere as it was deep. The brief speech in which the Chancellor announced to the Reichstag that the first Prussian Emperor was dead is the best proof of the grief that the national loss stirred within him. And even that official effort was too great a strain. For the first and the last time Bismarck broke down. He resumed his seat broken with emotion, after a few rugged sentences, in which both words and strength failed him. The failure was a far more impressive tribute to his royal and imperial master than any funeral oration. The simple Soldier-King and the mighty Minister-President of Prussia had worked together through a heroic epoch for great and heroic ends; and profoundly as they differed in character and gifts, sharp as had been on notable occasions the collision of their wills, the personal bond of loyalty, service, and affection, forged at Schloss Babenberg on September 22, 1862, had deepened and tightened with every year until it had become indissoluble, except by death. William I. never forgot that the two things in life which summed up his political creed—the House of Hohenzollern and the Prussian army—were the two things which his minister had saved from ruin and made the two most puissant and indisputable forces in Germany and Europe. Bismarck and Bismarck's policy had unified Germany, but unified it in such a way that the head of the House of Hohenzollern was the greatest sovereign on the Continent of Europe, while the power and stability of the dynasty rested on the unified nation in arms, of which the King-Emperor was the War-Lord by acknowledged right. In 1888 as he lay dying William could remember his mother Queen Louisa and Jena—he could remember 1848 and his brother, Frederick William IV.—only forty years ago. In the spring of 1888 'the March days' of '48 were as unthinkable as the recurrence of a Jena or the visit of a French conqueror to the tomb of Frederick the Great. William could die in peace, full of years, with a nation following him in mourning to his grave. The minister who had achieved was indeed mighty, but the sceptre and the prerogative that passed so rapidly to son and grandson were mightier than the minister, who had made them what they were. Within two years the Prussian Crown had broken the Chancellor. Bismarck could not work without the Prussian Crown : but the sequel showed that the Prussian Crown would and could work without Bismarck. And it was Bismarck who had made this possible.

Had fate decided differently, the strength of that Prussian Crown might have been convincingly exemplified in the reign of the Emperor Frederick. In December 1887, however, sentence of death had in reality been passed on the Crown Prince, and when the new Emperor arrived in Berlin on March 12 from San Remo —unable to reach his capital until three days after his father's death—he was a dying man. On June 8, Herr von Puttkamer, the reactionary Minister of the Interior ' resigned.' On June 15, the Emperor Frederick was dead. ' What a world is this, and how does fortune banter us ! '

It is a commonplace, but one of those commonplaces that enshrine notable truths, to pronounce the Emperor Frederick's reign to be a tragedy. The tragedy does not lie in the physical suffering, so heroically borne, nor in the premature death of one cut off in the prime of a superb manhood, but in the misery of frustrated purposes and baffled hopes. All his life, since the days of a generous and exultant youth, the Crown Prince had been inspired by high and noble purposes. Through the dreary 'era of conflict,' through Königgrätz, Wörth, Gravelotte, Sedan, and Versailles, through the *Kulturkampf* and the establishment of the Dual and Triple Alliance, the heir to the throne had cherished the ideal of proving to Prussia, Germany, and the world that a soldier-sovereign of the Hohenzollern House, who believed in the Prussian army and had played his part as became a Hohenzollern in the unification of Germany by victory in the field, could also be a liberal and constitutional ruler, whose duty it was to give to Prussia and Germany a government, a policy, and an outlook truly Liberal. And when at last Providence had placed the sceptre in his hands, and a great work awaited the new ruler which could only be done by a Liberal sovereign, fate struck him down impotent and tortured, yet haunted by the splendours of the ideal that had made his life an apprenticeship in self-suppression and a consecration to duty.

Death can be very bitter. Had Frederick's three months of rule been dogged by prolonged physical pain and the knowledge of failure to realise his dreams, they would have been a martyrdom; but to the bitterness of pain and defeat were added, in the mystery of human things, the rebellion and treachery of an ungrateful son, and the unpardonable tyranny of his Chancellor to all whom the Emperor loved or cared for—and his own helplessness to protect or to punish. Insolence, intrigue, defamation, and defiance are never so detestable as when they are employed against the dying and by those who reckon on the security that the Angel of Death at the door will bring to their authors. There are black pages in Bismarck's record and black places in his character, but the blackest that no extenuation can obliterate are recorded in the three months from March 13 to June 15, 1888. And it is fitting, perhaps, that the chapter and verse should be supplied in the amazing pages of Busch's chronicles,[1] though Busch's revelations are only a fragment of the evidence. Richter's speech in the Prussian Landtag (May 27), evoked by the infamous article on 'Petticoat Government,' was a scathing exposure of the campaign of libel opened (certainly with Bismarck's knowledge, probably at his inspiration) by the Conservative and National Liberal parties, and also of the intimidation and bribery practised by the government officials. It led to the Imperial rescript enjoining freedom at the elections, which caused Puttkamer's dismissal (June 8). Bismarck promptly paid a visit to, and then entertained the dismissed minister at a dinner at the Imperial Chancery (June 11).[2] The Emperor was known

---

[1] Busch, *Bismarck, Secret Pages*, see particularly iii. pp.163-189 (Eng. ed.). ' Circumstances here, notes Hohenlohe laconically on May 26, at Berlin, 'displeased me intensely. It is a pity that I could not retire now as a strong protest against all these goings on.' Hohenlohe was an honourable gentleman.

[2] There is considerable evidence that Bismarck really desired Puttkamer's dismissal, and characteristically placed the odium on the Emperor, taking care to represent it as an 'English' and 'feminine' intrigue.

to be dying—he could not be openly disobeyed, but he could be insulted and defied, with impunity. Such was Bismarck's gratitude for the three critical occasions in which the Emperor, as Crown Prince, in 1866, 1870, and 1879, had supported the Minister's policy against the obstinacy of the sovereign. The truth was, as Hohenlohe records (December 15, 1889); 'remarkable to me was the deep aversion which he (Bismarck) has for the Emperor Frederick. He declared him an egotistical, cold man, and said he had no heart.' Comment on such verdict is unnecessary. When, as so often, he was mastered by personal hate, which coincided with a fundamental political antagonism, there were no limits to Bismarck's unscrupulous brutality. One subject of bitter controversy, involving foreign policy, had arisen in these tragic three months—the proposed marriage between the Princess Victoria, the Emperor's daughter, and Prince Alexander of Battenberg. Since the secret Reinsurance Treaty, Bismarck was determined in every way to keep on good terms with the Tsar. The envenomed hostility of the Tsar to Prince Alexander had been proclaimed broadcast to the world in the preceding two years. In the summer of 1888 Prince Alexander no longer ruled in the united Bulgarias, and there was no chance of his ever being in authority again at Sofia. Bismarck vetoed the marriage, for the simple reason that it would stir such a ferocity of resentment in the Tsar as to endanger, if not snap, the *entente* of 1887. He chose to represent the proposal in the press and in official circles as a Machiavellian effort of England to control German policy for English ends, to embroil Germany and Russia for English ends, and to manipulate the destinies of Bulgaria for English purposes against the interests of Germany and Russia. The press under the Chancellor's control and in his pay had instructions to open a savage campaign against English interference in German affairs and in the Near East. And the instructions were obeyed with a scurrilous zest. If Bismarck did not know that this was untrue, he was very incompetent. But he was not incompetent, and the inference is obvious and indisputable. The marriage did not take place. But this was not a victory of an independent Germany over an intriguing and unscrupulous Great Britain. For, as we know now, the influence of Queen Victoria and Lord Salisbury were exerted precisely as Bismarck would have Germany believe they were not.

The accession of the Emperor William ii. on June 16, 1888—the year of the Three Emperors—opened up a wholly new situation. The new sovereign was in his twenty-ninth year, and teeming with energy, ideas, and masterfulness. Since 1887 he had been carefully instructed, at his grandfather's wish, in the mysteries of statecraft by Bismarck, and the effusive enthusiasm with which he proclaimed at the outset his desire to carry out his grandfather's (not his father's) policy with the aid of his grandfather's great Chancellor made the resignation that Bismarck had contemplated after the death of William i. superfluous. Germany was instructed to believe that the new sovereign would be in all things as obedient to Bismarck's advice and ripe experience as had been William i.

Bismarck himself believed it. A year later, in the autumn of 1889, when the Tsar was in Berlin and Bismarck emphasised his earnest desire that German policy should maintain a close co-operation with Russia, the Tsar pointedly asked, ' Are you sure of remaining in office ? ' ' Certainly, your Majesty,' Bismarck replied, ' I am absolutely sure of remaining in office all my life.' [1] That was on October 11. Five months later he had ceased to be Chancellor, and if any date must be selected for the commencement of the serious collision between Chancellor and Emperor it would be October 13,[2] two days after Bismarck's confident utterance, when a serious difference on foreign policy revealed itself. The publication by Geffcken (one of the Emperor Frederick's circle) of elaborate excerpts from the late emperor's diary in the *Deutsche Rundschau*, bearing particularly on the war of

---

[1] Bismarck related this to the *Neue Freie Presse*, which printed it in its issue of June 22, 1892. Down to the autumn of 1889, Hohenlohe repeatedly noted that the Emperor was 'entirely under the influence of the Chancellor.'

[2] In the conversation between the two, after the Tsar's departure, as recorded by Bismarck in the *Hamburger Nachrichten*, July 24, 1891.

1870, the foundation of the Empire and the Liberalism of the Crown Prince, created a great stir. Bismarck's 'Immediate Report' attacked the authenticity of the document, but as he admitted to Busch, whatever its authenticity, it must be treated as spurious because the record was damaging to the official version and the interest of the dynasty, and not least to Bismarck himself. Geffcken's prosecution was ordered, while Geffcken himself was arrested and sent to prison. 'The legend that the late Emperor was a Liberal, in sympathy with the Progressive party, was dangerous to the whole dynasty and must be destroyed.'

Geffcken's acquittal (January 4, 1882) by the Supreme Court was a damaging blow to Bismarck, which roused him to uncontrollable anger. He wished to institute 'disciplinary measures' against Geffcken in the University of Strasburg; or, in other words, to compel the University to deprive him of his chair. But, apart from this high-handed interference with academic and civic rights, how could a professor be dismissed for an alleged offence of which the highest tribunal in Germany had just acquitted him? The idea was proved to be legally impossible, but Bismarck's desire to crush Geffcken, as he had crushed Arnim, simply proved his intolerance of all opposition and all intellectual or political liberty. It proceeded from the same principles as the unrelenting pressure that he applied during 1888 and 1889 to the Swiss government in 'the Wohlgemüth affair,' to coerce the Federal authorities into collaborating with the German secret police, planted in Swiss territory, in hunting down German Socialists, driven out of Germany by the Anti-Socialist Law. The Swiss government very properly refused to comply with so unwarranted an intervention in the internal affairs of a Sovereign State. There followed a menacing correspondence in which Bismarck went so far as to threaten that Germany might decline to recognise any further the 'neutrality' of Switzerland defined by an international guarantee; but the Swiss, to Bismarck's anger, declined to be browbeaten by their powerful neighbour. 'He,' (Bismarck) Hohenlohe noted in the Geffcken affair, 'gave me the impression of a man not quite sound mentally' (January 25, 1889). He repeats the remark with reference to the Swiss. 'Even Herbert Bismarck,' he notes (June 24), 'said he could no longer understand his father, and many people were beginning to think that he was no longer quite sane.' The German soldier chiefs were seriously troubled. All their military plans for a war in which Germany might be involved with France were drawn on the assumption of a friendly and neutral Switzerland. Switzerland driven into the arms of France would dislocate the strategical ideas that the great General Staff, in its continuous study of the European situation, was always working out in the light of every fresh political development. Bismarck was, indeed, as sane as was Napoleon I. in his later years, but with both men uncontrolled power and overweening confidence in their genius brought out all the latent despotism that from the very first was embedded in their political principles and their interpretation of life ; and with both resentment concentrated in a personal hatred of the individual who symbolised the opposition. Bismarck only desired to treat Geffcken as Napoleon treated Mme. de Staël or the Duc D'Enghien. The world must be made safe for autocracy.[1]

The plain truth was that after June 1888 the conditions which had made the Bismarckian system workable and possible were suddenly reversed. Bismarck and Germany had grown accustomed to the rule of an emperor never fitted by his gifts to be a great master either of administration or of policy, who in 1871 was in his seventy-fourth year, and with every year was obliged to surrender more and more of power and control to the adviser whose

---

[1] No less characteristic of Bismarckian methods and manners and of the 'anti-English' campaign was the revival in the controlled German press of the charge that Sir R. Morier, then British Ambassador at Petersburg, had in 1870, when he was British minister at Darmstadt, betrayed to the French at Metz important military information damaging to the German operations. Morier publicly refuted this infamous and absurd libel, proving by a letter of Marshal Bazaine that it was a lie ; but Count Herbert Bismarck, though requested to do so, declined officially to disavow it, or, when challenged, to produce any evidence in its support; with the result that, to this day it is still believed in educated quarters in Germany.

genius, amazing capacity for work, and complete accord
with his sovereign in the general principles of government
inspired a deep confidence. Bismarck had thus syndicated
in himself both the formidable powers of the Imperial
Chancellorship and the still more formidable powers of the
Emperor and Prussian King. The new Emperor was
young, versatile, and fired by a devouring activity. Had
he been a constitutional sovereign he would not have
been prepared to step on to the shelf during the best years
of his life. But he was not a constitutional sovereign.
William II. had been born and bred in the militarist
atmosphere of the Hohenzollern Court, and he had been
trained in the theory, sedulously enforced since 1847 by
no one more than by Bismarck himself, that the Prussian
monarch personally governed, and that the Prussian
Crown was not the idle ornament of a constitutional
building, but the living and operative force in the mechanism of the State. 'If a lion knew its own strength,'
Wolsey remarked of the young Henry VIII., 'hard it were
to rule him.' There were, in fact, practically no limits
to what the Emperor, with the help of the Prussian Crown,
could do, if he chose to exercise to its full all the latent
power in the prerogative, prestige, and influence of the
Imperial and Prussian Monarchy. William II. took some
months to discover what an unexplored and inexhaustible
heritage had fallen to him—a heritage enriched by
Bismarck's efforts for a quarter of a century. Therein lay
the irony of the situation. Had Bismarck been the Parlia-
ment-made minister of a constitutional sovereign, whose
ministerial position rested on a national mandate expressed
through a representative assembly to which he was responsible, it would have been William II. not Bismarck who
must have given way. Bismarck had indeed the confidence
of the nation. A plebiscite in 1890 would have retained
him in office till death came. But the nation could not
save him in 1890, nor could it bring him back. Once he
had lost the support of the Crown he was powerless. He
could not appeal to the Reichstag nor to the Federal
Council, still less to the nation by a general election. He
must either resign or be dismissed. He could not even

advise his Imperial Majesty whom the Crown should invite to be its chief adviser in his place. And it is in the record that the man who all his life had fought against the conception of an electro-plated royalism, and against a kingship emasculated by English Liberalism, should later denounce this subservience to a personal monarchy as ' Byzantinism and Cæsar worship.'

There was also more even than this in the situation that was bitter. William II. was young. He could toil and travel as only the young can. Age has its compensations and its rewards, but not all its maturity of wisdom and experience can find a substitute for the recuperative vigour of manhood and womanhood in their prime. Bismarck could recall the felicity of the time when after a day at his desk he could swim in the moonlit waters of the Rhine, snatch a couple of hours of sleep, and then fling himself into work again or wear out a fiery horse in the exultant freshness of youth and the joy of life. He could do it no longer. He told the Reichstag in 1889 that he was obliged severely to limit his efforts and concentrate on the important and the essential. He now fought a losing battle with the Emperor—ebbing forces on the one side against vitality on the other. For all that, he was not prepared to let go. The more his grip slackened, the more fiercely did he demand submissive obedience to his autocratic will. It is a characteristic that history can exemplify fifty times over that the strong-willed who have long held unquestioned sway may lose, as the chariot of time drives remorselessly on, everything but the strength of their will. The appetite for domination waxes precisely as the capacity to gratify it wanes. The bitterest punishment indeed that the years can bring to some men and women is the fear and the resentment of rivals in power.

A new epoch had arrived in Germany which knew and reverenced Bismarck, but Bismarck neither knew nor reverenced it. William II. was a child of the new epoch. Bismarck had taught Germany to be strong and how to be strong. He had placed the Empire on the pinnacle of Continental power, and new worlds had swum into its

ken. The young Imperial Germany of 1888 desired to
prove that it was as strong, as great, as ambitious, and as
saturated with the realism of life as the Germany that had
overthrown Vienna and the Babylon of France. It was
grateful for Bismarck's achievements ; Bismarck summed
up for it all that was mighty in Germanism ; the ends
that Bismarck defined must pass with Bismarck himself ;
but Bismarckian methods and the Bismarckian gospel were
imperishable and could not be superseded. The profoundest homage that could be paid to the master was to
apply the principles and methods of Bismarckian statecraft to the problems of the future. The Bismarckian
Empire that was the State, incarnating Continental Power,
must be transformed into the World-Empire that incarnated World-Power. Nothing must happen in the world
within or without Europe in which Germany had not
the deciding voice. Bismarckianism not Bismarck was
the model. In the magician's magic more than in the
magician himself lay the essential secret of success. Round
the Emperor collected the new Germany. Fear, jealousy,
ambition, revenge—the human appetites and carnal forces
that find their most nourishing environment in the court
of a militarist personal monarchy added their unlovely
stimulus. Bismarck had made many enemies, whose enmity
was all the stronger because it had been so impotent.
The Chancellor was not popular at the Federated Courts—
neither at Stuttgart, Munich, Dresden, nor Karlsruhe—
the soldier ' demi-gods,' the Clericals, the anti-Semites,
the Lutheran Conservatives, the great industrials were
quite ready to salute as they saw the Chancellor depart ;
the Liberals and Radicals and Socialists had no reason
to love the Minister-President, for fate and Bismarck
had killed Liberalism. The German people alone was
Bismarck's most loyal ally, and the German people
through its representatives had been the accomplice in
the blunder by which the German people was excluded
from deciding in hours of crisis who should govern in
their name.

In the confidential circles of the monarchy and of the
official civil and military bureaucracy—the men who

governed and whom Bismarck had taught to regard the Reichstag as the House of Phrases, a statutory but useless appendage to the machinery of Power—it became clear that the iron Titan of Friedrichsruhe planned for the perpetuity of the Bismarckian autocracy. The House of Bismarck was to hold an unbroken mayoralty of the palace over, rather than under, the House of Hohenzollern. Count Herbert Bismarck, carefully trained in affairs of State, and since 1886 Foreign Secretary under the Chancellor, was obviously destined to sit in the Wilhelmstrasse in his father's chair. Herbert Bismarck had capacity and considerable powers of work. He modelled himself on his father as capable sons of great men are entitled to do. But he endeavoured to prove, not that he was a chip of the old block, but the old block itself by imitating and exaggerating with repellent fidelity all the worst defects in his father's character—his brutality, coarseness, dictatorial insolence, and unscrupulous disregard of the conventions of decent existence. His manners were insufferable and a byword.[1] Men were prepared to endure much from the Chancellor who had genius and achieved miracles. They were not prepared to endure the intolerable from one who was not a genius and had done nothing remarkable (except be outwitted in colonial negotiations by Lords Granville and Rosebery).

During 1888 and 1889 Bismarck was very little in Berlin. Most of his time was spent at Varzin and Friedrichsruhe, and it was at his country seats that the unending visitors found the Chancellor and did their business. His absence from the capital was not wholly the result of old age. In Herbert Bismarck at the Chancery the father had a devoted representative, and the Empire could be governed on Bismarckian lines almost as easily from Friedrichsruhe as from the Wilhelmstrasse. The Chancellor, however,

---

[1] 'I never go to Paris except in war time,' Herbert Bismarck is reputed to have replied to a French diplomatist. One of many examples can be cited. 'H. Bismarck had had the effrontery to say to the Prince of Wales that an emperor who could not talk was not fit to reign. The Prince had said that, had he not valued the good relations between England and Germany he would have thrown him out of the room.'—(*Hohenlohe Memoirs*, June 22, 1888). Herbert Bismarck's conduct in the controversy with Sir R. Morier is another good example of his insolence, boorishness, and dishonourable conduct.

did not realise that under a young Emperor, bent on probing into every department of State, and leaving an Imperial imprint upon it, the loss of touch with the personalities, the ministers and the forces of politics was a grave disadvantage. Nor did he appreciate the significance of the growing volume of criticism that found in these prolonged absences a substantial reason for a change.

Thus by the autumn of 1889 the whole Bismarckian system was being challenged—and by the Emperor. For William II. had inaugurated his reign by a series of travels. He was indefatigable in visiting all parts of Germany and learned much thereby. He went to Petersburg, Vienna, London, Athens, and most remarkable of all, to Constantinople, the first European sovereign to be received as a guest by an Ottoman Sultan. And in these visits what he learned about foreign policy caused him to think and think again. Bismarck resented these continuous journeys, and expressed his resentment in remarks that travelled to the travelling sovereign. They made the Emperor more important than Bismarck, and they did not assist the peculiar methods by which Bismarckian foreign policy was maintained. The old Emperor had been told just as much as the Chancellor thought fit ; the young Emperor was insisting on knowing what he thought fit—and he made discoveries, had ideas, and ' interfered.'

Bismarck's foreign policy was never easy to understand. It certainly needed a great deal of explanation in the last two years of his Chancellorship. Although Carnot's election to the Presidency and the slow pricking of the Boulanger bubble had greatly eased the situation in France, Bismarck had continued a deliberate policy of provocation. The new administrative order forbidding entry into Alsace-Lorraine except to those provided with a passport, viséd at the German embassy at Paris, coupled with the semi-official explanation that ' Germany did not desire war, but only more distant relations with France,' provoked a fresh Press campaign on both sides of the frontier. The order seemed to cool heads a wanton provocation. The tension in the Near East had also been relieved, though Russian resentment against Bulgaria continued unabated. But Russo-German relations showed no improvement, despite the secret reinsurance ; and the German Staff, impressed with the excellence of the French army and the completeness of French armaments, was very anxious about the outlook when the exhibition of '89 at Paris was over. Austrian policy was no less disquieting, for Austria desired to recognise Prince Ferdinand in Bulgaria, and this might lead to a rupture with Russia. The quotation of a Bulgarian loan on the Viennese exchange evoked an explosion of wrath at Petersburg that was very significant. Count Kalnoky's visit to Friedrichsruhe (November 3), shortly after the Tsar had visited Berlin, and while the Emperor William was at Constantinople caused justifiable speculation in every capital. A crisis had been reached alike in the relations of Austria and Germany and of Austria and Russia, and Bulgaria, as usual, was at the bottom of the trouble.

To the Emperor and his circle the position seemed to be very clear. They professed to be ' perplexed ' by the Chancellor's inexplicable leanings now to Austria, now to Russia, and they convinced themselves that Bismarck, if it came to a choice between Austria and Russia, would ' desert ' Austria, throw over the Dual Alliance, and let Austria fight alone with Russia while Germany stood by : whereas the Emperor was determined to stand by Austria, even at the cost of a war with both France and Russia. Bismarck's ' vacillations ' were interpreted as proofs either of senility or dishonesty. Things were being kept back from the Emperor—which is very probable.

The ' veerings ' may not have been due either to senility or to dishonesty. Since 1871 Bismarck's policy had turned on maintaining a very delicate equipoise between Austria and Russia, (just as since 1882 he had maintained a delicate equipoise between Italy and Austria) with Germany as the controller of the levers, and he had accomplished the difficult task by disregard of scruples, by prestige and an extraordinary intuition into the shifting phases of an ever-shifting situation. He had persistently refused to commit Germany by unlimited pledges to either side, and he was confident that no one but himself

could achieve the perpetual miracle of preventing a war
in the Near East. Nor could he have a partner in the
task—he must have *carte blanche* and unlimited trust from
his sovereign.

Apparently now he was ready to let Russia, if need be,
intervene in Bulgaria to reassert her waning authority,
while assuring to Austria her sphere of influence in Serbia.
But he was not ready either to provoke Russia by recognising Prince Ferdinand, or to give Vienna a free hand to
drag Germany in to cover Austria's blunders or to win
Austria's battles. The improved relations with Great
Britain, consequent on the Emperor's visit to London,
would result in shifting the odium of vetoing Russia from
Germany on to a joint *entente* between Great Britain and
Austria. 'We shall begin no war either with Russia or
France,' he explicitly told Prince Hohenlohe (December
15, 1889). Moreover, Bismarck was gravely perturbed
by the internal condition of Austria. The ' ally ' might
crack up internally, and where would Germany be then ?

It is tempting to infer that a new orientation of German
policy was taking definite shape in the Emperor's circle.
The dynastic connection, sealed by the marriage of the
Emperor's sister with the heir to the Greek throne, the
Duke of Sparta, the much advertised journey to Constantinople, with its hint of protection to Abdul Hamid
against all and sundry, and the recent completion of the
railways to Salonica and Constantinople, which laid direct
communication via Belgrade from Vienna both to the
Ægean and the Dardanelles, were the beginning of a new
epoch. The plan of substituting Germany for Russia
as the leading power at Constantinople, of drawing the
new Bulgaria slowly and surely into the German sphere
of influence, of assigning Salonica definitely as the Austrian
goal with Serbia under a benevolent Habsburg thumb,
and of a general German protectorate over the Balkans
with Athens as one of its bases and the Hohenzollern in
Roumania as another, had a beginning; and all the evidence
available supports the hypothesis that that beginning must
be placed in 1889. Such a policy, however tentative at
first, meant at some future date something like a breach

with Russia and a closer co-operation with Austria.   The
identification of Austrian and German objects would be
tolerably secure if it were accompanied by a clear understanding with Great Britain, with its reflex action on Italy,
and its reflex action upon Austria.   The Anglo-German
agreement of July 1, 1890, is on record, and Chancellor
Caprivi who concluded it refused to renew the Secret
Insurance Treaty of 1887.   What actually lay behind
these two significant facts is a matter of inference, not of
proof.   But the new policy was certainly not Bismarckian.
It was a reversal of Bismarck's policy.   His resistance to
it was inevitable, if for no other reason than that it was
an abandonment of Centralism as he understood it ;   and
it would lead straight to a Russo-French *entente*, culminating in an alliance.   Moreover Bismarck foresaw
that this ' world policy,' substituted for the Centralism
that he had created and maintained so successfully, would
lead, must indeed lead, if logically pursued, to an antagonism between Great Britain and Germany.   That was
fatal to the Bismarckian system.   Germany, which had
isolated both its friends and its foes, was thereby ensuring
its own isolation by provoking an anti-German coalition.[1]

The principles of Bismarck's home policy were no less
in grave danger.   The Chancellor's last speech in the
Reichstag (though neither he nor his audience dreamed
it would be his last) was on May 18, 1889, on the Old Age
Pension Bill.   The whole argument was a concentrated
indictment of Liberalism and Socialism, and a defence of
Conservatism, concluding with a menacing challenge to the

---

[1] Cp. the significant passage in *Hohenlohe Memoirs*, ii. p. 413 (March 31,
1890).   'The Emperor told the generals that Russia wished to begin a military
occupation of Bulgaria, and to assure herself of the neutrality of Germany in the
meantime.   He said that he had promised the Emperor of Austria to be a loyal
ally and he would keep his word.   The occupation of Bulgaria by the Russians
would mean war with Austria, and he could not leave Austria in the lurch.
. . . Bismarck was ready to abandon Austria. . . . From this point of view I
understand Bismarck's statement when he said that the Emperor was conducting
his policy in the manner of Friedrich William IV.   This is the black cloud on
the horizon.'   Cp. the entry for January 14, 1895 (ii. p. 462) : ' We (Bismarck
and Hohenlohe at Friedrichsruhe) talked . . . of the (secret) treaty with Russia
which Caprivi had not renewed because the policy it led to was too complicated
for him.   The difficulty of my position (Hohenlohe was about to become
Chancellor) lay in the sudden decisions of his Majesty.'

Liberal and Democratic parties : ' To the members of the
Conservative party alone—and I include the National
Liberals and the Centre in the Conservatives—to these
members alone have I explanations to offer : with all the
others I have to fight—that is another matter ; and I
would beg them especially to cut themselves adrift from
all common action with Socialists, Poles, Guelphs, Alsatian
Frenchmen, yes, and with the Liberals also.' The solid
cartel that gave him a majority was quite ready to act
on the advice ; it was prepared to vote for all repressive
measures and to fight with the Chancellor against every
form of Liberalism. What failed Bismarck now was not
the government majority but the Crown.

The Chancellor spent the autumn of 1889 in the country.
The anti-Socialist law was due for renewal ; and Bismarck
wished it to be made permanent, with added powers to
expel Socialist agitators and to suppress in perpetuity
Socialist papers. He was summoned by telegram from
Count Herbert Bismarck to return to the capital on
January 23, 1890, where he found the ministers very
uneasy at the strong opposition in the Reichstag to the
anti-Socialist law as drafted by the government. On
January 24 he resigned the Ministry of Commerce. The
Emperor desired conciliation with, and concessions to,
the Socialists, and two Imperial rescripts announcing this
policy, to be consummated by an international conference
on Labour and Social Problems, were ready for publication.
They were, in fact, a reversal of Bismarck's policy, and
had been prepared in his absence. When they appeared
they lacked the customary ministerial counter-signature
(February 4)—the first official documents for twenty-
seven years published without the counter-signature of
the Chancellor or Minister-President. On January 25
no official indication was given to the Conservative party
how to vote on the anti-Socialist Bill. The Conservatives,
regarding the measure, from which the expulsion clauses
had been struck out, as too lenient, went into the same
lobby as the Radicals and the Centre, and the anti-Socialist
law was rejected by 169 to 98 votes. All Berlin now knew
that it was confronted with a real ' Chancellor Crisis.'

Foreign policy, however, was the main cause of the collision. The explicit reports of Russian armaments and movements of troops perturbed Vienna and the German General Staff. The Emperor was determined to convince Austria that Germany was on her side—Bismarck stubbornly resisted any steps to support Austria and thereby alienate Russia : and the Emperor accused him of suppressing information in the Foreign Office.

The quarrel over home policy could have been settled, but the conflict over foreign policy cut down to fundamentals. A compromise was impossible. Bismarck's system was in issue. The general election, however, turned on the new Social and Labour policy. Bismarck declined to organise a governmental campaign ; he had quarrelled both with the Emperor and his colleagues, and the results were a rout for the cartel. The Conservatives lost 36, the National Liberals, 52 seats ; the Liberals gained 30, the Socialists, 24 seats. The cartel of 1887 was dissolved, although the Clerical Centre returned in undiminished strength. Bismarck now made a subtle move. Recognising that the Crown was undermining his presidential pre-eminence by uniting the ministers against him, he demanded that the Cabinet order of September 8, 1852, should be vigorously enforced. This order, requiring all ministers to submit their departmental business to the Minister-President before submitting it to the Crown, practically forbade all independent relations between the ministers and the Crown, and made the Minister-President the sole constitutional avenue of communication with the sovereign. Bismarck had always acted on it, though in the last ten years his frequent absences had required its relaxation. But such had been his prestige that the relaxation had not involved any real diminution of his authority in all essentials of governmental action. It was different now, when Bismarck realised that the King-Emperor aimed at uniting the ministerial cabinet against its constitutional chief. To the Emperor the order was an odious restriction on his prerogative. It meant that he could only confer with his ministers by and through a Minister-President, hostile to his policy and his ideas, alike in home and foreign affairs. Accordingly he demanded that the Minister-President should advise him to rescind the order. The dispute was a forcible illustration of Bismarck's warning to the Progressive Party in 1862 : ' Questions of right (*Rechtfragen*) in the long run become questions of might (*Machtfragen*).' The Emperor told Hohenlohe that February and March were for him ' a beastly time,' and that it had become ' a question whether the Bismarck dynasty or the Hohenzollern dynasty should rule.'

For Bismarck the issues were simple, but fundamental. His whole system was challenged. As Minister-President he was to be reduced to a position of equality with colleagues placed in complete independence in their relations with himself and with the Crown ; a policy in home affairs was to be carried out through the ministers of the Interior and Finance which reversed all his principles ; as Chancellor he was expected to carry out a foreign policy in flat contradiction to his convictions and ideas. The close connection between home and foreign policy—the keystone of his system and his success—was to be snapped ; alike in the Prussian Landtag and the Imperial Reichstag he would speak without any control over parties or any security that the votes would not be influenced by Imperial intrigues or ministerial pressure, unfavourable to himself. In the daily intercourse with the representatives of foreign governments he could no longer invite their confidence or express his own. Moltke had resigned his post as Chief of the General Staff. The new chief, Waldersee, in Bismarck's judgment was a second-rate soldier and an intriguing politician in the hands of a ' military ring ' bent on controlling the civil authority. In a word, the Chancellor and Minister-President would have lost all his rights to co-ordinate strategy and policy. The Emperor, he told more than one confidant, ' now wishes to reign alone —to be his own Chancellor and Minister-President.' It was impossible that Bismarck could accept after twenty-seven years of power a position that was a personal humiliation, a reversal of his policy, and a reduction to impotence. ' I cannot serve,' he said, ' on my knees ' (*Ich kann nicht mit Proskynesis dienen*). The final touch was given on March 14. Windthorst who wished to consult the Chancellor about the forthcoming session was received 'in audience' by Bismarck. What passed between them—whether Bismarck suggested a coalition between the shattered Conservatives and the Clericals, cemented by a final repeal of the May Laws—is uncertain and matters little. ' I come,' Windthorst observed, ' from the political deathbed of a great man.' The next day the Emperor in person demanded an explanation of what had passed, and Bismarck was dragged from his sleep to wait upon the unexpected visitor. ' It was all that Bismarck could do,' the Emperor subsequently related, ' to refrain from throwing the inkpot at my head.' Bismarck was no less certain that the Emperor lost his temper even more completely than he did himself. He refused to give the information demanded. The discussions with Windthorst or other leaders of parties were personal and confidential, and could not be controlled by the Crown, not even if the Crown commanded. According to one source, Bismarck drawing himself up to his full height asserted that he had received Windthorst as a gentleman had the right to receive his friends in his own house, and then he added that ' the orders of the Sovereign stopped at the door of the Princess's drawing-room.' The phrase may be an invention, but it exactly expressed Bismarck's attitude. The memorable conversation was not one between Minister and Emperor, but between the Prussian Junker of Schönhausen, Varzin, and Friedrichsruhe, and the Elector of Brandenburg whom the Junker had made German Emperor.

Repeatedly pressed, Bismarck at last submitted his resignation. On March 20 the official Gazette announced that the Emperor had been graciously pleased to accept with profound regret the Chancellor's request to be relieved of his offices, and in return for his ' imperishable services ' conferred upon him the title of Duke of Lauenburg and Colonel-General, with the rank of Field-Marshal in the army. *Punch*, in one of the most famous of its famous cartoons which, curiously enough, delighted both Bismarck and William II., summed up the event with unerring felicity. 'The Pilot' who had steered the ship through so many storms and so many shoals, 'was dropped.' The Emperor henceforward intended to be Captain and Pilot in one.

Official Berlin heard the news, expected for so many months, with a sigh of profound relief : [1] but to Germany and the German nation the Emperor's dismissal of the man who summed up German power and represented the Empire in the Councils of the world—the greatest German political figure since the Middle Ages—was received with consternation and genuine sorrow. The old Emperor was dead ; Moltke in his ninetieth year was no longer the brain of the German army ; and now Bismarck had gone, removed neither by death nor incapacitated by sickness. The German nation knew that in the political sphere there was no one in experience, strength of character, prestige, or intellect fit to tie the latchet of Bismarck's shoe. With March 20, 1890, the heroic age had indeed ended.

Bismarck refused the title of Duke of Lauenburg. ' I prefer,' he said, ' to bear for the future the name and the title that I have borne up till now.' He paid a final call on Moltke and on the Empress Frederick. Prince Hohenlohe tells us that ' when the Empress asked whether she could do anything for him he merely said : " I ask only for sympathy ! " ' In the evening of March 28, a carriage drove up to the Royal Mausoleum at Charlottenburg where the Emperor William I. was buried ; a tall figure alighted, with some roses in his hand, and paced in the dusk through the garden in solitary silence, then entered the Mausoleum and laid the roses on the Emperor's tomb. A long pause followed. The figure slowly left the sanctuary and drove away. It was Bismarck. He had come to say farewell to the dead master whom he had served. From that master's grandson he would not accept a dukedom ;

---

[1] 'Each separate personality,' notes Hohenlohe on June 18, 1890, 'is now conscious of his own value. Formerly the individual was oppressed and restricted by the dominant influence of Prince Bismarck, but now they have all swelled out like sponges placed in water. This has its advantages but also its dangers. There is no unity of will.' On March 24, 1890, he had written : 'Stosch told me much about his quarrel with Bismarck and was as chirpy as a wren that he could now speak openly and that the great man was no longer to be teared. This comfortable feeling is universal here (in Berlin).'

for his imperial honours he cared nothing. But for William I. he had the silence of memories that lay too deep for words or tears, memories and a handful of roses.

Next day, March 29, accompanied by his wife and his son Count Herbert, who had resigned with him, he left Berlin. Ambassadors, ministers, generals, and an enormous crowd, were at the station. Every one was aware that one personage was wanting—the Emperor—and nobody missed him, least of all the ex-Chancellor. Could William II. have been on the platform he would have learned from the homage of the people that emperors might come and go, but for Germany, indeed for Europe, there was only one Bismarck, and there never could be another.

If there could be any doubt that a fundamental difference of opinion on the principles, methods, and objects of foreign policy was the main, though not the sole, cause of the quarrel between Emperor and Chancellor the criticisms, denunciations, and warnings of Bismarck from the date of his dismissal practically till his last illness would convince the most obstinate sceptic. Sometimes made through interviews to journalists, carefully selected for the purpose, occasionally expressed in public replies to the addresses of ardent admirers or powerful organisations, but for the most part worked up in newspaper articles by ' inspired ' pens from material supplied by Bismarck in his solitude at Friedrichsruhe—these utterances constitute a ' Bismarck literature ' in themselves. They merit and repay a close study ; and German industry has facilitated in the volumes of Penzler and Hofmann their examination and collation. Every one in Germany was aware that in the columns of the *Leipziger Neueste Nachrichten*, the *Münchener Neueste Nachrichten*, and especially the *Hamburger Nachrichten* (under the able editorship of Julius Hartmeyer) the ex-Chancellor was speaking to the Germany that did not cease to regard him as the supreme oracle on all the affairs of Europe and of life. Veneration, gratitude, and affection heightened the homage to the fallen Titan in his lonely and morose grandeur.

The range of subjects is amazingly wide, and the treatment is rich in autobiographic reminiscences, in valuable additions to our historical knowledge, and in the matured criticism stamped with the unmistakable flavour and quality that personality tempered in the strife of a lifetime with great men and greater issues alone can impart— that specific flavour and quality which have given to Bismarck's letters and speeches a unique place in German literature. In many respects indeed the more weighty items in this remarkable collection strike a truer note and convey a more convincing sincerity than the Memoirs which, under pressure, Bismarck wrote late in life, and the value of which is somewhat impaired by faulty arrangement, omissions, contradictions, and, too often, slipshod displacement of dates and facts. From Penzler's and Hofmann's collections of Bismarckiana after March 1890, judiciously winnowed and critically pieced together, might easily be constructed a *Testament Politique*, picturing the statesman in his final stage, and epitomising the marrow and blood of his statecraft. Some day the scholar, it is hoped, will be found to confer the boon.

It is often asserted that Bismarck's judgments were inspired simply by hostility to his successors in the Wilhelmstrasse, and that this unquestionable jealousy and hatred deprive his criticisms of all weight. It would be truer to say that Bismarck was defending and explaining the principles of his policy from 1871 onwards, and that he viewed with profound misgiving the development of German policy under the ' New Course ' conducted by the Emperor and his advisers or instruments. He was deliberately providing a parallel and a contrast which is deeply instructive for the last decade of the nineteenth century. For example, shortly after his dismissal, the *Hamburger Nachrichten* (April 26, 1890) wrote :—

Austria cannot hope to obtain Germany's support for promoting her ambitious plans in the Balkan peninsula. These Austrian plans have never been encouraged by Germany as long as Germany's foreign policy was directed by Prince Bismarck. . . . Least of all is it Germany's business to support Austria's ambitions in the Balkans.

And again (September 29, 1890) :—

In the past, when the relations between Germany and Austria and between Germany and Russia were discussed, there were two points of danger : firstly, that German policy—or what would be worse, the German army—should be placed at the disposal of purely Austrian interests in the Balkans against Russia ; secondly, that Germany's relations with Russia should be endangered and brought to the breaking-point. . . . The Austro-German alliance does not demand that Germany should support Austria's Balkan interests against Russia. It only demands that Germany should assist Austria if her territories should be attacked by Russia.

And again (January 24, 1892) :—

The Austro-German alliance of 1879 contemplated only mutual defence against a possible attack. Hence Germany always pointed out in Vienna that the Austro-German alliance protected only the Dual Monarchy itself, but not its Balkan policy. With regard to the Balkans, Germany had unceasingly advised Austria to find protection by means of a separate treaty with the States interested in the Balkans, such as England and Italy. . . . By following the path upon which she has entered, Germany is in danger of gradually becoming dependent upon Austria, and in the end she may have to pay with her blood and treasure for the Balkan policy of Vienna. . . . Formerly the Triple Alliance existed as it does now, and its importance was increased by the fact that Germany had a free hand, directed it, and Europe. A crisis in Italy, a change of sovereign in Austria or the like may shake its foundations so greatly that, in spite of all written engagements, it will be impossible to maintain it. In that case Germany's position would become extremely serious, for in order not to become entirely isolated, she would be compelled to follow Austria's policy in the Balkans without reserve. Germany might get into the leading strings of another Power. . . .

These quotations might be indefinitely extended, but the point is admirably clear ; it is made still clearer by the following comment on the Triple Alliance (*Hamburger Nachrichten*, June 13, 1890) :—

The Austro-Italian Alliance is not equally favourable. Between Austria and Italy there are unadjusted differences, which are particularly to be found on the side of Italy, such as the anti-Austrian aspiration of the Irredentists. . . . The maintenance of the present relations between Austria and Italy must be the principal care of the diplomatists, especially as, if Italy for some reason or other should abandon the Triple Alliance, the Austrian army would be compelled to protect the Dual Monarchy against Italy . . . by the detachment of Italy, the Austro-German alliance would militarily lose so much that its value would become very problematical . . . as long as Germany, Austria-Hungary, and Italy are united in the Triple Alliance, and as long as these three States may reckon on the assistance of the English sea-power, the peace of Europe will not be broken. We must take care that friendly relations between Austria and Italy and between Italy and England shall be maintained. Besides, we must see that the Triple Alliance is restricted to its original scope, and that 'it is not allowed to serve those special interests which have nothing to do with it.

And again (May 18, 1892) :—

England's attitude towards the Triple Alliance depends not upon the Heligoland Treaty, but on Italy. If England is opposed to Germany, we can never reckon upon Italy's help.

In this connection, and also with reference to acute political controversies at the time (1895) Bismarck said in reply to an address :—

I wished to acquire Schleswig-Holstein, because unless we had that province we could not hope to have a German fleet. . . . I should consider it an exaggeration for Germany to compete with the French or the English navy. However, we must be strong enough on the sea to be able to deal with those second-rate powers which we cannot get at by land.

In September 1897, Maximilian Harden reproduced in his paper Die Zukunft, the following opinion from Bismarck :—

I have never been in favour of a colonial policy of conquest similar to that pursued by France. As far as one can see, the most important thing for Germany is a strong and reliable army, provided with the best weapons. I am of Moltke's opinion, that we shall have to fight on the continent of Europe for the possession of colonies.

And in one of the very latest of his pronouncements

(*Leipziger Neueste Nachrichten*, December 8, 1897)
Bismarck said :—

Nothing could be more strongly opposed to Germany's interest
than to enter upon more or less daring and adventurous enterprises,
guided merely by the desire to have a finger in every pie, to flatter
the vanity of the nation, or to please the ambitions of those who
rule it. To carry on a policy of prestige would be more in accordance with the French than the German character. In order to
acquire prestige, France has gone to Algiers, Tunis, Mexico, and
Madagascar. If Germany should ever follow a similar policy, she
would not promote any German interests, but would endanger the
welfare of the Empire and its position in Europe.

The reference to *Weltpolitik* and *Weltmacht* is unmistakable. Let it be simply noted that two years after
Bismarck's death Von der Goltz, who was not the victim
of journalistic Chauvinism but a scientific exponent of
policy, wrote :—

We must contradict the frequently expressed opinion that a war
between Germany and Great Britain is impossible . . . the
material basis of our power is large enough to enable us to destroy
the present superiority of Great Britain.

Von der Goltz only expressed what the advocates of
colonialism urged :—

The old century saw a German Europe. The new one shall see
a German world. . . . We do not require a fleet against France or
Russia. . . . We require a fleet only against England.

It is instructive to place such utterances beside those of
Bismarck in the Reichstag in 1885 and in 1889 (quoted on
page 420). The antithesis needs no comment. But if the
ex-Chancellor could fairly have said that the generation
which succeeded him had forgotten that Germany still
had to live in Europe with three or more neighbours, and
had disregarded his teaching, his principles, and his sense
of limits, the neo-Bismarckians could no less fairly retort
that they were only applying to new spheres the principles
and the methods that the master had taught were the only
successful and justifiable weapon of policy. Bismarckian
principles of statecraft and ends of policy cannot be limited

to a defined programme and then denounced as illegitimate, because they are held to be equally applicable to all spheres of action, in which the State is striving to secure the conditions on which it wishes to live with its neighbours. If Bismarck spent his years after 1890 in warning Germany against the dangers inherent in the doctrine and policy he had himself enforced, to that extent he did valuable service. But the young generation of the new Germany, felt by a true and inexorable logic which it had learned from the ex-Chancellor that if a State's needs constitute its rights, and if the realisation of those rights can only be achieved by force, a world-empire could be made, and only be made, by precisely the same methods as had made the German Empire, and by none other. The State that is the incarnation of Power ceases to lose its title to exist if it places limitations on Power derived from principles which are the negation of those on which it has been deliberately based. For power and force are, by implication, like the sovereignty defined by the jurist, intrinsically illimitable and indivisible, and provide, if at all, their own law and justification. Similarly in the warnings against the peril for Germany of Austria's Balkanism, Bismarck was largely responsible for the situation out of which Austrian Balkanism was created. There were mainly two causes in operation. The unification of Germany gave a tremendous impetus to Nationalism, which found its expression for South-Eastern Europe in the formula of ' The Balkans for the Balkan peoples.' But unless the Dual Monarchy controlled those Balkan nationalities their nationalism was dangerous, if not fatal, to the Austria-Hungarian Empire. Either Austria must subordinate Balkan nationalism to Austrianism or the nationalities would disintegrate the Habsburg Empire in the interests of Balkan, and particularly Slav, nationalism. The end of the Ottoman Empire in Europe meant the beginning of a new phase of the Austrian problem, and the most critical since the Ottoman Turk had crossed the Danube. Secondly, when Bismarck thrust Austria out of Germany, and also out of Italy, he made an Austrian expansion south-eastwards inevitable. Previously to 1866 Austria had always regarded the German

sphere as her chief concern. But after 1866, the diversion
of Austria was as essential to the maintenance of the
German Empire of 1871 as was the diversion of France or
of Russia. This is only another way of saying that when
Bismarck finally abandoned in 1859 the programme of the
Great Germany party, and adopted the programme of the
Small Germany party, he left unsolved the problem with
which Germany and Europe wrestled since the dissolution
in 1806 of the old Holy Roman Empire of the German
nation. Bismarck, as we have seen, convinced himself that
the Great Germany solution of the problem was not practicable, because it was incompatible with a Prussian supremacy in a united Germany—and on that argument it is
difficult to prove that his judgment erred—but the solution
which he achieved left the Germany that he had made still
confronted with the original and permanent difficulties.
The Germans in Austria had a broad common interest
with the Germany from which they were excluded; and
the German Empire which shut the Austrian Germans
out could not, on any argument of policy, interest,
nationalism, or safety, remain indifferent to the destinies
of a German Austria. Bismarck created a safety valve in
the Dual Alliance, which linked the Habsburg and Hohenzollern monarchies, and the divided Germans of the
Hohenzollern and Austrian empires in a united political
co-operation for common German ends. In reality, this
co-operation shelved rather than settled the problem, as the
sequel proved. The Central Europe that Bismarck created
was not purely Germanic. It rested not on German
nationalism, but on a German domination of a strategic
area. It included in its framework alien and suppressed elements alike in Schleswig-Holstein, Alsace-Lorraine, Prussian
Poland, and Austrian Galicia. Above all, in Hungary and
the relations of the Magyars to the non-Magyar and non-
German races in the Dual Empire, it avowedly identified a
German with a Magyar domination. The inevitable result
was that the safety of the complex and ill-knit Austrian
Empire became essential to the German Empire. Germany was confronted with the dilemma either of letting
Austria go her own independent way and thereby imperil-

ling both the western and eastern fronts of a united Germany, or of following Austria in a Balkan policy which entangled Germany in vast issues, outside of, and antagonistic to, her own specific German interests. To Bismarck's criticisms of German policy after 1890 there were not lacking in his own day powerful counter-critics, such as Holnstein, the silent *Éminence grise* of the Wilhelmstrasse, who pointed out that when Bismarck agreed to compensate Austria-Hungary with the occupation of Bosnia and Herzegovina he laid a mortgage on Germany which she could only repudiate by making Austria an open foe or only redeem by supporting Austrian Balkanism to the last reserves of the German army, if need be.

Nor were there lacking those who pointed out that Bismarck's ' moderation ' in 1866 was the original and decisive blunder. Two courses were open then, it was plainly argued after Bismarck's fall. The first was to have given the King and the soldiers *carte blanche* to roll Austria in the dust and to reduce the Habsburg sovereigns practically to the kingdom of Hungary, thereby making them the rulers of a non-German State outside a Greater Germany, with which an alliance, not an identity of interests, could have naturally followed. The second was to have retained German Austria, as before, in a reconstructed German confederation, in which the north, the south, and German Austria would have made a united but tripartite national polity. Such a confederation, it was suggested, would have kept all Germans in a single political organisation, so strong that all the groupings outside it of non-German States could not have affected either its stability or its capacity to exist as a power in Europe. What prevented the establishment of such a confederation was the refusal of Bismarck to dissolve Prussia in Germany, no less than his determination to impose Prussianism on as much of Germany as Prussian power could absorb and dominate. Hence the conclusion that Bismarck's solution was responsible for the difficulties that came to a head in 1890, and never ceased to be a wasting mortgage on Germany after Bismarck's fall.

Such criticism is not purely academic and dialectical;

however much it seems to ignore the practical difficulties
that its execution between 1862 and 1870 would have involved. It emphasises the historic truth that the Habsburg dynasty has been the gravest obstacle to the rational
and natural satisfaction of German Nationalism, as well as
to the formation of a truly German Empire from the age
of the Renaissance and the Reformation to the age of
Bismarck. The mediatisation of the particularist dynasties
in Hanover, Saxony, Württemberg, Baden, and Bavaria
was unquestionably essential to the creation of a federal
and national German State; but the mediatisation of
the Habsburg dynasty was still more essential, and would
have facilitated and federalised a national German State
even more effectually than the reduction of the Guelph,
Wittelsbach, or Saxon princely houses. Had the Austrian-
Hungarian Empire after 1866 been cut into two parts, and
the German part (deprived of its royal ruler) been associated with a new and greater Germany, while the non-
German parts were left to find a new and independent
existence on nationalist lines, Europe after 1866 might
well have had a happier life. It could certainly not have
had a less happy one than the course of things since 1871
provided. Be that as it may, the full consequences of the
Bismarckian solution of the German problem were only
working themselves out when Bismarck fell; nor can
Bismarck escape the full responsibility for those consequences, simply because he warned his successors that
they were making mistakes. It is not always the heirs
to a great legacy who mismanage the property. More frequently than is commonly supposed or admitted, the nature
of the property, the methods by which it has been acquired,
and the principles on which it has been administered prior
to the change of ownership impose obligations and involve
efforts, without which the inheritance itself must fall to
pieces. A generation which inherits what it has not made
by its own labours and self-sacrifice can be as reckless in the
ambition to spend as the heirs to a great estate, who have
been rocked, cradled, and dandled in the conviction that a
world they have not made exists for them, and not they for
the world. And in the case of Germany after 1890 the

heirs had been taught that to force, power, and reason of
State miracles were easy.

Bismarck's searchings of heart were by no means confined
to foreign policy. Earnestly meditating at Friedrichsruhe,
and convinced that the directors in the Reichskanzlerpalais
and at Imperial Headquarters were guilty of blunder after
blunder he diagnosed the causes of the mischief in two
plain conclusions—the royal autocracy and the complete
inability of a representative legislature to control policy.
The impotence of the Reichstag after 1890 was as conspicuous as the power of the imperial monarchy. In this
sphere, also, Bismarck pointed the moral very clearly in
more than one trenchant statement.

Thus (December 12, 1891) :—

The most disquieting feature for me is that the Reichstag has
abdicated its position. We suffer everywhere from the bureaucracy
. . . If the authority of the Reichstag declines, the bonds which
hold Germany together are weakened.

And still more emphatically (July 24, 1892) :—

To strengthen the Reichstag the responsibility of ministers
should be increased . . . the Chancellor's post may be abused to
such an extent that he becomes a mere secretary. . . . When I
became Minister, the Crown was threatened by the people. . . .
Hence I strove to strengthen the Crown against Parliament. Perhaps I went too far in that direction. We now require a balance of
power within Germany, and I believe that free criticism is indispensable to the monarchy. . . . If Parliament becomes powerless,
becomes a mere tool in the hands of the government, we return to
the régime of absolutism.

And again, in a reply to an address (July 30, 1892) :—

The basis of a constitutional monarchy is the co-operation of the
monarchical will with the convictions of the governed people. . . .
It is a dangerous experiment nowadays to strive after absolutism
in the centre of Europe . . . the wars which united Germany were
necessary . . . but Germany cannot conduct aggressive Cabinet
wars. Besides, a nation which can be forced into such wars does
not possess the right constitution . . . in building up the Empire
some kind of dictatorship was necessary, but that cannot be con-

sidered as a permanent feature. One's task can be completed only when Germany possesses a powerful Parliament which embodies our sense of unity.

Is this Saul among the prophets ? The young German of 1892 might pertinently ask, as he heard this passage : who made the Reichstag impotent ? who refused to allow ministerial responsibility to be established ? who made ' an aggressive Cabinet war ' in 1864, in 1866, and in 1870, and ' forced the nation into it ' because it did not ' possess the right constitution ' ? What indications were there in 1889 that the *empire autoritaire* created by Bismarck was intended by him to be a transient prelude to an *empire libéral* ? and finally, how could the Reichstag be made a truly effective political organ, except by rewriting the whole text of the Constitution imposed on Germany by Bismarck in 1866-7, and again in 1871 ? Was Bismarck suggesting in earnest that his whole work was to be undone and the fabric of the Empire reconstructed from top to bottom ?

The royal absolutism drew from the seer of Friedrichs-ruhe no less emphatic condemnation :—

Absolutism, he wrote in his *Memoirs*, would be the ideal form of government for a European State were not the King and his officials as other men to whom it is not given to reign with superhuman wisdom, insight, and justice. . . . If the King comes to any unfortunate decisions, no one can judge whether they are due to his own will or to the influences which various personalities of male and female gender—aides-de-camp, courtiers, and political intriguers, flatterers, chatterboxes, and tell-tales—may have upon the monarch. In the last resort the royal signature covers everything ; how it has been obtained no one ever knows.

On such a matter no one could speak with more intimate knowledge than Bismarck himself. Had he told us exactly how he obtained the royal signature between 1862 and 1888 the dark places in Prussian, German, and European history would be far less dark than they are. Or did he mean that autocracy was only useful when manipulated by a Bismarck ?

Sir Charles Dilke, who visited Friedrichsruhe, has recorded :—

As Bismarck mellowed with his pipes he told me that, though he was a high Tory, he had come to see the ills of absolutism, which to work well required the King to be an angel. 'Now,' he said, 'kings even when good have women round them, who, even if queens, govern them to their personal ends.'

And to Dilke he made another ' confession ' on the same point :—

People look on me as a monarchist. Were it all to come over again I would be republican and democrat ; the rule of kings is the rule of women ; the bad women are bad and the good are worse.

Allowance must be made for the bitterness of an old man, reflecting on the experience of a lifetime, who felt with justice that not once, but a dozen times, when it was in his power to have converted the Hohenzollern Crown into a constitutional and limited monarchy, he had resolutely fought to preserve intact the personal government and prerogatives of the Prussian Crown—and the power that he had preserved had been used to dismiss him and to reverse his policy. The ' confession,' apart from that, has the ring of the great Eldon's similar avowal. Unbending and stern Tory as he had been, Eldon avowed, in the old age that saw the triumphant passage of the Reform Act and the renaissance of Radicalism, that had he to begin all over again he would start as an ' Agitator.'

One other judgment of Bismarck's must find a place, in virtue of its penetrating intuition : ' Cavour, Crispi, even Krüger,' he told Dilke, ' were greater than myself. I had the State and the army behind me ; these men had nothing.' The fact emphasised is indisputable ; but had Bismarck explained how his predecessors in Prussia no less than himself had the State and the army behind them and had achieved nothing, he would have destroyed the truth of the conclusion. It was not the Prussian State nor the Prussian army, nor even the Prussian monarchy that made Bismarck's achievement what it was. If political genius could be so easily resolved into the instruments that it employs, history would shed not only its mysteries and riddles but all its power to inspire, to enthrall, and to instruct.

It is neither possible nor desirable here to embark further on the controversy that has divided Germany since Bismarck's death in 1898—the alluring question whether his successors deliberately departed from his policy, or whether their course from 1898 to 1914 was simply the logical and inevitable development of Bismarck's work. The issues raised are too complicated and too vast.

Even if the material and the perspective for framing an impartial judgment were available, a later generation will be able more dispassionately and with more utility to decide ; and a biographical study of statesmanship, that already belongs to the past, is obliged to avoid the danger of being warped by the introduction of arguments and controversies, however fascinating, urgent, and important, yet demonstrably irrelevant and misleading. So much will fairly be conceded by all students whether of Bismarck himself alone or of German policy under Caprivi, Hohenlohe, Bülow, and Bethmann-Hollweg. Of Bismarck the man and the statesman it is possible to write *sine ira et studio*. It is no less legitimate to conclude that with his fall from power a clearly marked epoch was closed, and to express the confident judgment that the historian of the future will see in the year 1890 the end of a period, as unmistakably as we can see now that with Richelieu, with Walpole, with Frederick the Great, and with Metternich, a system, and not merely a man, definitely ended. What the characteristics of that system were and how inextricably they were interwoven with the personality and principles of the man it has been the purpose of this biographical study to set forth. It is unnecessary to compile a laboured coda from characteristics sufficiently emphasised in the preceding pages. The import, even the value, of Bismarck's achievement will be very variously interpreted and judged by different observers ; nor is it possible for the critic, who does not belong to Bismarck's race and state, completely to

assimilate the point of view with which the German mind
is saturated. By Europe outside Germany, Bismarck will
always be viewed from an angle of vision different from that
of the German. The unification of Germany, the establishment of a German hegemony on the Continent, the Central
Europe, the armed peace imposed on and by Nationalism
in arms, the defeat of Liberalism and of democratic self-
government, the doctrine of the State as the representative
and incarnation of Might and Force, the principle that
policy is the expression of a national will for Power to
which all methods are legitimate, provided that they
achieve their end at a minimum of cost, the gospel that war
is an inevitable and necessary part of the struggle for existence, and that (in Moltke's famous words) the ideal of
universal peace is a dream, and not even a beautiful dream,
the principle that Reason of State transcends the code of
ethics, applicable in the social intercourse of individual
with individual—all these and many other characteristics
of the Bismarckian system and the Bismarckian interpretation of life and its values lie embedded in the period
of history which Bismarck made his own for the Germany
and the Europe in which he lived. So much is or ought
to be obvious to-day. It is no less obvious that Bismarck
did not succeed in securing their universal and unquestioned acceptance, even in the spheres where his immediate
success was greatest. If it be granted that he imprinted
them on Germany, and thereby solved for his own generation the problem to which he devoted his life, it is clear
that he had not solved the problem for other countries
even in his own lifetime, and that he bequeathed to the
Germany that followed him in veneration to his grave
riddles, no less formidable than those which he inherited,
and constituted his life's task to settle. His own solution,
too, by 1890 had called into existence and endowed with a
fresh vitality the forces both in thought and action which
challenged imperiously the permanent truth of his teaching and example. Bismarck, in brief, like other makers of
nations was either too successful or not successful enough.
Nor did he escape the peril of founding a school of disciples,
with its inevitable penalty, that the disciples either falsify

the master's precepts or are driven to employ them in destroying the master's work. One conclusion, however, will be readily accepted by all, irrespective of creed or race. No political figure in the nineteenth century leaves a more indelible impression of force—of that indefinable and unanalysable union of brain, will, and character—than Bismarck; and the closer he is studied, and the more remorselessly the historical microscope is applied, the more exigent and irrefutable is the impression. It is not easy to be moderate in estimating the sum of his positive achievement, for the Continent of Europe was his field, and the map and the State-system testify to what he wrought, and how he wrought it. But it is impossible to be moderate in the estimate of his personality. The force in the man himself surpassed the results that he stamped on the world. From the age of Luther onwards no other German political figure is his equal in titanic power. In German history Bismarck is, and is likely to remain, unique.

It is striking that like another Prussian genius—Frederick the Great—with whom he has so often been compared, Bismarck only seems to have grasped at the close of his life that with himself an epoch had ended and a new age had begun. Prince von Bülow, who can speak with authority, writes in his *Imperial Germany* :[1] 'It was Bismarck himself who pointed out the new way to us by bringing our old policy to a close. . . . It is certain that he did not foresee the course of this new development of Germany, nor the details of the problems of this new epoch. . . . We seek in vain in the conclusions of his practical policy for a justification of the steps which our international problems exacts from us.' And in a later chapter the ex-Chancellor relates how Bismarck was taken in his eightieth year to see the harbour of Hamburg. 'He stopped when he set foot on a giant steamboat, looked at the ship for a long time, at the many steamers lying in the vicinity, at the docks and huge cranes, at the mighty picture presented by the harbour, and said at last : " I am stirred and moved. Yes, this is a new age—a new world." '

[1] The edition of 1913, not the amended war edition of 1916.

It is always difficult for a man to recognise that the age in which he has lived has reached a terminus, and that the forces and ideas and ambitions which have made his world have changed their character, volume, and direction ; but when the man himself has been the most puissant expression and manipulator of those forces, ideas, and ambitions, the difficulty very nearly becomes an impossibility. The eight years of life that remained for Bismarck after his dismissal were not happy, nor did they add to his fame. Bismarck took with him to Varzin and Friedrichsruhe the profound sympathy, no less than the unstinted homage of the German people. The nation felt justly that the dismissal by a young Emperor of the servant whose loyalty to the Crown was beyond question, and whose services to the House of Hohenzollern were unexampled in their fidelity and magnitude, lacked both grace and gratitude. Bismarck was entitled, it must be frankly conceded, to be bitter and angry. But even his most unqualified admirers must admit that his subsequent behaviour provided his severest critics with material, ample and indisputable, for the harshest interpretation of his character.

He was not helped by those about him, relatives or henchmen. Love and loyalty forgot in the rancour of the situation the highest duty and interest of the chief; and Bismarck lent himself with a zeal and a readiness that admit of no extenuation to the playing of a part wholly unworthy of the claim that he had to the admiration and affection of the nation and the place that he had made for himself in his country's history. Of magnanimity, generosity, reticence, charity, or self-respect he exhibited no trace, and he seems almost to have rejoiced in exposing to the world every unlovely frailty and defect, and to desire to prove that he could only hate and neither forgive nor forget. ' Le roi me reverra,' he told Richter before he left Berlin ; but if he believed, as he probably did, that he was indispensable and that he would be recalled on his own terms, he did his best to break down all the bridges and to render a return to office impossible. In this, and in this alone, he succeeded. The Emperor, who after 1890 showed commendable self-restraint under intolerable provocation, said all that needs to be said in this connection : ' It is melancholy to think that such a man can sink so low.' And when Prince Hohenlohe (June 22, 1892) said point-blank, ' The only thing that people are afraid of is, that Bismarck will return.' ' They can make their minds easy,' replied the Emperor with a laugh, ' he will not return.' (*Memoirs*, ii. 432.)

For the first time Bismarck found himself at Varzin and Friedrichsruhe unemployed; yet the absolute leisure for which he had so often craved was framed in political isolation, and proved to be a curse. Had he been thirty years younger he could have flung himself, as he had often contemplated, into the duties of a great landowner, and found in Nature an outlet for his energies and an anodyne for the savage pain that ceaselessly tore his heart. To many statesmen the opportunity, before the final call comes, to remake the broken threads of intellectual interests and ambitions, or simply to sift and test in serene reflection the criticism of life matured by the golden sunshine of the ripening years, has been the boon they have valued most. For them old age, warmed by the recognition of a people's gratitude, has been a fruitful and satisfying climax. Through Leisure with Dignity the men of action have often taught their richest criticism of life. But Bismarck assuredly was not one of these. At seventy-six he could neither resume nor begin a contemplative and intellectual phase ; and his ebbing physical forces denied to him the power that he demanded for the mastery of nature. To him life without power and the contest for power lost all its savour. In his love of Nature, with all its keen appreciation of beauty —the dawn on dreaming woods, the blue witchery of distant hills, sunset on lush pastures, a mighty river wave —charmed by the earnest stars—can be detected from his boyhood an unconscious craving to make the beauty his own, and to bend the power it enshrined to his insurgent will. Nature now failed him, just because he was old and Nature was young, and could yearly repeat the miracle of renewing her youth. As he drove or walked on his estates, followed by his dogs as imperious and fierce as himself, Nature seemed to cry at every turn the mocking truth that no longer could he find the healing rest or the balm that had in the past always been the prelude to a mightier toil. In one place, and one alone,—the Reichskanzlerpalais in the Wilhelmstrasse—was the power that would satisfy. His favourite Goethe had said so truly that no young man can be a master. Knowledge, judgment, experience, the secrets of the Higher Command—these were not the prerogatives of youth but of a maturity, fired in the furnace of a life passed in great affairs. Bismarck knew that life had made him a master. Yet away there in Berlin the mastery was torn from him by ingrates and incompetents, mere novices and apprentices, compared with himself. The laceration of his heart poured out the pent-up passion in the revelation of State secrets and journalist denunciation.

It is not necessary here to follow the minute record. When Caprivi fell from power (1895), it was Prince Hohenlohe, not Bismarck, who succeeded to the Chancellorship. In 1892, when Herbert Bismarck was married and his father made a triumphal progress to Vienna, via Berlin, the German government was driven to forbid the German ambassador to be present at the wedding. In 1893, when Bismarck was seriously ill, there was, however, a temporary reconciliation with the Emperor; and in 1895 when the Reichstag refused to associate itself by vote with the national rejoicing to celebrate his eightieth birthday, the Emperor visited Friedrichsruhe, and repeated the visit in December of the same year on the eve of the celebrations for the ' silver wedding ' of the Empire (January 18, 1896). Bismarck, in the autumn of 1896, repaid the homage by publishing (October 24) the article that revealed the ' Reinsurance Treaty ' of 1887 and its non-renewal in 1890. He was entitled apparently to do with impunity what had ' justified ' the destruction of Arnim.

In 1894 he had suffered in the death of his wife (November 27) the personal bereavement that completed the solitude of these years of unquenchable resentment. The princess was buried at Varzin—the home that he made for her, and which was in itself a record of the achievement in which she had played a share, fully known only to Bismarck himself. Johanna von Puttkamer had been happy in the supreme gifts of love and life to a woman— the right to be the wife and ally of the mightiest German of her and his century ; and of that personal union both husband and wife could have said with truth that they had lived with distinction between the torch of marriage and the torch of death :

Viximus insignes inter utramque facem.

Varzin never beheld its bereaved master again, though to this day the peasantry tell how in the glades that Bismarck planted the lonely wayfarer in the dusk has suddenly been confronted with the familiar figure, now on horseback, now on foot—erect and superhuman in mien and stature, galloping or striding with the effortless majesty of power from one beloved haunt to another—and sometimes halting to turn on the awed spectator the penetration of eyes, once seen in life, never to be forgotten.

The end came on July 30, 1898, at Friedrichsruhe.

Nations that have beaten out their path through toil, failure, controversy, revolution, and civil war to the golden summits of victorious ambitions frequently anticipate the verdict of posterity even in the lifetime of the leader and in all the asphyxiating and blinding atmosphere of strife. The Germany of 1890 had already placed Bismarck along with the other three greatest of German figures since the Renaissance, with Luther, Frederick the Great, and Goethe. That first division of the first class, which nations intuitively limit with an unerring and jealous severity, Germany now opened to admit the Prussian statesman. It was aware that Bismarck, in common with the other three, had demonstrable and conspicuous defects. Canonisation, however, by a people is a more exacting inquest than canonisation by a church, for the duty assigned to the Devil's Advocate, who is none other than the nation itself, covers the vast field and infinite tests of that whole nation's endeavour. Hard as it unquestionably may be, it is easier to be a saint and to achieve a perfection of individual character and spirit than to sum up an epoch in a single personality, and thereby create an age in history. The title to be the maker of a nation and an epoch is, and always will remain, different from the accepted claims that distinguish the national saint or even the national hero. In the sanctuaries of a nation's Valhalla there will be niches without number for the heroes and the saints, and they will be perpetual shrines of honour, virtue, and praise ; but the corner reserved for the Makers of the Nation will be a scanty and awful plot. The few, the very few, who lie there, because they cannot lie in any other place, have made their grave for themselves from the blood, dust, passions, fears, hates, and dreams of their race, and their race cannot refuse the privilege, if privilege it be, in justice to itself rather than to them. Truth, not honour or reverence or praise, is the Makers' meed, and to such no tomb and no monument can pay the tribute of the final judgment. Over what they did, the good that they bequeathed and the evil that they wrought, men and women will wrangle as long as the nation that gave them birth retains its ambitions and can keep the flame of its conscience burning. On the hearts of all who come after is graven a testimony which words either falsify or mar, and from which there is and can be no appeal. Of the Makers the nation itself is the supreme judge. Germany or Europe may sternly reject or acclaim with enthusiasm Bismarck the man and Bismarck's achievement, but the Prussia and the Germany remain to which he gave himself with a passion and a loyalty that soar beyond all the doubts and all the praise, and the German people of the twentieth century faced the future as his memorial.

Bismarck himself knew it and was content. ' I do not,' he commanded when he was dying, ' I do not want a lying official epitaph. Write on my tomb,' he added, ' that I was the faithful servant of my master, the Emperor William, King of Prussia.' It was the bare truth. But something more was required, if justice was to be done. The dead Bismarck was happy in the felicity of those who made his grave at Friedrichsruhe. Set in the oaks and the beeches that he loved, far from the roaring Berlin that was for Germany but not for him the heart of the German Empire, was placed a simple chamber, yet massive with Prussian strength.   On the slab that marks his resting-place, beside the grave of his wife, ' who made him what he was,' is engraved but one word—and that is enough—' Bismarck.'

APPENDIX A

THE texts of (*a*) Abeken's dispatch to Bismarck, and (*b*) Bismarck's syncopated version for publication are printed in parallel columns below. It will be observed that the King left to Bismarck's discretion the public communication of his message, without sending any instructions as to the form that publication should take, should Bismarck decide upon this step.

Abeken to Bismarck

Ems, July 13, 1870.

3·40 P.M.

Bismarck's Version for Publication

His Majesty writes to me: 'Count Benedetti spoke to me on the promenade, in order to demand from me, finally in a very importunate manner, that I should authorise him to telegraph at once that I bound myself for all future time never again to give my consent if the Hohenzollerns should renew their candidature. I refused at last somewhat sternly, as it is neither right nor possible to undertake engagements of this kind *à tout jamais*. I told him that I had as yet received no news, and as he was earlier informed from Paris and Madrid than myself, he could see clearly that my government had no more interest in the matter.' His Majesty has since received a letter from Prince Charles

After the news of the renunciation of the hereditary Prince of Hohenzollern had been officially communicated to the Imperial government of France by the Royal government of Spain, the French Ambassador further demanded of his Majesty, the King, at Ems, that he would authorise him to telegraph to Paris that his Majesty, the King, bound himself for all time never again to give his consent, should the Hohenzollerns renew their candidature. His Majesty, the King, thereupon decided not to receive the French Ambassador again, and sent the aide-de-camp on duty to tell him that his Majesty had nothing further to communicate to the ambassador.

Anthony. His Majesty, having told Count Benedetti that he was awaiting news from the Prince, has decided, with reference to the above demand, on the suggestion of Count Eulenberg and myself, not to receive Count Benedetti again, but only to let him be informed through an aide-de-camp: 'That his Majesty has now received from the Prince confirmation of the news which Benedetti had already received from Paris, and had nothing further to say to the ambassador.' His Majesty leaves it to your Excellency to decide whether Benedetti's fresh demand and its rejection should be at once communicated to both our ambassadors, to foreign nations, and to the Press.

APPENDIX B

THE REINSURANCE TREATIES OF 1884 AND 1887

THE nature and contents of these secret undertakings, which form so decisive and interesting a feature of Bismarck's policy from 1883 to his dismissal in March 1890, still remain very obscure. The texts have never been officially or unofficially published, and inference from scattered and contradictory statements is all that is possible. Certain points, however, are quite clear. In 1884 Germany concluded with Russia a specific arrangement; in 1887, presumably because the arrangement of 1884 had terminated, Germany concluded a fresh arrangement with Russia. In 1890 the arrangement of 1887 was not renewed by Chancellor Caprivi. The public of Europe would probably have never known of the existence of 'the 1887 Compact' but for Bismarck's deliberate revelation of its existence and non-renewal in the *Hamburger Nachrichten* of October 24, 1896. It is noticeable that the revelation caused much excitement in Germany and a storm of indignant criticism in Austria. It was very embarrassing to the German government; whether it was as great a surprise to the Foreign Office in the Ball-Platz as it obviously was to the Austrian public is one of the points in controversy, on which precise information is still lacking. The Austrian public mind, as a study of the Viennese newspapers of November 1896 proves, was seriously upset, and there was much excited comment on Bismarck's betrayal of the Dual Alliance by the secret arrangements with Russia. But the Austrian government maintained an official discretion and reserved its indignation, if it felt any, for confidential communication to the Wilhelmstrasse at Berlin. Nor did the debate in the Reichstag (November 16, 1896) add anything to our knowledge. The official *Reichsanzeiger* had published (October 27) a curt note, pronouncing the 'revelation' to be a 'violation of the most confidential secrets of State which constituted a blow at the grave interests of the Empire'; but neither the Chancellor, Prince Hohenlohe, nor Foreign Secretary Baron Marschallv on Bieberstein, though they spoke at considerable length in reply to the interpellation of Graf Hompesch, gave any new information, except to admit the bare fact that a compact had been made in 1887 and not renewed in 1890. Prince Hohenlohe took refuge in the necessity of official secrecy and reasons of State. The Foreign Secretary indeed pointed out that a diplomacy which rested on a series of engagements, possibly conflicting in their terms, was of doubtful value, and that the worth of any single engagement was not increased by the number of other contracts. What the precise meaning of this cryptic utterance was, it is impossible to decide ; but it clearly was intended to convey—whether truly or not, we cannot say— that the German Foreign Office had not docketed in its cupboard other secret treaties of ' a reinsurance character,' together with an assurance for the world in general and Vienna in particular, that the German government of 1896 was, and intended to remain, free to fulfil loyally the terms of the Dual or Triple Alliance.

Both ministers, however, also spoke casually of ' negotiations between 1887 and 1890.' Negotiations with whom or for what they did not explain, but presumably they referred to negotiations with Russia between 1887 and 1890 for the renewal of ' the Compact of 1887 ' or a similar treaty. No explanation was offered of the reasons why Chancellor Caprivi did not renew the Compact of 1887—*e.g.* was it, as Hohenlohe suggests in his *Diary* (January 14, 1895, ii. 462), ' because the policy it led to was too complicated,' or because Russia raised her terms, or because the Emperor had embarked on a serious attempt in 1890 to bring Great Britain into the Triple Alliance, or because ' the reinsurance ' was judged to be a betrayal of Austria ? It is tempting to connect the non-renewal in 1890 with the dismissal of Bismarck ; for we know that Bismarck's policy was regarded as a betrayal of Austria by the Emperor and his military entourage. Another inference is still more tempting. Hohenlohe twice (*e.g.* ii. 429, and 452) succinctly states the contents of ' the reinsurance ' as he understood them to be (*i.e.* before he became Chancellor and had free access to confidential documents, when his silence is instructive) :

' When I told him (Caprivi) that Schuvaloff had described him as a *trop honnête homme*, he said that was because Bismarck had concluded a treaty with Russia, under which we guaranteed Russia a free hand in Bulgaria and Constantinople, while Russia undertook to observe a neutral attitude in the Franco-GermanWar. This treaty had lapsed when Caprivi assumed office, and he had not renewed it, because its publication would have shattered the Triple Alliance. I fear that Austria will not be grateful to us.' And to the same effect (ii. 452) : with the addition, ' Russia pledged herself to remain neutral in case of a war with France, even though Austria should lend a hand in the East.'

These passages are apparently explicit enough; in reality they are full of difficulties. Caprivi took office in March 1890; if, as we seem bound to assume, 'the reinsurance' was made in November 1887, it did not lapse when Caprivi *assumed* office, but ten months later. Are we to believe that 'the reinsurance' lapsed in March 1890, *i.e.* that it was made in March 1887 ? If so, what happened in November 1887 ? For if the Compact of 1884 was renewed in the spring of 1887, what is the explanation of the strained Russo-German relations from March to November 1887, and of the arrangement with the Tsar in that month at Berlin ? 'The publication' would have 'shattered the Triple Alliance' (*sic*)—but who was going to 'publish' it ? If it was a secret treaty, why should it be 'published' ? Did Hohenlohe intend to convey that Austria (as was probable) knew nothing of the 'reinsurance,' but that if she learned (from Russia or whom?) of its existence, the Triple Alliance would be shattered ? Why should 'Austria not be grateful?' Because she had been told (between 1890 and 1892) that she had been betrayed between 1887 and 1890, but would not be betrayed any more ? And how was 'Austria to lend a hand in the East,' detrimental to Germany ? By tearing up the Triple Alliance and attacking Germany ? By making an alliance with France or how ? Without the text of the document it is impossible to answer these and other conundrums. But if Hohenlohe is correct, the inference is certain that (*a*) 'the reinsurance' of 1887 at least was concluded behind Austria's back; (*b*) that its contents gravely imperilled the Dual and Triple Alliances; and (*c*) that the policy involved was condemned in 1890 and renounced.

What was that policy ? Clearly 'a free hand for Russia' in the Near East, and Bismarck said as much in his big speeches in 1887 and 1888, as noted in the text (see p. 446). That such 'a free hand' was in conflict with Austrian ambitions is no less certain. But, in 1890, the inference is irresistible that the Kaiser had already embarked on the *Weltpolitik* which aimed 'not at a free hand for Russia in Bulgaria and Constantinople' but 'at a free hand for Germany.' The heir to Constantinople, with Bulgaria as his washpot, was to be the German Emperor, not the Emperor of Russia; while, concurrently, Austria was to throw the Habsburg shoe over Serbia, the valleys of the Morava and Vardar and Salonica, meeting on a Macedonian frontier, to be delimited later, the Kaiser's brother-in-law, the Duke of Sparta, the 'Tino' of imperial telegrams and recent history. The non-renewal of 'the reinsurance' was the categorical pre-condition of such a policy, with which the Kaiser, flushed with super-Teutonic ambitions, returned from his pilgrimage in the East, to pledge himself to Austria and to dismiss Bismarck, who regarded ' the new course ' as midsummer madness. It is at any rate very noticeable that in 1896 neither Hohenlohe nor Baron Marschall attempted to meet the challenge of the *Hamburger Nachrichten*, that the Kaiser's and Caprivi's policy had driven Russia into the arms of France, and that the authors of the Franco-Russian alliance were the men who broke with Russia and supported Austria, *coûte que coûte*. It is no less certain that the non-renewal of the ' reinsurance ' was made with the full knowledge and approval of the Kaiser.

A writer, M. André Mévil, in the *Revue Hebdomadaire* for June 1907 gives a very confident and detailed account of the ' reinsurance ' treaties. He does not give his authorities, but he writes as if he had had access to information that could not be precisely stated. Briefly, according to M. Mévil, the first secret treaty was made at Berlin on February 24, 1884, and was verbally ratified (and not in writing, as not being necessary) in September 15, 1884, at Skierniewice. The contents were known to Austria, or Austria was a party to it. The Pan-Slav party under Katkoff worked unceasingly to prevent the renewal of the agreement, and in 1887 it was not renewed. This coincided with a dangerous crisis in Franco-German relations. Alexander declined to give a pledge to remain neutral in case of a war on the Rhine, and M. Mévil thinks that ' the Schnaebele incident ' was closed by Bismarck because he could not rely on Russian neutrality. Subsequently, when Bismarck had exposed certain forgeries misrepresenting Germany's policy in Bulgaria, the Tsar, when in Berlin, November 18, 1887, concluded the ' reinsurance ' which was not renewed in 1890. The agreement pledged Russia or Germany to neutrality in the event of either being attacked by a third party (*i.e.* presumably a Franco-German, or an Austro-German war). M. Mévil draws a clear distinction between the Compact of 1884, to which Austria was a party, and that of 1887, to which she was not. He asserts that it was Russia's unwillingness in 1887 to include Austria in the renewal that caused the Compact of 1884 to be dropped.

Hohenlohe spoke in the debate of November 16, 1896, ' of 1887 when Boulangism reached its height, and threatened a danger that disappeared with the disappearance of Boulangism,' *i.e.* a clear suggestion that the *raison d'être* of ' the reinsurance ' was the possibility of a Franco-German war, and the urgent desirability of securing Russia's neutrality against that eventuality (as was done by Bismarck in 1870).

The *Hamburger Nachrichten* also suggested (October 24, 1896) that the agreement was for six years, and M. Mévil seems to support this. But in view of the assertion in the same paper, that it had not been renewed in 1890, this seems impossible, unless it is meant that it was the treaty of 1884 which was for six years and that the agreement of 1887 was a separate convention, wholly independent of that of 1884—a hypothesis that only opens up fresh queries and difficulties.

Marschall and Hohenlohe positively asserted that the agreement, that was not renewed, was a secret one, to be kept secret. Against this the *Hamburger Nachrichten* of November 1, 1896, asserted that its tenor had been communicated both to Austria and to Italy! How in that case it could be a secret arrangement, and what value it would have, and why its non-renewal should have been such a grave blunder, and why the revelation of what was known both by the Austrian and Italian governments, as well as by the Russian government, should have caused the flurry of excitement in 1896 and been denounced as equivalent to a *lèse-majesté*, I confess I cannot understand.

In conclusion, I am driven to infer that : (1) the agreement of 1884 was for three years ; (2) Austria may have been a party to it ; (3) it pledged the signatories, possibly of three States, *i.e.* Bismarck, Szechenyi, and Sabouroff to a benevolent neutrality in the case of any of the three being attacked ; (4) this tripartite arrangement lapsed in 1887 ; (5) Bismarck, behind the back of Austria, concluded a secret and private ' reinsurance ' with Russia in 1887 ; (6) this ' reinsurance ' was for three years, and pledged each signatory to neutrality in the event of either being attacked by a third party, *i.e.* France or Austria ; (7) this was not renewed by Caprivi in 1890 ; (8) in consequence Russia felt isolated and gradually drifted into an *entente* and then an alliance with France.

It is noticeable, further, that the British *Standard* and the German *Zukunft* in 1884 duly notified their readers with the information that Germany had come to an understanding with Russia. So far as I know, no other newspaper discovered or published the fact. But the information passed practically unnoticed in 1884.

Secondly, German public criticism in 1896 represented Bismarck's ' reinsurance ' of 1887 as a masterpiece of German statecraft— that is to say, German public opinion hailed with enthusiasm the conclusion of a secret understanding by Germany with Russia, at the expense and behind the back of their ally, Austria ; and it regretted that Caprivi had failed to continue this Bismarckian method of pledging his country to one ally, while the value of the pledge was being secretly whittled away in favour of that ally's avowed enemy. Such a mental attitude is instructive in the thoroughness with which the German public had assimilated Bismarckian principles. What would German public opinion have said had Austria behind the back of Germany, and in violation of the Dual Alliance, made a secret reinsurance with Russia to the detriment of Germany ? Would that have been Austrian ' perfidy ' or a masterpiece of Austrian statecraft ?

The articles in the *Hamburger Nachrichten* and other papers, and a full report of the Debate of November 16, 1896, will be found in Penzler, *Bismarck nach seiner Entlassung*, vol. vii. and in vol. iii. of the *Bismarck Jahrbuch*. While this book was in the press, Professor Simpson's second article (*Nineteenth Century*, January 1918) on the Sabouroff Papers became available. Professor Simpson, unfortunately, does not throw any more light on the secret agreement of 1884, or of 1887—except to say (p. 75) : ' as a matter of fact the understanding became closer with Germany, especially as Bismarck was endeavouring to negotiate a " reinsurance " treaty with Russia, unknown to Austria, providing for neutrality in case either Power was attacked by a third. In this he succeeded. " Then came Caprivi in place of Bismarck "—the words are M. Sabouroff's—" and said that it was not necessary to make a separate treaty with Russia, because Germany was on good relations with her. Then followed still other councillors who began to smile towards France, but whether it began with Russia or with France I do not know." '

The main thesis of Professor Simpson's article is to summarise from the Sabouroff MSS. the negotiations by which Austria, Germany, and Russia came to conclude a treaty in 1881, arranging for an agreed policy in the Near East. This treaty was signed on June 18, 1881 : in 1884 ' it was renewed for a further term of three years, subject to one slight modification,' but not renewed in 1887. The whole article with the preceding one (*Nineteenth Century*, December 1917) fully bears out the general line of interpretation of Bismarck's policy and methods maintained in the text (chapter vi. §§ 3, 5, and 6). Some quotations are so relevant as to justify their presence here. ' Bismarck was a rough man even in politics, but his conservative convictions were very sincere ; he was opposed to Liberalism in any form. " There are five great Powers ; I must always strive," Bismarck said, " to be one of three against two." Gortschakov in 1870 " consulted the Emperor to take immediate steps, whatever the risk, to annul the clauses of the Treaty of Paris rather than wait the definitive victory of Prussia before doing so." In 1875 *à propos* of " the crisis " in May—" I confess that all my admiration went to Prince Gortschakov ; he showed himself superior in self-command, courtesy, precise and, I ought to add, breadth of view." The Grand Duke Nicholas in 1877 " did not occupy Constantinople in accordance with the instructions telegraphed to him, and the Emperor never forgave him." In 1880, Bismarck said : " Thus at last we shall be able to form that solid monarchical *bloc*, and feel no longer any concern about the internal convulsions with which the Western Powers may be troubled. The three Emperors are strong enough to defy all the agitations abroad, and sufficiently great lords to live content with the patrimony of their ancestors." '

Bismarck said on two occasions to M. Sabouroff : ' I do not share the prejudices of the other cabinets on the subject of the danger of handing over Constantinople to Russia ' : and again : ' I flatter myself that I was the first in Europe to break with the old tradition with which the Westerners inoculated all the Cabinets, viz., that a Russian Constantinople would be a European danger.' As to these utterances it is relevant to point out that Bismarck's *obiter dicta* and ' confessions ' are always interesting, but generally, unless confirmed by specific acts, wholly untrustworthy. Bismarckian thinking aloud, in the presence of another person, had invariably a concealed objective. Had Bismarck carried out all the ' confessions ' and ' thinking aloud ' that he made to Napoleon III. between 1858 and 1867, Central Europe would never have been reconstructed as it actually was. Napoleon, Lord Ampthill, M. Sabouroff, and many others learned that between Bismarck's ideas and confessions and Bismarck's acts there lay a substantial world of difference. Words with Bismarck were generally intended to mask his own, or unmask the thoughts of those with whom he conversed, and his alluring geniality was one of his finest and most deceptive diplomatic gifts. Hohenlohe records how Alexander III. after 1890 said that in doing business with Bismarck, even when the arrangement was satisfactory, he always felt ' qu'il me tricherait.'

Austria required much pressure in 1881 to come into the proposed arrangement. ' Throughout the Sabouroff *Memoirs*,' writes Professor Simpson, ' nothing is so obvious as the disdain that both the negotiators feel for " the ramshackle Empire," and yet it is always Bismarck who says the really brutal things.' ' It is abundantly clear, however, that the vital significance of the Dual Alliance had not been disclosed to the Tsar.' The arrangement of 1881 was for three years. ' When Austria,' Bismarck said, with one of his usual vivid touches, ' has worn that flannel next her skin for three whole years, she won't be able to take it off without running the risk of catching cold.' That was what happened in 1890 in the matter of the reinsurance treaties.

Caprivi threw off the flannel that Bismarck had made Germany wear next her skin for six years—and Germany caught cold. One other Bismarckian touch is too deliciously characteristic to be omitted.

'We shall make a mistake if we keep Austria from compromising herself by committing to writing these demands of hers (*i.e.* the annexation of Bosnia and Herzegovina, plus the Sandjak of Novi Bazar and some other acquisitions of a like character), which will only embroil her with the Western Powers, and furnish proofs of complicity with us in any future Eastern crisis.'

The negotiator who had lured Benedetti to state his proposals in writing, and then published them in *The Times*, knew well the value of promissory notes with the signature of the promissor attached. Bismarck liked a cupboard full of such compromising stuff—to be revealed, when he chose—and he took good care to leave as little of his own 'paper' in other persons' hands as possible. In Bismarckian ethics the morality of the betrayal of a confidence was decided by the difference between the betrayer and the betrayed. If you were the former, reason of State could administer a plenary absolution; but if you were the latter, then let the welkin ring with the iniquity of the act. But the best comment on Bismarckian methods and all of the same character was supplied by Bismarck himself to his wife, when he first became initiated in the grand diplomacy at Frankfort : 'Not even the most scoundrelly democrat or sceptic could conceive the charlatanry and fraud that lies in this diplomacy.'

BIBLIOGRAPHY

THIS Bibliographical Appendix is not, nor does it profess to be, a bibliography of German history for the period of Bismarck's lifetime. Such would require a separate volume. Nor does it profess to be an exhaustive bibliography of the historical literature on Bismarck himself. Attention here is necessarily confined to the chief *original* sources available, together with the leading secondary authorities, and brief critical comments based on the author's study. For a more complete catalogue reference should be made to Dahlmann-Waitz, *Quellenkunde der deutschen Geschichte* (8th edition, ed. Köhler, 1912), and R. Charmatz, *Wegweiser durch die Literatur der Österreichischen Geschichte* (1912), also to the bibliographies in vols. x., xi., and xii. of *The Cambridge Modern History* ; and to the bibliographies in Sir A. Ward's *History of Germany* (vols i. and ii.), the third volume of which, dealing with the period from 1871 onwards, has still to be published.

The chief original authorities that are indispensable are :
Bismarck Briefe (ed. Kohl), 1836-1872.
Neue Bismarckbriefe (ed. Poschinger).
Fürst Bismarck's Briefe an seine Braut u. Gattin (ed. H. von Bismarck) (Eng. transl., 1901).
Die Politischen Reden (ed. H. Kohl, 14 vols).
Briefwechsel zwischen Kaiser Wilhelm und Fürst Bismarck.
Briefwechsel mit dem Freiherrn von Steinitz.
Briefwechsel mit Leopold von Gerlach.
Bismarck, The Man and the Statesman (Eng. transl. of the *Gedanken und Erinnerungen*, cited as *The Memoirs* in the text). The German edition contains an ' Anhang' in two volumes. 1. Of Letters to the Emperor William. 2. Of other Letters and documents. This ' Anhang ' has not been translated.
Preussen in Bundestag (4 vols.). These contain the dispatches from Frankfurt, 1851-1859. They have been translated into French (ed. Funck-Brentano) but not into English.
Neue Berichte aus Frankfurt (ed. Poschinger. A supplement to the above).
The following also edited by Poschinger are collections of original sources :

506

Fürst Bismarck und der Bundesrat (2 vols).
Fürst Bismarck und die Diplomaten (2 vols).
Fürst Bismarck und die Parlamentarier (3 vols).
Fürst Bismarck als Volkswirt (5 vols., 2 of which are documents).
None of these have been translated.
The documents and letters in the *Bismarck Jahrbuch* (ed. H.
Kohl, 6 vols.), collected from many stray sources, make a valuable
collection. The various books by M. Busch are full of curious
information : *Tagebuchblätter* (3 vols.) ; *Bismarck, Some Secret
Pages of his History* (3 vols. Eng. transl.) ; *Unser Reichskanzler*,
(2 vols. Eng. transl.) ; *Bismarck in the Franco-German War*
(Eng. transl. 2 vols.). The official publication of original documentary material can be found in : *Ægidi, L. K.* and *A. Klauhold.*
Sammlung der offiziellen Aktenstücke, continued by L. Worthmann
and other editors (34 vols.). H. Kohl's *Fürst Bismarck Regesten
zu einer wissenschaftlichen Bibliographie* (2 vols.) is an indispensable aid to Bismarck's life.

Some very convenient monographs on sources are to be found
in the *Quellen Sammlung zur Deutschen Geschichte*, edited by
F. Brandenburger : e.g. *Briefe und Aktenstücke zur Geschichte
der Gründung des Deutschen Reiches* (ed. Brandenburger, 2 vols.) ;
Die Deutschen Parteiprogramme, 1844-1900 (ed. F. Salomon, 2 vols.) ;
Briefe u.s.w. zur Geschichte der Hohenzoll. Kandidatur (ed. R. Fester,
2 vols.) : with this latter should be placed R. Fester's *Neue Beiträge
zur Geschichte der Hohenz. Thronkandidatur* ; E. Marcks, *Bismarck
und die Hohenzollern Kandidatur*; and Delbrück's essay on the
subject in *Preuss. Jahrbücher*, vol. 82.

Of the numerous Biographies, that by E. Marcks will probably
be, when finished, the most complete ; but so far only one volume
(to 1848) has appeared. It contains much new and valuable
information with excerpts from many unpublished letters and documents. L. Hahn's *Biography* in five volumes is enriched with much
original documentary material, but is not very readable. M. Lenz's
Bismarck in one volume (a reprint of the article in the *Allgemeine
Deutsche Biographie*) is a masterly piece of work, but not very full
for the period after 1871. G. Egelhaaf's *Biography*, in one volume,
is a scholarly study, and much fuller on the period after 1871, but
not so well written as Lenz's book. Of the others, D. Klein-
Hattingen, *Bismarck und seine Welt*, is well worth reading. But the
best biography so far is that by P. Matter (in French, 3 vols.),
whose knowledge of the sources is complete—a book marked
by French artistry and scholarship and very judicial in tone and
judgment. In English there is a one volume biography by
G. W. Headlam, admirable, but unhappily not very full on the

period after 1871. The biography in two volumes by C. Lowe is readable, but not very critical, and now out of date. For some other aspects of Bismarck's work : A. Singer, *Bismarck in der Literatur* is indispensable. (This is a yearly register and catalogue of all the contemporary pamphlets, satires, and books bearing on Bismarck.) York, Graf von Wartenburg, *Bismarck's äussere Erscheinung in Wort und Bild* (with ninety portraits) is an interesting study of the portraits, etc. Grand-Carteret, *Bismarck en caricatures* (a study of the caricature literature) ; and with this should be examined G. Hochstetten, *Bismarck, Historische Karikaturen* (with text by Max. Harden) ; Senfft von Pilsach, *Aus Bismarck's Werkstatt* (a critical and stimulating study of Bismarckian principles) ; W. Blume, *Von Politik u. Strategie, Bismarck und Moltke* (a valuable study by a Prussian General of Bismarck's principles of policy in relation to strategy).

Apart from the criticism in the standard biographies, three monographs by well-known German historians on the historical value of Bismarck's reminiscences are real contributions to knowledge and scholarship : G. Kämmel, *Kritische Studien zu Fürst Bismarck's Gedanken* ; M. Lenz, *Zur Kritik der Gedanken, u.s.w.* : E. Marcks, *Versuch einer kritischen Würdigung der Gedanken, u.s.w.*

For the period after 1890 the following supply full material : P. Liman, *Bismarck nach seiner Entlassung* (2 vols) ; H. Hofmann, *Bismarck*, 1890-1898 (2 vols.) ; P. Penzler, *Fürst B. nach seiner Entlassung* (7 vols.).

On Bismarck's financial policy after 1878, see O. Schneider's monograph in *Schmoller's Jahrbuch* for 1910 and 1912 : for the Kulturkampf, see G. Goyau, *Le Kulturkampf*, P. Majunke, *Der Kulturkampf*, and Lefèbre de Behaine, *Léon XIII. et le Prince de Bismarck*.

For some other aspects of Bismarck, see H. Poschinger, *Die Tischgespräche des Reichskanzlers* (Eng. transl. with introd. by S. Whitman), and *Neue Tischgespräche* (1 vol.), and *Also sprach Bismarck* (2 vols.).

Of the secondary authorities for the period up to 1848, see the German history chapters in A. Stern, *Geschichte Europa's seit 1815* (vols. i.-vii.) ; and generally for the whole period, H. Oncken, *Das Zeitalter Kaiser's Wilhelm I.* ; H. v. Zweideneck-Südenhorst, *Deutsche Geschichte* (from 1806-1871) 3 vols. ; and H. Friedjung, *Der Kampf um die Vorherrschaft in Deutschland* (1857-1866), 2 vols.; H. v. Sybel (Eng. transl. by G. Perrin), *Die Begründung des Deutschen Reiches*, 7 vols. Sybel's work down to 1868 is based on material in the Prussian archives : it has been supplemented by Sybel himself in the later editions and criticised by various writers subsequently, but in spite of omissions, it remains indispensable. Of the works of H. v. Treitschke, the *Deutsche Geschichte* does not deal with the period of or after 1848 ; but his *Zehn Jahre deutscher Kämpfe* ; the *Histor. und politische Aufsätze* (2 vols.), the pamphlet *Was fördern wir von Frankreich*, and the *Politik* (Eng. transl.) are more than instructive ; they are essential for understanding the German point of view. Much the best history in English is that by Sir A. Ward, *Germany*, 1815-1871 (2 vols., Camb. Hist. Series—taking events down to 1871).

For the more recent history : H. Blum, *Das Deutsche Reich zur Zeit Bismarck's* ; G. Egelhaaf, *Geschichte der neuesten Zeit* ; H. Münz, *Von Bismarck bis Bülow* ; and P. Rohrbach, *Bismarck und Wir* ; and C. Andler (and others), *Les origines du Pangermanisme* (a series of volumes in French, which with their lengthy quotations from German writers, the critical annotations, and the scholarly bibliographies constitutes a valuable introduction to the later phases of German political development from 1870 onwards).

For the Schleswig-Holstein affair it must suffice to cite K. Jansen-K. Samwer, *Schleswig-Holstein's Befreiung*. (All the leading authorities deal with the copious controversial literature.) A brief statement of the Danish case will be found in a short Monograph by A. D. Jörgensen ; reference may also be made to W. R. Prior, *North Sleswick under Prussian Rule*. The standard biography of the Emperor William I. is that by E. Marcks, and of his son, ' the Crown Prince,' and Emperor Frederick III. by M. Philippson.

For the period 1870-1 and the making of the German Empire, I have found far the most useful W. Busch, *Die Kämpfe um Reichsverfassung und Kaisertum* ; to which may be added O. Lorenz, *Kaiser Wilhelm und die Begründung des Reiches*, 1866-1871, which contains much valuable original material—derived largely from the Grand-Duke of Baden and the unitarian group of which he was the head.

On Austrian history, the most useful general guides are two works by R. Charmatz, *Geschichte der auswärtigen Politik Österreich's im 19 Jahrhundert* (2 vols.) ; and *Österreich's innere Geschichte von 1848 bis 1907* (2 vols.) : two others may be mentioned, T. v. Sosnosky, *Die Balkanpolitik Österreich-Ungarns seit 1866* (2 vols.), and L. Eisenmann, *Le Compromis*. The well-known works by Chéradame and Seton-Watson do not specifically bear on Bismarck.

For general purposes K. Meinecke, *Weltbürgertum und National-Staat*, is an illuminating philosophical treatise in historical form on the development of political thought and principles in Germany from the French Revolution to Bismarck. It is not easy reading for those unacquainted with German philosophy, but its treatment is clear and masterly. P. Rohrbach, *Der Deutsche Gedanke in der Welt*, is a good statement of German ambitions in the period, 1871-1914.

Of the original Memoirs the following are invaluable : this selected list is intended to convey different points of view.

Keudell. (Personal recollections.) *Fürst und Fürstin Bismarck* (French transl., *Bismarck et sa Famille*).

Abeken. *Ein Schlichtes Leben* (also in an Eng. transl.). (Abeken was one of the most devoted of Bismarck's official staff.)

Wagener, H. *Erlebtes* (in 2 parts. Wagener was editor of the *Kreuzzeitung*).

Mittnacht, Freiherr von. *Erinnerungen an Bismarck.*

Beust, Count. *Drei viertel Jahrhunderten*, 2 vols. (Eng. transl. by Baron de Worms, 2 vols.) An entertaining and valuable contribution.

Roon, A. von. *Denkwürdigkeiten aus dem Leben* (absolutely invaluable). 3 vols.

Andrassy, Count Julius. *Sein Leben u. seine Zeit* (by E. von Wertheimer). 3 vols. This contains a great deal of original material, particularly in vols. 2 and 3.

Bernhardi, T. von. *Aus dem Leben T. v. B.*, 9 vols. (a work of great value, particularly after 1862).

Stosch, A. von. *Denkwürdigkeiten, Briefe und Tagebuch Blätter* (unfortunately does not go beyond 1872).

Unruh, H. V. von. *Erinnerungen* (ed. H. v. Poschinger).

Delbrück, R. *Lebenserinnerungen* (2 vols).

Bennigsen. *Life* by H. Oncken (with original papers and letters, not translated).

Simson E. v. *Erinnerungen.*

La Marmora. *Un po' più di Luce* (mainly on affairs in 1866).

Karl v. Rumanien. *Aus dem Leben König Karl's von Rumanien* (also in an Eng. transl.). Of great importance.

Ernst v. Sachsen-Coburg. *Aus meinem Leben und aus meiner Zeit* (gives the ' Coburg ' School point of view).

Lasker, E. *Aus E. Lasker's Nachlassungen.* Ed. W. Cahn. (The National Liberal who became a Radical.)

Bebel, A. *My Life* (Eng. transl. of the German autobiography).

Windthorst, L. *Ein Lebensbild* by P. Majunke. *Ausgewählte Reden*, ed. A. L. Meyer (4 vols.).

Richter, Eugen. *Im alten Reichstag, Erinnerungen.* (The leader of the South German Radicals.)

Tiedemann, C. *Erinnerungen.* (Tiedemann was Chef der Reichskanzlei under Bismarck for six years.)

Bamberger, L. *Erinnerungen.* (A leading National Liberal and

Secessionist.) Also his striking *Bismarck Posthumus* (published in 1899).

Freytag, G. *Erinnerungen* (Eng. transl. in 2 vols.); *Der Kronprinz und die Deutsche Kaiserkrone* (Eng. transl. in 2 vols.).

Gerlach, Leopold v. *Denkwürdigkeiten* (2 vols.).

Gerlach, E. Ludwig von. *Aufzeichnungen aus seinem Leben* (2 vols.).

Hohenlohe-Schillingsfürst. *Denkwürdigkeiten* (English transl. in 2 vols.).

Meding, O. *Memoiren zur Zeitgeschichte* (3 vols.).

Bucher, Lothar. *Leben und Werke* (by H. von Poschinger 3 vols.). (L. B. had a varied career from revolutionist to henchman of Bismarck.)

Stockmar, C. F. von. *Denkwürdigkeiten* (Eng. transl. 2 vols.).

Hansen, J. *Les Coulisses de la diplomatie.*

For the French side, the following original sources are indispensable : *Les origines diplomatiques de la Guerre de 1870-1* (a complete collection of the sources in the French archives, commencing with 1862, and critically edited and annotated. Ten volumes so far have been published, reaching July 12, 1866.) With these must be noted—Napoleon, *Les idées Napoléoniennes*; Rothan, G., *La Politique Française en 1866*; *Souvenirs diplomatiques*; *La France et sa politique extérieure en 1867* (2 vols.); *L'Allemagne et l'Italie*, 1870-1 (2 vols.), Count Benedetti, *Essais Diplomatiques*; *L'Empereur Guillaume et le Prince de Bismarck*; *Ma Mission à Ems*; *La Triple Alliance*; *La Paix Armée et ses Conséquences*; Gontaut-Biron, E. de, *La Mission de G. B. à Berlin* and *Dernières années de l'Ambassade à Berlin*; Duc de Gramont, *La France et la Prusse avant la guerre*; Thiers, A., *Notes et Souvenirs.* Valuable letters from General Le Flô were published in the *Figaro* for 1887 : the *Revue Historique* and the *Revue de Paris* contain many critical articles after 1880 on the period. Of the secondary authorities it is only necessary to cite here : P. de la Gorce, *Histoire du Second Empire* (7 vols.); Ollivier, E., *L'Empire Libéral* (16 vols.); Sorel, A., *Histoire Diplomatique de la Guerre Franco-Allemande* (2 vols.); Hanotaux, G., *Histoire de la France Contemporaine* (4 vols., with much original material from MS. sources; Eng. transl.); and Denis, E., *La Fondation de l'Empire Allemand* (a *chef-d'œuvre* of French historical scholarship); Deschaumes, E., *Gambetta, Le Grand Patriote*; and Débidour, *Histoire diplomatique de l'Europe*, 1814-1878 (a classical text book); the supplementary volume, 1878-1904 is useful, but somewhat disappointing, though its bibliographies, particularly of French sources, are valuable.

For the British side the following Parliamentary Papers and Blue Books contain diplomatic correspondence and other papers : Schleswig-Holstein, 1863, No. 74 ; 1864, Nos. 64 and 65 ; 1865, No. 57 ; Luxemburg, 1867, Nos. 74 and 415 ; 1870, No. 70 ; Africa, 1884-5, No. 54 ; 1890, No. 51 ; Poland, 1863, No. 75 ; 1864, No. 76 ; Russia, 1871, No. 72.

And the following biographies and memoirs : Morier, Sir Robert, *Memoirs and Letters*, 2 vols.; Lord J. Russell (*Life* by Sir S. Walpole) ; Acton, Lord, *Historical Essays and Studies* ('Essay on the Causes of the Franco-German War') ; Granville, Earl (*Life*, by Lord Fitzmaurice) ; *Clarendon, Earl, Life of*, by Sir H. Maxwell, in 2 vols. ; Crowe, Sir J. A., *Reminiscences* ; Loftus, Lord A., *Diplomatic Reminiscences*, second series ; Prince Consort, The, *Life*, by Sir T. Martin (particularly vols. 3-5) ; Vitzthum von Eckstädt, Count, *London, Gastein und Sadowa* ; Salisbury, Marquis of, *Essays on Foreign Policy* (reprinted from the *Quarterly Review*) ; Dilke, Sir C., *The Present Position of European Politics* (*i.e.* in 1886)— a most valuable study ; and *Life of Dilke*, by Miss Tuckwell, in 2 vols. ; *Lord Lyons, Life of*, by Lord Newton ; *Gladstone, W. E., Life of*, by Lord Morley.

The Annual Register throughout is very helpful ; and can be collated with Schulthess, H., *Europäischer Geschichts-Kalender* (annually produced after 1860). H. Egerton, *British Foreign Policy—A Rough Outline*, is very stimulating and helpful on the problems for British policy from 1850 onwards.

The following by W. H. Dawson are also very helpful : *German Socialism and F. Lassalle ; Bismarck and State Socialism ; The Evolution of Modern Germany ; German Fiscal Policy during the Nineteenth Century ; Social Insurance in Germany*, 1883-1911.

CHRONOLOGICAL TABLE

1815. April 1. Otto von Bismarck-Schönhausen born.
1821-27. Bismarck at Plamann's School in Berlin.
1827-30.　　„　at Friedrich-Wilhelms Gymnasium in Berlin.
1830-32.　　„　at the Gymnasium zum grauen Kloster.
1832.　　　„　a student at the University of Göttingen.
1834.　　　„　a student at the University of Berlin.
1835.　　　„　enters the State Civil Service.
1838.　　　„　serves for one year in the Garde-Jäger.
1839. Death of Bismarck's mother. He takes over (with his brother) the family estates.
1841. Bismarck settles at Kniephof.
1842-43. Travels in England, Switzerland, France, and North Germany.
1845. Death of Bismarck's father. Bismarck takes over Schönhausen.
1847. Bismarck attends the United Diet of the Estates (April 11).
Bismarck marries Johanna von Puttkamer.
1848-49. The years of Revolution in Germany.
1849. The Imperial Crown voted to the King of Prussia by the National Parliament at Frankfurt March (29), and rejected by him (April 28).
1850. Convention or Punctation of Olmütz.
1851. Re-establishment of the Federal Constitution of 1815 (May 16).
Bismarck appointed Minister Plenipotentiary for Prussia at Frankfurt (July 15).
1851-59. Bismarck Minister at Frankfurt.
1852. The Treaty of London settles the Danish Succession and the question of the Duchies (Schleswig-Holstein).
1854-56. The Crimean War. The Treaty of Paris (March 30, 1856).
1858. October 26. Prince William becomes Regent in Prussia.
1859. January 29. Bismarck transferred to the Embassy at Petersburg.
April 29. War between Austria and Piedmont (with France).
November 10. Treaty of Zürich ends the Italian War.
1860. May 5. Garibaldi's Expedition of 'The Thousand.'
1861. January 2. The Prince Regent becomes King of Prussia as William I.
1862. Bismarck appointed Ambassador at Paris (May 22).
September 23. Bismarck appointed Minister-President of Prussia. Rejection of the Military Budget. 'The Constitutional Conflict.'
1863 Rebellion in Poland. The Alvensleben Convention (February 8).
August 17. Congress of Princes at Frankfurt.
November 15. Death of Frederick VII. of Denmark. Opening of the Schleswig-Holstein Conflict.
1864. January 16. Alliance of Prussia and Austria.
April 25–June 25. Failure of the London Conference to settle the Schleswig-Holstein Question.
October 24. Treaty of Vienna. The Duchies ceded to Austria and Prussia.
1865. The Convention of Gastein (August 14).
1866. April 8. Prussia concludes an alliance with Italy.

1866.   June 14.   Prussia declares the Federal Diet dissolved.
        June 15.   Austria and Prussia at War.
        July 3.   Battle of Königgrätz.
        August 23.   Treaty of Prague.
        September.   The Constitutional Conflict ended.
        Bismarck is created a Count.
1867.   February 12.   The Constituent Reichstag of the North German
            Confederation meets.
        March and April.   The Luxemburg Question.
        May 11.   The Conference of London neutralises Luxemburg.
        July 1.   The Constitution of the North German Confederation comes
            into operation.
        July 14.   Bismarck appointed Federal Chancellor.
1868.   April 27.   The Customs Parliament for Germany meets.
        September.   Queen Isabella of Spain abdicates.
1869.   April 11.   Benedetti at Berlin inquires as to a Hohenzollern Candi-
            dature for the vacant Spanish Throne.
        The Vatican Council meets (December 8).
1870.   June 21.   King William agrees to the Hohenzollern Candidature.
        July 12.   The Hohenzollern Candidature abandoned.
        „   14.   Bismarck publishes the 'Ems telegram.'
        „   15.   Prussian mobilisation ordered.
        „   19.   France declares War on Prussia.
        „   25.   Bismarck publishes the Draft Treaty of August 1866.
        September 1.   Battle of Sedan.
        „   4.   Fall of the Second Empire.
        „   20.   Italian Troops enter Rome.
        October 27.   Surrender of Metz.
        „   31.   Russia denounces the Black Sea Articles of the Treaty
            of 1856.
1871.   January 18.   William I. proclaimed German Emperor at Versailles.
        Bismarck becomes Chancellor of the German Empire.
        March 13.   Conference at London revises the Treaty of 1856.
        April 1.   Bismarck created a Prince.
        May 10.   Treaty of Frankfurt.
1872.   Entente of the Three Empires and the Three Emperors (September).
        The Kulturkampf begins in Prussia.
1873.   May 15.   'The May Laws.'   The German occupation of France
            terminates.   Bismarck resigns the Minister-Presidency to Roon.
1874.   Increasing friction with France.
1875.   Franco-German Crisis.   Intervention of Russia and Great Britain
            (April to May).
        Revolts in Bosnia and Herzegovina.
1876.   Split in the Conservative Parties in Prussia.
        Serbia and Montenegro declare war on Turkey (July).
        Turkish Massacres in Bulgaria.
1877.   February 20.   Leo XIII. succeeds Pius IX. as Pope.
        Russia declares war on Turkey (April 24).
1878.   March 3.   Treaty of San Stefano.
        May 30.   Secret Convention between Great Britain and Russia.
        June 13.   Congress of Berlin.   The Treaties of Berlin (July 13).
1879.   The Dual Alliance between Germany and Austria (October 7).
        Bismarck commences to end the Kulturkampf and breaks with the
            National Liberals.
        Commencement of the New Protectionist and Socialist Policy.
1880.   A Liberal Ministry in Great Britain.
1881.   Assassination of the Tsar Alexander II. (March 13).

1881. Fall of the Gambetta Ministry in France.
1882. May 20. The Triple Alliance. Italy joins the Dual Alliance.
Foundation of *Die Deutsche Kolonial-Gesellschaft*.
1883. The New Socialistic Legislation in Germany.
1884. March. The Secret 'Reinsurance' Convention with Russia, confirmed (September) at Skierniewice.
Anglo-German Colonial friction. Germany acquires Togoland, the Cameroons, part of New Guinea, and other Colonies.
The Conference at Berlin to delimit spheres of the European Powers in Africa. Foundation of the Congo Free State.
Fall of the Ferry Cabinet at Paris (April).
Anglo-German Colonial Agreement.
Eastern Roumelia joins Bulgaria. War between Bulgaria and Serbia.
1886. January 7. Boulanger becomes Minister of War in France.
August 21. Alexander of Battenberg kidnapped in Bulgaria.
Russia and Austria-Hungary in prolonged disagreement over the Balkans.
1887. Renewal of the Triple Alliance.
Franco-German Crisis over 'The Schnaebele Incident' (April 20).
The Boulangist Movement at its height.
Pope Leo XIII. arbitrates between Germany and Spain. End of the Kulturkampf.
Great increase in German armaments. Renewal of the Reinsurance Treaty.
1888. February 6. Bismarck's Review of the European situation.
Death of the Emperor William I. (March 9).
Accession (March 9), and death of the Emperor Frederick III. (June 15).
Accession of the Emperor William II. (June 15).
1889. Commencement of the quarrel between Bismarck and the Emperor (September).
1890. March 20. Bismarck 'resigns' the Chancellorship.
General von Caprivi appointed Chancellor.
July 1. Anglo-German Colonial Agreement. The Emperor declares that 'our future lies on the water' (September).
1898. Death of Bismarck.
Foundation of the German Navy League.

INDEX

NOTE.—*Treaties, Battles,* and *Laws* are indexed under single collective headings

PRINTED IN GREAT BRITAIN BY
LOWE AND BRYDONE (PRINTERS) LTD., LONDON.